WHO'S WHO
IN THE
VOLUNTARY SECTOR

WHO'S WHO
IN THE
VOLUNTARY SECTOR

1997

·AURELIAN·

AURELIAN INFORMATION LTD 129 LEIGHTON GARDENS, LONDON NW10 3PS
Tel: 0181-960 7918/0171-794 8609

ABOUT *WHO'S WHO IN THE VOLUNTARY SECTOR*

WHO'S WHO IN THE VOLUNTARY SECTOR is an independent publication whose management is not affiliated to any charitable, voluntary, religious or political organization. The publication is compiled and produced under separate management from other Aurelian databases.

Information contained in each entry was supplied by the individual concerned. Whilst every care has been taken to ensure accuracy throughout, Aurelian Information Ltd can take no responsibility for the factual veracity of the contents.

The editors of this directory welcome all comments and suggestions from the users of
WHO'S WHO IN THE VOLUNTARY SECTOR. Our database coverage of the sector is expanding daily and other information packages are now available. If there is a specific subject area within the sector which you would like to see covered by a reliable information source, please do not hesitate to contact us.

Details of other Aurelian Information packages - hardcopy, disk and on-line versions - are available direct from:

AURELIAN INFORMATION, 129 Leighton Gardens, London NW10 3PS
Tel:0181-960 7918 Fax: 0171-794 8609 E-mail: aurelian@dircon.co.uk

WHO'S WHO IN THE VOLUNTARY SECTOR Copyright © 1996 Aurelian Information Ltd

Additional copyrights exist in articles as follows - Copyright © 1996:

Peter Chennell/Kim Worts; Joe Saxton; Howard Lake; Andrew Thomas; Hilary Blume.;

COPYRIGHT WARNING

The contents and presentation of **WHO'S WHO IN THE VOLUNTARY SECTOR** *are copyright in accordance with the terms of the Berne Convention. This information is for reference only, copying Hardcopy or Disks as a whole or in part is an act of theft. A reward will be offered to any person providing evidence to Aurelian Information Ltd leading to a successful prosecution for infringement under the Copyright Act.*

1111111111

ISBN 1 899247 07 6

Printed in Great Britain

ABOUT THE FOURTH EDITION ❑
A Word from the Editors

WHO *IS* WHO IN THE CHARITY WORLD?

Welcome to the fourth edition of **WHO'S WHO IN THE VOLUNTARY SECTOR**.

Once again, we would like to thank those who have helped to make this new edition possible - the contributors themselves who took the time to complete the questionnaires and responded so understandingly through a period punctured by postal and transport strikes. This year, the editors are particularly indebted for much-valued editorial advice from individuals on the grant-making side of the sector and for written contributions from specialists working in the increasingly important area of marketing for charities and voluntary organisations.

The issue of marketing within the voluntary sector is a broad and hotly debated one. For many the boundaries have blurred between communicating an idea or a cause, marshalling development funding for a major single project and selling T-shirts to fund the continued activities of a service charity. Definitions have been further distorted by the opportunities offered by the latest technology for new and more complete means of communicating with supporters, talking to donors, and publicising events and causes globally. As the pressure builds upon most charities to increase their funding levels, many are actively looking to explore new routes. While some are setting up Web sites and an electronic future, others are turning to tried and tested means and seeing what can be learnt from the current practitioners.

Whether you are considering restructuring your fundraising department, launching your cyber requests along the information highway, or setting up a full trading subsidiary, we hope the articles which follow will provide food for thought.

The views expressed in the articles featured in **WHO'S WHO IN THE VOLUNTARY SECTOR** are those of the individual authors. They do not necessarily represent either the viewpoints of the publishers nor a consensus of opinion among the authors themselves, who provided their texts independently from each other and free from editorial modification.

As in previous editions, the focus of the directory is primarily upon executives working for UK national, and UK-based international organisations. Additionally, a balanced view of what represents 'national' interests is supplied by representative figures from organisations which by nature operate locally or regionally, but form the working parts of a national movement. This year we are grateful for the participation of individuals from independent hospices and housing associations, medical research charities, heritage site and marine conservation organisations of national (or international) significance.

The Editors

CHARITIES ON DISK - *DATA DIRECT*

*IMMEDIATE ACCESS TO
7000+ UK National Charities
& Voluntary Organizations*

*Your instant database
- no research required*

*With monthly updates
- no need for you to revise*

*Categorised by subject
- easy to sort/search*

*Registered charity numbers
- positive identification*

*Phone, fax and address
at your fingertips*

*Runs on your in-house
database system*

DATABASE SERVICE - CHARITIES ON DISK

Information is continually checked and revised; subscribers receive full updated data disks every month.

Disks are issued in formats to fit all mainstream database systems and so can be loaded onto your own database to meet all your reference and mailing needs.

MAILING SERVICE

Mailing disks for your use can be prepared to your exact specifications. Alternatively, can place an insert in our regular mailings direct to *7000+* charities.

For all details & prices call Aurelian direct on 0181-960 7918/0171-794 8609.

CONTENTS ❑
WHO'S WHO IN THE VOLUNTARY SECTOR - 1997 EDITION

V	**ABOUT THE FOURTH EDITION**
IX	**VIEWS FROM THE SECTOR** Effective Marketing for Charities in a Changing Environment
IX	*Not Missing the Boat?* Peter Chennell
XII	*Time to Get Rid of Your Fundraising Director?* Joe Saxton
XIII	*Marketing on the Internet?* Howard Lake
XV	*Is There a Market Out There?* Andrew Thomas
XVII	*Marketing: An Appropriate Concept for Charity?* Hilary Blume
XVIII	**GLOSSARY OF ABBREVIATIONS**
1	**WHO'S WHO IN THE VOLUNTARY SECTOR**
154	**EXECUTIVE NOTICEBOARD** Training Sessions and Meetings for Charity Management in 1996/97
156	**MAGAZINES AND NEWSLETTERS** Specialist Charity Publications in the United Kingdom and Overseas
157	**CONSULTANTS AND SERVICES** Directory of Management & Development Resources for Charities
164	**INDEX BY ORGANISATION** Organisations listed A-Z with their Main Entry References

INTERNET-FOR-ALL

Publications:

Direct Connection's Guide to
FUNDRAISING ON THE INTERNET by Howard Lake

Local groups, national charities, community appeals - whether raising money for your school or your planet, this book shows how to use the Internet NOW.

'packed with ideas' **Professional Fundraising**
'earth-breaking guide ... largely written in words of one syllable - in some instances more pithily than others' **The Guardian**
' practical guide in non-technical language on how charities can use the Information Superhighway' **Charity Times**
'Thoroughly researched - easy to read - informative - inspirational' **Voluntary Voice**
'clear, non-technical language' **Update ICFM**

Paperback £12.99

Coming Spring 1997:
First Steps on the Internet: *the practical guide for the Voluntary Sector*
by Sandra Vogel

Should you start using the Internet? How will it help? Which service provider should you use? What modem do you need? Do you have to buy a new computer? Sandra Vogel answers all the first questions and gives a step by step guide to making the Internet work for you from the very beginning.

Paperback £12.99

THE VOLUNTARY SECTOR
☞ HANDS-ON ☜
INTERNET TRAINING SESSIONS

Courses are hosted at Internet Cafes. With a maximum of 2 people per PC you will learn through your own hands-on experience. As the cafes offer UK-wide public access to the Internet, you can continue to work on it even if your organization is not yet connected. Sessions include
FUNDRAISING ON THE INTERNET
GETTING YOUR MESSAGE ACROSS - INFORMATION PROVISION ON THE INTERNET
THE POWER OF E-MAIL

For details and dates of the courses in your area call   0181-960 7918

AURELIAN INFORMATION LTD, 129 Leighton Gardens, London NW10 3PS
Tel:0181-960 7918 Fax: 0171-794 8609 E-mail:aurelian@dircon.co.uk

VIEWS FROM THE SECTOR
Effective Marketing for Charities in a Changing Environment

Not Missing the Boat?

Peter Chennell

Peter Chennell came to run RNLI Sales Ltd from **Innovations,** *the ground breaking mail order group. His task was to streamline a venerable institution and maximise its considerable fundraising potential from trading. Having already achieved a demonstrable upturn in revenue, in the following article he has drawn on his experiences to advise other charities considering the advantages and pitfalls of setting up and running a trading arm.*

The RNLI targets an income of £62 million per annum: sourced from legacies, donations, subscriptions, fundraising activities and events organised by 2000 RNLI branches throughout the UK, and from RNLI Sales Ltd, the wholly owned trading subsidiary that generates the retail sales from 200 lifeboat station shops, merchandise sales from volunteer stalls at local events, and from goods supplied through *Watermark* - the multimillion pound generating mail order catalogue of the RNLI.

The proceeds from RNLI Sales Ltd go to the RNLI. This is the way a trading company operates alongside a charity. But the reality of the divide is much stronger and sharper than those simple words - we operate as a completely separate entity. This is dictated by both law and business necessity. Yet a purchase from our mail order catalogue goes towards the purchase of a lifejacket for one of our crew members. That is where the division blurs and from it we gain an edge over ordinary commercial companies.

We market our products to our target audience just as any other trading company would - but we offer an extra marketing incentive no non-charity can compete with. We save lives at sea - if you buy our goods then you are giving money to the brave crew who turn out day or night to rescue those in peril at sea. Call it emotional blackmail, or guilt transference (for the crew do what we cannot or dare not), but if we keep that message firmly in front of our audience then we are tipping the scales in our favour from the very beginning.

If you are going to run a successful business you have to run it in a businesslike fashion.

The company is run as a separate organisation from the RNLI charity. The size of the operation helps. The staff are separate, the accounts are, of course, separate, we even live in a separate building - directly opposite the main RNLI UK headquarters in Poole. It is important for us to act as a company, not a charity. When a decision has to be made I ask whether Slip Way Marketing would do it. The mythical Slip Way (the name is taken from our address) can be trusted to take only commercially valid decisions. If the answer is no, then I have to ask why we should be doing it. Usually this is the end of the discussion.

However, if the answer comes back that if we do not do it then the RNLI will lose 400 volunteers, then that seems to me to be a good reason and Slip Way has to take a back seat. We go ahead, we do it in order to keep the volunteers and so to benefit the RNLI, but we do record the reason that this unprofitable decision was made. It is not so much a matter of obeying two masters, as keeping the ultimate objective of assisting the RNLI before us at all times.

It is important to have someone working on the trading company whose experience is wholly commercial. Charities have different ways of operating: their detailed methods of checks and balances with committees and trustees and graduated decision-making does not translate easily into the commercial world. One of the main problems is timing. A commercial company needs to be able to react quickly, as quickly as the competition. Thus when setting up such a company a charity faces the immense difficulty of staffing it - and putting someone on to the job as a part-time secondment from within the charity is not a recipe for success. Yet to trust someone new from outside both the charity and the voluntary sector is a difficult and risky decision for the trustees to take.

How many staff you require is determined by whether any of the work of the company is sub-contracted out. At RNLI we deal with our own distribution and order fulfilment, we have our own merchandise buyers, our own warehouseing, and we rent mailing lists. All this infrastructure gives us the opportunity to monitor every facet of the quality of the

WHO'S WHO IN THE VOLUNTARY SECTOR - X

goods and the service we offer. To have such a level of control is a definite bonus. The fact that we have these resources is partly a historical accident, but the task of the nineties that we share with all other charity trading companies is to streamline the operation to ensure that each aspect works as efficiently and profitably as possible. If I can introduce a better piece of software that will cut £10,000 off the expenses of our order fulfillment centre in Thirsk, that puts £10,000 directly into the lifesaving work. That thought has to remain at the forefront of all decisions - money saved is as useful as money made.

My competitors are Pastimes, Scotts of Stow, Kaleidoscope, Innovations, everybody else - I don't see my competitor as Oxfam.

Once the company exists then the chosen trading activity should be targetted directly to the supporters the charity already holds. The best marketing advice I can give is - NEVER MIX THE MESSAGES.

Identify your supporters/buyers and talk directly to them. We save lives at sea. We have a recognisable lifeboat logo, we draw on emotional motifs relating to the perceived British traits of courage in adversity, the island race, the ordinary person capable of extraordinary sacrifice... we are supported by "middle England". Therefore we offer upmarket goods with a maritime flavour to appeal to their tastes. This year our catalogue is sprinkled throughout with short quotes from sea rescues, designed not simply to pull on the emotional heartstrings but also to keep the reader permanently aware of just what their money achieves.

In other respects our catalogue simply uses the best of the traditional mail order techniques in design and presentation, and in researching our lists and customers we have recently discovered the full benefits of profiling.

Working with the volunteers means providing them with total back up. I have recently introduced the new concept that actually we are a service company - we are serving our volunteers. The merchandise is always ours and they sell it on our behalf - but our job is to service their fundraising activities. We do that by providing them with the goods they want at the price they want. It is up to us to provide a commercial lead. I do not want the volunteers to be commercial - I want them to let me be commercial, so they can get on with what they are good at. We have street fundraisers who shake boxes and give out badges on flag days, branches that run fundraising events and sell our products on stands at fetes and shows, lifeboat centres that have gift and souvenir shops that may be open all year or simply for a few weekends in summer. What we have to do is work with the volunteers and not against them. The trick is not to demotivate them by being too commercial - and that is a balancing act we are constantly working on.

While the volunteers provide a variety of levels of enthusiasm, commitment and achievement, they also provide a very specific area of management problems. Each charity has its own structure of supporters. The RNLI operates through a network of guilds and branches. The hierarchy is fairly rigidly defined which can be helpful in mobilising high degrees of activity across a region but, equally, a problem at the top can lead to a lack of performance throughout. What we have to remember at all times is that we are dealing with volunteers, not paid staff. You might retain the services of a member of staff after telling them that their method of working has not been cost effective for the past five years, but tell that to a volunteer and you will either lose the volunteer completely or demotivate them so far as to make them ineffectual.

When we make changes to systems at RNLI Sales we shoulder the blame whether it exists or not. The morale of the volunteer force is a marketing asset that cannot be jeopardised. We try hard to communicate the need for changes, not simply demand them. However, if we meet major opposition to a change from an individual then reluctant co-operation is often achieved simply because the volunteer is willing to let their own views take a back seat for the good of the cause. Such loyalty usually comes from those who give many years of their lives to working for the RNLI and so is, to put it bluntly, an emotional advantage in working with volunteers only open to the older charities. Sad to say the 80/20 rule applies in our business as much as anyone else's - 80% of the income is generated by 20% of the volunteers and equally 80% of the problems are caused by (a different) 20% of the volunteer force.

Given our high profile, our corporate fundraising schemes are usually instigated by the commercial sector: they come to us offering sponsorship schemes, affinity marketing options, etc that will bring them more business while we receive the financial donations. When negotiating any use of your charity's logo you should have some idea of its value. Set a benchmark to aim for; you may not always actually get that amount but it will help maintain the value of what is most charities' most marketable asset. One word of warning: when calculating the predicted profit of any scheme - beware VAT, especially when dealing with the financial services sector.

Obviously our logo can be misused at times, but we have no specific system for monitoring this. Such instances are brought to our attention by word of mouth - a phone call from a supporter or colleague asking whether we know that the lifeboat logo is on X tour bus, or the posters for Y event. Corporate licensing in its various forms can bring in excellent returns with very little outlay - so the margins are obviously vastly better than in retail trading. Staffing levels are also low - the RNLI has a very small team covering all matters corporate. Yet when they set up a Give-As-You-Earn scheme we receive at least £62 per annum from each employee in the scheme - far more than we can expect to receive from each of our supporters, however committed.

In dealings with the corporate sector the question of ethics is often debated. The old chestnuts of taking tobacco and alcohol money are sometimes linked with many more taboos simply because of our charity connection. My view is fairly strongly that we should be governed no differently from Slip Way Marketing in making our decisions. A properly run company will have ethics imposed by law - as

WHO'S WHO IN THE VOLUNTARY SECTOR - XI

RNLB Hibernia; Arun Relief

regards pornography, etc, - and by its target audience. We are no different. It is counter-productive to enter into any agreement that will alienate the majority of your buyers, and knowing what will alienate them is a matter of obeying that first rule in trading - identify your market before you start. Do bear in mind that commercial decisions are made on the basis of numbers. To bow before every dissenting voice would lead to complete inertia. It is sometimes said in the charity world that you must take care never to offend anyone because you can never tell who may be the source of the next legacy. Commercial decisions cannot be governed by such random acts. At RNLI our apocryphal story is of the millions left to us by the man who changed his will after he looked out of his hotel room one rainy day in a seaside town and saw on the street corner opposite an RNLI collector, souwester dripping, shaking his lifeboat box on the empty wet street.

There are certainly some drawbacks to operating in a charity context. The public perception of the charity does make demands an ordinary trading company would not need to meet. We cannot be seen to give things away as incentives for purchasers. A charity that gives away free items, however valid the economic reasons may be, will be condemned as being too "clever" or too wasteful: "if they are doing so well they don't need our support ....". We have to keep the quality of our goods fairly high; even if rubbish sells, we cannot be seen to be selling it. Likewise, the profile of the RNLI supporter means that if we have too many products not made in the UK we are subject to criticism. I cannot rent out the RNLI members' list even though it is much in demand, it would be a breach of faith and the RNLI would suffer. Most importantly, whilst striving for the highest standards in terms of efficiency and service, we must avoid the appearance of slick commercialism, because that would blunt the RNLI's message, the emotional appeal that is intrinsic to our marketing success.

Despite my touchstone of Slip Way Marketing for the day-to-day decisionmaking, in deciding whether or not to set up a trading company each charity has to weigh the advantages that the endeavour may bring in more than simple balance sheet terms.

RNLI Sales Ltd is a fundamental part of the operation and success of RNLI. From the charity we gain certain advantages - our marketing is forged on the back of 200 years of courageous sea rescues; part of our sales is undertaken by a massive and committed volunteer force; our motivation is to make money for our brave volunteer crewman, which is much more uplifting for staff morale than simply putting extra profits into the pockets of private individuals however much one might admire their entrepreneurial spirit.

In return, the RNLI receives more than simply the trading profits: our mail order activity in a year brings in, separate from actual sales, around £150,000 in donations direct to the RNLI. Whilst I cannot sell the RNLI members' list, I do pass direct to the RNLI membership recruitment the names of any purchasers of goods - a warm lead is always better than a cool one. Selling the goods is the peg on which most of the fundraising and volunteer work hangs, it provides a focus for their involvement. Without the merchandise we would not have a presence at many events and shows, would not gather new recruits. At any gathering of RNLI supporters, what is the subject under most heated discussion? Our latest 1.5 million pound Severn lifeboat? Proposals for expenditure of thousands on new software? No - the subject that arouses most interest is the designs for tea-towels and Christmas cards. Perhaps we are all thwarted shopkeepers - but where would the RNLI be without the commitment of the fundraising volunteers?

Each charity has something different to gain and to offer if it chooses to enter the trading arena. But if you decide to go ahead then remember that you are starting a business, not another charity, and you are fighting for the pound in Mr Ordinary's pocket just like everybody else.

Peter Chennell, Managing Director, RNLI (Sales) Ltd
with Kim Worts, Aurelian Information Ltd.

WHO'S WHO IN THE VOLUNTARY SECTOR - XII

Time to get rid of your Fundraising Director?

Joe Saxton

Most charity chief executives and trustees would prefer to be able to do without their fundraisers. They are an inconvenient necessity reluctantly employed only when it is clear that legacies, investments and government handouts are no longer enough, and who are tolerated as long as they bring in the money. In a Faustian deal, most charities believe that fundraising amounts to selling their soul in exchange for the vital juices of corporate life: money. Fundraisers are tolerated, yet derided. Fundraisers, from a whole spectrum of charities, have told me that they feel undervalued, that the service providers (those who do 'the real work') see them as a necessary evil, if they see them at all. I know half a dozen fundraisers who left one major overseas charity because they were fed up with a culture and a chief executive who viewed them as second class citizens.

This attitude to fundraisers and fundraising permeates the entire charity world. How many fundraisers get to be Chief Executives? How many major charities have fundraisers as trustees? Fundraisers are expected to take the incoherent, unfocussed and expensive service-provision programmes that many charities have, and raise money for them. They are often allowed little information about the service itself, and are certainly 'banned' from suggesting that a different set of services might actually be more coherent.

How have we let this state of affairs develop, and more importantly how can we stop digging and even get out of the hole?

I believe that one of the main reasons for this situation is that charities are so service-driven. Up until the 1980s many charities never even needed to think about fundraising or income generation. So when they needed extra funds, charities did as little as they could in order to get the extra resources they desired. Fundraising was never seen as a legitimate discipline, merely as a means to an end. Fundraising was introduced reluctantly and piecemeal by people with service-provision backgrounds. Far from embracing and understanding the new discipline they ignored it and - ostrich-like - hoped it would bring in the funds. This attitude has now taken root and is endemic in the voluntary sector.

Yet fundraising has far more to offer than money. It can amount to a vote of endorsement of the charity's work. It can introduce ideas of performance measurement and accountability. It can provide a way in which an organisation can listen to a wider public and cease to be so introspective. More importantly, it is the vanguard of a whole new discipline: marketing. Where fundraising has failed, marketing can now succeed. Marketing can broadly be defined as the process of meeting people's needs. Where fundraising provided the brash, aggressive desire to sell people a cause no matter what, marketing enables organisations to understand who their audiences are and develop communications and services to meet the needs of those audiences. Where fundraising worked in isolation from the rest of a charity's communications, marketing can now create a coherent whole which both raises income and increases the organisation's effectiveness in the media, to service users and to a wider public.

Wherever you are in the development of fundraising, it's never too late to introduce the marketing process in your charity. What follows is my guide to introducing the marketing process into your organisation. It starts with your mission and ends with the demise of your fundraising director.

Why do you exist?
Perhaps this question sounds too navel-gazing, too zen, and above all irrelevant, but nothing could be further from the truth. Too many charities no longer know why they exist. They continue doing what they did last year and the year before, on the slow inexorable path to impotence and irrelevance. Every trustee, every staff member must know the answer to questions like: Why do we exist? What makes us different? What are we doing that nobody else does? I know charities large and small who can't satisfactorily answer these questions. Answer them and you will have gained a new sense of purpose.

How can you survive in a competitive world?
The world for charities is becoming more competitive every year, not just for money, but for share of voice and, worse still, in the provision of services. I believe there are four strategies for competitive advantage that charities can follow:

Niche Charities can attempt to find a small and defined area of service provision that they can address and 'own'. This niche can be geographical, for example accommodation for the homeless in a particular town. It can also be issue-specific, such as the only charity dealing exclusively with a particular medical condition.

Differentiation Charities who basically do very similar things to other organisations can make themselves different in the public mind. They can do this by appealing to a different audience (for example, a religious audience); by creating a different set of beliefs or way of working (we are the only animal charity who will never put down a healthy animal); by creating a new marketing or fundraising product (child sponsorship allows our supporters to have a real and direct link with third world communities).

Awareness There are about a dozen charities who try to be competitive by being better known than anyone else. This high level of awareness brings with it a range of benefits: spontaneous donations and legacies, media interest, and credibility in the public mind. Awareness is a risky strategy because the rewards are far lower for second place.

Externally-driven. This strategy is different from all the other approaches since it is not a strategy that could be rec-

WHO'S WHO IN THE VOLUNTARY SECTOR - XIII

ommended to any organisation trying to decide how to become competitive in today's world. It works for those organisations that, due often to their history, can survive on the fruits of external events beyond their control.

What is your brand?
Brand is just a fancy marketing term for image or personality. Every organisation has a brand, it is just that some brands are duller and more boring than others. You only need to look at the major cancer charities to see that big can mean dull and indistinguishable. Yet creating a brand is within the scope of every charity. What do you believe in? What messages do you want to get across? What words and phrases do you want associated with your work? Should you be seen as bold or innovative, passionate or caring and so on. You need to think in soundbites: 'We believe that children need parents, and parents need help'. Once you've heard the chosen phrases a thousand times the message may be starting to get home. Every communication needs to reinforce the brand. The agencies, the directors, the trustees need to understand their role in making sure that your communications are building a powerful brand.

Get your corporate identity right
Corporate identity is a small but important part of your brand. Think of it as the clothes that your brand wears. The clothes don't make the personality but they reflect it. It is often easier to spot a corporate identity that doesn't work: a typeface that looks out of date, a logo that is cluttered and complicated, colours that are hard to reproduce or indistinct. Most trustees would rather change their mission than their logo, but nonetheless corporate identity should overhauled at least once a decade. I know one charity that has six letterheads, numerous typefaces, three logos, and completely different styles for its direct marketing and for its advertising.

How are you talking to the world?
Everything talks: your shops, your switchboard, your press officers, your regional fundraising, your direct mail, and much else. The question is whether all this talking is saying the same thing and whether they are giving the right image. When you go to a supermarket and part with your hard-earned cash you are left with a basket of groceries. You can decide whether the cash provided value for money by consuming what you bought. When you part with your cash at a charity, you have no way of knowing directly whether the organisation is providing value for money and doing what they said they would. For this reason, people use incredibly trivial evidence to decide whether an organisation can be trusted: the length of time to bank a cheque, how a telephone is answered, an incorrect salutation, what their neighbour said and so on. These tiny 'moments of truth' can give people, for better or worse, their own personal version of your brand. Every time somebody is given an impression of your organisation your brand is being communicated and all these communications need managing.

Get ready to communicate
All the best strategic planning is wasted if you don't have the people in place and the expertise to provide each of the specific skills you need. Fundraising, design, public relations, internal communications, inquiries management, database, copywriting, spokespeople are all part of the armoury you need to market your organisation to the outside (and inside) world. In large organisations, you may need separate people, even departments for each of these skills. In small organisations, one person may take on many of the roles.

To head up all these communications a director is needed. A person who will understand the different skills that go to make up a communications or marketing strategy. A person who can put the cause of marketing across at the most senior level. A person who can create strategy and know whether it is working. A person who can spot communications opportunities and develop them. In short, the person who should sit on your board of directors is no longer a fundraiser, but a marketing or communications director. By looking at the whole picture, fundraising can change from being a derided poor relation to being an integral and successful part of a strategy that will make the whole organisation more effective, including its fundraising.

Joe Saxton
Consultant in brand, fundraising and strategy issues for nonprofit organisations.

Marketing on the Internet?

Howard Lake

Marketing on the Internet does not consist simply of transferring existing marketing material and practices. A far more subtle model has been adopted. This involves attracting and engaging consumers with relevant and helpful information with the possibility of developing some degree of relationship with the consumer that will produce at least one sale and preferably repeat purchases. Successful advertising on the Internet resembles far more the advertorials of print journalism than the static display advertisements. Nevertheless the same general marketing theories underpin Internet marketing. Burnett defines marketing as "finding out what consumers want or need and then supplying it at a profit". Research, strategy, product design, advertising, public relations, communication and even after-sales service are all part of marketing.

Fundraisers still have to determine and display on their online appeals their "URG" (Unique Reason to Give), Burnett's translation of the marketer's USP (Unique Selling Point) to the fundraiser's lexicon.

Michael Strangelove, author of *How to Advertise on the Internet*, puts the revolutionary nature of the Internet as an advertising medium into a historical perspective. First, the Internet has reversed the trend of "info-reduction", from text to sound to images, that has been the hallmark of the history of advertising, by allowing advertisers to provide more information. "With the exception of one-to-one personal interaction, every other medium familiar to advertisers restricted both the amount of information that could be transmitted and the degree of feedback that could be received".

Secondly, the Internet offers advertisers a global market presence for a very small capital outlay: "the cost of providing content on the Internet - when compared to the cost of communicating information through radio, print or television - is best described as trivial. Now $20-per-month Internet access can serve as the foundation for a global advertising campaign.

Thirdly, the implications for small businesses are therefore immense. "For the first time in history, the small-business world has affordable access to mass-communication and global markets through the Internet".

The WWW (World Wide Web) is not the only method of marketing one's product or service on the Internet. "Engaging Internet members through e-mail conversations and electronic newsletters is the most widely used, and by far the most effective, form of Internet advertising". For this reason small businesses can compete in many ways with large businesses who have many more resources at their disposal. The fact that "some of the most effective cybermarketing [can be] done merely by talking with people via e-mail" demonstrates the equalising and levelling effect of marketing on the Internet. Tom Tabor, online newsletter writer, wrote in *Internet World* "Today, I think e-mail is the killer app[lication]... E-mail is still the communications tool for the overwhelming majority of the network". Early successes and failures in for-profit marketing on the Internet have already produced useful guides and rules of thumb: for example, a marketer's site "must be appealing, relevant, and current". Bill Washburn, formerly executive director of the Commercial Internet Exchange (CIX), advises that the entertainment value of a resource is also important.

New marketing approaches are required for the Internet. The straight reproduction of a printed colour brochure to a Web page for example fails to capitalise on the dynamic and interactive nature of the WWW. John Hegarty, Chairman of advertising agency Bartle Bogle Hegarty, argues convincingly that advertising on the Internet involves a reversal of the traditional roles of advertiser and consumer, away from the broadcast paradigm. "You are going to have to buy actively into the advertisement. It will have to be something you want to watch because it is interesting, not something you had to watch because it was there".

Strangelove argues that "a solid understanding of the nature of the Net as a new form of human communication, consumer behaviour, and virtual culture is the key to success in this revolutionary medium". This understanding can only be gained, he argues, if one's company becomes part of the virtual community of its consumers and potential consumers and maintains an active presence. He concludes that "success will go to those who enter fully into the new paradigm and transform their marketing messages into an interactive, dynamic community presence". The early successes and failures of online fundraising appeals would seem to confirm this view.

An essential aspect of entering this new paradigm is the practice of marketing a nonprofit's online presence. Simply creating a Web page is not enough: the marketing effort has itself to be marketed. Existing donors have to be informed of the site's existence, possibly through the traditional supporters' newsletter or on letterhead paper. Potential donors have to be encouraged to visit the site. This can be done in a number of ways but the most basic and essential is registering the new site with the various Internet search engines and directories. If this isn't done then it will prove very difficult for a nonprofit's site to be found. Fundraisers must also then ensure that their WWW site is linked hypertextually to other related sites, thereby encouraging greater traffic.

At the same time the site should be announced on the various relevant e-mail discussion and mailing lists and on relevant Usenet newsgroups. In a sense this marketing of the online site should be an iterative process. Fundraisers must also be aware that, as new relevant sites are created, their owners should also be asked to add a link to the nonprofit's page. Most importantly new Internet users are appearing all the time, so a system should be planned and implemented for posting appropriate updates and announcements of any changes to the nonprofit's WWW site to relevant e-mail lists and Usenet newsgroups.

The implications for nonprofit fundraisers are clear. The Internet is a marketplace which can be entered at very low cost. It is one in which two-way relationships with customers are essential and indeed unavoidable, and therefore in line with fundraisers' commitments to relationship fundraising. Significantly it is a marketplace where novelty, integrity, currency and compelling content are the ingredients of success. These attributes should sound very familiar to successful fundraisers who employ them in all their other traditional fundraising activities.

Howard Lake is a professional fundraiser, currently for Amnesty International, and the author of **Direct Connections's guide to Fundraising on the Internet.**

Are you following the latest marketing trends in the Not-For-Profit sector?

**Read the specialist magazines worldwide when you access them across the Internet.
See journals listed p. 156**

WHO'S WHO IN THE VOLUNTARY SECTOR - XV

Is There a Market Out There?

Andrew Thomas

Not many voluntary organisations have a problem in knowing if there is a market for their services. If there was no market for our cause most of us would look for another job tomorrow. We may have to market ourselves to ensure that the most needy groups know we are here, but there is a larger issue for most of us: where is the market to pay for our service?

Recently the voluntary sector has turned to marketing people to solve its funding problems. Many organisations now have marketing directors instead of fundraising directors, direct marketing departments instead of appeals to send out the begging letters, and marketing strategies instead of fundraising plans.

Some of my friends remember when *public relations, communications* and *development* were also euphemisms for those who preferred anything to the rather coarse business of asking people to give money. A few of my friends argue that marketing is just another set of the Emperor's new clothes, and there may be some truth in that. Certainly, from our surveys of job advertisements, a number of Directors of Fundraising posts now seem to reappear as Directors of Marketing, but there is more to it than that.

Quite what the extra ingredient is may be worth exploring if your organisation is about to embark on some form of marketing to raise more resources. Often it arises because there is a funding panic. Maybe statutory sources are drying up, a lottery bid needs matching funding, or you may be in a growth phase. Marketing has something to offer but, as I hope to demonstrate, it is not the whole story.

To start with, marketing is probably not much use if you need money tomorrow. It may be fine in theory but getting money in a hurry is a case of all hands on telephones to ask supporters for help, or fixing appointments with people who can open a few new doors; that is selling, not marketing.

The only people able to use marketing in an emergency are those cynical but brave souls who work for third world organisations and know that the media can usually manage one or two emergencies in Rwanda or Bosnia at least once a year before they start running the story about compassion fatigue in 1997.

Marketing really comes into its own as a proper discipline when an organisation starts planning strategically over "-5 years. Now that the recession may be easing a bit for some people, longer term planning is coming back into fashion and strategic plans, corporate plans and the like are starting to pop up on trustees' agendas.

The trouble is that marketing is often invited in too late. Time after time, as Charity Consultants Ltd, we are asked to devise marketing and funding strategies for organisations which have already written their strategy before they do any work to see if there is a donor constituency or customer base to support their grandiose schemes. Often the strategy has a few lines in a 20-50 page document talking about where the resources needed to finance the plans might come from. Just as frequently there is almost nothing about how the marketing strategy is to be financed; presumably from non-existent reserves or cutting services to clients.

Most strategies start with some forward plans which cost more than projected income but few go to the next step of drafting a proper development plan to say:

- what makes up that funding gap?
- how big is it?
- who might be interested in helping to pay for our services?
- how do we make them aware of the problem?
- how do we reach them with a proposition which solves the problem?

Yet without answering these questions marketing will inevitably address the wrong issues. The first two points, about content and scale of the funding gap, are usually answered by the chief executive, trustees, and the finance director. Thank goodness more finance directors get involved in marketing and fundraising issues instead of being the bad guy who just says NO to all budget requests. But the last three points are a real marketing challenge which need more attention from senior managers, not just the fundraisers.

Let me start with who might be interested in supporting you. It amazes me that business-like boards and managers from industry agree marketing strategies without understanding the market they are in, do any market research to identify the size and source of potential funding markets, or understand concepts of a marketing mix or cycle. All of this is essential.

If you do not have experience internally, look for a volunteer, a trustee or, if the job is large enough, a consultant to guide you through the maze of information available. No business would ever invest in some of the marketing schemes I have seen without also investing in market research; no army would ever commit reserves without time spent on reconnaissance. Money and time invested now saves scarce time and money later.

Parts of the funding market are worth re-appraising. Statutory sources still give more than private fundraising according to *Dimensions in the Voluntary Sector*. Public companies and trusts are reaching saturation unless you have a special offering. New direct mail supporters are hard to come by but maybe some traditional supporters could give a lot more. Fees may be crucial but vulnerable, the lottery may be your saviour or a waste of time and so on. This marketing assessment needs to be done analytically perhaps through a marketing study or a thorough fundraising audit. In preparing the marketing analysis it is important to consider internal as well as external markets. At its most basic any marketing approach needs to assess whether your staff, volunteers and present supporters are open to this new approach.

There is not much point in opening up new markets if your approach alienates present supporters. Similarly there may be an internal marketing job to be done to convince people the organisation really needs to fundraise. Perhaps you need to have large reserves but supporters forget that you will need them to repair buildings 10 years after they were built. Many of us are managing organisations with a strong public sector legacy and which still believe that the state really ought to fund them to provide the service their clients need.

Once we know where the market is, it becomes easier to focus on how to make the market aware that we exist and have a fundraising need. Britain has some enormous organisations which the public rarely thinks need money. Housing associations often have huge capital assets but may need money for the social services in order to dramatically improve the quality of service to their clients. An organisation like Motability may be able to offer 99% of its customers a perfectly good service but severely disabled customers may need expensive adaptations to their car which can only be paid for from new charitable funds. In both these cases large organisations use marketing to create an awareness of the need.

Here you are in exactly the same position as any company trying to offer a product which nobody needs to buy. You are not in the business of selling the staple foods of bread, milk and vegetables. You are in the slightly more upmarket of wine and chilled foods. When I go to Tesco's I do not need to buy wine but I might, if I fancy the idea and I have the money to spare, think it would impress the supper guests . Then I have the fun task of selecting which bottle to buy when there are almost as many varieties to choose from as there are charities. At least if you are a large charity some people will have heard of you but for small or start up organisations just getting donors to know that you exist or that you have a funding problem is the real marketing challenge.

So our first task is to create a marketing proposition which identifies our client's problem to society. For most of us this means taking a fresh look at how we present ourselves to donors, funders and commercial partners. Sometimes it involves going back to the basic reasons of why we exist. If we cannot explain that to people in simple language then our friends and competitors in other causes will win our market from us.

This may just mean repackaging the service or product we offer or occasionally completely restructuring what we do. Whilst the last thing we want to do is let our funders dictate policy, we should not forget that we may have funding problems precisely because we too eagerly accepted public funders' priorities rather than building up a market of diversified funders. If we had a market we might not be in our present predicament. Better a flock of conflicting donor priorities than one government policy which could be changed at the next election.

The second challenge is to create a product which meets our objectives and those of potential supporters. In doing this too many people assume that donors are broadly the same in their needs and aspirations. They also tend to think of them solely as organisations whereas at the end of the day we have to convince individuals to believe in us.

This involves not just producing a proposal that meets your needs but one that fits funders or donors as well. After all, how would you like it if I tried to offer the same consultancy solution to you as I had to 20 other Chief Executives!

ANDREW THOMAS is Chief Executive of Charity Consultants Ltd, a network of not-for-profit consultants which specialises in strategic planning, marketing and fundraising issues. Charity Consultants Ltd offer a free half day consultancy to Chief Executives and Chairs of not-for-profit organisations. He can be reached on 01734 -401016.

Looking for an outside expert?
- see pp. 157-163

Marketing: An Appropriate Concept for a Charity?

Hilary Blume

Is marketing an appropriate concept for charity? Is it helpful to see supporters and beneficiaries as buyers of a charity's services? Are beneficiaries to become the photogenic advertising aids in the charity's marketing plan? There are those who would argue the case in favour, referring to the discipline it brings to the work, its more 'scientific' approach. But marketing is only one way of looking at things, and no more interesting than analysing one's organisation in historic terms, or as an instrument for societal change, or by bench marking.

Why have UK charities over the last 20 years rushed to embrace 'marketing' and the jargon of the business school? Why does one hear the plea for charities to become more businesslike, when British business is so palpably second rate?

Organised charitable endeavour is increasing. There are around 150 thousand charities in the UK. Over the last 20 years the numbers employed in the voluntary sector have risen and the income of charities has multiplied. Yet the percentage of our population who are poor is increasing. It is not merely a question of rising expectations. For many people their quality of life, measured on virtually any scale, has worsened. So what has been the outcome of all this charitable effort? As a sector we have no cause for complacency and perhaps some for shame.

Perhaps we charity workers are using the wrong concepts. Marketing, strategic planning, monitoring and evaluation; professionalisation; business planning; quality assurance - perhaps we should have been looking at the old biblical synonyms of charity - justice and righteousness? Those concepts would perhaps inject a sense of urgency into our work, and keep the end users in sight. The trouble with 'marketing' as a method is that we begin to see people for what we can get out of them, and in the charity context this means too much attention is concentrated on the potential donor and too little on the needy recipient.

Use of the jargon of the business school has been very excluding. It cows people, making them feel ill-informed, and unable to challenge even the silliest schemes. To counteract this well-observed phenomenon, the grant giving charities have even come up with training programmes to teach would-be applicants, often those actually caring for the beneficiaries, how to use the jargon. They describe with pride their teaching a local community worker how to draw up a marketing plan or a 3-year business plan. They never question whether their money and the time of that community worker could be better spent. They argue that these skills are needed. By and for whom? Teaching charity workers marketing skills provides work and income for those providing the training; it does not necessarily benefit any poor or disadvantaged person.

Because the world is so evidently unjust, and the condition of most of its inhabitants so pitiful, perhaps we turn away from the large issues of justice and righteousness, and provide ourselves with manageable activity, like preparing marketing plans. Perhaps it is too painful to any but the most lax conscience to look at our fellow men except as buyers and sellers.

Hilary Blume
of Charities Advisory Trust

Turn the pages to find:

Computer services - 157
Conference/Exhibition Facilities - 157
Design & Print Services - 158
Direct Mail Services - 158
Financial Services - 159
Fundraising Consultants - 159-160

Information Providers - 160
Internet Services - 161
Legal Advisers - 161
Management Services - 162
Promotional Goods - 162
Publications - 163

WHO'S WHO IN THE VOLUNTARY SECTOR - XVIII

GLOSSARY OF ABBREVIATIONS

Accts	- Accountants/Accounts	Inst	- Institute/Institution
Addits	- Additional Information	Int/Internat	- International
Adv	- Advisor/Advisory	Jnl	- Journal
Brd/Bd	- Board	LA	- Local Authority
Brit	- British	LB	- London Borough
Bus	- Business	Leg	- Legislation
Chair	- Chairman/Chairwoman	Mbr	- Member
Cmty	- Community	Mngmt	- Management
Cncl	- Council	Nat	- National
Co-Chair	- Co-Chairman/woman	Org	- Organization
Commr	- Commissioner	PO	- Probation Officer
Con	- Conservation	Pres	- President
Cttee	- Committee	Prog	- Programme
Devmt	- Development	Pty	- Party
Disab	- Disabled	Res	- Research
Env	- Environment	Serv	- Service
Equit	- Equitable	Soc	- Social
Fed	- Federation	Sch	- School
Fndtn/Fdn	- Foundation	Sols	- Solicitors
Gall	- Gallery	Stud	- Studies/Study
Gp	- Group	Tres	- Treasurer
HA	- Housing Association	Trng	- Training
Ind	- Industrial	Trnr	- Trainer
Indep/Ind	- Independent	VP	- Vice President

SAMPLE ENTRY:

INDIVIDUAL Name of Job Title **NAME OF ORGANISATION** SUBJECT OF ORGANIZATION Type: Activity Undertaken. Address and Telephone/Fax details. **Expertise** This lists the individuals's particular specialisation (administration, child care, counselling, etc.) **Prev Posts** Listing of the last 2-3 posts held; also any posts running concurrently. **Prof Background** Relevant educational training and qualifications. **Awards/Research** Awards received (OBE, etc); Major publications or general areas of research undertaken. **Pres Committees** Current list of main committees, boards and trusteeships **Past Committees** Listing of most important committees and boards previously attended. **Media Experience** Level of media activity and co-operation including any specific regular broadcasts or press contributions. **Addits** Any additional information of relevance to the career of the individual.

WHO'S WHO IN THE VOLUNTARY SECTOR 1997

AARONSON Michael Director General **SAVE THE CHILDREN FUND, THE** CHILDREN/YOUTH Type: Fundraiser; Service provider; Development organization. Mary Datchelor House, 17 Grove Lane, Camberwell, London SE5 8RD Tel:0171-703 5400 Fax:0171-793 7466.

ABEL Christine Chief Executive **BROOK HOSPITAL FOR ANIMALS** ANIMAL Type: Service provider. Broadmead House, 21 Panton St, London SW1Y 4DR Tel:0171-930 0210 Fax:0171-930 2386 **Expertise** Third world development; management; programme and project design. **Prev Posts** World Bank 1973-86; PAT Group International 1986-89; Field Director, Save the Children Fund - Nepal 1989-91, Sri Lanka 1991-94. **Prof Background** MSc Administration; BA Modern Languages; Diplome Superieur des Etudes Francaises. **Pres Committees** Advisory Director, WSPA; Secretary, Friends of St Mary's.

ABRAHAM Dr Peter Executive Director **MEDICAL COUNCIL ON ALCOHOLISM** MEDICAL/HEALTH Type: Service provider. 3 St Andrews Place, London NW1 4LB Tel:0171-487 4445 Fax:0171-935 4479 **Expertise** Psychiatry; Clinical Neurophysiology. **Prev Posts** Consultant at Addiction Unit 1992-93; Medical Council on Alcoholism 1992-today. **Prof Background** Psychiatry; Encephalography. **Awards/Research** Officer Brother of the Order of St John of Jerusalem; Research/articles: Electroencephalography; Schizophrenia; Sleep loss. Jt chapter of textbook. **Pres Committees** Management Committee, Journal of the Royal Army Medical Corps; Medical Advisory Cttee, Brit Members Cncl of the World Veterans Federation; Medical Committee, Alcohol Concern. **Media Experience** Occasional broadcasts and interviews.

ADAMS C.S. Chief Executive **HYDE HOUSING ASSOCIATION** SOCIAL Type: Service provider; Grant maker; Campaigning. Leegate House, Burnt Ash Rd, London SE12 8RR Tel:0181-297 1500 Fax:0181-297 3878 **Expertise** Housing; care; job creation. **Prev Posts** Regional Director, Housing Corporation 1990-93. **Prof Background** Architect. **Pres Committees** Hyde Charitable Trust; Hyde Pension Fund. **Media Experience** Various radio/press/TV interviews. **Addits** School Governor 1986-92.

ADAMS John Director **LANGLEY HOUSE TRUST** SOCIAL Type: Service provider. 46 Market Square, Witney, Oxon OX8 6AL Tel:01993-774075 Fax:01993-772425 **Expertise** Offenders; justice issues; housing; mental health; substance misuse. **Prev Posts** Probation service manager 1983-93. **Prof Background** CQSW. **Awards/Research** Organizations and Negotiation in the Probation Service, Bristol Univ unpub, 1987; regular articles in Church press and jnls. **Media Experience** Radio & TV feature progs, news, current affairs, phone-ins.

ADAMSON Hugh Secretary General/Director **NATIONAL SPIRITUAL ASSEMBLY OF THE BAHAIS OF THE UK** RELIGIOUS 27 Rutland Gate, London SW7 1PD Tel:0171-584 2566 Fax:0171-584 9402 **Expertise** General management/administration; public relations. **Prev Posts** Chairman/MD, Continental Can UK Ltd 1980-84; Chairman/MD, Adamson Business Microsystems Ltd 1984-86. **Prof Background** BA; MA (History and Philosophy Comparative Religion); MBA (Finance and Management); Fellow: Institute of Directors; Institute of Management. **Pres Committees** Dir, Int Inst for Healing of Racism; Chair:Assoc for Bahai Studies, English Speaking Europe; Exec Cttee Bahai Publ Trust; Vice Chair, World Congress of Faiths; Hon Vice Pres, United Nations Assoc. **Media Experience** Broadcasts inc: BBC Wld Service; Prayer for the Day; various TV appearances. **Addits** Patron, Wld Conf for Religions of Peace; Mbr, Exec Cttee Wyndham Place Trust.

ADEBOWALE Victor O. Chief Executive **CENTREPOINT** SOCIAL Type: Service provider. Bewlay House, 2 Swallow Place, London W1R 7AA Tel:0171-629 2229 Fax:0171-409 2027 **Expertise** Management; housing. **Prev Posts** Regional Dir, Ujima Housing Assoc; Permanent Property Co-ord, Patchwork HA; Area Housing Manager, LB Newham; Dir, Alcohol Recovery Project 1990-94. **Prof Background** Henley Management Courses. **Pres Committees** Chair, SITRA; Exec Cttee, ACENVO; Alcohol Concern; Phoenix HA; Frontline Housing Advice; Nat Fed of Housing Assocs, Housing Care & Support Sub-Cttee. **Media Experience** Interviews on BBC Radios 1 & 4; ITN TV; National print & broadcasting.

AL QADHI Samia Director **BREAST CANCER CARE** MEDICAL/HEALTH Type: Service provider. Kiln House, 210 New Kings Road, London SW6 4NZ

WHO'S WHO IN THE VOLUNTARY SECTOR - 2

Tel:0171-384 2984 Fax:0171-384 3387 **Prev Posts** Admin Manager, Riverside Health Promotion Service 1986-1987; Head of Centre Support Services, London Lighthouse 1987-1994. **Prof Background** MSc. Management Development and Social Responsibility, University of Bristol; Dip. Counselling Skills - University of London; BA (Hons) History - University of Sussex. **Awards/Research** Auth: Managing Death & Bereavement: a framework for caring organisations, Policy Innovations, Policy Press 1996.

ALDERSON Lawrence Director **RARE BREEDS SURVIVAL TRUST - RBST** ANIMAL/WILDLIFE Type: Service provider. National Agricultural Centre, Kenilworth, Warwickshire CV8 2LG Tel:01203-696551 **Expertise** Animal breeding; genetic conservation programmes. **Prev Posts** Technical Consultant, RBST 1973-90. **Prof Background** MA, Cambridge University; Post-grad. Genetics and Education. **Awards/Research** Auth: The Chance to Survive; Ed Vol 1, Co-Ed Vol 2: Genetic Conservation of Domestic Livestock; several other books, papers and articles. **Pres Committees** Chair: Countrywide Livestock Ltd; Rare Breeds International. Member: Global Animal Data Bank Cttee. **Past Committees** Director, PSB Ltd; Chair, Combined Flock Book. **Media Experience** Frequent participant.

ALEXANDER-PASSE Anita Director **BRITISH FRIENDS OF RAMBAM MEDICAL CENTRE** MEDICAL/HEALTH Type: Fundraising. 34-36 Maddox St, London W1R 9PD Tel:0171-495 8849 Fax:0171-495 8859 **Expertise** Fundraising, public speaking. **Prev Posts** Operation Wheelchairs Committee, Chairman (Concurrent). **Pres Committees** Chairman, Operation Wheelchairs Committee. **Past Committees** Board of Deputies of British Jews; National Chairman - Na'Amat/Pioneer Women.

ALKER Doug Chief Executive **ROYAL NATIONAL INSTITUTE FOR DEAF PEOPLE - RNID** DISABILITY Type: Fundraiser; Service provider. 19-23 Featherstone Street, London EC1Y 8SL Tel:0171-296 8000 Fax:0171-296 8199 **Prev Posts** RNID: Director of Community Services 1982-90, Director of Research & Development 1990-94. **Prof Background** MBA; BSc Mathematics; First elected Deaf Trade Union Official in Britain. Hon Degree, University of Lancaster **Pres Committees** RNID Committees; Board of Trustees; Finance; Policy and Research; External Relations; Human Resources; Services; East Lancashire Deaf Society. **Media Experience** Channel 4, People's Parliament, 1994; BBC, See Hear.

ALLATT C.S. Honorary Secretary **SCHOOLS' ASSOCIATION FOOTBALL INTERNATIONAL BOARD** CHILDREN/YOUTH Type: Fundraiser; Service provider; Professional Association. 1 Croxall Drive, The Green, Shustoke, Warks B46 2BH Tel:01675-481175 Fax:01675-481175 **Expertise** Physical Education; School Administration; Football Administration. **Prev Posts** Headmaster, Holte School, Birmingham 1978-81; Headmaster, George Dixon School, Birmingham 1981-85; General Secretary, English School Football Association 1985-91. **Prof Background** St Peter's College; Birmingham Carnegie College, Leeds; Birmingham University. **Pres Committees** Trustee, St Peter's Urban Village Trust, Birmingham; St Peter's College, Old Salts Association. **Media Experience** Series of broadcasts for the World Service, on the laws of Association Football.

ALLEN Anthony Chief Executive **NATIONAL HOUSE BUILDING COUNCIL** SOCIAL Type: Service provider; Campaigning; Industry Association. Buildmark House, Chiltern Ave, Amersham, Bucks HP6 5AP Tel:01494-434477 Fax:01494-728521 **Expertise** New house building industry. **Prev Posts** Dept Town Clerk, LB of Southwark 1973-76; Chief Exec: LB of Hammersmith & Fulham 1976-86; Chief Exec, Berkshire CC 1986-93. **Prof Background** Solicitor LL.B (Hons) **Awards/Research** CBE. **Pres Committees** London Youth Games Ltd 1976-to date; BSI 1992-95. **Past Committees** Chaired: DISASTERS Working Party for Dept of Health 1989/90.

ALLEN Godfrey Chief Executive **APEX TRUST** SOCIAL Type: Service provider; Campaigning. St Alphage House, Wingate Annexe, 2 Fore Street, London EC2Y 5DA Tel:0171-638 5931 Fax:0171-638 5977 **Expertise** Urban policy; economic and organisational development. **Prev Posts** Race Equality Off, Ealing Race Equality Cncl 83-87; Fullemploy Training: Reg Mnger 87-89, Chief Exec 89-90;MD, OPP Int Ltd 90-93;Task Force Leader, Birmingham Task Force 93-95. **Prof Background** Magistrate; Mbr, British MENSA; Mbr, Institute of Directors. **Pres Committees** Chair, OPP Int Ltd; Governor, South Thames College Corporation. **Media Experience** Radio/TV/Press interviews.

ALLEN Graham S. Director **CHARITY FORUM** SOCIAL/TRAINING Type: Umbrella Organisation. Stovolds, 191 The Street, West Horsley, Surrey KT24 6HR Tel:01483-281 766 Fax:01483-281 767 **Expertise** Purchasing & Administration. **Prev Posts** Executive Officer, British Geriatrics Society, 1993-95; Senior Buyer, British-American Tobacco Co Ltd, 1985-93; Buyer, British-American Tobacco Co Ltd 1968-85. **Prof Background** Industrial Purchasing.

ALLEN Mrs Sibyl R. Administrator **SAINT MARTIN IN THE FIELDS CHRISTMAS APPEAL FUND** SOCIAL Type: Fundraiser; Grant maker; Trust. 6 St Martin's Place, London WC2N 4JJ Tel:0171-930 0089 Fax:0171-839 5163 **Expertise** Fundraising to assist those in need & administering funds. **Prev Posts** Church Secretary 1972-92. **Pres Committees** Christmas Appeal Fund.

ALLSOP Douglas T. Executive Director/Secretary **SCOTTISH COUNCIL ON ALCOHOL, THE - SCA** SOCIAL Type: Service provider. 2nd Floor, 166 Buchanan Street, Glasgow G1 2NH Tel:0141-333 9677 Fax:0141-333 1606 **Expertise** Finance and organizational structures. **Prev Posts** Scottish Regional Director, Slater and Walker Ltd 1972-76; Glasgow Cncl on Alcohol 1978. **Prof Background** Banking and finance. **Awards/Research** MBE 1991 for services to SCA. **Pres Committees** Board of Int Council on Alcohol and Addictions. **Past Committees** Min of Transport Drink, Driving Rehab Cttee; Min Of Ag/F/F, Unit Labelling Cttee; Scottish Health Education Co-ordinating Cttee. **Media Experience** Frequent participation in all media.

WHO'S WHO IN THE VOLUNTARY SECTOR - 3

ALLUM Cliff Director **SKILLSHARE AFRICA** SOCIAL Type: Service provider. 3 Belvoir Street, Leicester, Leics LE1 6SL Tel:0116-254 1862 Fax:0116-254 2614 **Expertise** Education, training, development, management, industrial relations. **Prev Posts** Education Wker, Coventry Trades Cncl Unemployed Worker Project 1983-86; Tyseley Training & Cmty Resource Centre: Cmty Development Officer 1986-87; Centre Director 1987-93. **Prof Background** BA (Hons) Econ/Politics, Univ of Kent; Univ of Warwick: MA and PhD, Industrial & Business Studies. **Awards/Research** Doctorate: Labour Process & Trade Union Organisation; Various publications on industrial relations, education, training and community development 1978-86. **Pres Committees** Chair, West Mercia District Workers Educational Association; MSF West Midlands Regional Council. **Past Committees** MSF Cttees: Nat Educ, W. Mids Reg Educ; TUC Cttees: Mids Reg Educ, Mids Reg Training; Coventry Trades Council. **Media Experience** Various radio/TV/video and press.

ALSTEAD Allan Chief Executive **SCOTTISH SPORTS COUNCIL** SPORTS/SOCIAL Type: Fundraiser; Service provider; Grant maker. Caledonia House, South Gyle, Edinburgh EH12 9DQ Tel:0131-317 7200 Fax:0131-317 7202 **Expertise** Sports administration. **Prev Posts** Commander 51 Highland Brigade, 1984-86; NATO Research Fellow, Edinburgh Univ 1986-87; NATO Reinforcement Co-Ordinator 1987-90. **Prof Background** Glasgow Academy; Royal Military Academy, Sandhurst; Royal Naval Staff College; Joint Services Staff College; University of Wales (M Phil). **Awards/Research** CBE. Ten in Ten? The Reinforcement of Europe for War; Deputy Lieut, City of Edinburgh. **Pres Committees** Gov, Moray Ho Inst; Trustee, King's Own Scot Bordrs; Pres, SSAFA Edin & Midlothian; Exec, Scot Cncl Devt & Ind; Dep Col, City of Edin Univ OTC; Mbr, Lowland TAVRA; Gov, Glasgow Acad. **Past Committees** NATO Executive Working Group; NATO Senior Logisticians Committee; Highlands TAVRA. **Media Experience** TV, radio interviews, press conferences & interviews with journalists. **Addits** Trustee, Seagull Trust.

AMPHLETT Sue Director **PARENTS AGAINST INJUSTICE - PAIN** FAMILIES/CHILDREN/YOUTH Type: Service provider; Infl childcare policy/practice; Info to media/public. 10 Water Lane, Bishop's Stortford, Herts CM23 2JZ Tel:01279-656564 Fax:01279-655220 **Prev Posts** Flight Lt, Princess Mary's Royal Air Force Nursing Service 1972-77; Snr Nursing Officer, Occupational Health 1977-80. **Prof Background** State Registered Nurse; Occupational Health Certificate. **Awards/Research** Auth: Working in Partnership (coping with an investigation of alleged abuse/neglect). Papers: The Parents' Dilemma; Strategic Management in Child Protection. **Pres Committees** Member of various national working parties; county forums; Trustee of National Council of Voluntary Child Care Organisations (NCVCCO). **Past Committees** Voice for the Child in Care (VCC). **Media Experience** Frequent - documentaries/news items/press conferences/articles/profiles. **Addits** Papers presented at nat/internat conferences; training.

ANDERSON Mrs J. Chairman **ARTHROGRYPOSIS GROUP - TAG** MEDICAL/HEALTH Type: Support Group. 1 The Oaks, Gillingham, Dorset SP8 4SW Tel:01747-822655 Fax:01747-822655 **Expertise** Organization of research programme; putting the group on a more professional standing. **Prev Posts** TAG: Research Sec 1983-91; Vice Chair 1991-92. **Prof Background** B Ed (Hons); Teacher. **Media Experience** Interviews: BBC for Children in Need 1989; BBC Bristol West/Bristol Radio 1993.

APPLEBY Eric Director **ALCOHOL CONCERN** MEDICAL/HEALTH Type: Grant maker; National umbrella body. Waterbridge House, 32-36 Loman St, London SE1 0EE Tel:0171-928 7377 Fax:0171-928 4644 **Prev Posts** Nat Organizer, Nat Fed of Vol Literacy Schemes 1979-88; Div Dir, Services and Professional Education, Alcohol Concern 1988-90. **Prof Background** BA (Hons) Modern and Mediaeval Languages, Cambridge Univ. **Pres Committees** Mental Health Foundation: Community Services Development Committee (grant giving). **Past Committees** Adult Literacy and Basic Skills Unit Mngmnt Cttee 1980-88; Chr, MHF Expert Wkng Gp on Persistent Street Drinkers. **Media Experience** Regular news and current affairs pieces on radio and TV. **Addits** Past Cttee: Royal Coll of Phys: Alcohol & Young People.

APPLETON Martin Director General **KING GEORGE'S FUND FOR SAILORS** SOCIAL Type: Fundraiser; Grant maker. 8 Hatherley Street, London SW1P 2YY Tel:0171-932 0000 Fax:0171-932 0095 **Expertise** Financial and administrative management. **Prev Posts** Royal Navy, 1957-93; Commodore in Command, HMS Centurion, 1991-93; Dir of Appts (WRNS & Supply), MOD, 1988-91; Chf Staff Off (Prsnnl & Logistics) to Submarine Command 1986-88. **Prof Background** Graduation BRNC Dartmouth 1959, Commissioned into Supply & Secretariat specialisation Royal Navy. **Pres Committees** Director, Merchant Navy Welf Bd; Officer's Assoc, Trustee; Annual Seafarers Service St Paul's, Trustee; Confed Brit Service & Ex-Service Orgs, Exec Cncl Mbr; John Cornwell VC Nat Memorial, Trustee.

ARCHER Susan Registrar **HAEMOPHILIA SOCIETY** MEDICAL/HEALTH Type: Service provider. 123 Westminster Bridge Rd, London SE1 7HR Tel:0171-928 2020 Fax:0171-620 1416 **Expertise** Financial management; personnel management; company secretary. **Prev Posts** Administrator, Oak Foundation (UK) Ltd 1988-89; Administrator, AIDS Prevention Unit, IPPF 1989-91. **Prof Background** BSc (Hons) Environmental Sciences; Part-completed MA - Management Development in Voluntary & Community Organisations. **Awards/Research** Part-complete research study into the impact of HIV on the management of voluntary organizations.

ARMITAGE Eric D Group Chief Executive **NORTH BRITISH HOUSING ASSOCIATION** SOCIAL Type: Service provider. 4 The Pavilions, Portway, Preston, Lancs PR2 2YB Tel:01772-897200 Fax:01772-202436 **Prev Posts** Financial Controller, NBHA 1973-83. **Prof Background** Chartered Accountant. **Awards/Research** OBE. **Pres Committees** Member, Social Housing Agency Ltd. **Past Committees** Chair:Nat Fed of HAs;HAs Consult/Adv Serv;Fndr Mbr: NFHA Finance Wkng Gp.

WHO'S WHO IN THE VOLUNTARY SECTOR - 4

ARMSON Simon Chief Executive **SAMARITANS, THE** SOCIAL Type: Service provider. 10 The Grove, Slough SL1 1QP Tel:01753-532713 Fax:01753-819004 **Expertise** Overall management of the organization. **Prev Posts** Deputy District Administrator, Milton Keynes Health Authority 1982-84; Asst General Sec. Samaritans, 1984-90 **Prof Background** Denstone College. **Awards/Research** Fellow, Royal Society of Arts 1993; Companion, Institute of Management 1995. **Pres Committees** Council of Childline; Chair, Telephone Helplines Group. **Past Committees** Chair, Telephone Helplines Group: 1993-1996. **Media Experience** Contributor to numerous radio/TV programmes; frequent press articles.

ARMSTRONG George Chief Executive **ACTION FOR M.E.** MEDICAL/HEALTH Type: Service provider; Campaigning charity. PO Box 1302, Wells, Somerset BA5 2WE Tel:01749-670799 Fax:01749-672561.

ASH Ms. J. Director **SOUTHAMPTON COUNCIL OF COMMUNITY SERVICE** SOCIAL Type: Local development agency/umbrella organisation. 18 Oxford Street, Southampton, Hants SO14 3DJ Tel:01703-228291 Fax:01703-222929 **Expertise** State policy, voluntary sector, management, development, housing & social care. **Prev Posts** Chief Officer, Eastleigh Council of Community Service 1980-84; Consultancy 1985-89; Co-ordinator, Resettlement Unit Replacement Implementation Group 1989-92. **Prof Background** MA, State Policy & Social Change; BA (Hons) Social Studies; CCETSW Accredited Practice Teacher for Social Work. **Awards/Research** Contributor to Priority Setting in Action (Redcliffe Medical Press); Research into Young Homelessness; Women & Homelessness & Advice Service for Disabled People. **Pres Committees** Hyde Housing Association; Society of St Dismas.

ASHBROOK Kate General Secretary **OPEN SPACES SOCIETY** CONSERVATION/ENVIRONMENT Type: Service provider. 25a Bell Street, Henley-on-Thames, Oxon RG9 2BA Tel:01491-573535 **Prev Posts** Hon Secretary, Dartmoor Preservation Association 1981-84. **Prof Background** BSc (Hons) Biology, Exeter University. **Awards/Research** Auth: Our Common Right,1987; Commonplace No More, 1983; Contrib: Walks of South East England, 1975; Severnside, A Guide to Family Walks, 1976; Res. Ramblers' Assoc pamphlet. **Pres Committees** Chairman, Ramblers' Assoc; Exec Cttee, Cncl for National Parks; Chairman, Central Rights of Way Cttee. **Past Committees** Common Land Forum; Open Spaces Society Cttee. **Media Experience** Regular press releases; radio/TV interviews; articles in The Countryman. **Addits** Editor of Open Space since 1984.

ASHBY Robert Executive Director **BRITISH HUMANIST ASSOCIATION** SOCIAL Type: Service provider. 47 Theobalds Rd, London WC1X 8SP Tel:0171-430 0908 Fax:0171-430 0908 **Expertise** General charity management, policy and media. **Prev Posts** Public Affairs Officer, National Deaf Children's Society 1988-93; Coordinator, Sainsbury Management Fellows & Consultant, Gatsby Charitable Foundation 1993-95. **Prof Background** BSc Hons. (Chemistry), Durham; FRSA. **Awards/Research** Articles on belief and theology, 'glue ear', and child safety. **Pres Committees** Director, Pemberton Publishing Company Ltd; British Digestive Foundation Publishing Committee; Centre for Critical Studies Programme Committee, Westminster College, Oxford. **Past Committees** Commission of Enquiry into Human Aids to Communication (1991). **Media Experience** News broadcasts TV/radio; Talk UK phone-in shows; religious programmes. **Addits** Consultant to 3 production companies; many press features.

ASHCROFT Michael Chairman **NATIONAL ASSOCIATION FOR PATIENT PARTICIPATION - NAPP** MEDICAL/HEALTH Type: Campaigning. PO Box 999 Nuneaton CV11 6ZS Tel:01203-641331 **Expertise** Promoting Patient Participation Groups/Self help groups in primary health care. **Prev Posts** President Nuneaton Round Table 1994-95; Press & public relations officer, Children's Care Campaign since 1993. **Pres Committees** Steering committee Patients Forum; Governors Forum (Warwickshire Schools). **Media Experience** Several appearances on TV/Radio; numerous interviews in press.

ASHTON Pauline Executive Director **GUIDE ASSOCIATION SCOTLAND** CHILDREN/YOUTH Type: Educational youth work. 16 Coates Crescent, Edinburgh EH3 7AH Tel:0131-226 4511 Fax:0131-220 4828 **Expertise** Adult education and management. **Prev Posts** Teacher, Newcastle-upon-Tyne 1984-86; Training Manager, Girl Guides Association 1984-89. **Prof Background** B.Ed; Girl Guides Assoc Training Licence. **Pres Committees** Community Education, Validation and Endorsement (CeVe) Cttee of the Scottish Community Education Council.

ASTON Anthony Director Community Services Division **ROYAL NATIONAL INSTITUTE FOR THE BLIND - RNIB** DISABILITY Type: Fundraiser; Service provider; Grant maker. 224 Great Portland Street, London W1N 6AA Tel:0171-388 1266 Fax:0171-388 2034 **Expertise** Vocational, residential, holiday, health, community services;vol agencies for blind/part sighted people. **Prev Posts** Extensive career with RNIB. **Prof Background** Engineering background; vocational services and management training; FIMgt. **Awards/Research** OBE. **Pres Committees** Chairman, European Blind Union Rehab Commission; DPTAC; World Blind Union Cttee on Rehabilitation and Employment; Jnt Cttee, Mobility of Blind & Partially Sighted People. **Past Committees** Prince of Wales' Advisory Group. **Media Experience** Radio/press experience. **Addits** Envir issues affecting/improving overseas servs for the visually impaired.

ATHERTON Mr J.K. Hon. Secretary **BRITISH CARTOGRAPHIC SOCIETY** CONSERVATION/ENVIRONMENT Type: Learned Society. c/o Royal Geographical Society, 1 Kensington Gore, London SW7 2AR Tel:01703-781519 Fax:01703-781519 **Awards/Research** Auth: The Cartographic Journal (bi-annl); Directory of Freelance Cartographers; Directory of UK Map Collections.

ATKINSON Jane Director **LADY HOARE TRUST FOR PHYSICALLY DISABLED CHILDREN** DISABILITY Type: Service provider. 4th Floor, Mitre House, 44-6 Fleet Street, London EC4Y 1BN Tel:0171-583 1951

WHO'S WHO IN THE VOLUNTARY SECTOR - 5

B

Fax:0171-583 1391 **Prev Posts** Gen Sec, Pre-school Playgroups Assoc 1976-85. Co-ordinator: ICA Campaign 1985-86; National Rubella Cncl 1987-88; Caring Costs 1989-91. **Prof Background** Administration background and training; BA (Hons) Open Univ.

ATKINSON Geoffrey C. Director **BEN-MOTOR AND ALLIED TRADES BENEVOLENT FUND** SOCIAL Type: Fundraiser; Service provider; Industrial/professional benevolent fund. Lynwood, Sunninghill, Ascot, Berkshire SL5 0AJ Tel:01344-20191 Fax:01344-22042 **Expertise** Industrial and related fundraising; PR; residential and nursing care management. **Prev Posts** Director, Petrol Retailers' Assoc 1970-78. **Awards/Research** Articles in care and industrial jnls. **Pres Committees** Chairman, OBFA (Occupat Benev Funds Allnce); VOICES (Vol Orgs Involved in Caring for the Elderly Sector). **Media Experience** Extensive participation.

ATTENBOROUGH Jane Director **DANCE UK** SOCIAL Type: Service provider; Campaigning; Professional Body. 23 Crisp Road, London W6 9RL Tel:0181-741 1932 Fax:0181-748 0186 **Awards/Research** Dance UK News, Quarterly News Letter; Handbook for Dance Floors; Look Before You Leap; (all Dance UK Publs). **Pres Committees** Mngmt Liaison Gp (Small/middle scale dance Co Managers); Nat Dance Co-ord Cttee; Nat Campaign Co-ord Cttee (Large scale dance Co Managers); Nat Campaign for the Arts Cncl; Cncl for Dance Educ & Training.

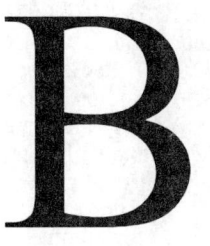

BAGNALL Pippa Director **QUEEN'S NURSING INSTITUTE** MEDICAL/HEALTH Type: Professional body. 3 Albemarle Way, London EC1V 4JB Tel:0171-490 4227 Fax:0171-490 1269 **Expertise** Nursing. **Prev Posts** Riverside Health Authority, Professional Head of School Nursing 1990-91; Neighbourhood Nurse Manager 1991-92. **Prof Background** RN; BA Psychology; currently undertaking an MHM. **Awards/Research** Numerous articles published; consultant editor British Journal of Community Health Nursing; research undertaken for QNI and Dept of Health. **Pres Committees** Chairman, Jnt Cttee for Professional Nursing Midwifery & Health Visiting Assocs (England); Trustee & Mbr of Brd of Mngmnt, National Asthma Campaign; Trustee, Edith Cavell & Nation's Fund for Nurses. **Past Committees** Vice-Chair, HVA 1990-92. **Media Experience** Radio/TV & press experience.

BAGULEY Frank S. Honorary Secretary **NATIONAL CAVING ASSOCIATION - NCA** SOCIAL Type: Service provider; Conservation and Recreation. Monomark House, 29 Old Gloucester St, London WC1N 3XX Tel:01639-849519 **Expertise** Access and Conservation. **Prev Posts** Secretary: Cambrian Caving Council; Chairman: Outdoor Pursuits Group of the Welsh Sports Association (of the Sports Council for Wales) 1972-95. **Prof Background** Dental Surgeon. **Awards/Research** Monthly Newsletter & Annual Journal for Cambrian Caving Council (Wales). Sports Council for Wales, Sports Administrator of the Year. **Pres Committees** Welsh Sports Assoc: Exec Cttee; Chair, Outdoor Pursuit Gp; Brec Beacons NP Access Recr Gp; Wales Wildlife & Countryside Link; Wales Mntn Leadership Training Brd; C'side Cncl for Wales Access Forum. **Past Committees** Nature Conservancy Council Cave Management Committee.

BAILEY Gordon Chief Executive **SCHOOLS OUTREACH** CHILDREN/YOUTH Type: Fundraiser; Service provider. 10 High St, Bromsgrove, Worcs B61 8HQ Tel:01527-574404 Fax:01527-577803 **Expertise** Management, Recruitment, Training & Fundraising. **Prev Posts** Film Editor, ITV 1956-59; Commercial Manager 1959-62; School-based Pastoral Care Worker 1962-88. **Prof Background** BA (Hons). **Awards/Research** Contributor to: 7 books containing collections of writings 1971-89; Variety of educational & religious publications. **Media Experience** Regular part-time broadcaster on TV & radio over the past 24 years. **Addits** Lecturer & part-time trainer with ref to work with children & young people.

BAILLIE Kate General Secretary **BRITISH LEAGUE**

WHO'S WHO IN THE VOLUNTARY SECTOR - 6

AGAINST RHEUMATISM MEDICAL/HEALTH Type: Umbrella Group. 41 Eagle Street, London WC1R 4AR Tel:0171-242 3313 Fax:0171-242 3277 **Prev Posts** Currently: General Secretary, Brit Society for Rheumatology. **Prof Background** NHS Admin - graduate trainee. BA Russian & Soviet Studies; MA Philosophy and Healthcare. **Pres Committees** Trusteeships: Vice Sec Gen, Euro League Against Rheumatism, Social Leagues; Member, Open Section Council, Royal Soc of Medicine.

BAIN Prof George S. Principal **LONDON BUSINESS SCHOOL** SOCIAL/TRAINING Type: Service provider; Educational establishment. Sussex Place, Regent's Park, London NW1 4SA Tel:0171-262 5050 Fax:0171-724 3881 **Expertise** Industrial Relations; Trade Unions. **Prev Posts** Econ Lectr, Manitoba Univ 62-3; Res Fellow, Nuffield Coll, Oxford 66-9; Frank Thomas Prof Ind Rels, UMIST 69-70;Dep Dir/Dir, Warwick Univ 70-81;Chm Sch Ind & Bus Studies 83-89. **Prof Background** BA; MA; Univ of Manitoba; DPhil, Oxford Univ; Univ Lecturer in Economics/Ind Rels. Consultant to UK and Canada Governments on Industrial Relations; often arbitrator in ind disputes. **Awards/Research** Jt publ inc: Union Growth & The Business Cycle, 1976; Bibliography of Brit Ind Relations, 1979; Ind Relations in Britain, 1983. Numerous articles & contribs. **Pres Committees** Dir, Basil Blackwell; The Economist; Canada Life Assurance. **Past Committees** Nat Forum Mngmt Educ & Devlpmt; Dir, Amer Assembly Coll Schls of Business; Cncl,IMgt; Trustee/V Pres, Eur Fndtn for Mngmt Devlmnt. **Addits** Prev: Trustee/Vice Pres, Snr Salaries Revw Bdy; Int Cncl, Amer Mngmt Assoc.

BAINER Mrs Susan Director **JOINT EDUCATIONAL TRUST - JET** CHILDREN/YOUTH Type: Fundraiser; Grant maker. Clove Building, 4 Maguire Street, Butlers Wharf, London SE1 2NQ Tel:0171-378 1391 Fax:0171-403 0062 **Expertise** Personnel management; corporate fundraising. **Prev Posts** Restaurant Owner 1967-75; Housemistress, St James Girls School 1975-80; Asst to Dir-Gen, US Chamb of Commerce 1980-83; Pers Mngr: ENI Chem UK Ltd 1983-87, Savills Estates 1987-89. **Prof Background** Private High School 8 years; Open Univ, computers and company business training; IPD; Member of BIM, IPD and ICFM. **Pres Committees** Trustee, Island Health Trust, Isle of Dogs; Govnr, IoD Jnr Sch. **Media Experience** You and Yours, 1992.

BAINES Stephen Chief Executive **HOCKEY ASSOCIATION** SOCIAL Type: Service provider; Grant maker; Sport Governing Body. The Stadium, Silbury Boulevard, Milton Keynes, Bucks MK9 1HA Tel:01908-241100 Fax:01908-241106 **Expertise** International Sport; Sports Marketing; Development of Sports Facilities. **Prev Posts** Director of Marketing, National Association of Boys' Clubs, 1983-86; Sports Marketing Consultant (Canada), 1981-83; Executive Director, Canadian Rugby Union, 1975-81. **Prof Background** Certificate in Education, Avery Hill College 1969; BSc & MSc Recreation Administration, University of Oregon, 1973-75. **Awards/Research** Presented a number of papers at International Sports Conferences; Frequent contributor of articles to publications. **Pres Committees** Secretary & Trustee, National Hockey Foundation; Secretary, Hockey Association Youth Trust; Vice Chairman, British Institute of Sports Administration. **Media Experience** Given a number of interviews on Radio and Television. **Addits** Mbr, Advisory Group to the British Sports Council on Int Affairs.

BAIRD Anthony Director **INSTITUTE FOR COMPLEMENTARY MEDICINE** MEDICAL/HEALTH Type: Fundraiser; Service provider. PO Box 194, London SE16 1QZ Tel:0171-237 5165 Fax:0171-237 5175 **Expertise** Administration 1982-today. **Past Committees** District Council for 17 years; Community Health Council for 8 years. **Media Experience** Extensive.

BAIRD Nicola Director **FOREST MANAGEMENT FOUNDATION - FMF** CONSERVATION/ENVIRONMENT Type: Fundraiser. 47c Aubert Park, London N5 1TR Tel:0171-359 7183 Fax:0171-359 7183 **Expertise** Environment, promoting small-scale, community forest projects; South Pacific; Development issues; Training **Prev Posts** Fundraiser for New Statesman & Society magazine, 1993. **Prof Background** BA Politics, University of York. **Awards/Research** Author: Setting Up & Running a School Library (Heinemann/VSO) 1994; 1995 David Thomas essay prize - Does free trade threaten the environment? - Run by Financial Times. **Pres Committees** Member of Forest Stewardship Council's press & publicity, UK working group. **Past Committees** Media Association of Solomon Islands (MASI) (1990-92). **Media Experience** Print Journalist.

BAISDEN Carole Chief Executive **PARENTLINE** CHILDREN/YOUTH Type: Telephone counselling. Endway House, Endway, Hadleigh, Benfleet, Essex SS7 2AN Tel:01702-554782 Fax:01702-554911 **Expertise** Staff management; fundraising support for membership; management of national charity. **Prev Posts** Personal Assistant to Managing Director 1980-87. **Prof Background** Personnel; administration. **Past Committees** Parentline Board of Trustees. **Media Experience** Radio, TV and press participation.

BAKER Alan H. Clerk to the Trustees **QUEEN MARY'S ROEHAMPTON TRUST** MEDICAL/HEALTH Type: Grant maker. 13 St George's Road, Wallington, Surrey SM6 0AS Tel:0181-395 9980 Fax:0181-395 9980 **Expertise** Services & benefits for the war disabled and war widows. **Prev Posts** Head, War Pensions Policy, DSS 1990-92. **Prof Background** Civil Servant, DSS 1959-92. **Pres Committees** Trustee, Leopardstown Park Hospital Trust (Dublin); Trustee, Far East Prisoners of War Association.

BAKER Jenny Group Co-ordinator **NORTHERN CONCORD** SOCIAL Type: Service provider. P.O. Box 258, Manchester M60 1LN **Expertise** Helping transvestites & transsexuals & their families (for the last 10 years). **Awards/Research** Cross Talk Magazine. **Pres Committees** Trustee, The Beaumont Trust. **Media Experience** Experience in radio, press & TV.

BALDERSTONE David President **ADVENTIST BUSINESS & PROFESSIONALS ASSOCIATION** SOCIAL Type: Professional Association. BUC Offices, Stanborough Park, St Albans Road, Watford, Herts Tel:01923-675009 **Expertise** Driving trucks to Sarajevo.

Prev Posts Transport Manager for charity ADRA (UK) 1992-93; Vice President, ABPA 1993-95. **Prof Background** Landscape Gardening. **Awards/Research** ADRA (UK) for Humanitarian Aid. **Pres Committees** Chair, Garston Gardens (Watford) Ltd; Dir, Isoma Process Engineers (UK) Ltd; Eurobeat Services Ltd; Transport Manager, ADRA (UK). **Media Experience** Radio/Press.

BALDWIN Clarissa Chief Executive Officer **NATIONAL CANINE DEFENCE LEAGUE - NCDL** ANIMAL/WILDLIFE Type: Fundraiser; Service provider. 17 Wakley Street, London EC1V 7LT Tel:0171-837 0006 Fax:0171-833 2701 **Expertise** PR; journalism. **Prev Posts** With NCDL since 1974. **Prof Background** St Agnes and St Michaels School, East Grinstead; held posts in Cambridge Press, Evening Standard and in PR for three years. **Pres Committees** Cttee and Brd, Hearing Dogs for the Deaf; Assoc of Brit Dogs Homes; Pet Advsry Cttee; Trustee, Pet Plan Charit Trust; Adv Dir, World Soc for the Protection of Animals; Secrtrt, Dangr Dogs Act Rfm Gp. **Media Experience** All forms of media on many occasions. **Addits** Judge:Veterinary Nurse of the Year Awds; Bounce Superdogs; Westminster Dog of the Year.

BALFOUR Doug General Director **TEAR FUND** SOCIAL Type: Fundraiser; Service provider; Grant maker; Overseas. 100 Church Rd, Teddington, Middx TW11 8QE Tel:0181-977 9144 Fax:0181-977-9144 **Expertise** Relief & Development Agency. **Prev Posts** Relief Director, MedAir 1991-92; Commercial Manager, Lucas 1992-95. **Prof Background** BSc (Hons) Geology; MBA.

BALL Dr Chris Voluntary Sector National Secretary **MSF - THE UNION FOR SKILLED AND PROFESSIONAL PEOPLE** SOCIAL Type: Trade Union. MSF Centre, 33-37 Moreland Street, London EC1V 8BB Tel:0171-505 3054 Fax:0171-505 3282 **Expertise** Personnel management; Industrial relations and employment matters. **Prev Posts** Divisional Officer, Assoc of Scientific Technical and Managerial Staffs 1979-88; Snr Advisor, Greater London Enterprise Board 1983-85; London Regional Officer, MSF 1988-93. **Prof Background** Teacher/Lecturer; Doctorate from London School of Economics, Department of Industrial Relations. **Awards/Research** Research on employment law; employment issues. Fmr Ed, MSF's Vol Sect Newsltr; Curr Ed Common Ground, Vol Sec Mag. Publ: Articles, pamphs, eg Trade Unions and Eql Opps Employers. **Media Experience** Contrib: The Guardian, The Independent and Community Care; TV and Radio.

BALL Graham Director **SOUTH WEST HERTS HOSPICE CHARITABLE TRUST (THE PEACE HOSPICE)** MEDICAL/HEALTH Type: Service provider; Information/support charity providing hospice care. The Peace Hospice, Cassiobury Drive, Watford, Herts WD1 3AD Tel:01923-221109 **Expertise** Patient Empowerment, strategic planning. **Prev Posts** Deputy Director: National Eczema Society 1992-95; The MSD Foundation 1988-92. **Awards/Research** Main articles on patient needs and evaluation techniques.

BALL Maria Director **ASSOCIATION FOR RESEARCH IN THE VOLUNTARY AND COMMUNITY SECTOR - ARVAC** SOCIAL Type: Information provider. 60 Highbury Grove, London N5 2AG Tel:0171-704 2315 Fax:0171-704 2315.

BALL Patricia A.L. General Secretary **ALLIANCE OF PARENTS & SCHOOLS** CHILDREN/YOUTH Type: Fundraiser; Service provider; Campaigning. 91 Saffron Close, Wootton Bassett, Wiltshire SN4 7JD Tel:01793-848435 Fax:01793-848442 **Expertise** Help, advice & support for parents/PTA's and Home School Associations. **Prof Background** Sales & Marketing Manager for Management Consultants; educated in Ryde, Isle of Wight. **Pres Committees** National Association for Small Schools; Wiltshire Education & Business Partnership. **Past Committees** Trustee, National Confederation of PTA's; Trustee, Wiltshire Federation of PTA's. **Media Experience** Radio & Press.

BANTON Sue Director and General Secretary **NATIONAL ASSOCIATION FOR CHILDREN WITH LOWER LIMB ABNORMALITIES - STEPS** MEDICAL/HEALTH Type: Fundraiser; Service provider. 15 Statham Close, Lymm, Cheshire WA13 9NN Tel:01925-757525 **Expertise** Children and family health issues **Prev Posts** Hospital play specialist; teacher. **Prof Background** Diploma Art and Design; Post Graduate Certificate in Education; Hospital Play Specialist Certificate; Business Enterprise Certificate (Salford School of Business). **Awards/Research** Whitbread Community Care Award 1987; Guardian Jerwood Award; 1994; editor of STEPS Publications. **Pres Committees** Steering Committee; Medical Research Council Hip Trial; Trustee, Manchester & District Transport for Sick Children. **Past Committees** Chair, Publications Committee, National Association of Hospital Play Staff. **Media Experience** Interviews: Woman's Hour & local radio; Action for Sick Children (NAWCH) video. **Addits** Founder of STEPS.

BARCHARD Betty Secretary **LEAGUE OF REMEMBRANCE** SOCIAL Type: Fundraiser; Service provider. 55 Great Ormond Street, London WC1N 3HZ Tel:0171-242 5660 **Prev Posts** Senior Nursing Officer, Sheffield Children's Hospital 1969-74; Chief Nursing Officer, Hospital for Sick Children, Gt Ormond St 1975-94. **Prof Background** RGN, RSCN. **Awards/Research** OBE. **Pres Committees** The League of Friends, Gt Ormond St. **Past Committees** Board of Governors, The Hosp for Sick Children; City & Hackney District Health Authority. **Media Experience** Minimal.

BARCUS Shona Director **SCOTTISH ASSOCIATION FOR MENTAL HEALTH** DISABILITY Type: Fundraiser; Service provider; Raising awareness; public education; campaigning. Atlantic House, 38 Gardner's Crescent, Edinburgh EH3 8DQ Tel:0131-229 9687 Fax:0131-229 3558

BARING Tessa (Teresa Anne) Commissioner **CHARITY COMMISSION** SOCIAL Type: Statutory Body. St Albans House, 57-60 Haymarket, London SW1Y 4QX Tel:0171-210 4425 Fax:0171-210 4604 **Expertise** General Voluntary Sector/Grant-giving Child Care. **Prev Posts** Chair, Barnardo's Council 1987-93; Director, St Michael's Fellowship 1981-87. **Prof Background** Sociologist. **Awards/Research** Parental Choice in Education. **Pres Committees** Nat Lottery Charities Brd;

WHO'S WHO IN THE VOLUNTARY SECTOR - 8

Assoc of Charitable Foundations; Council for Charitable Support; Barnardo's, Baring Foundation, St Michael's Fellowship; Adv Grp for NCVO. **Past Committees** Chair Deregulation Taskforce for the Voluntary Sector.

BARKER Adrian Director of Trading **NATIONAL DEAF-BLIND AND RUBELLA ASSOCIATION - SENSE** DISABILITY Type: Fundraiser; Service provider. Unit 2, Murray Business Centre, Murray Rd, Orpington, Kent BR5 3RE Tel:01689-827030 Fax:01689-821577 **Expertise** Charity Retailing; Trading activities in general. **Prev Posts** Shops Department, Spastics Society, Area Manager 1978-84; Regional Manager 1985-87. **Awards/Research** Articles in charity based magazines. **Past Committees** All internal shop based committees in Spastics Society; Charity Retailing Statistics Group; Charity Shops Group. **Media Experience** Numerous in past 16 years.

BARLOW Joy Senior Manager **ABERLOUR CHILD CARE TRUST** CHILDREN/YOUTH Type: Service provider. 36 Park Terrace, Stirling, Central, Scotland FK8 2JR Tel:01786-450335 Fax:01786-473238 **Expertise** Chemical dependency/addictive behaviour in women, effects upon their children; HIV/AIDS and families. **Prev Posts** Dept/Year Head, Beaconsfield High Schl, Bucks 1974-79; Drugs Project Off, Scottish Episcopal Church 1984-88; Devmt Off, Aberlour CCT 1987-88. **Prof Background** BA, Theology and Philosophy, London Univ; Cert of Ed; worked in education 1972-79, involved in issues of drug misuse/counselling/bereavement/loss; Mngmt training; training on the issues of HIV/AIDS. **Awards/Research** Auth: Grit and Diamonds - A Decade of Scottish Women; Women Talking About AIDS, 1990; Contrib: Women, HIV and Drugs- Practical Issues, 1990; Working with Women and AIDS, 1992. **Pres Committees** Adv Council, Misuse of Drugs Prevention Wking Grp; Adv Council, Misuse of Drugs; AIDS Prevention Co-ordinating Group for Scotland; Scottish Advisory Cttee on Drug Misuse. **Past Committees** Ministerial Task Force: on AIDS, Scott Off 91/92, on Drugs, Scott Off 94;Chair, Lothian AIDS Forum 89/91;Trustee, Nat AIDS Trust. **Media Experience** Frequent radio/TV news and press. TV inc. Heart of the Matter, 1992. **Addits** Presentations to nat/internat confs on HIV/Drug Misuse/Women and Children.

BARLOW Sue Director **COMMUNITY DESIGN FOR GWENT - CDG** CONSERVATION/ENVIRONMENT Type: Service provider; Community Technical Aid. Pill Box, Church Street, Newport, Gwent NP9 2BY Tel:01633-250271 Fax:01633-221985 **Prev Posts** Local Authority Architect 1978-79; Freelance Architect 1979-85. **Prof Background** BSc BArch, Welsh School of Architecture UWCC; Registered with Architects Registration Council of UK (ARCUK). **Awards/Research** Publ: Ideal Homes, 1992; Design Services for Community Action, 1994. **Pres Committees** Assessment Panel, RIBA Comnty Proj Fund; Exec Ctte, Gwent Assoc Vols Orgs; Gwent Gp, Prince of Wales Ctte; Gwent Environment Forum; Jt Wkg Pty, Torfaen BC; Policy Adv Gp, Wales Cncl of Vol Orgs. **Past Committees** Chair (1990-92), Board Mbr (1988-92), Assoc of Community Technical Aid Centres; Nat Womens Sub-Ctte - TASS Trade Union 1980-85. **Media Experience** Experience in radio interviews, press and a TV broadcast.

BARNES Rosie Chief Executive **CYSTIC FIBROSIS TRUST** MEDICAL/HEALTH Type: Fundraiser; Service provider; Grant maker. Alexandra House, Blyth Road, Bromley, Kent BR1 3RS Tel:0181-464 7211 Fax: 0181-313 0472 **Expertise** Market/image/policy research and interpretation; policy; dev and pres; rep spec int grps;PR priv lobbying. **Prev Posts** Trainee Mngr, Research Bureau Ltd, Unilever, 1967-9; Product Mngr, Yardley 1969-72; Teacher 1972-73; Mkt/Soc Researcher Corps/Charities; 1973-87; MP Greenwich SDP 1987-92; Director, Wellbeing 1992-96. **Prof Background** Bilborough Grammar School, Notts; BSocSc (Hist), Birmingham Univ 1967; SDP offices: Polit Sec; Chair, Ed Policy Dev Cttee (ILEA area). **Awards/Research** Lectures/debates on various political and social issues throughout UK. **Past Committees** Parl Cttees (Bills): Health and Medicines; Soc Security 1988-89; Maintenance Enforcement 1990-91; Child Support 1990-91. **Media Experience** All media inc Question Time; Any Questions; Woman's Hour; C4 Comment. **Addits** Initiated 2 Priv Mbrs Bills, inc Stillbirth Definition Act, now law.

BARNETT Paul College Secretary **ROYAL COLLEGE OF OBSTETRICIANS AND GYNAECOLOGISTS** MEDICAL/HEALTH Type: Fundraiser; Service provider; Grant maker; Professional Association. 27 Sussex Place, Regent's Park, London NW1 4RG Tel:0171-262 5425 Fax:0171-723 0575 **Expertise** Management and personnel. **Prev Posts** RCOG Examination Secretary 1974-76; RCOG Deputy College Secretary 1976-86. **Prof Background** Diploma in Management Studies. **Pres Committees** WellBeing: Council; Finance. RCOG: Trustee, Pension Scheme, all Committees/Council.

BARNETT Trisha Director **TOURISM CONCERN** ENVIRONMENT Type: Service provider; Membership organization. Southlands College, Wimbledon Parkside, London SW19 5NN Tel:0181-944 0464 Fax:0181-944 6583 **Expertise** Environmental and social impacts of Tourism, especially on third world destinations. **Awards/Research** Contrib: In Focus Magazine.

BARON Judith General Manager **BRITISH ASSOCIATION FOR COUNSELLING - BAC** SOCIAL Type: Umbrella organization. 1 Regent Place, Rugby, Warwickshire CV21 2PJ Tel:01788-550899 Fax:01788-562189 **Expertise** Counselling and assisted reproduction treatments **Prev Posts** Social Worker 1967-88; 1988 Regional/Training Mngr, (Midlands) Retirement Security Ltd 1989-91; Manager, British Epilepsy Assoc. **Prof Background** Social work; BA (Hons) Sociology; MSc (Oxon) Applied Social Studies; CQSW; BAC Fellow. **Awards/Research** Dissertation: Helping Infertile Couples; Contrib: Mental Health Casework, Manchester University Press. **Pres Committees** BAC Advertising Ltd, Director and Secretary; BAC Management Committee, Company Secretary. **Past Committees** BAC: past chair and board member since 1982. **Media Experience** Often for BAC and Counselling, formerly for British Epilepsy Assoc.

BARRELL John Chief Executive **INSTITUTION OF OCCUPATIONAL SAFETY & HEALTH** MED-

ICAL/HEALTH Type: Service provider. The Grange, Highfield Drive, Wigston, Leics LE18 1NN Tel:0116-257 1399 Fax:0116-257 1451 **Expertise** Company Law and Administration; Environmental Law. **Prev Posts** Commissioned Officer, Regular Army, 1956-78. **Prof Background** Chartered Secretary (FCIS); LLB. **Awards/Research** Environmental Law (various). Awards: OBE. Territorial Decoration (TD) for Service in Territorial Army. **Pres Committees** Executive Committee Member (Director), Royal Society for Prevention of Accidents; Chairman, IOSH Publishing Limited. **Past Committees** BSI Tech Cttee HS/I, Occ Health & Safety Mngmt; UK Steering Cttee, European Year of Safety & Health Protection at Work.

BARRIE David Director **NATIONAL ART COLLECTIONS FUND** CONSERVATION/ENVIRONMENT Type: Service provider. Millais House, 7 Cromwell Place, South Kensington, London SW7 2JN Tel:0171-225 4800 Fax:0171-225 4848 **Expertise** Work of John Ruskin. **Prev Posts** HM Diplomatic Service 1975-87; Cabinet Office 1988-89; Executive Director, Japan Festival 1991, 1989-92. **Prof Background** MA (Hons) Oxford, Philosophy and Experimental Psychology. **Awards/Research** Ed: Modern Painters, by John Ruskin; various articles and reviews. **Pres Committees** Director, Guild of St George (founded by John Ruskin). **Media Experience** Interviews given on radio, TV and press.

BARROW Valerie J. Secretary **ASSOCIATION OF CHARITY OFFICERS - ACO** SOCIAL Type: Umbrella body liaising with registered charities. Beechwood House, Wyllyots Close, Potters Bar, Herts EN6 2HN Tel:01707-651777 Fax:01707-651777 **Expertise** Health and social services; charity admin via member funds and their beneficiaries in all areas. **Prev Posts** Centre for Policy on Ageing (NCCOP) 1972-76; Principal Off LB Waltham Forest SS (Elderly People & Learning Disabilities) 1976-87; Hon Sec, ACO 1975-87. **Prof Background** BA (Hons) Russian and French. Career: 3yrs computing ind and market info, 4yrs charity resid care mngmt/grant aid admin; 11yrs govt SS mngmt; 24 yrs charity mngmt; part-time consultancy in vol sect. **Awards/Research** Initiated and supervised research on work of charities, inc. ACIOG report with ACO 1991/2, on effect on the VS of fees shortfall funding elderly people in residential care. **Pres Committees** Counsel and Care; Outward Housing Group; local Abbeyfield Management Cttee; The Relatives Association. **Media Experience** Magazine style programmes related to work of charities, inc You and Yours, PM.

BARUCH Geoffrey Director **BRANDON CENTRE** CHILDREN/YOUTH Type: Counselling & psychotherapy for young people. The Brandon Centre, 26 Prince of Wales Rd, London NW5 3LG Tel:0171-267 4792 Fax:0171-267 5212 **Expertise** Young people, adolescents, psychotherapy, psychoanalysis. **Prev Posts** Staff Member: Brent Consultation Centre. **Prof Background** PhD Medical Sociology; Mbr: British Psycho-Analytical Soc; trained in child psychoanalysis. **Awards/Research** Auth: Psychiatry Observed; var articles on adolescence. **Pres Committees** Brit Psycho-Analytical Soc: Chair Research Cttee, Book Club; Internat Jnl of Psycho-Analysis, Edit Bd.

BASS Neville Chief Executive **CHARITY CHRISTMAS CARD COUNCIL** SOCIAL Type: Service provider. 221 St John Street, London EC1V 4LY Tel:0171-336 7476 Fax:0171-490 8288 **Expertise** Charity Trading (Marketing & Law). **Prev Posts** Rank Organisation, West End Theatres, Asst Premiere Controller 1964-66; Ever Ready (GB) Ltd, Asst to MD 1966-70; Field Studies Cncl, Development Secretary 1970-73. **Prof Background** MA (Hons); RC; FRSA; Member, Institute of Management (MIMgt); Member, Institute of Directors (MInstD). **Pres Committees** Foundation Governor, St Vincent's RC School, London W1. **Media Experience** Experience of all media, appearances on News, Chatshows etc.

BATEMAN John Chief Executive **YOUTH CLUBS UK** CHILDREN/YOUTH Type: Service provider. 11 St Bride Street, London EC4A 4AS Tel:0171-353 2366 Fax:0171-353 2369 **Expertise** All matters relating to social needs of young people. **Prev Posts** National Sports Officer, Youth Clubs UK; Director of Youth Work, Youth Clubs UK. **Prev Posts** Qualified teacher and youth and community worker. **Pres Committees** Grants Panel, CAF; Exec Mbr, Nat Cncl for Voluntary Youth Serv; Trustee, Fndtn for Outdoor Adventure; Pres, Euro Confed of Youth Clubs; Cncl for Env Educ Youth Wk Cttee. **Media Experience** Radio/TV and press contrib. **Addits** Mbr: CAF East/West Links Group.

BATEMAN Richard Executive Secretary **GEOLOGICAL SOCIETY** CONSERVATION/ENVIRONMENT Type: Service provider; Professional association; Learned society. Burlington House, Piccadilly, London W1V 0JU Tel:0171-434 9944 Fax:0171-439 8975 **Expertise** Management and administration. **Prev Posts** Asst Sec, Chamber of Shipping of the UK 1969-75; Asst Manager, General Council of British Shipping 1975-80. **Pres Committees** Assoc of European Geological Societies (Pan European Body); Jt Assoc for Petroleum Exploration Courses. **Media Experience** Press.

BATES Dr Paul Jeremy J. Director **HARRISON ZOOLOGICAL MUSEUM** ANIMAL/WILDLIFE Type: Zoological museum. Bowerwood House, 15 St Botolph's Rd, Sevenoaks, Kent TN13 3AQ Tel:01732-742446 Fax:01732-742446 **Expertise** Zoology, mammals, bats, systematics, conservation, Asia, Africa, Arabia, biodiversity studies. **Prof Background** MA, Keble College, Oxford University; PhD, Royal Holloway College, London University. **Awards/Research** The Bats of The Indian Subcontinent (demonstration CD-ROM), University of Amsterdam; The Mammals of Arabia (co-auth David Harrison). **Media Experience** Consultant: BBC Natural History Unit, Bristol; Guest speaker BBC Radio Kent.

BATES Terry N. Administration and Development Director **NATIONAL CRICKET ASSOCIATION** SPORTS Type: National governing body for cricket. Lord's Cricket Ground, London NW8 8QZ Tel:0171-289 4405 Fax:0171-289 5619.

BATTEN Dr John R. Director **ACTIONAID** SOCIAL Type: Fundraiser; Service provider; Campaigning; Overseas Development. Hamlyn House, Macdonald Road, Archway, London N19 5PG Tel:0171-281 4101 Fax:0171-263 4613 **Expertise** Education;

Community/Organisational Development; Training; Organisational Management; Project Management. **Prev Posts** Founder Dir, PACE Priory Adult Coll of Educ, Jamaica 1971-77; Dir, Int Training, IIRR Philippines 1978-85; Training Adv, CARE Int 1986-89; County Dir, Actionaid Kenya 1989-95. **Prof Background** PhD Educational Adminstration/Supervisor 1978; MA Elementary Education 1975; Teaching Cert. Secondary Education 1969. **Awards/Research** MBE 1996. Research: Cost Benefit Analysis of Adult Basic Education 1978. **Past Committees** Mbr: NGO Coord Board, Kenya 93-95; VADA Board, Kenya 88-95; NGO Cncl, exec cttee, Kenya 91-95; Chair: EARRA Brd, Kenya. **Addits** Chair, Org Cttee E African Fundraising Workshop 1993-95.

BATTERSBY Neil Chief Executive **ACTION WATER** SOCIAL Type: Fundraiser; Service provider. Mount Hawke, Truro, Cornwall TR4 8BZ Tel:01209-715385 Fax:01209-715385 **Expertise** Management of unique charity that refurbishes water tankers and drilling rigs, mainly for Africa. **Prev Posts** Sales Manager, British Leyland. **Prof Background** FRGS. **Media Experience** Frequent.

BEALE James Executive Director **OCKENDEN VENTURE** SOCIAL/TRAINING Type: Fundraiser; Service provider; Grant maker. Constitution Hill, Woking, Surrey GU22 7UU Tel:01483-772012 Fax:01483-750774 **Expertise** NUO management and overseas programme devmt; Economics. **Prev Posts** Sight Savers: Programme Manager Asia/Pacific (UK) 1988-93, Regional Director, East Asia/Pacific (Thailand) 1993-95. **Prof Background** MSc Agricultural Economics University of Reading;BA Geography (School of Oriental/African Studies, University of London). **Media Experience** Radio/press.

BECKETT Elsa Co-ordinator **GEMMA** SOCIAL Type: Self-help Friendship; Support Group. BM Box 5700, London WC1N 3XX Tel:0171-485 4024 **Expertise** Co-ordinating group activities. **Prev Posts** Co-ordinator, Gemma since 1976. **Awards/Research** Gemma Newsletter. **Pres Committees** Cttee Mbr, Newham Association of Disabled People; Cncl Mbr, S.P.O.D.; Cttee Mbr, Action & Rights of Disabled People. **Past Committees** Committee Mbr, British Council of Organisations of Disabled People.

BECKETT Fran Chief Executive **SHAFTESBURY SOCIETY** SOCIAL Type: Service provider. 16 Kingston Rd, South Wimbledon, London SW19 1JZ Tel:0181-239 5555 Fax:0181-239 5580 **Expertise** Professional social care & community work. **Prev Posts** Social Work Adviser, Shaftesbury Society 1988-91; Community Care Coordinator, Shaftesbury Society 1991-93; Urban Action Director, Shaftesbury Society 1993-95. **Prof Background** Cert. Qual in Social Work; Religious Studies Diploma; MSc, Voluntary Sector Organisations. **Awards/Research** Author of: Called To Action (Harper Collins); Love In Action (The Shaftesbury Society); various articles on social care, community work & church activity in community development. **Pres Committees** Board Member, Christian Impact (education/training institute); Council Member, Evangelical Alliance (coordinating/umbrella body); Board Member, London Bible College (theological college). **Media Experience** Religious affairs programmes (radio & TV); column, New Christian Herald.

BEECHER John Director **ADVOCACY PARTNERS** SOCIAL Type: Advocacy Provider. 6 Lind Road, Sutton, Surrey SM1 4PJ Tel:0181-643 7111 Fax:0181-643 7111 **Expertise** Advocacy; Organisational Development, Staff Development, Information Technology. **Prev Posts** IT Management 1980-93, Freelance Consultant, Investors in People 1994-95. **Prof Background** BSc Hons. Mathematics. **Pres Committees** Trustee of Ealing and Harrow Citizen Advocacy.

BEETHAM Tony Director **CHRISTIAN ENQUIRY AGENCY** RELIGIOUS Type: Fundraiser. Inter-Church House, 35-41 Lower Marsh, London SE1 7RL Tel:0171-620 4444 Fax:0171-728 0010 **Expertise** Management and planning. **Prev Posts** Director & General Mngr, City of Oxford Bus Company 1969-73; Group Executive & National Bus Company 1974-82; Executive Director, National Bus Company 1983-88. **Prof Background** BSc (Econ) London School of Economics; Fellow of Chartered Institute of Transport; Oxford Ministry Course (leading to ordination 1975). **Awards/Research** FCIT. **Pres Committees** Council of Christian Enquiry Agency (CEA); Management Committee of CEA; Council of Road Operators Safety Council. **Past Committees** National Bus Company Management Board; Council of Confederation of Passenger Transport. **Media Experience** Radio & TV interviews; Press relations. **Addits** Non-Stipendiary Minister, Church of England.

BEETON David Christopher Chief Executive **HISTORIC ROYAL PALACES** CONSERVATION/ENVIRONMENT Type: Heritage attraction. Hampton Court, E. Molesey, Surrey KT8 9AU Tel:0181-781 9751 Fax:0181-781 9754 **Expertise** As Chief Executive all areas are covered. **Prev Posts** Chief Executive, Bath City Council 1973-85; Secretary, National Trust 1985-89. **Prof Background** Qualified Solicitor. **Pres Committees** London Tourist Board. **Media Experience** Frequent interviews on radio and TV.

BEGG Patrick Director **COUNCIL FOR SCOTTISH ARCHAEOLOGY** CONSERVATION/ENVIRONMENT Type: Service provider. c/o National Museums of Scotland, York Bldgs, 1 Queen Street, Edinburgh EH2 1JD Tel:0131-225 7534 Tel:0131-557 9498.

BELL Graham Director **SCOTTISH PERMACULTURE** CONSERVATION/ENVIRONMENT Type: Service provider; Education/Design information sharing. c/o Earthward, Tweed Horizons, Newtown St Boswells Melrose, Roxburghshire TD6 0SG Tel:01835-82212 **Expertise** Land usage, sustainable transport,rural regeneration, appropriate energy. **Prev Posts** Director, Good Earth Limited 1985-88; Director, Neatwork 1988-to date. Director, Earthward 1994-to date. **Prof Background** MA (Oxon) 1977; C.Inst M 1979; Dip Perm Inst 1989. **Awards/Research** Permaculture Community Service Awd 1989; Tweed Horizons Awd 1994. Auth: The Permaculture Way, 1992; The Permaculture Garden, 1994; Ed. Permaculture News; numerous articles. **Pres Committees** Trustee, Borders Forest Trust. **Past Committees** Permaculture UK Council 1989-91. **Media Experience** Various inc. World Service, Tomorrows World, Grow

Your Greens, Great Outdoors.

BELL Margaret Chief Executive **NATIONAL COUNCIL FOR EDUCATIONAL TECHNOLOGY - NCET** SOCIAL Type: NDPB. Milburn Hill Rd, Science Park, Coventry CV4 7JJ Tel:01203-416994 Fax:01203-411418 **Expertise** IT: learning;organisational development. **Prev Posts** Head of Distance Learning BT 1990-92;Head of Computer Based Learning CCC. **Prof Background** CERT ED. City of Birmingham Coll. of Ed; BA First class OU; Freeman of City of London. **Awards/Research** Various publications on the use of IT in training and education. **Pres Committees** RSA Exams/Assess Fndtn;Chair: Forum Tech Based Trnng;Exec Mbr Parl Info Tech Cttee;Mbr: RSA Lrng Soc Exchange;IoD;Court,Univ Warks; Multimedia Adv Bd, Wolverhampton Univ; Mbr Tile Hill Coll Corp Coventry. **Past Committees** Saturn; Director, Women Into Technology. **Media Experience** World Service interview BBC Radio 95; Educational press. **Addits**: Mbr: Prof Brd,Uni Warwick; FEFC Learning/Tech Cttee; Mbr COMMITT, Netherlands.

BELLRINGER Paul Director **UK FORUM ON YOUNG PEOPLE & GAMBLING** CHILDREN/YOUTH Type: Service provider. PO Box 5, Chichester, W Sussex PO19 3RB Tel:01243-538635 Fax:01243-538365 **Expertise** Yng people and gmblng; pub awareness of issues/treatment facils fr prob gamblers;trnr/gmblng;cncllg techs **Prev Posts** Probation Officer, West Sussex 1983-85; Senior Probation Officer, West Sussex 1985-90; **Prof Background** CQSW 1975; Professional Diploma in Management (Dip. Man [Open]) 1989. **Awards/Research** Publ: Working with Young Problem Gamblers: Guidelines to Practice (1991); Probation Service Training Manual: Working with Problem Gamblers. **Pres Committees** Gamblers Anon. General Services Board; Mbr, Gordon House Ctte; Co-opted Mbr, Assoc of Chief Officers of Probation; Advisor, CONCERN and Centre for Gambling and Commercial Gaming, Univ of Salford.

BELSEY Hugh Curator **GAINSBOROUGH'S HOUSE SOCIETY** ARTS Type: Fundraiser; Service provider; Museum. Gainsborough's House, 46 Gainsborough Street, Sudbury, Suffolk CO10 6EU Tel:01787-372958 Fax:01787-376991 **Expertise** Academic interest in Thomas Gainsborough & 18th century Florence and the Grand Tour. **Prev Posts** Curator, Bowood House, Calne, Wilts 1979-80. **Prof Background** BA in History of Art, Manchester University; MLitt in Fine Arts, Barber Institute, Birmingham University; Dip in Art Gallery & Museum Studies, Manchester University. **Awards/Research** Articles in Burlington Magazine, Apollo & other specialist journals; Art gallery catalogues, etc. **Pres Committees** Council member, Association of Independent Museums; AIM representative, Standing Conference, Archives & Museums; Council member, Walpole Society. **Media Experience** Press & TV appearances.

BENFIELD Graham Director **WALES COUNCIL FOR VOLUNTARY ACTION/CYNGOR GWEITHREDU GWIRFODDOL CYMRU - WCVA** SOCIAL Type: Umbrella charity, advocacy, service, development. Llys Ifor, Crescent Road, Caerphilly, Mid-Glamorgan CF83 1XL Tel:01222-869224 Fax:01222-860627 **Prev Posts** Asst Soc Dev Off, Skelmersdale Dev Corp 1974-77; Sr Lect Plymouth Poly, Co-ord Virginia House Settlement 1977-83; Dir, West Glam Cmty Serv Cncl 1983-9. **Prof Background** BA (Hons) Politics/Philos 1972, MA 1986 St Catherines Coll, Oxford; Dip Soc Admin, York Univ 1974; Dip Appl Soc Studies/CQSW 1982, MSc 1988, Univ Coll, Swansea. **Awards/Research** Auth: Okehampton Rural Community Development Project 1983; Rural Deprivation and Community Work 1989. **Pres Committees** Mbr: Volunteering in Wales Fund; Community Projects Foundation-Welsh Policy Comm; National Council of Voluntary Organizations.

BENNETT Margaret Chief Executive **NATIONAL LIBRARY FOR THE BLIND - NLB** DISABILITY Type: Service provider. Cromwell Road, Bredbury, Stockport SK6 2SG Tel:0161-494 0217 Fax:0161-406 6728.

BENNETT Susan Executive Director **DISABLED LIVING FOUNDATION - DLF** DISABILITY Type: Service provider. 380-84 Harrow Road, London W9 2HU Tel:0171-2896111 Fax:0171-2662922 **Prev Posts** Director of Services, DLF 1992-94. **Prof Background** Post Graduate Diploma in Mngmt Studies; Diploma in Occupational Therapy, Psychiatric Nursing.

BENTHALL Jonathan Director **ROYAL ANTHROPOLOGICAL INSTITUTE** SOCIAL Type: Fundraiser; Service provider; Grant maker; Learned Society; Publisher. 50 Fitzroy Street, London W1P 5HS Tel:0171-387 0455 Fax:0171-383 4235 **Prev Posts** Secretary, Institute of Contemporary Arts, London, 1971-73. **Prof Background** English MA, Cambridge. Member, Association of Social Anthropologists. **Awards/Research** Disasters, Relief and the Media (IB Tauris, London, 1993); Numerous artics & 3 ed bks. Ed, Anthropology Today; Hon Research Fellow, Univ Coll Lond Dept Anthrop 1995-. **Pres Committees** Various Committees of Save the Children Fund (UK) since 1980. **Past Committees** International Broadcasting Trust, 1992-95. **Media Experience** Anthropology in the Media Award, American Anthropological Assoc. 1993. **Addits** Chevalier de L'Ordre des Arts et des Lettres (France) 1973.

BERMAN E.D. Founder/Chief Executive/Trustee **INTER-ACTION TRUST** SOCIAL Type: Res & Development of model, transferable projects. HMS President (1918), Victoria Embankment, London EC4Y 0HJ Tel:0171-583 2652 Fax:0171-583 2840 **Expertise** New project & programme development, and writer. **Prev Posts** Seconded as Special Advisor on Inner City & Vol Sector to Sec of State for Environment 1982-83. **Prof Background** Harvard Graduate; Rhodes Scholar to Oxford. Theatre, director, playwright, author, Artistic Director, CEO of charities, training company, educational equipment. **Awards/Research** MBE. 6 yrs post-grad research on educ methods & creativity. Breaks for Young Bands 86; Which Software? Which Hardware? for Vol Agencies 87; Healthy Learning Songs & Activities 89. **Pres Committees** Trustee: Community Education Trust; Social Enterprise Foundation; CEO: Inter-Action Social Enterprise Trust Ltd; Dir: Social Enterprise Projects Ltd; Options Training Ltd. **Media Experience** Ed TV, magazine pieces; prod dir video/audio cassettes & plays (inc

TIE). **Addits** Auth: New Game Songs & Activities 89; Democracy Handbook 94.

BERRY Jane Manager **WREN TELECOTTAGE (WARWICKSHIRE RURAL ENTERPRISE NETWORK)** SOCIAL Type: Fundraiser; Service provider; Educational Charity (Small Business Support). Stoneleigh Park, Warwickshire, CV8 2RR Tel:01203-696986 Fax:01203-696538 **Expertise** Training and enterprise, small business devt teleworking and telecottages. **Prev Posts** TEFL Teacher (o\s); Freelance Trainer/writer/translator. **Prof Background** BA Hons French/Russian; NVQ Assessors Award; NVQ4 Business Counselling. **Awards/Research** Numerous articles/Presentations on Teleworking/Telecottages (eg.The Methdlgy of Supporting Small Bus Creation in Rural Areas); Contributor to Case Studies on Good Practice. **Pres Committees** Director Coventry and Warks Small Business Consortium. **Media Experience** Frequent radio guest/TV interviewee; video scripting/apppearing. **Addits** WREN has achieved nomination for EC sponsored Cridel Local Devt Award 1994.

BERRY Lynne Executive Director **CHARITY COMMISSION** SOCIAL Type: Service provider; Grant maker; Regulator and Advisor. St Albans House, 57-60 Haymarket, London SW1Y 4QX Tel:0171-210 4477 Fax:0171-210 4604 **Expertise** Soc policy esp povty/soc justice; user rights/participtn iss; snr mngmt staff & org devt; VS polcy/mngmt. **Prev Posts** Incl: Director, FWA; Head of continuing education and social policy, Nat Institute for Social Work 1984-89; Inspector, General Policy Group, Social Services Inspectorate, 1989-91. **Prof Background** Professional training in Social Work and Social Policy; Management; Higher Education: BA English and History; CQSW; Dip Social Work; M Phil/PhD Social Policy. **Awards/Research** Mbr Commsn on Future of VS; Auth: Whose Social Services, 1988; Open to Complaints, 1989; Co-auth: Social Work in Europe, 1992. Numerous articles in professional and national press. **Pres Committees** Trusteeship: NVCO; IYF 1994. **Past Committees** National Children's Bureau; NCVCCO; Trustee, Pregnancy Advisory Service; Association of Community Workers. **Media Experience** Freq contr TV/Radio; Adviser: Soc Policy Press; Edit Bd, Comty Devmt Jnl. **Addits** FRSA; Mbr, Brit-Amer Successor Generation Project.

BERRY Sally Clinical Director **WOMEN'S THERAPY CENTRE - WTC** MEDICAL/HEALTH Type: Service provider. 6-9 Manor Gardens, London N7 6LA Tel:0171-263 7860 Fax:0171-281 7879.

BERRY Simon Director **NATIONAL RURAL ENTERPRISE CENTRE - RASE** SOCIAL Type: Service provider; Community/Economic Development. National Rural Enterprise Centre, Stoneleigh Park, Warks CV8 2RR Tel:01203-690691 Fax:01203-696770.

BERRY Tessa Administrator **SOCIETY FOR RADIOLOGICAL PROTECTION** SOCIAL Type: Professional Association. Ramillies House, 1-9 Hills Place, London W1R 1AG Tel:0171-287 4955 Fax:0171-287 4906.

BERRY Trevor President **FAMILIES NEED FATHERS** SOCIAL Type: Service provider; Initiator of research projects. 134 Curtain Road, London EC2A 3AR Tel:0171-613 5060 Fax:0171-613 5060 **Expertise** Family law and practice (private law). **Prev Posts** Retired from career in government service; chairman of Families Need Fathers 1981-94. **Prof Background** Chartered Engineer (C. Eng) **Awards/Research** Co-auth: Children and Family Breakdown - Custody and Access Guidelines, 1987; numerous articles on children, divorce and custody in legal and social work journals and national press. **Pres Committees** Regular communication with government, eg. appeared before House of Commons Social Security Committee on Changes in Maintenance Arrangements. **Media Experience** Frequent contrib radio and TV. Also letters in national press.

BERWICK I. H. Chairman **UNITED KINGDOM VINEYARDS ASSOCIATION** ENVIRONMENT Type: Fundraiser; Service provider; Campaigning. Church Road, Bruisyard, Saxmundham, Suffolk IP17 2EF Tel:01728-638080 Fax:01728-638442.

BESAG Dr F.M.C. Medical Director **ST PIERS LINGFIELD** MEDICAL/HEALTH Type: Service provider. Educational/residential. St Piers Lane, Lingfield, Surrey RH7 6PW Tel:01342-832243 Fax:01342-834639 **Expertise** Medical practitioner in epilepsy and psychiatry. **Prev Posts** Honorary Consultant, Maudsley Hospital 1985-today; Chief Exec/Medical Dir, St Piers Lingfield 1985-96;Hon Snr Lecturer,Inst of Psychiatry & Inst of Child Health 1989-today **Prof Background** BSc (Physics); Msc; PhD; MB; ChB; MRCP (UK); FRCP; DCH; FRCPsych; Mbr, Brit Paediatric Assoc. **Awards/Research** Longterm research/articles/books on all aspects of epilepsy. Presently involved in drug co. trials of new antiepilepsy drugs. **Pres Committees** UK rep, Int League against Epilepsy Comm on Paediatrics; Trustee, Epilepsy Res Fndtn; Mgmt Cmtee Mbr/Mbr, Medical & Scientific Adv Cmtee, Epileptology Inst. **Past Committees** Int League against Epilepsy (Brit Chapter). **Media Experience** Interviews on local/nat/int radio/press; nat TV; several videos.

BESSE Dr Christopher Chief Executive **MEDICAL EMERGENCY RELIEF INTERNATIONAL (MERLIN)** MEDICAL/HEALTH Type: Fundraiser; Service provider; Professional Association. 1a Rede Place, Chepstow Place, London W2 4TU Tel:0171-229 4560 Fax:0171-243 1442 **Expertise** Medical Emergency Relief. **Prev Posts** Hospital Medicine 1981-85; General Practice 1985-90; Humanitarian Aid MSF WHO 1990-96. **Prof Background** Physician.

BEST Keith Chief Executive **IMMIGRATION ADVISORY SERVICE** SOCIAL Type: Fundraiser; Service provider. County House, 190 Great Dover Street, London SE1 4YB Tel:0171-357 7511 Fax:0171-403 5875 **Expertise** Management, fundraising, PR. **Prev Posts** Direct Mail Consultant, NCH Action for Children 1987-89; Director, Prisoners Abroad 1989- 93. **Prof Background** Barrister MA (Oxon) Jurisprudence; Member of Parliament. **Awards/Research** Territorial Decoration; Auth: Write Your Own Will; The Right Way to Prove a Will. **Pres Committees** Executive Chairman, World Federalist Movement. **Media Experience** Radio, TV, video and press experience.

BEST Richard Director **JOSEPH ROWNTREE FOUNDATION** SOCIAL Type: Service provider; Grant maker. The Homestead, 40 Water End, York YO3 6LP Tel:01904-629241 Fax:01904-620072 **Expertise** Housing. **Prev Posts** Dir, British Churches Housing Trust 1968-73; Dir, National Federation of Housing Associations 1973-88. **Prof Background** Degree - Social Administration. **Awards/Research** OBE; Numerous articles on housing; some on charity/voluntary sector. **Pres Committees** Commissioner, Rural Development Commission; Housing Assoc Cttees; Chairman, UK National Council for the UN City Summit. **Past Committees** BBC/IBA Jt Appeals Adv Cttee; Exec Cttee, ACF; IBM Cmty Affrs Adv Panel; HA Cttees; Adv, H of Commons Select Cttee on the Envir 1993 **Media Experience** Numerous appearances on radio and TV. **Addits** Secretary, Duke of Edinburgh's Inquiry into British Housing 1984-91.

BICKELL John Director of Community Affairs **ALLIED DUNBAR CHARITABLE TRUST** SOCIAL Type: Grant maker; Advisory body. Allied Dunbar Centre, Swindon, Wilts SN1 1EL Tel:01793-514514 Fax:01793-506982

BILLINGTON Andrew Director **WINGED FELLOWSHIP TRUST** DISABILITY Type: Service provider. Angel House, 20-32 Pentonville Road, London N1 9XD Tel:0171-833 2594 Fax:0171-278 0370 **Expertise** Personnel; fundraising; general management. **Prev Posts** Forte 1972-74; John Grooms Association 1979-89. **Prof Background** Bachelor of Theology; Fellow, Institute of Personnel Managers; Member, the Hotel and Catering Institutional Managers Association. **Pres Committees** Chair, WFT Stationers Ltd. **Past Committees** V Chair, ACENVO; Director, The London Hotel for Disabled People; Exec Mbr, ICFM (Inst of Charity Fundraising Managers). **Media Experience** Radio and TV programmes; publications.

BINGHAM Dee Information Officer **TIDY BRITAIN GROUP** ENVIRONMENT Type: Fundraiser; Service provider; Campaigning; Information Provider. The Pier, Wigan WN3 4EX 0942-824620 0942-824778 **Expertise** Litter: legal issues, general information and advice. **Prev Posts** Tidy Britain Group: Project Officer 1990-92; Exec Asst 1992-93. **Prof Background** Member of Institute of Administrative Management; Affiliate Member of Library Association. **Awards/Research** Leaflets: Litter and the Law; Dog Fouling and the Law;various information sheets on litter issues. **Pres Committees** British Cleaning Council - Board Member. **Past Committees** Civic Trust Committee. **Media Experience** Press releases and press enquiries.

BINNIE Prof Frank Chief Executive **CALEDONIAN FOUNDATION** SOCIAL Type: Fundraiser; Service provider; Grant maker; Campaigning; Charity - Foundation Company Ltd by Guarantee. 9 Lynedoch Crescent, Glasgow G3 6QE Tel:0141-3325668 Fax:0141-3325673 **Expertise** Sales, marketing, funding, operations in the private, public & voluntary sectors. **Prev Posts** Director/Company Secretary, Midlothian Enterprise Trust 1985-88; Managing Dir, Perkins H & G (Coxmore plc) 1988-90; Chief Executive, Design Council/Scottish Design 1990-96. **Prof Background** Clothing & Textile Technology; Professor of Engineering Design, University of Strathclyde; Fellow, Royal Society Arts Design & Manufacturing; Fellow, Chartered Society of Designers. **Pres Committees** Mbr, Coutts Scot Advisory Cttee on Employment; External Assessment Cttee MBA, Univ of Westminster; Chair, Fashion Product Design Marketing Grp, The Textile Inst. **Past Committees** Chair, Scotvec Cttee on Design; Board Member, 1999 City of Architecture & Design; Chairman, UK Cttee on Clothing & Textiles. **Media Experience** Experience in radio, TV, video & press. **Addits** Company auditor ISO9000.

BLAIR Mr David B. N. Publicity Convener **SCOTTISH BEEKEEPERS ASSOCIATION** SOCIAL Type: Service provider; Promotion of beekeeping within Scotland & beyond. 44 Dalhousie Rd, Kilbarchan, Renfrewshire PA10 2AT Tel:01505-702680 **Expertise** Beekeeping. **Prof Background** Expert Beemaster & Honey Judge. **Awards/Research** Scottish Beekeeper (Monthly Magazine); An Introduction To Bees & Beekeeping (Handbook). **Pres Committees** Executive Committee (SBA).

BLAKE Eleanor Marketing Manager **BANKSIDE GALLERY** ARTS Type: Arts & Cultural; Educational. 48 Hopton Street, London SE1 9JH Tel:0171-928 7521 Fax:0171-928 2820 **Expertise** Marketing; public relations; publicity. **Prev Posts** Marketing Asst, Shamrock Peat 1990-92; Marketing/PR, Stradivarium 1992-1994. **Prof Background** BA (Hons) History, Southampton University; CIM Diploma (Marketing) UWE. **Past Committees** Mgt Cttee, Stradivarium. **Media Experience** Press releases and media generally.

BLASHFORD-SNELL John Chairman **SCIENTIFIC EXPLORATION SOCIETY** CONSERVATION/ENVIRONMENT Type: Service provider; Scientific Exploration. Expedition Base, Motcombe, Dorset SP7 9PB Tel:01747-853353 Fax:01747-855411 **Expertise** Archaeology, natural history, youth work. **Prev Posts** British Army 1955-91. **Prof Background** RMA Sandhurst Staff College. DSc (Hon) Durham University; Inst of Royal Engineers, Gold Medal. **Awards/Research** OBE. Bks inc: Operation Raleigh:The Start of an Adventure; Adv Challenge (Jt Auth); Adv Unlimited (Jt Auth); Something Lost Behind the Ranges; Mammoth Hunt: A Taste for Adventure **Pres Committees** Chairman, British Chapter, The Explorers Club; Co-Chair, Operation New World. **Past Committees** Dir of Operations, Operation Drake; Dir Gen, Operation Raleigh; Outward Bound Council. **Media Experience** Frequent. **Addits** Freeman, City of Hereford; Darien, Livingstone (RSGS), Fnders Medals (RGS).

BLUNT Anthony Director General **HEARING DOGS FOR THE DEAF - HDFD** DISABILITY Type: Fundraiser; Service provider. The Training Centre, London Road (A40), Lewknor, Oxford OX9 5RY Tel:01844-353898 Fax:01844-353099 **Expertise** All roles of the chief executive. **Prev Posts** Police officer, Thames Valley Police 1954-82. **Prof Background** Police; dog trainer/instructor (specialist); administrator; volunteer organiser; lecturer. **Pres Committees** Director, Hearing

Dogs for the Deaf Trading Co; President, Assistance Dogs International; Chair, Assistance Dogs (UK) Assoc. **Media Experience** Frequent to promote society on TV, radio, video and press. **Addits** Founder member of HDFD.

BODELL Derek Director **NATIONAL AIDS TRUST** MEDICAL/HEALTH Type: Fundraiser. Policy Development; Sector Support. New City Cloisters, 188/196 Old Street, London EC1V 9FR Tel:0171-814 6767 Fax:0171-216 0111 **Prev Posts** Director, Prevention Program New York 1986-88; Snr Prog Officer, Health Educ Authority 1988-92; S Thames RHA Regional HIV/AIDS Prog Mgr 1992-95. **Prof Background** Degree Applied Social Studies; CQSW; Social Work. **Pres Committees** N.E.C. Family Planning Assoc; Projects Committee CRUSAID.

BODMER Sir Walter Fred Principal **HERTFORD COLLEGE, OXFORD** MEDICAL/HEALTH Type: Scientific research. Oxford OX1 3BW (also: c/o IMM, John Radcliffe Hospital, Headington, Oxford OX3 9DU) Tel:01865-279407 Fax:01865-279437 **Expertise** Human genetics; cancer research; molecular biology. **Prev Posts** Prof, Dept Genetics, Stanford Univ 1968-70; Prof Genetics, Ox U 1970-79; Dir Res, 1979-91 Dir-Gen 1991-96 Imp Cancer Res Fund 1979-91. Curr:Hd,Can Genets & Imlgy Lab, Inst Mol Med **Prof Background** BA (Mathematics), Clare College, Cambridge Univ 1956; PhD (Genetics) Clare College, Cambridge Univ 1959. FRS; Numerous Hon Fellow/memberships inc Royal College of Surgeons & Physicians. **Awards/Research** Knight Bachelor, 1986; 11 Hon DScs; 515+ jnl contribs; co-auth: The Genetics of Human Populations; Our Future Inheritance - Choice or Chance; Genetics, Evolution and Man; Book of Man. **Pres Committees** Incl - Pres, EACR 1994-96; Vice Pres, Brit Assoc for Advancement of Science (Chair of Council, 1996-); Parliamentary and Sc Cttee;(Hon), Research Defence Society; Chancellor, Univ of Salford 1995-. **Past Committees** Pres:HUGO 90-92; Brit Soc Histocompat & Immunogenetics 90-92;Assoc Sci Ed 89-90;Royal Statist Soc 84-85;Org of Euro Canc Inst 90-93 **Addits** 1994: Faraday Awd; Dr Honoris Causa, Masaryk Univ, Brno;Harv Orat,RCPhys,London.

BONDS John Charity Commissioner **CHARITY COMMISSION** SOCIAL Type: Statutory Body. St Albans House, 57-60 Haymarket, London SW1Y 4QX Tel:0171-210 4540 Fax:0171-210 4604 **Expertise** Finance & Accountancy. **Prev Posts** Finance Director, Norske Shell 1983-86; Vice-President, Shell Internationale Petroleum 1986-93. **Prof Background** MA (Oxford University); FCCA (Certified Accountant). **Pres Committees** Charity Commission Board. **Past Committees** Director of Several Shell Group Companies.

BONNET P.R.F Major General Chief Executive **OFFICER'S PENSIONS SOCIETY (WIDOW'S FUND)** SOCIAL Type: Fundraiser; Service provider; Grant maker; Campaigning. 68 South Lambeth Road, London SW8 1RL Tel:0171-820 9988 Fax:0171-820 9948 **Expertise** Assistance to widows of Ex-Servicemen; Pensions for Ex-Servicemen/women, widows, widowers, dependants. **Prev Posts** Army career, 1958-92. **Prof Background** Army Officer; BSc; MPhil. **Awards/Research** International Terrorism: Its Nature and Ways, 1985; Short History of the Royal Regiment of Artillery, 1994; CB (1991) MBE (1975). **Pres Committees** Army Benev Fund: Exec Cttee & Chair Grants Cttee; Mbr, Cncl of Legal Practice Course Cent Appl Brd; Civil Serv Pensioners' Jt Consult Cttee; Publ Serv Pens' Cncl: Gen Purps Cttee & Exec Cttee. **Addits** Current Cttee: Colonel Commandant, Royal Regiment of Artillery.

BONSER Jeff General Secretary **CHURCHES ADVISORY COUNCIL FOR LOCAL BROADCASTING - CACLB** RELIGIOUS Type: Service provider. PO Box 124, Westcliff-on-Sea Essex, SS0 0QU Tel:01702-348369 Fax:01702-348369 **Expertise** Radio and TV broadcasting. **Prev Posts** General Manager of commercial radio station Essex Radio 1980-89. **Awards/Research** Author of several newspaper & magazine articles on broadcasting and the churches. **Pres Committees** Christian Media Trust, owners of Premier Radio; Helping Hands, Essex Radio Charity. **Media Experience** Radio Broadcasting and Management.

BOON Barbara Senior Administrative Officer **BRITISH ASSOCIATION FOR EARLY CHILDHOOD EDUCATION - BAECE** CHILDREN/YOUTH Type: Service provider. 111 City View House, 463 Bethnal Green Road, London E2 9QY Tel:0171-739 7594 Fax:0171-613 5330 **Prev Posts** Mother/Housewife; Secretarial 1965-70. **Prof Background** Foster-parent; Childminder; Playgroup Organiser. **Pres Committees** Executive Committee, AAUEF (Assoc of Advisers for Under Eights and their Families).

BORG Dr Alan Director **VICTORIA & ALBERT MUSEUM** ARTS/CULTURAL South Kensington, London SW7 2RL Tel:0171-938 8504 Fax:0171-938 8477 **Prev Posts** Director General, Imperial War Museum, 1982-95; Keeper, Sainsbury Centre for Visual Arts, 1978-82; Assistant Keeper, Royal Armouries, Tower of London, 1970-78. **Prof Background** Educ:Westminster School & Brasenose College Oxford, BA (Hons); London University, PhD History of Art; Courtauld Institute, Modern History & MA History of Art. **Awards/Research** Auth/Joint: Architectural Sculpture in Romanesque Provence(1972); European Swords & Daggers in the Tower of London (1974); Torture & Punishment (1975); Heads & Horses (1976). **Pres Committees** Governor, Thomas Coram Foundation; Army Museums Ogilby Trust; Chevening Estate; Public Records Advisory Cttee. **Addits** Auth/Joint: The Vanishing Past (1981); War Memorials (1991).

BOS Frances Director of Public Relations **BRITISH HORSE SOCIETY - BHS** ANIMAL/WILDLIFE Type: Service provider. British Equestrian Centre, Stoneleigh Park, Kenilworth, Warks CV8 2LR Tel:01203-696697 Fax:01203-696867 **Expertise** Marketing; press; publicity. **Prev Posts** Press Officer, Plymouth Arts Centre 1988-90; Press Officer, Horse Trials Group 1990-93. **Prof Background** BA (Hons) Drama & Theatre Studies; Chartered Inst of Marketing Exams; RSA Qualifications in typing and word processing. **Awards/Research** Research into BHS membership; editorial liaison on British Horse Magazine; created Horse Trials Followers Group. **Pres Committees** Specialist Writers UK. **Media Experience** 5 years experience at national and local level.

BOURN Douglas Director **DEVELOPMENT EDUCATION ASSOCIATION** SOCIAL Type: Service provider. 29-31 Cowper St, London EC2A 4AP Tel:0171-490 8108 Fax:0171-490 8123 **Expertise** Development and environment educ; History of educ theory; Youth work training; culture of voluntary orgs. **Prev Posts** National Secretary, Woodcraft Folk 1983-1990; Head of Local Groups Dept, Friends of the Earth 1990-1993. **Prof Background** BA (Hons) Keele University; PhD Keele, on Labour Party and Education. **Awards/Research** Articles on education for social change; history of Woodcraft Folk; Chapter in book on 1945 Labour government and education policies. **Pres Committees** International Broadcasting Trust Board; British Overseas NGO's for Development Executive Committee. **Past Committees** UK2000 Brd; Commonwealth Youth Exchange Cncl Exec Ctte; Nat Cncl for Vol Youth Servs Exec Ctte; Cncl for Envir Educ Youth Cttee. **Media Experience** Radio/TV interviews; produced promotional video for Woodcraft Folk. **Addits** Former mbr: Youth Exchange Centre; Co-op Union Educ Exec.

BOWEN Rev Roger General Secretary **CROSSLINKS** RELIGIOUS Type: Mission Agency. 251 Lewisham Way, London SE8 4JL Tel:0181-691 6111 Fax:0181-694 8023 **Expertise** Missiology.

BOWER Joanne Honorary Secretary **FARM AND FOOD SOCIETY - FAFS** ANIMAL/WILDLIFE Type: Service provider; Educational/Lobbying/Agricultural Interests. 4 Willifield Way, London NW11 7XT Tel:0181-455 0634.

BOWLER David Director **SCOTTISH URBAN ARCHAEOLOGICAL TRUST LTD - SUAT** CONSERVATION/ENVIRONMENT Type: Service provider. 55 South Methven Street, Perth PH1 5NX Tel:01738-622393 Fax:01738-631626 **Expertise** Roman archaeology in Britain, urban archaeology in Scotland. **Prev Posts** Deputy Director, SUAT 1985-93. **Prof Background** BA Hons Classics, McGill; MPhil Roman Archaeology, Oxford. **Awards/Research** Articles on Perth's medieval harbours and excavations in Perth; Research on development and topography of Scottish medieval town. **Media Experience** Interviewed on local radio programmes.

BOYD Brenda Chair **CHARITY FORUM COUNCIL** SOCIAL Type: Service provider. 8 Templemere, Weybridge, Surrey KT13 9PB Tel:01982-847696 Fax:01982-847696.

BRACEGIRDLE Hilary Director **NATIONAL HORSERACING MUSEUM** SPORTS Type: Museum. 99 High Street, Newmarket, Suffolk CB8 8JL Tel:01638-667333 **Expertise** Museum & business management. **Prev Posts** Staff Development Officer, Victoria & Albert Museum 1989-91; Head of Picture Library V & A Museum 1992-93; Registrar, V & A Museum 1983-96. **Prof Background** Museum Studies, Master of Business Administration. **Past Committees** UK Registrars Group.

BRADLEY Anna Director **INSTITUTE FOR THE STUDY OF DRUG DEPENDENCE - ISDD** SOCIAL Type: Fundraiser; Information provider. Waterbridge House, 32-36 Loman St, London SE1 0EE Tel:0171-928 1211 Fax:0171-928 1771 **Expertise** Management; Information Strategy. **Prev Posts** Consumers Assoc: Head of Food and Health 1988-91, Dep Research Director 1991-93. **Prof Background** BA (Philosophy); MBA. **Past Committees** Patients Association. **Media Experience** Extensive experience of all types.

BRADLEY Christine Ann Company Secretary **MCCARTHY FOUNDATION** THE ELDERLY Type: Fundraiser; Grant maker. Homelife House, 26 Oxford Rd, Bournemouth, Dorset BH8 8EZ Tel:01202-315064 Fax:01202-315064 **Expertise** Older people, crime prevention. **Prev Posts** Present position held since 1989. **Prof Background** Member of: Institute of Management; ACENVO; ICFM. **Pres Committees** Regional Committee Member, Sovereign Housing Association; Executive Committee member, New Forest Marathon Association. **Media Experience** Press.

BRAHAM Margaret Louise Managing Editor **RIGHT OF WAY LAW REVIEW** CONSERVATION/ENVIRONMENT Type: Service provider; Information Service. The Granary, Charlcutt, Calne, Wiltshire SN11 9HL Tel:0124-9740286 Fax:0124-9740404 **Expertise** Law relating to public rights of way & general land law. **Prev Posts** Barrister & law tutor; Chairman & Chief Eexecutive, Byways & Bridleways Trust 1979-94; Managing Editor, Rights of Way Law Review (RWLR) 1990-. **Prof Background** MA, BCL (Oxon); Barrister, Middle Temple; Law Tutor, Somerville & St Hugh's Colleges, Oxford. **Awards/Research** Public rights of way law; Author of all unsigned legal articles until 1994 in Byway & Bridleway; Edited all articles published in RWLR. **Pres Committees** Central Rights of Way Committee; Rights of Way Review Committee. **Past Committees** Trustee, Byways & Bridleways Trust 1979-94; various Countryside Commission Committees since 1972. **Addits** Farming (sheep).

BRANDON Heather Chairman - World Board **WORLD ASSOCIATION OF GIRL GUIDES AND GIRL SCOUTS** CHILDREN/YOUTH Type: Fundraiser; Service provider. World Bureau, Olive Centre, 12c Lyndhurst Rd, London NW3 5PQ Tel:0171-794 1181 Fax:0171-431 3764 **Expertise** Development of girls and young women; gender issues; international agency. **Prev Posts** Chief Commissioner, Girl Guides Assoc of S Africa 1986-92; Vice Chair, Pax Lodge Hostel 1991-93; World Board Member 1993-96. **Prof Background** Headmistress; career in education & adult leader training. **Awards/Research** Awds: J&B Achievers Award; Silver Springbok; GGSA Silver Fish; Medal of Merit. Research: Development of girls & young women. **Pres Committees** Brd Mbr, Donaldson Trust; Exec, Independent Schools Council (Junior Primary); Johannesburg Soroptimists. **Past Committees** National Scout Council; Womens Coalition; SABC Broadcasting Board. **Media Experience** Extensive.

BREWSTER Richard Chief Executive **SCOPE** DISABILITY Type: Fundraiser; Service provider; Grant maker; Campaigning. 12 Park Crescent, London W1N 4EQ Tel:0171-636 5020 Fax:0171-436 0931 **Expertise** Fundraising & Public Relations. **Prev Posts** Products Manager, ICI 1976-86; National Appeals Manager, Oxfam 1986-89; Director of Marketing, SCOPE 1989-95. **Prof**

Background BA (Hons) Classics; General Commercial Management in Chemical Industry. **Pres Committees** Open University Voluntary Sector Management Advisory Board. **Past Committees** ICFM (Institute of Charity Fundraising Managers Executive). **Media Experience** Experience with interviews for radio, TV, video and press.

BRIAN Mr R. K. Chairman **BRITISH HYPNOTHERAPY ASSOCIATION - BHA** MEDICAL/HEALTH Type: Service provider; maintains register of qualified practitioners. 1 Wythburn Place, London W1H 5WL Tel:0171-723 4443 **Expertise** Emotional and/or relationship problems; parenthood; psychosexual development; utilization of potential. **Prof Background** Educated at Westminster College; registered psychotherapist and hypnotherapist. **Awards/Research** Numerous publ inc: Choosing a Hypnotist; Enjoy Marriage; Enjoy Parenthood; British Medical Hypnotists and the General Medical Council; How to Assess Therapy Organizations **Media Experience** BBC TV and radio; numerous press articles. **Addits** Prev editor of 2 jnls: Psychotherapy Review and You.

BRIER Norma Executive Director **RAVENSWOOD FOUNDATION** DISABILITY Type: Fundraiser; Service provider. Broadway House, 80-82 The Broadway, Stanmore, Middx HA7 4HB Tel:0181-954 4555 Fax:0181-420 6800 **Expertise** Care and education of children and adults with learning disabilities. **Prev Posts** Lecturer in Sociology and Counselling Skills; Director of Community Services, Ravenswood. **Prof Background** BA Hons (Sociology); MSc Social Policy and Social Work Studies; CQSW **Awards/Research** 1994 Public Mngmt Leadership Award. Research: employment problems for ex-prisoners; patient attitudes to staff in psychiatric hospitals; articles on long stay hospitals. **Pres Committees** Trustee, SENSE.

BRIER Sam Executive Director (Resources) **NORWOOD RAVENSWOOD** CHILD/FAMILY SERVICES CHILDREN/YOUTH Type: Service provider. Broadway House, 80-82 The Broadway, Stanmore HA7 4HB Tel:0181-954 4555 Fax:0181-420 6800 **Expertise** Childcare policy in Jewish community; strategic decision making in vol sector. **Prev Posts** LB Harrow Social Services Dept: Team Leader 1976-80; Area Dir 1980-84. **Prof Background** CQSW, North London Polytechnic 1970-72; MA, Public and Social Administration, Brunel Univ 1988-90; PhD, LSE 1991- current (part time). **Awards/Research** A study of organizational change in Victorian charity - From Isolation To Integration - 1989. **Pres Committees** Council of Nat Council of Voluntary Child Care Organizations; Executive of Council of Jewish Social Services. **Past Committees** Area Review Committee, LB Harrow. **Media Experience** Frequent spokesperson in Jewish and local media. **Addits** Expertise on marketing/fundraising esp of the Community Chest.

BRIERLEY Dr Peter Executive Director **CHRISTIAN RESEARCH** RELIGIOUS Type: Fundraiser; Grant maker. 4 Footscray Road, Eltham, London SE9 2TZ Tel:0181-294 1989 Fax:0181-294 0014 **Expertise** Data analysis & interpretation; teaching & applying vision building; editing UK Christian Handbook. **Prev Posts** Statistician, Cabinet Office 1970-78; Programme Director, Bible Society 1978-83; European Director, MARC Europe 1983-93. **Prof Background** Honors Degree in Statistics (University of London); Diploma of Theology (University of London); Hon. Doctorate, Greenwich University 1995. **Awards/Research** English Church Census 1979,1989 (published as Christian England); Scottish Church Census 1984,1994 (published as Prospects for Scotland 2000); Reaching and Keeping Teenagers 1993. **Media Experience** Various interviews, frequent consultations. **Addits** Auth: Priorities, Planning & Paperwork, 1993; Vision Building.

BRIGGS Dr Peter Executive Secretary **BRITISH ASSOCIATION FOR THE ADVANCEMENT OF SCIENCE - BA** SOCIAL Type: Fundraiser; Service provider. 23 Savile Row, London W1X 2NB Tel:0171-973 3500 Fax:0171-973 3051 **Expertise** Public understanding of science. **Prev Posts** BA: Education Manager 1980-86; Public Affairs Manager 1986-90. **Prof Background** Sussex Univ: BSc (Chemistry) 1966; DPhil (Theoretical Chemistry) 1969. **Pres Committees** Trustee, Rutherford Trust for Public Understanding of Science; COPUS - Cttee on the Public Understanding of Science. **Media Experience** Occasional interviews.

BRODIE David Director **TAXAID** SOCIAL Type: Service provider. Linburn House, 342 Kilburn High Rd, London NW6 2QJ Tel:0171-624 5216 Fax:0171-624 5248 **Expertise** Tax advice specialist & financial writer. **Prev Posts** Manager, Stoy Hayward (Accountants) 1984-86; Tax Consultant 1986-91. **Prof Background** BSc Mathematics; BA (Hons) Law; FCA Chartered Accountant. **Awards/Research** Author of: Taxation of Marriage & Marriage Breakdown (Tolley Publishing Co Ltd 1988). **Pres Committees** Member, Tax Law Review Committee; Member, Self-Assessment Consultative Committee. **Past Committees** Board Member, Friends of the Earth; Treasurer, Campaign for Work. **Media Experience** Articles for The Guardian (personal finance); Radio interviews (tax matters).

BROOKING Barry A. Chief Executive **PARKINSON'S DISEASE SOCIETY OF UK** MEDICAL/HEALTH Type: Medical Charity. 22 Upper Woburn Place, London WC1H 0RA Tel:0171-383 3513 Fax:0171-383 5754 **Expertise** Senior Management; Education; Training. **Prev Posts** Commissioned Officer, Royal Navy 1965-81; Business Administrator, Medical Protection Society 1981-91; St John Ambulance 1991-95. **Prof Background** BA; MA; ACP; Qualified Teacher; MInst M; MIPD. **Awards/Research** MBE (Military). Publ: The Production of Effective Instructional Text. **Pres Committees** Deputy Chairman N and E Division Surrey Magistrates Bench; Chairman, The Brooking Society. **Past Committees** Surrey Probation Committee; Magistrates Courts Committee, Surrey. **Media Experience** Extensive MRTS. **Addits** JP for County of Surrey.

BROOKS Mrs Liz Executive Director/Chair Bursary Fund **DYSLEXIA INSTITUTE, THE** DISABILITY Type: Fundraiser; Service provider; Grant maker; Bursary. 133 Gresham Road, Staines, Middlesex TW18 2AJ Tel:01784-463851 Fax:01784-460747 **Expertise** Teaching; management; fundraising and PR. **Prev Posts** Dyslexia Institute: Teacher 1982-83; Area Principal (South

East) 1984-87; Director (Administration) 1987-91. **Prof Background** Certificate of Education, London University; Dip. Dyslexia Institute; MA School and College Management. **Pres Committees** Chair, Bursary Fund; Council Mbr, CReSTeD (schools for dyslexia students); Council, British Dyslexia Association. **Media Experience** Numerous interviews national and local TV and Radio. Regular press interviews.

BROOKS Marilyn Managing Director **PILKINGTON RETIREMENT SERVICES LTD** SOCIAL Type: Service provider. Chalon Way, St Helens, Merseyside WA10 1AU Tel:01744-457901 Fax:01744-454410 **Expertise** Management. **Prev Posts** Community Care Department Manager 1986-90; Field Services Manager 1990-91. **Awards/Research** Welfare Officer;Institute of Welfare Officers; Ashridge Management College. **Pres Committees** Pilkington Retirement Services Ltd; Age Concern (St Helens); Pilkington plc Grants Committee; United Voluntary Organisations. **Addits** Justice of the Peace; Fellow, Royal Society of Arts.

BROPHY Michael Chief Executive **CHARITIES AID FOUNDATION - CAF** SOCIAL Type: Service provider; Grant maker; Operating UK and overseas. Kings Hill, West Malling, Kent ME19 4TA Tel:01732-520000 Fax:01732-520001 Chief Executive since 1982. **Pres Committees** Secretary of the Council for Charitable Support; Vice Chairman of the European Foundation Centre.

BROWN Ann UK Secretary **FALKLANDS CONSERVATION** CONSERVATION/ENVIRONMENT Type: Fundraiser; Service provider. 1 Princes Avenue, Finchley, London N3 2DA Tel:0181-343 0831 Fax:0181-343 0831 **Expertise** Charity administration, wildlife conservation. **Prev Posts** BTCV Company Secretary 1964-77; Finance Director, London Wildlife Trust 1985-92. **Prof Background** Business Studies. **Awards/Research** Auth:Organising a Local Conservation Group (BTCV). **Pres Committees** BTCV Resources Committee; LB Barnet Environment Forum; Treasurer/Trustee, 22nd Finchley Scout Group; Chair, London Wildlife Trust (Barnet Group). **Past Committees** BTCV Local Groups Committee.

BROWN John General Secretary **AIRLINE AVIATION AND AEROSPACE CHRISTIAN FELLOWSHIP** RELIGIOUS Type: Fundraiser; Service provider; Campaigning, Professional association. 103 Ambleside Rd, Lightwater, Surrey GU18 5UJ Tel:01276-472724 Fax:01276-472724 **Expertise** General Secretary from 1971 onwards. **Prof Background** RAF; BOAC. **Awards/Research** Newline; Crossway; Christian Support for Christian Standards in the Aviation Professions. **Media Experience** Video.

BROWN Peter M. Chairman **GABBITAS EDUCATIONAL CONSULTANTS** CHILDREN/YOUTH Type: Service provider. Carrington House, 126-130 Regent Street, London W1R 6EE Tel:0171-734 0161 Fax:0171-437 1764 **Expertise** Leadership. **Prof Background** FCA; FCIM; FIOD; MIL; FMRS; MIPM. **Pres Committees** Chairman: Charity Appointments, Hyde Park Estate Association, Top Pay Research Group, Dawson Holdings Plc. **Past Committees** Vice President, Thomas Coram Foundation; Trustee, Charities Effectiveness Review Trust 1984-89. **Media Experience** Contributes articles to national papers and magazines.

BROWN Sandra Chief Administrative Officer **LEUKAEMIA CARE SOCIETY** MEDICAL/HEALTH Type: Service provider; Grant maker; Supportive Charity (Self-Funding). 14 Kingfisher Court, Venny Bridge, Pinhoe, Exeter EX4 8JN Tel:01392-464848 Fax:01392-460331 **Expertise** Administration. **Prev Posts** Leukaemia Care Society: Clerical Assist 1984-87; Administrative Officer 1987-90; Finance Officer 1991-93; Chief Administrative Officer 1994-. **Prof Background** No formal training in the charity field.

BROWN Mrs Sheila Executive Director **BIRTH DEFECTS FOUNDATION** DISABILITY Type: Fundraiser; Grant maker; Campaigning. Chelsea House, West Gate, London W5 1DR Tel:0181-862 0198 **Expertise** Prevention of inborn handicap, special needs children, disability rights, medical & scientific research. **Prev Posts** Director, Grapevine for Special Families; Director, Noonan Syndrome Society. **Prof Background** Voluntary sector, administration & counselling. **Awards/Research** Author of articles & booklets. **Pres Committees** Hon. Director/Trustee, Noonan Syndrome Society; Trustee, Grapevine; Board Member, Housing Association; World Alliance of Birth Defect Prevention Organisations. **Past Committees** Committee Member, Cheslyn Hay Youth Club; Board Member, Kaleidoscope Theatre; School Governor, Special School Staffordshire. **Media Experience** Wide range of media experience especially with radio & TV. **Addits** Consultant, speaker & contributor to journals, newsletters & campaigns.

BROWNLIE Thomas **BRITISH FEDERATION OF FILM SOCIETIES - BFFS** SOCIAL Type: Fundraiser; Service provider; Grant maker. PO Box 1DR, London W1A 1DR Tel:0171-734 9300 Fax:0171-734 9093 **Expertise** Film exhibition and administration. **Prev Posts** Administrator 1982-85; Teacher 1985-87. **Prof Background** MA Glasgow Univ; Teaching Cert, Jordanhill College; DMS, City of London Polytechnic. **Pres Committees** Exec Cttee, International Federation of Film Socs (IFFS).

BRUCE Professor Ian Director-General **ROYAL NATIONAL INSTITUTE FOR THE BLIND - RNIB** DISABILITY Type: Fundraiser; Service provider; Grant maker. 224 Great Portland Street London W1N 6AA Tel:0171-388-1266 Fax:0171-388 2034 **Expertise** Management generally, marketing in particular. **Prev Posts** Mkgt Mngr,Unilever; Appeals/PR Officer then Asst Dir, Age Concern England 1970-74; Dir, Volunteer Centre UK 1975-81; Asst Chief Exec, LB Hammersmith & Fulham 1981-83. **Prof Background** Companion, (Brit) Inst of Mngmt; Hon Doctorate, Univ of Birmingham. **Awards/Research** Co-auth:Blind & Partially-sighted Adults in Britain, 92; Managing & Staffing Britain's Largest Charities, 92; Management for Tomorrow, 93;Meeting Need - Successful Charity Mkting 94. **Pres Committees** Nat Advisory Cncl on Employment of Disabled People; Co-chair, Disability Benefits Consortium; Dep Chair, Central London TEC. **Past Committees** Adv

Cncl, Centre Policies on Ageing 79-83;IBA Educ Adv Cncl 81-83;Exec Cttee, Age Concern Eng 85-91; Exec Cttee, NCVO 90-94. **Media Experience** Numerous appearances on all media. **Addits** Hon Dir, VOLPROF, Centre for Vol Sect Mngmt, City Univ Business School.

BRUEGGEMANN Ingar Secretary General **INTERNATIONAL PLANNED PARENTHOOD FEDERATION - IPPF** MEDICAL/HEALTH Type: Fundraiser; Service provider; Grant maker. Regents College, Inner Circle, Regents Park, London NW1 4NS Tel:0171-486 0741 Fax:0171-487 7950.

BRUNWIN Rick Director **SIR OSWALD STOLL FOUNDATION** SOCIAL Type: Service provider. 446 Fulham Road, London SW6 1DT Tel:0171-385 2110 Fax:0171-381 8274 **Expertise** Housing Management and Development. **Prev Posts** Area Housing Manager 1980-86; Royal Borough of Kensington and Chelsea. **Prof Background** BA Professional Qualification in Housing. **Pres Committees** Director, Shepherds Bush Housing Assoc & Old Etonian Housing Association; Chairman and Director, Keep Warm (Care and Repair Hammersmith & Fulham).

BRYANT John LEAGUE AGAINST CRUEL SPORTS ANIMALS/WILDLIFE Type: Fundraiser; Service provider; Grant maker; Campaigning. 83-87 Union Street, London SE1 1SG Tel:0171-403 6155 Fax:0171-403 4532 **Expertise** Wildlife Protection; Animal Welfare Legislation; Animal Rights Movement. **Prev Posts** Manager, Ferne Animal Sanctuary 1976 -83; Cncl Mbr, RSPCA 1972-79; Chairman, Animal Aid Cncl 1983-87. **Prof Background** Aircraft Engineer. **Awards/Research** Fettered Kingdoms - An Examination of the Animals Rights Ethic 1982; Grey Squirrels - No Black & White Issue - League Against Cruel Sports Pub 1994. Numerous articles on foxhunting. **Pres Committees** Campaign for the Protection of Hunted Animals, Joint campaign group: RSPCA, Intl Fund for Animal Welfare, League against Cruel Sports. **Past Committees** Coalition for Badgers (A coalition of several wildlife protection & conservation bodies) 1990-91. **Addits** Draughtsman of sev Parliamentary bills for protection of wild mammals.

BRYER David Ronald William Director **OXFAM** SOCIAL Type: Fundraiser; Service provider; Grant maker; Relief and development overseas. 274 Banbury Road, Oxford OX2 7DZ Tel:01865-311311 Fax:01865-312317 **Prev Posts** OXFAM - Field Director, Middle East 1975-79; Co-ordinator of Africa Programme 1981-84; Director of Overseas Programme 1984-91. **Prof Background** BA/MA Middle East Studies, Worcester College, Oxford 1966; D.Phil. Oxford (The Origins of the Druze Religion) 1972; Dip Ed Manchester Univ 1967. **Awards/Research** CMG; Various articles on Middle East, especially Druze, and Development matters. **Pres Committees** VSO Council; Eurostep; Chair, Steering Committee for Humanitarian Response (Geneva). **Past Committees** ACORD; British Refugee Council; ICVA. **Media Experience** Frequent participation.

BUBB S J Director of Personnel & Administration **NATIONAL LOTTERY CHARITIES BOARD** SOCIAL Type: Grant maker; Statutory Body. St Vincent House, 30 Orange Street, London WC2H 7HH Tel:0171-747 5272 Fax:0171-747 5210 **Expertise** Personnel. **Prev Posts** Head of Personnel, AMA, 1987-95; Executive Secretary, METRA, 1989-1995; Negotiations Officer NUT 1980-87 **Prof Background** MA, Christchurch, Oxford; FRSA; Mbr, IPM. Juvenile Court Magistrate. **Awards/Research** Books on TUPE, ARD and TUPE, Brussels Sprouting. **Pres Committees** Director, Oval House; Committee Member, Christ Church Association; Member (and Founder), The Landmark & South London Aids Action. **Past Committees** Chair, City of Oxford Orchestra (1994-95); many other voluntary sector bodies over the last 15 years. **Media Experience** Extensive media experience.

BUCHANAN Dr Mary Chairman **WOMEN'S NATIONWIDE CANCER CONTROL CAMPAIGN - WNCCC** MEDICAL/HEALTH Type: Service provider; Health education. Suna House, 128-130 Curtain Rd, London EC2A 3AR Tel:0171-729 4688 Fax:0171-613 0771 **Expertise** Breast and cervical cancer. **Prev Posts** Principal in family practice; medical posts in gynaecology, family planning, paediatrics. **Prof Background** Medical training at Manchester Univ. **Awards/Research** In-house reports and publications; Jt auth (w. A Oakley, G Bendelow, J Barnes, O Husain) Health and Cancer Prevention: Knowledge and Beliefs of Children and Young People (1993). **Pres Committees** Chair, Cancer Educn Co-ordng Gp; Bd Mbr of women's prison; Internat Proj Liaison, Soroptimist Internat; Mbr, Bd of UK Nat Breast Cancer Coalit; Mbr UK Forum of Europa Donna. **Media Experience** Radio and press contrib/interviews.

BUCK Michael Honorary Secretary **HALLIWICK ASSOCIATION OF SWIMMING THERAPY** DISABILITY Type: Fundraiser; Service provider; Educational. 26 Stone Grove, Edgware, Middlesex HA8 7UA Tel:0181-958 1642 Fax:0181-958 1642 **Expertise** Training as lecturer for Halliwick courses **Prev Posts** RAF(Medical Branch) 1954-76; Provisions Officer, American Medical International 1975-80. **Pres Committees** Harry Brown 'Bus Society (Voluntary Transport Service for Disabled People).

BUCKLEY Dr E.G. Executive Director **SCOTTISH COUNCIL FOR POSTGRADUATE MEDICAL AND DENTAL EDUCATION** MEDICAL/HEALTH Type: Statutory Body. 12 Queen Street, Edinburgh EH2 1JE Tel:0131-2254365 Fax:0131-2255891 **Expertise** Post Graduate Medical Education. **Prev Posts** General Practitioner 1974-93; Editor, British Journal of General Practice 1983-89. **Prof Background** Medicine, MD Edinburgh. **Awards/Research** Fellow: Royal College of General Practitioners & Royal College of Physicians of Edinburgh; Author of Articles & Chapters on medical education, care of the elderly & medical audit. **Pres Committees** Secretary, Association for the Study of Medical Education (ASME). **Past Committees** Cncl Mbr, European Academy of Teachers in General Practice (EURACT) 1993-6; Cncl Mbr, Medical & Dental Defence Union of Scotland.

BULL David Director **AMNESTY INTERNATIONAL (UK)** SOCIAL Type: Fundraiser; Campaigning. 99-119 Rosebery Ave, London EC1R 4RE Tel:0171-814 6200

Fax:0171-833 1510 **Prev Posts** Public Affairs Unit Officer, Oxfam 1979-84; Director, Environment Liaison Centre Int 1984-87; General Sec World University Service (UK) 1987-90. **Prof Background** BA Economics (Sussex); MSc Development Studies (Bath). **Awards/Research** A Growing Problem: Pesticides & the 3rd World Poor (Oxfam 1982); The Poverty of Diplomacy: Kampuchea & the Outside World (Oxfam 1983). **Pres Committees** Executive Cttee, ACENVO; Board, The Pesticides Trust. **Media Experience** Extensive media experience.

BULLIVANT Mrs Barbara J.P. Hon. Secretary **HOME AND SCHOOL COUNCIL** CHILD/YOUTH Type: Service provider; Umbrella for parent organisations. 40 Sunningdale Mount, Sheffield, S. Yorkshire S11 9HA Tel:0114-2364181 Fax:0114-2364181 **Expertise** Has run council for 25 yrs; secretarial work; sales of booklets; service subscribers & postal sales. **Prev Posts** Hon. Secretary, Campaign for State Education 1971-80; Hon. Secretary, National Association of Governors & Managers 1980-89. **Prof Background** Trained social worker, University of Sheffield & Liverpool; Home Office training; Much of voluntary work has been as a parent. **Awards/Research** Numerous training booklets: You Are The Governor & New Governors Guide, etc.; Children & Young People in Trouble; co-author of Helping Children at Home & Parents & Young People. **Pres Committees** Sheffield Magistrates Court, Youth, Domestic & Adult Benches; Member, S Yorks Police Authority (20 years); School Governor (15 schools over 26 yrs); Chair, HSC Trust. **Past Committees** Advisory Centre for Education, Executive Cttee, Nat Children's Bureau; CASE Cttee, Nat Assoc of Governors & Managers (founder mbr). **Media Experience** Many radio broadcasts (Woman's Hour, etc.); Granada TV series on Education.

BUNCE Colin Chief Executive **GARDENERS' ROYAL BENEVOLENT SOCIETY - GRBS** THE ELDERLY Type: Fundraiser; Service provider; Grant maker. Bridge House, 139 Kingston Road, Leatherhead KT22 7NT Tel:01372-373962 Fax:01372-362575 **Expertise** Provision and maintenance of sheltered residential and nursing housing. **Prof Background** Military; ACIS.

BUNTING Mrs Sylvia P. National Secretary **GIRLS' BRIGADE NATIONAL COUNCIL FOR ENGLAND AND WALES** CHILD/YOUTH Type: Service provider. Girls' Brigade House, Foxhall Road, Didcot, Oxon OX11 7BQ Tel:01235-510425 Fax:01235-510429 **Expertise** Youth work, social work. **Prev Posts** Medical social worker, Doncaster Royal Infirmary 1971-73; Fieldwork Group Leader, Doncaster MBC Social Services 1973-79. **Prof Background** BA (Hons) Latin/French, University of Reading; Dip in Social Services, University of Southampton; Dip in Applied Social Studies, University of Newcastle. **Past Committees** Girls' Brigade International Management Committee 1989-92.

BURGE Mr Richard Director General **ZOOLOGICAL SOCIETY** ANIMAL/WILDLIFE Type: Service provider. Regents Park, London NW1 4RY Tel:0171-449 6207 Fax:0171-449 6283 **Expertise** Management of public bodies & mammal ecologist. **Prev Posts** Ass Dir, The Brit Cncl in Nigeria 1986-90; Head of European Union & World Bank Contracts, The Brit Cncl 1992-93; Head of Africa & Middle East Operations, The Brit Cncl 1993-95. **Prof Background** BSc (Hons) Zoology, University of Durham; Commonwealth Research Scholar, University of Peradeniya. **Pres Committees** ACENVO Policy & Research Task Group; Friend's of Regent's Park Committee. **Media Experience** Contributions to TV & radio (current affairs in UK & Africa).

BURGESS Jacquelin Chairperson **LANDSCAPE RESEARCH GROUP** CONSERVATION/ENVIRONMENT Type: Fundraiser; Service provider; Grant maker. c/o Dept of Geography, University College London, Gower St, London WC1E 6BT Tel:0171-387 7050 Fax:0171-380 7565 **Expertise** Landscape researcher; qualitative work with general public of relevance to policy makers. **Prev Posts** University College London: Lecturer in Geography 1975-91; currently Reader in Geography. **Prof Background** BA and PHD, Hull Univ. **Awards/Research** Many publ related mainly to landscape/nature conservation and countryside issues. **Pres Committees** Steering Group, Lee Valley Community Outreach Project. **Media Experience** Consultant to TV documentaries on landscape meanings & values.

BURKE Henry Artistic & Managing Director **NORWICH PLAYHOUSE** ARTS Type: Fundraiser; Service provider; Arts venue & professional producing theatre. 42-58 St George's Street, Norwich, Norfolk NR3 1AB Tel:01603-612580 Fax:01603-617728 **Expertise** Theatre Director; Businessman. **Prev Posts** Director, Brahams (Gt. Yarmouth) Ltd. 1967-81; Chairman & Director, Seymour-Burke Ltd 1983 to date. **Prof Background** Ed: Cambridge University 1951-53. **Pres Committees** Member, The Directors' Guild of Great Britain. **Past Committees** Sewell Barn Theatre Trust, Norwich; St George's Trust, Gt. Yarmouth. **Media Experience** Experience in TV (BBC TV, Tyne Tees TV, Anglia TV).

BURKEMAN Steven Trust Secretary **JOSEPH ROWNTREE CHARITABLE TRUST** SOCIAL Type: Grant maker. The Garden House, Water End, York YO3 6LP Tel:01904-627810 Fax:01904-651990 **Expertise** Democratic process; corporate responsibility; South Africa. **Prev Posts** Dir, Check, Rights Centre, Liverpool 1971-74; Special Assistant, Area Management Unit, Liverpool City Council 1974-77; Secretary, Central Birmingham CHC 1977-82. **Prof Background** LL.B (Hons), Manchester University; PGCE, York University; M.Soc.Sc, Birmingham University; currently undertaking doctoral research at York University. **Awards/Research** Publ:Funding for Change in South Africa (ed), pub. by Assn of Char. Foundations; Truth & Integrity in Voluntary Organisations in Questions of Integrity, LYM 1993. **Pres Committees** Company Dir, FunderFinder; Brd Mbr, Interfund; Adv. Cncl, Public Concern at Work; Sch Governor; Governor & Mbr, Mgmt Cttee, The Retreat; & others. **Past Committees** EIRIS; New Consumer; Euro Citizen Action Service & others.

BURMAN Rickie Director **JEWISH MUSEUM - LONDON'S MUSEUM OF JEWISH LIFE** CONSERVATION/ENVIRONMENT Type: Service provider. 129-131 Albert Street, London NW1 7NB Tel:0171-284 1997 Fax:0171-267 9008 **Prev Posts** Research Fellow,

Manchester Polytechnic 1979-84; Co-ordinator, Manchester Jewish Museum 1982-84; Curator, London Museum of Jewish Life 1984-95. **Prof Background** MA Archaeology and Anthropology; M.Phil Social Anthropology, Cambridge University. **Awards/Research** Articles on changing role of Jewish women and on Jewish heritage in Britain. **Past Committees** Radio and press interviews.

BURMAN Michael Administrative Director **UNION OF LIBERAL & PROGRESSIVE SYNAGOGUES - ULPS** RELIGIOUS Type: Service provider; Grant maker; Campaigning; Communal org. The Montagu Centre, 21 Maple Street, London W1P 6DS Tel:0171-580 1663 Fax:0171-436 4184 **Expertise** Administration & Religion. **Prev Posts** Senior Teacher, Tollington Park School 1970-79; Senior Deputy Head Teacher, Whitmore High School, Harrow 1979-95. **Prof Background** BSc (Hons) Geography, University of London; PGCE, University of London; FRGS; OFSTED Inspector of Schools; Certificate in Therapy & Counselling. **Awards/Research** Author of articles on Joint Jewish/Geographical topics. **Pres Committees** Governor, The Akiva School; Project Coordinator, The Shalom School; Educational Consultant, The Anne Frank School; Numerous ULPS Committees. **Past Committees** Board of Deputies of British Jews; Association of Jewish Teachers; The New North London Synagogue; Barnet Community Relations Council. **Media Experience** Experience with radio and as consultant on Jewish issues.

BURNELL Jan Director (until winter 1996) **NATIONAL COUNCIL OF VOLUNTARY CHILD CARE ORGANISATIONS - NCVCCO** CHILDREN/YOUTH Type: Service provider. Unit 4, Pride Court, 80-82 White Lion Street, London N1 9PF Tel:0171-833 3319 Fax:0171-833 8637 **Expertise** Child care. **Prev Posts** Registered Childminder 1979-84; Under-7s Co-ordinator, LB Haringey 1984-87; Director, National Childminding Assoc 1987-93. **Prof Background** BA (Hons) History with Philosophy. **Past Committees** Advisory Group, NCB Early Childhood Unit; Law Reform for Children's Day Care; Childcare Umbrella; NCVCCO General Purposes Cttee. **Media Experience** Interviews on TVAM, Woman's Hour, You and Yours, LBC. **Addits** Member of ACENVO (Assoc of Chief Execs of Nat Vol Orgs).

BURNHAM Reverend Anthony G. General Secretary **UNITED REFORMED CHURCH, THE** RELIGIOUS Type: Church 86 Tavistock Place, London WC1H 9RT Tel:0171-916 2020 Fax:0171-916 2021 **Expertise** Minister of Religion. **Prev Posts** Minister, South West Manchester Group of Churches, URC 1973-81; Moderator, North Western Province of the URC, 1981-92. **Prof Background** BA (Admin) Manchester Univ; trained for Congregational ministry at Northern College, Manchester. **Media Experience** Regular broadcaster of religious programmes for BBC radio and TV.

BURNIE Mrs PA Director **LIMBLESS ASSOCIATION** DISABILITY Type: Service provider. 31 The Mall, Ealing, London W5 2PX Tel:0181-579 1758.

BURNS Anthony Michael James Executive Director/Secretary **CORONARY ARTERY DISEASE RESEARCH ASSOCIATION, THE - CORDA** MEDICAL/HEALTH Type: Fundraiser; Grant maker. PO Box 9353, 121 Sydney St, London SW3 6ZA Tel:0171-349 8686 Fax:0171-349 9414 **Expertise** General management and fundraising. **Prev Posts** Retail Marketing Executive for major grocery, pharmaceutical and toy companies, 1967-80; Asst Appeals Director, Imperial Cancer Research Fund 1980-84. **Prof Background** Bexhill Grammar School; Dip. Management Studies, Hatfield Polytechnic. **Awards/Research** Various articles dealing with heart disease, fundraising and retail marketing. **Pres Committees** Managing Director, CORDA Cards Ltd; Secretary to CORDA Research Grants Cttee. **Media Experience** Principal spokesperson for CORDA; writer/producer of promotional videos.

BURTON Lt Col B. M. Administrator **ADA COLE MEMORIAL STABLES** ANIMAL/WILDLIFE Type: Equine Rescue. Broadlands, Broadley Common, Nazeing, Essex EN9 2DH Tel:01992-892133 Fax:01992-893841 **Expertise** Fulfil all roles as only paid manager for the charity. **Prev Posts** Army Officer 1966-94. **Prof Background** BA MSc (Econ). **Pres Committees** NEWC. **Media Experience** Editor, Services Newspaper Cyprus.

BURTON Gerald Chief Executive **WOMEN'S ROYAL VOLUNTARY SERVICE** WOMEN Type: Fundraiser; Service provider. 234-244 Stockwell Road, London SW9 9SP Tel:0171-416 0146 Fax:0171-416 0148 **Expertise** Finance, Management Structure and Strategy. **Prev Posts** Partner & Senior Partner, Kidsons Impey (Chartered Accountants), 1955-92. **Prof Background** Chartered Accountant. **Pres Committees** Bethlem & Maudsley NHS Trust; Bradford & Bingley London Regional Board; Regent House Properties; Trustee of Various Family Trusts. **Media Experience** Experience in radio, TV and press.

BURTON John A. Chief Executive **WORLD WIDE LAND CONSERVATION TRUST** ANIMAL/WILDLIFE Type: Fundraiser; Service provider; Grant maker. Blyth House, Bridge Street, Halesworth, Suffolk IP19 8AB Tel:01986-874422 Fax:01986-874425 **Expertise** Wildlife; Conservation **Prev Posts** Wildlife Consultant, Friends of the Earth 1970-75; Exec. Secretary, Fauna & Flora Preservation Society 1975-88. **Awards/Research** Over 25 books mostly on natural history, including several field guides & books on endangered species. **Pres Committees** Library Cttee; Linnean Society; Edit Bd, Fauna & Flora Preservation Soc; Conservation Committee, Suffolk Wildlife Trust; Environmental Advisory Board, Trustee Savings Bank; Mbr Emeritus IUCN/SSC. **Past Committees** Int Council for Bird Preservation (UK), Otter Trust. **Media Experience** Extensive radio/TV and press.

BURTON Neil Secretary **GEORGIAN GROUP** CONSERVATION/ENVIRONMENT Type: Fundraiser; Grant maker; Campaigning, Statutory Consultee. 6 Fitzroy Square, London W1P 6DX Tel:0171-387 1720 Fax:0171-387 1721 **Expertise** Historic Buildings/Architectural Conservation. **Prev Posts** Historian. GLC Historic Buildings DIV, 1973-88. English Heritage: Church Inspector for North England 1988-1991, Historic Buildings Inspector East Midlands 1991-1994.

Prof Background BA(HONS) Mod History/Oxford, Diploma History Art. (Edinburgh), Historian/GLC Historic Bldgs Divn. Inspector/English Heritage. **Media Experience** Some media experience.

BURTON Virginia Chair **PARENTLINE** SOCIAL Type: Fundraiser; Service provider. Endway House, Endway, Hadleigh, Benfleet, Essex SS7 2AN Tel:01702-554782 Fax:01702-554911 **Expertise** VS Policy & Mngmt, youth pol & volunteering; chld/fam suppt; chld's rghts/abuse/prtctn, esp. sex ab/dom violnce **Prev Posts** Unit manager, Thurrock Family Service Unit 1983-88; Training development adviser, NCVCCO 1988-93; Adviser, Dept Nat Heritage, Voluntary & Community Division 1994-present. **Prof Background** BSc (Soc); CQSW; social work practice and management: children and families; voluntary sector policy. **Awards/Research** Auth: Numerous articles in professional journals. **Pres Committees** Independent Persons Service Advisory Gp, Voice for the Child in Care; Advisory Gp, Who Cares? Trust; Advice, Guidance, Counselling & Psychotherapy Lead Body Bd; Observer status on other boards. **Media Experience** Radio/TV and press comments on variety of related issues.

BUSH Geoffrey Group Community Relations Director **GRAND METROPOLITAN PLC** SOCIAL Type: Grant maker. 64-65 North Road, Brighton BN1 1YD Tel:01273-570170 Fax:01273-679523 **Expertise** Charity, Foundation and Business Management: organization, administration and leadership skills. **Prev Posts** GrandMet Trust: Managing director 1990-96. **Prof Background** Fellow, Institute of Chartered Accountants; Fellow, RSA; Fellow, British Institute of Management; Master of Science (Business Administration). Auth: Grand Met Community Involvement. **Pres Committees** Chair, Grand Metropolitan Charitable Trust, GrandMet Int Fndtn. Corp Responsibility Gp; Bridge Gp; Cities in Schools UK; Foyer Fed for Youth; Project Fullemploy; Troubleshooters Ltd. Mbr: Gateway Educational Trust; Tomorrow's People; Nat Child Labor Cttee (USA).

BUSHBY Rob Co-ordinator **VENTURE SCOTLAND** CHILDREN/YOUTH Type: Service provider. Bonnington Mill, 72 Newhaven Rd, Edinburgh EH6 5QG Tel:0131-5535333 Fax:0131-5535333 **Expertise** Personal development using the outdoor environment and management. **Prev Posts** Assistant, Oil Control Division, British Petroleum, London 1985-86; Tutor, Outward Bound Australia 1988-89; Tutor, Outward Bound Ullswater 1991-94. **Prof Background** BSc (Hons) Business Studies; various outdoor qualifications; National Certificate in Training Practice. **Pres Committees** John Muir Award Steering Group.

BUTLER Mr R.F. Director **BEAFORD CENTRE** CONSERVATION/ENVIRONMENT Type: Service provider; Arts Development Agency. Beaford, Winkleigh, Devon EX19 8LU Tel:01805-603201 Fax:01805-603202 **Expertise** Arts; marketing. **Prev Posts** Director, Colway Theatre Trust 1986-90. **Prof Background** BA Hons Social Policy and Administration. **Pres Committees** Secretary, Devon Arts Forum. **Media Experience** Frequent contributions all media.

BUTLER David Chief Executive **PRINCESS ROYAL TRUST FOR CARERS** SOCIAL Type: Fundraiser; Service provider. 16 Byward St, Tower Hill, London EC3R 5BA Tel:0171-480 7788 Fax:0171-481 4729 **Expertise** Strategic management, personnel, finance. **Prev Posts** Director, Personnel/Finance, HM Treasury 1986-89; Deputy Director, National Savings 1989-90; Director, National Savings 1990-95. **Prof Background** Public administration, general management.

BYRNE Anthony J. Chief Executive **ROYAL SOCIETY OF HEALTH - RSH** MEDICAL/HEALTH Type: Professional Association. RSH House, 38a St George's Drive, London SW1V 4BH Tel:0171-630 0121 Fax:0171-976 6847 **Expertise** Health policy. **Prev Posts** Int Market Mgr, Glaxo 1982-84; Marketing Consultant, Milpro 1984-86; Independent Healthcare Assoc 1986-91; Dir, Governance, Parliamentary Consultant 1991-94. **Prof Background** Pharmacist, Pharmaceutical Industry; Marketing Management. **Pres Committees** North Down Community NHS Trust Board. **Past Committees** European Union of Private Hospitals; Kings Fund Accreditation Scheme; Conservative Medical Society Executive. **Media Experience** Radio/TV/video/press.

C

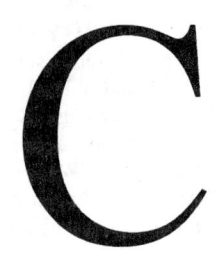

CAFFREY Kevin Director & Company Secretary **FATHER HUDSON'S SOCIETY** SOCIAL Type: Fundraiser; Service provider. Coventry Rd, Coleshill, Birmingham, B46 3ED Tel:01675-463187 Fax:01675-466607 Professional, administrative management. **Prev Posts** Snr Social Worker 1973-75; Snr Training Officer 1975-78; Area Social Services Manager 1978-91. **Prof Background** Qualified Social Worker, CQSW; BA Politics; MA Human Resource Management. **Pres Committees** Trustee, Catholic Child Welfare Council; Chair, Mngmt Brd - Voluntary Residential Care Home; Primary School Governor. **Past Committees** Member, Nottingham Dioceses Social Care Commission **Media Experience** Occasional press, radio.

CALDWELL Neil Director **PRINCE'S TRUST - BRO** SOCIAL Type: Fundraiser; Service provider; Grant maker. 4th Floor, Empire House, Mount Stuart Square, Cardiff, CF1 6DN Tel:01222-471 121 Fax:01222-482 086 **Expertise** Rural, Landscape, Environment, Welsh Language, Community Development. **Prev Posts** National Trust 1982-88; Campaign for the Protection of Rural Wales, 1988-94. **Prof Background** BSc (Hons) Geography, University of Wales; PhD Coastal Geomorphology, Polytechnic of Wales. **Awards/Research** Past Editor: Rural Wales; Contributor to: The Green Agenda (Wales), A Parliament for Wales. **Pres Committees** Vice Ch, Wales Wildlife & Countryside Link; Mbr, NRA Wales Rivers Cttee, UK Mbrs Group European Environmental Bureau, Welsh Language Board, Wales Rural Forum, Chair, Environmental Wales Strategy Grp. **Past Committees** Council for National Parks; Institute for Welsh Affairs. **Media Experience** Considerable media experience. **Addits** Fellow, RSA.

CALLIS Sidney Chairman of Trustees **BLIND BUSINESS ASSOCIATION CHARITABLE TRUST - BBA** DISABILITY Type: Fundraiser; Service provider; Grant maker; Campaigning, Professional association. The Old School House, School Lane, Buckingham, Bucks MK18 1HB Tel:01280-813267 Fax:01280-813267 **Expertise** Management Consultancy, Finance/Communication skills. **Prev Posts** Self Employed since 1968. **Prof Background** FCA; FIPD. Conference speaker eg Multi-media Nov 94, Polish Blind Assoc Conference July 1996. **Awards/Research** Numerous articles in management/training journals; Training Manual: Effective Writing for Business Publ 1994 **Pres Committees** Trusteeships: BBA Charitable Trust. **Past Committees** Blind Business Association Ltd, Committee Member/Treasurer. **Media Experience** Frequent broadcast BBC World Service/TV/Frequent press contact.

CAMP Anthony J. Director **SOCIETY OF GENEALOGISTS** SOCIAL Type: Educational Charity. 14 Charterhouse Buildings, Goswell Road, London EC1M 7BA Tel:0171-251 8799 **Expertise** Genealogical research. **Prev Posts** Society of Genealogists: Research Asst 1957-59, Director of Research, 1962-79; Director and Secretary since 1979. **Prof Background** BA Hons, University College, London; Mbr of Council, Association of Genealogists & Record Agents 1968-75, (Chairman 1973-5, Vice-Pres since 1980). **Awards/Research** Award of Merit, Nat Geog Soc 1984; Freeman of City 1984. Publ inc: Everyone has Roots, 1978; Index to Wills proved in the Prerogative Court of Canterbury 1750-1800, 6 vols 1976-92. **Pres Committees** Mmbr of Cncl of British Record Society 1967-71, 1983-; Friends of Public Record Office 1988-; of Marc Fitch Fund 1991-. **Past Committees** Cncl Mbr, Eng Genealogical Congress (Pres 91-2); Pres, Herts Family & Pop History Soc; Vice-Pres, Assoc Genealogists & Record Agents **Media Experience** Monthly Diary in Family Tree Magazine since 1984.

CAMPBELL Allan Chief Executive **COMUNN NA GAIDHLIG** ARTS/CULTURAL Type: Fundraiser; Service provider; Grant maker. 5 Mitchell's Lane, Inverness IV2 3HQ Tel:01463-234138 Fax:01463-237470 **Expertise** Broadcasting, Marketing, Economic Development. **Prev Posts** BBC Radio, Programmes Producer 1980-84; Area Economic Dev Manager, Highland Reg/Council 1984-85; BBC Radio Station Manager 1985-91. **Prof Background** Postgraduate in Marketing in Food Industry, University of Aberdeen; 8 years management in industry. **Pres Committees** Trustee, Sabhal Mor Ostaig (Gaelic College); Director, Balnain House Trust (Music Heritage Centre); Director, Comhairle nan Sgoiltean Araich (National Gaelic Playgroup Council).

CAMPBELL David Executive Director **FARM-AFRICA** OVERSEAS Type: Fundraiser; Service provider; Operational agricultural development NGO in Africa. 9-10 Southampton Place, London WC1A 2EA Tel:0171-430 0440 Fax:0171-430 0460 **Expertise** Agricultural development in Africa; agricultural journalism. **Prev Posts** Business Editor, Farmers Weekly 1971-75; Oxfam Field Director, Bangladesh 1976-80; Oxfam Field Director, East Africa 1981-85. **Prof Background** Diploma Agric Science, Royal Agricultural College, Cirencester; MSc Agric Extension, Reading University. **Awards/Research** Under 30's Fisons Award 1967; Fisons Travel Scholarship for Investigative Reporting 1974; IPC Award for Innovative Journalism 1975. Publ: FARM-Africa Newsletter and Annual Review. **Pres Committees** SOS Sahel Cncl. **Past Committees** Cape Land Development Trust, South Africa 1993-96. **Media Experience** Reporter, Farmers Weekly 1966-69; Features Writer 1969-71; Bus Editor 1971-75.

CAMPBELL Douglas Executive Director **DISABLED DRIVERS ASSOCIATION** DISABILITY Type: Fundraiser; Service provider. National HQ, Ashwellthorpe, Norwich, Norfolk NR16 1EX Tel:01508-489449 Fax:01508-488173 **Expertise** Mbr Support & Serv; External & Media Relations; Campaigning; Servicing Main Cttees; Administration. **Prev Posts** Honorary National Treasurer, 1993-95; Honorary National Chairman, 1990-93; Member of

Management Committee, 1987-90 (all with The Disabled Drivers Association). **Prof Background** Qualified Chartered Accountant, worked in this capacity before joining The Disabled Drivers Association. **Awards/Research** FCA. **Pres Committees** Joint Committee on Mobility for Disabled People. **Media Experience** Occasional contributor to radio & specialist media.

CAMPBELL George National Organiser **CHRISTIAN ENDEAVOUR UNION OF GREAT BRITAIN AND IRELAND** RELIGIOUS Type: Youth Training. Wellesbourne House, Walton Road, Wellesbourne, Warwickshire CV35 9JB Tel:01789-470439 Fax:01789-470439 **Expertise** Admin/Training/International Fellowship. **Prev Posts** Deputation Secretary, African Evangelical Fellowship 1965-73; General Secretary, Scottish Christian Endeavour 1973-74; Christian Endeavour 1975-85. **Prof Background** Trained in the Printing Industry - Works Manager. **Pres Committees** World Christian Endeavour; Evangelical Alliance (Children) Cttee. **Media Experience** Radio Programmes while working in Africa.

CAMPBELL Susan Chief Executive **YOUTH SPORT TRUST** CHILDREN/YOUTH Type: Fundraiser; Service provider. Rutland Building, Loughborough University, Loughborough, Leicestershire LE11 3TU Tel:01509-228 293 **Prev Posts** Loughborough Univ, PE Dept Lecturer 1975-79; Sports Council, East Midlands, 1979-83; Chief Exec, Nat Coaching Foundation 1983-95. **Prof Background** PE Teacher; Masters Degree; Honorary Doctorate. **Awards/Research** Published 3 books on coaching Netball; Talent Identification Systems across the World; Published 24 articles in various journals & magazines. **Pres Committees** Mbr, Sports Council's Task Force on Young People; Mbr of European group looking at harmonisation of coaching standards across Europe. **Past Committees** Mbr, SPRITO, Ind Training Org for Sport & Recreation; Mbr of numerous working parties relating to coaching issues in sport. **Media Experience** TV Commentator; appeared on a number of TV & Radio programmes. **Addits** England Netball & Athletics Int Snr Coach.

CAREY Conan Director General **HOME FARM TRUST LTD, THE** DISABILITY Type: Service provider. Merchants House, Wapping Road, Bristol BS1 4RW Tel:01179-273746 Fax:01179-225938 **Prev Posts** Senior Management Posts in Government. **Prof Background** Belvedere College, Dublin; Royal Military Academy, Sandhurst; Royal Military College of Science, Shrivenham; Staff College, Camberley. Acquired: FCIT, FBIM, FIPM, FRSA and Psc. Mbr, Inst of Dirs. **Pres Committees** HFT Management Board; Association of Residential Care Board; Vol Orgs Disability Gp. **Media Experience** Occasional.

CAREY Peter Director **NATIONAL ASSOCIATION FOR GIFTED CHILDREN** CHILDREN/YOUTH Type: Service provider; Training; Welfare. Park Campus, Boughton Green Road, Northampton, NN2 7AL Tel:01604-792300 Fax:01604-720636 **Expertise** In-Service training of teachers and parents, addressing branches, liaison with related agencies. **Prev Posts** Head of Upper Sch, Sch of St David & St Katharine, London 1976-79; Dep Head, Radcliffe Sch, Milton Keynes 1980-94; Professional Tutor, Oxford Univ Dept of Educ Studies 1990-93. **Prof Background** BA (Hons) History, Bristol; PGCE King's College, London; Special Diploma in Education, Oxford. **Awards/Research** Auth: Articled Teachers Scheme, 1992; Education articles in NAGC journal & Looking to their Future. **Pres Committees** Screening Cttee, Joint Educational Trust; Adviser, ACENVO Manual of Basic Guides to Good Practice; OFSTED Advisory Group for High Ability Children. **Media Experience** Regular items for radio, television and the press. **Addits** Amateur violinist and conductor of orchestras and choral societies.

CARINE James Registrar/Secretary **ARAB HORSE SOCIETY** ANIMAL Type: Service provider; Horse breeding and Welfare Association. Windsor Hse, Ramsbury, Marlborough, Wilts SN8 2PE Tel:01672-520782 Fax:01672-520880 **Expertise** General Manager with particular responsibility for stud book and racing. **Prev Posts** Commodore in Command HMS Drake 1988-89; Rear Admiral Chief of Staff, Naval Home Command 1989-91, Royal Navy 1951-1991. **Prof Background** King William's College, Isle of Man 1945-50; Fellow Chartered Institute of Secretaries (FCIS) 1980. **Awards/Research** Knight of St. Gregory the Great (Civil Division) KSG 1981 (Papal Award); Professional Magazine Articles. **Pres Committees** Director, United Services Trustee 1995; Senior Warden, Worshipful Company of Chartered Secretaries 1996. **Media Experience** Radio & TV interviews in America while in Royal Navy.

CARLETON-SMITH Major General M.E. Director General **MARIE CURIE CANCER CARE** MEDICAL/HEALTH Type: Fundraiser; Service provider. 28 Belgrave Square, London SW1X 8QG Tel:0171-235 3325 Fax:0171-823 2380 **Expertise** General management. **Prev Posts** British army 1949-85. **Prof Background** RMA Sandhurst; Army Staff College; Joint Services Staff College; National Defence College; Royal College of Defence Studies; FBIM. **Awards/Research** CBE 1980, MBE 1966, DL 1992. **Pres Committees** Chair, Marie Curie Trading Co Ltd; Vice-Chair, National Hospice Council. **Past Committees** Cabinet Contingencies Unit. **Media Experience** Fairly extensive.

CARLING Christine Director **NATIONAL ASSOCIATION OF COUNCILS FOR VOLUNTARY SERVICE - NACVS** SOCIAL Type: Service provider, specific to cncls for vol service & local vol orgs. 3rd Floor, Arundel Court, 177 Arundel Street, Sheffield S1 2NU Tel:0114-278 6636 Fax:0114-278 7004 **Expertise** Charity management; umbrella bodies; social and public policy issues. **Prev Posts** Co-ordinator, Children's Centre 1986-87; Manager, Citizen's Advice Bureau 1987-90. **Prof Background** BA (Hons); MBA. **Awards/Research** Contribs to newsletters. **Past Committees** Exec Cttee, NCVO. **Media Experience** Occasional press/radio interviews.

CARLOWE Melvyn I. Chief Executive **JEWISH CARE** RELIGIOUS Type: Service provider. Stuart Young House, 221 Golders Green Road, London NW11 9DQ Tel:0181-458 3282 Fax:0181-455 7185 **Expertise**

Management and leadership. **Prev Posts** Jewish Welfare Board: Chief Welfare Officer 1967-72, Executive Director 1972-89. **Prof Background** Social Work, Birmingham Univ, 1959-63. **Pres Committees** Hon Sec/Vice Chair, Central Cncl for Jewish Community Services; Trustee/Cncl/Exec Chair, North London Hospice; London & Quadrant Housing Assoc; NE Thames Liaison Cttee; Charity Tax Reform Group. **Past Committees** Federation of Jewish Family Services.

CARMICHAEL Brother Michael Director of Trust **MALT HOUSE TRUST** SOCIAL Type: Service provider. The Malt House, Church St, Uckfield, E Sussex TN22 1BS Tel:01825-761226 **Expertise** Working with ex offenders, substance abuses etc. **Prev Posts** Social Worker 1963-65;self employed in various businesses. **Prof Background** Training in Bereavement/HIV/AIDS/Drug Abuse. **Media Experience** Press articles; Broadcasting.

CARNEY Lynne Director **NATIONAL ASSOCIATION OF YOUTH THEATRES - NAYT** CHILDREN/YOUTH Unit 1304, The Custard Factory, Gibb Street, Digbeth, Birmingham B9 4AA Tel:0121-608 2111 Fax:0121-608 2333 **Expertise** Administration; fundraising and financial control; strategic planning and policy implementation. **Prev Posts** Administrator, Gazebo T.I.E. 1987-90; Administrator, Big Brum T.I.E. 1990-94; **Prof Background** BA (Hons) Humanities (Drama Specialism). **Addits** Specialization in Theatre-in-Education.

CARNIE Fiona National Coordinator **HUMAN SCALE EDUCATION** SOCIAL Type: Fundraiser; Service provider; Campaigning. 96 Carlingcott, Nr Bath, Avon BA2 8AW Tel:01761-433733 Fax:01761-433733 **Expertise** Small schools, Holistic education, Relationships in schools. **Prev Posts** British Council, Programme coordinator 1983-86. **Prof Background** BSc (Hons) Bristol; MA in Education Open Univ. **Awards/Research** Publ: Freeing Education (ed w. M Tasker & M Large) 1996; Articles in Guardian Mar 96, Resurgence 91, 92, 93. **Pres Committees** Associate Director, Education Now; Trustee, Bath small school; On the board of European Forum for Freedom in Education (Germany). **Media Experience** Various radio and television interviews. **Addits** Video produced: Education on a Human Scale.

CARNWATH Francis Adviser **NATIONAL HERITAGE MEMORIAL FUND** CONSERVATION Type: Grant maker. 10 St James Street, London SW1A 1EF Tel:0171-930 0963 Fax:0171-930 0968 **Expertise** Heritage, Arts, Business, Administration, Charity Trustee. **Prev Posts** Director, Baring Brothers & Co Ltd 1979-89; Deputy Director: Tate Gallery 1990-94; Acting Director, Nat Heritage Mem Fund 1995, Adviser, 1996- **Prof Background** Banking and Finance. **Pres Committees** Whitechapel Gallery, Trustee (since 1994); London Advisory Cttee, English Heritage (since 1990); Phillimore Estates, Trustee (since 1983); Spitalfields Historic Building Trust (since 1981). **Past Committees** Treasurer: Friends of Tate Gallery (1985-90), Voluntary Service Overseas (1981-85). **Media Experience** Occasional.

CARR Isabel Anne General Secretary (Scotland) **YOUNG WOMENS CHRISTIAN ASSOCIATION OF GB SCOTTISH NATIONAL COUNCIL - YWCA** SOCIAL Type: Fundraiser; Service provider; Advocacy. 7 Randolph Crescent, Edinburgh EH3 7TH Tel:0131-225 7592 Fax:0131-467 7008 **Expertise** General Management; Fundraising; PR; Public Speaking; Overseas/Devt Education; Training & Education. **Prev Posts** Church of Scotland Missionary 1981-85; Christian Aid, Area Secretary, 1985-92. **Prof Background** Community Education Certificate BA. **Past Committees** Church of Scotland, Middle East Committee; Youth Education Committee; Scottish Christian Women's Consultative Committee. **Media Experience** Various Radio interviews; Local/Nat Press; Articles in Church Press.

CARR Sally Development and Training Manager **CITIZEN ADVOCACY INFORMATION AND TRAINING** SOCIAL Type: Service provider. Unit 2K, Leroy House, 436 Essex Road, London N1 3QP Tel:0171-359 8289 Fax:0171-704 2227 **Expertise** Citizen advocacy. **Prev Posts** Education Officer, NACRO 1980-83; Literacy Scheme Co-ord, Soc of Vol Associates 1980-83; Co-ord, Advocacy Alliance 1983-87; Co-ordinator, National Citizen Advocacy 1987-94. **Prof Background** Graphic Design, Art Teaching. **Awards/Research** Auth: Bridging the Gap (NACRO); A Powerful Partnership (NCA). **Past Committees** Treasurer, International Childcare Trust; Trustee, White Lion Street Free School Ltd. **Media Experience** Interviews on national radio and TV.

CARRINGTON Lucie Editor **MUSEUMS JOURNAL** CONSERVATION/ENVIRONMENT Type: Service provider. Museums Association, 42 Clerkenwell Close, London EC1R 0PA Tel:0171-250 1834 Fax:0171-250 1929.

CARTER Jane Director **UNITED NATIONS ASSOCIATION FOR INTERNATIONAL SERVICE - UNAIS** OVERSEAS Type: Fundraiser; Service provider; Campaigning & International Organisation. Suite 3a Hunter House, 57 Goodramgate, York, N Yorks YO1 2LS Tel:01904-647 799 Fax:01904-652 353 **Expertise** Overseas Development, Human Resource Management. **Prev Posts** Secretary, El Salvador Solidarity Campaign, 1982-84. **Prof Background** BA. **Media Experience** TV, radio, video and press experience.

CASS Mrs Ruth Hon Correspondence Secretary **JOSEPHINE BUTLER SOCIETY & J.B. EDUCATIONAL** SOCIAL Type: Grant maker; Campaigning; Educational trust. 60 Rotherwick Road, London NW11 7DB Tel:0181-455 1664 **Expertise** Hospital social work. **Prev Posts** Retired 1982. **Prof Background** BSc (Econ) A1 MSW. **Pres Committees** Josephine Butler Soc. Cttee.

CAYTON Harry Executive Director **ALZHEIMER'S DISEASE SOCIETY** MEDICAL/HEALTH Type: Fundraiser; Service provider; Grant maker; Carer's Organization. Gordon House, 10 Greencoat Place, London SW1P 1PH Tel:0171-306 0606 Fax:0171-306 0808 **Prev Posts** Director, National Deaf Children's Society 1982-91. **Prof Background** BA; BPhil; Dip. Anth. **Awards/Research** Canadian Commonwealth Fellowship, 1982 **Pres Committees** Trustee: Hearing Research Trust; Mbr, Sec of State for Health's YTS Adv Gp; Gov:Ovingdn Hall Sch; Mental Health Review Panel, Parkside HA; DoH

Standing Cttee on Consumer Involvement in NHS R&D. **Past Committees** Vol Cncl for Handicapped Children; Nat Children's Bureau; Euro Fed of Parents of Hearing Impaired Children; CERT; Age Concern Exec. **Media Experience** Regular TV and radio; articles for specialist press. **Addits** Hon life member, Euro Fed of Deaf Children's Assocs.

CHADWICK Dr Derek J Director **CIBA FOUNDATION** SOCIAL Type: Service provider, Grant maker. 41 Portland Place, London W1N 4BN Tel:0171-636 9456 Fax:0171-436 2840 **Prev Posts** Prize Fellow, Magdalen Coll Oxford, 1973-77; Lecturer and Snr Lecturer, Liverpool Univ, 1977-88. **Prof Background** DPhil; CChem, FRSC 1982, MACS 1989. **Awards/Research** Auth/contrib: Aromatic & Heteroaromatic Chemistry 1979; Comprehensive Heterocyclic Chemistry 1984; The Research and Academic Users' Guide to the IBM PC 1988; Pyrroles Pt 1 1990. **Pres Committees** Mbr: Sci Cttee, Louis Jeanter Fndn, Geneva 1989-; Hague Club of Euro Foundn Dirs 1989- (Sec 1993-); Sci Adv Cttee 1990-95; Exec Cncl 1991-96 (Vice Chm 1994-96); Assoc of Med Res Charities; Mbr Soc of Apothecaries 1990. **Addits** Ed of vols in Ciba Fndtn Symposium series; papers in Chemistry.

CHAIR KENRIC SOCIAL Type: Service provider; Lesbian social organisation. BM KENRIC, London WC1N 3XX **Expertise** A subscribed lesbian voluntary organisation providing social activities/networking facilities for members. **Awards/Research** KENRIC is frequently used by researchers into lesbian issues. **Media Experience** KENRIC is happy to comply with request for speakers. **Addits** Please address any correspondence to the Chair.

CHALMERS Robert Development Worker, Company Secretary **COMMUNITY SELF-BUILD SCOTLAND** SOCIAL Type: Fundraiser; Service provider. 72 Newhaven Road, Edinburgh EH6 5QG Tel:0131-467 4675 Fax:0131-538 7223 **Expertise** Community architecture, timber-fame design. **Prev Posts** Community Architect, ECDS (Edinburgh Community Design Service) 1989-95. **Prof Background** BSc (Hons) in Architectural Studies, BArch, ARIAS. **Awards/Research** All Action Research such as the Self-Build Working Group with Scottish Homes; feasibility work for Self-Build Groups Community Buildings. **Pres Committees** Scottish Homes Advisory Committee on Housing Information and Advice (Homepoint); Reforesting Scotland (Board of Directors). **Past Committees** Assoc. of Community Technical Aid Centres. **Media Experience** Regular press releases; irregular radio interviews.

CHANDLER Paul General Secretary **SOCIETY FOR PROMOTING CHRISTIAN KNOWLEDGE - SPCK** RELIGIOUS Type: Grant maker; Religious publisher/bookseller. Holy Trinity Church, Marylebone Road, London NW1 4DU Tel:0171-387 5282 Fax:0171-388 1947 **Expertise** General management; strategic planning; retail management. **Prev Posts** Strategic Planning Manager, Barclays Bank 1987-1989; Assistant Personal Sector Director, Barclays Bank 1989-1992. **Prof Background** MA (Hons) Modern History, St John's College, Oxford (1983); Associate Chartered Institute of Bankers (1985); MBA - Henley Management College (1987). **Pres Committees** Trustee: All Saints Educational Trust, Harold Buxton Trust, Richards Trust. Mbr: Partnership for World Mission, Gen Synod's Brd of Mission Brd, Indian SPCK; SPCK USA, SPCK Australia; SPCK New Zealand. **Past Committees** Seconded to Church Urban Fund 1987. **Media Experience** Radio and press interviews. **Addits** Governor, St Martin in Field's High School for Girls.

CHAUDHRY Mr B.A. Chairman **LEAGUE OF BRITISH MUSLIMS UK** RELIGIOUS Type: Service provider; Advice on immigration/housing/welfare benefits. 124 Betchworth Rd, Seven Kings Ilford, Essex IG3 9JG (Community Centre, Eton Rd, Ilford, Essex IG1 2UE) Tel:0181-514 0706 **Prev Posts** Chairman, Council of Racial Equality, Barking; Secretary, Pakistan Welfare Association. **Prof Background** BSc, B.Ed. **Pres Committees** Trustee, Ilford Muslim Community Centre. **Past Committees** School Governor; Executive Member Police Consultative Group, CRC, CVS; Chair, Customer Complaints Committee, Redbridge.

CHAUDHRY Brigitte Founder and National Secretary **ROADPEACE** SOCIAL Type: Service provider; Campaigning, Professional association. PO Box 2579, London NW10 3PW Tel:0181-964 9353 **Expertise** Needs of road traffic victims, road traffic law, inquests. **Prev Posts** National Secretary since founding in 1992-to date. **Prof Background** Padagogische Hochschule in Germany, followed by 20 years as teacher in England. **Awards/Research** UK co-ordinator of Research into Impact of Road Death and Injury on Victims/victim Families, for European Federation of Road Traffic Victims (funded by Commission for European Union). **Pres Committees** RoadPeace; UK delegate with European Federation of Road Traffic Victims (UN delegate in Vienna); Victims' Voice/Steering Committee. **Past Committees** Road Death Working Party. **Media Experience** Radio/TV/press interviews during past 5 years, film for Channel 4.

CHAUDHRY Shaheen Director **MATERNITY AND HEALTH LINKS** MEDICAL/HEALTH Type: Service provider. The Old Co-op, 38-42 Chelsea Road, Easton, Bristol BS5 6AF Tel:01179-558495 Fax:01179-558495 **Expertise** Social sciences and health.

CHEAL Susanna Director **WHO CARES? TRUST** CHILDREN/YOUTH Type: Service provider; Campaigning to improve the care system. 5th Floor, Kempe House, 152-160 City Road, London EC1V 2NP Tel:0171-251 3117 Fax:0171-251 3123 **Expertise** Health care and education; families; children. **Prev Posts** Management Recruitment Consultancy Div, J Walter Thompson 1971-75; Teacher, LB Barnet 1976-78; Chair (Vol role only), BLISS 1979-90. **Prof Background** BSc (Hons) Social Sciences; Dip Personnel Management; Postgraduate Cert. in Education; Mbr Institute of Public Relations. **Awards/Research** MBE, 1992 (for services to charities, inc. development of BLISS - Baby Life Support Systems - from beginning). **Pres Committees** Vice-President, BLISS; Founder/Director, Working For A Charity (provides training for those transferring to Voluntary Sector); Adviser on boards of SCA clients. **Past Committees** Founder/Chair of BLISS 1979-90. **Media**

Experience Featured in press, TV/radio interviews; organized media campaigns, inc videos.

CHESTERMAN David Acting Director **BRITISH COUNCIL FOR PREVENTION OF BLINDNESS** DISABILITY Type: Fundraiser; Grant maker. 12 Harcourt Street, London W1H 1DS Tel:0171-724 3716.

CHICKEN Mr B.W.O Secretary to the Trustees **FESTINIOG RAILWAY TRUST** ARTS Type: Fundraiser; Grant maker; Cultural. 28 Grove Way, Esher, Surrey KT10 8HL Tel:0181-398 2932 **Expertise** Finance & administration. **Prof Background** Chartered Accountant.

CHILDS David J. Director **WORLD MEMORIAL FUND FOR DISASTER RELIEF** SOCIAL Type: Fundraiser; Grant maker. Europa House, 13/17 Ironmonger Row, London EC1V 3QN Tel:0171-250 1700 Fax:0171-250 1511 **Expertise** Military involvement in disaster relief. **Prev Posts** Royal Navy 1965-93; Currently: Director, National Memorial Arboretum. **Awards/Research** Auth: British Forces Plan for Disaster Relief Operations. **Media Experience** Occasional articles and press interviews.

CHITHAM Robert Chairman **INTERNATIONAL COUNCIL ON MONUMENTS AND SITES - ICOMOS UK** CONSERVATION/ENVIRONMENT Type: Research & Education. 10 Barley Mow Passage, Chiswick, London W4 4PH Tel:0181-994 6477 Fax:0181-747 8464 **Prof Background** RIBA Architect.

CHURCHILL James Chief Executive **ASSOCIATION FOR RESIDENTIAL CARE - ARC** DISABILITY Type: National umbrella charity. ARC House, Marsden St, Chesterfield, Derbyshire S40 1JY Tel:01246-555043 Fax:01246-555045 **Expertise** Residential Care; learning disability; care in the community. **Prev Posts** Director, ELS 1976-80; Director, United Response 1980-88. **Prof Background** BA, MA (Theology); PGCE; Teacher. **Awards/Research** Press articles on residential care; Auth: Introductory Reader in Philosophy of Religion; Co-ed:It Could Never Happen Here! 1996;There Are No Easy Answers 1996;Competence in Care 1995. **Pres Committees** Trustee, United Response; Vice Chair, VOICE Bd of Trustees; Mbr: Mansell Advisory Cttee, Panel of Experts of Registered Homes Tribunal Residential Forum. **Media Experience** Close involvement with professional press for social work and vol sector. **Addits** Ed:Managers in the Middle 1996.

CHURCHILL Viscount Managing Director. **CCLA INVESTMENT MANAGEMENT LTD - CCLA** SOCIAL Type: Service provider. St Alphage House, 2 Fore Street, London EC2Y 5AQ Tel:0171-588 1815 Fax:0171-588 6291 **Expertise** Investment Management. **Prev Posts** Morgan Grenfell and Co, Ltd (Asst. Dir. 1971-4) 1958-1974; Investment Mngr COIF 1974-1995; Central Board of Finance of CBF C of E Funds. **Prof Background** Eton; MA, New College, Oxford. **Pres Committees** Non-Exec Dir, Kleinwort Charter Inv Trust plc; Schroder Split Fund plc; Foreign and Colonial Income Growth Inv Trust plc. Trustee: Royal Fndn of St Katharine; Stained Glass Museum Trust, Ely.

CLARE John Andrew Secretary **SCOTTISH HISTORIC BUILDINGS TRUST** CONSERVATION Type: Building Preservation Trust. Saltcoats, Gullane, E. Lothian EH31 2AG Tel:01620-842757 Fax:01620-842757 **Expertise** All aspects of financing the repair and re-use of historic buildings. **Prev Posts** Civil Servant 1968-85. **Prof Background** MA (Natural Sciences) Cambridge. **Pres Committees** Deputy Chairman, Association of Preservation Trusts; Director (trustee), Cockburn Conservation Trust. **Past Committees** Member, Council of the Cockburn Association (The Edinburgh Civic Trust).

CLARK Andrew C. General Secretary **QUAKER PEACE & SERVICE** SOCIAL Type: Fundraiser; Service provider. Friends House, Euston Road, London NW1 2BJ Tel:0171-387 3601 Fax:0171-388 1977 **Expertise** Peace and reconciliation programmes; Rural community development. **Prev Posts** Team Leader, Relief & Rehab in SE Nigeria, Quakers 1968-70; Consultant to Buddhist Groups in Vietnam, Oxfam 73-75; Rural Cmty Dev progs India Mnger & Consultant, Oxfam 1976-82. **Prof Background** B.Soc. Science; Dip. Community Development; M.Ed.(Rural Development); Dip. Ag. Eng. (Soil & Water). **Awards/Research** Research on Social/educational change in S. Indian villages using Sarvodaya/Gandhian ideals. Contrib: Encyclopaedia Britannica, Social Conditions in Bangladesh 1972. **Pres Committees** Exec Ctte, Refugee Council; Council of Churches of Britain & Ireland, International Affairs Liaison Group; Governor, Leighton Park School. **Past Committees** Oxfam, Asia Committee. **Media Experience** Occasional radio interviews.

CLARK Malcolm B. Director **QUEEN ELIZABETH'S FOUNDATION FOR DISABLED PEOPLE** DISABILITY Type: Service provider. Leatherhead Court, Woodlands Road, Leatherhead, Surrey KT22 0BN Tel:01372-842204 Fax:01372-844072 **Prev Posts** Managing Director, Bush Boake Allen Ltd 1975-80. **Prof Background** PhD Chemical Engineering.

CLARK Rodney Chief Executive **NATIONAL DEAF-BLIND AND RUBELLA ASSOCIATION - SENSE** DISABILITY Type: Service provider. 11-13 Clifton Terrace, London N4 3SR Tel:0171-272 7774 Fax:0171-272 6012 **Expertise** Voluntary sector management; health and social services administration. **Prev Posts** Project Administrator, RNID 1978-81. **Pres Committees** Chair: Sign, The Anastasia Soc for Deaf People; Governor, Whitefield School and Centre, LB Waltham Forest.

CLARKE Angela General Secretary **INSTITUTE OF HORTICULTURE, THE** ENVIRONMENT Type: Professional association. 14-15 Belgrave Square, London SW1X 8PS Tel:0171-245 6943 Fax:0171-245 6943.

CLARKE Peter Coordinator **CHOICES IN CHILDCARE** CHILDREN/YOUTH Type: Umbrella organisation for children's info service. Holly Building, Holly Street, Sheffield S1 2GT Tel:0114-2766881 Fax:0114-2766881 **Prev Posts** Civil Service including Equal Opportunities 1964-94; Coordinator for Youth Access 1994-96 . **Prof Background** Diploma in Management Training; Associate Member of Institution of Occupational Safety & Health.

CLATWORTHY Michael James Executive Member **NATIONAL ASSOCIATION OF FIELD STUDY OFFICERS - NAFSO** ENVIRONMENT Type: Professional Association. 1 Hornbeam Drive, Northfields, Oxford OX4 5UU Tel:01865-716635 **Expertise** Environmental Field Studies;Geography, Environmental Consultancy. **Prev Posts** Field Centre Head 1977-96;Geog. Teacher/Field Centre Head 1969-77;Co-ed Teacher of Geog. 1966-69. **Prof Background** Cert.Ed. Teaching 30 years; Environmental Fieldwork 27 years;Cert. Archaeology. **Awards/Research** Environmental fieldwork; contributor NAFSO Journal and other publications; Fieldwork in Action series for the Geographical Assoc; co-auth: Our World - Our Responsibility. **Pres Committees** Sec, Field Studies working group of Geog Assoc; Exec Member Council: Environmental Education;Outdoor Education/Recreation/Training. **Past Committees** Founder Member: Outdoor Council; 15 years: NAFSO;FSWG;CEE. **Media Experience** Articles for press; conference organiser with Oxford Poly. **Addits** Involvement as judge with John Kettley in nat comp run by Fisons.

CLAYTON Dr Anthony Head of Research **INSTITUTE FOR POLICY ANALYSIS AND DEVELOPMENT** ENVIRONMENT/CONSERVATION Type: Service provider. 60 Cumberland Street, Edinburgh EH3 6RE. Tel:01578-760248 Fax:01578-760248 **Expertise** Sustainability/sustainable devmt; systems dynamics; cleaner technology; ind symbiosis; soc & econ policy. **Prev Posts** Environmental consultant; director of 7 different environmental charities and projects. Also currently: Environmental Co-ordinator, Edinburgh University. **Prof Background** MA (Hons); PhD Psychology. Hon Fellow, Faculty of Science & Engineering. **Awards/Research** Auth:Sustainability In Green Values 1993;Sustainability: A Systems Approach 1994;Sustainability: Guide for Decision Makers 1994; Strategies for Maintenance of Natural Capital 1994. **Pres Committees** Int Assoc, Centre for Soc & Envir Accounting Research, Dundee Univ. **Past Committees** Energy Action Scotland; Lothian Energy Group; Edinburgh Heatcare. Lothian & Edin Partnership; Lothian & Borders Energy & Env Netwk. **Media Experience** Experience in radio, television and press. **Addits** Auth of studies/reports on sustainability, energy, housing & env issues.

CLAYTON Charles Executive Director **WORLD VISION UK** RELIGIOUS Type: Fundraiser; International relief and development. 599 Avebury Boulevard, Milton Keynes MK9 3PG Tel:01908-841000 Fax:01908-841014 **Expertise** Leadership; management; theology; church relations. **Prev Posts** Scottish Area Director, The Navigators 1980-84; Sabbatical Study, Philadelphia 1984-86; Assistant UK Director, The Navigators 1986-89. **Prof Background** BSc (Hons) Civil Engineering; MA Theology; Leadership development. **Awards/Research** Publ:Who's Who among Students in American Universities, 1986; Let the Reader Understand, 1994; theological research for the Women's Commission of World Vision International. **Pres Committees** Secretary to the Board of Trustees, World Vision UK; Vice President, World Vision International; Social Responsibility Committee, St Andrews Church, Oxford. **Past Committees** UK Leadership Team and Internat Access Committee, Navigators; Advisory Board, Cygnet Business Development; NewsVision Board, London. **Media Experience** News and current affairs interviews on radio, TV and press. **Addits** Church of Scotland Session and Congreg Brd; active mbr CofE; frq conf spker.

CLEMENTS Judi National Director **NATIONAL ASSOCIATION FOR MENTAL HEALTH - MIND** DISABILITY Type: Fundraiser. Granta House, 15-19 Broadway, Stratford, London E15 4BQ Tel:0181-519 2122 Fax:0181-522 1725 **Expertise** Management - general/specific. **Prev Posts** Asst Dir Housing, LB Camden 1982-87; Deputy Dir Housing, Brighton Cncl 1987-91; Head, Mngmt Practice, Local Gov Mngmt Brd 1991-92. **Prof Background** LL.B. Birmingham Univ 1974; MA Public and Social Administration, Brunel Univ 1979; Professional qualification of Institute of Housing; London Executive Programme, London Business School 1986. **Past Committees** Homeless Action, Cttee Mbr 1981-86, Chair 1984-86; Founding mbr, Women in Local Gov Network; Mbr, Comm for Local Democracy, Sep 1994 **Media Experience** Fairly frequent interviewee on radio/TV news/current affairs programmes.

CLEVERDON Julia Chief Executive **BUSINESS IN THE COMMUNITY - BITC** SOCIAL Type: Service provider. 44 Baker Street, London, W1M 1DH Tel:0171-224 1600 Fax:0171-486 1700 **Expertise** Corporate comty involvement; campaigns - business involvement in educ, econ devmt, employee volunteering. **Prev Posts** Division Dir, Industrial Society 1981-88; BITC: Dir, Education Unit 1988-89; Managing Dir, Development 1990-92. **Prof Background** Newnham College, Cambridge. **Awards/Research** CBE **Pres Committees** Prince's Trust Volunteers; Trident Trust Gifts in Kind UK. **Past Committees** School Curriculum Development Cttee; National Curriculum Council. **Addits** Exp in business to business campaigns on env/race/women's career devmt.

CLIFFORD Sue Co-Director **COMMON GROUND** CONSERVATION/ENVIRONMENT Type: Service provider; Education/awareness raising. Seven Dials Warehouse, 44 Earlham St, London WC2H 9LA Tel:0171-379 3109 Fax:0171-836 5741 **Expertise** Promoting the cultural significance of everyday surroundings; combining conservation and the arts. **Prev Posts** Researcher, Ministry of Housing and Local Government 1970; Senior Lecturer, Central London Polytechnic 1970-74; Lecturer, University College London School of Architecture 1975-90. **Prof Background** BSc (Hons) Geography, Dip. Town Planning (Edinburgh); 30 years in practice and education on rural and natural resource planning, and conservation. **Awards/Research** MBE (1994). Co-auth/ed: Holding Your Ground, 1985; Trees Be Company, 1989; Local Distinctiveness,1993; From Place to Place, maps & parish maps, 1996. **Past Committees** New Nat Forest Adv Bd; Friends of the Earth Bd 1972-81; Earth Resources Res Bd 1976-86; Arts Cncl Special Proj Adv Cttee 1990-92. **Media Experience** News/feature participation in all media. **Addits** Promoting Local Distinctiveness project/Cmty Orchards/Apple Day/parish maps.

CLOUGH Richard General Secretary **SOCIAL CARE**

ASSOCIATION - SCA SOCIAL Type: Professional Association. 23a Victoria Road, Surbiton, Surrey KT6 4JZ Tel:0181-390 6831 Fax:0181-399 6183 **Expertise** Residential Care. **Prev Posts** Head of Residential Home 1972-78; General Secretary SCA 1978-to date. **Prof Background** Trained in child care. Assoc Mbr, Chartered Inst of Arbitrators (chaired/involved on 9 committees of enquiry). **Awards/Research** MBE (1979); OBE (1993). **Pres Committees** All Party Parliamentary Panel on Personal Social Services; Chief Exec, Social Care Association (Education). **Past Committees** CCETSW 1978-84; Home Life Working Party 1983; Warner Committee 1993; Residential Forum Code of Practice (1994-95). **Media Experience** Frequent dealings with radio, TV and press.

COBBE Alec Founder & Director **COBBE FOUNDATION** in association with the National Trust CONSERVATION/ENVIRONMENT Type: Service provider; Dissemination of musical knowledge. Hatchlands Park, East Clandon, Guildford, Surrey GU4 7RT Tel:01483-222787 **Expertise** Foundation has one of the world's largest groups of composer-associated keyboard instruments. **Prev Posts** Museum picture conservator; Historic buildings consultant; Museum designer and artist. **Awards/Research** Numerous publications on musical instruments.

COBBOLD Richard Director **ROYAL UNITED SERVICES INSTITUTE FOR DEFENCE STUDIES** SOCIAL Type: Service provider; Academic research. Whitehall, London SW1A 2ET Tel:0171-930 5854 Fax:0171-321 0943 **Expertise** Defence & International Security. **Prev Posts** Director, Defence Concepts 1987-88; Captain, 2nd Frigate Squadron 1989-90; Asst Chief of Defence Staff (Operational Requirements) 1991-94. **Prof Background** Royal Navy 1960-94; Seaman Specialist, Aviation Sub-Specialist; Education: Bryanston School, Britannia Royal Naval College Dartmouth, Royal Naval Staff College, Royal College of Defence Studies. **Awards/Research** CB & FRAeS; Author of: The World Reshaped; 50 Years After The War In Europe (Vol 1); and In Asia (Vol 2); Macmillan 1996; various articles & contributions. **Media Experience** Experience with TV and radio. **Addits** Co-author: The Royal Navy Today & Tomorrow, 1995 (with J. Oswald).

COCKE Thomas Hugh Secretary **COUNCIL FOR THE CARE OF CHURCHES - CCC** CONSERVATION Type: Grant maker. Fielden House, Little College Street, London SW1P 3SH Tel:0171-222 3793 Fax:0171-222 3794 **Expertise** History of Building restoration, medieval buildings. **Prev Posts** Lecturer, Art History Manchester Univ 1973-76; Investigator, Royal Commission on Historical Monuments 1976-90. **Prof Background** Scholar at Pembroke College; History Tripos; Courtauld: MA/PhD **Awards/Research** FSA;Articles in learned journals;Salisbury Cathedral Perspectives on the Architectural History 1993;900 years; Restorations of Westminster Abbey 1995. **Pres Committees** Fellow of Darwin College, Cambridge;Mbr: Executive Cttee Georgian Group;Council, Royal Archaeological Institute. **Past Committees** Extra Member of Court, Skinners Company. **Media Experience** Regular briefings.

COFFEY Revd David R. General Secretary **BAPTIST UNION OF GREAT BRITAIN, THE - BUGB** RELIGIOUS Type: Religious denomination. Baptist House, PO Box 44, 129 Broadway, Didcot, Oxfordshire OX11 8RT Tel:01235-512077 Fax:01235-811537 **Expertise** Mission & evangelism; Church music; Church & society; Gospel & culture. **Prev Posts** Baptist Church Minister: Whetstone 1967-72; North Cheam 1972-80; Upton Vale, Torquay 1980 -85; Sec for Evangelism, BUGB 1988-90; Pres, BUGB 1986-7; Vice Pres, Eur Bapt Fed 1995-97. **Prof Background** BA; Minister of religion trained at Spurgeon's College, South London. **Awards/Research** Auth: Build that Bridge: Conflict resolution in the local Church. **Pres Committees** Bapt Uni Cncl;Free Church Fed Cncl;Church Reps Meet, Steering Cttee Cncl Churches for Brit & Ireland;Evang Alliance Cncl;Bapt Mission Soc Gen Cttee;Keswick Conv Cncl;Chair, BWA Evang & Educ Div. **Past Committees** President, Spurgeon's College Conference 1982; Chair, Baptist World Alliance Worship Commission 1990-95. **Media Experience** BBC Radio 4 & 5 and local; World Service; BBC1 & ITV Morning Service. **Addits** Major conference/convention speaker in Europe/North America/Australasia.

COHEN Dr Bronwen Director **CHILDREN IN SCOTLAND** CHILDREN/YOUTH Type: Nat membership agency for child/family in Scotland. Prince's House, 5 Shandwick Place, Edinburgh EH2 4RG Tel:0131-228 8484 Fax:0131-228 8585 **Expertise** Social policy; childcare; disability/special needs. **Prev Posts** Head of Policy Devmt and Euro Liaison, Equal Opportunities Commission 1983-89; Snr Research Fellow, Dept Soc Policy & Soc Wk 1989-90. **Prof Background** BSc Hons; MA; PhD. **Awards/Research** Co-Auth: Childcare in a Modern Welfare System, Inst Pub Pol Res 1991; Auth: Childcare in Partnership CEC 1993; Childcare Service for Rural Families CEC 1995. **Pres Committees** Vice Pres, Confed Fam Orgs in Euro Un; UK Mbr, Euro Commsn Ntwk on Child & Other Measures to reconcile Empl & Fam Responsibilities; Dir, Caledonian Fndtn; Mbr, Mngmt Gp Garvald Ctre. **Past Committees** Nat Cncl for One Parent Families. **Media Experience** Radio, TV & press. **Addits** Co-Ed, Children's Services: Shaping up for the Millenium.

COLEMAN Don Director **ROYAL PHILANTHROPIC SOCIETY** CHILDREN/YOUTH Type: Service provider. Rectory Lodge, High Street, Brasted, Westerham, Kent TN16 1JE Tel:01959-561611 Fax:01959-561891 **Expertise** Child care; Organisational development; Project development & management; Voluntary child care sector. **Prev Posts** Asst. Divisional Dir, Barnardo's (North West) 1976-82; Divisional Dir, Barnardo's Irish Division 1982-86. **Prof Background** Senior Certificate in Residential Care, Children & Young People; Diploma in Social Work Administration; MA in Social Service - Planning. FRSA. **Awards/Research** Churchill Fellow. Research subjects inc. pluralism in welfare, intermediate treatment, partnership. Numerous articles during the past 20 years. **Pres Committees** Trustee St. Anthony of Padua Fndtn for the Disabled. **Media Experience** Articles; TV/radio interviews. **Addits** Hon Sec, Euromet Childcare Alliance. Trustee, Young Builders Trust.

COLES Ruth Director **ACTION FOR DYSPHASIC ADULTS - ADA** DISABILITY Type: Information and support service. 1 Royal Street, London SE1 7LL Tel:0171-261 9572 Fax:0171-928 9542 **Expertise** Aphasia therapy. **Prev Posts** District Speech Therapy Manager (Locum); Aphasia Specialist (Locum) Milton Keynes 1991. **Prof Background** Dipl, College of Speech and Language Therapists; MSc Clinical Communication City University. **Awards/Research** Co-Auth; Practical Activities for Stroke Groups, 1981; Housing Project Good Practice Guide 1988. **Pres Committees** British Aphasiology Society Cttee; MIND, St Albans District Cttee. **Past Committees** Chair, MIND St Albans District.

COLLECTIVE RIGHTS OF WOMEN SOCIAL Type: Service provider. 52-54 Featherstone Street, London EC1Y 8RT Tel:0171-251 6577 Fax:0171-608 0928 **Expertise** Policy and research. **Prof Background** Rights of Women is run as a collective comprising academics, lawyers, advice workers and researchers. **Awards/Research** Publ: Wide variety of publications produced by the collective on subject of women and the law. **Past Committees** Various Law Commission working parties. **Media Experience** Frequent contrib to all media.

COLLETT David Advisor on the Voluntary Sector SOCIAL 14 Fourth Avenue, Hove, E Sussex, BN3 2PH Tel:01273-772121 Fax:01273-772121 **Expertise** Third world development; running of voluntary organisations; strengthening of volunteering. **Prev Posts** Adviser on Social Development, ODA 1969-72; Director, VSO 1973-80; Director, WaterAid 1981-94. **Prof Background** BA (Hons) Keele 1956; Hon Doctorate, Heriot Watt University, Edinburgh; Hon Fellow, Chartered Inst of Water and Environmental Management. **Awards/Research** OBE. **Pres Committees** Chairman, Board of Governors, National Centre for Volunteering; Chairman, Board of Directors, Contact a Family; Trustee, Child Hope.

COLLIN Rosalind Director **JEWISH AIDS TRUST** MEDICAL/HEALTH Type: Service provider; Grant maker; Educational/counselling and support. HIV Education Unit, Colindale Hospital, Colindale Ave, London NW9 5HG Tel:0181-200 0369 Fax:0181-905 9250 **Expertise** Director. **Prev Posts** Vice-Chair, Exodus; Reform synagogues of GB, Soviet Jewry Campaign 1981-1987; Chair, 1987-1990. **Prof Background** Business Studies Degree (HND); ex Merchandiser for M&S. **Past Committees** Hon. Secretary, National Council for Soviet Jewry.

CONNON Joyce Scottish Secretary **WORKERS' EDUCATIONAL ASSOCIATION: SCOTLAND** SOCIAL Type: Service provider; Adult education. Riddle's Court, 322 Lawnmarket, Edinburgh EH1 2PG Tel:0131-226 3456 Fax:0131-220 0306 **Prev Posts** District Secretary, WEA; Tutor Organiser, Lothian WEA.

CONWAY Mike Chief Executive **NATIONAL ASSOCIATION OF LEAGUES OF HOSPITAL FRIENDS** MEDICAL/HEALTH Type: Central support/advice service for member leagues. 2nd Floor, Fairfax House, Causton Rd, Colchester, Essex CO1 1RJ Tel:01206-761227 Fax:01206-560244

COODE-ADAMS Giles Chief Executive **ROYAL BOTANIC GARDENS KEW FOUNDATION** CONSERVATION/ENVIRONMENT Type: Fundraiser. Royal Botanic Gardens (Kew), Richmond, Surrey, TW9 3AB Tel:0181-332 5911 Fax:0181-332 5901 **Prev Posts** Partner, L. Messel & Co. 1968-1986; Managing Director, Lehman Brothers 1986-to date. **Prof Background** Investment banker. **Awards/Research** Deputy Lieutenant of Essex. **Past Committees** Council, University of Essex; Governor, Brentwood School.

COOK Andrea Director **NEA (THE NATIONAL ENERGY ACTION CHARITY)** SOCIAL Type: Service provider; Policy development. National Office, St Andrews House, 90-92 Pilgrim St, Newcastle upon Tyne NE1 6SG Tel:0191-261 5677 Fax:0191-261 6496 **Expertise** Governmental relations; Corporate affairs; Energy efficiency initiatives to assist low income households. **Prev Posts** Head of Community & Health Service Training 1980-84; Head of Development & Training, Neighbourhood Energy Action 1984-88. **Prof Background** BA (Hons) Social Policy/Anthropology; MA (Ed);Further Education Teaching Certificate. **Awards/Research** OBE (1991);JP. **Pres Committees** Chairman, Eaga (Ltd Co); Mbr: UK Govt Round Table on Sustainable Devmt;DTI Renewable Energy Advisory Cttee; Non-Exec Dir, Friends Provident Ethical Investment Trust; Brd Mbr, Energy Action Scotland. **Past Committees** Honorary Sec, Northumbrian Fed of Community Organisations 1980-84, Trustee, NCVO 1988-93. **Media Experience** Extensive experience on local and national news and current affairs programmes.

COOKE-PRIEST Rear Admiral Colin National Director **TRIDENT TRUST** SOCIAL Type: Service provider. Saffron Court, 14b St Cross St, London EC1N 8XA Tel:0171-242 1616 Fax:0171-430 2975 **Prev Posts** In Command Second Frigate Squadron 1987-89; Maritime Advisor to Supreme Allied Commander Europe 1989-90; Flag Officer Naval Aviation (Head of Fleet Air Arm) 1990-93. **Prof Background** Career Naval Officer 1957-1993; Marlborough College; Royal Naval College, Dartmouth. **Awards/Research** CB (New Years Hons 1993); Elected Fellow, Royal Aeronautical Society 1992. **Pres Committees** Trustee, Trident Transnational. **Past Committees** Chair of Trustees, Fleet Air Arm Memorial Church; Fleet Air Arm Museum; Fleet Air Arm Benev Trust; Mbr, Ships Names & Badges Cttee.

COOMBES Lt Cdr I.M.P. Secretary **ASSOCIATION OF ROYAL NAVY OFFICERS** SOCIAL Type: Fundraiser; Service provider; Grant maker. 70 Porchester Terrace, Bayswater, London W2 3TP Tel:0171-402 5231 Fax:0171-402 5231 **Prev Posts** Royal Navy 1955-88. **Prof Background** Open University Courses in Philosophy and Psychology; Winter expedition leader and langlauf ski instructor. **Awards/Research** Editor, ARNO Yearbook 1989-96.

COOPER Deborah Director **SKILL: NATIONAL BUREAU FOR STUDENTS WITH DISABILITIES** DISABILITY Type: Service provider; Campaigning. 336 Brixton Rd, London SW9 7AA Tel:0171-274 0565 Fax:0171-274 7840 **Expertise** Disability in relation to post-compulsory education, training & employment. **Prev Posts** Community Worker, Milton Keynes 1980-84; Community Servs Officer, Milton Keynes Develmnt

Corporation 1983-84; Assistant Director, SKILL 1984-89. **Prof Background** English degree; PGCE; MEd, Special Education, Teaching, Community Work, Work in Voluntary Sector. **Awards/Research** Hon. Degree, Open University; Auth: Post Compulsory Education & Training; Several books & articles. **Pres Committees** Coll Gov Body; FEFC Learning Diffs and/or Disabilities Cttee; Nat Cncl for Vocational Q'fications' Forum of Fair Assessment & Equal Opps; TEC Nat Cncl sub-group on equal opps & spec training needs. **Media Experience** Regular media contact.

COOPER J. Neville Trustee and Chief Executive **COOPER ATKINSON CHARITABLE TRUST FOR INDIA** OVERSEAS Type: Fundraiser; Grant maker. Crane Court, 302 London Rd, Ipswich, Suffolk 1P2 OAJ Tel:01473-216994 Fax:01473-231276 **Expertise** Relief of poverty in Southern India including the advancement of education and the Christian Faith. **Prev Posts** Senior Partner, Ballams, Chartered Accountants. **Prof Background** Chartered Accountant and Member of the Institute of Taxation. **Pres Committees** National Council of YMCAs; Prospect Housing Trust (Trustee); Ipswich YMCA (Trustee). **Past Committees** Chairman of Anglia Region of National Council of YMCAs 1988-1993 **Media Experience** Radio interviews and Press coverage; BBC Hearts of Gold appearance April 1996.

COOPER Libby Director **CHARITIES EVALUATION SERVICES - CES** SOCIAL Type: Service provider. 4 Coldbath Square, London, EC1R 5HL Tel:0171-713 5722 Fax:0171-713 5692 **Expertise** Research, evaluation, advising funders on evaluation and monitoring approaches. **Prev Posts** Teaching 1976-82; Director, Community Research Advisory Centre, N London Univ 1982-90. **Prof Background** BA Soc Sc; Teaching Certificate; Unfinished PhD. **Awards/Research** Research/articles on community research and evaluation studies associated with community activities ie. disability, crime, race, housing, domestic violence. OU chapter on evaluation. **Pres Committees** Trustee, Co-operation for Development. **Past Committees** ARVAC, Women's Centre. **Media Experience** Various articles.

COOPER Michael J. Director General **BRITISH DIABETIC ASSOCIATION - BDA** MEDICAL/HEALTH Type: Fundraiser; Service provider; Grant maker. 10 Queen Anne Street, London W1M 0BD Tel:0171-323 1531 Fax:0171-637 3644 **Expertise** Business management; international activities. **Prev Posts** Marketing Dir, Panoceanic Anco Ltd 1970-79; Managing Dir, Panoceanic Anco Ltd 1980-83; Dir, Burmah Castrol Plc 1983-91. **Prof Background** BA, Exeter Univ; MBA, IMD Switzerland. **Pres Committees** Member, Brighton & Hove Health Authority; Visiting Professor, University of Westminster. **Past Committees** Dir: Energy Transportation Corp Inc. NY; Pakistan Petroleum Ltd, Karachi; Burmah Castrol Plc; Premier Consolidated Oilfields Plc.

COOPER P. Chief Executive **COMMUNITY TRANSPORT** CONSERVATION/ENVIRONMENT Type: Fundraiser; Service provider. Vauxhall Industrial Estate, Greg Street, Reddish, Stockport SK5 7BR Tel:0161-477 2962

COOPER Tim Chairman **CHRISTIAN ECOLOGY LINK** ENVIRONMENT Type: Fundraiser; Service provider; Educational charity. 20 Carlton Road, Harrogate, N Yorks HG2 8DD. Tel: 01423-871616 **Expertise** Economics, Environmental Politics. **Prof Background** Senior Lecturer in Consumer Studies, Sheffield Hallam University. **Awards/Research** Green Christianity, Hodder 1990; Beyond Recycling: The Longer Life Option, New Economics Foundation, 1994. **Pres Committees** Trustee, Create; Trustee, Christian Ecology UK Ltd. **Media Experience** Substantial experience with TV, radio and press.

COOPER Steven A. Head of Corporate Planning & Evaluation **ROYAL NATIONAL INSTITUTE FOR THE BLIND-RNIB** DISABILITY Type: Fundraiser; Service provider; Grant maker; Campaigning; Research & Development. 224 Great Portland Street, London W1N 6AA Tel:0171-388 1266 Fax:0171-383 0508 **Expertise** Corporate strategy, planning, mngmt process, marketing, organisational developmnt, research & developmnt. **Prev Posts** Research Fellow, Policy Studies Institute 1978-85; Dep. Director, Greater London Council 85-88. **Prof Background** BA Geography 1976; MSc Planning & Development 1978; MPhil Organisational Behaviour 1985. **Awards/Research** Substantial publications record (most recently in areas of housing, assistive technology and media for visually impaired people). **Pres Committees** Member, Strategic Planning Society, Member, Chartered Institute of Marketing. **Addits** Visiting Lecturer, City University Business School.

COPE Prof David R. Executive Director **UK CENTRE FOR ECONOMIC AND ENVIRONMENTAL DEVELOPMENT UK - CEED** CONSERVATION/ENVIRONMENT Type: Research Institute. 3E King's Parade, Cambridge CB2 1SJ Tel:01223-367799 Fax:01223-367794 **Expertise** Environmental economics, energy & environment, land use, pollution control, transport policy, East Asian environment. **Prev Posts** Lecturer, Nottingham University 1971-81; Environmental Team Leader, Int Energy Agency 1981-86; Exec Dir, UK CEED 1986-Today. **Prof Background** MA Cambridge, MSc (Econ) London. **Awards/Research** Large number of books, reports and articles. **Pres Committees** Packaging Standards Council. **Past Committees** Standing committee on Environment, Cabinet Office Council, National Society for Clean Air, Environmental Development Advisory Panel. **Media Experience** Frequent radio/TV/press contributor.

COPLAND Dr Geoffrey Vice-Chancellor **UNIVERSITY OF WESTMINSTER** SOCIAL/TRAINING Type: Service provider. University 309 Regent St, London W1R 8AL Tel:0171-911 5000 Fax:0171-911 5103 **Expertise** University management & physics. **Prev Posts** Physics Lecturer, University of London 1971-80; Dean of Studies, Goldsmiths' College 1981-87; Deputy Rector, University of Westminster 1987-95. **Prof Background** PhD Physics. **Awards/Research** Author of various research papers in Physics. **Pres Committees** CVCP; Governor, University of Westminster; Governor, Greenhill College; Thomas Wall Trust.

CORBETT Mary Chief Executive **MARRIAGE CARE**

SOCIAL Type: Service provider; Education Training. Clitherow House, 1 Blythe Mews, Blyth Rd, London W14 0NW Tel:0171-371 1341 Fax:0171-371 4921 **Expertise** Impact of social issues on personal development; Evolving Nature/ Structure of Family. **Prev Posts** Social & Pastoral Action 1982-89; Dir, HAPAS Hertfordshire Alcohol Problems Advisory Service, 1989-93. **Prof Background** Medieval Historian; Anthropology; Counselling. **Awards/Research** The Role of the Apinase Tribe in an Evolving Brazil; Education & Cultural Imperialism. **Pres Committees** Trustee/Bd Management, Family Research Trust. **Past Committees** CENFI-PETROPOLIS, Brazil. **Media Experience** Radio: Woman's Hour, Radio 5 Live.

CORDEN Julie Aerobiologist/Administrator **MIDLANDS ASTHMA & ALLERGY RESEARCH ASSOCIATION** MEDICAL/HEALTH Type: Fundraiser; Service provider; Grant maker. 12 Vernon St, Derby, Derbyshire DE1 1FT **Expertise** Aerobiology, asthma & allergy research. **Prev Posts** Research Assistant, MAARA 1964-71; Tutor 1971-85; Aerobiologist, MAARA 1985-94. **Prof Background** BSc. **Awards/Research** Papers published on aerobiological research. **Media Experience** Interviewed for radio, TV & press.

CORDY Tim Director **TOWN AND COUNTRY PLANNING ASSOCIATION - TCPA** CONSERVATION/ENVIRONMENT Type: Advocacy Group. 17 Carlton House Terrace, London SW1Y 5AS Tel:0171-930 8903 Fax:0171-930 3280 **Prev Posts** Chief Executive, Royal Society for Nature Conservation; 15 years in Local Government. **Prof Background** Planning, environment and local government. **Pres Committees** Trustee, Environmental Training Organisation 1996. **Past Committees** Trustee, Volunteer Centre UK 1990-96; UK 2000 1987-94.

CORKISH Norma Director **OVERCOMING SPEECH IMPAIRMENTS - AFASIC** CHILDREN/YOUTH Type: Fundraiser; Service provider. 347 Central Markets, Smithfield, London EC1A 9NH Tel:0171-236 3632 Fax:0171-236 8115 **Prev Posts** AFASIC: Fundraiser 1982-87; Assistant Director 1987-89. **Prof Background** BSc Social Sciences Administration; Member, Royal Soc of Arts (RSA). **Pres Committees** Communications Forum. **Past Committees** DES Steering Cttee for Development of Distance Taught Course for Teachers on Speech/Language Impairments.

CORNFORD James Director **PAUL HAMLYN FOUNDATION** SOCIAL Type: Grant maker. Sussex House, 12 Upper Mall, London W6 9TA. Tel:0181-741 2812 Fax:0181-741 2263 **Expertise** Politics, Constitutional reform. **Prev Posts** Director, Outer Circle Policy Unit 1976-80; Director, Nuffield Foundation & Secretary to Commonwealth Relations Trust 1980-88; Director, Inst for Public Policy Research 1989-94. **Prof Background** Lecturer/Professor of politics at Edinburgh University; Prize Fellowship at Trinity College 1960; Harkness Fellow of the Commonwealth Fund 1961-62. **Awards/Research** Numerous articles/contributions inc. On writing a Constitution, 1991; Towards a Constitutional Equation? 1991; Wholesale Reform, 1993 and reports on public policy. **Pres Committees** Chairman, Political Quarterly Publishing Co; Director, Job Ownership Ltd; Chairman of the Council, Campaign for Freedom of Information; Trustee/Chair, South African Adv Education Project. **Past Committees** Lit Ed, Political Quarterly; Mbr, CoI into Educ of Children of Ethnic Minorities; Chair/V-Pres, RIPA; Adv Bd, Constit Reform Centre.

CORNWELL Mary Director of Education **WILDLIFE TRUSTS** CONSERVATION/ENVIRONMENT Type: Habitat conservation; educ on environment issues. The Green, Witham Park, Lincoln LN5 7JR Tel:01522-544400 Fax:01522-511616 **Expertise** Environment education. **Prev Posts** Primary school teacher 1976-84; Senior Lecturer, Primary Science 1984-89. **Prof Background** BEd (Hons) Special Biology; MPhil Environmental Education; Member, Institute of Biology, Chartered Biologist; Fellow of RSA. **Awards/Research** Many publications and articles. **Pres Committees** Wildlife Link - Education Cttee; Council for Environmental Education Executive. **Addits** Education Cttee, Institute of Biology. **Media Experience** Participated in all branches of media.

CORRY Stephen Director General **SURVIVAL INTERNATIONAL** SOCIAL Type: Fundraiser; Human rights. 11-15 Emerald Street, London WC1N 3QL Tel:0171-242 1441 Fax:0171-242 1771 **Expertise** Tribal peoples.

CORSAR Bill Development Director **NATIONAL SOCIETY FOR EPILEPSY - NSE** MEDICAL/HEALTH Type: Fundraiser; Service provider. Chalfont St Peter, Gerards Cross, Bucks SL9 0RJ Tel:01494-873991 Fax:01494-871927 **Expertise** Relationship marketing; TQM; HR; patient education/information and general medical issues. **Prev Posts** Direct Marketing Manager, Glaxo Pharms 1988-1993; Business Consultant 1993-1994. **Prof Background** Diploma Direct Marketing 1992. **Pres Committees** Management Committee.

COTTERILL Annette Director, (Chief Exec & Co Sec) **LEARNING THROUGH ACTION** SOCIAL Type: Fundraiser; Service provider. The Learning Through Action Centre, Cumberland Rd, Reading, Berks. RG1 3JY Tel:01734-665556 Fax:01734-669746 **Expertise** Active learning method, advanced training of teachers, interactive behavioural education. **Prev Posts** Senior Lecturer, Education (Univ. of Reading) 1967-84. **Prof Background** MA, LRAM, ADB, CERT. ED. University of Leeds, Bristol Old Vic Theatre School, Univ. London Ins. of Education. **Awards/Research** Functionality of Educational Theatre - University of Leeds. Author/Editor over 20 books and learning resources packs. Gulbenkian Award for Innovation in Museum Education 1993. **Media Experience** Wide experience of radio & TV, press & public relations & fund raising. **Addits** Lecturing/course leader.

COULTER Angela Director **KING'S FUND DEVELOPMENT CENTRE** MEDICAL/HEALTH Type: Grant maker; Development Agency. 11-13 Cavendish Square, London, W1M 0AN Tel:0171-307 2693 Fax:0171-307 2810 **Expertise** Health services development and research. **Prev Posts** Oxford Univ: Research Off, Public Health and Primary Care Dept 1983-86; Dir, Primary Care Research, Clinical Epidemiology Unit 1986-91; Dir, Health Services Research Unit 1991-93. **Prof Background** BA (Hons)

Applied Social Studies; MSc (thesis) Health Services Research; PhD Health Services Research. **Awards/Research** Author of about 100 academic papers and articles. Co-ed: Hospital Referrals, 1992. **Pres Committees** NHS R&D Standing Group on Health Technology Assessment; MRC Health Services Research & Public Health Grants Cttee; BUPA Medical Fndtn; Intensive Care National Audit & Research Cttee. **Media Experience** Occasional radio and TV interviews.

COULTER Jim Chief Executive **NATIONAL HOUSING FEDERATION** SOCIAL Type: Rep body for HAs & nonprofit social landlords. 175 Grays Inn Road, London WC1X 8UP Tel:0171-278 6571 Fax:0171-955 5696 **Prev Posts** Director, Leeds Federated Housing Assocs 1976-88. **Prof Background** BA History; Career in trade union world until 1976. **Media Experience** Regular participant as spokesperson for housing associations.

COURTNEY Angela Regional Management Co-ordinator **NORTHERN IRELAND WOMEN'S AID FEDERATION** WOMEN Type: Fundraiser; Service provider; Campaign/training;Co-ord body for Affiliated Mbrs. 129 University St, Belfast BT7 1HP Tel:01232-249041 Fax:01232-239296 **Expertise** Domestic Violence; Organisational Mgmt. **Prev Posts** Volunteer Co-ordinator/Resource Team Mgr 1986-94; Regional Development Worker 1994-95. **Prof Background** Voluntary Sector/Women's Movement Activist. **Awards/Research** Edited NIWAF Info & Training Pack on Domestic Violence; Edited & contributed to Foam Sprite Book of Poetry to commemorate 15 years of Women's Aid. **Pres Committees** Ulidia Housing Assoc Mgmt Cttee; Regional Forum on Domestic Violence. **Past Committees** NI Cncl for Voluntary Action (NICVA); NI Cncl for the Homeless. **Media Experience** Radio, TV, Video, Press.

COWAN Michael General Secretary **BRITISH ASSOCIATION FOR LOCAL HISTORY** SOCIAL Type: Service provider; Representative body. 24 Lower Street, Harnham, Salisbury, Wiltshire SP2 8EY Tel:01722-332158 Fax:01722-413242 **Expertise** Charity management. **Prev Posts** Project management for local branches of Relate and Mencap; Museum and Arts Festival Administration. **Prof Background** Military; managerial. **Awards/Research** History; archaeology; environment.

COX Edward R. Secretary **AIR LEAGUE EDUCATION TRUST** SOCIAL Type: Service provider. 4 Hamilton Place, London W1V 0BQ Tel:0171-491 0470 Fax:0171-499 7261 **Expertise** Senior manager; professional navigator. **Prev Posts** Directing Staff, Royal College of Defence Studies 1984-86; Air Branch Director, HQ Allied Forces Southern Europe, Naples 1987-90; Branch Dir, International Military Staff, NATO HQ. **Prof Background** RAF College Cranwell; RN Staff College Greenwich; Royal College of Defence Studies. **Awards/Research** New NATO Command Structure; Air Operations in Former Yugoslavia. **Pres Committees** Council of the Air League. **Past Committees** NATO Military Committees. **Media Experience** Mainly press and radio.

COX Peter Chief Executive **INSTANT MUSCLE LTD** SOCIAL Type: Service provider. Springside House, 84 North End Rd, London W14 9ES Tel:0171-603 2604 Fax:0171-603 7346 **Expertise** Working with unemployed, ex-offenders, homeless. **Prev Posts** ITT Data Systems 1975-85; Alcatel Business Systems, 1985-91; Langley Trust 1991. **Prof Background** Commercial, operations, counselling. **Pres Committees** Trustee of Homeless Charity.

CRAGGS Vic Director **COMMONWEALTH YOUTH EXCHANGE COUNCIL** CHILDEN/YOUTH Type: Fundraiser; Service provider; Grant maker; Youth organisation; Educational charity. 7 Lion Yard, Tremadoc Rd, London SW4 7NQ Tel:0171-498 6151 Fax:0171-720 5403 **Expertise** Youth development; International understanding & development. **Prev Posts** Careers Officer, Hertfordshire County Council 1974-76; VSO Volunteer in Papua New Guinea 976-79; Development Officer, Commonwealth Youth Exchange Council 1980-88. **Prof Background** Honours Degree in History, University of Warwick 1972; Diploma in Careers Guidance 1974. **Pres Committees** Advisory Council, National Youth Agency, England; Council Member (Trustee), British & Foreign School Society; Commonwealth Sub-Committee, Prince's Trust.

CRAIGIE Andrew John The Bursar **SALISBURY CATHEDRAL SCHOOL** CHILDREN/YOUTH Type: Fundraiser; Service provider; Grant maker; Educational. 1 The Close, Salisbury, Wilts SP1 2EQ Tel:01722-322652 Fax:01322-410910 **Expertise** Administration. **Prev Posts** HM Forces 1959-87; Bursar, Mount House School, Tavistock 1987-90. **Prof Background** HM Forces. **Awards/Research** OBE. **Pres Committees** Board of Directors, Close Harmony Ltd (Trading Arm of Salisbury Cathedral).

CREIGHTON Robert Chief Executive **GREAT ORMOND STREET HOSPITAL FOR CHILDREN NHS TRUST** CHILDREN/YOUTH Type: Fundraiser; Service provider. 49 Great Ormond Street, London WC1N 3JH Tel:0171-813 8330 Fax:0171-813 8218 **Expertise** Health, international education, young people. **Prev Posts** Department of Health 1988-95, Principal Private Secretary and other posts; United World Colleges 1978-88, International Secretary. **Prof Background** MA (History); PGCE; Civil Service. **Pres Committees** Council; Fairbridge; Waterford Kamhlaba UK Trustees. **Past Committees** Chair, UK Standing Conference on Education for International Understanding. **Media Experience** Occasional.

CRICK Ronald Pitts Chairman **INTERNATIONAL GLAUCOMA ASSOCIATION** MEDICAL/HEALTH Type: Fundraiser; Service provider; Grant maker. c/o Kings College Hospital, Denmark Hill, London SE5 9RS Tel:0171-737 3265 Fax:0171-737 3265 **Expertise** Ophthalmology with special interest in glaucoma and epidemiology. **Prev Posts** Surgeon, Royal Eye Hospital 1950-69; Consultant Ophthalmic Surgeon, King's College Hospital 1950-82; Hon Consultant Ophthalmic Surgeon, King's College Hospital 1982-present. **Prof Background** King's College Hosp Medical School (Open Science Scholarship) 1934-39; Surgeon Lieut. RNVR 1939-46; Registrar King's College Hosp & Royal Eye Hosp, 1946-50. Alim Memorial Lecture 1992. **Awards/Research** Duke-Elder Glaucoma Awd, 1985. Medical jnl papers

1953-94; books inc: The Computerised Monitoring of Glaucoma, 1979; A Textbook of Clinical Ophthalmology (jt auth) 1987, 2nd Ed 1996. **Pres Committees** Council of the International Glaucoma Association; Visiting Research Fellow, Dept of Biomedical Engineering, Sussex Univ 1976-. **Past Committees** Member Ophthalmic Speciality Committee, SE Thames RHA 1970-82; Chairman, Ophthalmic Training Committee, SE Thames RHA 1973-82. **Media Experience** Much radio, some TV & video work on glaucoma. **Addits** Collab UK geneticists/US molecular biologists to search for glaucoma genes.

CRICK Rev W. Director **RADIANT LIFE MINISTRIES** RELIGIOUS Type: Service provider. 47 Gloucester Road, Akrington, Middleton, Manchester M24 1HT Tel:0161-653 3040 **Expertise** Christian ministry, mainly in the area of marriage enrichment through seminars. **Prof Background** Supervisory skills; called into full-time Christian ministry in 1991. **Awards/Research** Seminars: Superb Marriage (for couples); What Every Wife Wants Her Husband To Know (for husbands); Understanding Your Husband (for wives) & Enriching Second Marriage.

CRIPPS Alan Director **HOUSING SERVICES AGENCY** SOCIAL Type: Fundraiser; Service provider. 140 Camden St, London NW1 9PF Tel:0171-284 0293 Fax:0171-482 1260 **Expertise** General Management/Strategy. **Prev Posts** Housing Development Officer, NACRO; Director, Ducane Housing Association 1986-94. **Prof Background** BA (English), Oxford; MBA Univ. of Westminster. **Pres Committees** Supported Housing Sub-committee, National Federation of Housing Associations; Executive Committee, London Federation of Housing Associations. **Past Committees** Chair Board of Directors, Centrepoint 1985-93; Chair Management Committee, NACRO Housing in London 1993-95.

CRIPPS Diana Executive Director **WOMEN'S ENVIRONMENTAL NETWORK** WOMEN Type: Service provider; Campaigning. Aberdeen Studios, 22 Highbury Grove, London N5 2EA Tel:0171-354 8823 Fax:0171-354 0464 **Expertise** Organisational development, fundraising & charity management. **Prev Posts** Supervisor, Urban Spaces Scheme 1986-87; Senior Supervisor, Urban Spaces Scheme 1987-85; Centre Manager, London Ecology Centre 1988-95. **Prof Background** BSc (Hons) Environmental Science. **Pres Committees** Executive Committee, UNED-UK; Steering Committee, ALG Agenda 21. **Media Experience** Varied media experience.

CRIPPS Mr N. Administrator **VOICE OF THE PEOPLE TRUST** SOCIAL Type: Fundraiser; Service provider; Grant maker. 42 Sunnybank Road, Sutton Coldfield, W. Midlands B73 5RE

CROMPTON Mrs Hazel General Secretary **GIRLS FRIENDLY SOCIETY - GFS** SOCIAL Type: Service provider. Townsend House, 126 Queen's Gate, London SW7 5LQ Tel:0171-589 9628 Fax:0171-225 1458 **Expertise** Housing management and development; special needs housing; youth and community projects management. **Prev Posts** Housing Manager/Deputy Director, Aldwyck HA 1977-81; Director of Housing, GFS 1982-85.

Prof Background Associate, Incorporated Society of Valuers and Auctioneers (rtd); Theology Diploma, Kent Univ. **Past Committees** Rochester Diocesan Synod and Board of Finance. **Media Experience** Radio experience.

CROOK Frances Director **HOWARD LEAGUE FOR PENAL REFORM** SOCIAL Type: Campaigning; Penal reform. 708 Holloway Road, London N19 3NL Tel:0171-281 7722 Fax:0171-281 5506 **Expertise** Young people and crime; politics and criminal justice; women in prison; human rights. **Prev Posts** Campaign co-ordinator, Amnesty International 1980-86. **Prof Background** Teacher. **Past Committees** Hansard Society Commission into Legislative Process 1992. **Media Experience** Regular contrib to local and national media. **Addits** Labour party councillor, Barnet 1982-90.

CROSBIE John Centre Director **CALVERT TRUST, KESWICK** DISABILITY Type: Service provider. Adventure Centre, Little Crosthwaite, Underskiddaw, Keswick, Cumbria CA12 4QD Tel:01768-772254 Fax:01768-773941 **Expertise** Outdoor education. **Prev Posts** Deputy Warden, Calvert Trust 1991-93. **Prof Background** B Ed (Hons) Outdoor Education. **Pres Committees** Sailability (Sailing for People with Disabilities); Disability Cttee, British Canoe Union. Flyability Cttee (Para & Hangliding for People With Disabilities).

CROSSETT Tom Secretary General/Chief Executive **NATIONAL SOCIETY FOR CLEAN AIR AND ENVIRONMENTAL PROTECTION** CONSERVATION/ENVIRONMENT Type: Service provider. 136 North Street, Brighton BN1 1RG Tel:01273-326313 Fax:01273-735802 **Expertise** Environmental science, policy and management. **Prev Posts** Min of Ag/Fish/Food: Sci Liaison Off (Horti/Soils) 1978;Head, Food Sci Div 1984,Chief Scientist 1985-89; Nat Power:Head Env Policy 1989-90, Env Dir, 1990-91; Currently: Dir Gen, Int Union Air Pollution Assocs 1996-. **Prof Background** BSc BAgr, Queen's Univ Belfast; DPhil, Lincoln College, Oxford. **Awards/Research** Auth: Papers on plant physiology, marine biology, food science and environmental management. Mbr, UK Roundtable on Sustainable Development; Chair, Southern Region Environmental Protection Advisory Cttee of the Environment Agency. **Past Committees** UK Delegate, Tripartite Meetings on Food & Drugs 1985-88; Mbr NERC 1985-89; AFRC 1985-89; Cttee on Medical Aspects of Food Policy.

CROWTHER-HUNT Elizabeth National Director **PRINCE'S TRUST VOLUNTEERS, THE** CHILDREN/YOUTH Type: Fundraiser; Service provider; Grant maker. 18 Park Square East, London NW1 4LH Tel:0171-543 1234 Fax:0171-543 1367 **Expertise** Young people; community service; volunteering. **Prev Posts** Division Director, The Industrial Society; Chief Executive, South East Training; Asstnt to Chief Executive, London Borough of Southwark. **Prof Background** BA Hons, Geographical Tripos, Newnham College, Cambridge 1966-69; Diploma in Social Administration, University of York 1969-70. **Awards/Research** Auth: Inner Cities Inner Strengths. **Pres Committees** Trustee: National Volunteering Centre; Associate, Newnham College, Cambridge.

CROXON Roy Chief Executive **CASTEL FROMA HOME FOR PEOPLE WITH PHYSICAL DISABILITIES** DISABILITY Type: Fundraiser; Service provider. 93 Lillington Road, Leamington Spa, Warks CV32 6LL Tel:01926-427216 Fax:01926-885479 **Expertise** Management of resources. **Prev Posts** 31 years in Royal Army Medical Corps Medical Administration 1959-90. **Awards/Research** B.E.M. **Pres Committees** Chief Executive Castel Froma Trustees. **Past Committees** Numerous Army Boards, Promotion, Welfare and Mobility Planning. **Media Experience** Many TV interviews as Commander Medical during Ambulance strikes; press.

CRUICKSHANK Diana Secretary **DOLMETSCH HISTORICAL DANCE SOCIETY - DHDS** ARTS Type: Service provider; Professional Assoc. c/o Hunters Moon, Orcheston, Salisbury, Wilts SP3 4RP Tel:01980-620339 **Expertise** European Social Dance from 15th-19th centuries, working from original sources.

CULWICK David Chief Executive **SPURGEONS CHILD CARE** CHILDREN/YOUTH Type: Service provider; Operating England, Romania, Uganda. 74 Wellingborough Road, Rushden, Northants NN10 9TY Tel:01933-412412 Fax:01933-412010 **Expertise** Development of partnership schemes - children & families between Vol & State Sector incl church based. **Prev Posts** Principal Officer, Child Care 1972-84; Asst Director, Children - Salford SSD 1984-89.

CUNNINGHAM Michael Managing Director **SCOTTISH EUROPEAN AID** SOCIAL Type: Fundraiser; Service provider; Awareness. 18 Hanover Street, Edinburgh EH2 2EN Tel:0131-2254456 Fax:0131-2263106 **Expertise** Architect, post-war reconstruction, general management. **Prev Posts** Salaried Architect 1988-91; Partner in Architects Practice 1991-93. **Prof Background** Architect, Liverpool Polytechnic; Masters, York University. **Awards/Research** Author of: Aid in Former Yugoslavia (paper), Luton University; Architects & Aid (article) Architects Journal. **Past Committees** Board of Scottish European Aid. **Media Experience** Experience with various interviews for TV, radio and press. **Addits** Lecturer.

CUNNINGHAM Miss Phyllis M. Chief Executive **ROYAL MARSDEN NHS TRUST** MEDICAL/HEALTH Type: Service provider; Specialist hospital (cancer). Royal Marsden Hospital, Fulham Rd, London SW3 6JJ Tel:0171-352 8171 Fax:0171-376 4809 **Expertise** General management. **Prev Posts** Planning Off, Royal Free Hosp, London 1964-74; Dep Hse Gov & Sec to the Board, Royal Marsden SHA 1974-80; Chief Exec, Royal Marsden Hosp Special Health Authority 1980-89. **Prof Background** Healthcare management. **Awards/Research** Awarded Business Woman of the Year, 1991; Fellow RSA. **Pres Committees** Mbr, Hosp Officers Club; Gov, Christ's Sch, Rchmond; Dir, Royal Marsden NHS Trust; Dir, The RHM Cancer Fund Trading Co Ltd; Sec to Trustees, Royal Marsden Hosp Cancer Fund. **Past Committees** St. Anne's Church, Kew: Mbr, Parochial Church Council; Mbr, Finance Committee; Mbr, Restoration Committee. **Media Experience** Substantial media experience promoting Royal Marsden & fundraising. **Addits** Member, Council of Management, Institute of Cancer Research.

CURTIS Hilary Executive Director **BMA FOUNDATION FOR AIDS** MEDICAL/HEALTH Type: Service provider; Educational and Advocacy Organisation. BMA House, Tavistock Square, London WC1H 9JP Tel:0171-383 6345 Fax:0171-388 2544 **Expertise** Ethical, social, policy and human rights aspects of HIV/AIDS. **Prev Posts** Research Student, Cambridge University 1982-85; Research & Projects Officer, British Medical Association 1985-88. **Prof Background** Trained as a Research Chemist: MA, PHD (Cambridge University). **Awards/Research** Auth: Promoting Sexual Health, 1992. Various articles on AIDS healthcare and prevention. **Past Committees** Scientific co-ord, Org Cttee 2nd Int Wkshp on Prev of Sexual Transmission of HIV & other STDs; Tres, UK NGO AIDS 3rd Wld consortium. **Media Experience** Interviews on news/current affairs programmes. **Addits** Former consultant to WHO on Human Rights, Ethics and AIDS.

CURTIS-PRIOR Dr Peter Gen Secretary of Trust;Dir of Institute **CAMBRIDGE RESEARCH INSTITUTE, THE BETHANY TRUST** MEDICAL/HEALTH Type: Grant maker; Biomedical Education, Res/Development/Consultation. Bethany House, Histon, Cambridge, CB4 4HG Tel:01223-233053 Fax:01223-233053 **Expertise** Therapeutics; Medicinal Plants; Contraception; Neuropsychology. **Prev Posts** Head of Biosciences Research Napp Research Centre, Cambridge 1984-87;Scientific Director, Institute Henri Beaufour, Paris, France 1981-84. **Prof Background** BSc; PhD. 1964-72 academic medical research Dept of Experimental Medicine, Guys Hosp, London;1972-87 Drug research in the pharmaceutical industry in England and France. **Awards/Research** TD. Ed:(series) Biochemical Pharmacology of Metabolic Disease States, vol 1 Obesity 1983;Prostaglandins-Biology/Chemistry of Prostaglandins and Related Eicosanoids 1988. **Pres Committees** Chair: Cambridge Group, Prison Fellowship;President: Full Gospel Businessmen's Fellowship Int'l (Cambridge) and Field Representative for E Anglia Region. **Media Experience** Thought of the Day, local radio; Radio interviews; Christian videos; Press releases **Addits** Contributed over 100 articles to professional journals.

CUTHBERT Neil Director **OPPORTUNITY TRUST** Type: Fundraiser; Grant maker; Overseas development. 103 High Street, Oxford OX1 4BW Tel:01865-794411 Fax:01865-295161 **Prev Posts** Director Sales & Marketing, Lion Publishing U.S. 1990-95; Publisher, Sovereign World Inc 1995-96.

D

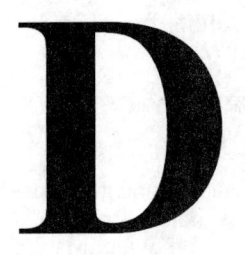

DALES Mike Access & Conservation Officer **MOUNTAINEERING COUNCIL OF SCOTLAND - MCofS** SPORTS Type: Fundraiser; Service provider; Grant maker; Campaigning. 4A St. Catherine's Road, Perth PH1 5SE Tel:01738-638227 Fax:01738-442095 **Expertise** Footpath management; visitor surveys; Scottish mountain issues; active mountaineer & sea kayaker. **Prev Posts** Outdoor Ed Tutor, Cranedale Study Ctre 1985-89; Visitor Monitoring Off, Countryside Commission For Scotland 1991-92; Recreation & Access Off, Scottish Nat Heritage 1992-95. . **Prof Background** B.Ed, Outdoor Education; Postgraduate Diploma, Tourism Management. **Awards/Research** Part-author, part-editor, The SNH Visitor Monitoring Training Manual. **Pres Committees** Scottish Wildlife & Countryside Link Uplands Working Group; British Mountaineering Council Access & Conservation Cttee; MCofS Access & Conservation Cttee; Scottish Canoe Assoc Touring Cttee.

DALLEY Gillian Director **CENTRE FOR POLICY ON AGEING** THE ELDERLY Type: Research, Policy & Information. 25-31 Ironmonger Row, London EC1V 3QP Tel:0171-253 1787 Fax:0171-490 4206 **Expertise** Health Services Research; Social Gerontology. **Prev Posts** Research Fellow, Policy Studies Institute 1989-91; Regional Quality Manager, S.E. Thames Regional Health Authority 1991-94. **Prof Background** PhD Social Policy; MA(Econ) Social Anthropology; BA Anthropology. **Awards/Research** Ideologies of Caring: rethinking community and collectivism, Macmillan. 1996 (2nd edn); Many papers, articles on community care, health services. **Pres Committees** Phoenix Committee, Nuffield Foundation. **Past Committees** Barking & Havering Family Health Services Authority. **Media Experience** Experience in radio, TV, video and press.

DALTON Dorothy Director **ASSOCIATION OF CHIEF EXECUTIVES OF NATIONAL VOLUNTARY ORGANISATIONS - ACENVO** SOCIAL Type: Professional association. 31-33 College Rd, Harrow on the Hill, Middlesex HA1 1EJ Tel:0181-424 2334 Fax:0181-426 0055 **Prev Posts** Head, Northwood College 1986-91; Chief Executive, PHAB 1991-92. **Prof Background** BSc (Hons) 1st Class, Mathematics; MSc Mathematics. **Pres Committees** Chair of Trustees of the JOLT Trust; Governor, Orley Farm School; Council Member, The Harrow Club; Trustee, Charities Evaluation Services. **Addits** Founder of The JOLT Trust.

DANBY Keith Chief Executive **SEND THE LIGHT LTD** RELIGIOUS Type: Service provider; Grant maker. Distributor. Po Box 300, Kingston Town Broadway, Carlisle, Cumbria CA3 0QS Tel:01228-512512 Fax:01228-514949 **Expertise** General Management Strategy; Financial Administration Policy. **Prev Posts** Managing Director, Home improvement 1978-87; MD management services company 1976-79. **Prof Background** Chartered Secretary, Financial Administration; BIMgt Diploma in management. **Awards/Research** Many articles on Christian literature distribution. Send the Light won Cumbrian Business of Year Award 1994. **Pres Committees** Thana Trust, Trustee; Wesley Owen Ltd, Director; Evangical Alliance, Advisory Board. **Past Committees** Operation Mobilisation UK, Board; Capernwray Hall Ltd, Board. **Media Experience** All Media

DANIELS Barbara Secretary **CLUB FOR ACTS AND ACTORS** (incorp Concert Artistes Association). SOCIAL Type: Members club for actors/entertainers/stage people. 20 Bedford St, London WC2E 9HP Tel:0171-836 3172 **Expertise** Secretarial; Singing. **Prev Posts** Sec to Dir of Soc Servs Inspectorate, Civil Service 1984-86; Sec for corporate procurement dept of Marriot Hotels 1986-90; Temping in various fields inc medical 1990-92. **Prof Background** 4 years training as a singer/teacher of singing at the Royal Academy; Further training as singer; Secretarial Courses; Professional singer. **Awards/Research** LRAM - singing teaching; ARCM - singing performing. **Addits** Singing on radio & TV inc religious progs; Acting on many TV progs.

DANIELS Susan T. Chief Executive **NATIONAL DEAF CHILDREN'S SOCIETY** DISABILITY Type: Fundraiser. 15 Dufferin St, London EC1Y 8PD Tel:0171-250 0123 Fax:0171-251 5020 **Expertise** Education of deaf people. **Prev Posts** Lecturer, Deaf Education 1984-88; Higher Education Development Officer 1988-89; Head of Education, Training and Employment, RNID 1989-92. **Prof Background** BA (Hons) History and Politics; Certificate in Education (FE/HE); Certificate in Education of Deaf Children. **Awards/Research** Auth: Top-Up Loans - Implications For Students With Disabilities 1990; FEHE Bill- Legislation and Its Potential Impact on Deaf People; Co-Auth: Deaf Students in HE. **Pres Committees** Mbr, Governing Cncl of SKILL, NBSD; Prince of Wales Disability Wking Party; Snowdon Award Trust; Non-Exec Dir, S. Daniels Plc. **Past Committees** NATED;CVCP Equal Opportunities Working Party; VOADL. **Addits** Paper at NATED Open Day April 1990: Deaf Students and Access to HE.

DARLEY Gillian Director (part-time) **LANDSCAPE FOUNDATION** ENVIRONMENT Type: Campaigning; Contemp landscape design. c/o 14 Doughty St London WC1N 2PL Tel:0171-242 3301 Fax:0171-430 1672 **Expertise** Architecture and landscape design; writing/journalism. **Prev Posts** Always freelance but Architectural Correspondent for The Observer 1990-93. **Prof Background** Art history (BA hons); Politics & Administration (MSc). **Awards/Research** Regular contributor to many professional journals (architecture) and Financial Times. Author or co-author of 6 books including Villages of Vision (1975) Octavia Hill (1990). **Pres Committees** Vice chairman, Society for the Protection of Ancient Buildings; Vice Chairman, Friends of St George's

Gardens. **Past Committees** Development sub-cttee New Islington & Hackney HA 1984-90; SAVE Britain's Heritage 1976-81; TCPA Exec Cttee 1975-79. **Media Experience** Radio/TV/press. **Addits** Awards: BP Arts journalism 1988.

DARLEY Sylvia Founder & President **MALCOLM SARGENT CANCER FUND FOR CHILDREN** MEDICAL Type: Fundraiser; Service provider; Grant maker. 15 Abingdon Road, London W8 6AH Tel:0171-937 5740 Fax:0171-376 1193 **Expertise** Concert organisation & management. **Prev Posts** Sir Malcolm Sargent's Manager 1947-67; Chief Executive, Malcolm Sargent Cancer Fund for Children since 1967. **Awards/Research** OBE. **Pres Committees** Director, Malcolm Sargent Festival Choir. **Past Committees** Chairman, Charity Christmas Card Council; Chairman, Friends of Queen Charlotte's Hospital. **Media Experience** Radio, Television & Press.

DARNBROUGH Ms Ann Chief Executive **NATIONAL INFORMATION FORUM** DISABILITY Type: Service provider. Post Point 228, BT Proctor House, 100-110 High Holborn, London WC1V 6LD Tel:0171-404 3846 Fax:0171-404 3849 **Expertise** Disability information. **Prev Posts** Secretary, Community Health Council; Co-Director, AHRTAG (Appropriate Health Resources & Technologies Action Group). **Prof Background** Much experience. **Awards/Research** Author of: Directory for Disabled People, Motoring & Mobility for Disabled People, The Sex Directory & many more. **Pres Committees** Viscount Nuffield Auxiliary Fund Selection Committee; BBC Appeals Committee; Snowdon Award Scheme Selection Committee; Board of Trustees, Tripscope. **Media Experience** Varied media experience.

DART John Director **DYSTROPHIC EPIDERMOLYSIS BULLOSA RESEARCH ASSOCIATION - DEBRA** MEDICAL/HEALTH Type: Service provider; Medical research/information. Debra House, 13 Wellington Business Park, Duke's Ride, Crowthorne, Berkshire RG11 6LS Tel:01344-771961 Fax:01344-762661 **Expertise** Physical disability. **Prev Posts** Welfare Administrator, MS Society 1983-87; Director, Westminster Mencap 1987-89. **Prof Background** BSc (Hons) Sociology; Diploma in Applied Social Sciences/CQSW **Pres Committees** Vice Chair, Genetic Interest Group; Joint Co-ordinator, DEBRA Europe; Mbr Disab Appeal Trib; Tres, European Alliance of Genetic Support Groups. **Past Committees** Crossroads Care National Executive Cttee, 1983-87; Patient Services Cttee, International Federation of Multiple Sclerosis Societies. **Media Experience** Numerous press and radio interviews. **Addits** Ind mbr/ch, Berks Soc Servs Dept, Complaints Review Panel since 1992.

DARTINGTON Lord Young of Director **INSTITUTE OF COMMUNITY STUDIES** SOCIAL Type: Research institute. 18 Victoria Park Square, Bethnal Green, London E2 9PF. Tel:0181-980 6263 Fax:0181-981 6719 **Expertise** Families. **Prev Posts** Lecturer, Cambridge University, 1959-66. Chairman, National Consumer Council 1985-88. **Prof Background** Economics, Law. Hon Fellow, British Academy; Hon Fellow, RIBA. **Awards/Research** Numerous publ inc: Family & Kinship in E London, (jt) 1957; Rise of the Meritocracy, (jt) 1958; The Metronomic Society, 1988; Life after Work, 1991. **Media Experience** Press Articles. **Addits** Royal Society for the Arts Albert Medal awarded 1992.

DAVEY John Chief Executive **TRINITY COLLEGE LONDON** CHILDREN/YOUTH Type: Service provider. 16 Park Crescent, London W1N 4AP Tel:0171-323 2328 Fax:0171-323 5201 **Expertise** Strategic planning & management of international examinations board. **Prev Posts** Head of Science, Roedean School 1970-74; Senior Master, Roedean School 1974-78; Headmaster, St Brandons School 1978-90. **Prof Background** Hon. FTCL; FRSA; BSc (Hons) Chemistry, Kings College, London 1957-60. **Pres Committees** Chairman of Governors, Burgess Hill School; British Council's English Teaching Advisory Committee (ETAC). **Past Committees** Common Entrance Board. **Addits** JP in Avon and earlier in East Sussex.

DAVID Ernest Director **ASSOCIATION OF JEWISH REFUGEES IN GREAT BRITAIN** RELIGIOUS Type: Service provider. 1 Hampstead Gate, 1a Frognal, London NW3 6AL Tel:0171-431 6161 Fax:0171-431 8454 **Prev Posts** Airline Manager, British Airways 1966-1991. **Prof Background** Barrister at Law LL.B (Hons).

DAVIDSON John Chief Executive **GROUNDWORK FOUNDATION** CONSERVATION/ENVIRONMENT Type: Environmental charity. 85-87 Cornwall Street, Birmingham B3 3BY Tel:0121-236 8565 Fax:0121-236 7356 **Expertise** Environmental Regeneration. **Prev Posts** Acting Director, Countryside Commission 1984; Regional Dir and Policy Dir, Countryside Commission 1974-84. **Prof Background** Degrees and diplomas in geography, conservation and ecology, and town planning. **Pres Committees** Member of: Newpin Board (New Parent Infant Network); Acting Chair, UK 2000 Board, Bridge Group; Commission on Environmental Strategy and Planning - IUCN. **Addits** Fellow: Royal Society of Arts; Royal Town Planning Institute; D.Univ - (uct).

DAVIES David G. Chief Executive **BRAINWAVE** DISABILITY Type: Fundraiser. Marsh Lane, Huntworth Gate, Bridgwater, Somerset TA6 6LQ Tel:01278-429089 Fax:01278-429622 **Expertise** Fundraising, Media, Marketing. **Prev Posts** Marketing/Finance Manager, Barclays Bank International 1971-87; Regional Manager, Save the Children 1987-95. **Prof Background** International banking UK and overseas; Associate Institute of Banking; MICFM. **Media Experience** Radio interviews; (general press contacts).

DAVIES Elsa Director **NATIONAL PLAYING FIELDS ASSOCIATION** CHILDREN/YOUTH Type: Service provider. 25 Ovington Square, London SW3 1LQ Tel:0171-584 6445 Fax:0171-581 2402 **Expertise** Fundraising and general management. **Prev Posts** Head Teacher, Surrey CC 1974-83; Head Teacher, LB Hillingdon 1983-87; Manager of Education and Vocational Liaison, BIMgt 1988-91. **Prof Background** Teachers Cert, Univ Wales 1965; BA Open Univ 1976; Dip Ed 1978; MA Mgmt London Univ 1980; Page Scholar, ESU 1981; FIMgt; FRSA. Mbr, English Speaking Union. **Awards/Research** Articles, chapters and reviews in educational publ (topics range from education management to work experience); School awards for communications with parents; 3 Industry Year awards. **Pres Committees** National Lottery Advisory Group; Hon Advisor (former Chair), World Education Fellowship - GB Section; member Glamorgan County Cricket Club, ACENVO. **Past Committees** Numerous inc Nat Cic Wkg Gp on Design and Tech; 2 CNAA Brds; Chair, Adv Centre for Educ;Central Bureau for Educ Visits & Exchanges. **Media Experience** Television, radio, video and press interviews. **Addits** Mbr: London Businesswomen's Netwk;Westminster Dining Club;Lady Taverners.

DAVIES Hywel Chief Executive **ROYAL HIGHLAND AND AGRICULTURAL SOCIETY OF SCOTLAND - RHASS** CONSERVATION/ENVIRONMENT Type: Service provider; Grant maker. Royal Highland Centre, Ingliston, Edinburgh EH28 8NF Tel:0131-333 2444 Fax:0131-333 5236 **Expertise** General management and administration. **Prev Posts** Army Officer 1967-88; Consultant 1988-91. **Prof Background** Magdalene College, Cambridge. **Pres Committees** Director, Scottish Assoc of Agriculture; Director, Scottish Agricultural & Rural Development Centre.

DAVIES J. Secretary **ANGLICAN FELLOWSHIP IN SCOUTING AND GUIDING** RELIGIOUS Type: Fundraiser; Service provider; Working within scouting and guiding. 31 Loseley Rd, Farncombe, Godalming Surrey GU7 3RE Tel:01483-428876 **Expertise** Training of Adult Leaders; Producing resource material for their use within the Scout & Guide Promise. **Prev Posts** Hon Sec from foundation of Fellowship 1983. **Prof Background** Leader in Scouting since 1972. **Awards/Research** Prayer Book: Prayers for Uniformed Youth; 52 Resource sheets for adult leaders in Youth Church Organisations. **Pres Committees** Trustee, Anglican Fellowship in Scouting & Guiding; Parochial Church Cncl; Deanery Synod Secretary; Mbr, Diocesan Synod (Church of England Positions). **Past Committees** Parochial Church Council; Deanery Synod Secretary; Member of Diocesan Synod (Church of England Positions). **Media Experience** Radio/TV: some experience.

DAVIES Dr Mary Director **PRE-RETIREMENT ASSOCIATION OF GB & NI** THE ELDERLY Type: Service provider. 26 Frederick Sanger Rd, Surrey Research Park, Guildford GU2 5YD Tel:01483-301170 Fax:01483-300981 **Expertise** Management in the voluntary sector; education; training. **Prev Posts** University Lecturer, London; Educ Officer for a National Charity 1986-89. Freelance Trainer/Consultant, Open Univ NHS Training Authority, MSD Foundation etc. **Prof Background** BSc; PhD Certificate in Psychology. **Awards/Research** Contrib: Sexuality and the Physically Disabled 1983; Sex Therapy in Britain 1988. Auth: Sex Educ for Physically Disabled Young People 1983; many articles/teaching aids. **Pres Committees** SAGA Magazine Editorial Board; REACH Council. **Past Committees** British Association for Service to the Elderly Executive (BASE). **Media Experience** Radio interviews inc: You & Yours, Surrey local radio. **Addits** Honorary Editor of Action Baseline for short period.

DAVIES Peter R.C.B. Director General **ROYAL SOCIETY FOR THE PREVENTION OF CRUELTY TO ANIMALS - RSPCA** ANIMAL/WILDLIFE Type: Fundraiser; Service provider; Grant maker. Protection agency/Parliament and EC Adviser. The Causeway, Horsham, Sussex RH12 1HG Tel:01403-264181 Fax:01403-241048 **Expertise** General leadership. **Prev Posts** HM Forces: Commander 12 Armoured Brigade; BAOR Commander Communications 1987-90; GOC Wales. **Prof Background** HM Forces Maj. Gen. (Ret'd) 1991; psc+; RCDS; CIMgt; FIPD; FZS. **Pres Committees** Exec Dir, Eurogroup For Animal Welfare 1992-; Exec Dir, WSPA 1992-; Trustee, Llandovery College 1991-; Chair, Freedom Food Ltd 1993-.Exec Cttee, Forces Help Society & Lord Roberts Workshops 1994-. **Addits** Col, King's Regiment 1986-94; Col Comdt, Royal Signals 1991-.

DAVIES W J Chief Executive **RIDING FOR THE DISABLED ASSOCIATION** DISABILITY Type: Service provider. Avenue R, National Agricultural Centre, Kenilworth, Warwickshire, CV8 2LY Tel:01203-696510 Fax:01203-696532 **Expertise** Charity Management; Fundraising; Finance. **Prev Posts** Management Consultant, 1993-95; Financial Advisor in Banking, 1969-93.

DAVIS Andrew Director **ENVIRONMENTAL TRANSPORT ASSOCIATION** ENVIRONMENT Type: Service provider. 10 Church St, Weybridge, Surrey KT13 8RS Tel:01932-828882 Fax:01932-829015 **Expertise** Environmental transport. **Pres Committees** ETA Trust. **Media Experience** Experience with radio, TV and press.

DAVISON Geoffrey M. Chief Executive/Founder **BREAK** SOCIAL Type: Service provider. 7a Church St, Sheringham, Norfolk NR26 8QR Tel:01263-822161 Fax:01263-822181 **Prev Posts** Assistant Company Secretary, Lotus Car Group 1962-64; Assistant General Secretary, Brit Epilepsy Association 1964-66; Assistant Director, Brit Heart Foundation 1966-76. **Prof Background** Queen Elizabeth I Grammar School, Darlington; Kings College, University of Durham; Member: ICFM (Institute of Charity Fundraising Managers); ACENVO. **Pres Committees** Joint Charity Card Associates PLC. **Past Committees** Sec, Assoc for Res Mental Care; Insp Advisory Cttée of Norfolk Social Services; Gen Purposes Cttee, Nat Cncl of Vol Child Care Orgs. **Addits** Senior Officer, Scout Association, Norfolk; Queens Scout.

DAVISON Judith Ann Executive Officer **BREAK** SOCIAL Type: Service provider. 7a Church Street, Sheringham, Norfolk NR26 8QR Tel:01263-822161 Fax:01263-822181 **Expertise** Residential social work, including family assessments. **Prev Posts** Teacher 1964-69; with BREAK since 1969. **Prof Background** Teaching Certificate.

DAWES Jenny Director **ST KATHARINE & SHADWELL TRUST** SOCIAL Type: Fundraiser; Grant maker. Campaigning PO Box 1779, London E1 8NL Tel:0171-782 6962 Fax:0171-782 6963 **Expertise** Origination, establishment, and direction of charitable and campaigning grps. **Prev Posts** On-going self-employed consultancies and directorships. **Prof Background** Charity consultant, instigator and devisor of strategies. **Pres Committees** The City Endowed Clerks Forum; Brd Mbr Tower Hamlets Educational Business Partnership; Summer University Steering Committee; Admin London

Music Hall Trust. **Past Committees** Committees, campaigns and projects for arts, education, racial equality, crime, urban regeneration and literacy.

DAY William Director **CARE INTERNATIONAL** SOCIAL Type: Fundraiser; International humanitarian aid. 36-38 Southampton St, London WC2E 7AF Tel:0171-379 5247 Fax:0171-379 0543 **Expertise** African aid issues; small enterprise development. **Prev Posts** Field Dir, Save The Children Fund 1985; Prod, Focus on Africa, BBC Wld 1986-87; Relief Co-ord, OXFAM 1987-88; Dir, Charity Projects 1988-94; Dir, Opportunity Trust 1994-96. **Pres Committees** BBC Central Appeals Advisory Cttee; Director, South Kent NHS Hospital Trust. **Past Committees** CAF Grants Council.

DAYSH Mrs Zena Executive Vice Chair **COMMONWEALTH HUMAN ECOLOGY COUNCIL - CHEC** SOCIAL Type: Service provider; International NGO, charity status; educational. 57-58 Stanhope Gardens, London SW7 5RF Tel:0171-373 6761 Fax:0171-244 7470 **Expertise** Organiser/admin/lobbyist; conferences/wkshops & cttees; catalyst for grassroots self-reliance activities. **Prev Posts** Founder of the Committee on Nutrition in the Commonwealth, 1951; founder & chief administrator of CHEC, 1969-present. **Prof Background** Physiotherapist; nutritionist; applied research & human ecological devmt in the Commonwealth; Scholarly Achievement Award 1992, Inst of Oriental Philosophy, Tokyo; Honoured Guest 1993, Rotary Int Ed. **Awards/Research** Co-ed: Human Ecology - Indian Perspective, 1985; Human Ecology, Env Educ & Sustainable Devmt, 1991; Commonwealth & Env Mngmt, 1992; Dialogue of Cultures for Sustainable Devmt, 1992. **Pres Committees** Commonwealth Professional Association; Habitat International Council; V-Pres. of several national CHECs. **Media Experience** Occasional TV; int newspaper articles; co-ed CHEC journal. **Addits** Most Distinguished Fellowship 1992, Delhi School of Non-Violence.

DEANE Kathryn L. Chief Executive **SOUND SENSE** DISABILITY Type: Service provider. Riverside House, Rattlesden, Bury St Edmunds, IP30 0SF Tel: 01449-736287.

DE'ATH Erica Chief Executive **NATIONAL STEPFAMILY ASSOCIATION - STEPFAMILY** SOCIAL Type: Service provider; Campaigning; membership organization. Chapel House, 18 Hatton Place, London EC1N 8RU Tel:0171-209 2460 Fax:0171-209 2461 **Expertise** Child and family welfare; parent education; stepfamilies; family centres; self help. **Prev Posts** Snr Dvmt Off, Nat Children's Bureau 1981-86; Dept Head, Children's Soc 1985-88; Chief Exec, Foundation for Study of Infant Deaths 1988-90. Currently NCVCCO Director Designate. **Prof Background** BA (Hons) Psychology, 1st class; Business leadership, Ashridge Coll. Mbr: Assoc for Family Therapy; Assoc of Child Psychologists and Psychiatrists; ACENVO; Brit Psychological Soc. **Awards/Research** Auth: Changing Families 1991; Ed: Stepfamilies: What do we Know?.. 1992; Co-ed: Working Towards Partnership in the Early Years 1989; Parenting Threads: Caring for Children.. 1992. **Pres Committees** Management Board, National Children's Bureau. **Past Committees** Chair, Nat Stepfamily Assoc; Vice Chair, Internat Conference on Children and Death; Chair, Thames Telethon Children's Panel. **Media Experience** Feature progs/news/current affairs/phone-ins; contrib/consult/auth support mat. **Addits** Co-author: Confident Parents, Confident Children, 1994.

DE GROOT Richard Director **COMMUNITY HEALTH UK (NATIONAL COMMUNITY HEALTH RESOURCE)** MEDICAL/HEALTH Type: Fundraiser; Service provider; Grant maker. Community health project development & networking. 6 Terrace Walk, Bath BA1 1LN Tel:01225-462680 Fax:01225-484238 **Expertise** Community health; primary health care; education and training. **Prev Posts** Headteacher, Shaftesbury School 1981-85; Consultant/Education and Training Manager in the Voluntary Sector 1985-91. **Prof Background** MA, Oxon; PGCE. **Awards/Research** Publ inc: Student Centred Learning and Appraisal; Alcohol Education.

DENBIGH Alan Executive Director **TELEWORK TELECOTTAGE AND TELECENTRE ASSOCIATION - TCA** SOCIAL/TRAINING Type: Fundraiser; Service provider. The Other Cottage, Shortwood, Nailsworth, Glos GL6 0SH Tel:01453-834874 Fax:01453-836174 **Prev Posts** ACRE Teleworking Advisor (1990-93); Bluebird Software Product Consultant (1987-90); Metier Application Devt Exec (1983-87). **Prof Background** Professional Engineer BSc Hons (Bristol). **Awards/Research** Teleworker Magazine; Teleworking Handbook. **Pres Committees** EC Fourth Framework Programme Advisory Cttee. **Media Experience** Extensive experience.

DEVINE Wing Commander D. Assistant Director **EX-SERVICES MENTAL WELFARE SOCIETY** MEDICAL/HEALTH Type: Fundraiser; Service provider. Hollybush House, Hollybush, By Ayr KA6 7EA Tel:01292-560214 Fax:01292-560871

DICKENS Joy Founder/Director **PARENTS' FRIEND** SOCIAL Helpline (National), Support Group (Local). c/o Voluntary Action Leeds, Stringer House, 34 Lupton Street, Hunslet, Leeds LS10 2QW Tel:0113-267 4627 **Expertise** Helping parents understanding/accepting their child's sexuality. **Awards/Research** A Guide for Parents who have Lesbian, Gay or Bisexual Children; Leaflets, relevant articles, reading list. **Media Experience** Great deal of experience on radio and TV.

DIEHL Caroline Director **MEDIA TRUST** SOCIAL Type: Media resource centre; TV & video production. 56 Whitfield Street, London W1P 5RN Tel:0171-637 4747 Fax:0171-637 5757 **Expertise** Media, Voluntary sector. **Prev Posts** CSV Media - Manager. **Media Experience** TV production and training.

DIGBY Susan Principal **VOICES FOUNDATION** ARTS/CULTURAL Type: Service provider. 21 Earls Court Square, London SW5 9BY Tel:0171-370 1944 Fax:0171-370 1874 **Expertise** Primary music education; Choir director; Childrens' choir trainer; Piano; Singing; Conducting. **Prev Posts** Head of Junior Choral Studies, Academy for Performing Arts, HK; Taught musicology, HK University; Head of Music, Diocesan Girls Junior School, HK. **Prof Background** King College, London, BMus(Hons); Kecskemet, Hungary studied choral conducting. **Awards/Research** Awarded: Churchill Fellowship (1990). **Past Committees** Hong Kong Ballet; Director, Wessex FM. **Media Experience** Extensive news media coverage including hosting programmes for radio & TV.

DIPLOCK Mrs Shelagh Director **FAWCETT SOCIETY, THE** SOCIAL Type: Campaigning organisation. 5th Floor, 45 Beech Street, London EC2Y 8AD Tel:0171-628 4441 Fax:0171-628 2865 **Expertise** Gender and disability issues; management of change; local service development; political lobbying. **Prev Posts** Manager, Robinsons Bookshop, Brighton Polytechnic 1984-87; Co-ord, Brighton and Hove Fed of the Disabled 1988-92. **Prof Background** BA (1st Class Hons) International Politics, History and Economics; MSc International Relations, LSE 1988; Fellow RSA. **Pres Committees** Chair, National Council, World Development Movement.

DIXEY Judy Director **BANKSIDE GALLERY** ARTS Type: Service provider. 48 Hopton St, London SE1 9JH Tel:0171-928 7521 Fax:0171-928 2820 **Prev Posts** Assistant Director (resources) 1985-89; Administrator Bournemouth International Festival 1991. **Prev Posts** Chartered Accountant, MA (Hons) Oxon. **Pres Committees** Gemini (trustee). **Past Committees** Forum for Initiatives in Reparation & Mediation (Treasurer).

DIXIE David General Secretary **BRIB - working with blind people** DISABILITY Type: Fundraiser; Service provider. 24 Wood Lane, Harborne, Birmingham B17 9AY Tel:0121-428 5000 Fax:0121-428 5008 **Expertise** Strategy and Coordination; Finance; Central Administration. **Prev Posts** Diocese of N Argentina, Financial Sec 1973-81; Selly Oak Colleges, Chief Admin Officer 1982-91. **Prof Background** Chartered Accountant.

DIXON Brigadier A.K. Director **EX-SERVICES MENTAL WELFARE SOCIETY - COMBAT STRESS** MEDICAL/HEALTH Type: Fundraiser; Service provider. Broadway House, The Broadway, London SW19 1RL Tel:0181-543 6333 Fax:0181-542 7082 **Prev Posts** Army Service 1952-88. **Prof Background** Royal Military Academy, Sandhurst 1953-55; Royal Naval Staff College, Greenwich 1966; National Defence College 1971-72; Staff College, Camberley 1972-4; Henley Management College 1978. **Pres Committees** Hon Sec, British Mbrs Council, World Veterans Federation;Exec Cttee, Confed British Service & Ex-Service Organizations; Central Advisory Cttee on War Pensions; Trustee, Queen Mary's Roehampton Trust. **Past Committees** Trustee, Charities Effectiveness Review Trust; Exec Cttee, Surrey Council for Mental Health.

DOBSON Jane Secretary/Administrator. **ASSOCIATION OF INNER WHEEL CLUBS IN GREAT BRITAIN AND IRELAND.** SOCIAL Type: Women's organization raising money; Providing help locally. 51 Warwick Square, London SW1V 2AT. Tel:0171-834 4600.

DODDS Felix Co-ordinator **UNITED NATIONS ENVIRONMENT & DEVELOPMENT UK UNED-UK** CONSERVATION/ENVIRONMENT Type: Service provider; Facilitate work on Agenda 21 in the UK. 3 Whitehall Court, London SW1A 2EL Tel:0171-930 2931 Fax:0171-930 5893 **Expertise** United Nations; Agenda 21; Local Agenda 21. **Prev Posts** Chair of Young Liberals 1985-87; Regional Officer, UN Association 1987-91; Head of UNA Sustainable Development Unit 1991-today. **Prof Background** Scientist; Teacher. **Awards/Research** Contrib, Politics of Rio, 1994. Auth: Into the 21st Century - An Agenda for Political Realignment, 1988; Three Years Since the Rio Summit (with Tom Bigg); Habitat ll Papers (ed). **Pres Committees** Advisor to UK Govt: UN Gen Assembly 92, UN Econ Social Cncl 93; UN Commission on Sustainable Devmt 93; Greenwich Millenium Brd; Ed Brd TCPA, CSD; NGO Steering Cttee; Adv to UK Govt UN CSD 1994-96. **Past Committees** Liberal Party Cncl; Liberal Party Defence Panel; Co-ord, Green Voice; Chair, Nat League of Young Liberals. **Media Experience** All TV news broadcasts; all quality newspapers. **Addits** Past Cttee:Ed Brd Cntr for Our Common Future, Green Magazine Global Forum 94.

DOGGETT T.S. Executive Director **COTTAGE AND RURAL ENTERPRISE LIMITED - CARE** SOCIAL Type: Fundraiser; Service provider. 9 Weir Road, Kibworth, Leicestershire LE8 0LQ Tel:01162-793225 Fax:01162-796384 **Expertise** General management of the charity, building work. **Prev Posts** Director of Fundraising & PR, CARE 1984-90; Technical Director Sketchley Cleaners Ltd 1978-84; Other posts at Sketchley Plc 1958-78. **Prof Background** Natural Sciences Tripos (Hons) M.A. Cambridge. **Media Experience** Some Radio & Press.

DORRANCE Dr Richard C. Chief Executive **COUNCIL FOR AWARDS IN CHILDREN'S CARE AND EDUCATION** CHILD/YOUTH Type: Service provider; Awarding Body. 8 Chequer Street, St Albans, Herts AL1 3XZ Tel:01727-847636 Fax:01727-867609 **Expertise** Education, National Curriculum, Assessment. **Prev Posts** Asst Chief Executive, Nat Curriculum Council 1989-91; Dep Chief Executive (Acting CE 1991-92) of School Examination & Assessment Council 1991-93. **Prof Background** BSc (Hons) Chemistry, University of East Anglia 1969; PhD, University of East Anglia 1972; PGCE, London University 1974; Fellow of the Royal Society of Chemistry (elected). **Awards/Research** Numerous magazine articles. **Pres Committees** Care Sector Consortium Awarding Body Forum; NVQ Steering Committee for Review of Child Care and Education Awards; Royal Society of Chemistry Thames Valley Education Committee. **Past Committees** Advisory Cttee for Wales (SEAC); Curriculum Cncl for Wales (Observer); Cncl for the Accreditation of Teacher Education (Observer). **Media Experience** Press & radio interviews; videos about Nat Curriculum for teachers & parents. **Addits** Sat on FEU Committee on Assessment in an Ethnically Diverse Society.

DOTTRIDGE Mike Director **ANTI-SLAVERY INTERNATIONAL** SOCIAL/OVERSEAS Type: Research; Campaigning. The Stableyard, Broomgrove Rd, London SW9 9TL Tel:0171-924 9555 Fax:0171-738 4110 **Expertise** Human rights campaigning, Managing change, Human rights in Central Africa, Child labour. **Prev Posts** Amnesty International (Intl Secretariat), 1977-95; Head of Amnesty's Africa Unit 1987-95. **Prof Background** Human rights (both civil/political and economic/social) specialising in French-speaking countries.

DOUGAL Andrew Patrick Chief Executive **NORTHERN IRELAND CHEST HEART & STROKE ASSOCIATION** MEDICAL/HEALTH Type: Fundraiser; Service provider; Grant maker. 21 Dublin Road, Belfast BT2 7FJ Tel:01232-320184 Fax:01232-333487 **Expertise** PR; advocacy/lobbying; organizat/mngmt devlopment; personnel mngmt; media training; fundraising. **Prev Posts** Registrar, St Louise's Comprehensive College, Belfast 1975-83. Currently: Non-Exec Dir, NI Chest Heart & Stroke Enterprises Ltd. **Prof Background** BA (Classics), Postgrad Dip (Business Admin), Queens Univ, Belfast; Postgrad Dip (Personnel Mngmt), Ulster Poly; Mbr: IPD, IOD. **Awards/Research** OBE **Pres Committees** V Chair, Cttee of Mgmt of Share Centre (disab hols); Non-Exec Dir, Hugh O'Kane & Co (Funeral Dirs); Mbr, NI Coronary Prev Gp; Mbr, NICREST Cttee on Hypertension; Tres, Int Soc & Fed of Cardiology. **Past Committees** Chair, NI branch IPM 91-93; Educ Off, NI branch, IPR; BBC NI Educ Broadcasting Cncl 87-89; Non-Exec Dir, Belfast Cmnty Radio 89-92. **Media Experience** Regular broadcasts: BBC NI, Ulster TV, radio & all aspects of the press. **Addits** Lay reader.

DOUGILL Dr J.W. Chief Executive & Secretary **INSTITUTION OF STRUCTURAL ENGINEERS IStructE** CONSERVATION/ENVIRONMENT Type: Professional Institution. 11 Upper Belgrave St, London SW1X 8BH Tel:0171-235 4535 Fax:0171-235 4294 **Expertise** Institution management. **Prev Posts** Professor of Concrete Structures, Imperial College; Director of Engineering, Institution Structural Engineer. **Prof Background** Structural/civil engineering. **Awards/Research** Baker Medal, Institution of Civil Engineering. Auth: papers in engineering mechanics, materials and structures. **Pres Committees** Member of Court of the Whitgift Foundation. **Past Committees** NEDO Research Strategy Committee; Chairman, SERC Civil Engineering Committee. **Addits** Secretary General, Federation International de la Precontrainte.

DOUGLAS Carolyn Director **EXPLORING PARENTHOOD** CHILDREN/YOUTH Type: Service provider. 4 Ivory Place, 20a Treadgold St, London W11 4PB Tel:0171-221 6681 Fax:0171 221 4471 **Expertise** Individual, group and family therapy; organizational psychology. **Prev Posts** Senior Psychiatric Social Worker, St Bartholomew's Hospital 1972-82; Senior Social Worker Family Therapist, Parkside Clinic 1982-89. **Prof Background** Hons Degree, Psychology and Social Administration; Dip. Mental Health. **Awards/Research** Regular publications on issues of parenthood. **Pres Committees** International Year of the Family (IYF) Council; Mgmt Cttee, Bayswater Homeless Families Project. **Media Experience** Regular contributions to radio and TV.

DOVE Claire Director **WOMEN'S EDUCATIONAL TRAINING TRUST/WOMEN'S TECHNOLOGY SCHEME - WETT** SOCIAL Type: Fundraiser; Service provider. Blackburne House Centre for Women, Hope St, Liverpool L1 9JB Tel:0151-709 4356 Fax:0151-709 8293 **Expertise** Women's education & training, emphasis on black women. **Prev Posts** Communications Manager, United Way of America 1980-81; Director, Charles Wootton College 1981-83. **Prof Background** BA Hons; MA. **Awards/Research** MBE. Articles for various women's publications. **Pres Committees** University of Liverpool Council; City of Liverpool Community College Board; Womens Training Network; Co-ordinate Iris II for European Commission; Granby Toxteth Community Trust. **Media Experience** Papers presented Europe/UK on women; local/nat/internat radio, TV & press.

DOW Rear-Admiral Douglas Director **NATIONAL TRUST FOR SCOTLAND** CONSERVATION/ENVIRONMENT Type: Conservation charity. 5 Charlotte Square, Edinburgh EH2 4DU Tel:0131-226 5922 Fax:0131-243 9501 **Expertise** Management and leadership. **Prev Posts** Joined Royal Navy 1952; Sec to Controller of Navy 1981; Captain, HMS Cochrane 1983; Commodore, HMS Centurion 1985; RCDS 1988; Dir-Gen, Naval Personal Servs 1989-92. **Prof Background** Royal Naval College Dartmouth; FBIM.

DOWER Michael Secretary General **EUROPEAN COUNCIL FOR THE VILLAGE AND SMALL TOWN - ECOVAST** CONSERVATION/ENVIRONMENT Type: Networking/Pressure Group. c/o CCRU, Cheltenham & Gloucester College, Swindon Rd, Cheltenham, Glos GL50 4AZ Tel:01242-544031 Fax:01242-543273 **Expertise** Rural development; protection of the rural heritage. **Prev Posts** Director, Dartington Institute 1967-85; Director, Peak District National Park 1985-92; Director General, Countryside Commission 1992-96. **Prof Background** Chartered Town Planner; Chartered Surveyor. **Awards/Research** Auth: Strategy for Rural Europe, 1991 (updated 1994); European Landscape Convention (non-legal draft) 1996. **Pres Committees** ECOVAST International Committee; Council of Europe Working Group on European Landscape Convention. **Past Committees** Rural Voice (alliance of national organizations representing rural communities in England). **Media Experience** Frequent media participation.

DOYLE Colin P. Chief Executive **COUNTRYWIDE HOLIDAYS** SOCIAL Type: Fundraiser; Service provider. Grove House, Wilmslow Road, Didsbury, Manchester M20 2HU Tel:0161-448 7112 Fax:0161-448 7113 **Expertise** Marketing and developing products for the leisure industry. **Prev Posts** Freelance Marketing Communications Consultant 1990-91; Director/Gen Manager, Rainbow European Travel House 1991-92. **Prof Background** CWS Snr Management, Manchester Business School; HND Mkting & Ind Eng (Dist), Blackburn College of Technology; Fellow, Tourism Society. **Awards/Research** Various articles for trade jnls. **Past Committees** Chair, BITOA Reg Liaison Cttee; ABTA UK Tourism Cttee; Director, North West Tourist Board.

DRAKE Madeline Chief Executive **RICHMOND FELLOWSHIP** DISABILITY Type: Fundraiser; Service provider. 8, Addison Road, London W14 8DJ Tel:0171-603 6373 Fax:0171-602 8652 **Expertise** Special needs housing managment; policy research; European housing. **Prev Posts** Exec Officer, Newham Commty Dev Proj (HO) London 1972-73; Principal Scientific Officer, Centre for Env Studies 1973-80; Housing Consult, London 1980-85. **Prof Background** BA (Hons) French/Russian;

Diploma in Social Science, Birmingham; Housing. **Awards/Research** Reports on homelessness, child care, housing, Europe. Notably: Single and Homeless HMSO 1981; Managing Hostels NFHA 1986. Contrib: Faces of Homelessness, 1995. **Pres Committees** Shelter Board, Circle Thirty Three Housing Trust: (Vice Chair 1988-94); Audit sub-committee; Supported Housing Sub-committee, Main committee. **Past Committees** National Federation of Housing Assoc Council 1987-93; Strategy & Finance sub-committee; Chair Standards & Practices sub-committee. **Media Experience** TV/radio interviews, newspapers articles. **Addits** Consultancy on housing & homelessness in Australia, Russia, Bulgaria.

DRURY Martin Director-General **NATIONAL TRUST** ENVIRONMENT Type: Conservation charity. 36 Queen Anne's Gate, London SW1H 9AS Tel:0171-222 9251 Fax:0171-222 5097 **Prev Posts** Deputy Director General 1992-95; Historic Buildings Secretary 1981-95; Historical Buildings Representative (SE Furniture Adviser) 1973-81.

DUCHESNE P. Robin Secretary General **ROYAL YACHTING ASSOCIATION** SPORT Type: Fundraiser; Service provider; Campaigning; Professional Association; Membership Association. RYA House, Romsey Road, Eastleigh, Hampshire SO50 9YA Tel:01703-627400 Fax:01703-629924 **Expertise** Chief Executive. **Prev Posts** British Army 1955-84; D/Commander and Chief of Staff UN Forces in Cyprus 1984-86. **Prof Background** Leadership and Management Team Leader, Army Staff College; Military & Sporting Admin to 1984; Sports Admin to date. **Awards/Research** OBE. **Pres Committees** Chairman, Marine Con Soc; Chairman, Int Sail Training Assoc; Member UK Nat Olympic Cttee. **Media Experience** Considerable. Regular Interviews.

DUCKETT Richard Chief Executive **ROYAL AGRI-CULTURAL BENEVOLENT INSTITUTION - RABI** SOCIAL Type: Fundraiser; Service provider; assists disab/retired/disadv farmers & families. Shaw House, 27 West Way, Oxford OX2 0QH Tel:01865-724931 Fax:01865-202025

DUNCAN Geoffrey General Secretary **CHURCH OF ENGLAND BOARD OF EDUCATION** RELIGIOUS Type: Service provider. Church House, Great Smith Street, London SW1P 3NZ Tel:0171-222 9011 Fax:0171-233 1094 **Expertise** Education. **Prev Posts** Teacher/lecturer 1964-72; LEA Officer 1972-82; Church of England Schools Officer 1982-90. **Prof Background** BSc Econ. London University 1959. MA Exeter University, 1972. **Awards/Research** MA Thesis: Church and Society in Early Victorian Torquay. **Pres Committees** Various cttees of the General Synod; The National Society; Gov Cncl of Coll of St Mark and St John (Plymouth); Brd, Urban Learning Foundation. **Media Experience** Press articles and various appearances on TV and radio. **Addits** Gen Sec. National Society (CofE) For Promoting Religious Education.

DUNCAN Kathleen N. Director General **TSB FOUNDATION FOR ENGLAND & WALES** SOCIAL Type: Grant maker. PO Box 140, St Mary's Ct, 100 Lower Thames St, London EC3R 6HX Tel:0171-204 5272 Fax:0171-204 5275 **Expertise** Grant making; Fundraising; Marketing; Communications. **Prev Posts** Int Marketing Dir, Boosey & Hawkes Music Publs 1983-86; Marketing Dir, The Order of St John 1986-89; Marketing Cnslt, Performing Rights Society 1989-90. **Prof Background** Christ's Hospital School; St Aidan's College, Durham University; School of Management Studies; The Polytechnic of Central London. **Pres Committees** Cncl of Almoners, Christ's Hospital Sch; Exec Cttee, Assoc of Charitable Foundations; Deputy Chairman, Crime Concern Board.

DUNCAN Dr William Executive Secretary **ROYAL SOCIETY OF EDINBURGH** CONSERVATION/ENVIRONMENT Type: Service provider; Grant maker; Educational. 22-24 George Street, Edinburgh, EH2 2PQ Tel:0131-225 6057 Fax:0131-220 6889

DUNION Kevin Director **FRIENDS OF THE EARTH SCOTLAND** CONSERVATION/ENVIRONMENT Type: Fundraiser; Campaigning/membership. Bonnington Mill, 72 Newhaven Rd, Edinburgh EH6 5QG Tel:0131-554 9977 Fax:0131-554 8656 **Expertise** Overseas aid; sustainable development; campaigning. **Prev Posts** Campaigns Manager, Oxfam in Scotland 1984-1991. **Prof Background** MA (Hons) Modern History; MSc African Studies. **Awards/Research** A Scottish Parliament and Overseas Aid, 1992; contributor of articles to various papers and magazines. Editor, Radical Scotland Magazine 1982-85; Living in the Real World, 1995. **Pres Committees** Treasurer, Friends of the Earth International; Board Mbr, Scottish Educ & Action for Devmt; Lothians & Edinburgh Environmental Partnership; Sec of State's Advisory Group on Sustainable Devmt. **Media Experience** Frequent contributor on Scottish environmental issues. **Addits** Chair, Scottish Env Forum.

DUNN-MEYNELL Hugo Executive Director **INTERNATIONAL WINE & FOOD SOCIETY** SOCIAL Type: Service provider. 9 Fitzmaurice Place, London W1X 6JD Tel:0171-495 4191 Fax:0171-495 4172 **Expertise** Appreciation of quality in food and wine production. **Prev Posts** Advertising 1957-1980. **Prof Background** FRGS; FIPA. **Awards/Research** Gold medal of International Wine & Food Society. Publ: A Wine Record, 1953; The Wine & Food Society Menu Book (with Alice Wooledge Salmon), 1983. **Media Experience** Experience in radio, TV, press and videos.

DUNNING Norman Director **ENABLE** DISABILITY Type: Service provider. 7 Buchanan Street, Glasgow G1 3HL Tel:0141-226 4541 Fax:0141-204 4398 **Prev Posts** Leader, Overnewton Centre 1978-87; Divisional Manager, RSSPCC 1987-91. **Prof Background** BA Oxford University; CQSW. **Awards/Research** Child and Family Research Project at Glasgow University - Joint Director 1981-85. **Pres Committees** Director/Trustee: Enable Homes Ltd; Scotcap Ltd; Care Cards Ltd; SSMH Trustee Services Ltd; Enable Services Ltd; Sam Trust; Key Trust. **Past Committees** Chair/Vice Chair, BASPCAN; Childline Advisory Council. **Media Experience** Regular spokesperson.

E

EAMES Lady (Christine) World-Wide President **MOTHERS' UNION** RELIGIOUS Type: Fundraiser; Grant maker; Campaigning; Christian Educational. The Mary Sumner House, 24 Tufton Street, London SW1P 3RB Tel:0171-222 5533 Fax:0171-222 1591 **Expertise** The family in The World-Wide Christian Church. **Prev Posts** Diocesan President 1988-94; Central Executive Member 1988-94. **Prof Background** LL.B (Hons); M.Phil (Medical Ethics & Law).

EASTWOOD Mike Chief Executive **DIRECTORY OF SOCIAL CHANGE - DSC** SOCIAL Type: Information provider. Federation House, Hope Street, Liverpool L1 9BW Tel:0151-708 0136 Fax: 0151-708 0139. **Prev Posts** With DSC for 9 years as researcher before taking up current post in 1995.

EDMOND Brian General Secretary **ROYAL ASSOCIATION IN AID OF DEAF PEOPLE - RAD** DISABILITY Type: Fundraiser; Service provider. 27 Old Oak Road, London W3 7HN Tel:0181-743 6187 Fax:0181-740 6551 **Prev Posts** Marketing Director, BUPA Health Services Ltd; various marketing and sales appointments with Glaxo and May & Baker Ltd. **Prof Background** Mill Hill School; Qualified pharmacist at School of Pharmacy and Biomedical Sciences, Portsmouth Univ; MRPharmS. **Pres Committees** Vice Chair, Governors of the Royal School for Deaf Children Margate; Mbr, Gov Body, UK Cncl on Deafness; Mbr, Cttee for Ministry among Deaf People; Mbr: Royal Overseas League; Rotary International. **Past Committees** Board Member, BUPA Health Services Ltd. **Addits** Freeman, Worshipful Company of Gardeners.

EDWARDS A.W.(Tony) Chief Executive **ROYAL SOCIETY FOR THE PREVENTION OF ACCIDENTS** MEDICAL/HEALTH Type: Fundraiser; Service provider. Campaigning. Edgbaston Park, 353 Bristol Road, Birmingham B5 7ST Tel:0121-248 2000 Fax:0121-248 2001 **Prev Posts** Managing Director, Hartz International 1974-80; Chairman, Hartz Holdings Ltd 1981-90; Chief Executive, Association for International Cancer Research 1992-93. **Prof Background** MA (Hons) St Andrews; FIMgt. **Pres Committees** St. Andrews University Giving Clubs Advisory Board.

EDWARDS Dave Director **FAMILY RIGHTS GROUP - FRG** SOCIAL Type: Service provider. The Print House, 18 Ashwin Street, London E8 3DL Tel:0171-923 2628 Fax:0171-923 2683 **Expertise** Families and child protection procedures; local authority care; family support services. **Prev Posts** Child Protection Co-ordinator & team manager, Wandsworth Social Services, 1989-95; Deputy Regional Director, The Rainer Foundation, 1995-96. **Prof Background** Qualified social worker. **Media Experience** Occasional.

EDWARDS Helen Acting Director General **NATIONAL ASSOCIATION FOR THE CARE & RESETTLEMENT OF OFFENDERS - NACRO** SOCIAL Type: Fundraiser; Service provider; Campaigning; Policy Devmt; Research & Information. 169 Clapham Road, London SW9 0PU Tel:0171-582 6500 Fax:0171-735 4666 **Expertise** Causes of Crime & Crime Prevention; Young Offenders; Crime and the Media. **Prev Posts** Director & Assistant Director, NACRO, 1986-96; Deputy Project Director, Save the Children Fund, 1980-83; Social Worker, East Sussex County Council, 1976-80. **Prof Background** BA (Hons) University of Sussex; MA University of Warwick; CQSW (Social work Qualification); Critical Reader for the Open University. **Awards/Research** Numerous NACRO Publications; Articles in Journals & Professional Publications; Auth: Crime & Social Policy, report of the Donnison Committee. **Pres Committees** Awaiting appointment of Permanent Director General of NACRO. **Past Committees** Morgan Committee; Crime & Social Policy Committee; Home Office Committee on Juvenile Crime. **Media Experience** Extensive mainly news & current affairs, TV, radio & press.

EDWARDS Jennifer Director **NATIONAL CAMPAIGN FOR THE ARTS - NCA** SOCIAL Type: Campaigning. Francis House, Francis Street, London SW1P 1DE Tel:0171-828 4448 Fax:0171-931 9959 **Expertise** The arts. **Prev Posts** Policy Researcher for Jo Richardson MP, Shadow Minister for Women 1989-91; Snr Policy Officer, LB Camden 1991-93. **Prof Background** BA Archaeology & Anthropology, Girton College, Cambridge Univ. Fellow, Royal Society for the Encouragement of Arts, Manufacture and Commerce. **Awards/Research** Produced magazine and booklets for Shadow Ministry for Women and CND; articles for NCA News. **Past Committees** Soc Servs/Grants Cttee, Westmin City Cncl. Exec: Age Concern Westmin;Westmin Women's Aid. CND Nat Cncl. Parkside Cmty Health Cncl. **Media Experience** Regular contact with all media. **Addits** Dep Leader of the Opposition, Westminster City Cncl 1990-93.

EDWARDS Miss Jenny General Secretary **DISABLED CHRISTIANS FELLOWSHIP** RELIGIOUS Type: Fundraiser; Service provider. 211 Wick Rd, Brislington, Bristol, Avon BS4 4HP Tel:0117-9830388 Fax:0117-9830388 **Expertise** Offering Christian fellowship to all disabled with day care, holidays, magazine, tape fellowhip. **Prev Posts** Previously worked as nurse at Bristol Children's Hospital before becoming disabled (paraplegic). **Prof Background** NNEB, RSCN. **Awards/Research** The Vital Link Magazine (monthly). **Pres Committees** Disability Coalition of Evangelical Alliance; Executive Committee Disabled Christians Fellowship; Holidays for the Disabled (D.C.F.). **Media Experience** Experience with TV and radio (especially local as interviewee).

EDWARDS Linda Director **NATIONAL OSTEOPOROSIS SOCIETY** MEDICAL/HEALTH Type:

WHO'S WHO IN THE VOLUNTARY SECTOR - 43

Service provider. PO Box 10, Radstock, Bath, Avon BA3 3YB Tel:01761-471771 Fax:01761-471104 **Expertise** Professional Communication & Media Skills. **Prev Posts** Post Office, Reg Press & Publicity Office 1971-82; Own Public Relations Consultancy 1982-86. **Prof Background** BA (Hons) English Literature; Dip CAM; MIPR. **Awards/Research** A wide range of booklets & leaflets explaining osteoporosis to both lay and professional audiences. **Pres Committees** Trustee, European Foundation for Osteoporosis; Royal College of Physicians Committee on Fractures in Elderly People. **Past Committees** Advisory Group on Osteoporosis (Dept of Health Cttee); School Governor. **Media Experience** Nat, Reg, Local Press; TV & Radio, News at Ten, Today, Ladykillers hlth series.

EDWARDS Neil Executive Director **INLAND WATERWAYS ASSOCIATION** ENVIRONMENT Type: Campaigning. 114 Regents Park Road, London NW1 8UQ Tel:0171-586 2510 Fax:0171-722 7213 **Expertise** Campaign; Environment issues; Financial; Legal; Media; Volunteer Recruitment. **Prev Posts** BZW (merchant banking). **Awards/Research** Regular columnist in the waterways press. **Pres Committees** Directorships: Elected mbr of Cncl of the National Trust (since 1987); Co Sec, East Anglian Waterways Assoc; Director, Waterway Recovery Gp Ltd; Co Sec, IWA (Sales) Ltd.

EDWARDS Robert Jack Henderson National Director **CHRISTIAN CHILDREN'S FUND OF GREAT BRITAIN - CCF GB** CHILDREN/YOUTH Type: Fundraiser; Service provider. 4 Bath Place, Rivington St, London EC2A 3DR Tel:0171-729 8191 Fax:0171-729 8339 **Expertise** Accountancy and financial services; investment mngmt; banking; theology; history; languages; politics. **Prev Posts** Posts in audit/industry/merchant banking 1960-69; Senior Mngr audit group with Farrow Middleton 1969-76;. Sec, British Red Cross Society 1976-83. **Prof Background** Nottingham High School 1945-54; Practising Chartered Accountant, trained Nottingham 1955-60; Received into Roman Catholic Church 1985. **Awards/Research** Contributor to various religious/theological jnls; ed: Childworld GB magazine. **Pres Committees** Tres, Natural Family Planning Educat Foundation;NGO/UNICEF Co-ord Cttee for Children in E Europe.Mbr: City Livery Club, Cricketers Club; Liveryman, Worshipful Co Of Pattenmakers. **Past Committees** Trustee/Chair, Invest Cttee, Pension Trust for Charities and Vol Orgs; Gen Synod CofE until 1980; Chair, SPUC; Exec Cttee, ACENVO. **Media Experience** None. **Addits** Previously: Pres, Catenian Assoc, London; Chair, Leigham Dist Scout Assoc.

EGGINTON-METTERS Ian Director **NATIONAL FEDERATION OF CITY FARMS - NFCF** SOCIAL Type: Service provider; Membership organization. The Green House, Hereford St, Bedminster, Bristol BS3 4NA Tel:0117-923 1800 Fax:0117-923 1900 **Expertise** Community management of voluntary agencies. **Prev Posts** Leader, Manchester Crisis Centre 1983-85; Asst General Secretary, NFCF 1986-88. **Prof Background** BSc Agriculture. **Pres Committees** National Food Alliance, Growing Food in the Cities. **Past Committees** RVA (Returned Volunteer Action); BACEN (Bristol & Avon Community Enterprise Network).

EISENSTADT Naomi Chief Executive **FAMILY SERVICE UNITS** SOCIAL Type: Service provider. 207 Old Marylebone Road, London NW1 5QP Tel:0171-402 5175 Fax:0171-724 1829 **Expertise** Social policy, family policy, voluntary sector governance and management. **Prev Posts** Cntre Leader, Moorland Children's Cntre 1978-83; Lecturer, Sch of Education, Open Univ 1983-86; Asst Dir Staff Dev, Save the Children Fund 1986-92; Dir, Mbr Servs NCVO 1992-96. **Prof Background** BA Sociology; MSc Social Policy. **Pres Committees** Governing Cncl London Lighthouse; Trustee, Brd Charities Evaluation Serv; Trustee, Brd Nat Cntre for Volunteering; Trustee, Brd Milton Keynes Cmty Trust; Mbr, Charities Aid Fndtn Grants Cttee. **Past Committees** Advisory Cttee, Open Univ Bus Sch; Advisory Cttee, Norwood Childcare; Training Cttee, Nat Cncl of Voluntary Childcare Orgs. **Addits** Chair of Governors, Moorland First School.

EL-RAYES Mary Director **STILLBIRTH AND NEONATAL DEATH SOCIETY - SANDS** MEDICAL/HEALTH Type: Fundraiser; Service provider; Professional Advisory Service. 28 Portland Place London W1N 4DE Tel:0171-436 7940 Fax:0171-436 3715 **Expertise** Health Service Management. **Prev Posts** Gen Manager, St John & St Elizabeth Hospital 1989-91; Manager, Child Health Directorate 1991-94. **Prof Background** Registered Nurse/Health Visitor; Dept Health Service Management. **Pres Committees** Joint Committee Nursing & Health Visiting Assoc; Health Visiting Assoc; Parliamentary Food & Health Forum, World Council Health Care Workers. **Past Committees** Public Health Alliance.

ELLIOTT Michelle Director/Founder **KIDSCAPE** CHILDREN/YOUTH Type: Service provider. 152 Buckingham Palace Road, London SW1W 9TR Tel:0171-730 3300 Fax:0171-730 7081 **Expertise** Prevention - child sexual abuse, bullying. **Prev Posts** Educational psychologist, American School in London NW8 until 1984. .**Prof Background** Educational psychologist; teacher; author. **Awards/Research** Winston Churchill Res Fellowship 1991. Auth - Feeling Happy Feeling Safe 1990; Bullies meet Willow Street Kids 1992; 501 Ways to Be a Good Parent; training manuals/kits. **Pres Committees** Childline Advisory Committee; British Board of Film Classification. **Past Committees** Chaired WHO and Home Office working groups on child sexual abuse prevention. **Media Experience** Frequent guest on news, information and counselling TV/radio programmes. **Addits** Ed:Bullying: A Practical Guide.. for Schls; Female Sex Abuse of Chldrn 1993.

ELLISON Jane Chairperson **TWINS AND MULTIPLE BIRTHS ASSOCIATION - TAMBA** MEDICAL/HEALTH Type: Service provider. PO Box 30, Little Sutton, South Wirral L66 1TH Tel:0151-348 0020 Fax:0151-200 5309 **Prev Posts** Hon Treasurer, TAMBA 1980-86; Promotional Sales Coordinator, TAMBA 1987-89; Budget Controller, TAMBA Twinline 1991-95; Chair TAMBA Twinline 1995-96; Vice Chair TAMBA 1995-96. **Prof Background** BSc (Econ) Hull University; currently a JCC & JF manager for a health authority; previously accountancy work in NHS Trust, local govt and EMGB. **Pres Committees** Mbr, COMBO, International (Society of Twins Studies); Chair, TAMBA

Management Cttee; Mbr, TAMBA Twinline Sub-Cttee; Trustee, TAMBA; Mbr, Telephone Helpline Assoc for TAMBA. **Addits** Parent of boy/girl twins born 1977.

ELLISTON Tony Project Director **YOUTH ACTION 2000** YOUTH Type: Service provider. The Support Office, Phoenix Youth Centre, Hawes Lane, West Wickham, Kent BR4 9AE Tel:0181-777 7350 Fax:0181-777 1914 **Expertise** Youth service provision and management. **Prof Background** Certificate in Youth & Community Studies. **Past Committees** Trustee, Race Equality Council; Chair, Bromley Police Community Consultative Group. **Media Experience** Experience with local radio.

ELSY Stephanie Director **POSITIVELY WOMEN** MEDICAL/HEALTH Type: Service provider. 347-349 City Road, London EC1V 1LR Tel:0171-713 0444 Fax:0171-713 1020 **Expertise** HIV; women; drug misuse and disability. **Prev Posts** Director & Administrator, Greater London Assoc for Disabled People 1986-89; Director, Phoenix House 1989-92. **Prof Background** BA (Hons) English Language and Literature, University of Liverpool. **Pres Committees** Board of Management, City Roads. **Media Experience** Experience in TV and press.

EMMERSON David Chief Executive **ELIZABETH FITZROY HOMES** DISABILITY Type: Fundraiser; Service provider. Caxton House, Station Approach, Haslemere, Surrey GU27 2PE Tel:01428-656766 Fax:01428-643262 **Expertise** Management; learning disabilities. **Prev Posts** Senior managerial posts in Government. **Awards/Research** CBE. **Pres Committees** Chair, Association for Residential Care. **Media Experience** Various interviews on radio and television.

ENDICOTT Grattan Secretary to the Trustees **FOUNDATION FOR SPORT AND THE ARTS** ARTS/SPORT Type: Grant maker. P O Box 20, Liverpool L13 1HB Tel:0151-259 5505 Fax:0151-230 0664 **Expertise** Knowledge of the gambling market and gambling modes; reduction of bureaucracy. **Prev Posts** Imperial Chemical Ind, Personnel Asst 1946-57;Littlewoods Pools, Head of Product Services (as well as other roles previous to this) 1957-89. **Awards/Research** European Bridge League Commentary on the Laws of Duplicate Contract Bridge. **Pres Committees** World Bridge Federation Laws Committee, Vice Chairman. **Past Committees** European Bridge League Laws Committee, Chairman.

ENNALS Paul Director of Education & Employment **ROYAL NATIONAL INSTITUTE FOR THE BLIND - - RNIB** DISABILITY Type: Service provider. 224 Great Portland Street, London W1N 6AA Tel:0171-388 1266 Fax:0171-383 4921 **Expertise** Children with special educ needs; policy development, campaigning, management of services overseas. **Prev Posts** Director of Welfare and Information, SENSE 1983-89. **Prof Background** Psychology degree; mobility instructor for blind. **Awards/Research** Regular articles in journals/newspapers. **Pres Committees** Chair: Council for Disab Children; Special Educational Consortium. Board: Nat Childrens Bureau; Contact-a-Family; Sight Savers. **Past Committees** Chair, Disability Alliance. **Media Experience** Regular with all branches.

EPSTEIN Joyce Secretary General **FOUNDATION FOR THE STUDY OF INFANT DEATHS** MEDICAL/HEALTH Type: Fundraiser; Service provider; Grant maker. 14 Halkin St, London SW1X 7DP Tel:0171-235 0965 Fax:0171-823 1986 **Expertise** Health and consumer affairs. **Prev Posts** Senior research consultant, Research Institute for Consumer Affairs 1979-88; Dep Dir, ASH 1988-91. **Prof Background** MA Psychology. **Awards/Research** About 20 articles, mainly on consumer issues.

ETHERINGTON Stuart Chief Executive **NATIONAL COUNCIL FOR VOLUNTARY ORGANISATIONS - NCVO** SOCIAL Type: Service provider; Umbrella Group. Regent's Wharf, 8 All Saints St, London N1 9RL Tel:0171-713 6161 Fax:0171-713 6300 **Expertise** Strategy. **Prev Posts** Dir, Good Practices in Mental Health 1985-87; RNID: Dir, Public Affairs 1987-90, Chief Executive 1991-94. **Prof Background** BSc Politics, Brunel University; MA Social Services Planning, Essex University; MBA, London Business School. **Awards/Research** Auth:Housing and Mental Health; Toward the Sensitive Bureaucracy; regular contributor to health and social service magazines. **Media Experience** Appearances on TV and radio.

EVANS David Chief Executive **ROYAL ARTILLERY MUSEUMS LTD/HERITAGE CAMPAIGN** ARTS/CULTURAL Type: Fundraiser; Museum/Educational. Royal Artillery Barracks, Woolwich, London SE18 4BH Tel:0181-855 7755 Fax:0181-855 7100 **Expertise** Running large Projects/Events; Fundraising Worldwide. **Prev Posts** Chief of Staff RSA (Colonel), 1988-91; Research/Staff Appointments (Lt Col/Col), 1980-91; Regimental Commanding Officer (Lt Col), 1977-80. **Prof Background** Bedford Modern School, Sandhurst; Staff College, National Defence College. **Awards/Research** Regimental Heritage. **Pres Committees** Royal Artillery Museums Ltd Board/Project/Design/Budget Committee. **Past Committees** Numerous Committees ranging from Sports to Heritage including Chairman School Board of Governors. **Media Experience** TV, radio & press articles and interviews.

EVANS Helen Co-Ordinator **BOOTSTRAP ENTERPRISES** SOCIAL Type: Service provider. The Print House, 18 Ashwin Street, London E8 3DL Tel:0171-254 0775 Fax:0171-275 9914.

EVANS John A. Chairman **BRITISH ORGAN DONOR SOCIETY - BODY** MEDICAL/HEALTH Type: Service provider. Balsham, Cambridge CB1 6DL Tel:01223-893636 **Prev Posts** Development Engineer 1960-65; Production/Industrial Engineer 1965-74; Managing Director, Pottery since 1974. **Prof Background** BSc Physics; PhD Semi-Conductors. **Awards/Research** PhD Thesis and 3 papers. **Media Experience** Several local/national TV and radio broadcasts, videos and press articles.

EVANS Martyn Chief Executive **CITIZENS ADVICE SCOTLAND - CAS** SOCIAL Type: Service provider. 26 George Square, Edinburgh EH8 9LD Tel:0131-667 0156

Fax:0131-668 4359 **Expertise** Social welfare; law. **Prev Posts** Deputy Director, Shelter Scotland 1983-87; Director, Shelter Scotland 1987-92. **Prof Background** BA (Hons); MA (Econ). **Awards/Research** Visiting Professor, Law, Strathclyde University. **Pres Committees** Non-exec Director, SCVO; Trustee, Hamish Allen Trust; Member, STV Action 2000. **Media Experience** Extensive experience.

EVANS Nancy Director **SOCIETY FOR THE PREVENTION OF SOLVENT AND VOLATILE SUBSTANCE ABUSE, THE - RE-SOLV** MEDICAL/HEALTH Type: Fundraiser; Service provider; Grant maker. 30A High Street, Stone, Staffordshire ST15 8AW Tel:01785-817885 Fax:01785-813205 **Prev Posts** Training manager, Walsall Chamber of Commerce and Industry 1987-91;MD Mid Wales Training 1990-91. **Prof Background** Postgraduate Dip Management Studies 1990; MBA Business Administration 1993. **Awards/Research** MBA Dissert: Marketing by Charities in UK. Study projects: USA Soc marketing by nonprofit orgs, 1993 & Human Resource Devmt for EC, 1990; Managing Change in Russian Econ, Moscow 1990. **Pres Committees** Service - The All Party Group on Solvent and Volatile Substance Abuse; DTI Industry Forum. **Past Committees** Mid Wales CBI Cttee; Powys Schls Indust Liaison Cttee; Walsall Trng & Entrprse Cncl Devmt Plan Subcttee; Adv Cncl Misuse of Drugs. **Addits** Guardian Jerwood Awards commended for individual excellence.

EVANS Pam Professional Director **ROYAL COLLEGE OF SPEECH AND LANGUAGE THERAPISTS** MEDICAL/HEALTH Type: Professional Association. 7 Bath Place, Rivington Street, London EC2A 3DR Tel:0171-613 3855 Fax:0171-613 3854 **Expertise** Speech therapy management. **Prev Posts** Head of Speech and Language Therapy, Barnet, Herts 1989-95. **Media Experience** Appeared on Radio/Video/Press.

EVANS Stephen General Secretary & Chief Executive **SOCIETY AND COLLEGE OF RADIOGRAPHERS** MEDICAL/HEALTH Type: Service provider. 2 Carriage Row, 183 Eversholt St, London NW1 1BU Tel:0171-391 4500 Fax:0171-391 4504 **Prev Posts** Director of Marketing, Ipswich Hospital, 1992-95; Director of Contracting, Ipswich Hospital, 1990-92; Head of Diagnostic Imaging, Ipswich Hospital, 1988-90. **Prof Background** Diagnostic Radiographer; Teacher; Manager; DCR; HDCR; TDCR; MSocSc.

EVANS Dr T. J. Chief Executive and Secretary **INSTITUTION OF CHEMICAL ENGINEERS** SOCIAL Type: Professional Association. Davis Building, 165-189 Railway Terrace, Rugby, Warwickshire CV21 3HQ Tel:01788-578214 Fax:01788-560833 **Prev Posts** CSIR, Pretoria 1968-69; Ford Motor Company 1972-73. **Prof Background** BSc (Eng) Chemical Engineering, University College London 1968; PhD 1972. **Awards/Research** Kurnakov Memorial Medal 1991; Titanium Achema Plaque. **Pres Committees** Ed Adv Brd, Ullmann's Encyclopaedia of Ind Chem; Exec Cttee, Commonwealth Engineers' Cncl; Science Adv & Exec Brds, Euro Fed of Chem Engineering; Steering Gp, Action for Eng Prog (DTI). **Past Committees** Brd of Cncl of Science & Tech Insts 1976-87; Process Ind Manpower Study Gp (DTI).

EWINGTON John General Secretary/Secretary to Council **GUILD OF CHURCH MUSICIANS - GCM** ARTS Type: Professional Association. St Katharine Cree, 86 Leadenhall St, London EC3A 3DH Tel:0171-247 5433 **Expertise** Church Musician/Administrator. **Prev Posts** Guild Of Church Musicians for past 20 years. **Prof Background** Archbishops' Cert Church Music; Dip.Ch.Music (Uni. London); Fellow Guild of Church Musicians; Hon Fellow Cambridge Schl of Music; Dir, City Singers; Organist & Choirmaster, Blechingley P.C.. **Awards/Research** OBE **Pres Committees** Academic Board Guild Church Musicians; CHIME (Churches' Initiative in Music & Education);Vice Chairman of Govns Oxted County School. **Media Experience** Broadcasts and T.V. with City Singers.

F

FAGAN Dr Austin National President of England and Wales **ST VINCENT DE PAUL SOCIETY ENGLAND & WALES** SOCIAL Type: Fundraiser; Service provider; Charitable society of vol mbrs helping the needy. Damascus House, The Ridgeway, London NW7 1EL Tel:0181-906 1339 Fax:0181-906 4119.

FAIRCLOTH Kenneth G. Chairman **AA FOUNDATION FOR ROAD SAFETY RESEARCH** SOCIAL Type: Campaigning. Norfolk House, Priestley Rd, Basingstoke, Hants RG24 9NY Tel:01256-493280 Fax:01256-492092 **Expertise** Road safety. **Prev Posts** AA: Managing Director 1985-89, Deputy Director General 1989-94. **Prof Background** BSc (Econ); Business. **Awards/Research** OBE. AA Foundation Reports - approx 2 per year. **Pres Committees** Chair: AA FRSR; European Road Safety Federation. Trustee, CAF. **Past Committees** AA Ltd. **Media Experience** Spokesman for AA on TV, radio & press.

FARAM L. Honorary Director **TRANSPORT ON WATER ASSOCIATION** CONSERVATION/ENVIRONMENT Type: Service provider; Campaigning; Professional Assoc. Basin South Gate 14, Woolwich Manor Way, London E16 2QY Tel:0171-476 2424 **Expertise** Rivers/Canals.

FATEH Mr Eenasul Executive Director **LEAVENERS** SOCIAL/TRAINING Type: Service provider. 8 Lennox Road, Finsbury Park, London N4 3NW Tel:0171-272 5630 Fax:0171-272 8405 **Expertise** Mngmt cnsltntcy;strategic planng; proj mngmt; community work; PR, fundraising; prod/dir, live arts/TV. **Prev Posts** Cncl Mgmnt & mrchnt bnkng consltncy 1980-90; Frlnce Soc Dev Advr/prdcr 1990-92;Projt Mn /Dir, NYCD Prjct, Cambridge House 1992-95; Mgmt Cnsltnt/prod, Outsider Arts 1995-96. **Prof Background** BSc Econ (Hons) LSE 1977-80; Research, LSE (Econs and Internat Rels) 1980-84; short courses: counselling/groupwork, physical theatre, charity management. **Awards/Research** Auth: Bailing or Enabling? Responses to Young Adults in Challenging Need in the Inner City - based on survey, Lond Boro Southwark, Cambridge Ho 1995; Var res and consltncy pprs LSE. **Pres Committees** Chair: Black Mime Theatre Co, London; Entelechy/New Moves, London; Bd Mbr & Chr of Fundrsng/Mktng/PR Subcttee Lond Cyrenians Housing; Ptnr/Fndtn Mbr, Euro Forum for Youth Culture & Social Action. **Media Experience** BBC Radio 1; Spectrum Radio, Lond Network Radio; Carlton TV; CH4;ID Mag. **Addits** Perf artist/magician; 1st Prize Int Alt Arts Fest Lond; Nat Rev of Live Arts.

FAULKNER Helen Secretary **MUSICIANS BENEVOLENT FUND** Type: Fundraiser; Service provider; Grant maker. 16 Ogle Street, London W1N 8JB Tel:0171-636 4481 Fax:0171-637 4307 **Expertise** Music Administration. **Prev Posts** Academic Posts 1976-85; Manager, BBC Music Libraries 1985-94. **Prof Background** M Mus, London University. **Awards/Research** Frequent reviewer; Contributor The Musician's Handbook 1996; Fontes Artis Musicae; Delius Society Journal. **Pres Committees** Board, British Music Info Centre; Liveryman, Musician's Company; RVW Trust Cttee; Delius Trust Board. **Past Committees** Board, Int Assoc of Music Libraries. **Media Experience** Radio & TV contributor; script writer; dir/producer & frequent interviewee.

FEATHERSTONE Godfrey Director **KENWARD TRUST** MEDICAL/HEALTH Type: Service provider. Kenward House, Yalding, Kent ME18 6AH Tel:01622-814187 Fax:01622-814187 **Expertise** Drug & alcohol rehabilitation, work with homeless and prisoners. **Prev Posts** Senior Engineer, L.B. Bromley 1970-73. **Prof Background** BA (Psychology/Sociology); Dip CE; Cert. Counselling CSCT; Chartered Engineer. **Pres Committees** Trustee, Tower Hamlets Mission; Chairman, Mid Kent Drug Reference Group. **Media Experience** Some experience in radio.

FERRAN Brian Chief Executive **ARTS COUNCIL OF NORTHERN IRELAND** ARTS Type: Statutory Body. 185 Stranmillis Rd, Belfast BT9 5DU Tel:01232-381591 Fax:01232-661715 **Expertise** Public service management, arts management & professional visual artist. **Prev Posts** Visual Arts Director, Arts Council of Northern Ireland 1966-91. **Prof Background** BA (Hons) Art History, Courtauld Institute, London University; PostGrad Dip, Business Administration, Queen's University, Belfast. **Awards/Research** Author of: Basil Blackshaw - Painter (Nicolson & Bass Ltd 1995); various journal reviews & journals. **Pres Committees** Visiting Arts Unit of GB; Alice Berger Hammerschlag Trust; Thomas Dammann Jr Memorial Trust; Nat Self-Portrait Collection; Burren College of Art; North-West Arts Trust; CEO, ACNI Cttee & Brd. **Past Committees** Brit Cncl Fine Art Cttee; Crafts Cncl of GB Intl Cttee; Ulster Museum Fine Art Cttee; Irish Exhibition of Living Art. **Media Experience** Frequent interviews with radio, TV and press. **Addits** CEO, Cttee & Brd, Nat Lottery Arts Fund; Arts Manager & Practising Artist.

FIELDING Mr Holroyd Director/Secretary **BEACON CENTRE FOR THE BLIND** DISABILITY Type: Fundraiser; Service provider; Grant maker; Specialist Accommodation. Wolverhampton Rd East, Wolverhampton, West Midlands WV4 6AZ Tel:01902-880111 Fax:01902-671889 **Expertise** Employment of people with disabilities; Voluntary body administration (visual impairment). **Prev Posts** Works Manager, British Castors Ltd. Tipton West Mids 1974-80; General Manager, Beacon Industries, Wolverhampton 1980-88. **Prof Background** Industrial Engineering; Chartered Engineer, C. Eng. MIEE. **Pres Committees** Wolverhampton CHC; Wolverhampton/Walsall CEPD; National Association of Supported Employment. **Media Experience** Limited media experience. **Addits** Member of

Rotary Club of Wolverhampton.

FILMER-SANKEY William Director **VICTORIAN SOCIETY** CONSERVATION/ENVIRONMENT Type: Service provider; Campaigning, Statutory Consultee. 1, Priory Gardens, Bedford Park, London W4 1TT Tel:0181-994 1019 Fax:0181-995 4895 **Expertise** Victorian Churches; 19th century archaeology; current legislation on protecting 'built environment'. **Prev Posts** Doctoral Student 1985-89; Archaeological Consultant 1990-93. **Prof Background** Degree in Modern History; Doctorate in Early Medieval Archaeology; Worked in archaeology before joining Victorian Society in 1993. **Awards/Research** All relating to Anglo-Saxon archaeology. **Pres Committees** Hon Secretary, British Archaelogical Association. **Media Experience** Small scale involvement with all media (except video). **Addits** Member of the Institute of Field Archaeologists (MIFA).

FILOCHOWSKI Julian Director **CATHOLIC FUND FOR OVERSEAS DEVELOPMENT - CAFOD** SOCIAL Type: Fundraiser; Grant maker. 2 Romero Close, Stockwell Road, London SW9 9TY Tel:0171-733 7900 Fax:0171-274 9630 **Expertise** Development economics; Latin America; Church and social action. **Prev Posts** Central America co-ordinator, Brit Volunteer Programme 1969-73; Latin America Secretary, CIIR 1973-82. **Prof Background** MA Mathematics and Economics, Cambridge University. **Pres Committees** Euro-CIDSE; Cttee for Int Justice and Peace, Catholic Bishops Conf; CCBI; Chair, Caritas Internationalis Commission on Aids; Trustee, Catholic Agency for Social Concern. **Past Committees** Board, Christian Aid; CIIR Exec Committee; Pontifical Cncl COR UNUM (Rome); EC NGO Liaison Cttee, Brussels.

FINESTONE Eric Head of Services **ASSOCIATION FOR JEWISH YOUTH** CHILDREN/YOUTH Type: Service provider. Norwood House, Harmony Way, off Victoria Rd, London NW4 2BZ Tel:0181-203-3030 Fax:0181-202-3030 **Expertise** Jewish Youth Service. **Prev Posts** Director, Brady Maccabi Jewish Youth & Community Centre 1979-82; District Youth Officer, L.B. Barnet 1982-88; Principal Youth Officer, L.B. Barnet 1988-95. **Prof Background** Qualified Youth & Community Worker, Jordanhill College of Education. **Pres Committees** Member, Jewish Youth Service Partners Group; Member, Jewish Youth Fund. **Past Committees** Standing Conference of Principal Youth Officers (South East).

FISHER F.J. Secretary **SOCIETY FOR THE PROMOTION OF HELLENIC STUDIES** ARTS/CULTURAL Type: Service provider; Grant maker; Learned Society. 31-34 Gordon Square, London WC1H 0PP Tel:0171-387 7495 Fax:0171-387 7495

FISHER Harold Director **PHOBICS SOCIETY** Type: Fundraiser; Service provider. 4 Cheltenham Rd, Chorlton-cum-Hardy, Manchester M21 9QN Tel:0161-881 1937 **Expertise** Anxiety disorders including panic attacks, phobias & obsessional compulsive disorders & assoc depression. **Prev Posts** Army Service 6 years, Warrant Officer 1952-58; Transport Manager 20 years 1960-80. **Prof Background** Psychologist/Hypnotherapist.

Awards/Research Self-help pack (anxiety disorders); Quarterly report. Greater Manchester Whitbread Community Care Award 1989; National Whitbread Community Care Award 1989. **Media Experience** Local & national TV/radio for 15 years.

FISHER Michael J. Chairman **JOINT ASSOCIATION FOR PETROLEUM EXPLORATION COURSES (UK)** CONSERVATION/ENVIRONMENT Type: Fundraiser; Service provider; Grant maker. The Geological Society, Burlington House, Piccadilly, London W1V 0JU Tel:0171-434 9944 Fax:0171-439 8975 **Expertise** Exploration Geology; Skills Management; Risk Analysis. **Prev Posts** Exploration Manager, Britoil Plc 1982-85; New Ventures Manager, Britoil Plc 1985-89; Director, Nevis Associates Ltd since 1989. **Prof Background** Graduate, Geology; Post-Graduate, Geology. **Awards/Research** Over 30 Scientific Publications & Education Publications. **Pres Committees** Children's Panel Advisory Committee; Monitoring, recruiting etc for administration of 1968 Social Work (Scotland) Act. **Media Experience** Open University films, TV/radio interviews.

FISHER Michael Robert Chairman **WEST HAUGH CENTRE FOR DISABLED CHILDREN** DISABILITY Type: Treatment for disabled children. Newbridge, Edinburgh EH28 8LA Tel:0131-3334515 **Expertise** Proprietor in business; construction; guest house. **Prof Background** Construction industry & guest house ownership. **Pres Committees** Chairman, The West Haugh Centre Trust. **Media Experience** West Haugh Centre for Disabled Children filmed for BBC Children in Need.

FISHER Thelma Director **NATIONAL FAMILY MEDIATION - NFM** SOCIAL Type: Service provider; Professional and PR assoc of 66 services. 9 Tavistock Place, London WC1H 9SN Tel:0171-383 5993 Fax:0171-383 5994 **Expertise** Mediation of family disputes, particularly in separation and divorce; family transition. **Prev Posts** Co-ordinator, Swindon Family onciliation Service 1981-85; Lecturer in Social Work, Bath Univ 1985-89. **Prof Background** English graduate, trained in social work in postgraduate course. **Awards/Research** Ed: Family Conciliation within the UK, 1992; Co-ed: The Fundamentals of Family Mediation, 1993; Auth: Towards a Model of Co-Working in Family Conciliation, Brit Jnl of Soc Work 1986. **Pres Committees** Management Committee, National Family Mediation; Management Committee, Council for Family Proceedings. **Media Experience** Appears on TV, radio and press representing National Family Mediation.

FITZDUFF Dr Mari Director **COMMUNITY RELATIONS COUNCIL (NI)** SOCIAL Type: Service provider; Grant maker. 6 Murray Street, Belfast BT1 6DN Tel:01232-439953 Fax:01232-235208 **Expertise** Conflict resolution. **Prev Posts** Co-ordinator, Community Conflict Skills Project 1988-90. **Prof Background** Social psychology, conflict resolution work. **Awards/Research** Community conflict skills (1988); Beyond Violence (UN series on conflict & governance 1996). **Pres Committees** NI Voluntary Trust, Peace Institute (Limerick); Common Purpose (Belfast). **Media Experience** Considerable experience with radio, TV, video and press.

FITZGERALD Julie Director **NATIONAL FEDERATION OF GATEWAY CLUBS** DISABILITY Type: Fundraiser; Service provider; Campaigning; people with learning disability. 123 Golden Lane, London EC1Y 0RT Tel:0171-696 5590 Fax:0171-608 3524 **Expertise** Service management; campaigning; lobbying. **Prev Posts** Leader, Camden Council 1990-93; Director, New Horizon, Euston 1993-95. **Prof Background** BA Linguistics; City/Guilds Upholstery. **Awards/Research** Articles in Local Government Journals. **Pres Committees** Vice-Chair Arlington Housing Assoc. **Past Committees** Assoc: London Auth;Metropolitan Auth; London Fire/Civil Defence Auth; Great Ormond Street Hosp Brd; Hampstead Health Auth. **Media Experience** BBC; GLR; Newsnight; Local/national press.

FITZHERBERT Luke **DIRECTORY OF SOCIAL CHANGE - DSC** SOCIAL Type: Information provider. 24 Stephenson Way, London NW1 2DP Tel:0171-209 0902 Fax:0171-209 4130 **Expertise** Voluntary sector funding. **Prev Posts** Teacher 1972-82; Industrial Marketing Manager 1961-72 **Awards/Research** Editor: Guide to the Major Trusts; Joseph Rowntree Fndtn: The Impact of the Lottery, 1995; numerous other DSC books.

FITZMAURICE Jon Director **HOUSING CAMPAIGN FOR SINGLE PEOPLE - CHAR** SOCIAL Type: Housing campaign for single people. 5-15 Cromer Street, London WC1H 8LS Tel:0171-833 2071 Fax:0171-278 6685 **Expertise** Housing Association activity/fundraising/campaigns. **Prev Posts** Head of London Region, National Federation of Housing Associations 1982-87; Planning and Information Director, London and Quadrant Housing Trust 1987-91. **Prof Background** BSc (Social Science) Southampton Univ 1967-70; Research, Reading Univ 1970-72. **Pres Committees** NCVO Board; Roof Magazine Editorial Board; St Mungos Housing Assoc Management Committee; Empty Homes Agency Management Cttee. **Media Experience** Interviews:Today, Thames, LBC Radio, You and Yours.

FLOOD Tom Chief Executive **BRITISH TRUST FOR CONSERVATION VOLUNTEERS - BTCV** CONSERVATION/ENVIRONMENT Type: Service provider. 36 St Mary's Street, Wallingford, Oxfordshire OX10 0EU Tel:01491-839766 Fax:01491-839646 **Expertise** Undertaking practical conservation with volunteers. **Prev Posts** Marketing Manager, 3M UK 1972-86; BTCV: Marketing director 1986-90; Deputy chief executive 1990-92. **Prof Background** BA (Hons) English and Philosophy; Fellow: Brit Inst Mngmt; Fellow: RSA. **Pres Committees** Chair, Trustee: Tree Council and Age Resource; Trustee, Red Admiral Project.

FLOUD Roderick Provost **LONDON GUILDHALL UNIVERSITY** CHILD/YOUTH Type: University. 31 Jewry Street, London EC3N 2EY Tel:0171-320 1310 Fax:0171-320 1390 **Expertise** Economic History. **Prev Posts** Professor of Modern History, Birkbeck College, London 1975-88; Visiting Professor, Stanford University 1980-81. **Prof Background** MA, D.Phil (Oxon). **Awards/Research** Hon. Fellow, Birkbeck College; Co-author: Height, Health & History (1990), The Economic History of Britain since 1700 (1994). **Pres Committees** Cncl Mbr & Chair of Research Resources Bd, Economic & Social Research Council. **Past Committees** Advisory Council on Public Records (1978-83).

FLOWER Antony John Frank Consultant to the Trust **JOSEPH ROWNTREE REFORM TRUST** Type: Grant maker. 18 Victoria Park Square, London E2 9PF Tel:0181-983 4246 Fax:0181-981 6719 **Prev Posts** Co-founder (w Lord Young of Dartington) & Gen Sec Tawney Society 1982-88;Dir Research Inst for Economic & Social Affairs 1982-92;Dir Argo Trust 1986-95. **Prof Background** BA Hons Phil and Soc; MA Soc; PhD Mass Communications Leicester. **Awards/Research** FRSA. Auth:(jt) Starting to Write; (jt ed) The Alternative; Young at Eighty; (Conslt ed) Guide to Pressure Grps. **Pres Committees** Co-ord Argo Venture;Assoc:Open Coll Arts;Redesign Ltd;Nicholas Lacey J&P (Archtcts);Adv Bd & Spec Advr Earth Ctre;Constnt:Rocklabs Geochem Anal CC;Family Cov Assoc. Trustee: Gaia Inst and others. **Past Committees** Dir Hlthline Hlth Info Serv;Dir, Trustee Hlth Info Trust;Co-ord Campng for Educ Choice;Assoc Inst for Public Pol Rsch. **Addits** Patron: Nat Space Science Cntr. Co-fndr, Ed Samizdat magazine.

FORD Colin John Director **NATIONAL MUSEUMS & GALLERIES OF WALES/AMGUEDDFEYDD AC ORIELAU CENEDLAETHOL CYMRU** CONSERVATION/ENVIRONMENT Type: Museum. Cathays Park, Cardiff CF1 3NP Parc Cathays, Caerdydd CF1 3NP Tel:01222-397951 Fax:01222-373214 **Expertise** Lecturer, writer and broadcaster on films, theatre and photography; exhibition organizer. **Prev Posts** Keeper of Film and Photography, National Portrait Gallery 1972-81; Director, National Museum of Photography, Film and TV 1982-93. **Prof Background** MA, University College, Oxford. Hon MA, University of Bradford. **Awards/Research** CBE. Auth/Co-auth articles/publ inc: Early Victorian Album 76; Rediscovering Mrs Cameron 79; Portraits 83; A 100 Years Ago (Britain in the 1880s) 83; Story of Popular Photography 88. **Pres Committees** Governor, Raymond Mander & Joe Mitchenson Theatre Collection; Patron, Julia Margaret Cameron Trust; Trustee, E. Chambre Hardman Trust; Board Memb, Wales Film Council; Bd Memb: Museums Association. **Media Experience** Radio presenter: Kaleidoscope; Third Ear; Night Waves; Third Opinion, etc.

FORD Miss J. General Secretary & Administrator **BEAVERBROOK FOUNDATION** SOCIAL Type: Grant maker. 11 Old Queen Street, London SW1H 9JA Tel:0171-222 7474 Fax:0171-222 2198

FORD John N P Director of Administration **SCOTTISH CIVIC TRUST, THE** CONSERVATION/ENVIRONMENT Type: Service provider. Campaigning; Statutory Body. 24 George Square, Glasgow G2 1EF 041-221 1466 041-248 6952 **Expertise** Administration. **Prev Posts** MD, Grange OCS Cleaning Servs Ltd Belfast 1977-92; Director, Office Cleaning Services Ltd 1975-92; Chair, Office Cleaning Servs (Scotland) Ltd 1988-92. **Prof Background** Commerce/Service Industry;Fellow Inst. of Directors. **Awards/Research** Tidy Britain Group - Queen Mothers Award 1992. **Pres Committees** Chair: Princes Scottish Youth Business Trust, Glasgow area; Chair, Order of St John, Glasgow; Trustee, New Lanark Conservation Trust. **Past Committees** Deacon Convener; Trades House of

Glasgow 1991-92; Governor, Hutchesons Educational Trust 1986-96. **Media Experience** Interviews on TV and radio.

FOSTER Dr A. Chief Executive Officer **GLASGOW & WEST OF SCOTLAND SOCIETY FOR THE BLIND** Type: Fundraiser; Service provider; Campaigning. 2 Queen's Crescent, St George's Cross, Glasgow G4 9BW Tel:0141-332 4632 Fax:0141-353 2981 **Expertise** Sensory impairment; Adult education & training; Cmty dev; Marketing; Communications; Research; Finance. **Prev Posts** Tutor 1981-83; Project Leader, Save the Children 1983-86; Development Officer, Save the Children 1986-89. **Prof Background** MA Philosphy; PhD Philosophy; MEd; MBA; FRSA; ICFM. **Awards/Research** Bridge Alliance Marketing Award. **Pres Committees** Chair, Nat Assoc of Local Societies for the Visually Impaired; UK Cttee for Prevention of Visual Impairment. **Past Committees** Woodlands Cmty Dev Trust; Dep Chair, Scottish Mobile Projects Assoc. **Media Experience** Occasional. **Addits** Andrew Skirving Gold Medal.

FOX Andrew J.A. General Manager **H.M. FRIGATE UNICORN** CONSERVATION/TRAINING Type: Fundraiser; Visitor attraction/museum/training organisation. Victoria Dock, Dundee DD1 3JA Tel:01382-200900 **Prev Posts** H.M. Frigate Unicorn 1987-92; Project Supervisor, H.M. Frigate Unicorn 1992-95. **Prof Background** MA (ord), Aberdeen University 1976; Dip in Secondary Education, Dundee College of Education 1979. **Awards/Research** Books of poems: The Oceanographers (1985), Darkness and Snowfall (1990) & For Everything Must Be Returned (1996); also many poems published in international magazines. **Pres Committees** Board of Scottish PEN (Poets, Essayists, Novelists), currently serving second term (three years per term). **Media Experience** Interviews with press in connection with professional & literary activities. **Addits** Has given frequent readings in public.

FOX Daniel Director **SOS CHILDREN'S VILLAGES UK** CHILDREN/YOUTH Type: Fundraiser; Grant maker; Overseas. 32a Bridge Street, Cambridge CB2 1UJ Tel:01223-365589 Fax:01223-322613 **Expertise** Direct marketing; capital appeals; trading. **Prev Posts** Head of Appeals, MENCAP 1986-88; Deputy Dir, Wishing Well Appeal 1988-89; Fundraising Dir YMCA 1989-90. **Prof Background** Institute of Marketing Foundation Course; Member, Institute of Charity Fundraising Managers. **Pres Committees** ICFM East Anglia Region Cttee.

FOX Tina Chief Executive **VEGETARIAN SOCIETY UK LTD** Type: Fundraiser; Service provider; Campaigning and Educational. Parkdale, Dunham Road, Altrincham, Cheshire WA14 4QG Tel:0161-928 0793 Fax:0161-926 9182 **Expertise** Management, particular focus on customer care, public speaking, media, writer. **Prev Posts** Local Government for 22 years 1973-1995; various departments and roles. **Prof Background** Certificates and Diploma of Public Administration, Liverpool University. **Awards/Research** Number of published articles on Vegetarian issues. Regular articles on Animal Folklore. **Pres Committees** Secretary to the Society's Board of Directors; Company Secretary of VSUK Ltd; Patron, Wirral Green Alliance. **Past Committees** Management Teams for Liverpool City Council Planning and also Highways. Co-Ordinator Green Party Animal Rights working group. **Media Experience** Radio. Television and general press work.

FRAMJEE Pesh Co-ordinator **CHARITY FINANCE DIRECTORS' GROUP** SOCIAL Type: Service provider; Membership group; Advisory. Binder Hamlyn, 20 Old Bailey, London EC4M 7BH Tel:0171-489 6140 Fax:0171-489 6288 **Expertise** Charity finance, tax law, governance and management. **Prev Posts** Finance director, Save the Children Fund 1987. Currently, Head of Charity Unit, Binder Hamlyn. **Prof Background** Visiting Fellow, Charity Accounting & Audit, South Bank University; Fellow, Institute of Chartered Accountants in England and Wales. **Awards/Research** Jt Auth, Charities: The Law & Practice; Auth: Charities & Trading 96. Over 70 published articles, regular lectures, contrib to Charity Finance Handbook, NGO Finance, Charity World. **Pres Committees** Charity Comm: Charity Accts Review Cttee & Charity Monitoring Cttee; Mngng Cttee, Charities Strategic Mngmnt Forum; Charity Accts Wkg Pty, ICAEW; Resources Cttee, ICFM; Charity Law Advisory Gp, NCVO; Fiscal Affairs Wkng Gp, NCVO. **Past Committees** Charity Comm/NCVO, On Trust report wkng pty; Dep Chair, Strategic Planning Society charities gp;briefing to Charities Bill HoL Cttee **Media Experience** TV, radio & press interviews.

FRAMPTON Lt Cdr Richard M. General Secretary **MARINE SOCIETY, THE** SOCIAL Type: Service provider; Grant maker. 202 Lambeth Road, London SE1 7JW Tel:0171-261 9535 Fax:0171-401 2537 **Expertise** General management. **Prev Posts** Administrator, Birmingham and W Midlands Soc of Chartered Accts 1976-78; The Marine Soc: Deputy Sec 1978-79; Sec 1980-86. **Prof Background** Royal Navy. **Awards/Research** Auth: Sea Careers; Articles on Merchant Shipping; Seafarers; Sea Training. Ed: Sea Charmed Voices. Co-Auth: Full Ahead, Meteorology for Seafarers. **Pres Committees** Chairman: The World Ship Trust; Cncl Mbr: HMS Trincomalee Trust; Foudroyant Trust; Thames Nautical Training Trust;John Slater Memorial Trust; Merchant Navy Welfare Board. **Past Committees** Astrid Trust; London Nautical School. **Media Experience** As required.

FRANKEL Maurice Director **CAMPAIGN FOR FREEDOM OF INFORMATION** SOCIAL Type: Pressure group. 88 Old Street, London EC1V 9AX Tel:0171-253 2445 Fax:0171-608 1279 **Prev Posts** Social Audit 1973-83. **Prof Background** BSc Biology. **Pres Committees** Trustee, Public Concern; Secretary, Social Audit.

FREEMAN Jennifer M. Director **HISTORIC CHAPELS TRUST** CONSERVATION/ENVIRONMENT Type: Fundraiser; Service provider. 29 Thurloe St, London SW7 2LQ Tel:0171-584 6072 Fax:0171-225 0607 **Expertise** Architectural writer, historian, developer specialising in historic buildings. **Prev Posts** Secretary, Victorian Society 1982-1985; Writer on historic buildings 1976-1996; Chair, Freeman Historic Properties Ltd 1992-today. **Prof Background** BA (Hons); Diploma in Building Conservation; 25 years experience in historic buildings field. **Awards/Research** Reports for Save Britain's Heritage; Articles: Country Life, etc. Auth: W.D. Caroe: His Architectural Achievement. Co-auth: Save The City: A Conservation Study of the City of London. **Pres Committees** London Advisory Ctte, English Heritage; Council for the Care of Churches; Chair, Kensal Green Cemetery Chapels Restoration Ctte; Save Britain's Heritage. **Past Committees** Victorian Society. **Media Experience** TV & Radio; press contributor; lecturer. **Addits** Organiser, 1991 exhibition on work of W.D. Caroe at RIBA Heinz Gallery.

FREESTONE Patrick Principal **MARY WARD CENTRE** SOCIAL Type: Fundraiser; Service provider; Educational and community services. 42 Queen Square, London WC1N 3AQ Tel:0171-831 7711 Fax:0171-430 1986 **Expertise** Community and adult education; youth work; voluntary organisations. **Prev Posts** Head of Centre, George Greens School E14 1975-80; Community Education Co-ordinator, Tower Hamlets Inst of Adult Educ 1980-86. **Prof Background** BA (Hons); PGCE; education management; teaching; detached youth and community work. **Awards/Research** Publ: Pictorial History of East London. **Pres Committees** Mary Ward Legal & Financial Advice Centre; Holborn Community Assoc; Mary Ward Youth Club; Trustee, South Islington Mothers & Babies Fund; College Companies. **Past Committees** Tower Hamlets Youth Committee. **Media Experience** Editor of community newspaper.

FREMANTLE Edward V.E. Trust Secretary/Head of Finance & Admin. **ANIMAL HEALTH TRUST** ANIMAL/WILDLIFE Type: Service provider. PO Box 5, Newmarket, Suffolk CB8 7DW Tel:01638-661111 Fax:01638-665789 **Expertise** Management; finance. **Prev Posts** Kleinwort Benson Ltd, corporate finance/banking 1969-88; Head of Corporate Finance, Rathbone Brothers Plc 1989-90. **Prof Background** MA Oxford University; FCA Price Waterhouse 1964-69.

FRIEND Julie Chief Executive **MEDIC ALERT FOUNDATION** MEDICAL/HEALTH Type: Service provider. 12 Bridge Wharf, 156 Caledonian Road, London N1 9UU Tel:0171-833 3034 Fax:0171-278 0647 **Expertise** Emergency identification (Bracelets/Necklets) for people with hidden medical conditions. **Prev Posts** PR Officer, Medic Alert, 1993-94, Customer Services Supervisor, Medic Alert, 1992-93; Director, Pink Noise Limited, 1990-92. **Media Experience** Guest, Time & Place, Jan 94, Live Radio & Press interviews.

FRIES Richard Chief Charity Commissioner **CHARITY COMMISSION** SOCIAL Type: Statutory regulator. St Albans House, 57-60 Haymarket, London SW1Y 4QX Tel:0171-210 4465 Fax:0171-210 4604 **Expertise** Head of department. **Prev Posts** Home Office 1965-92. **Prof Background** Administrative civil servant.

FROST G.B.J. Secretary **ST DUNSTANS FOR MEN AND WOMEN BLINDED IN THE SERVICES** DISABILITY Type: Service provider; Grant maker. PO Box 4XB, 12-14 Harcourt Street, London W1A 4XB Tel:0171-723 5021 Fax:0171-262 6199

FRY Tam Mr Honorary Chairman **CHILD GROWTH FOUNDATION - CGF** MEDICAL/HEALTH Type: Service provider. 2 Mayfield Avenue, London W4 1PW Tel:0181-995 0257 Fax:0181-995 9075 **Expertise** Child growth. **Prev Posts** Production, Peter Davies Ltd 1959-60; Production, Hodder and Stoughton Ltd 1960-63; Producer, BBC TV 1963-88. **Prof Background** TV Producer.

FULFORD Myra Director **MANIC DEPRESSION FELLOWSHIP** MEDICAL/HEALTH Type: Fundraiser; Service provider; Self-help; Advice and information. 8-10 High Street, Kingston-upon-Thames, Surrey KT1 1EY Tel:0181-974 6550 Fax:0181-974 6600 **Expertise** Management and fundraising. **Prev Posts** Adult Education Co-ordinator, Sparkhill Adult Education Inst 1976-82; Co-ord, Wandsworth Volunteer Bureau 1982-86; Gen Sec, Kingston Council for Voluntary Service 1986-92. **Prof Background** BA (Hons); Postgraduate Business Studies, London University; 1 year Counselling skills, South London Polytechnic; 1st year of MSc Policy Studies, Bristol University. **Past Committees** Advance; NAVBX; Local Development Agencies Fund; A-Z Training and Executive Council.

FULLER R.A. Dr Honorary Secretary **INSTITUTION OF ENVIRONMENTAL SCIENCES** Type: Professional Association. 14 Princes Gate, Hyde Park, London SW7 1PU Tel:01778-394846 Fax:01778-394846 **Expertise** Built Environment **Prof Background** Chartered Surveyor & Project Manager. **Awards/Research** Space Utilisation in University Development; Economics of Town Planning. **Pres Committees** Council, IES and Trusteeship IES.

FUNNELL Christina M. Chief Executive **SKIN CARE CAMPAIGN/NATIONAL ECZEMA SOCIETY** MEDICAL/HEALTH Type: Service provider; Advocacy, health & dermatology policy. 163 Eversholt Street London NW1 1BU Tel:0171-388 5655 Fax:0171-388 5882 **Expertise** Policy development; patient advocacy; external relationships of the organization. **Prof Background** BA Special Hons, Social Administration; sociology; psychology; social structures. **Pres Committees** Chair/fndng mbr, Long-Term Med Conditns Allnce; Jt Mangng Dir, internat newsltr The Patient's Network; NHS Patient Partnrshp Strategy Strng Gp; Stndng Adv Gp on Consumer Involvement in NHS R&D Prog. **Media Experience** Regular participant in all branches of media. **Addits** Cttees:RCPhys Ptnt Liasn Gp;Cnsmr Ntwk UK Cochrane Clbn;BAD Lon Derm Plnng Gp.

G

GAFFIN Jean Executive Director **NATIONAL COUNCIL FOR HOSPICE AND SPECIALIST PALLIATIV CARE SERVICES** MEDICAL/HEALTH Type: Co-ordinating and rep body/information provider. 59 Bryanston Street, London W1A 2AZ Tel:0171-611 1216 Fax:0171-724 4341 **Expertise** Management; Health and social policy in general and for the terminally ill. **Prev Posts** Exec Sec, Brit Paediatric Assoc 1982-87; Chief Exec, Arthritis Care 1988-91; Dept of Hlth Working Grp on Admission to & Discharge from Intensive Care & High Dependency Units 1996. **Prof Background** BSc (Econ); MSc (Soc Admin), LSE. **Awards/Research** OBE; Auth:Services for People who are Terminally Ill, NHS Hndbk, NAHAT 1994,95 & 96; Co-Auth:Caring & Sharing (Co-op Wmn's Gld Hist) 1993. Artics/reviews on health/soc policy issues. **Pres Committees** Chair, Oftel Adv Cttee on Telecommunications for Eld/Disab; RSM Open Sect Cncl. **Past Committees** Sutton & Merton FHSA 1974-80; Parl Cncl on Trans Safety, Treas 1982-89; Cncl, Child Acc Prev Trst 1985-91. **Media Experience** Extensive local and national radio/TV interviews. **Addits** Magistrate; Dept of Transport Streetworks Advisory Cttee 1987-95.

GAILEY Dr Lorraine Director **LINK CENTRE FOR DEAFENED PEOPLE** DISABILITY Type: Service provider. 19 Hartfield Road, Eastbourne, E Sussex BN21 2AR Tel:01323-638230 **Expertise** Psychology of deafness, adult acquired hearing loss, speech therapy in acquired hearing loss. **Prev Posts** Snr course tutor, BSc Speech and Language Therapy Ulster University 1980-88. **Prof Background** Psychology, counselling, speech & language therapy. **Pres Committees** College Speech and Language Therapists Academic Board. **Past Committees** E Sussex, Physical & Sensory Disability Planning Group.

GAMBLE Rev David Secretary, Family & Personal Relationships **METHODIST CHURCH** RELIGIOUS Type: Service provider. 2 Chester House, Pages Lane, London W10 1PR Tel:0181-444 9845 Fax:0181-365 2471 **Expertise** Childrens work; Family Life Education. **Prev Posts** Minister, York Central Methodist Church 1981-87; Childrens Work Secretary, Methodist Division of Education/Youth 1987-95; General Secretary 1995-96. **Prof Background** LL.B. (Hull) 1968;M.A. (Cantab) 1974. **Awards/Research** One - an introduction to all age worship 1991; Step Carefully (Ed) 1995. **Pres Committees** Barnardos: Council;Executive Finance Cttee (Chair);Chair: Churches Together for Families;Stepfamily Management Cttee. **Past Committees** Chair: Barnardo Adoption Sub Cttee 1987-93;Consultative Group on Ministry among Children (moderator 1993-95). **Media Experience** BBC Radio York-Contributor/Producer, Religious Broadcasts.

GAMBLE R.M. Trust Director **SALISBURY CATHEDRAL TRUST** CONSERVATION Type: Fundraiser. The Kings House, 65 The Close, Salisbury, Wilts SP1 2EN Tel:01722-332004 Fax:01722-323564 **Expertise** Management of charity. **Prof Background** Ex Army Officer. **Media Experience** Radio, TV & press experience (conservation & repair of Salisbury Cathedral).

GANDY Mrs Mary C. General Secretary **CATHOLIC CHILD WELFARE COUNCIL - CCWC** CHILDREN/YOUTH Type: Federation of Catholic childcare agencies. 120 West Heath Road, London NW3 7TY Tel:0181-731 8028 Fax:0181-731 8028 **Prev Posts** Gen Sec, Assoc of Genealogists and Record Agents 1979-85; Publications and Conferences Manager, Soc of Genealogists 1986-92. **Prof Background** BA (Hons) Social Studies, Kent University 1970; CQSW, LSE 1972.

GARDNER Dr Rita Director **ROYAL GEOGRAPHICAL SOCIETY - RGS** ENVIRONMENT/CONSERVATION Type: Fundraiser; Service provider; Grant maker; Learned Society. 1 Kensington Gore, Kensington, London SW7 2AR Tel:0171-589 5466 Fax:0171-584 4447

GARLAND Mrs Elizabeth Manager **ASSOCIATION FOR THE PROTECTION OF RURAL SCOTLAND - APRS** CONSERVATION/ENVIRONMENT Type: Planning, land use and landscape protection. 3rd Floor, Gladstone's Land, 483 Lawnmarket, Edinburgh EH1 2NT Tel:0131-225 7012 Fax:0131-225 6592 **Expertise** Town and country planning, land use issues. **Prev Posts** Farming and land management experience; provision of affordable housing; Branch Technical Secretary, CPRE. **Prof Background** BA Hons (Geography). **Media Experience** Press, radio and TV.

GARNHAM Diana General Secretary **ASSOCIATION OF MEDICAL RESEARCH CHARITIES - AMRC** MEDICAL/HEALTH Type: Charities association. 29-35 Farringdon Road, London EC1M 3JB Tel:0171-404 6454 Fax:0171-404 6448 **Prev Posts** Administrative Sec, Council on Christian Approaches to Defence and Disarmament 1985-87; Executive Officer, AMRC 1987-89. **Prof Background** BA Leicester Univ; MA War Studies, Kings College, London Univ; Postgrad research, Univ Coll of Wales, Aberystwyth. **Pres Committees** BBC Appeals Advisory Committee; Board Mbr, Groundwork Southwark; Trustee, Cae Dai Trust. **Past Committees** Executive Committee, Association of Charitable Foundations; Member, ACF Committee of Enquiry on National Lottery Distribution; Executive Committee, Charity Strategic Management Foundations. **Media Experience** Various.

GARROD Trevor General Secretary **RAILWAY DEVELOPMENT SOCIETY** CONSERVATION/ ENVIRONMENT Type: Campaigning, voluntary body. 15, Clapham Rd, Lowestoft, Suffolk NR32 1RQ Tel:01502-581721 **Awards/Research** RDS Publ inc: Europe beyond the Tunnel; East Anglia by Rail (and other titles in same series); A-Z of Rail Reopenings, Life beyond Cars. **Media Experience** TV, radio, press: interviews; articles.

GARSON Mother Mary Prioress Gen/Dir Hse of Hospitality **BENEDICTINE SISTERS OF OUR LADY OF GRACE & COMPASSION/HOUSE OF HOSPITALITY** Type: Fundraiser; Service provider. 1 Manor Rd, Kemp Town, Brighton, East Sussex BN2 5EA Tel:01273-680720 Fax:01273-680527 **Expertise** Leader of this religious congregation; psychologist. **Prev Posts** Industrial psychologist, Philips 1946-49; Educational psychologist, East Sussex County Council 1949-55; Head, Benedict Sisters/Hse of Hospitality 1954-. **Prof Background** MA Psychology, Aberdeen University; (Associate of British Psychological Society - ABPsS). **Pres Committees** Internal committees of: Board of Directors, House of Hospitality Ltd (under whose auspices the Sisters' work is conducted); General Council, Sisters of Our Lady of Grace and Compassion etc. **Media Experience** Radio and Televison interviews.

GATWARD John Group Chief Executive **HANOVER HOUSING ASSOCIATION** Type: Service provider. Hanover House, 18 The Avenue, Egham, Surrey, TW20 9AD Tel:01784-438361 Fax:01784-431830 **Expertise** General Management; Finance. **Prev Posts** Director of Programme, The Housing Corporation 1981-91; Registrar, The Housing Corporation 1991; Group Chief Exec. Hanover Housing Association 1992-Today. **Prof Background** MA (Cantab), FCA. Lead role in introducing private finance initiative for Housing Associations (from 1986). **Pres Committees** Sached Educational Trust; Sached Educational and Training Charitable Trust. **Past Committees** Review of Co-operative Housing (1989) Dept of Environment. **Media Experience** Occasional interviews. **Addits** Lead responsibility for incorporating The Housing Finance Corporation.

GAULDIE Alison Company Director **CLEAN BREAK THEATRE COMPANY LTD** ARTS Type: Fundraiser; Service provider; Touring Company. 37-39 Kings Terrace, London NW1 0JR Tel:0171-383 3786 Fax:0171-388 7252 **Expertise** Corp, trust, statutory fundraising, organisational dev for small orgs, high profile grant giving in cmty. **Prev Posts** Trust Secretary, Thames/LWT Telethon 1987-91; Corporate/Trust Fundraiser, Action for Blind People 1991-92; Director, Youth Adventure 1993-95. **Prof Background** BA (ORD); Memberships: ICFM, Assoc of Arts Fundraisers (Committee), Women in Fundraising Dev; Training: ICFM, deaf signing, disability awareness; background in media & labour relations. **Awards/Research** Award for spinally injured sports people. **Pres Committees** Association of Arts Fundraisers (Committee). **Past Committees** The Thames Help Trust. **Media Experience** Frequent radio, TV & broadsheet interviews; Assoc of Indep Radio Contractors. **Addits** Consultancies: Children in Need; Employers Forum on Disability.

GAUSSEN Sam Appeal Secretary **NATIONAL EYE RESEARCH CENTRE** MEDICAL/HEALTH Type: Fundraiser; Grant maker; Campaigning. Bristol Eye Hospital, Lower Maudlin St, Bristol BS1 2LX Tel:0117-9290024 Fax:0117-9251241 **Expertise** Fundraising and administering medical research. **Prev Posts** Army Officer 1952-87. **Prof Background** Army Officer (retired as Colonel); Passed Staff College Member (ICFM). **Pres Committees** Trustee, National Eye Research Centre & National Eye Research Centre Scientific Advisory Panel. **Past Committees** Chairman, Cotswold Hunt.

GEAR Alan Chief Executive **HENRY DOUBLEDAY RESEARCH ASSOCIATION, THE - HDRA** CONSERVATION/ENVIRONMENT Type: Service provider; Organic gardening, farming and food. Ryton Organic Gardens, Ryton-on-Dunsmore, Coventry, Warwickshire CV8 3LG Tel:01203-303517 Fax:01203-639229 **Expertise** Organic horticulture and agriculture. **Prev Posts** With HDRA for 20 years. **Prof Background** BSc/MSc Civil Engineering. **Awards/Research** Thorsons Organic Consumer Guide; Regular column in The Guardian. **Pres Committees** Director, Brogdale Horticultural Trust; Director, Organic Enterprises Ltd; Director, Congelow Organic Education Trust; Judge, Environment City. **Past Committees** British Organic Standards Committee. **Media Experience** Ch4 TV Series All Muck and Magic, and sequal; regular contrib R4 Farming Today.

GEAR Mrs Jackie Executive Director **HENRY DOUBLEDAY RESEARCH ASSOCIATION - HDRA** CONSERVATION/ENVIRONMENT Type: Service provider; Organic gardening, farming and food. Ryton Organic Gardens, Ryton-on-Dunsmore, Coventry, Warwickshire CV8 3LG Tel:01203-303517 Fax:01203-639229 **Expertise** Fundraising; marketing; strategic thinking. **Prev Posts** Research and development manager in private industry before joining HDRA in 1973. **Prof Background** BSc Zoology. **Awards/Research** Auth: Thorson's Organic Consumer Guide; Thorson's Organic Wine Guide; Your Organic Questions Answered; Chilli & Pepper Cookbook (1995). **Pres Committees** Director: HDRA Sales Ltd; Organic Enterprises Ltd; Training and Enterprise Council. **Media Experience** Regularly appears on national and local TV and radio. **Addits** Runs Egon Ronay listed organic restaurant.

GEEKIE Peter Chairperson **WANDSWORTH OASIS AIDS SUPPORT CENTRE AT SALVATION ARMY** MEDICAL/HEALTH Type: Fundraiser; Service provider; Self help group. 547 Battersea Park Road, London SW11 3BL 1TR Tel:0171-228 8331.

GEM Dr Richard David H. Secretary **CATHEDRALS FABRIC COMMISSION FOR ENGLAND** CONSERVATION Type: Grantmaker; Statutory Body. Fielden House, Little College St, London SW1P 3SH Tel:0171-222 3793 Fax:0171-222 3794 **Expertise** Architectural history and archaeology with particular reference to religious buildings. **Prev Posts** Inspector of Ancient Monuments, DoE 1970-80; Research Officer, Cncl for the Care of Churches 1981-88. **Prof Background** Eastbourne College; Peterhouse, Cambridge (archaeology and history of art); FSA; MIFA. **Awards/Research** Many publications in learned journals on medieval architecture. **Pres Committees** Royal Commission on the Historical Monuments of England. **Past Committees** Ancient Monuments Committee, English Heritage; Past-President, British Archaeological Association.

GEORGESON Ray Director **WASTEWATCH** CONSERVATION/ENVIRONMENT Type: Fundraiser; Campaigning. Gresham House, 24 Holborn Viaduct,

London EC1A 2BN   Tel:0171-248 1818 Fax:0171-248 1404 **Expertise** Recycling, Waste management, environmental audit, education, community business. **Prev Posts** Development Manager, Community Recycling Network, 1995-96; Dvlpmt Officer, Waste Watch, 1992-95; Project Manager, Halton Recycling, 1990-92. **Prof Background** Lancaster University, BA(Hons) Urban Policy; former lecturer in Geography & Urban Policy; previous background in Industry (textiles).   **Awards/Research** Auth: Community Recycling (Waste Watch 1994). **Pres Committees** Chair of Trustees, Create Charitable Trust Ltd; Executive Cttee of National Recycling Forum. **Media Experience** Extensive regional TV, radio, press experience on env. issues.

GIBSON Alan General Secretary **BRITISH EVANGELICAL COUNCIL** RELIGIOUS Type: Service provider; Regional Organisation. 113 Victoria St, St Albans, Herts AL1 3TJ   Tel:01727-855655   Fax:01727-855655 **Expertise** Church relationships, theology. **Prev Posts** Pastor, North London 1958-63; Pastor, Winchester 1963-77; Pastor, Canterbury 1977-82. **Prof Background** London University, Bachelor of Divinity. **Awards/Research** Editor, The Church and its Unity, IVpress 1992; Numerous articles in evangelical journals. **Pres Committees** Various evangelical coalitions, committees. **Media Experience** Occasional local radio, press articles.

GIFFORD Barry Thomas Director of Finance and Administration **ROYAL NATIONAL INSTITUTE FOR THE BLIND - RNIB** DISABILITY Type: Fundraiser; Service provider; Grant maker. 224 Great Portland Street, London W1N 6AA   Tel:0171-388 1266 Fax:0171-388 2034   **Prev Posts** Mott Hay & Andersen 1961-70; Sharkland Cox (Int Firm of Architects and Planners) 1970-79. **Prof Background** Assoc, Inst of Chartered Secretaries. **Pres Committees** Trustee, Gift of Thomas Pocklington, Charity Tax Reform Group. **Past Committees** Chair (until July 1992), Charity Tax Reform Group. **Media Experience** Radio and TV.

GILLETT Rev Canon David Principal **TRINITY COLLEGE, BRISTOL** RELIGIOUS Type: Theological College. Stoke Hill, Bristol, Avon BS9 1JP Tel:0117-9682803   Fax:0117-9687470 **Expertise** Spirituality, Pastoral Theology & Mission. **Prev Posts** Lecturer, St John's College Nottingham 1974-79; Education Officer, Rostrevor Ecumenical Centre, N. Ireland 1979-82; Vicar, St. Hugh's, Luton 1982-88. **Prof Background** BA; M.Phil; Academic Theologian/Anglican Clergyman. **Awards/Research** Author of: The Darkness Where God Is (Kingsway 1982); Trust and Obey (Dalton, Longman & Todd 1993). **Pres Committees** General Synod, The Church of England; Church of England Cttee for Minority Ethnic Concerns; Church of England Advisory Board of Ministry. **Past Committees** Church of England, Interfaith Consultancy Group 1990-95; Church of England, Board of Mission 1990-95.

GILLIS Richard Clerk to the Council & Company Secretary **UNIVERSITY OF DERBY** SOCIAL/TRAINING Type: Service provider;University. Kedleston Road, Derby, Derbys DE22 1GB   Tel:01332-622 222 Fax:01332-622 299 **Expertise** Charity, Commercial & Company Law. **Prev Posts** Secretary, ABB Transportation Holdings Ltd, 1985-95; Assistant to the Secretary, TI Group plc, 1981-85. **Prof Background** Solicitor (admitted 1975).   **Awards/Research** Auth/Joint Pub: Secretary; Justice report on perjury. **Pres Committees** Chairman, Property Committee, Derbyshire Council of the Order of St John; Member, Stakeholders' Forum, Derby City Challenge. **Past Committees** Vice Chairman, Crewe Devlpmt Agency; Member, CBI East Midlands Regional Council; Trustee, ABB Transportation Pension Plan.

GIMINGHAM Alison   Director **SCOTTISH FIELD STUDIES ASSOCIATION: KINDROGAN FIELD CENTRE**   CONSERVATION/ENVIRONMENT Type: Service provider; Educational; Professional and school. Kindrogan Field Centre, Enochdhu, Blairgowrie, Perthshire PH10 7PG Tel:01250-881286 Fax:01250-881433 **Expertise** Environmental Education. **Prev Posts** Head of Ecology, Cranedale Centre 1985-94. **Prof Background** BSc Hons Ecological Science; PGCE Rural and Enviromental Science C1 Biol. **Pres Committees** British Ecological Soc, Educ and Careers Cttee; Scottish Wildlife & Countryside Link.

GODDARD George Ferguson Secretary **ROYAL SOCIETY FOR THE RELIEF OF INDIGENT GENTLEWOMEN OF SCOTLAND**   THE ELDERLY Type: Service provider; Grant maker.   14 Rutland Square, Edinburgh EH1 2BD Tel:0131-229 2308 Fax:0131-229 0956 **Prev Posts** Partner, Chartered Accountancy Practice 1965-today.   **Prof Background** Chartered Accountant. **Awards/Research** MBE.

GOEDKOOP Mrs Gail Director **HELEN ARKELL DYSLEXIA CENTRE**   DISABILITY Type: Service provider. Frensham, Farnham, Surrey GU10 3BW Tel:01252-792400 Fax:01252-795669 **Expertise** Specific learning difficulties & dyslexia; training teachers. **Prev Posts** Specialist teacher 1976-83; Director of Courses, HADC 1984-87. **Prof Background** BA (Hons), Wellesley College, Massachusetts (Durant Scholar); M.Ed, Harvard Graduate School of Education, Cambridge, Massachusetts. **Awards/Research** Member of SIGMA X1 International Scientific Society; Article, Neuro-linguistic Programming, Benefits for Teachers in Sp & D. **Pres Committees** Accreditation Board for Training Courses, BDA (British Dyslexia Association). **Past Committees** Royal Society of Arts Working Party for Diploma in Specific Learning Difficulties.

GOGGINS Paul National Co-ordinator **CHURCH ACTION ON POVERTY - CAP** SOCIAL Type: Education; campaigning. Central Buildings, Oldham Street, Manchester M1 1JT   Tel:0161-236 9321 Fax:0161-237 5359 **Expertise** Poverty, unemployment, homelessness and related issues. **Prev Posts** Social Work - Project leader, Alternatives to Custody for Juvenile Offenders 1984-89. **Prof Background** Professional social work training, also training in theology. **Awards/Research** Auth:Impact of Poll Tax, 1990; various magazine and newspaper articles on poverty and related subjects. **Pres Committees** CAP Executive Committee; Churches National Housing Coalition Co-ordinating Committee; Catholic Bishops' Conference Committee on Community Relations. **Media Experience** Involved in current affairs programmes on radio, TV, video and press.

GOLDER John National Organiser **REMAP (SCOTLAND)** DISABILITY Type: Design/produce aids for physically/mentally disab people. Maulside Lodge, Beith, Ayrshire KA15 1JJ Tel:01294-832566 **Expertise** Mechanical engineering. **Prev Posts** Senior Management positions in Engineering & Production, I.C.I. plc 1947-79. **Prof Background** ARTC; BSc (Mechanical Engineering); C.Eng.; F.I.Mech.E.

GOOCH Peter Chief Executive **PHAB ENGLAND** DISABILITY Type: Fundraiser; Service provider; Grant maker; Campaigning. Summit House, Wandle Road, Croydon CR0 1DF Tel:0181-667 9443 Fax:0181-681 1399 **Expertise** Fundraising, Motivation, Finance. **Prev Posts** Chief Executive, Surrey Assoc of Youth Clubs & Surrey PHAB 1981-94. **Prof Background** Certificates: Youth & Community Work; Tutoring Young People. **Awards/Research** Extensive list of publications; Awarded: Surrey County Cncl Award for Achievement. **Pres Committees** SS Advisory Cttee, Children in Need. **Media Experience** Various local radio, BBC ITV.

GOODMAN Mike Director **RELEASE** SOCIAL Type: Service provider; National drugs and legal helpline. 388 Old Street, London EC1V 9LT Tel:0171-729 9904 Fax:0171-729 2599 **Expertise** Strategic management; social policy; media and communications; public sector direction and leadership. **Prev Posts** Mngr, NACRO Central London Cmty Prog 1983-85; Policy and Projects Head, London Disab Cttee 1987-91; Council Leader, LB Hamm and Fulham 1988-91. **Prof Background** Qualified barrister, mbr Grays Inn. Praised for successful handling of legal aftermath by Independent Enquiry into Hammersmith and Fulham Interest Rates Swops Activities. **Awards/Research** Contrib: The Release White Paper on Reform of the Drug Laws; various policy and management papers. **Past Committees** Law Centres Federation; Brunel University Senate. **Media Experience** Frequent TV/radio: BBC/ITN News, Newsnight, Business Prog, Today prog, Newsbeat; You Decide.

GOODWIN Jennifer **NATIONAL MUSIC COUNCIL** ARTS Type: Service provider; Campaigning. Francis House, Francis St, London SW1P 1DE Tel:0181-347 8618 Fax:0181-347 8618

GORDON Christopher Chief Executive **ENGLISH REGIONAL ARTS BOARDS - ERAB** ARTS Type: Service provider. 5 City Road, Winchester, Hants SO23 8SD Tel:01962-851063 Fax:01962-842033 **Expertise** Arts/Cultural policy in UK & Continental Europe. **Prev Posts** County Arts Officer, Hampshire CC 1977-85; Executive Officer, Council of Regional Arts Associations 1985-92. **Prof Background** MA Classics, St Andrews University; Arts Administration, Polytechnic of Central London. **Awards/Research** UK Arts Press, UNESCO, Council of Europe. **Pres Committees** Southampton University Arts Centre; Hampshire Sculpture Trust; Portsmouth Theatre Royal Trust. 94/95 Council of Europe Rapporteur for Evaluation of Italian Cultural Policy. **Past Committees** Governor, Winchester School of Art 1981-89; Bournemouth Orchestras Brd 1981-91; Arts Cncl Planning Brd; Cncl of Europe Project Team. **Media Experience** General - radio, TV and press. **Addits** Univ of Warwick-external examiner.

GORDON MCVIE Prof J Director General **CANCER RESEARCH CAMPAIGN** MEDICAL/HEALTH Type: Fundraiser; Grant maker. 10 Cambridge Terrace, London NW1 4JL Tel:0171-224 1333 Fax:0171-224 2399 **Expertise** Cancer Research & Cancer Medicine. **Prev Posts** Head Clinical Res Unit, Netherlands Cancer Inst, 1980-84; Clinical Res Director, 1984-89, Netherlands Cancer Inst; Scientific Director, Cancer Res Campaign, London 1989-96. **Prof Background** University of Edinburgh BSc Hons; MB; ChB; MD 1978; MRCP; FRCP 1981; FRCPS 1987. **Awards/Research** Contributes to bks/jnls on Anti-cancer drug devmt/cancer medicine. Books: Clinical & Experimental Pathology & Biology of Lung Cancer (1985); Microspheres & Drug Therapy (1984); **Pres Committees** Pres, EORTC;Chair, UICC Fellowships Prog;Chair Ed Brd, Euro Soc for Med Oncol;Cancer Res Campaign Phase 1 New Drugs Cttee;Med Res Cncl Cancer Therapy Cttee UK;Examr: Royal Col Phys & Surgs, Edinburgh. **Past Committees** Immunomods Min of Health, Netherlands; Sci Rev Cttee, Ludwig Inst, Melbourne; Chair, ESO;Int Mtng Drug Resist; var RC Phys London. **Media Experience** Mbr Ed Brd incl: Jnl of NCI; Tumori; Cancer; C. Therapy Rpts; Annals of Oncol.

GORMAN Mark Acting Chief Executive **HELPAGE INTERNATIONAL** THE ELDERLY Type: Service provider. 67-74 Saffron Hill, London EC1N 8QX Tel:0171-404 7201 Fax:0171-404 7203

GOVENDIR Ian Chief Executive **BRITISH LUNG FOUNDATION** MEDICAL/HEALTH Type: Fundraiser; Service provider; Grant maker. 78 Hatton Garden, London EC1N 8JR Tel:0171-831 5831 Fax:0171-831 5832 **Expertise** Marketing, Management, Fundraising. **Prev Posts** Head of Direct Marketing, British Red Cross 1992-94. **Prof Background** HND in Business and Finance; Masters Degree in Marketing. **Awards/Research** ICFM/DMA. **Pres Committees** RSA; CND Advisory. **Media Experience** Experience with TV and press.

GRAHAM Andy Artistic Director **SNAP PEOPLES THEATRE TRUST** ARTS Type: Service provider. Unit A Causeway Business Centre, The Causeway, Bishops Stortford, Herts CM23 2UB Tel:01279-504095 Fax:01279-501472 **Expertise** Producer, Director & Educational Drama Specialist. **Prev Posts** Director, The Shifrin Foundation (Liverpool, Jewish Youth Community) 1977-78; Artistic Director, SNAP Theatre Company 1979-97. **Prof Background** Trained Teacher, Youth Leader, Actor, Director. **Awards/Research** Awarded Prince Michael Award for Road Safety (Snap Theatre Company). **Pres Committees** Chairman, East Herts Leisure Sub-Committee; Chairman, Bishops Stortford Leisure Committee; East Herts Policy & Finance Committee; Bishops Stortford Planning Committee. **Past Committees** Snap Peoples Theatre Trust; Rainbow Theatre for the Deaf; Eastern Arts Board.

GRAHAM Cathy Executive Director **SOCIETY FOR THE PROMOTION OF NEW MUSIC** ARTS Type: Service provider. Francis House, Francis Street, London

SW1P 1DE Tel:0171-828 9696 Fax:0171-931 9928 **Prev Posts** Teacher, Vocal Coach & Repetiteur, Sweden 1978-92; Assistant Administrator, English Contemporary Opera Studio 1993; Artists' Manager 1993-94. **Prof Background** B.Mus, Birmingham University; Post Grad Studies: Royal Northern College of Music. **Pres Committees** National Music Council.

GRANT Allan Director **PRISON FELLOWSHIP SCOTLAND** RELIGIOUS Type: Service provider. Religious PO Box 366, 101 Ellesmere Street, Glasgow G22 5QS Tel:0141-332 8870 Fax:0141-332 8870 **Prev Posts** Prog Mgr, MV LOGOS 1985-87; Scottish Rep, Operation Mobilisation 1987-90; Field Director, Operation Mobilisation, Japan 1992-94. **Prof Background** BSc Aeronautical Engineering.

GRANT Duncan Director **SAVE & PROSPER EDUCATIONAL TRUST** SOCIAL Type: Grant maker. Finsbury Dials, 20 Finsbury Street, London EC2Y 9AY Tel:0171-417 2332 Fax:0171-417 2122 **Prev Posts** Senior Teacher; Charity Manager. **Prof Background** Sir Walters St Johns, Leicester University (BSc); Keele University (PGCE), CPS and ICSA (foundation). **Pres Committees** Board Mbr, Palace Theatre Trust; Trustee, Southend Youth Wind Band. **Media Experience** Interviews and articles for local and national media.

GRANT Mrs Margaret T.J. Founder **BRITTLE BONE SOCIETY** MEDICAL/HEALTH Type: Fundraiser. 112 City Road, Dundee, Tayside, Scotland DD2 2PW Tel:01382-667603 **Expertise** Helping sufferers of osteogenesis imperfecta. **Prev Posts** Founder then Honorary Secretary of Brittle Bone Society since 1968. **Prof Background** A sufferer of osteogenesis imperfecta. **Awards/Research** Ed: Society newsletter 3 times per annum. **Pres Committees** National Committee, Brittle Bone Society; Dundee Access Group (highlighting need for access for disabled people). **Media Experience** TV and radio appeals, and Society video. Frequent press coverage. **Addits** Craft making for fundraising.

GRANT Tony Regional Manager **SUSTRANS SCOTLAND** SOCIAL Type: Fundraiser; Service provider; Grant maker. 53 Cochrane Street, Glasgow, G1 1HL Tel:0141-5528241 Fax:0141-5523599 **Expertise** Design, promotion & construction of cycle facilities. **Prev Posts** Marketing Manager, Brown Boveri & Cie, Baden, Switzerland 1968-82. **Prof Background** C.Eng; DiplHWU; MIMechE; RSA. **Awards/Research** Author of numerous reports on cycle provision in Scotland. **Pres Committees** The Scottish Viaducts Committee; Scottish Transport Forum.

GRAY Linda Director **SCOTTISH EDUCATION AND ACTION FOR DEVELOPMENT - SEAD** SOCIAL Type: Campaigning, Publ, Exchange visits with Scotland. 23 Castle St, Edinburgh EH2 3DN Tel:0131-225 6550 Fax:0131-226 6384 **Expertise** Democracy in decision making in Scotland & Third World; Poverty; Social exclusion. **Prof Background** Graduate of University of Edinburgh. **Media Experience** Various interviews and contributions to radio and Scottish press.

GREASLEY Andrew Chair **HANDIGOLF FOUNDATION** DISABILITY Type: Fundraiser; Service provider. Stone Cottage, Launton Road, Stratton Audley, Oxon OX6 9BW Tel:01908-655102 Fax:01908-653858 **Expertise** Competitive golf for physically disabled people. **Prof Background** University lecturer in Engineering. **Awards/Research** Disabled Golfers Yearbook, First Edition 1995. **Media Experience** Extensive experience; Presenter/Author of several educational videos.

GREEN G. David Director **VOLUNTARY SERVICE OVERSEAS - VSO** SOCIAL Type: Fundraiser; Service provider. 317 Putney Bridge Road, London SW15 2PN Tel:0181-780 2266 Fax:0181-780 1326 **Expertise** Education; training; personnel management; general management. **Prev Posts** Teacher 1972-76; Dir, Children's Relief Internat 1976-79. Dir Personnel and Admin, Save The Children Fund 1979-90. **Prof Background** Leys Sch Cambs; Cert Ed Keswick Hall Coll of Ed, Norwich; BEd, Trinity Hall, Cambs; FRSA; FRGS. **Awards/Research** Auth: Chorus, 1977. **Past Committees** Dir/Cncl Mbr: Council for Colony Holidays for School Children 1970-80. Mbr, Laurence Olivier Awds panel 1984-85. **Addits** VSO Vol in Pakistan 1967-68.

GREEN Mrs J. Founder **ACCEPTANCE HELPLINE FOR PARENTS OF LESBIANS AND GAY MEN - ACCEPTANCE** SOCIAL Type: Service provider; Helpline; meetings/information/support service. 64 Holmside Avenue, Halfway Houses, Sheerness, Kent ME12 3EY Tel:01795-661463 **Prof Background** Personal experience as parent. **Media Experience** Many appearances on nat TV/radio to promote Acceptance & help other families.

GREEN Penny National Administrator **DOWN'S HEART GROUP** MEDICAL/HEALTH Type: Fundraiser; Self-help and support. 17 Cantilupe Close, Eaton Bray, Dunstable, Beds LU6 2EA Tel:01525-220379 Fax:01525-221553 **Expertise** Down's syndrome with associated congenital heart defects. **Prof Background** Background in banking. But in relation to Down's Heart Group work - most important, I am a parent. **Media Experience** Experience with radio and TV interviews (Radio 5, BBC3 Counties, Sky News).

GREENE Dr J. Patrick Director **MUSEUM OF SCIENCE & INDUSTRY IN MANCHESTER** ARTS Type: Museum Liverpool Rd, Castlefield, Manchester M3 4FP Tel:0161-8322244 Fax:0161-8332184 **Expertise** Museum management & development. **Prev Posts** Director, Norton Priory Museum, Cheshire 1971-82. **Prof Background** BSc & PhD, Leeds University. **Awards/Research** OBE 1991; Author of: Norton Priory (Cambridge University Press 1989) & Medieval Monasteries (Leicester University Press 1992). **Pres Committees** Pres, ICOM/CIMUSET (Inter Cttee of Museums of Science & Tech); Trustee/Jdge, Europ Museum of the Year Award; Chair, Greater Manchester Visitor & Convention Bureau; Brd Mbr, Marketing Manchester. **Past Committees** Brd Mbr, London Transport Museum; Founder Secretary, Assoc of Indep Museums. **Media Experience** Wide-ranging experience in interviews & articles for radio, TV and press.

GREENFIELD Tanya Lottery Officer Head of Unit **ARTS COUNCIL OF NORTHERN IRELAND** ARTS Type: Service provider; Grant maker. Statutory Body. 181(A) Stranmillis Road, Belfast BT9 5DU Tel:01232-667000 Fax:01232-664766 **Expertise** Lottery. **Prev Posts** Publishing Admin, Circa Publications, Belfast 1988-89; Admin, Arts Theatre, Belfast 1989-90; Partner, Hanna Greenfield Theatrical Agency, Belfast 1990-94. **Prof Background** Arts Administration; Postgrad Dip in Arts Admin, University College, Dublin. **Past Committees** TMA Theatre Awards Panel; Director, Dubbeljoint Theatre Co. **Media Experience** Interviewee only.

GREENGROSS Sally (Lady) Director General **AGE CONCERN ENGLAND - THE NATIONAL COUNCIL ON AGEING** THE ELDERLY Type: Fundraiser; Service provider; Grant maker. Covers all areas of work connected with ageing. 1268 London Road, London SW16 4ER Tel:0181-679 8000 Fax:0181-679 6069 **Expertise** General social, political and economic policy esp. related to older people. **Prev Posts** Age Concern:Asst Dir 1977-82; Dep Dir 1982-87. **Prof Background** London School of Economics; FRSH; FRSA. Career as linguist; industrial executive; researcher; lecturer. **Awards/Research** OBE 1993. UK Woman of Europe 1990. D Litt Ulster (Hon); Hon DUniv Kingston & St Georges. Publ bks, articles. Ed incl:Ageing, An Adventure in Living; The Law & Vulnerable Elderly People; Jt Ed:Living Loving & Ageing. **Pres Committees** Fndr,Sec-Gen Eurolink Age;JE Ch Bd Age Concern Inst of Geront K Coll Lond;V Pres Int Fed on Ageing;UN Network on Ageing;Adv Cttee Sec State DOE on Older Workers; Adv Cncl Euro Movement. **Past Committees** Int Sec-Gen(Eur) Int Fed Ageing;Mbr Stndng Adv Cttee Trsprt for Disab & Eld Pple;Adv Cttee:Carnegie Inq 3rd Age;Euro Yr Older Pple; Bd World Org for Care in Home & Hospice. **Media Experience** Very frequent.Cnsultnt, Jnl of Ed Gerontology; Ed Adv to Home Care **Addits** Pres,Action on Elder Abuse.

GREENHALGH Bob Trustee **FRIEDREICH'S ATAXIA GROUP** MEDICAL/HEALTH Type: Service provider; Research. The Stable, Wiggins Yard, Bridge St, Godalming, Surrey GU7 1HW Tel:01483-417111 Fax:01483-424006

GREENWOOD Gillian Patricia National Director **ALEXANDRA ROSE DAY** Type: Fundraiser; Service provider; Grant maker; Campaigner. 2A Ferry Road, Barnes, London SW13 9RX Tel:0181-748 4824 Fax:0181-748 3188 **Expertise** Projects undertaken for Fundraising, Underprivileged Children & Children's Hospice Movement. **Prev Posts** National Association Welfare of Children in Hospital 1983-85; Children's Country Holidays's Fund 1985-89; Alexandra Rose Day 1988-95. **Prof Background** Further Education Teachers Certificate; Certificated Member Conservative Agents. **Awards/Research** Parliamentary Research; Contribution to Charity Publications. **Pres Committees** Chairman & Trustee, Teme Valley Youth Club. **Past Committees** Nat Conservative Educ Advisory Cttee; Governing Bd, Wigmore Comprehensive Sch; Church Council of Wigmore Abbey, Herefordshire. **Media Experience** Radio: BBC & local; TV: Thames, current affairs; reg contrib local press. **Addits** Mbr:Inst Supervisory Mngmt, Inst Charity Officers, ICFM.

GREGG Andy Director **WORLD UNIVERSITY SERVICE WUS (UK)** SOCIAL Type: Fundraiser; Service provider; Grant maker; Campaigning; Refugee Education & Training. 14 Dufferin Street, London EC1Y 8PD Tel:0171-426 5802 Fax:0171-251 1314 **Prev Posts** London Development Officer, NFCO 1987-89; General Sec, Islington Voluntary Action Council 1989-1996. **Prof Background** BA; MA in Philosophy. **Pres Committees** Exec Cttee, LVSC; Mngmt Bd, Community House Information Centre; Mngmt Cttee, British Eritrean Association; Safer Islington Trust; London Voluntary Sector Resource Centre. **Media Experience** Ex freelance journalist & editor.

GREGORY Roger General Manager **PRAMACARE** SOCIAL/DISABILITY Type: Fundraiser; Service provider; Homecare. 1551 Wimborne Road, Kinson, Bournemouth, Dorset BH10 7AZ Tel:01202-599199 Fax:01202-477914 **Expertise** General Management & Company re-engineering. **Prev Posts** ICI (Plc), 1966-90; Director of WMEC Ltd, Chichester; Director, The Management Experience Ltd, Wimborne. **Prof Background** BSc & Internal ICI Management Training. **Awards/Research** BSc. **Pres Committees** Trustee, The McDougal Trust.

GREGORY-JONES G. Chief Executive **BRITISH UNIVERSITIES SPORTS ASSOCIATION** SOCIAL Type: Service provider; Grant maker. 8 Union Street, London SE1 1SZ Tel:0171-357 8555 Fax:0171-403 0127 **Expertise** Student Sport. **Prev Posts** College Registrar, 1972-89. **Prof Background** BSc University of London; Postgrad Dip, Education Administration, University of London. **Pres Committees** Amateur Rowing Association, Executive Council.

GRENIER Paola Director **MYALGIC ENCEPHALOMYELITIS ASSOCIATION** MEA MEDICAL/HEALTH Type: Fundraiser; Service provider. Stanhope House, High Street, Stanford le Hope, Essex SS17 0HA Tel:01375-642466 Fax:01375-360256.

GRIEVE William Director **ABERLOUR CHILD CARE TRUST** CHILDREN/YOUTH Type: Service provider. 36 Park Terrace, Stirling, Scotland FK8 2JR Tel:01786-450335 Fax:01786-473238 **Expertise** Juvenile Justice Systems, especially Scottish Children's Hearing System. **Prev Posts** Reporter,Children's Panel, Strathclyde Region 1977-84; Asst Div Dir, Save The Children Fund (Scotland) 1984-94. **Prof Background** MA Hons Psychology Edinburgh; Diploma in Social Work, Glasgow University.

GRIFFITH Richard J. Director **EDINBURGH NEW TOWN CONSERVATION COMMITTEE** CONSERVATION/ENVIRONMENT Type: Grant maker. 13a Dundas Street, Edinburgh EH3 6QG Tel:0131-5575222 Fax:0131-5566355 **Expertise** Registered architect; Architectural conservation. **Prev Posts** G.L.C. Historic Building Division 1979-86; English Heritage, London Region 1986-94. **Prof Background** MA (Cantab); DIPARCH (Cantab); RIAS.

GRIFFITHS Mr K. Secretary **WARWICKSHIRE INDUSTRIAL LOCOMOTIVE TRUST** CONSERVATION Type: Fundraiser; Service provider; Grant maker. 143 Queslett Road East, Sutton Coldfield, W. Midlands B74 2AL.

GRIMES Chris Chief Executive **HEALTHCARE FINANCIAL MANAGEMENT ASSOCIATION** MEDICAL/HEALTH Type: Professional Association. 3 Robert St, London WC2N 6BH Tel:0171-543 5659 Fax:0171-543 5789 **Expertise** National Health Service Financial Management. **Prev Posts** Deputy Regional Dir of Finance, S.E Thames RHA 1974-77; Dir of Finance, West Glamorgan Health Authority 1977-89. **Prof Background** Accountant, Fellow of ACCA; Member Chartered Inst of Public Finance and Accountancy (CIPFA). **Pres Committees** UK Central Council for Nursing, Health Visiting and Midwifery; Chairman of Finance Committee of UKCC.

GRIMSHAW John Executive Director **SUSTRANS** CONSERVATION/ENVIRONMENT Type: Service provider. 35 King St, Bristol BS1 4DZ Tel:0117-9268893 Fax:0117-9294173 **Expertise** Civil Engineering. **Prev Posts** Engaged for 15 years in the establishment and direction of Sustrans. **Prof Background** BA (Cantab); MICE. Awards inc: several RIBA/Community enterprise schemes, RICS, Scottish Development Agency/RIAS; several UK 2000 Kitemarking awards, AA environment award. **Awards/Research** MBE. Arts Council/British Gas Award 1992. Auth: Disused Railways in England and Wales; Potential Cycle Routes, 1982. Approx 300 reports on pedestrian/cycle provision in GB & Ireland. **Media Experience** Documentaries; innumerable radio and press interviews. **Addits** Designed/constructed 400 miles of paths for pedestrians, cyclists & disabled.

GRIMSON Dermot Director **RURAL FORUM SCOTLAND** CONSERVATION/ENVIRONMENT Type: Service provider; Grant maker. Highland House, 46 St Catherines Road, Perth PH1 5RY Tel:01738-634565 Fax:01738-638699 **Expertise** Rural policy. **Prev Posts** Planner, Renfrew District Cncl 1977-80; Planner, Banff & Burton District Cncl 1980-87. **Prof Background** Mbr, Royal Town Planning Institute. **Pres Committees** Secretary, Trans European Rural Network; Board Member: Enterprise Music Scotland; Local Breadabane. **Past Committees** Perth Civic Trust; Forum on the Environment; Countryside Around Towns Forum.

GROVES Colin National Director **NABC - CLUBS FOR YOUNG PEOPLE** CHILDREN/YOUTH Type: Fundraiser; Service provider. 371 Kennington Lane, London SE11 5QY Tel:0171-793 0787 Fax:0171-820 9815 **Expertise** General & Charge Mgmt; Training; Operational Planning. **Prev Posts** Commander Training Support Command 1990-93; Commander Initial Training Group 1993-94. **Prof Background** Regular Army Officer 1963-96; FIPD; FIMgt; MInstD. **Pres Committees** Nat Cncl for the Voluntary Youth Services; Interested Organisations CCPR; Board of Trustees NABC - Clubs for Young People. **Media Experience** Interviews/articles/letters in/on national & local TV/Radio/Press.

GRUBB David H. W. Executive Director **CHILDREN'S AID DIRECT** CHILDREN/YOUTH Type: Fundraiser; Private Limited Company International Aid Agency. 82 Caversham Rd, Reading, Berks RG1 8AE Tel:0118-9584000 Fax:0118-9588988 **Expertise** Child development & education, fundraising & innovation management. **Prev Posts** National Director, Barnardo's, General Appeal 1986-90. **Prof Background** Cert.Ed (Culham College); M.Ed (Exeter University). **Awards/Research** Author of The Gifted Child at School (Oxford Society for Applied Studies in Education 1985); Editor of Journal of Applied Educational Studies (OSASE). **Media Experience** Experience in TV and letters in all major newspapers.

GRUNFELD Rabbi J. National Director **PROJECT SEED EUROPE** RELIGIOUS Type: Fundraiser; Service provider. Middlesex House, 29-45 High St, Edgware, Middlesex HA8 7UU Tel:0181-381 1555 Fax:0181-381 1666 **Expertise** Rabbi, lecturer, educator. **Prof Background** Rabbinic degree. **Awards/Research** First Chief Rabbinate Award for Excellence in Jewish Adult Education, 1993. Res: Talmud.

GUNNELL Jonathan Charles Bursar/Secretary **ROYAL SCHOOL FOR DEAF CHILDREN** DISABILITY Type: Service provider; Education of deaf children. Victoria Road, Margate, Kent CT9 1NB Tel:01843-227561 Fax:01843-227637

GUTCH Richard Chief Executive **ARTHRITIS CARE** DISABILITY Type: Service provider; Campaigning. 18 Stephenson Way, Euston, London NW1 2HD Tel:0171-916 1500 Fax:0171-916 1505 **Expertise** Relations with government, contracting, voluntary sector policy. **Prev Posts** Asst to the Chief Executive, LB Brent 1980-85; Asst Dir, NCVO 1985-92. **Prof Background** BA Moral Sciences and History of Architecture and Fine Arts; MPhil Town Planning. **Awards/Research** NCVO: Getting in on the Act 1987, Partners or Agents 1990, Contracting Lessons from the US 1992; Arthritis Care: Countdown to Community Care 1992; Community Care One Year On, 1994. **Pres Committees** Vice-chair, ACENVO. **Past Committees** Chair, Consortium on Opportunities for Volunteering, 1990-92; Chair, Long Term Medical Conditions Alliance. **Media Experience** Letters to all main nat papers; interviews/articles on radio/TV, press/jnls. **Addits** Conference speaker.

GUY John G. Chairman **WORLD ORTHOPAEDIC CONCERN (UK)** MEDICAL/HEALTH Type: Fundraiser; Service provider. 35-43 Lincoln's Inn Fields, London WC2A 3PN Tel:01905-421997 Fax:01905-420856 **Expertise** Orthopaedic education & care in developing countries. **Prev Posts** Committee Member, World Orthopaedic Concern (UK) 1988-91; Fundraising Chairman, World Orthodpaedic Concern (UK) 1991-95. **Prof Background** Consultant Trauma & Orthopaedic Surgeon. **Awards/Research** Awarded 'C' Merit Award; Author of various articles on WOC (UK). **Pres Committees** Tropical Health & Education Trust; Member, International Health Consortium; Lorey Trustee, Lusaka Zambia. **Past Committees** Member, Education Sub-Committee British Orthopaedic Association 1986-90. **Media Experience** Experience in TV and radio (health matters).

GWILLIAM Michael C Director **CIVIC TRUST** CONSERVATION/ENVIRONMENT Type: Fundraiser; Service provider; Grant maker. 17 Carlton House Terrace, London SW1Y 5AW Tel:0171-930 0914 Fax:0171-321 0180 **Expertise** Planning, transport, conservation, sustainable development, urban policy and regeneration. **Prev Posts** County Planning Officer, Bedfordshire (1988-96); Chief Planner, Leicestershire (1985-88). **Prof Background** M.A. Oxford Univ; Planning Diploma UCL; Management Diploma De Montfort; Member of Royal Town Planning Institute; Fellow of RSA. **Pres Committees** Urban Villages Forum Council. **Past Committees** Reg Bd Princes Youth Business Trust; Luton Dunstable P'ship Bd; Leics Coalfield P'ship; Bedford P'ship Bd; Marsten Vale P'ship. **Media Experience** Frequent media contact.

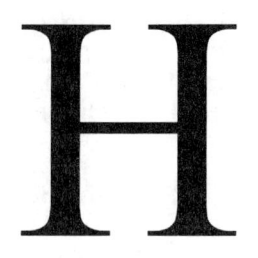

H

HAIGH Nigel Director **INSTITUTE FOR EUROPEAN ENVIRONMENTAL POLICY, LONDON - IEEP** CONSERVATION/ENVIRONMENT Type: Service provider. 158 Buckingham Palace Rd, London SW1W 9TR Tel:0171-824 8787 Fax:0171-824 8145 **Expertise** EC environmental policy. **Prev Posts** Civic Trust 1973-1980; IEEP 1980-today. **Prof Background** Read engineering at Cambridge University 1958-1961; practiced as a chartered patent agent 1962-1972; Visiting Research Fellow, Imperial College, London 1991-today. **Awards/Research** OBE. Manual of Environment Policy: The EC and Britain, 1992. **Pres Committees** Chairman, The Green Alliance; Mbr,Board of Environment Agency. Editorial Board, International Environmental Affairs. **Past Committees** Vice President, European Environmental Bureau 1975-79; UK National Committee for European Year of the Environment 1987-88.

HAIGH Dr Paul Chairman **SCOUT AND GUIDE GRADUATE ASSOCIATION - SAGGA** CHILDREN/YOUTH Type: Fundraiser; Service provider; Grant maker. 22 Hatherley Court Road, Cheltenham, Glos GL51 5AG Tel:01242-572493 **Expertise** Nuclear Power in Eastern Europe. **Prev Posts** Treasurer, Scout & Guide Graduate Association 1990-94. **Prof Background** BSc, MSc, PhD (Chemical Engineering), Manchester University 1961-68. **Pres Committees** Council of Institution of Chemical Engineers; FIChemE; C.Eng. **Media Experience** Experience with various TV & radio interviews.

HALDANE Duncan Director **JOHN S COHEN FOUNDATION** SOCIAL Type: Grant maker. 85 Albany St, London NW1 4BT Tel:0171-486 1117 Fax:0171-486 1118 **Expertise** The arts, particularly visual arts & Islamic art; disability (including visual impairment and the arts). **Prev Posts** Dep Keeper, Nat Art Library, V & A Museum 1980-89; Chief Ass, Policy & Planning Unit, BBC 1989-91; Ass Dir, Sainsbury Family Charitable Trusts 1991-93. **Prof Background** MA Arabic, University of Edinburgh; PhD Islamic Painting, University of Edinburgh; MA Arts Administration, City University London. **Awards/Research** Mamluk Painting, Warminster 1979; Islamic Bookbindings, London 1982; Many articles in Apollo, Connoisseur, Encyclopedia Iranica, etc.; Art & Visually Impaired People, London 1986. **Pres Committees** Trustee, Living Paintings Trust; Secretary, Patsy Hardy Trust; Hon. Research Fellow, University of Exeter. **Past Committees** BBC Middle East Representative 1976-77. **Media Experience** Wide experience with radio as interviewer/presenter & scriptwriter.

HALL Keith Founder **ASSOCIATION FOR ENVIRONMENT CONSCIOUS BUILDING** CONSERVATION/ENVIRONMENT Type: Service provider; Campaigning; Professional association. Nant-Y-Garreg, Saron, Llandysul, Carmarthenshire SA44 5EJ Tel:01559-370908 Fax:01559-370908 **Expertise** Greener, more ecologically acceptable building. **Prev Posts** Self employed. **Prof Background** Carpenter & joiner; Professional builder. **Awards/Research** Editor of Building for a Future Magazine; Coauthor of Greener Building Products & Services Directory. **Pres Committees** AECB. **Media Experience** Experience with radio, TV, video and press.

HALL Martyn Director **ELIMINATION OF LEUKAEMIA FUND - ELF** MEDICAL/HEALTH Type: Fundraiser. 17 Venetian Road, Denmark Hill, London SE5 9RR Tel:0171-737 4141 Fax:0171-737 7009 **Expertise** Fundraising; policy development; lobbying; consultancy. **Prev Posts** Policy Development Officer, London Vol Serv Cncl 1985-86; Director, Nat Out of School Alliance 1987-88. **Prof Background** MA (Philosophy, Politics & Economics), Oxford Univ. **Past Committees** Cancerlink Cttee 1981-84; SHAPE 1980-83; Patients Assoc 1981-83; ACENVO 1988-93. **Media Experience** Mainly press experience, some TV and radio.

HALL Michael Registrar **COUNCIL FOR PROFESSIONS SUPPLEMENTARY TO MEDICINE** MEDICAL/HEALTH Type: Charitable trust. 184 Kennington Park Rd, London SE11 4BU Tel:0171-582 0866 Fax:0171-820 9684 **Expertise** Administrator. **Prev Posts** Chief Executive & Secretary, British Association & College of Occupational Therapists. **Prof Background** Army, Royal Military College of Science, Army Staff College. **Media Experience** Contributor to radio, TV, video and press.

HALLIDAY Eunice Chair **NETWORK OF ACCESS AND CHILD CONTACT CENTRES - NACCC** Type: Fundraiser; Service provider; Umbrella Group for other service providers. St Andrews with Castlegate Ch, Goldsmith St, Nottingham NG1 5JT Tel:0115-948 4557 **Expertise** Information and advice to organisations. **Prev Posts** Information officer at NACCC 1992-95. **Prof Background** Solicitor. **Pres Committees** Coventry Childrens Contact Centre Management Committee.

HAMILTON Richard Secretary General **INTERNATIONAL FEDERATION OF MULTIPLE SCLEROSIS SOCIETIES** MEDICAL/HEALTH Type: Fundraiser; Service provider; Federation of 34 national MS societies. 10 Heddon Street, London W1R 7LJ Tel:0171-734 9120 Fax:0171-287 2587 **Expertise** Board & institutional development for non-profit organisations, fundraising, marketing. **Prev Posts** Managing Director, Craigmyle Consultants 1975-80; WWF International: Dir of Fundraising 1981-90, Dir of Institutional Development 1991-95. **Prof Background** MA, Consulting and Staff experience since 1963. **Pres Committees** Maritime Trust, Council Member; World Fund Raising Council, Board Member. **Media Experience** Usual interview experience.

HAMMOND Celia Founder and Trustee **CELIA HAMMOND ANIMAL TRUST - CHAT** ANIMAL/WILDLIFE Type: Fundraiser; Service provider; Campaigning charity; Professional association. High St, Wadhurst, East Sussex TN5 6AG Tel:01892-783820 Fax:01892-784882 **Expertise** Rescue, re-homing & neutering animals, mainly feral cats. Establishment of low-cost neuter clinics. **Pres Committees** RSPCA Committee. **Media Experience** Radio/TV/video/press.

HAMPSON Clare Executive **INSTITUTE OF PAPER CONSERVATION** CONSERVATION Type: Fundraiser; Service provider; Grant maker; Campaigning; Professional association. Leigh Lodge, Leigh, Worcs WR6 5LB Tel:01886-832323 Fax:01886-833688 **Expertise** Paper conservation; business manager. **Prof Background** Paper conservator; business management.

HAMPTON Ruth Scottish Director **CRUSE BEREAVEMENT CARE SCOTLAND** SOCIAL Type: Fundraiser; Service provider;Training for those who work in death and dying. 18 South Trinity Road, Edinburgh EH5 3PN Tel:0131-551 1511 Fax:0131-551 3058 **Expertise** Administration **Prev Posts** Sec, Institute of Acoustics 1979-81; Administrator MSc Course, Heriot Watt University 1981-84. **Prof Background** Business Admin Course, Edinburgh. **Awards/Research** Papers: 3rd Int Conference on Bereavement, Australia 1991; 4th Int Conference on Bereavement, Stockholm 1994. **Pres Committees** Vice Pres, Scottish Society for Autistic Children; Sec, Lords Taveners (Scotland) Lady Tavener. **Past Committees** Nat Autistic Soc; Scottish Cncl Single Parents; SCVO; Chair, Scottish Soc for Autistic Children; Confed Scottish Cnselling Agencies. **Media Experience** BBC Scotland; Radio Forth; Shetland Radio; STV: Time & Place; Scottish Women.

HANBURY-TENISON Robin Chief Executive **BRITISH FIELD SPORTS SOCIETY** Type: Fundraiser; Service provider. 59 Kennington Rd, London SE1 7PZ Tel:0171-928 4742 Fax:0171-620 0842 **Expertise** Lobbying on behalf of countryside, wildlife management and field sports. **Prof Background** Environmentalist, Human rights campaigner, Author. **Awards/Research** OBE; RGS Gold Medal; Krug Award for Excellence; Hon. Doctorate; 14 books on tribal people, rainforests, expeditions, long distance horse rides & children's fiction. **Pres Committees** President, Survival International; Council Member, Royal Geographical Society; Trustee, Ecological Foundation. **Past Committees** President, Cornwall Wildlife Trust 1958-95. **Media Experience** Many Broadcasts & TV films.

HANCOCK Christine General Secretary **ROYAL COLLEGE OF NURSING - RCN** MEDICAL/HEALTH Type: Nursing; Campaigning, Trade Union, Charity & Educ Institute. 20 Cavendish Square, London W1M 0AB Tel:0171-409 3333 Fax:0171-355 1379 **Expertise** State Registered Nurse, Midwifery Training, Family Planning Training. **Prev Posts** District Gen Mgr, Waltham Forest Health Authority(H.A.), 1985-89; Chief Nursing Officer, Bloomsbury H.A, 1982-85; Area Nursing Officer, Camden & Islington H.A., 1979-82. **Prof Background** University of London, Economics (Hons); London Business School, London Executive Prog (PG); King's Fund College, Management Devmt Prog. **Awards/Research** Auth/Joint: A future for Ward-based Nursing Officers; The Special

Industrial Relations(IR) Problems in Nursing in IR in the NHS, A Search for a System; Managing Nurses. **Pres Committees** Inst of Employment Studies Cncl; King's Fund Mngmt Cttee; Health Advisory Cttee; Cncl Member, Ash; Vice Chair, Nurses & Midwives Negotiating Cncl; Trustee, Public Mngment Fndtn. **Past Committees** Chair, Oct Club; Chair, Mind Study Team on Qlty in Comm Care; Member, Civil Serv Occupat Health Cttee; Member, Taskforce Nursing Res; Econ & Soc Res Cncl. **Media Experience** Extensive experience: nat/regional print & broadcast media. **Addits** Jt Auth: Giving advice at Work: A Guide for Ward Sisters & Charge Nurses. Pres, Standing Cttee of Nurses of Euro Union.

HANCOCK Robert M. Chief Executive and Company Secretary. **DAVID LEWIS CENTRE** MEDICAL/HEALTH Type: Fundraiser; Service provider. Mill Lane, Warford, Nr Alderley Edge, Cheshire SK9 7UD Tel:01565-872613 Fax:01565-872829 **Expertise** Committee mngmt, special education, international developments. **Prev Posts** Dir of Operations,Scope (formerly Spastic Society); Chief Inspector, Birmingham Local Authority; Senior Staff Inspector (I.L.E.A). **Prof Background** Head Teacher/Head of Psychology Service. **Awards/Research** Teachers Appraisal Industrial Compacts; 16 children's text books, research on special educational needs, further education and management. **Pres Committees** Director, National Primary Trust; Visiting Fellow Keele University, International Dir of the Peto Inst, Budapest. **Past Committees** Many in education and special education. **Media Experience** Regular national TV/radio, local radio, special affairs documentaries.

HAND Peter Administrator **GREAT BRITAIN SASAKAWA FOUNDATION - GBSF** SOCIAL Type: Grant maker. 43 North Audley Street, London W1Y 1WH. Tel:0171-355 2229 Fax:0171-355 2230 **Expertise** Japan **Prev Posts** Regional Director, Pacific Basin ANZ Grindlays Bank 1980-87. **Prof Background** Banker. **Pres Committees** Council of Japan Society; UK-Japan 2000 Group - Education Committee; Japanese Language Association - Bath; Tavistock Language College; Governor of Fairfield School.

HANNAH Liz Co-ordinator **SPARE TYRE THEATRE COMPANY** WOMEN Type: Service provider. West Greenwich House, 141 Greenwich High Road, London SE10 8JA Tel:0181-305 2800 **Expertise** Theatre training, arts education. **Prev Posts** Teaching English in Secondary Schools 1986-90;Education Project worker, Woolwich Citizens Gallery, Greenwich Festival 1991. **Prof Background** Diploma in Arts Management, City University 1991; PGCE English & Drama Southampton University 1986. **Awards/Research** English & French B.A. (joint Hons) Leeds University 1985 **Pres Committees** Performing Arts Advisory Board; NEWVR sixth form college; Mgt Cttee, W Greenwich House Community Centre.

HANRECK Carla Secretary/Company Secretary **EQUITY TRUST FUND** SOCIAL Type: Fundraiser; Service provider; Grant maker. Suite 222, Africa House, 64 Kingsway, London WC2B 6AH Tel:0171-404 6041 Fax:0171-831 4953 **Expertise** Administration, organising offices and committees. **Prev Posts** Secretary, Brook Advisory Centres 1987-89; Secretary, British Heart Foundation 1990-91. **Pres Committees** Entertainment Charities Fund (main governing Body);Occupational Ben. Funds Assoc-delegate;Assoc Charity Officers-delegate.

HARDING James Owen Glyn, (Jim) Director and Chief Executive **NATIONAL SOCIETY FOR THE PREVENTION OF CRUELTY TO CHILDREN - NSPCC** CHILDREN/YOUTH Type: Fundraiser; Service provider. National Centre, 42 Curtain Road, London EC2A 3NH Tel:0171-825 2500 Fax:0171-825 2525 **Prev Posts** RB Ken & Chelsea:Child Care Officer/Snr Child Care Officer 68-71;Area Officer/Asst Dir, Soc Serv Dept 71-85; NSPCC:Dir of Child Care 86-89;Dep CE & Dir of Children's Serv 89-95. **Prof Background** Pinner Grammar Sch;University of Sussex (BA);University of Exeter (Home Office Letter of Recognition in Child Care). **Awards/Research** A Child in Mind (part auth);media experience;Journals on social work and children's issues. **Pres Committees** Trustee of National Council of Voluntary Child Care Organisations. **Past Committees** Commission of Inquiry on the death of Kimberley Carlisle;Howard League Commission of Inquiry into Violence in Penal Institutions. **Addits** Sch governor; bereavement counsellor for the church.

HARDING Esq K. R. K. Secretary General **CHARTERED INSTITUTE OF ARBITRATORS** SOCIAL Type: Service provider; Professional association. 24 Angel Gate, City Road, London EC1V 2RS Tel:0171-837 4483 Fax:0171-837 4185 **Expertise** Administration & Dispute Resolution means other than litigation. **Prev Posts** Infantry Officer 1956-78; Executive Secretary, The Glass & Glazing Federation 1987-81. **Prof Background** MIPD; MInstD; FRSA; FCIArb. **Awards/Research** Author of articles on the process of arbitration. **Pres Committees** Executive Board, The Chartered Institute of Arbitrators Board, Arbitration Services Ltd. **Media Experience** Experience with press & radio.

HARDWICK Nick Chief Executive **BRITISH REFUGEE COUNCIL** SOCIAL Type: Service provider; Campaigning. Bondway House, 3-9 Bondway, London SW8 1SJ Tel:0171-582 6922 Fax:0171-582 9929 **Prev Posts** Regional Manager, NACRO 1980-86; Chief Executive, Centrepoint 1986-95. **Prof Background** BA Eng Lit. **Pres Committees** Board Member, Stonebridge HAT; Mbr, Soc Security Adv Cttee. **Past Committees** Var housing orgs incl: Big Issue, Princes Trust Homelessness Cttee, Homeless Netwk, Lond Connection,; Chair, Lond Reg Carr Gomm Soc. **Media Experience** Various.

HARDWIDGE Martin Executive Officer **FRONTIER YOUTH TRUST** CHILDREN/YOUTH Type: Fundraiser; Service provider; Training and support. 4th Floor, 70-74 City Road, London EC1Y 2BJ Tel:0171-336 7744 Fax:0171-324 9900 **Expertise** Fundraising, Finance, Supporter, Communication. **Prev Posts** General Secretary, Coke Hole Trust 1980-89; Assistant Manager, St Petrocs's Housing 1989-90. **Prof Background** Teaching; Sociology. **Past Committees** Vice Chair, Resettlement of Offenders, Co-ordinating committee; Evangelical Coalition on Drug and Substance Abuse.

HARPER Malcolm Director **UNITED NATIONS ASSOCIATION UK - UNA UK** SOCIAL Type: All

Party Parliamentary Lobby Group on UN Issues. 3 Whitehall Court, London SW1A 2EL Tel:0171-930 2931 Fax:0171-930 5893 **Prev Posts** PA to the Anglican Archbishop of Cape Town 1961-62; Oxfam (in UK and abroad) 1963-81. **Prof Background** MA History and Theology. **Awards/Research** UNESCO Einstein Gold Medal 1995. Articles for magazines on UN/International issues. **Pres Committees** Gov, Int Students House, London; Chair, Int Broadcast Trust; Chair, Cttee for Free & Fair Referendum W Sahara; Exec Cttee, Refugee Cncl; Exec Cttee, Friends of UNESCO; Exec/Finance Cttees Wld Fed UNA. **Past Committees** Oxfam Africa Cttee 1984-90. **Media Experience** Considerable **Addits** Chair, Burford School Govs, Oxon, Charlbury Cricket Club.

HARRIS Anne Gertrude Director **CAMPHILL VILLAGE TRUST** DISABILITY Type: Service provider. College and Rehabilitation Centre, Delrow House, Hilfield Lane, Aldenham, Watford WD2 8DJ Tel:01923-856006 Fax:01923-858035 **Expertise** Provision for people with special needs. **Prev Posts** Current Dir: Camphill Fndtn; C. Milton Keynes Cmty; Wm Morris Cmty; Dir/Chair: C. Devon Cmty; Dir: C. East Anglia. **Prof Background** Trained under founder Karl Konig; founder mbr of first cmtys in England. Worked with Camphill Commmunities since 1946. **Awards/Research** MBE, 1984. **Pres Committees** Mbr: Natwide Counselling Serv, Nat Assoc for Rehab of Offenders, Nat Schiz Fellowship; Assoc Resid Cmtys; Assoc Therapeutic Cmtys. Cttee Housing Assoc for Single People, Islington. **Past Committees** Mbr, Disablement Advisory Cttee. **Addits** Speaker to Rotarians, Womens Institutes, Soroptimists.

HARRIS Toby Director **ASSOCIATION OF COMMUNITY HEALTH COUNCILS FOR ENGLAND AND WALES - ACHCEW** MEDICAL/HEALTH Type: Statutory Consumer Body. 30 Drayton Park, London N5 1PB Tel:0171-609 8405 Fax:0171-700 1152 **Expertise** Health; social policy. **Prev Posts** Deputy Director, Electricity Consumers Council. **Prof Background** BA (Hons), Cambridge Univ. **Awards/Research** Jt Ed: Energy and Social Policy, 1983. Contrib: Rationing in Action, 1993; Whistleblowing in the Health Service, 1994. **Pres Committees** Ch:Assoc of London Gov; Leader,Haringey Council; Mbr, HO Adv Cncl on Race Relats; Cttee of Regions/European Union; Trustee, Help for Health Trust; Jt Ch London Pride Partnership; Ch Local Gov Anti-Poverty Unit **Past Committees** Chair, AMA Social Services Cttee; LBTC - Training for Care; Gov, Nat Inst for Social Work.

HARRISON Hereward Donald McKaig Director of Counselling **CHILDLINE UK** CHILDREN/YOUTH Type: Fundraiser; Service provider; Free phone counselling of children/young people. 2nd Floor, Royal Mail Building, Studd Street, London N1 0QW Tel:0171-239 1000 Fax:0171-239 1001 **Expertise** Directing policy/practice/training for work with children & young people;training/management of volunteers **Prev Posts** Senior Supervisor, Children's Aid Society of Penna, Philadelphia USA 1979-84; Principal Social Worker (Teaching) Guy's Hospital 1984-88. **Prof Background** HND Business Studies; BSc Sociology; Dip. Applied Soc Studies; Psychotherapy for Social Workers, Tavistock Clinic. **Awards/Research** Articles for ChildLine on: Bullying, Female Sexual Abusers, Satanist Abuse, Telephone Counselling (of children and young people). **Pres Committees** Various advisory groups on services for children & young people,Executive Committee of Telephone Helplines,British Asscn of Counselling Advisory Council. **Media Experience** Frequent on behalf of users of ChildLine. **Addits** Assistance and advice to indivs/orgs asking ChildLine for help.

HARRISON Margaret Director **HOME-START UK** CHILDREN/YOUTH Type: Service provider. 2 Salisbury Road, Leicester LE1 7QR Tel:0116-233 9955 Fax:0116-233 0232 **Expertise** Creating, developing and sustaining a voluntary organization from local to international operation. **Prev Posts** Priv Sec to Labour Attache, Spanish Embassy, London 1957-59; British Consulate, New York 1959-61;Volunteer & Vol Work Co-ord, Leicester Children's Dept/SSD 1969-73. **Prof Background** MA; Social Studies Certificate (Distinction), Leicester University 1966-69; Churchill Travelling Fellowship 1973; Council of Europe Award 1981. **Awards/Research** OBE. **Pres Committees** Chair, International Initiative for Children, Youth & Families; Chair, steering committee, Home-Start International. **Past Committees** Assessor, Dip in Policy Studies, Co-operative Coll, Loughborough; Mgmt Cttee, NCB; Brd of Visitors, HMP Leicester. **Addits** Formerly Trustee, Leicester Grammar Sch and Educ & Training Cttee, RELATE.

HARRITY Sara Director **BOOK AID INTERNATIONAL** SOCIAL/OVERSEAS Type: Service provider. 39-41 Coldharbour Lane, London, SE5 9NR Tel:0171-733 3577 Fax:0171-978 8006

HARROWER Neil Scottish Co-ordinator **INTERNATIONAL VOLUNTARY SERVICE - IVS** SOCIAL Type: Service provider. 7 Upper Bow, Edinburgh EH1 2JN Tel:0131-226 6722 Fax:0131-226 6723 **Prev Posts** Scottish Co-ordinator, International Voluntary Service 1986-today. **Prof Background** University of Aberdeen. Currently studying for MBA - Open University Business School. **Addits** Wide experience at local level.

HART Frances Administrator **ALL-PARTY WATERWAYS GROUP** CONSERVATION/ENVIRONMENT 5 Cambridge Drive, Ruislip HA4 9JS Tel:0181-866 5352 **Expertise** Parliamentary and media. **Prev Posts** Press Officer, British Waterways 1974-77; Dir, P Moon & Son 1977-84; Secretary, Inland Waterways Amenity Advisory Council (Exec Man) 1984-90; Chief Executive, Inland Waterways Assoc 1991-96. **Prof Background** University of Exeter European Studies degree. **Awards/Research** Publ inc: Canal Architecture in Britain; Inland Waterways Guide 1979-89; Waterways Users' Companion; Sharpness Centenary; Safety on the Waterways; Angling for the Disabled. **Pres Committees** Administrator, Parliamentary Waterways Gp. **Past Committees** Secretary to Inland Waterways Amenity Advisory Council; Mbr, London Assoc of Regional Press; Man Cttee of Inland Waterways Assoc. **Media Experience** Extensive media experience.

HARTOG Martin Chair **MEDICAL ACTION FOR GLOBAL SECURITY - MEDACT** MEDICINE/HEALTH Type: Campaigning. 601 Holloway Rd, London N19 4DJ Tel:0171-272 2020

Fax:0171-281 5717 **Expertise** General physician with specialist interests in diabetes and endocrinology. **Prev Posts** Reader in Medicine, Bristol University; Hon. Consultant Physician, Southmead Hospital Bristol 1976-96. **Prof Background** BM; BCh; DM; FRCP. **Awards/Research** Research publications on topics related to diabetes, endocrinology and serum lipids (in relation to cardiovascular disease). **Past Committees** Chair, Specialist Advisory Cttee Diabetes & Endocrinology; Royal College of Physicians; President, W. Country Physicians 1992-96. **Addits** President, Bristol Division BMA 1994-95.

HARVEY A.W. Admin & Finance Trustee/Assoc Co Sec **SWIMMING TEACHERS ASSOCIATION/CHARITABLE TRUST** SOCIAL Type: Service provider; Professional association. Anchor House, Birch St, Walsall, West Midlands WS2 8HZ Tel:01922-645097 Fax:01922-720628 **Expertise** Aquatics - specifically teaching swimming & education/training of swimming teachers. **Prev Posts** Association Council member since 1986; Association President 1991-92; Member, Associations Board of Trustees since 1993. **Prof Background** Schoolmaster, Secondary Sector; Psychology Degree, Open University. **Awards/Research** Contrib to Associations publications (newsletter and magazine). **Pres Committees** Teacher Governor; Sandwell Link School's Governor; Sandwell Central Health & Safety at Work Cttee.

HASLAM Geoff Executive Director **COMMUNITY DESIGN SERVICE - CDS** CONSERVATION/ENVIRONMENT Type: Service provider; Community technical aid centre. The Maltings, East Tyndall Street, Splott, Cardiff, S. Glamorgan CF1 5EA Tel:01222-494012 Fax:01222-456824 **Expertise** Participatory design in architecture and urban design. **Prev Posts** Director, Hull Architecture Workshop 1981-84; Environmental Education Officer, Avon County Council 1984-87. **Prof Background** Architect, Manchester Polytechnic and Hull School of Architecture. **Media Experience** Radio and press interviews.

HASLER Frances Director **GREATER LONDON ASSOCIATION OF DISABLED PEOPLE** DISABILITY Type: Service provider; Campaigning. 336 Brixton Road, London SW9 7AA Tel:0171-274 0107 Fax:0171-274 7840 **Expertise** Independent living for disabled people; equal opportunities. **Prev Posts** Welfare Officer, Spinal Injuries Assoc. 1980-85; Organiser, Islington Disablement Assoc. 1985-90. **Prof Background** BA Hons English Lit. Sussex University 1977. **Awards/Research** Contributions to several books on social policy/disability; reviews and articles. **Pres Committees** Project Advisory Gps for Jos Rowntree Fndtn; Mngmt Cttee Apna Ghar Housing Assoc. **Past Committees** Assoc of Carers Mngmt Cttee; Islington Community Health Council. **Media Experience** TV and radio interviews/phone-ins. **Addits** Founding nat persnl assist serv; trng/conslt eql opps/disab.

HASSELL Barry Chief Executive **INDEPENDENT HEALTHCARE ASSOCIATION** MEDICAL/HEALTH Type: Fundraiser; Service provider; Services to ind hosps, nursing homes et al. 22 Little Russell Street, London WC1A 2HT Tel:0171-430 0537 Fax:0171-242 2681 **Expertise** Healthcare, disability, social, development, services and policy. **Prev Posts** Special Projects Exec, Spastics Society 1974-85; Chief Executive, Tadworth Court Trust 1983-92. **Prof Background** London Business School (LEP), Management Consultant. **Pres Committees** Tadworth Court Childrens Hospital Appeal Fund; Union of European Priv Hosps (UEHP). **Past Committees** Project Bombay; Action India. **Media Experience** Frequent.

HAWKINS Nigel JOHN MUIR TRUST CONSERVATION/ENVIRONMENT Type: Fundraiser; Conservation charity, conserving wild places. 13 Wellington Place, Leith, Edinburgh EH6 7JD Tel:0131-554 0114

HAY Jocelyn Chairman **VOICE OF THE LISTENER TRUST** SOCIAL Type: Voluntary consumer/citizen body. 101 King's Drive, Gravesend, Kent DA12 5BQ Tel:01474-352835 **Expertise** Media, broadcasting, PR for voluntary orgs, freelance writer & broadcaster. **Prev Posts** Head of Press & PR, Girl Guide Assoc 1973-78; Principal, Jocelyn Hay Assoc, Public Relations 1978-92; Director, London Media Workshops, Media Training Agency 1978-94. **Prof Background** BA (Hons) Social Science, Open University. **Awards/Research** Author of many articles & features for national & local magazines & newspapers. **Pres Committees** Examiner, CAM Diploma in Public Relations Practice; Chairman, Voice of the Listener & Viewer. **Past Committees** Institute of Public Relations Council & Education Committee; Society of Women Writers & Journalists Council. **Media Experience** Extensive experience in all media over the past 30 years.

HAYNES Gillian Chief Executive **NATIONAL CHILDMINDING ASSOCIATION** CHILD/YOUTH Type: Service provider; Campaigning. 7 Masons Hill, Bromley, Kent BR2 9EY Tel:0181-464 6164 Fax:0181-290 6834 **Expertise** Campaigning; training; organisation development; equal opportunities. **Prev Posts** Staff Development Advisor, GLC 1984-86; Personnel Officer, London Residuary Body 1986-88; Equal Opportunities/Personnel Officer, East Sussex C.C. Education Dept. 1988-93. **Prof Background** BA Hons (Philosophy); Training Officer (LGMB); OU Certificate in Industrial Relations. **Awards/Research** Author of various articles. **Pres Committees** Chair, CACHE (Council for the Awards in Children's Care & Education). **Past Committees** Deputy Leader, Brighton Council; Chair, Personnel/Housing/Police Committee(s); Director, Brighton Buses; School Governor. **Media Experience** Extensive media experience as parliamentary candidate (1992) & in current post.

HAYNES Nigel Director **FAIRBRIDGE** CHILDREN/YOUTH Type: Service provider. 1 Westminster Bridge Road, London SE1 7PL Tel:0171-928 1704 Fax:0171-928 6016 **Prev Posts** HM Forces until 1993. **Prof Background** Aid projects in Far East and Middle East. Worked with young people leading expeditions and skippering sail training vessels. **Awards/Research** CBE.

HAYS Chris D. Chief of Operations **INTERNATIONAL RELIEF FRIENDSHIP FOUNDATION** SOCIAL Type: Fundraiser; Service provider. 164 Empire Court,

Northend Rd, Wembley Park, Middlesex HA9 0AJ Tel:0181-903 5779 Fax:0171-724 2262 **Expertise** Project management in Eastern Europe. **Prev Posts** Project(s) Manager, Senior NGO Balkan Desk 1991-94. **Prof Background** A.A/B.A degree. **Awards/Research** Research & articles on strategic project management on Russian elections & Bulgarian non-profit sector. **Pres Committees** Common Bonds, UK 1995-96; International Cultural Foundation (ICF) 1994-96. **Past Committees** ACENVO. **Media Experience** Experience with press as foreign correspondent for world & foreign news. **Addits** Volunteer for Oxfam.

HAYWOOD Sir Harold Chairman Grants Council/Trustee **CHARITIES AID FOUNDATION - CAF** SOCIAL Type: Service provider; Grant maker. 114-118 Southampton Row, London WC1B 5AA Tel:0171-831 7798 Fax:0171-831 7798 **Prev Posts** General Secretary Educational Interchange Council 1974-78; Director Royal Jubilee & Princes Trust 1978-88. **Prof Background** College of Education 1948; FRSA. Mbr: Y Care Exec; Civil Service Club; Bell Educational Trust, Camb. Hon Life Mbr: Anglo-Austrian Soc; Assoc of Charitable Fndtns.Patron: CSV; Youth Clubs UK. **Awards/Research** KCVO; OBE. **Pres Committees** Ed Brd, Directory of Grant-Making Trusts; Chair; Action for Age. Vice-Pres: Int Science Forum; YMCA's Nat Cncl.

HAYZELDEN K.J. Chief Executive **NATIONAL FENCING TRAINING AUTHORITY** TRAINING Type: Industry training organisation. IMEX Business Park, Shobnall Rd, Burton on Trent, Staffordshire DE14 2AU Tel:01283-512611 Fax:01283-515049 **Expertise** Strategic planning for all aspects of the provision of training & advisory serv to the fencing industry. **Prev Posts** Training Off, Heavy Engineering 1962-66; Group Training Manager, Construction Industry 1966-91. **Prof Background** BA (Hons) Spanish; FIPD. **Pres Committees** BSI Fencing Standards Revision (General Fencing), Vehicle Safety Fencing Sector Scheme Advisory Committee. **Past Committees** CITB Civil Engineering Committee.

HEAD Christopher Development Director **CANCER AND LEUKAEMIA IN CHILDHOOD - CLIC-UK** MEDICAL/HEALTH Type: Fundraiser; Service provider; Grant maker. 12-13 King Square, Bristol BS2 8JH Tel:0117-924 8844 Fax:0117-924 4505 **Expertise** Fundraising; marketing; business development; strategic planning; personnel. **Prof Background** MA (Cantab); MICFM.

HEALY B.J.P. Chief Executive **ST ANDREW'S AMBULANCE ASSOCIATION** MEDICAL/HEALTH Type: Fundraiser; Service provider; Campaigning; Professional association. St Andrew's House, 48 Milton St, Glasgow G4 0HR Tel:0141-332 4031 Fax:0141-332 6582

HEARLE Marie Head of Campaigns **OXFAM IN SCOTLAND** SOCIAL Type: Campaigning and supporter development. Floor 5, Fleming House, 134 Renfrew Street, Glasgow G3 6ST Tel:0141-331 2724 Fax:0141-331 2264 **Expertise** General management; Fundraising; Charity retailing; Working with Volunteers. **Prev Posts** Area Organiser, Oxfam Shops 1984-1986; Director, Oxfam in Scotland 1986-1992; Head of Campaigns, Oxfam in Scotland 1992-today. **Awards/Research** Papers on In-house Training; Volunteer Development; Staff Development. **Pres Committees** Chair, International Development Education Association of Scotland; Chair, Scottish Development Education Centre. **Media Experience** Press, radio and video. **Addits** Overseas field trips to Bangladesh, El Salvador and Nicaragua.

HEARN Donald P. Secretary **ROYAL HORTICULTURAL SOCIETY** SOCIAL Type: Service provider. Learned Society. 80 Vincent Square, London SW1P 2PE Tel:0171-834 4333 Fax:0171-630 6060 **Expertise** Finance; legal and representative. **Prev Posts** Finance Director since 1986. **Prof Background** FCA; MA Cambridge University. **Pres Committees** Chairman, Audit Cttee, Imperial College; Mbr, F&GP Cttee, Royal PG Med Sch;Gen Commissioner of Taxes. **Media Experience** Some experience.

HEATH Michael Stuart Director General **ENGINEERING COUNCIL** SOCIAL Type: Service provider. 6th Floor, 10 Maltravers Street, London WC2R 3ER Tel:0171-240 7891 Fax:0171-240 1528 **Expertise** Electrical Engineering and senior management. **Prev Posts** Commander Maintenance, British Army of the Rhine 1989-91; Director General of Equipment Support (Army) 1991-93. **Prof Background** Army officer and Chartered Engineer. **Awards/Research** CB; CBE. **Pres Committees** General Committee of Lloyds' Register. **Past Committees** Learmont Inquiry into Prison Security (1994).

HEDLEY Gill Director **CONTEMPORARY ART SOCIETY** ARTS Type: Fundraiser; Service provider; Arts & culture. 20 John Islip St, London SW1P 4LL Tel:0171-821 5323 Fax:0171-834 0228 **Expertise** Contemporary British art; exhibition curator. **Prev Posts** Curator, Southampton City Art Gallery; Exhibition Curator, British Council 1988-93. Currently also Director, Contemporary Arts Society Projects Ltd. **Prof Background** BA Hons, Courtauld Institute of Art; Museums Association Diploma; FRSA. **Awards/Research** Publications on English landscape painting, gardening and theory. Exhibitions: Francis Bacon, Moscow 1988; Richard Hamilton, Venice Biennale 1993. **Pres Committees** AXIS National Campaign for the Arts; National Touring Exhibitions Advisory Board. **Past Committees** Chair, Visual Arts Advisory Panel, Southern Arts; History of Art and Design, Advisory Bd, CNAA. **Media Experience** Reviews in art press; local TV and national radio.

HEHIR Lesley Secretary **SOCIETY FOR THE INTERPRETATION OF BRITAIN'S HERITAGE - INTERPRET BRITAIN** Type: Professional Association. 12 The Grove, Benton, Newcastle-upon-Tyne NE12 9PE Tel:0191-266 5804 **Expertise** Environmental interpretation. **Prev Posts** Education Officer, Newcastle Architecture Workshop Ltd 1984-90; Team Leader, Countryside North Tyneside 1990-91; Prof Asst Interpretation Durham County Cncl, 1991 to present. **Prof Background** Planner; Teacher. **Awards/Research** Articles in SIBH Journal; Joint Author: Our Built Environment, Design Technology Interactions, Publ by Stanley Thornes.

HEMMINGS Gwynneth Director **SCHIZOPHRENIA ASSOCIATION OF GREAT BRITAIN** MEDICAL/HEALTH Type: Service provider; Research Information. Bryn Hyfryd, The Crescent, Bangor, Gwynedd LL57 2AG Tel:01248-354048 Fax:01248-354048 **Prof Background** Science degree **Awards/Research** Auth: Inside Schizophrenia; Ed: Biological Aspects of Schizophrenia and Addiction; Biochemistry of Schizophrenia & Addiction; The Biological Basis for Schizophrenia.

HENDERSON Leslie Coultas Chief Executive **DISABLED CHILDRENS FOUNDATION** CHILDREN/YOUTH Type: Fundraiser; Service provider; Grant maker. 21/23 Royal Cambers, 110 Station Parade, Harrogate, North Yorkshire HG1 1EP Tel:01423-509863 Fax:01423-569020 **Expertise** Assisting disabled people; especially children's disability. **Prev Posts** Arthritis Care, 1967-86; Lady Hoare Trust 1986-91. **Prof Background** Commercial, the food trade in particular. Knowledge of disability acquired over the years as a volunteer in various disabled charities. Vis MS local Disabled Clubs etc: EX RT **Pres Committees** Director of the trading companies of DCF; Director of Housing Association. **Past Committees** Various committees of Arthritis Care. **Media Experience** Have appeared on radio talks ref. arthritis. TV on Social Programme.

HENDRY Jim Chief Executive **BRITISH CYCLING FEDERATION - BCF** SOCIAL Type: Service provider. National Cycling Centre, Stuart Street, Manchester M11 4DQ Tel:0161-230 2301 Fax:0161-231 0591 **Prev Posts** Housing Manager, 1975-79; Director of Racing, BCF 1979-87. **Prof Background** Local authority housing posts; former professional cyclist and national cycling coach. **Awards/Research** Awds: David Saunders Memorial 1980. Auth: Guide to Fitness and Training, 1986; BCF Training Manual, 1987; Take Up Cycle Racing, 1989. **Pres Committees** Olympic Solidarity (UCI) Didactic Commission. **Media Experience** Interviewee for most media.

HEPWORTH G. Anthony Chief Executive **LISTENING LIBRARY, THE** DISABILITY Type: Fundraiser; Service provider. 12 Lant Street, London SE1 1QH Tel:0171-407 9417 Fax:0171-403 1377 **Prev Posts** Industry & Commerce 1952-86; Fundraiser, Inst of Obstetrics & Gynaecology 1987-89; Fundraising Director then Exec Director, NLL 1989-today.

HERBERT Katharine Chief Executive **ENGLISH TOURING OPERA** ARTS Type: Fundraiser; Service provider, Opera Company. W121 Westminster Business Square, Durham Street, London SE11 5JH Tel:0171-820 1131 Fax:0171-735 7008 **Expertise** General Administration; Planning and Programming. **Prev Posts** English National Ballet 1982-92, Company Manager 1985-89; Assist/General Administrator, 1989-91. **Prof Background** BA (Hons), Music & History of Art; Mbr of the Institute of Directors. **Pres Committees** Siobhan Davies Dance Company, Board Member.

HERINGTON Michael Director **GREATER LONDON FUND FOR THE BLIND** DISABILITY Type: Fundraiser; Service provider; Grant maker. 12 Whitehorse Mews, 37 Westminster Bridge Rd, London SE1 7QD Tel:0171-620 2066 Fax:0171-620 2016 **Pres Committees** Trustee & Treasurer, Young Musicians Symphony Orchestra; Governor, Ravenscourt Park Preparatory School.

HERMAN Marc National Director **UNION OF MACCABI ASSOCIATIONS IN GREAT BRITAIN AND NORTHERN IRELAND** RELIGIOUS Type: Fundraiser; Service provider. Gildesgame House, 73a Compayne Gardens, London NW6 3RS Tel:0171-328 0382 Fax:0171-328 9118 **Expertise** Youth Work, Community Action, Drugs and Young People, Training, Youth Leadership, Management Skills. **Prev Posts** National Education Officer, Maccabi Union GB, 1993-1995. **Prof Background** Qualified Youth and Community Worker; Certificate in Training, Goldsmiths College. **Pres Committees** Mngmt Cttee of Kadimah Victoria Youth Club; Kenton Maccabi; LE'AN Jewish Youth Theatre Company. Deputy at The Board of Deputies of British Jews. **Media Experience** Many radio interviews, press releases.

HESLOP Michael Director **SHELTERED HOUSING AND WORKSHOPS PROJECT - SHAW** DISABILITY Type: Service provider. Kielder Avenue, Beacon Lane, Cramlington, Northumberland NE23 8JT Tel:01670-733966 Fax:01670-590115 **Expertise** Finance, administration, public relations, marketing and fundraising. **Prev Posts** Associate Partner, David Sheppard Management Consultants 1986-91. **Prof Background** Fellow, ICAEW. **Pres Committees** Chairman, Northumbrian Educational Trust Ltd. **Media Experience** Radio interviews; regular contrib to press.

HESSLEGRAVE Caroline Director **CHILDLINK ADOPTION SOCIETY** CHILDREN/YOUTH Type: Service provider; Approved Voluntary Adoption Agency. 10 Lion Yard, Tremadoc Rd, London SW4 7NQ Tel:0171-498 1933 Fax:0171-498 1791 **Expertise** Adoption, domestic, inter-country. **Prev Posts** London Boro of Lambeth, Social Worker 1982-85; Westminster: Adoption & Fostering 1985-86; Team Leader (Fostering) 1986-88; Childlink, Inter-Country Adoption Co-ordinator 1991-92. **Prof Background** MA (Honours) Degree (Politics); CQSW (Certificate on Qualification in Social Work). **Pres Committees** Overseas Adoption Helpline Steering Board; British Advisory Board on Inter-Country Adoption. **Media Experience** Radio/TV appearances on the subject of Inter-Country Adoption.

HEWITT Rex Chief Executive **TURNING POINT** SOCIAL Type: Fundraiser; Service provider. 1456 New Loom House, 101 Backchurch Lane, London E1 1LU Tel:0171-702 2300 Fax:0171-702 1456 **Expertise** Community Development. **Prev Posts** Development Officer, Community Projects Foundation 1979-84; Director, Mencap, Wales 1984-89; Assistant Director of Social Services, S. Glamorgan County Council 1989-96. **Prof Background** MA Policy Studies; Trained as Social Worker & Teacher of people with learning disabilities. **Pres Committees** Cartrefi Cymrii. **Past Committees** Secretary of State for Wales; All Wales Advisory Panel for the Development of Services for People with Learning Disabilities. **Media Experience** Experience with TV, radio and press.

HICKS Barbara Joint National Organiser **NATIONAL WOMEN'S REGISTER** WOMEN Type: Service provider. 3a Vulcan House, Vulcan Rd North, Norwich, Norfolk NR6 6AQ Tel:01603-406 767 Fax:01603-407 003 **Expertise** Management of office, contact with members. **Prev Posts** Regional Organiser & National Grp Member, 1994-96; Volunteer Fundraiser, Barnardo's, 1989-96. **Prof Background** Secretary; Cert in Personnel Management. **Awards/Research** Awarded: Silver Volunteer Award (5 yrs).

HIGGINS Dr Andrew James Director **ANIMAL HEALTH TRUST** ANIMAL/WILDLIFE Type: Fundraiser; Service provider; Grant maker; Independent veterinary institute. PO Box 5, Newmarket, Suffolk CB8 8JH Tel:01638-661111 Fax:01638-665789 **Expertise** Veterinary science and medicine. **Prev Posts** Comssnd RAVC 1973; Vet Officer, Oman, 1975-76; Vet Adv, Middle East/N Africa, Wellcome Foundation 1977-82; Consult, Food and Agric Org 1981-. **Prof Background** BVetMed 1973, PhD 1985 London Univ; MSc, Edinburgh Univ 1977. Mbr Royal Coll of Vet Surgeons 1993;CBiol.FIBiol 1993;Gov St Edmunds Hosp,Bury St Edmunds;Trustee,Pet Plan Charitable Trust. **Awards/Research** Lond Univ Laurel 1971;Ciba-Geigy Prize for Res in Animal Health 1985;Equine Vet Jnl Open Awd 1986;Centrl Vet Soc Centenary Prize 1987;B Vet Jnl G. Fleming Prize 1987. Auth, bks/jnls. **Pres Committees** Cncl Soc for Prot of Animals Abroad; Ethics Cttee, Zoological Soc London; Hon Vet Adviser to Jockey Club; Hon Sci Adviser, Internat Equestrian Fed (FEI). **Media Experience** Ed,Brit Vet Jnl 1991-;Adv Brd,Equine Vet Jnl 1985-;pubs in scientific journals. Ed The Equine Manual 1995.

HIGGS John Executive Director (UK) **ACROSS TRUST** SOCIAL Type: Service provider. Bridge House, 70-72 Bridge Rd, East Molesey, Surrey KT8 9HF Tel:0181-783 1355 Fax:0181-783 1622 **Expertise** Non-Profit Marketing, Non-Profit Management. **Prof Background** MA Kingston University; BA (Hons) South Bank University. **Awards/Research** Thesis on Non-Profit Marketing, pub date late 1995.

HILBORNE Stephanie Principal Officer **WILDLIFE AND COUNTRYSIDE LINK** ANIMAL/WILDLIFE Type: Liaison Service. 246 Lavender Hill, London SW11 1LJ Tel:0171-924 2355 Fax:0171-223 4235 **Prof Background** BSc. Biology Hons First Class Bristol University; MSc Conservation, UCL.

HILL Julie Director **GREEN ALLIANCE** CONSERVATION/ENVIRONMENT Type: Non-profitmaking group for environmental policy. 49 Wellington Street, London WC2E 7BN Tel:0171-836 0341 Fax:0171-240 9205 **Expertise** Biotechnology and environmental institutions. **Prev Posts** Deloitte Haskins Sells 1982-83; Wld Food Assembly 1984-85; Green Alliance: Administrator 1985-87; Parliamentary Officer 1987-91; Dir of Policy 1991-92. **Prof Background** Degrees: English and Philosophy, Leeds Univ; Western European Politics, LSE. Ecology and Conservation Certificate, London Univ. **Awards/Research** Co-Auth: Ethics Environment and the Company, 1990; Towards Good Environmental Practice - A Book of Case Studies, 1992. **Pres Committees** HM Gov Advisory Cttee on Release to the Environment (of genetically modified organisms); Advisory Gp, Pesticides Trust; Core Group, Genetics Forum; Advisory Cttee, Environmental Law Foundation. **Media Experience** Radio, TV and press interviews.

HILL Mr R. W. President **BRITISH CARTOGRAPHIC SOCIETY** Type: Service provider; Learned Society. c/o Royal Geographical Society, 1 Kensington Gore, London SW7 2AR Tel:01703-871519 Fax:01703-781519 **Expertise** Commercial Cartography. **Prev Posts** Council Member until 1994; Vice President, BCS 1994-96. **Prof Background** Joint Managing Director of Lovell Johns Ltd.; Privately owned cartographic service company; Diploma in Cartography 1972, Oxford Polytechnic. **Pres Committees** Board of Lovell Johns Ltd. (Company). **Past Committees** BCS Council.

HINCHLIFFE-WOOD Mieke Director **HERTFORDSHIRE & MIDDLESEX WILDLIFE TRUST** ANIMAL/WILDLIFE Type: Fundraiser; Service provider; Wildlife conservation. Grebe House, St Michaels Street, St Albans, Herts AL3 4SN Tel:01727-858901 Fax:01727-854542 **Expertise** Management & organisational development, marketing, volunteer development. **Prev Posts** Co-ordinator, Bedfordshire Against Nuclear Dumping 1984-88; Director, National Library Campaign 1988-90; Development Officer, Council for the Protection of Rural England 1990-92. **Prof Background** Educated in Holland; social work qualification; psychology credits. **Awards/Research** Various articles published in library journals. **Past Committees** Britain Opposed to Nuclear Dumping (B.O.N.D). **Media Experience** Comprehensive national and international media experience.

HINES Vince National Director **BLACK EUROPEAN COMMUNITY DEVELOPMENT FEDERATION - BECDF** SOCIAL Type: Fundraiser; Service provider; Nat. Rep. Umbrella Organisation est. 1975. 150 Townmead Road, London SW6 2RA Tel:0171-384 2876 Fax:0171-371 8105 **Expertise** Organisation development; consultancy; training; community development; advocacy and the media. **Prof Background** MA; DSc (Soc). **Awards/Research** Publ: 3 bks on race relations, youth and community development. Ed: Self-Help News; The Advocate Magazine. Many articles on policy & practice of community development in inner cities. **Pres Committees** Community Education & Training Services; Marcus Garvey College; Management, Administrative & Support Services. **Past Committees** Mngmt Ctte, LDA Development Fund 1986-87; Mngmt Ctte, London Voluntary Servs Cncl; Chair, NFSHO 1975-1985; Chair, CAND 1990-1992. **Media Experience** Trained journalist/broadcaster. **Addits** BECDF has incorporated NFSHO - Nat Fed of Self-Help Orgs.

HINKES The Revd. Sidney Chairman **ANGLICAN PACIFIST FELLOWSHIP - APF** RELIGIOUS Type: Religious and educational. 11 Weaver'S End, Hanslope, Milton Keynes, Buckinghamshire MK19 7PA Tel:01666-825249 **Expertise** Theology of peace; Christian Peace Organisations. **Prev Posts** Chairman, Christian CND 1964-66; Secretary, APF 1975-93; Missioner, APF New

Zealand 1991. **Prof Background** BA History, Ethics, Theology 1950; BD Christian Ethics 1970. **Awards/Research** Budapest Seminars on Theology of Peace 1984/87 (Steering Committee); Publ: Let's Love Russia; The Teaching of Jesus. **Pres Committees** Week of Prayer for World Peace. **Past Committees** Oxfordshire Council for Community Relations; Oxford Peace Council; Oxford Round Table of Religions. **Media Experience** Radio interviews; press: articles and sermons.

HIRST Jenny Trustee **INSULIN DEPENDENT DIABETES TRUST** MEDICAL/HEALTH Type: Service provider; Information & education. PO Box 294, Northampton NN3 2BN Tel:01604-721325 Fax:01604-721325 **Expertise** Advocacy, representation, self-help & support for people with diabetes and their families. **Prev Posts** Trustee, British Diabetic Association 1985-93; Self-employed Optometrist in Industry 1985-96; Vice Chair, British Diabetic Association 1992-93. **Prof Background** Educated at Wakefield High School for Girls; Bradford University; Fellow, College of Optometrists. **Awards/Research** Editor of The Insulin Dependent Diabetes Trust Quarterly Newsletter; Various Articles in The British Diabetes Association Journal, Balance. **Pres Committees** Trustee, Insulin Dependent Diabetes Trust. **Past Committees** Board of Trustees, Brit Diabetic Assoc; Mbr, Internat Team supported by Rockefeller Foundation (produced the Bellagio Report 1996). **Media Experience** Radio & TV experience (related to patients & carers who live with diabetes). **Addits** Co-founder of Tadpole for Children with Diabetes.

HITHERSAY Medora Ann Director **ST CHRISTOPHERS FELLOWSHIP** CHILDREN/YOUTH Type: Fundraiser; Service provider. 217 Kingston Rd, Wimbledon, London SW19 3NL Tel:0181-543 3619 Fax:0181-544 1633 **Expertise** Voluntary sector; child care; housing for homeless young people; management education. **Prev Posts** Director of Regions, Spastics Society 1989; Project Director, Spastics Society 1989-91. Currently Tutor, Open University Voluntary Sector Management Programme. **Prof Background** MBA Ashridge 1989. **Pres Committees** NCVCCO Trustee Board; Founder Trustee, Children's Trust. **Past Committees** Chair, Committee Distributing Department Health Training Grants to Voluntary Sector. **Media Experience** Little. **Addits** Tutor, Open University Voluntary Sector Management Programme.

HOBBS Michael Director **OUTWARD BOUND TRUST** CHILDREN/YOUTH Type: Service provider. PO Box 1219, Windsor, Berks SL4 1XR Tel:01753-730060 Fax:01753-810666 .

HODGKIN Rachel Principal Policy Officer **NATIONAL CHILDREN'S BUREAU - NCB** CHILDREN/YOUTH Type: Research/Practice Development 8 Wakley Street, London EC1V 7QE Tel:0171-843 6013 Fax:0171-278 9512 **Expertise** Policy development for children. **Prev Posts** Law Centre worker, Camden Law Centre 1974-79; Advice/Policy Dev. Children's Legal Centre 1979-92. Currently: Clerk to the All Party Parliamentary Group for Children. **Prof Background** BA Eng Literature, Cambridge University. **Pres Committees** Exec. Cttee, UNICEF; Management Council: Children's Rights Development Unit; Assoc to Protect All Children (APPROACH). **Past Committees** Management Cttee, Rainer Foundation.

HODGKINS Chris Director **JAZZ SERVICES** ARTS/CULTURAL Type: Service provider; Campaigning. 5th Floor Africa House, 64-78 Kingsway, London WC2B 6BD Tel:0171-405 0737 Fax:0171-405 0828 **Prev Posts** Prof Musician 1971-83; Dir, Welsh Jazz Soc 1978-80; Dir, Welsh Jazz Festival 1974-81; Mng Dir, Jazz Services, The Nat Org for Jazz in UK 1985-. **Prof Background** Higher Nat Dipl in Business & Finance 1985; MBA London 1990; Dipl Mktg, Ch Inst Mktng 1991. **Pres Committees** Bd of Dirs, Welsh Jazz Soc 1978-; Nat Mus Cncl of GB 1978-, Hon Treas, 1986-;Mbr, Nat Jazz Fndn Archive, Sec 1988-; Assoc Brit Jazz Musicians, Sec 1988-.

HOLLAND Raymond Reginald General Secretary **BRITISH LIMBLESS EX SERVICEMEN'S ASSOCIATION - BLESMA** DISABILITY Type: Service provider. Frankland Moore House, 185-187 High Road, Chadwell Heath, Romford, Essex RM6 6NA Tel:0181-590 1124 Fax:0181-599 2932 **Expertise** Administration and general management. **Prev Posts** Military Career, retired early as Lt Col; Commanding Army Stores Depot 1980-83; BLESMA: Deputy General Secretary 1983-89. **Prof Background** Command and Logistics Course; Senior Management Course. **Awards/Research** Editor, BLESMAG; author of numerous articles in charitable magazines. Awds: BEM 1964; MBE 1974; OBE 1995. **Pres Committees** Ch,Essex War Pensions Cttee;Mbr:Govmt Cent Adv Cttee/War Pensions;Scot Adv Cttee/Prosthetics;Cncl/Brit Serv & Ex Serv Orgs;MOD Med Discharge & After Care Cttee;Mbr,Jt Cttee/Mobility for Disabled People. **Past Committees** Chair, Herts & Essex Borders Branch BIM; Mbr, Welsh Common Services Agency Adv Gp; Nat Adv Gp on Casework Co-operation. **Media Experience** TV and video appearances.

HOLLANDS Clive Secretary **COMMITTEE FOR THE REFORM OF ANIMAL EXPERIMENTATION - CRAE** ANIMAL/WILDLIFE Type: Lobbying group. 10 Queensferry Street, Edinburgh EH2 4PG Tel:0131-225 6039 Fax:0131-220 6377 **Expertise** Animal Welfare. **Prev Posts** Royal Navy 1946-53; Marine Personnel Officer, Caltex Trading and Transport 1953-66; Asst Sec 1966-70, Dir 1970-88, Scot Soc for Prevent of Vivisect. Co Sec, St Andrew Anml Fund 1970-94. **Prof Background** St Clement Dane's School, London; St Mary's College, Liverpool. **Awards/Research** OBE. Auth: Compassion is the Bugler - the Struggle for Animal Rights, 1980; contrib/author many titles on animal welfare, eg. In Defence of Animals, 1985. **Pres Committees** Farm Anml Welfare Cncl; Hon Assoc, Brit Vet Assoc; Trustee, Farm Anml Care Trust; Jane Goodall Inst. **Past Committees** Chair, Animal Welfare Year 1976-77; Vice-President, RSPCA 1980-82; Secretary, GECCAP 1978-9. **Media Experience** On a regular basis 1973-94. **Addits** Patron, Zoo Check, Born Free Foundation, Felix Cat Rescue.

HOLLOWAY Christine Director **LONDON VOLUNTARY SERVICE COUNCIL** SOCIAL Type: Service provider, CVS. 356 Holloway Rd, London N7 6PA Tel:0171-700 8107 Fax:0171-700 8108 **Expertise** Social policy, organisational & management development. **Prev Posts** Fellow, Strategic & Analytical Studies, Off for Public Mngmt 1991-93; Dir, Field Support 1993-95 & Dir, Policy & Public Affairs 1995-96: Nat Assoc of Citizens Advice Bureau. **Prof Background** Degree; MA Organisational Behaviour. **Awards/Research** Getting Organised, NCVO 1985. **Pres Committees** Director, Child Poverty Action Group (Charity); Chair, Pan-London Community Regeneration Consortium. **Past Committees** Board of CHAR (Campaign For Single Homeless People); Board of SHAC (London Housing Aid Centre).

HOLMES Chris Director **NATIONAL CAMPAIGN FOR HOMELESS PEOPLE - SHELTER** SOCIAL Type: Fundraiser; Service provider; Campaigning. 88 Old St, London EC1V 9HU Tel:0171-505 2124 Fax:0171-505 2169 **Prev Posts** Director, CHAR 1982-87; Consultant, Priority Estates Project 1988-90; Housing Director, LB Camden 1990-95. **Prof Background** MA Economics, Clare College, Cambridge; Diploma in Industrial Administration, Bradford University. **Past Committees** Chair: National Young Homelessness Group 1983-85; Campaign for Bedsit Rights 1982-86. **Media Experience** Substantial experience in radio, TV & press interviews.

HONEYBALL Mary General Secretary **ASSOCIATION OF CHIEF OFFICERS OF PROBATION** SOCIAL Type: Membership organisation. 212 Whitechapel Rd London E1 1BJ Tel:0171-377 9141 Fax:0171-375 2100 **Expertise** Criminal juctice; social policy; public relations. **Prev Posts** General Sec, Newham Voluntary Agencies Council 1986-90; Service Manager, The Spastics Society 1990-91; Chief Executive, Gingerbread 1991-94. **Prof Background** MA Modern History, Somerville College, Oxford University 1972-75. **Pres Committees** Governor London Schools:Deptford Green School, SE14. **Past Committees** Councillor, LB Barnet Council 1978-86; Exec. Cttee, London Voluntary Service Council 1988-90; Chair, Docklands Forum 1987-89. **Media Experience** Freq participant Radio/TV eg.Today, You and Yours, Woman's Hour, World Tonight.

HOODLESS Elisabeth A. Executive Director **COMMUNITY SERVICE VOLUNTEERS - CSV** SOCIAL Type: Volunteer and training agency. 237 Pentonville Road, London N1 9NJ Tel:0171-278-6601 Fax:0171-833 0149 **Expertise** Volunteer management. **Prev Posts** CSV: Asst Director 1963-72; Deputy Director 1972-75. **Prof Background** Social Work; BA Durham University 1962; Dip Applied Soc Studies, LSE 1963; Qualified Social Worker. Volunteer in Israel & Kent. **Awards/Research** CBE 1992; Fellowships: Churchill 1966; Commonwealth Youth 1974; Global Family Award 1990, Int Assoc of Vol Effort. Auth: Encouraging Citizenship 1991; Education for Citizenship, 1992. **Pres Committees** Chair, Hackney Youth Court (JP Inner London 1969); Governor: Sevenoaks Schl; Elizabeth Garratt Anderson Schl; President, Volunteurope; Regional Chair (Europe) Assoc of Volunteer Administration. **Past Committees** Dep Chair, Speaker's Commission on Citizenship, 1988-90. **Media Experience** TV/Radio: Any Questions, Question Time, News at One, PM etc; press comment. **Addits** Co-launch:VISTA-Vols in Serv To America;Jamaica Nat Serv Prog.

HOOPER Cheryl Associate Director **ACTION FOR SICK CHILDREN** CHILDREN/YOUTH Type: Campaigning. Argyle House, 29-31 Euston Road, London NW1 2SD Tel:0171-833 2041 Fax:0171-837 2110

HORNSBY Timothy Chief Executive **NATIONAL LOTTERY CHARITIES BOARD** SOCIAL Type: Grant maker. St Vincent House, 30 Orange Street, London WC2H 7HH Tel:0171-747 5201 Fax:0171-747 5213 **Expertise** Management. **Prev Posts** Director General, Nature Conservancy Council 1988-91; Chief Executive, Royal Borough of Kingston upon Thames 1991-95. **Prof Background** Oxford University, MA, 1st Class Hons, Modern History. FRSA. **Awards/Research** Various articles on management & change. **Past Committees** Various. **Media Experience** Wide media experience.

HORNSBY Valerie Director/Hon. Secretary **ROMANIAN AID FUND** SOCIAL Type: Fundraiser. 1 Catherine Court, Page Hill, Buckingham MK18 1OG Tel:01280-814361 Fax:01280-816334 **Expertise** Experienced co-ordinator for support sent to evangelical Christian ministries in Romania. **Prof Background** BSc (Hons); PGCE. **Awards/Research** Romanian Aid Fund; Guides for Christians travelling to Romania.

HORROCKS, Christiana Director **VOICE** DISABILITY Type: Advice and Information Provider; Campaigning. PO Box 238, Derby DE1 9JN Tel:01332-519872 Fax:01332-521392.

HORSNELL Graham J. Chief Executive **BARNABAS TRUST** CHILDREN/YOUTH Type: Fundraiser; Service provider. Carroty Wood, Higham Lane, Tonbridge, Kent TN11 9QX Tel:01732-354690 Fax:01732-360429 **Expertise** Health ind -Civil Serv, NHS, Priv health care sect; admin & gen mngmt;church pastoral wk; o'seas mission. **Prev Posts** Snr Civil Serv, Dept Health -1986; Asst Reg Gen Mnger/Dir Com Servs, SE Thames Reg HA 1986-90; Contracts Mnger/Dir Mngmt Servs, Saudi Medicare 1990-93. **Prof Background** Mbr, Inst Health Services Servs Mngmt. Training (O'seas) in contracts mngmt.Contract/Staff recruit experience in Far/Middle East & India. Church mission wk in E Europe & Africa. **Pres Committees** Eldership Team of Battle Baptist Church; Dir: Christian Solidarity Int; No Frontiers (Int Literature Outreach).

HORWICH Alan Dean/Professor of Radiotherapy **CANCER RESEARCH, INSTITUTE OF** MEDICAL/HEALTH Type: Medical Research. 15 Cotswold Rd, Sutton, Surrey SM2 5NG Tel:0181-642 6011 Fax:0181-643 8809 **Expertise** Radiotherapy and Oncology. **Prev Posts** Registrar, Royal Marsden Hospital 1979-81; Institute of Cancer Research Lecturer 1981-83, Senior Lecturer 1984-6; MRC Senior Grade Scientist, MRC Radiobiology Unit 1983-4. **Prof Background** MBBS 1971; MRCP 1974; PhD 1981; FRCR 1981. **Awards/Research** Ed: The Management of Testicular Cancer (1991); Combined Chemotherapy and Radiotherapy in Clinical Oncology (1992). **Pres Committees** Cancer Research Campaign Scientific Cttee. **Past Committees** BIR Council; Chair, MRC Testicular Working Party.

HORWITE Brian Chairman **NEWSTRAID BENEVOLENT SOCIETY** SOCIAL Type: Fundraiser; Service provider; Trade charity. PO Box 306, Great Dunmow, Essex CM6 1HY Tel:01371-874198 Fax:01371-873816 **Expertise** Senior management. **Prev Posts** The Sun: Circulation Manager, 1972-80; Circulation Director, 1981-90. General Manager, News International Newspapers Ltd 1990-94. **Pres Committees** Executive Committee, Newstraid Benevolent Society. **Media Experience** Extensive media experience.

HOWARD F. Trustee **VEGFAM - FEEDS THE HUNGRY WITHOUT EXPLOITING THE ANIMALS** SOCIAL Type: Fundraiser; Grant maker. The Sanctuary, Nr Lydford, Okehampton, Devon EX20 4AL Tel:01822-820203 Fax:01822-820203 **Expertise** Feeding people with plant foods without exploiting animals and without damaging the environment. **Prev Posts** Chartered Engineer, Anglian Water Authority 1976-89; Chartered Engineer, National Rivers Auhority 1989-93. **Prof Background** Civil Engineer, Water Resources & Supply. **Pres Committees** Find Your Feet (Leaf for Life, London SE); Concern Universal (Chatham Kent). **Media Experience** Documentary TV Programme.

HOWARD Roger Director **STANDING CONFERENCE ON DRUG ABUSE - SCODA** SOCIAL Type: National co-ordinating and representative body. Waterbridge House, 32-36 Loman St, London SE1 0EE Tel:0171-928 9500 Fax:0171-928 3343.

HOWARTH David Chief Executive **BRITISH WHEELCHAIR SPORTS FOUNDATION** Type: Fundraiser; Service provider; Grant maker. Guttmann Road, Stoke Mandeville, Bucks, HP21 9PP Tel:01296-84848 Fax:01296-24171 **Expertise** Sport and leisure charity management. **Prev Posts** General Manager, Celtworld, Ireland 1991-93; Chief Executive, Endeavour, Derbyshire 1993-96. **Prof Background** Graduate of PE & English, London University; Postgraduate (MSc) Recreation Management, Loughborough University. **Past Committees** Irish Tourism Committee; Young People Now. **Media Experience** Experience in radio, TV, video and press.

HOWARTH Valerie Chief Executive **CHILDLINE** CHILDREN/YOUTH Type: Fundraiser; Service provider. 2nd Floor, Royal Mail Building, Studd Street, London N1 0QW Tel:0171-239 1000 Fax:0171-239 1001 **Expertise** Organizational management; child care. **Prev Posts** Assistant DSS, Lambeth 1969-82; Dir of Soc Servs, Brent 1982-86. **Prof Background** Social Work; Business Training. **Awards/Research** Child care; homelessness. **Pres Committees** Independent Cttee for the Supervision of Telephone Standards ICSTIS; John Grooms for Disabled People; European Forum for Child Welfare; Lucy Faithfull Foundation; Sieff Foundation. **Past Committees** Numerous. **Media Experience** Frequent.

HOWE Jackie Office Co-ordinator and Hon Treasurer **NATIONAL ASSOCIATION FOR PREMENSTRUAL SYNDROME - NAPS** MEDICAL/HEALTH Type: Support for sufferers and families. PO Box 72, Sevenoaks, Kent TN13 1XQ Tel:01732-459378 **Expertise** Co-ordinating national office and overseeing finance/fundraising; training of self-help group leaders. **Prev Posts** Teaching. **Prof Background** BA History, University of Sussex; MA International Relations, University of Sussex. **Awards/Research** Jt Publ: Young Person: Guide to Premenstrual Syndrome. **Pres Committees** NAPS Executive Committee; NAPS Scientific Committee and Education Committee. **Media Experience** Kilroy, This Morning; Radio; The Guardian 1993; various women's magazines.

HOWETT Kevin National Officer **MOUNTAINEERING COUNCIL OF SCOTLAND** CONSERVATION/ENVIRONMENT Type: Service provider; Grant maker; Campaigning; National Body. 4a St Catherine's Road, Perth PH1 5SE Tel:01738-638227 Fax:01738-442095 **Prof Background** Degree in Zoology - Exeter University; PGSE, Bangor, N Wales; climber for 20 years. **Awards/Research** Auth: Rock climbing in Scotland, 1990. **Pres Committees** Aberfoyle Forest Environmental Panel.

HOWLAND Guy Director **PATIENTS ASSOCIATION** MEDICAL/HEALTH Type: Advisers/represents patients' interests. 8 Guilford St, London WC1N 1DT Tel:0171-242 3460 Fax:0171-242 3461

HOWLETT Michael Director **ZITO TRUST** MEDICAL/HEALTH Type: Fundraiser; Service provider; Campaigning. PO Box 265, London WC2H 9JD Tel:0171-240 8422 Fax:0171-240 8422 **Expertise** Mental health law, psychiatry & hist, community care (mental health), risk assessment, criminal justice. **Prev Posts** Therapeutic Staff, Peper Harow, Surrey 1990-93; Secretary to The Special Hospitals Service Authority 1993-94; Part-time lecturer, Criminal Justice Studies & Criminal Law. **Prof Background** Law Degree, LLM (Hons), Cambridge University. **Awards/Research** Author of articles on patients' rights, risk assessment, community care, bullying in schools (book review), disturbed adolescents & thematic review of women patients in special hosps. **Past Committees** Special Hospitals Service Authority Board. **Media Experience** Wide-ranging experience in radio, TV and press (national & local).

HOYLE Neil Chief Executive **INCORPORATED SOCIETY OF MUSICIANS** ARTS Type: Service provider; Professional association. 10 Stratford Place, London W1N 9AE Tel:0171-629 4413 Fax:0171-408 1538 **Expertise** General administration, policy making, drafting government, management of people and projects. **Prev Posts** Head of Public Transport, Metropolitan Branch, Dept of Transport 1985-87; Private Secretary to Secretary of State for Transport 1987-89. **Prof Background** Bachelor of Music with Hons, Edinburgh University 1969-73; Postgraduate Certificate in Education with Distinction, Cambridge University 1974-75. **Pres Committees** General Sec to Council of Incorporated Society of Musicians;Director, Educational Recording Agency Ltd;Director, St Cecilia Enterprises Ltd;Royal Concert Cttee. **Past Committees** Executive Cttee, National Music Council.

HUFF John Director **EURO BUREAU** SOCIAL Type: Service provider. 9 Bower Street, Stoke-on-Trent, Staffs ST1 3BH Tel:01782-266712 **Expertise** Work of the

European Parliament. **Prof Background** Community work. **Awards/Research** Power in the European Parliament.

HUGHES Elizabeth Honorary Secretary **BRITISH RECORDS ASSOCIATION** Conservation Type: Pressure Group. 18 Padbury Court, London E2 7EH Tel:0171-729 1415 Fax:0171-729 1415 (From Jan/Feb 1997: Greater London Record Office, 40 Northampton Rd, London EC1R 0HB).

HUNT John Chief Executive **BRITISH DENTAL ASSOCIATION - BDA** MEDICAL/HEALTH Type: Professional Association 64 Wimpole St, London W1M 8AL Tel:0171-935 0875 Fax:0171-487 5232 **Expertise** Oral health policy. **Prev Posts** Dental Ref Officer, DHSS 1984-88; Dept of Health: Dental Officer 1988-89; Senior Dental Officer 1989-93; Hon Lecturer, Dept Child Dental Health, London Hospital 1989-93. **Prof Background** BDS, Guy's Hospital; LDS, Royal College of Surgeons. **Media Experience** Radio, TV, press - significant experience.

HURST Rachel Director **DISABILITY AWARENESS IN ACTION** DISABILITY Type: International Disability Information Network. 11 Belgrave Road, London SW1 1RB Tel:0171-834 0477 Fax:0171-821 9539 **Expertise** Human rights of disabled people; Independent living. **Prev Posts** Chair, Greenwich Association of Disabled People 1981-90; Chair, British Council of Disabled People 1985-87. **Prof Background** Dip/Ed, Rose Bruford Training College of Speech & Drama, 1960. **Awards/Research** Hon Doct Univ Greenwich 1996;OBE 1995;Freedom of London Boro Gr 1990. Many contribs to jt auth pubs incl Choice & Empowerment-Lessons from Eur;Internat Perspectives & Sols. **Pres Committees** Chair, Disabled Peoples' International, European Region; V-C GRAEAE Theatre Co; Trustee Action on Disability & Devt; Bd Mbr IMPACT; Mngmt Cttee Christchurch Forum. **Past Committees** Resourcer dvt Seminars Zimbabwe, Zambia, Brazil; DPI rep to EV HELIOS Prog. **Media Experience** Interviewer/Narr: Letters from our Lives, 1992 Ch4; var interviews incl LINK. **Addits** Spkr UN Gen Assembly;World Summits on Hum Rts & Soc Devt.

HUSAIN Dr M. Hasanat Chair Person **GREATER SYLHET DEVELOPMENT & WELFARE COUNCIL** SOCIAL Type: Community organisation. Suda House, 100 Mile End Road, London E1 Tel:0171-702 8120 Fax:0171-702 8120 **Expertise** Teaching Physics at Intermediate, Graduate and Post Graduate Level at Universities and Colleges. **Prev Posts** Chairman, Sussex University Bangladesh Association, Associate Professor, University of Sebha, Zambia, Dhaka, Associate, Int Centre for Theoretical Physics, 1977-80. **Prof Background** PhD, Exeter; Royal Soc Post Doctoral, Sussex; Assoc Prof of Physics at various Universities; C Phys (Chartered Physicist); M Inst P (Member Institute of Physics). **Awards/Research** Bangladeshis in UK & In Tower Hamlets (GSC Publ); Growth of Single Crystal of Adamantane (Netherlands); Ultrasonic Studies of Materials (UK); Applying Hydrostatic Pressure (India). **Pres Committees** Exec Mbr, National Governers Council (UK); Trustee, UK-Bangladesh Education; Consultant, Bangladesh Caterers Assoc in GB; Chair of Governors, London Borough of Tower Hamlets. **Past Committees** Governors' Forum, LB Tower Hamlets;Bangladeshi & Asian Welfare, Chester;Bangladesh Assoc of Oldham;Secondary Transfer Wkng Gp, LBIH. **Media Experience** Appeared at many press conferences. **Addits** Asian Film Academy Award 1995 for Community Services in UK.

HUTTON Ceri Director **IMMUNITY LEGAL CENTRE** SOCIAL Type: Service provider; Advocacy; Policy. 32-38 Osnaburgh Street, London NW1 3ND Tel:0171-388 6776 Fax:0171-388 6371 **Expertise** Policy, HIV/AIDS, campaign strategies, human rights. **Prev Posts** Overseas Project Officer, IYSH 1986-88; Policy Researcher, AIDS Policy Unit 1988-89; Head of Policy, National AIDS Trust 1989-94. **Prof Background** Monmouth School for Girls; Oxford University (Brasenose);10 years in Voluntary Sector in PO. **Awards/Research** Human Rights in Europe;Women & AIDS;Parliamentary briefings on wide number of topic areas. **Pres Committees** AIDS & Housing Project;UK Forum on HIV & Human Rights, Ch;Pan London Providers' Consortium. **Past Committees** Homeless International;Brook Advisory Centres;UN International Women/Shelter Network;Galop (Gay London Policing) Stonewall Group. **Media Experience** Appearances on Newsnight/Moral Maze & many more.

HUXFORD Robert Manager **ASSOCIATION OF MUNICIPAL ENGINEERS - AME** CONSERVATION/ENVIRONMENT Type: Public sector civil engineering & technical servs. Institution of Civil Engineers, 1 Great George St, London SW1P 3AA Tel:0171-665 2210 Fax:0171-222 7722 .

HYSLOP David S. Director and Chairman of Trustees **BREAKTHROUGH TRUST DEAF/HEARING INTEGRATION** DISABILITY AND HANDICAP Type: Service provider. Birmingham Centre, 998 Bristol Road, Selly Oak, Birmingham B29 6LE Tel:0121-472 6447 Fax:0121-471 4368 **Expertise** Communication between deaf/hearing children/youth/adults. **Prev Posts** Children's Integration Officer 1972-76; Co-Director, Breakthrough Birmingham Centre 1977-79. Total Communication Tutor. **Prof Background** Profoundly deaf since birth; Spring Hill School for the Deaf, Northants 1937-45; School Cert, Oxford; Market gardening; Apprentice/master jeweller; qualified in training adult education. **Awards/Research** OBE 1996. CACDP's Outstanding Service Award (Joseph Maitland Robinson Award) 1991;Leslie Edwards Memorial Lecture, Leicester University;Rotary International Research Scholarship 1979. **Pres Committees** Chair: Longwill School for the Deaf Board of Governors; CACDP. Mbr/V-Chair, Mngmt Cttee TAG-Diel/OFTel. **Past Committees** DTI's Visicom Project - Hasicom Project; GB's representative for the Home Office to USSR in 1983 (provision for deaf people). **Media Experience** BBC See Hear;Forum - Listening Eye, ITV; BBC Pebble Mill at One. **Addits** 1st deaf UK user telephone/text; 1st transatlant relay call (Jack Ashley).

I

IMRAY Sir Colin Secretary General **ORDER OF ST JOHN, THE** SOCIAL Type: Service provider; Co-ordinator. St John's Gate, St John's Lane, Clerkenwell, London EC1M 4DA Tel:0171-253 6644 Fax:0171-490 8835 **Expertise** Management. **Prev Posts** High Commissioner Bangladesh & Tanzania 1986-93; Diplomatic Service 1957-93. **Prof Background** BA Oxford (Balliol) Politics Philosophy Economics 1957. **Awards/Research** KBE; CMG; KStJ. **Pres Committees** All St John Order Committees; Patron, Friends of the Centre for the Rehabilitation of the Paralysed (Bangladesh). **Past Committees** Numerous during diplomatic service career. **Media Experience** Occasional - in the diplomatic service.

INGHAM Sylvia Chief Executive **ROY CASTLE CAUSE FOR HOPE FOUNDATION** MEDICAL/HEALTH Type: Fundraiser; Grant maker; Campaigning. 12th Floor, 100 Old Hall St, Liverpool L3 9TA Tel:0151-2273636 Fax:0151-2272128 **Expertise** Public Relations & Fundraising. **Prev Posts** Administrator, Border TV's Telethon Appeal 1992-93. **Awards/Research** Awarded Professional Fundraiser of the Year 1996.

IRVING Mrs Karen Director **PARENTS FOR CHILDREN** CHILDREN/YOUTH Type: Service provider. 41 Southgate Road, Islington, London N1 3JP Tel:0171-359 7530 Fax:0171-226 7840 **Expertise** Adoption and fostering. **Prev Posts** Snr Social Worker, Adoption and Fostering 1979-86; Teencare Co-ordinator, Herts 1991-92. **Prof Background** BA (Hons), Sussex Univ; CQSW & Diploma in Social Administration, Goldsmiths College; FRSA. **Awards/Research** Articles published in social work journals. **Media Experience** Various TV and radio programmes.

IVES Cyril Director Of Education **LANTERN TRUST** MEDICAL/HEALTH Type: Service provider; Educational charity. 72 Honey Lane, Waltham Abbey, Essex EN9 3BS Tel:01992-714900 **Expertise** Arts Therapies; loss and bereavement; death education. **Prev Posts** Principal Officer, Elderly N. Ireland 1974-82; Principal Officer, Elderly North Yorks SSD 1982-1985. **Prof Background** Residential Social Work Management; Bereavement Counselling Training; Arts Therapy Diploma; currently completing Masters Degree in Education. **Awards/Research** Post-graduate research, Birmingham, Caregivers attitudes to HIV/AIDS; published resource pack Positive Care 1989. **Pres Committees** Chair of Lantern Trust Academic Board. **Past Committees** Carers Nat Assoc Mngmt Board; St Clare Hospice Planning Team; Chair, Waltham Abbey Cruse; Chair, NI Branch of Social Care Assoc. **Media Experience** Contrib to professional jnls; Channel 4 programme on Gay/Lesbian bereavement.

IVES Graham Appeals Director **TELEPHONES FOR THE BLIND** DISABILITY Type: Fundraiser; Service provider; Grant maker. 56 Knole Rd, Dartford, Kent DA1 3AW Tel:01322-225828 Fax:01322-225828 **Expertise** Fund raising. **Prev Posts** Accountant with BT 1960-1990 **Prof Background** Training in accountancy & computer applications. **Awards/Research** Awards in Athletics. **Pres Committees** Telephones for the Blind; Sports Foundation for the Disabled; Dartford Lions; Dartford Volunteer Bureau. Committee member of two national running associations. **Media Experience** TV; Appeal for Telephones for the Blind (1993); Various local radio appeals. **Addits** Heavily involved in athletics, long distance.

J

JACKSON Jim Executive Director **ALZHEIMER SCOTLAND - ACTION ON DEMENTIA** MEDICAL/HEALTH Type: Service provider; Public Advocacy. 8 Hill Street, Edinburgh EH2 3JZ Tel:0131-225 1453 Fax:0131-225 8748 **Expertise** Community care policies & performance indicators. **Prev Posts** Consultant, Home Office Voluntary Service Unit 1981-84; Asst Director, Scottish Council for Voluntary Organizations 1984-93. **Prof Background** BA Hons (Open Univ). **Awards/Research** Publ inc: Voluntary Care and Caution, 1992; Dials or Tin Openers: Role of Performance Indicators in the Voluntary Sector, 1990; Financial Management Initiatives, 1985. **Pres Committees** Convener,Care in the Community Scottish Working Group. **Past Committees** Unemployed Voluntary Action Fund 1986-93;Crossroads Care Attendant Schemes,Scotland. **Media Experience** Occasional interviews/contrib.

JACKSON Mr John M. National Director **INTERSERVE SCOTLAND** RELIGIOUS Type: Fundraiser; Service provider; Christian mission. 12 Elm Avenue, Lenzie, Glasgow G66 4HJ Tel:0141-7762943 Fax:0141-7778146 **Prev Posts** Teacher of Physics, Paisley Grammar School 1974-79; Assistant Principal Teacher of Physics, Aberdeen Grammar School 1979-81; North of England Coordinator, Tear Fund 1981-95. **Prof Background** Physics & Mathematics - Teaching, BSc Hons Glasgow University. **Pres Committees** International Council of Interserve.

JACKSON Mr M. I. Director **SAINT JOHN'S WINCHESTER CHARITY** THE ELDERLY Type: Service provider. 32 St John's South, The Broadway, Winchester, Hants SO23 9LN Tel:01962-854226 Fax:01962-840602 **Expertise** Continuing care for older people (legal, spiritual & holistic & needs of those with dementia). **Prev Posts** Solicitor in private practice 1976-86. **Prof Background** Solicitor. **Awards/Research** Awarded Winston Churchill Travelling Fellowship 1988; wrote consultation paper 1993: Longstay Care for the Elderly Mentally Infirm in Winchester (prepared for Winchester EMI forum). **Pres Committees** Executive Committee, the National Association of Almshouses; Associate Manager, The Mental Health Act for Winchester & Eastleigh Healthcare Trust. **Past Committees** Chair, Age Concern 1988-90, Winchester; Exec Cttee, Age Concern, Hampshire 1989-91; Dir, Winchester & District Samaritans 1991-94. **Media Experience** Experience with media interviews as Director of The Samaritans. **Addits** Clerk to The Governors, Twyford C of E Primary School 1990-95.

JACKSON Margaret National Co-ordinator **NATIONAL KIDNEY FEDERATION (NAT FED OF KIDNEY PATIENT ASSOCS) - NFKPA** MEDICAL/HEALTH Type: Service provider. 6 Stanley Street, Worksop, Nottinghamshire S81 7HX Tel:01909-487795 Fax:01909-481723 **Expertise** PR; education; advice; counselling. **Prev Posts** Company Secretary 1970-81; Training Co-ordinator 1981-83. **Prof Background** Business administration; teaching/youth training; charity administration; FTC; CSoc.St. **Pres Committees** TIME (Transplants in Mind) Council. **Past Committees** Time/Dept of Health Education Subcommittee (Transplantation). **Media Experience** Editor: Kidney Life.

JACKSON Richard Smith Honorary Chairman **RESCARE - NAT SOC FOR MENTALLY HANDICAPPED PEOPLE IN RESIDENTIAL CARE** DISABILITY Type: Relief/welfare of the mentally handicapped. Rayner House, 23 Higher Hillgate, Stockport, Cheshire SK1 3ER Tel:0161-474 7323 Fax:0161-480 3668 **Expertise** Help, support, information, advice and lobbying ministers/departments re mentally disabled people. **Prof Background** C.Eng; MIMechE; M.InstM. **Awards/Research** MBE. **Past Committees** Various charitable committees regarding people with a mental handicap. **Media Experience** Limited.

JACKSON Tessa Director **ARNOLFINI** ARTS Type: Service provider; International Centre for Contemporary Arts. 16 Narrow Quay, Bristol, Avon BS1 4QA Tel:0117-929 9191 Fax:0117-925 3876 **Prev Posts** Art Editor, Oxford Univ Press 1979-80; Curator, Collins Gallery Univ of Strathclyde 1982-88; Visual Arts Officer Glasgow 1990, 1988-91. **Prof Background** Fine Art BA (Hons); Museum Studies Diploma. External examiner, Bath College of Higher Education. **Pres Committees** Advisory Board, Tate Gallery St Ives; Forest of Dean Sculpture Trust; Bristol Cultural Development Partnership; Arnolfini Collection Trust. Bd of Dirs, Bristol Cent for Performing Arts; Govr, Falmouth Coll of Arts.

JAMES Gareth Director **CANOLFAN IAITH GENEDLAETHOL** SOCIAL Type: Service provider. National Welsh Language Centre, Nant Gwrtheyrn, Llithfaen, Pwlheli, Gwynedd LL53 6PA Tel:01758-750334 Fax:01758-750335 **Expertise** Administration; financial control. **Prev Posts** Organizer, Youth Festival 1983-89; Director, European Centre 1989-91. **Prof Background** Management of youth associations and Welsh language, culture and promotion; university education. **Pres Committees** WJEC - Adult Education; North Wales Forum on Rural Development; UK Sec, Euro Bureau for Lesser Used Languages. **Media Experience** Interviews given.

JAMES Gwen Director **VOICE FOR THE CHILD IN CARE** CHILDREN/YOUTH Type: Service provider. Unit 4, Pride Court, 80-82 White Lion St, London N1 9PS1 Tel:0171-833 5792 Fax:0171-833 8637 **Expertise** Complaints procedures, independent representation, advocacy, children's rights. **Prev Posts** Area Officer, Children's Dept Haringey 1968-71; Area Officer, Haringey Social Services 1971-75; Principal Social Worker (Haringey) 1975-85. **Prof Background** Teaching Certificate; Diploma in Social Work (1961); Home Office Letter of Recognition (1962).

JAMES John D. Chief Executive **WOODLAND TRUST** CONSERVATION/ENVIRONMENT Type: Fundraiser. Autumn Park, Dysart Road, Grantham, Lincolnshire NG31 6LL Tel:01476-581111 Fax:01476-590808 **Expertise** Marketing. **Prev Posts** Marketing Dept, Geest Industries 1969-71; Marketing Dept, John Player and Sons 1971-77. **Prof Background** Mbr Institute of Directors,Institute of Charity Fundraising Managers;Fellow,Royal Society of Arts. **Awards/Research** OBE. Nottingham Roosevelt Scholar 1975; Churchill Travelling Fellowship 1980. **Media Experience** Producer, BBC2 Open Door documentary on Woodland Rescue 1980.

JAMES Mary Director **INDEPENDENT ADOPTION SERVICE - IAS** CHILDREN/YOUTH Type: Service provider, Adoption agency. 121-123 Camberwell Road, London SE5 0HB Tel:0171-703 1088 Fax:0171-277 1668 **Expertise** Child and family welfare; training, adoption practice and policy. **Prev Posts** Local Authority: Area Children's Officer 1968-73; Principal Social Worker 1970-73. **Prof Background** Cert in Soc Science, Sheffield Univ; Home Office Letter of Recognition, Birmingham Univ; Executive Development, Aston Univ. **Awards/Research** Articles on adoption and fostering in prof jnls and chapters in text books. Mbr, DHSS Cttee Guide to Foster Care, etc. **Pres Committees** LB Southwark Adoption Panel;Dep Ch, Single Person Adoption Research Adv Gp;Brit Agencies for Adoption & Fostering Mngmt Cttee. **Past Committees** City of Westminster Adoption Panel; Consortium of Vol Adoption Agencies Wkng Pt **Media Experience** Radio/TV interviews; press statements issued.

JARMAN Richard General Director **SCOTTISH OPERA** ARTS Type: Service provider. 39 Elmbank Crescent, Glasgow G2 4PT Tel:0141-248 4567 Fax:0141-221 8812 **Expertise** General management. **Prev Posts** General Administrator, English National Ballet 1984-90; Festival Administrator, Edinburgh International Festival 1978-84. **Prof Background** MA (Oxon) English Language & Literature. **Awards/Research** Publ: History of Sadler's Wells/English National Opera; History of New Opera Company; History of London Coliseum Theatre. **Pres Committees** Scottish Opera Ltd; Scottish Opera Theatre Royal Ltd; National Opera Studio; SALVO; Chair, TMA Opera Negotiating Cttee. **Past Committees** Society of West End Theatres;Chair, TMA Ballet Negotiating Cttee.

JARVIS Averil Director **CINNAMON TRUST** ELDERLY Type: Service provider. Foundry House, Foundry Square, Hayle, Cornwall TR27 4HH Tel:01736-757900 Fax:01736-757010 **Expertise** Pets & the elderly; care of geriatric animals. **Prev Posts** Self-employed 1970-84. **Prof Background** BSc Physiology & Biochemistry. **Awards/Research** 1983-85 Res into importance of pets to elderly people and identification of anxieties, negative aspects etc; care homes for elderly which accept pets. **Past Committees** Trustee, The Cinnamon Trust, 1985-87. **Media Experience** Interviewed by all media, and pivotal role in CT Video.

JASPER Mr Lee Director **1990 TRUST** SOCIAL Type: Fundraiser; Service provider; Charitable trust. Southbank Technopark, 90 London Rd, London SE1 6LN Tel:0171-717 1579 Fax:0171-717 1585 **Expertise** Black rights, policy resrch & dev, evaluation, fundraising, cmty dev, advocacy, human rights, policing. **Prev Posts** Director of Development, Mangrove Trust 1989-92; Senior Policy Adviser, ILEA 1988-89. **Prof Background** BA (Hons) Social Science; MA Social Policy. **Awards/Research** Awarded Black Male of the Year 1995 (Progressive African Co-operative Economics (PACE). **Pres Committees** Chair, Nat Black Alliance; Mbr, Black/Jewish Forum; V Chair, Nat Assembly Against Racism; Cncl Mbr, Charter 88; Spokesperson, Nat Black Caucus; Chair, Mangrove Cmmty Assoc; Exec Mbr, Brixton Law Cnt. **Media Experience** Widespread experience (commentator, press contributor & documentary producer).

JAZAIRY Idriss Executive Director **AGENCY FOR COOPERATION AND RESEARCH IN DEVELOPMENT - ACORD** SOCIAL Type: Fundraiser; Service provider; Campaigning. Francis House, Francis Street, London SW1P 1DE Tel:0171-828 7611 Fax:0171-976 6113 **Expertise** Overseas development. **Prev Posts** Ambassador of Algeria to Belgium & European Communities 1989-92; Roving Ambassador of Algeria 1992-93; Pres, The International Fund for Inter Dev (UN Specialised Agency) 1984-93. **Prof Background** MA Political Science, Oxford University; MA Public Administration, Harvard University; Ancien Eleve, Ecole Nationale d'Administration, Paris. **Awards/Research** Awards:Comm Wissam Alaouite (Morocco);Off Nat Order Merit(Mauritiania);Grand Off Order Merit (Italy);Medal Indep Jordan(1st class).Publ incl:State of World Rural Pov 1992;Non-Alignment **Pres Committees** Member, Board of Overseers & Board of Directors, CARE (U.S.A.); President, Emir Abd El-Kader Foundation (Algeria). **Past Committees** Mbr, Advisory Grp to UN Sec Gen Boutros-Ghali on 4th World Conference on Women; President of Board of Governors, African Dev Bank. **Media Experience** Wide range of articles published in world press in English, French & Arabic.

JELL Leslie J. Director of Finance & Administration **HOSPICE OF OUR LADY AND ST JOHN** Type: Fundraiser; Service provider; Association of Hospice Administrators. Manor Farm, Milton Rd, Willen, Milton Keynes, Bucks MK15 9AB Tel:01908-663780 Fax:01908-695717 **Expertise** Administration; Finance; Fundraising. **Prev Posts** Buckinghamshire Red Cross: Day Care Administrator 1977-87, Branch Director 1987-89. **Prof Background** Spurgeons College, London, Theology for Baptist Ministry; Various Management Courses. **Pres Committees** Vice Chair: Milton Keynes General NHS Trust; Secretary, Oxford Regional Palliative Care Council; Trustee, Navigation Cruising Club. **Past Committees** Milton Keynes, Relate; Milton Keynes CAB; Past President Rotary Club of Bletchley.

JENKINS David Director/Co-ordinator **COED CYMRU** CONSERVATION/ENVIRONMENT Type: Service provider. The Old Sawmill, Tregynon, Newtown, Powys SY16 3PL Tel:01686-650777 Fax:01686-650696 **Expertise** Forestry and environment policy; hardwood products habitat restoration. **Prev Posts** Senior Fisheries Officer, Thames Water.

JENKINS Emyr Chief Executive **ARTS COUNCIL OF**

WALES CONSERVATION/ENVIRONMENT Type: Grant maker. 9, Museum Place, Cardiff CF1 3NX Tel:01222-394711 Fax:01222-221447 **Prev Posts** Programme planning organiser, BBC Wales 1971-78; Director, Royal National Eisteddfod of Wales 1978-93; Director, Welsh Arts Council 1993-94. **Prof Background** B.Sc. (Physics) University of Wales. **Awards/Research** Honorary MA, University of Wales; FRSA. Media contribs on arts topics in Wales. **Media Experience** Compere/Commentator, Radio/TV; Anchorman nightly news TV prog; R3 concerts.

JOHANSON Captain Philip Chief Secretary **CHURCH ARMY, THE** SOCIAL Type: Fundraiser; Evangelism and social action. Independents Road, Blackheath, London SE3 9LG Tel:0181-318 1226 Fax:0181-318 5258 **Expertise** Chief executive ie. organization and leadership. **Prev Posts** Church Army: Head of Missions 1975-83, Director of Evangelism 1983-90. **Prof Background** Alderman Cogan Church of England School, Hull; Church Army Wilson Carlile College of Evangelism, London. **Pres Committees** Church Army; African Pastors Fellowship; Evangelical Alliance.

JOHNSON David Director **WAVERLEY CARE TRUST** CHILDREN/YOUTH Type: Fundraiser; Service provider. 4a Royal Terrace, Edinburgh EH7 5AB Tel:0131-556 3959 Fax:0131-556 5045 **Expertise** HIV/AIDS; Child care issues **Prev Posts** Principal Training Officer, Barnardos Scotland 1990-94; Unit Manager Edinburgh Family Service Unit 1984-90. **Prof Background** Qualified social worker (C.Q.S.W); Diploma in Social Administration. **Pres Committees** Barnardo's Scotland Adoption Committee; Scottish Adoption Management Committee.

JOHNSON Brigadier Peter Dunbar General Secretary **OFFICERS' ASSOCIATION, THE - OA** SOCIAL Type: Service provider; Grant maker. 48 Pall Mall, London SW1Y 5JY Tel:0171-930 0125 Fax:0171-930 9053 **Expertise** Armed services. **Prev Posts** Senior Service Appointments, Army, until 1985. **Prof Background** Army.

JOHNSTON T.L. President **ROYAL SOCIETY OF EDINBURGH** CONSERVATION/ENVIRONMENT Type: Service provider; Grant maker; Educational. 22-24 George Street, Edinburgh EH2 2PQ Tel:0131-225 6057 Fax:0131-220 6889 **Expertise** Economics, industrial relations, arbitration and mediation. **Prev Posts** Chairman, Manpower Services Cttee for Scotland 1977-80; Principal & Vice Chancellor, Heriot-Watt University 1981-88.

JONES Prof Arthur Stanley Principal **ROYAL AGRICULTURAL COLLEGE** ENVIRONMENT Type: Fundraiser; Campaigner. Cirencester, Gloucestershire GL7 6JS Tel:01285-652531 Fax:01285-650219 **Expertise** Education, agriculture & land use. **Prev Posts** Dep Dir, Rowett Research Inst 1983-87; Strathcona-Fordyce Prof of Agric, Univ of Aberdeen; Head of Sch of Agric; Principal, N. of Scotland Coll of Agriculture 1987-9 . **Prof Background** BSc; PhD; CBiol; FIBiol; FBIM; FIAgrM; FRSA; Nutritional Biochemistry; career in research, specialising in nutrition. **Awards/Research** Over 100 publications in Scientific Journals. **Pres Committees** Governing Cncl, Henley Mgmt College; Chair, Academic Advisory Cncl, Henley Mgmt Coll; Cncl Mbr, Royal Agricultural Soc of Eng; Mbr, The Trehane Trust; Chair, Royal Agricultural Coll Enterprises Ltd. **Past Committees** Dir, Arable Research Cntrs; Gov, Rowett Research Inst; Gov, Aberdeen Centre for Land Use; Mbr, AFRC Research Consultative Cttee. **Media Experience** Experience in radio, TV and press. **Addits** Member, Geoffrey Cragghill Memorial Trust.

JONES Brian Chief Executive **INVALID CHILDREN'S AID NATIONWIDE - I CAN** CHILDREN/YOUTH Type: Fundraiser; Service provider; Specialist schools/nurseries/training. Barbican City Gate, 1/3 Dufferin St, London EC1Y 8NA Tel:0171-374 4422 Fax:0171-374 2762 **Expertise** Special education; Educational management, voluntary sector partnership. **Prev Posts** Deputy Head Teacher 1983-86; Principal, Special F.E. College 1986-89. **Prof Background** BSc (Hons) Architecture; P.G.C.E. **Pres Committees** Trustee of Communications Forum. **Media Experience** Radio/TV/video/press.

JONES Revd Canon Glyndwr Secretary General **MISSIONS TO SEAMEN, THE** RELIGIOUS Type: Missionary Society of the Anglican Church. St Michael Paternoster Royal, College Hill, London EC4R 2RL Tel:0171-248 5202 Fax:0171-248 4761 **Expertise** Priest of the Anglican Church. **Prev Posts** Missions to Seamen: Chaplain, 1972-81; Auxilliary Ministries Secretary 1981-85; Asst Gen Secretary 1985-90. Chaplain to Lay Sheriff, City/London 1993-94. **Prof Background** Dip Theology, St Michael's Theological College, Llandaff, University Of Wales. Member of Royal College of Chaplains. **Awards/Research** Freeman of the City of London, 1990. Hon Member of Honorable Company of Master Mariners, 1990. **Pres Committees** Cncl mbr: Merchant Navy Welfare Brd; Marine Soc; Partnership for World Mission; Int Christian Maritime Assoc. Chaplain, Worshipful Companies - Information Technologists, Farriers, Carmen, Innholders. **Addits** Hon Canon, St Michael's Cath, Kobe, Japan.

JONES Ian Huntley Director **BRITISH PREGNANCY ADVISORY SERVICE - BPAS** MEDICAL/HEALTH Type: Service provider. Austy Manor, Wootton Wawen, Solihull, West Midlands B95 6BX Tel:01564-793225 Fax:01564-794935 **Prev Posts** Family Planning Assoc 1971-76; NHS Management, Birmingham Area Health Authority 1976-82. **Prof Background** Associate, Inst. of Personnel Management; Associate, Inst. of Health Service Management; Henley Management College. **Pres Committees** Board of Directors and Pension Fund trustees, BPAS; Joint Action Cttee on Families, Inter-Parliamentary Group; Donors Cttee, Birth Control Trust. **Past Committees** Nat Council/Regional Exec cttees, FPA; West Midlands RHA Fertility Strategy Group; North Birmingham Community Health Council. **Media Experience** Lead role in media activity for charity.

JONES Prof John Gwynfryn Director **FRESHWATER BIOLOGICAL ASSOCIATION** ENVIRONMENT Type: Service provider; Grant maker; Educational. The Ferry House, Far Sawrey, Ambleside, Cumbria LA22 0LP Tel:015394-42468 Fax:015394-46914 **Expertise**

Freshwater microbiology. **Prev Posts** Principal Scientific Officer 1975-86; Senior Principal Scientific Officer, 1986-87; Director, Institute of Freshwater Ecology 1989-93. **Prof Background** 1983, CBiol, FIBiol; 1982, DSc; 1968, PhD, University of Wales; 1965, BSc University of Wales. **Awards/Research** Over 100 scientific papers. Awards: Project Urquart; BOC Foundation; NERC; Leverhulme Trust; TESCO; EC; Fishmonger's Company; Esmee Fairburn Trust Fund. **Pres Committees** Scientific Dir, Project Urquhart; Cttee Mbr: IOB Environment Cttee; Baikal Int Ctr for Eco Res (BICER); Int Cttee for Microbial Ecology; DTI LINK Prog; NERC RACS; NERC TIGER II Wking Gp. **Media Experience** TV/Radio experience Re: Freshwater research, Campaigns in Loch Ness. **Addits** Ed: Advances in Microbial Ecology; Freshwater Forum.

JONES Hugh Secretary **RWANDA DEVELOPMENT TRUST** OVERSEAS Type: Fundraiser; Grant maker. P.O. Box 566, Bromley, Kent BR1 3WZ Tel:0181-290 5103 Fax:0181-290 5103 **Expertise** Providing & maintaining a channel for financial assistance to precise region of Central Africa.

JONES Revd Keith G. Deputy General Secretary **BAPTIST UNION OF GREAT BRITAIN, THE - BUGB** RELIGIOUS Type: Religious denomination. Baptist House, PO Box 44, 129 Broadway, Didcot, Oxfordshire OX11 8RT Tel:01235-512077 Fax:01235-811537 **Expertise** Historian; religious trust management; international conflict resolution. **Prev Posts** Minister, Baptist Church Centre, Barnoldswick 1975-80; General Sec, Yorkshire Baptist Assoc 1980-90. **Prof Background** Qualified Inst of Transport, passenger transport management; Northern Baptist College; BA (Theology) Manchester Univ; MA Peace Studies, Bradford Univ; Ruschlikon Seminary Zurich Univ. **Awards/Research** Auth:Our Heritage, Lancs and Yorks Baptists, history 1647-1987; Authority of the Trust Deed, EA Payne Memorial Essay Prize 1988; MA Thesis 1980: Ind Rev and Dissenters in NW England. **Pres Committees** Baptist Union Cncl & Brd of the Baptist Union Corporation; Mbr, Christian Aid Board 1991 to date, Exec Cttee, 1994 to date; Church Representatives Meeting, Cncl of Churches of Britain and Ireland. **Past Committees** West Yorkshire Ecumenical Council; Northern Church Leaders Consultation; Yorkshire Baptist Association Council. **Media Experience** Pennine Radio religious news presenter 1982-88; BBC R2 Morning Prayers 1989-91.

JONES Margaret A. Chief Executive **BROOK ADVISORY CENTRES** MEDICAL/HEALTH Type: Service provider, Education. 165 Grays Inn Road, London WC1X 8UD Tel:0171-833 8488 Fax:0171-833 8182 **Expertise** Birth control services for young people. **Prev Posts** Manager & Resources Officer, Health Education Authority Family Health Programme 1974-88. **Prof Background** MSc; PhD in Chemistry. **Past Committees** Board member:Tacade; Mental Health Film Council; Maternity Alliance.

JONES Roy Director **RESEARCH INSTITUTE FOR THE CARE OF THE ELDERLY** THE ELDERLY Type: Fundraiser; Service provider, Medical and allied research. St Martins Hospital, Bath, Avon BA2 5RP Tel:01225-835866 Fax:01225-840395 **Expertise** Medical research; memory impairment, dementia and Alzheimer's Disease; elderly people. **Prof Background** Physician. **Awards/Research** Articles on: Dementia, Memory Impairment and the Clinical Pharmacology of Old Age. **Media Experience** BBC & Commercial Radio & TV; Programmes including Videos; Press interviews.

JONES Russell Chief Executive **NATIONAL FEDERATION OF MUSIC SOCIETIES - NFMS** SOCIAL Type: Service provider; Grant maker. Training and lobbying. Francis House, Francis Street, London SW1P 1DE Tel:0171-828 7320 Fax:0171-828 5504 **Expertise** Music administration. **Prev Posts** Orchestra Manager, Royal Liverpool Philharmonic Orchestra 1981-86; Concerts Manager, Scottish Chamber Orchestra 1986-86; Admin, Haydn Orchestra since 1986. **Prof Background** BA (Hons) British Government Politics & History, University of Kent at Canterbury. **Pres Committees** Ch,Nat Music Cncl/GB;Cncl Mbr,Hon Sec/Treasurer,Vol Arts Network;Mbr,Steering Ctte,Nat Music Day;Cncl Mbr,Nat Fed/Young Choirs;Lon Symphony Chorus Cncl 96-;Mbr,Musicians Ben Fund Proms & Friends Cttee **Past Committees** Cncl Mbr, Amateur Music Association 1987-89; London Symphony Chorus Board 1987-89/1991-94.

JONES Sydney Chief Executive/Brigade Secretary **BOYS' BRIGADE, THE** CHILDREN/YOUTH Type: Service provider. Felden Lodge, Felden, Hemel Hempstead, Herts HP3 0BL Tel:01442-231681 Fax:01442-235391 **Expertise** Residential care of children in care and young offenders; staff training and development; youth work. **Prev Posts** Dep Head, Approved Schools 1967-73; Head, Community Homes with Education (CHE) 1973-88. **Prof Background** Qualified teacher; graduate in education and social work. **Awards** OBE 1995.

JORDAN June Nat Helpline Co-ord. & Training Officer **CRY-SIS SUPPORT GROUP** CHILDREN/YOUTH Type: Fundraiser; Service provider; Support Group with helpline. 28 Nine Acres Road, Cuxton, Kent ME2 1EL Tel:01634-710913 **Expertise** Volunteer Management Administration. **Prev Posts** Regional Co-Ordinator (Kent), CRY-SIS, 1988-89; Regional Co-Ordinator (S.E. England), CRY-SIS, 1989-92. **Prof Background** Pre-School Playgroups Assoc - Foundation Course, 1990 Started up and supervised the Beehive Playgroup, 1973-84 Bank Clerk, Barclays Bank Plc. **Awards/Research** Assist publication of Cry-sis booklets; write & publish Newsletter. **Pres Committees** CRY-SIS Management Committee - Non Voting. **Media Experience** Radio, newspapers, magazines.

JOSEPH Peter Director **KARUNA TRUST** RELIGIOUS Type: Fundraiser. St Mark's Studios, 16 Chillingworth Rd, London N7 8QJ Tel:0171-700 3434 Fax:0171-700 3535 **Prev Posts** Teacher 1985-87; Centre Director, Auckland Buddhist Centre 1989-90. **Prof Background** Arts degree; Primary & EFL teacher. Teacher of Buddhism & meditation. **Awards/Research** 3 months study tour in India, 1 year study in Buddhism. **Pres Committees** Trustee, Oxford Buddhist Centre. **Past Committees** Auckland Buddhist Centre

JULIENNE Louis Director **FEDERATION OF BLACK HOUSING ORGANIZATIONS - FBHO** SOCIAL Type: Service provider. 374 Gray's Inn Road, London WC1X 8BB Tel:0171-837 8288 Fax:0171-278 1867 **Expertise** Housing management; race equality; community development; project development. **Prev Posts** Housing manager; director of FE establishment. **Prof Background** BA (Hons).

JUPE Miss E.A. Founder & Manager **BROOMFIELD HORSE SANCTUARY** ANIMAL/WILDLIFE Type: Rescue centre for horses & ponies. Holly House, 25 Nancherrow Terrace, St Just-in-Penwith, Cornwall TR19 7LA Tel:01736-788320 **Expertise** Animal welfare & care. **Prev Posts** Self-employed antique restorer and groom. **Prof Background** Grammar School education with 'O' Levels; British Horse Society Training in Horse Management. **Media Experience** Experience with radio & press regarding The Broomfield Horse Sanctuary.

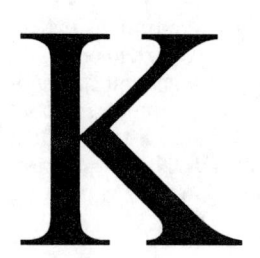

K

KANABUS Annabel Director **AIDS EDUCATION AND RESEARCH TRUST - AVERT** MEDICAL/HEALTH Type: Fundraiser. 11 Denne Parade, Horsham, West Sussex RH12 1JD Tel:01403-210202 Fax:01403-211001 **Expertise** AIDS. **Prof Background** Science degree then worked mainly in computer industry. **Awards/Research** Co-author of various AVERT publications on AIDS.

KAUFMANN Dr Georgia Director **UNITED KINGDOM JEWISH AID AND INTERNATIONAL DEVELOPMENT - UKJAID** SOCIAL Type: Service provider. 33 Seymour Place, London W1H 6AT Tel:0171-723 3442 Fax:0171-723 3445 **Expertise** Social anthropology; population issues; reproductive issues. **Prev Posts** Fellow, Inst of Development Studies, Univ of Sussex 1992-96; Fellow, Harvard Center for Population & Development Studies 1994-95. **Prof Background** DPhil Social Anthropology, Oxford Univ; MSc Population Studies, LSE; BA Anthropology, Cambridge Univ. **Awards/Research** Numerous book & journal articles on kinship structures, marriage systems & socio-economic gender roles. **Media Experience** Radio Sussex & Radio 5 Live - panel talk shows.

KAUFMANN Julia Chief Executive **BBC CHILDREN IN NEED APPEAL** CHILDREN/YOUTH Type: Grant maker. BBC Broadcasting House, Portland Place, London W1A 1AA Tel:0171-765 4151 Fax:0171-765 4183 **Expertise** Grant making; self-help organizations; administration. **Prev Posts** Cllr, Pregnancy Advisory Service 1970-72; Teaching Post 1973-75; Co-director, Centre for Social Education 1976-78; Gingerbread: Info Officer 1978-79; Chief Exec 1979-87. **Prof Background** SRN; B.Ed; Dip. Social Administration. **Awards/Research** Auth: Self Help Day Care Schemes, 1979; A Handbook for Self Help Groups, 1981. **Pres Committees** Assoc. of Charitable Foundations; Mbr, National Lottery Charities Board; Mbr, Broadcast Appeals Consortium. **Past Committees** Exec Cttees: Family Forum; Nat Cncl for Vol Child Care Orgs; Nat Out of School Allnce. Adv Cttee: Internat Yr of the Child 1979. **Media Experience** Contribs to radio and TV; script-writing for children's TV.

KAUSSARI Shala Founder/Executive Director **AFRICA NOW** SOCIAL Type: Fundraiser; Service provider; Grant maker. 4 Rickett Street, London SW6 1RU Tel:0171-386 5200 Fax:0171-386 5910 **Expertise** Programme development; monitoring and evaluation; international development and strategic planning. **Prev Posts** Commercial Marketing and Management 1970-74; Social Marketing Specialist 1974-79; International Development Consultant

1979-83. **Prof Background** BSc Economics; MBA (Master of Business Administration). **Awards/Research** Awds: Allied Chemical Fellowship. Articles and research on application of social marketing in development; Global marketing series. **Pres Committees** Exec Cttee, British Overseas NGOs for Development (BOND); Wharton Alumni Assoc. **Past Committees** Social Marketing International Association.

KAY Janet General Manager **SAINT LEONARDS HOSPICE** MEDICAL/HEALTH Type: Fundraiser; Service provider. 185 Tadcaster Rd, York, N. Yorks YO2 2QL Tel:01904-708553 Fax:01904-704337 **Prev Posts** Macmillan Nurse 1981-84. **Prof Background** BA; RGN; HVCert; ENB 100; ENB 931.

KAY Judy Executive Director **BABY LIFE SUPPORT SYSTEMS - BLISS** MEDICAL/HEALTH Type: Fundraiser; Grant maker. 17-21 Emerald Street, London WC1N 3QL Tel:0171-831 9393 Fax:0171-404 3811 **Expertise** Corporate promotions; direct mail; membership fundraising; telemarketing. **Prev Posts** Appeals Director, Association for Spina Bifida and Hydrocephalus, 1978-85; Appeals Director, Chest, Heart and Stroke Association 1985-87. **Prof Background** Fundraising and public relations. **Awards/Research** Chapter on telemarketing in: Charities and Advertising, by Directory of Social Change. **Past Committees** Executive, ICFM (Inst of Charity Fundraising Managers); Controlling Board, Cashcade Lottery (Ex Ladbrokes). **Media Experience** Experienced broadcaster on TV/radio/video; also scriptwriting and journalist.

KEARY Anne Marie Chairperson **NATIONAL ABORTION CAMPAIGN** SOCIAL Type: Campaigning. The Print House, 18 Ashwin St, London E8 3DL Tel:0171-923 4976 Fax:0171-923 4979 **Expertise** Education and reproductive rights. **Prev Posts** Welfare Officer, University College Dublin 1988-89; Deputy President, Union of Students in Ireland 1989-90; Religious Education Teacher, Archway School 1990-95. **Prof Background** BA; Higher Diploma in Education. **Awards/Research** NAC Publ: Facts & Figures on Abortion; Christianity & Abortion. **Pres Committees** Trustee, Education for Choice; Steering Cttee, Pro-Choice Alliance; Chair, NAC's Management Cttee. **Past Committees** Chair, USI Welfare Cttee; Mbr, Irish Council for Overseas Students. **Media Experience** Discussed abortion issues in all media.

KEEGAN Catherine Director **CAF CERT CONSULTANCY SERVICES** SOCIAL Type: Service provider. Charities Aid Foundation, 114-118 Southampton Row, London WC1B 5AA Tel:0171-400 2300 Fax:0171-404 1331.

KEELING Preston Chief Executive **MYASTHENIA GRAVIS ASSOCIATION** DISABILITY Type: Fundraiser; Service provider. Keynes House, Chester Park, Alfreton Road, Derby DE21 4AS Tel:01332-290 219 Fax:01332-293641 **Expertise** Fundraising; Strategic Planning; Telemarketing; Lotteries; Note: Chair ICFM Lottery Panel. **Prev Posts** General Manager, Commercial Development and Telemarketing, SCOPE, 1974-84. **Prof Background** Member, Institute of Executives & Managers within the Service Industry; Member, Institute of Sales & Marketing Managers; Member, Institute of Charity Fundraising Managers. **Awards/Research** Acknowledged Authority on Lottery Law/Operation. **Pres Committees** Trustee, The Neurological Alliance; Chair, ICFM Lottery Panel; Nat Exec, ICFM. **Media Experience** Wide experience as interviewer/interviewee while Parliamentary Candidate. **Addits** Member, ACENVO.

KEIGWIN Mr R. T. Chief Executive **YORKSHIRE AGRICULTURAL SOCIETY** Type: Fundraiser; Service provider; Grant maker. Gt Yorkshire Showground, Harrogate, N. Yorks HG2 8PW Tel:01423-561536 Fax:01423-531112 **Expertise** General management. **Prev Posts** Military Service (Lt. Col) 1963-92. **Prof Background** Fellow, The Institute of Management. **Media Experience** Experience with radio, TV and press.

KELLEHER Colette Director **DAYCARE TRUST/NATIONAL CHILDCARE CAMPAIGN** CHILDREN/YOUTH Type: Advocacy, research, child daycare/parent needs. 4 Wild Court, London WC2B 4AU Tel:0171-405 5617 Fax:0171-831 6632

KELLY Lesley General Secretary **NATIONAL FEDERATION OF THE BLIND OF THE UNITED KINGDOM** Type: Fundraiser; Campaigning; Self help organization. Unity House, Westgate, Wakefield, W Yorks, WF1 1ER Tel:01924-291313 Fax:01924-200244 **Expertise** Improving the living standards of blind/partially sighted, and helping them live independently.

KELLY Roger Director **CENTRE FOR ALTERNATIVE TECHNOLOGY - CAT** CONSERVATION/ENVIRONMENT Type: Service provider. Machynlleth, Powys SY20 9AZ Tel:01654-702400 Fax:01654-702782 **Expertise** Integrated environmental planning; ecological design; co-operative management. **Prev Posts** Lecturer, Hull School of Architecture 1977-79; Self-employed architect/researcher 1979-87 **Prof Background** Dip.Arch; Registered Architect. **Awards/Research** Publications and articles on rural resource management; ecological design; sustainable development. **Pres Committees** Centre for Alternative Technology Plc; Machynlleth & District Civic Society. **Past Committees** BT Environmental Advisory Panel; Urban Centre for Appropriate Technology; National Ecology Centre, Ireland. **Media Experience** Frequent radio, television and press interviews.

KELMANSON Andrea Director **NATIONAL CENTRE FOR VOLUNTEERING, THE** SOCIAL Type: Promotional and developmental agency. Carriage Row, 183 Eversholt St, London NW1 1BU Tel:0171-388 9888 Fax:0171-388 0448 **Expertise** Volunteering, management in the voluntary sector. **Prev Posts** Programme Manager, Community Service Volunteers 1969-88; Deputy Director, National Aids Trust 1988-92. **Prof Background** Dip. Fine Art (Painting); BA (1st) Management and Organization Development. **Pres Committees** Trustee, Jewish Aids Trust. **Media Experience** Normal activity as per job demands. **Addits** Extensive experience of the criminal justice system.

KEMPTON James Secretary **COLLEGE OF PAEDIATRICS & CHILD HEALTH** Type: Professional Association. 5 St. Andrews Place, Regent's Park, London

NW1 4LB Tel:0171-486 6151 Fax:0171-486 6009 **Prev Posts** Executive Secretary, General Medical Services Committee BMA 1985-89; Head of Central Secretariat, Royal College of General Practitioners 1989-96. **Prof Background** Eltham College; University of York, History and Politics. **Pres Committees** Councillor for Holloway Ward LB Islington; Islington Community Health Council.

KENDALL Jeannie Director/Co-ordinator **MANNA COUNSELLING SERVICE** SOCIAL Type: Fundraiser; Service provider. 147-149 Streatham High Rd, London SW16 6EG Tel:0181-769 1718 Fax:0181-769 1718 **Expertise** Trained psychodynamic counsellor; trained teacher; counselling; training & all aspects of administration. **Prev Posts** Teacher, Camberwell 1976-79; Head of Religious Studies, Grey Coat School, Westminster 1979-82. **Prof Background** B.Ed (1976); Counselling: 3 yrs, Sutton Pastoral Foundation; 2 yrs, Goldsmiths College, Advanced Diploma Psychodynamic Counselling.

KENNARD Alan Secretary **BLUE CROSS, THE** ANIMAL/WILDLIFE Type: Fundraiser; Service provider. Shilton Road, Burford, Oxfordshire OX18 4PF Tel:01993-822651 Fax:01993-823083 **Expertise** Effective use of publicly donated resources to improve human, animal and natural environmental welfare. **Prev Posts** Snr Mngr, Coopers and Lybrand 1965-72; accountancy practice Plymouth 1972-76; Asst Treasurer, Lady Margaret Hall, Oxford 1976-89. **Prof Background** Chartered Accountant (FCA). **Awards/Research** MBE. **Media Experience** Chair, Jnt Cttee for Conservation of the Large Blue Butterfly; Jnt Cttee for Conservation of Brit. Insects; Hon Sec/Council Mbr, Berks, Bucks and Oxon Naturalists Trust; Blue Cross Trading Co Ltd.

KENNETT R J Director **ROYAL AERONAUTICAL SOCIETY** SOCIAL Type: Service provider; Grant maker. 4 Hamilton Place, London W1V 0BQ Tel:0171-499 3515 Fax:0171-499 6230 **Expertise** Engineering & Management. **Prev Posts** Lucas Aerospace Ltd, Chief Engineer (10 Years); Power Systems Division, Quality Assurance Manager (2 Years). **Prof Background** Engineering & Management. **Awards/Research** Awards: FIMgt, FInstD, FCIT, AFAIAA, FRAES, FRSA. **Media Experience** Frequent radio & TV broadcasts.

KENT Alastair Director **GENETIC INTEREST GROUP - GIG** MEDICAL/HEALTH Type: Service provider; Info/awareness raising campaigning/umbrella body. Farringdon Point, 29-35 Farringdon Rd, London EC1M 3JB Tel:0171-430 0090 Fax:0171-430 0092 **Expertise** Policy and service development. **Prev Posts** RNID 1986-89; Action for Blind People 1989-93. **Prof Background** Special Educ. Service development with disabled people. Policy work, advocacy, campaigning. **Awards/Research** Res: M.Phil; Occupational Choice in Schl Leavers with Learning Difficulties. **Pres Committees** Trustee: MD Group; Skill: Nat Bureau for Students With Disab; United Response. **Past Committees** IYDP Emp Cttee;RADAR,Educ & Employment Cttee;HASICOM;ACENVO Exec Cttee;CHANGE:Cncl for People with Learning/Sensory Disabilities. **Media Experience** Local/nat interviews; contrib/consult progs and articles, etc.

KENT Howard Director **YOGA FOR HEALTH FOUNDATION** MEDICAL/HEALTH Type: Service provider. Ickwell Bury, Biggleswade, Beds SG18 9EF Tel:01767-627271 Fax:01767-627266 **Expertise** Remedial Yoga (chronic conditions);preventative health measures. **Prev Posts** Held current post since 1972. **Prof Background** Education: Whitgift;former newspaper journalist/Film/Stage/TV Producer. **Awards/Research** Unity in Yoga Award (U.S.)1995;Books: Day-By-Day Yoga, My fun with Yoga, Key Facts: Yoga, Yoga for the Disabled, Complete Yoga Course. **Pres Committees** International Advisory Council: Assoc of Yoga Therapists; Unity in Yoga; International Integrated Health Assoc. **Media Experience** Number of TV/Radio appearances.

KERBEY Alan National Director **CRUSADERS** CHILDREN/YOUTH Type: Service provider; Christian Youth Organisation. 2 Romeland Hill, St Albans, Herts AL3 4ET Tel:01727-855422 Fax:01727-848518 **Expertise** Regulation of Intermediary Metabolism; Christian Youth Work. **Prev Posts** University Research Scientist, University of Oxford, 1982-92; Lecturer in Biochemistry, Trinity College, Oxford, 1985-92. **Prof Background** Biochemistry (Universities of Bristol & Oxford),PhD; Post-Doctoral Training, Oxford & Sydney. **Awards/Research** Scientific: The Biochemistry & Physiology of Diabetes (60 publications); Religion: 1 book & articles in Christian periodicals. **Pres Committees** Evangelical Alliance Youth Committee; Joint Consultative working group with 3 other youth organisations. **Media Experience** Radio, Press.

KERR Ruby Joint National Organiser **NATIONAL WOMEN'S REGISTER** WOMEN Type: Service provider. 3a Vulcan House, Vulcan Road North, Norwich NR6 6AQ Tel:01603-406 767 Fax:01603-407 003 **Expertise** Responsible for finance & conferences. **Prev Posts** Regional Organiser & National Grp Member, 1994-96; Field worker & voluntary fundraiser for local hospice. **Prof Background** Business Training, Caledonia University; Sales; Postmistress; Managerial Training; Personnel Admin; Managed small business. **Media Experience** TV & radio discussions.

KILBRIDE Peter Director **RSI ASSOCIATION** MEDICAL/HEALTH Type: Fundraiser; Service provider; Campaigning. Chapel House, 152-156 High Street, Yiewsley, West Drayton, Middlesex UB7 7BE Tel:01895-431134 Fax:01895-431134 **Expertise** Administration, Fundraising, Advice & Support. **Prof Background** Banking & Business. **Media Experience** Experience in radio, TV and press.

KILN Dr Matthew Principal in Gen Practice/Co-Chairman **INSULIN DEPENDENT DIABETES TRUST** MEDICAL/HEALTH Type: Fundraiser; Information & Education. PO Box 294, Northampton NN3 2BN Tel:01604-721325 Fax:01604-721325 **Expertise** Diabetes Mellitus & Human Insulin; Views of patients in the NHS; Sports; Medicine. **Prev Posts** School Doctor, Dulwich College 1980-96; Medical SHO 98-86; GP 1986-96. **Prof Background** Doctor. **Awards/Research** MBBG; ORCOG; FRSH; Many publications on diabetes and sport in Nature, Lancet, BMJ. **Pres Committees** Child Health Care Group, King's College Hospital; Sports

Working Party; British Diabetic Association; Rockefeller Foundation, April 1996. **Past Committees** Loss of Warnings Task Force; British Diabetic Association. **Media Experience** Experience with press (national) and TV (Newsnight & several shows).

KIMBER Charles Peter Chief Executive **SCRIPTURE UNION - ENGLAND** RELIGIOUS Type: Service provider; Christian Evangelistic Movement. 207-209 Queensway, Bletchley, Milton Keynes MK2 2EB Tel:01908-856000 Fax:01908-856005 **Expertise** Bible reading promotion, children's Christian education. **Prev Posts** Assistant Director, Scottish Examination Board 1987-93; Deputy Chief Executive & Director of Development, Scottish Examination Board 1993-96. **Prof Background** St Lawrence College, Ramsgate; MA, English Language & Literature, Oxford Univ; Dip Ed, Aberdeen Univ; MEd, Glasgow Univ; Pilot Officer, Royal Air Force; Meteorologist, Brit Antarctic Survey. **Awards/Research** Various occasional articles in educational journals. **Pres Committees** Cttee on Testing: 5-14, Scot Off Ed & Industry Dept (SEOID); Curriculum & Assessment Grp (SOEID); Qualifications & Marketing Cttee, Scot Vocational Ed Cncl; Chair, Brit & Irl Reg Cncl, Script Union. **Media Experience** Radio & TV appearances; arts for press (ref: exams, assessment & Christianity).

KING Angela Co-Director **COMMON GROUND** CONSERVATION/ENVIRONMENT Type: Service provider; Education/awareness raising. Seven Dials Warehouse, 44 Earlham Street, London WC2H 9LA Tel:0171-379 3109 Fax:0171-836 5741 **Expertise** Making links between culture and place. **Prev Posts** Friends of the Earth's (first) wildlife campaigner 1971-75;Joint co-ordinator Otter Haven Project 1975-79; Earth Resources researcher (wildlife habitat loss) 1979-80. **Awards/Research** Arts/environmental articles in popular/professional journals; auth: Paradise Lost? 1980; Co-auth/ed: Whale Campaign Manual 2 1974; The Declining Otter 1976; Holding Your Ground 1985. **Past Committees** Friends of the Earth Wildlife Advisory Group 1986-88; The Green Alliance Board 1989-92. **Media Experience** Press. **Addits** Promoting Local Distinctiveness Project.

KING Charles Chief Executive **ROYAL SCHOOL OF CHURCH MUSIC - RSCM** ARTS Type: Service provider. Cleveland Lodge, Westhumble, Dorking, Surrey RH5 6BW Tel:01306-877676 Fax:01306-887260 **Expertise** Administration; accountancy. **Prev Posts** MD, Wheelers Restaurants 1984-88; MD, City Jeroboam 1988-91. **Prof Background** Accountant (FCMA); retailing background.

KING Diana Chief Executive **ENGLISH SKI COUNCIL** SPORTS Type: Fundraiser; Service provider; Grant maker; Sports governing body. Area Library Bldg, Queensway Mall, The Cornbow, Halesowen, West Midlands B63 4AJ Tel:0121-501 2314 Fax:0121-585 6448 **Expertise** Sports Administration, Management & Development. **Prev Posts** Solicitor, Pinsent & Co., Birmingham 1983-85. **Prof Background** Solicitor, qualified 1979; BA (Law) Sheffield University; Currently reading for MBA at Aston University. **Pres Committees** Central Council of Physical Recreation Executive Committee. **Past Committees** British Gliding Association Executive Committee 1983-93.

KING Peggy Anne Administration Director **BRITISH ORT** SOCIAL Type: Service Provider. British ORT House, 126 Albert St, London NW1 7NF Tel:0171-446 8520 Fax:0171-446 8654 **Expertise** Administration; function organization; fundraising. **Prev Posts** B'Nai Brith Hillel Foundation 1992-94; Lecturer, London University Extra Mural Dept. **Prof Background** BA Hons: PGCE. **Pres Committees** Association of Jewish Communal Professionals.

KING Robert Artistic Director **KING'S CONSORT, THE** ARTS Type: Fundraiser; Service provider. 34 St Mary's Grove, Chiswick, London W4 3LN Tel:0181-995 9994 Fax:0181-995 2115 **Expertise** Classical music. **Prev Posts** Artistic Director, The King's Consort since 1980. **Prof Background** MA (Cantab). **Awards/Research** Editor of much pre-1750 music (some published by Faber Music); Henry Purcell, biography (pub. Thames & Hudson). **Pres Committees** PAMRA. **Media Experience** Considerable experience in all media, esp recording industry, radio & TV.

KING Stephen P. Director TCS Division **ROYAL NATIONAL INSTITUTE FOR THE BLIND - RNIB** DISABILITY Type: Service provider. Bakewell Road, Orton Southgate, Peterborough PE2 0XU Tel:01733-370777 Fax:01733-391865 **Expertise** Communications (publishing, library services), daily living (aids/equip), production, distribution. **Prev Posts** Fontana Pbk mngr, Wm Collins 1972-82; Ops Mngr, RCA Columbia Video 1982-85; Ops Dir, Athena Internat 1985-88; Consult, Business Ops. 1988-90. **Prof Background** Manager in Business MBA - operations, marketing and finance. **Pres Committees** British Wireless Fund for the Blind; Director: Big Print Ltd; ETNA Ltd; IFLA - Section for Libraries for the Blind. **Addits** Bringing modern management effectiveness methods/style to Vol Sect.

KIRKWOOD James K. Scientific Director **UNIVERSITIES FEDERATION FOR ANIMAL WELFARE - - UFAW** ANIMAL/WILDLIFE Type: Technical, scientific & educational. 8 Hamilton Close, South Mimms, Potters Bar, Herts EN6 3QD Tel:01707-658202 Fax:01707-649279 **Expertise** Health, welfare & conservation of captive & free-living wild animals. **Prev Posts** Research Fellow, Hawk Trust 1977-78; Rsrch Fellow, Bristol Univ 1981-84; Snr Veterinary Off & Head of Veterinary Science Grp, Inst of Zoology, Zoological Soc of London 1984-96. **Prof Background** BVSc; PhD; MRCVS. **Awards/Research** Author of 1 book and over 100 papers in scientific literature (aspects of diseases, medicine, management, welfare & conservation of wild animals). **Pres Committees** Visiting Research Fellow, Inst of Zoology; Dir, Inst of Zoology/Royal Veterinary Coll Master's Course in Wild Animal Health; Chief Examiner, Royal Coll of Veterinary Surgeons Zoological Medicine Brd. **Past Committees** Pres, Brit Vet Zoolgcl Soc 1994-95; Tres, Brit Wildlife Rehab Cncl Steering Gp 1991-96; Mbr, Sci Adv Cncl of Wild & Wetlands Trust. **Media Experience** Various, with TV, radio & press. **Addits** Dept of the Environment Zoo Inspector.

KITCHING H.S. Secretary **INSTITUTION OF STRUCTURAL ENGINEERS BENEVOLENT FUND** SOCIAL Type: Fundraiser; Grant maker. 11 Upper Belgrave Street, London SW1X 8BH Tel:0171-235 4535 Tel:0171-235 4294

KNOX John National General Secretary **YMCA SCOTLAND** CHILDREN/YOUTH Type: Service provider; Voluntary Youth Organisation. 11 Rutland Street, Edinburgh EH1 2AE Tel:0131-228 1464 Fax:0131-228 5462 **Expertise** Management; Development; Youth work and youth work policy. **Prev Posts** Gen Sec, Irish Methodist Youth Dept 1969-78; Assoc Sec, Irish Cncl of Churches 1978-82; Chief Officer, Scottish Standing Conf of Vol Youth Org 1982-92. **Prof Background** Methodist Minister; BA, Queens University, Belfast; BD, London University. **Awards/Research** Author of publications & articles on youth work and education; Peace Education publications & articles. **Pres Committees** Trustee, Unemployed Voluntary Action Fund; Hon Director, Youthlink Scotland; Member, Scottish Youth Work Partners Group; Sundry church and youth work committees. **Past Committees** CEVE (Community Ed Validation & Endorsement); Peace Ed Network; Nat Youth Cncl of Ireland Executive; Scottish Comty Ed Youth Cttee. **Media Experience** Radio & TV on Youth Work/Relig Affairs/Crnt Issues; BBC, ITV, Lcl Radio.

KOE Brigadier M.R. Chief Executive **PROGRESSIVE SUPRANUCLEAR PALSY (PSP EUROPE) ASSOCIATION** MEDICAL/HEALTH Type: Fundraiser; Service provider; Grant maker; Campaigning; promote research into PSP. The Old Rectory, Wappenham, Towcester, Northants N12 8SQ Tel:01327-860342 Fax:01327-860242 **Expertise** Concerned with research into cause, treatment & cure of PSP; support & info for patients & their carers. **Prev Posts** Military (Retired 1984); Defence Security Consultant since 1984. **Prof Background** BSc (Eng); (PSc JSSC); Military, Regular Army Officer. **Awards/Research** OBE. **Pres Committees** Trustee & Executive Committee Member, Progressive Supranuclear Palsy Association. **Past Committees** Military Committees & Joint Intelligence Committee (Germany). **Media Experience** Experience with local media.

KUMAR Harpal S. Chief Executive **PAPWORTH TRUST** DISABILITY Type: Fundraiser; Service provider. Head Office, Papworth Everard, Cambridge CB3 8RG Tel:01480-830341 Fax:01480-830781 **Expertise** Voluntary/special needs sector; finance; organisational management; manufacturing industry. **Prev Posts** Healthcare Specialist/Engagement Manager, McKinsey & Co. Inc. (Management consultants) 1987-93. **Prof Background** M.A., M.Eng - 1st class Hons (Chemical Engineering), St. John's College, Cambridge; MBA Harvard Business School. **Awards/Research** Duke of Edinburgh Award (Gold). **Pres Committees** Brd Mbr, CambsTEC, Camb (Training & Enterprise Cncl); Mbr, South Cambs Consultative Grp; Business Sub-Group; Mbr, Ed Strategy Forum; Mbr, Special Needs Sub-Group; Exec Grp Mbr, NATWHAG. **Media Experience** Experience in national & local television, radio and press.

KYRKE-SMITH Neville National Director **AID TO THE CHURCH IN NEED - ACN** RELIGIOUS Type: Fundraiser; Grant maker. 1 Times Square, Sutton, Surrey SM1 1LF Tel:0181-642 8668 Fax:0181-661 6293 **Expertise** Religions; marketing. **Prev Posts** Graduate Management Trainee, Sales & Marketing, Bass M&B 1979-81; Clergyman, CofE, Oxford & London 1983-90. **Prof Background** MA (Oxon);Sales & Marketing Training (Bass M&B); Pastoral & Management Responsibility (CofE), Cert Theol (Oxon). **Awards/Research** Theology, esp Catholic Church in E Europe;articles on Catholicism. **Pres Committees** Churches' East-West European Relations Network; Church Liturgy Committee;International Directors Conference (Germany). **Past Committees** Church Advisory Board; School Governor/Chairman. **Media Experience** Radio and press interviews.

L

LAIDLAW Bruce Administrative Secretary **ROYAL SCOTTISH ACADEMY** ARTS Type: Art Gallery. The Mound, Edinburgh EH2 2EL Tel:0131-225 6671 Fax:0131-225 2349 **Expertise** Administration, project organisation & committee management. **Prev Posts** Public Service, Edinburgh City 1966-74; Elections Officer, Lothian Regional Council 1975-79; Public Service, Lothian Regional Council 1980-95. **Prof Background** Company Secretary (ACIS). **Pres Committees** Chairman, Lothian Friends of ARMS.

LAMB Robert Director **TELEVISION TRUST FOR THE ENVIRONMENT - TVE** CONSERVATION/ENVIRONMENT Type: Fundraiser; Service provider. Prince Albert Road, London NW2 4RZ Tel:0171-586 5526 Fax:0171-586 4866 **Prev Posts** UN Envir Prog: Science Writer/Policy Adviser, 1982-84; Consultant to Exec Dir, 1984-92, Communications Dir, Int Union for Conservation of Nature & Natural Resources. **Prof Background** Sorbonne, Paris (1970) Advanced Certificate in French; Cambridge BA (History), Gladstone Scholarship, MA (1979). **Awards/Research** Articles in over 70 mass circ newspapers worldwide; Auth/co-auth:BOOT, Saddle to Horse (Cobett's Rural Rides revisited) 1977, State of the Planet - Ed 1982, Earth Matters - Ed 1984. **Pres Committees** Chair, Agenda 21 Helsinki Group; Co-Chair Global Television Network;Mbr Prix Leonardo, Adv Bd People & the Planet, IUCN Education Commission;Chair and Pres,TVE (USA),Chair,TVE Netherlands; Bd TVE Japan **Past Committees** Exec Consultant to EC Med Media prog,Officer OUTREACH TVE's info to schs in dev countries. **Addits** Auth: Env Film Guide 1986, Burke to Band Aid.

LAMBERT Bobby REDR - REGISTERED ENGINEERS FOR DISASTER RELIEF SOCIAL Type: Service provider. 1-7 Great George St, London SW1P 3AA Tel:0171-233 3116 Fax:0171-222 0564

LAMPLUGH Diana Director/Founder **SUZY LAMPLUGH TRUST, THE** SOCIAL Type: Fundraiser; Service provider; Research/education/campaigning for safer lives. 14 East Sheen Avenue, London SW14 8AS Tel:0181-392 1839 Fax:0181-392 1830 **Expertise** Personal safety. **Prev Posts** Founder/Director, British Slimnastics Association. **Prof Background** City and Guilds 730, Teaching Adult Education (Double Distinction, 1980) **Awards/Research** OBE. Auth: Beating Aggression, 88; Without Fear, 91; Personal Safety for Schools, 96; training manuals on personal safety while travelling, violence in workplace, missing persons. **Pres Committees** HM Gov: Health and Safety Exec's Cttee on Violence; Dept of Transport, Wking Pty on Minicabs; HSE Cttee on Violence, Financial Sector; BT Police Cttee; Chair, HO Cttee for Personal Safety for Disabled. **Past Committees** Central Cttee, Physical recreation; International Stress and Tension Control Soc. **Media Experience** Frequent/unlimited experience of all media; training/talks given to orgs.

LANCASTER Mike Director of External Relations **ROYAL NATIONAL INSTITUTE FOR THE BLIND RNIB** DISABILITY Type: Service provider; Campaigning. 224 Great Portland Street, London W1N 6AA Tel:0171-388 1266 Fax:0171-388 2034 **Expertise** Marketing; fundraising; PR. **Prev Posts** British Rail (1970-89) senior marketing positions, Marketing Manager Intercity (British Railways Board) 1985-89. **Prof Background** BA (Hons) Social Sciences, Kent University 1970; MBA (Business Administration) City University 1980; Dip. Market Research Soc 1980; Mbr Institute of Charity Fundraising Managers 1989. **Pres Committees** Hon Treasurer, ICFM, & Chair, Resources Cttee, ICFM; Director, Cards for Good Causes Ltd (The 1959 Group of Charities). **Past Committees** Governor, St Mary's College, Twickenham. **Media Experience** Considerable experience. **Addits** Led/joined Parent Action Gps - for blind and/or disab children.

LANE Barry John Secretary General **ROYAL PHOTOGRAPHIC SOCIETY, THE** Type: Service provider; Campaigning; Membership society. The Octagon, Milsom Street, Bath, Avon BA1 1DN Tel:01225-462841 Fax:01225-448688 **Expertise** Photography; New Technology; Public Sector Funding; Publishing Exhibitions; Archives & Collections. **Prev Posts** Photography Officer, Arts Council 1973-91; Head of Photography, Arts Council, 1991-95. **Prof Background** BA (Oxon), Philosophy & Psychology. **Awards/Research** 1972 Kodak Award. **Pres Committees** British Photographers Liaison Committee;AXIS-Visual Arts Inf Serv;SW Arts Adviser;British Photographic Association;Wells Museum Trustee.

LANE J.E.J Executive Secretary **ROYAL ASTRONOMICAL SOCIETY** ENVIRONMENT Type: Professional Association. Burlington House, Piccadilly, London W1V 0NL Tel:0171-734 4582 Fax:0171-494 0166 **Expertise** Administrator; Personnel. **Prev Posts** Regular Army Officer (Colonel) retired 1954-91. **Prof Background** RMA Sandhurst; Army Staff College Camberley (psc); National Defence College (ndc). **Pres Committees** All Society Cttee; Mayfair and St James Association; Point of Contact for various Scientific wkng gps. **Past Committees** Service (Army) Administration, Training, Operations; International (NATO) Military Cttees. **Media Experience** Some media experience.

LANE John Director/Secretary **ST MUNGO ASSOCIATION CHARITABLE TRUST** SOCIAL Type: Fundraiser; Grant maker - Grants to St Mungo Housing Assoc only. Atlantic House, 1-3 Rockley Rd, London W14 0DJ Tel:0181-600 3000 Fax:0181-600 3079 **Expertise** General management and fundraising. **Prev Posts** Director, Peckham Settlement 1972-77; National PRO, YWCA of GB 1977-79; Director/Secretary St Mungo Housing Assoc

1980-94. **Prof Background** Anglican priest, Dip Theol; MSc Motivation of Professionals to work in Vol Agencies, Cranfield. **Awards/Research** Int Editor, Homelessness in Industrialised Countries. **Pres Committees** Meeting Point Community Development Project Cttee SE15. **Past Committees** Int Fed/Housing/Planning Cttee on Homelessness;Ch,Frobisher Adult Educ Inst.Mbr,Rowntree Trust Res Body on Homelessness. **Media Experience** Contrib to radio/TV and press. **Addits** Mbr, Euro Fed of Nat Orgs Working with the Homeless.

LANE Jon Director **WATERAID** OVERSEAS Type: Service provider; Overseas Development. Prince Consort House, 27-29 Albert Embankment, London SE1 7UB Tel:0171-793 4500 Fax:0171-793 4545 **Expertise** Civil engineering relating to overseas development and disaster relief. **Prev Posts** Civil Engineer, Ove Arup Partnership 1979-86; Country Representative, Wateraid, Nepal 1987-91; Director, RedR 1991-94. **Prof Background** MA (Cantab); Member of the Institution of Civil Engineers. **Awards/Research** Various articles relating to water and sanitation in developing countries. **Media Experience** Interviews given.

LANE Paddy Executive Officer **NATIONAL RETREAT ASSOCIATION** RELIGIOUS Type: Service provider; Info and resources about Christian retreats. The Central Hall, 256 Bermondsey St, London SE1 3UJ Tel:0171-357 7736 Fax:0171-357 7724 **Expertise** Administration; Ecumenical. **Prev Posts** Finance Officer for Childrens Charity 1979-86; Adminstration Public Sector 1989-94. **Media Experience** Occasional articles.

LANKESTER Dr Ted Director **INTERHEALTH** MEDICAL/HEALTH Type: Service provider. Partnership House, 157 Waterloo Road, London SE1 8US Tel:0171-902 9000 Fax:0171-902 0927 **Expertise** Travel medicine, Community health in developing countries; Church-related holistic health care. **Prev Posts** Principal in General Practice 1974-81; Founder-Director, SHARE Community Health Programme, N. India 1984-88. **Prof Background** Medical, Hospital, General Practice, Developing Countries. Education: St Thomas's Hospital, Trinity Hall Cambridge, St John's College Nottingham. **Awards/Research** Author of Setting up Community Health Programmes, Macmillan 1991; Good Health Good Travel, Hodder & Stoughton 1995. **Pres Committees** Brd Mbr & Mbr Personnel Cttee, Tear Fund; Mbr, Overseas Service Cttee Christian Medical Fellowship; Editorial Brd, Footsteps Newspaper (Tear Fund); Trustee, Taj Trust; Asst Ed, Tropical Medicine. **Addits** Community Health Advisor to Medical Services International.

LANSDALE Susan Director **BRITISH FEDERATION OF YOUNG CHOIRS - BFYC** CHILDREN/YOUTH Type: Fundraiser; Service provider; Grant maker; Campaigning. 37 Frederick St, Loughborough, Leics LE11 3BH Tel:01509-211664 Fax:01509-233749 **Expertise** Specialised Arts Management; Marketing; Publicity. **Prev Posts** Company Secretary/Administrator, Cambridge Symphony Orchestra Trust Ltd 1978-83; Administrator, Airline Computer Services Ltd 1985-86. **Prof Background** BA (Hons) Music; PGCE Music; MA (Arts Administration). **Awards/Research** MA Thesis - Orchestral Music Provision in East Anglia; Churchill Fellowship Report, Children's Choir Training in Europe; Various published articles. **Media Experience** TV/radio: mainly news reports; press articles.

LANSDELL Nick Team Leader **YMCA SCOTQUEST** Type: Service provider; Voluntary sector. 11 Rutland Street, Edinburgh EH1 2AE Tel:0131-228 1464 Fax:0131-228 5462 **Expertise** Outdoor education. **Prev Posts** Outdoors Instructor, University of Edinburgh 1993-94; Team Leader, Princes Trust Volunteers 1994-95. **Prof Background** MA Religious Studies, Edinburgh University; PGCE, R.E. Secondary; DPSE, Outdoor Education. **Media Experience** Experience in TV, local Radio & press interviews.

LASHBROOKE Ian Chief Executive & Commandant **ROYAL STAR & GARTER HOME FOR DISABLED SAILORS, SOLDIERS & AIRMEN** DISABILITY Type: Fundraiser; Service provider. The Royal Star & Garter Home, Richmond Hill, Richmond, Surrey TW10 6RR Tel:0181-940 3314 Fax:0181-940 1953 **Expertise** Fundraising & Administration. **Prev Posts** Director of Appeals, Royal Masonic Hospital, 1982-84; Chief Executive, Royal Masonic Hospital 1984-87; Director of the Appeals, Royal Star & Garter Home, 1987-92. **Prof Background** Fleet Air Arm Engineer 1960-82. Member, ICFM. **Awards/Research** Various articles, Charity Magazine. **Pres Committees** F&GP Cttee;Fundraising Cttee;Care & Development Cttee;Dir of Pharmacy Trading Co.(All at Royal Star & Garter Home);Cncl Mbr,Royal British Legion Poppy Factory. **Past Committees** Executive & Finance Committee, Royal Masonic Hospital; Fundraising Committee, Royal Masonic Hospital. **Media Experience** Extensive Radio & TV Interviews.

LAURENZI Carlo Executive Director **PRISONERS ABROAD** SOCIAL Type: Service provider. 82 Rosebery Avenue, London EC1R 4RR Tel:0171-833 3467 Fax:0171-833 3460 **Prev Posts** Director, Policy & Research, National Deaf Children's Society; also worked in the City, local government and as a consultant. **Prof Background** Member of public body, DLAAB.

LAVERY Christine Director **SOCIETY FOR MUCOPOLYSACCHHARIDE DISEASES - MPS** MEDICAL/HEALTH Type: Service provider; Grant maker; Training days/personal workshops for parents. 55 Hill Avenue, Amersham, Bucks HP6 5BX Tel:01494-434156 Fax:01494-434252 **Expertise** Support to parents of children with rare life threatening diseases; bereavement support. **Prev Posts** Training for Specific Disease Co-ordinator, Mental Health Foundation grant 1983-87; Nat Dev Officer for Specific Condition Gps, Contact a Family 1987-93. **Prof Background** Nursing skills acquired from accompanying husband on postings in diplomatic service: volunteering in Japan; parent of child who died from MPS. **Awards/Research** Whitbread Award 1986;Jerwood Guardian Award 1995;10 yr study of incidence of MPS;Auth:Contact a Family Directory of Specific Diseases & its Support Network; Pre-Natal Diagnosis and Termination of Fetal Abnormality (Kings Fund). **Pres Committees** Trustee,Lawrence Moon Biedl Cttee;Trustee,ACT (Action for Children with Terminal Illness);DOH Advisory Cttee on Genetic Testing (ACGT). **Past Committees** V-Ch,Genetics Interest Gp;Pilot Projects for Life-Limiting Diseases;Dept/Health Grant Giving Board;V-Ch of Progress. **Media Experience** Many news/features: After Simon; Help Prog; BBC Children in Need; News, Jeans for Genes Campaign. **Addits** Organised 4-day internat conf on MPS, 28 nations and 630 delegates.

LAWES Glen Chief Executive **IRONBRIDGE GORGE MUSEUM TRUST** CONSERVATION Type: Museum, Educational Charity. Ironbridge, Telford, Shropshire TF8 7AW Tel:01952-433522 Fax:01952-432204 **Expertise** Management. **Prev Posts** General Management, British Petroleum 1979-91. **Prof Background** Degree in Engineering. **Pres Committees** Ironbridge Gorge Museum Trading Co.; Severn Gorge Countryside Trust; Ironbridge Institute. **Media Experience** Experience with radio (local broadcaster) & press (one-time weekly journalist).

LAWSON Andrew J. Unit Director **TRUST FOR WESSEX ARCHAEOLOGY LTD** Type: Service provider. Old Sarum Park, Salisbury, Wilts SP4 6EB Tel:01722-326867 Fax:01722-337562 **Expertise** Archaeology. **Prev Posts** Deputy County Field Archaeologist, Norfolk County Council 1973-83. **Prof Background** BSc (Hons) University of Wales; MSc, University of London. **Awards/Research** Author of more than 50 articles & books on prehistory & British archaeology. **Pres Committees** Mbr, Ancient Monuments Advisory Cttee (English Heritage); Mbr, Reg Advisory Cttee (S & W) (Forestry Commission); Mbr, Contract Archaeology Cttee (Inst of Field Archaeologists). **Past Committees** Cncl, Prehistoric Society; Cncl for British Archaeology; Cncl, Soc of Antiquaries; Science based Archaeology Cttee (SERC/NERC). **Media Experience** Experience in national and local radio & TV. **Addits** Fellow of The Society of Antiquaries.

LAWSON Isobel Director **STEPPING STONES IN SCOTLAND** SOCIAL Type: Service provider. 55 Renfrew St, Glasgow G2 3BD Tel:0141-3312828 Fax:0141-3311991 **Prev Posts** Development Worker, Strathclyde Regional Council 1977-87; Development Worker, Stepping Stones in Scotland 1987-88. **Prof Background** Social work & community development. **Pres Committees** Board Member, Children in Scotland; Executive Member, Scottish Network; Executive Member, Strathclyde Early Years Forum; Board Member, The Wynd Centre. **Media Experience** Experience in interviews & articles for radio, TV and press.

LAYLAND Dr W. Ralph Vice-President **BRITISH PSYCHO-ANALYTICAL SOCIETY,THE/INSTITUTE OF PSYCHO-ANALYSIS,THE** Type: Professional association. 63 New Cavendish Street, London W1M 7RD Tel:0171-580 4952 Fax:0171-323 5312 **Expertise** Psychoanalysis. **Prof Background** Psychoanalyst; MD; MRCPsych; DPM.

LEACH R.C.F. Registrar **CORPORATION OF THE SONS OF THE CLERGY** RELIGIOUS Type: Grant maker. 1 Dean Trench Street, London SW1P 3HB Tel:0171-799 3696 Fax:0171-233 1913 **Prev Posts** HM Services (Army) 1955-75; Deputy Registrar, Corporation of the Sons of the Clergy 1975-82. **Prof Background** RMA Sandhurst & Service.

LEAR Stephen Director **ROYAL LIFE SAVING SOCIETY UK, THE - RLSS UK** SOCIAL/CHILDREN/HEALTH Type: Fundraiser; Service provider. Mountbatten House, Studley, Warwickshire B80 7NN Tel:01527-853943 Fax:01527-854453 **Expertise** Management, especially human resources, team development, managing strategic change. **Prev Posts** Director, management consultant. Personnel & line management at Shell, BOC & NHS. **Prof Background** BSc Sociology; FIPD.

LEE Philip Chief Executive **BRITISH EPILEPSY ASSOCIATION** MEDICAL/HEALTH Type: Fundraiser; Service provider; Grant maker; Campaigning. Anstey House, 40 Hanover Square, Leeds, W Yorks LS3 1BF Tel:0113-243 9393 Fax:0113-242 8804 **Expertise** Fundraising; volunteer services; general management/charity administration. **Prev Posts** BEA: Marketing Manager; Development Director. **Prof Background** BA Hons History (Wales); Company Secretary. **Awards/Research** Auth: many articles in national and international epilepsy journals. **Pres Committees** Joint Epilepsy Council (JEC) Management Committee Member; Director BEA Trading Ltd; Member of International Bureau for Epilepsy European Committee. **Media Experience** Numerous and regular interviews/contributions.

LEE Stephen Director **INSTITUTE OF CHARITY FUNDRAISING MANAGERS TRUST - ICFM** SOCIAL Type: Professional Institute. 5th Floor, Market Towers, No 1, Nine Elms Lane, London SW8 5NQ Tel:0171-627 3436 Fax:0171-627 3508 **Prev Posts** Deputy Director, Charities Advisory Trust 1984-86; Commercial Director, Family Welfare Association 1986-88. **Prof Background** BA (Hons) Humanities, Huddersfield Polytechnic; MSc (Econ) International Relations, LSE. **Awards/Research** Numerous. **Pres Committees** Over 25. **Past Committees** NCVO Nathan Report on efficiency and effectiveness of Voluntary Sector; Charity Commission/NCVO On Trust, wking pty on trustee role. **Media Experience** Frequent appearances on national and regional TV and press. **Addits** 150 plus conf/after dinner speeches on fundraising/charitable sector yearly.

LENG Alan Executive Director **DYSTONIA SOCIETY, THE** MEDICAL/HEALTH Type: Fundraiser; Service provider; Welfare. Weddel House, 13-14 West Smithfield, London EC1A 9HY Tel:0171-329 0797 Fax:0171-329 0689 **Expertise** Charity administration; marketing; fundraising. **Prev Posts** Director, Cyclists' Touring Club 1981-89; Marketing, PR and Fundraising Director, Mary Rose Trust 1989-91; Appeal Director, Froebel Institute College 1991-92. **Prof Background** BA (Hons) French and Spanish; Postgraduate Certificate in Education. **Pres Committees** Trustee/Dir, The Neurological Alliance. **Past Committees** Director, Mary Rose Trading Co; Clerk to the Trustees, Cycle Touring and Countryside Trust. **Media Experience** Interview experience with all media; planning input on TV/radio programmes.

LERMAN Antony Executive Director **INSTITUTE FOR JEWISH POLICY RESEARCH - JPR** SOCIAL Type: Policy Research Institute. 79 Wimpole Street, London W1M 7DD Tel:0171-935 8266 Fax:0171-935 3252

Expertise Public policy issues affecting Jews and Jewish communities worldwide. **Prof Background** University of Sussex; London School of Economics. **Pres Committees** Executive Committee, Jewish Council for Racial Equality. **Media Experience** Articles for press; BBC TV news, Newsnight, Channel 4 News, BBC World TV. **Addits** BBC Radio 4 broadcasts: Today, PM, World at One; BBC World Serv Radio.

LESIRGE R. Chief Executive **COTTAGE HOMES** SOCIAL Type: Fundraiser; Service provider; Grant maker. HQ Marshall Estate, Hammers Lane, London NW7 4EE Tel:0181-201-0111 Fax:0181-959-4425 **Expertise** Trade benevolent organisation to the fashion & stores trade; Core business: eldercare, residential estate. **Prev Posts** Principal Ad. Ed. Institute 1989-92. **Prof Background** Education, Adult education, medical education, management training. **Awards/Research** BBC publication, adult literacy, education publications for Macmillan, NEC, etc. **Pres Committees** Executive Committee Member, ACENVO; Governor, Hendon FE College; Governor, Secondary School. **Past Committees** Chair, Barnet Bereavement Project (1992-96); Barnet School Music Centres Association. **Media Experience** Radio writing and presenting; TV writing. **Addits** Churchill Fellow; Commonwealth Trust Bursar.

LETTS Melinda Chief Executive **NATIONAL ASTHMA CAMPAIGN** MEDICAL/HEALTH Type: Fundraiser; Medical Research/Information/Support. Providence House, Providence Place, London N1 0NT Tel:0171-226 2260. Fax:0171-704 0740 **Expertise** Management of charities;campaigning;planning of IT installations. **Prev Posts** VSO: Admin Manager 1985-86, Programme Funding Manager 1986-87, Regional Manager South Asia/Middle East 1987-89; McKinsey And Co. Staffing Manager 1989-91. **Prof Background** BA (Hons) Literae Humaniores, St Anne's, Oxford;MIMgt - Member of the Institute of Management. **Pres Committees** Board of Directors, Asthma Enterprises Ltd;Trustee,Long Term Medical Conditions Alliance. **Past Committees** CND: Council, Executive, Finance and General Purposes Committee, Publications Committee; Board of Directors, Books for a Change Ltd.

LETTS Rosa Maria Chairman & Founder **EUROPEAN ACADEMY FOR THE ARTS/ ACCADEMIA ITALIANA** ARTS Type: Fundraiser; Display & Promo; Italian & European Art & Culture. 8 Grosvenor Place, London SW1X 7SH Tel:0171-235 0303 Fax:0171-235 0404 **Expertise** Art History, Rennaisance, Baroque, Impressionism Law (Univ Rome); Int Law (Brandeis Univ. Massachussetts) **Prev Posts** Cultural Councillor, Italian Embassy, London, 1992-95; Panel Lecturer, V & A Education Dept, 1975-82; Lecturer, University of London, Extra Mural Dept, Hist of Art, 1966-80. **Prof Background** Law Degree, Rome Univ; Int Law MA, Brandeis Univ, Mass (USA); European Hist Art, Courtauld Inst London; Hist Studies of Rennaissance, M Phil Hons, Warburg Inst, Uni London; Fulbright Scholarship. **Awards/Research** The Renaissance; Italia Ao Luar; Numerous exhibition catalogue essays & artwork including; Giambattista Tiepolo, Arturo Martini, The Scale of Space. **Pres Committees** Judge on the Committee of SBS European Art Competition 1995; Juror of the European Design Award organised by RSA. **Past Committees** Chairman of the Ball - Star & Garter Homes; Chairman of the Ball, British Italian Society. **Media Experience** Several interviews for Italian and English TV, Radio, Newspapers & Magazines. **Addits** Cavaliere Officiale of the Italian Republic.

LEVETT Mrs Sally Chief Executive **FRIENDS OF THE ELDERLY** ELDERLY Type: Fundraiser; Service provider; Grant maker. 42 Ebury St, London SW1W 0LZ Tel:0171-730 8263 Fax:0171-259 0154 **Expertise** Fundraising, Administration, Personnel. **Prev Posts** Fundraising Mngr, Mission Aviation Fellowship 1982-89; Appeal Dir, Robert Menzies Trust 1989-90; Dep to CEO & Dir of Fundraising John Grooms Assoc for Disabled People 1990-94. **Prof Background** Educated to University entrance with 'A' levels, etc.; Member of ICFM. **Pres Committees** Voices Committee (voice of voluntary sector providers of residential care for the elderly).

LEVVY George Chief Executive **MOTOR NEURONE DISEASE ASSOCIATION - MNDA** MEDICAL/HEALTH Type: Service provider. PO Box 246, Northampton NN1 2PR Tel:01604-250505 Fax:01604-24726 **Prev Posts** Jnr Hosp Dr 77-78/79-83;Camphill Rudolf Steiner Schls Vol, 78-79;Excerpta Medica Tokyo: Medical Dir 84-86, Consult 87-88;Countrywide Comms 88-91;Brit Red Cross, Mktg Hd 91-4. **Prof Background** Robert Gordon's College, Aberdeen, 1963-71; MBChB, Edinburgh University, 1971-77.

LEWIS Miriam Executive Director **RESCUE FOUNDATION FOR THE BRAIN INJURED INFANT** MEDICAL/HEALTH Type: Research and development. Portland House, Trefin, Dyfed, Wales SA62 5AX Tel:01348-837778 Fax:01348-837503 **Expertise** Research and child studies. **Prev Posts** Paul Sartori Foundation 1984-86; Independent Researcher 1986-90. **Prof Background** BA (Open), MIINFSci., MA INFO (Brighton). **Awards/Research** National Family Study (Brain Injury) 1992-1993; National Professional Study (Brain Injury) 1992-1993. **Media Experience** Radio, television and press.

LEWIS Jenny Coordinator, Wales **BBC CHILDREN IN NEED** CHILD/YOUTH Type: Fundraiser; Grant maker. BBC Broadcasting House, Llandaff, Cardiff CF5 2YQ Tel:01222-572383 **Expertise** Grant making to the Welsh voluntary sector concerned with disadvantaged children. **Prev Posts** Project wkr, Barnardo's Family Link Project 1987-89; Project leader, NCH Llanrumney Community Project 1989-90; Training/Development Officer, S Wales Practice Centre 1990-91. **Prof Background** BA (Hons) Psychology & German (Cardiff) 1970; Dip, Applied Soc Studies (Swansea) 1986; C.Q.S.W. (Swansea) 1986; Qualified soc worker with varied background in soc servs & the voluntary sec in Wales. **Awards/Research** Respite Care Parental Choices & An Evaluation of Family Based Respite Care, published as Barnardo's practice papers 1989. **Pres Committees** S.C.O.V.O; Steering Committee of the Charitable Trust for Wales; Exec Mbr, WCVA. **Media Experience** Many radio & TV interviews (as BBC's corporate charity).

LEWIS Martin Exec Director **ST JOHN AMBULANCE**

MEDICAL/HEALTH Type: Service provider. 1 Grosvenor Crescent, London SW1X 7EF Tel:0171-235 5231 Fax:0171-235 0796

LIDDELL Donald J. Chief Executive **SCOTTISH SOCIETY FOR AUTISTIC CHILDREN** CHILDREN/YOUTH Type: Fundraiser; Service provider; Campaigning. Hilton House, Aloa Business Park, Whins Road, Alloa FK10 3SA Tel:01259-720044 Fax:01259-720051 **Prev Posts** Chief Executive (East Kilbride District Council) 1988-93;Director of Administration/Legal Services (Clydesdale District Council) 1984-88. **Prof Background** LLB (Hons), Glasgow University 1971.

LINDEN Ian Executive Director **CATHOLIC INSTITUTE FOR INTERNATIONAL RELATIONS - CIIR** RELIGIOUS/OVERSEAS Type: Fundraiser; Service provider. Unit 3, Canonbury Yard, 190a New North Road, Islington, London N1 7BJ Tel:0171-354 0883 Fax:0171-369 0017 **Expertise** Development and third world issues; Personal specialisation - third world theology, Rwanda. **Media Experience** Channel 4 News; BBC World Service; Articles for press.

LINDSAY Colonel Oliver J.M. Trust Director/Secretary to Trustees **TRELOAR TRUST** YOUTH/DISABILITY Type: Fundraiser; Service provider; Disabilities. Upper Froyle, Alton, Hampshire GU34 4JX Tel:01420-22442 Fax:01420-23957 **Prev Posts** Regular Army officer in Grenadier Guards, retired 1993 in rank of Colonel. **Prof Background** Eton; RMA Sandhurst; Staff College Camberley; National Defence College Latimer; FRHistS; MICFM. Awarded: Freedom of the City of London. **Awards/Research** CBE. Auth:At the Going Down of the Sun - HK & SE Asia 1941-5, 1981;Ed: A Guards' General-Memoirs of Maj Gen Sir Allan Adair, 1986;Once a Grenadier - history of Grenadier Guards, 1996. **Past Committees** Governor, Victoria League for Commonwealth Friendship 1986-91; Governor, Commonwealth Trust 1988-90. **Addits** Mbr, Queen's Body Guard for Scotland (Royal Company of Archers).

LING Brenda Administrative Director **INSTITUTE OF GROUP ANALYSIS** SOCIAL Type: Service provider. 1 Daleham Gardens, London NW3 5BY Tel:0171-431 2693 Fax:0171-431 7246 **Expertise** Administration; Training courses in group psychotherapy. **Pres Committees** Council; Board of Auditors. **Past Committees** IGA Council; Finance Committee.

LITTLE Mrs Isabel Administrator & Foundation Secretary **EPILEPSY RESEARCH FOUNDATION** MEDICAL/HEALTH Type: Fundraiser; Grant maker. PO Box 3004, London W4 1XT Tel:0181-995 4781 Fax:0181-995 4781 **Expertise** Charity administration. **Prev Posts** Organiser, Warwickshire Assoc for the Blind 1977-80; Director, Berkshire Council on Alcoholism 1980-87. **Prof Background** Language graduate; Accredited Counsellor. **Pres Committees** Vice-Chairman, Joint Epilepsy Council. **Past Committees** Chair, Association of Directors of Councils on Alcoholism 1985-87. **Media Experience** Experience with radio, TV, video and press. **Addits** Magistrate.

LITTLEWOOD Cyril Founder & Director **YOUNG PEOPLE'S TRUST FOR THE ENVIRONMENT & NATURE CONSERVATION - YPTENC** CHILDREN/YOUTH Type: Service provider; Environmental Education. 8 Leapale Road, Guildford, Surrey GUI 4JX Tel:01483-39600 Fax:01483-301992 **Expertise** Education of Children; Natural History; Mammals & Endangered Species. **Prev Posts** Director of Youth Services, WWF, 1962-80; Director YPTENC, since 1981. **Prof Background** Layman Naturalist with 48 years experience. **Awards/Research** MBE (1971); OGA (1994). Auth: The World's Vanishing Mammals; The World's Vanishing Birds. **Media Experience** 150+ TV appearances, regular radio interviews etc.

LIU Sato Executive Director **NATURAL MEDICINES SOCIETY - NMS** MEDICAL/HEALTH Type: Fundraiser; Grant maker; Consumer organisation. Market Chambers, 13a Market Place, Heanor, Derbyshire DE75 7AA Tel:01773-710002 Fax:01773-533855 **Expertise** Alternative and complementary medicine; administration; marketing. **Prev Posts** Joined Natural Medicines Society in 1989. **Pres Committees** Nat Cncl of Women of GB; Medicines Advisory Research Cttee (NMS); Advisory Cttee of the Parliamentary Gp for Alternative & Complementary Medicine; Trustee, Foundation for Traditional Chinese Medicine. **Media Experience** Some experience in radio and press.

LIVINGSTONE Michael G. Secretary/Finance Director **BRITISH HEART FOUNDATION - BHF** MEDICAL/HEALTH Type: Fundraiser; Grant maker. 14 Fitzhardinge Street, London W1H 4DH Tel:0171-935 0185 Fax:0171-486 5820 **Expertise** Corporate and financial strategy and management in a commercial environment. **Prev Posts** Finance director, Wigham Poland Ltd 1972-86; Chief Executive, BMS Investment Holdings Ltd 1986-91. **Prof Background** Chartered Accountant (1952). **Pres Committees** Non-executive director of a number of companies. **Past Committees** Trustee of various pension funds, educational and youth club trusts. **Addits** Chairman, Seal Partners Ltd (general and financial consultancy).

LLEWELLYN Timothy David Director **HENRY MOORE FOUNDATION** ARTS Type: Service provider; Grant maker; Exhibition Maker, Publisher. Dane Tree House, Perry Green, Much Hadham, Herts SG10 6EE Tel:01279-843333 Fax:01279-843647 **Expertise** Visual arts. **Prev Posts** Old Master Paintings Dept, Sotheby's 1969-84; Managing Director, Sotheby's 1984-94. **Prof Background** Art History, Cambridge University. **Pres Committees** Courtauld Institute (art); Elgar Foundation (music).

LOCHRIE Robert General Secretary **WORKERS' EDUCATIONAL ASSOCIATION - WEA** SOCIAL Type: Service provider; Adult education charity. Temple House, 17 Victoria Park Square, London E2 9PB Tel:0181-983 1515 Fax:0181-983 4840.

LOCKHART Dr Bill Director **EXTERN ORGANISATION** SOCIAL Type: Service provider. Graham House, 1-5 Albert Square, Belfast BT1 3EQ Tel:01232-240900 Fax:01232-331498 **Expertise** Criminological research;

crime prevention; management of multi-agency initiatives. **Prev Posts** Senior Psychologist, Lisnevin Training School 1974-83; Deputy Director, Extern 1987-94. **Prof Background** AFBPsS Chartered Forensic Psychologist; BA (Hons) Psychology and Philosophy; Postgraduate Diploma Counselling; PhD Counselling Psychology. **Awards/Research** Many publ inc: Remands in Custody Revisited, for Standing Advisory Commission on Human Rights 1994; Current joint research on crime trends in Ireland since World War II. **Pres Committees** Exec Ctte, British Society of Criminology; Chair, Northern Ireland Branch of British Society of Criminology; Editorial Board, Howard Journal of Criminal Justice. **Media Experience** Radio and TV at local and national levels.

LOGAN Colin Chief Executive **YOUTH HOSTELS ASSOCIATION (ENGLAND AND WALES) - YHA** SOCIAL Type: Service provider. Trevelyan House, 8 St Stephen's Hill, St Albans, Hertfordshire AL1 2DY Tel:01727-855215 Fax:01727-844126 **Expertise** General management. **Prev Posts** YHA: Regional Director, Northern England 1986-89; Director of Operations 1989-92. **Prof Background** Regular Army 1958-77 (Staff College 1969/70); Overseas Civil Service (Hong Kong) 1977-1980. **Pres Committees** Development Cttee, British Tourist Authority; NCVO, Board of Trustees; Marketing Task Group, Int Youth Hostels Federation. **Media Experience** Occasional appearances.

LOMAS Sarah E. Executive Officer **INVALIDS-AT-HOME** DISABILITY Type: Grant maker. 17 Lapstone Gardens, Kenton, Harrow HA3 0EB Tel:0181-907 1706 **Expertise** Grant making; administration; information supply to clients and advisers. **Prev Posts** Occupational Therapist, Whittington Hospital 1968-70; Disabled Living Foundation: Info Officer 1970-80, Deputy Director 1978-80. **Prof Background** Occupational therapist. **Past Committees** BSI Wheelchair Committee; Joint Committee for Mobility for the Disabled. **Media Experience** Not recently.

LONGFIELD Anne Director **KIDS' CLUBS NETWORK** CHILD/YOUTH Type: Fundraiser; Service provider; Grant maker; Training & resource. Bellerive House, 3 Muirfield Crescent, London E14 9SZ Tel:0171-512 2112 Fax:0171-512 2010 **Expertise** Childcare, children's play and development, quality development, commmunity development, lobbying. **Prev Posts** Development Group, Wandsworth Latchkey Development Group 1984-87; Senior Development Officer, Kids' Club Network 1987-91; Head of Development, Kids' Club Network 1991-93. **Prof Background** BA (Hons) History, Newcastle Upon Tyne University. **Awards/Research** Range of pubs at Kids' Club Network: Next Step for School Age Childcare, Summer's Here - Let's Play, Quality Assurance Programme, Kids Play - Get Active & Out of School - in School. **Pres Committees** Trustee, Nat Childrens Bureau; Tres, Nat Play Cncl; Mgmt Grp, NVCCO-VOCS; Acenvo Policy Dev Cttee; Chair, Childcare Umbrella, All Party Cttee on Parenting; 4 Nations Out Of School Care Group. **Media Experience** Regular TV & radio interviews (news items, women's & children's features. **Addits** Has also written numerous articles in trade press.

LONGSTAFF Lisa Spokeswoman **WOMEN AGAINST RAPE** SOCIAL Type: Service provider; campaigning. Crossroads Womens Centre, PO Box 287, London NW6 5QU Tel:0171-482 2496 Fax:0171-209 4761 **Expertise** Counselling, support, legal advice, information.

LOPEZ-JONES Nina Spokeswoman/Point of Reference **ENGLISH COLLECTIVE OF PROSTITUTES - ECP** SOCIAL Type: Service provider; Campaigning; voluntary organization. Crossroads Womens Centre, PO Box 287, London NW6 5QU Tel:0171-482 2496 Fax:0171-209 4761 **Expertise** Prostitution laws and their implementation. **Prof Background** Fluent French/Italian/Spanish (native); regular consultant: trade unions, health auths, AIDS orgs, lawyers, politicians, women's/lesbian/gay civil rights community gps. Speaker 1990 USA/Canada. **Awards/Research** Auth: Who's a Good Girl Then? Contrib: Sex Work, 1988; Network (ECP Newsletter); Guide to the Rules of the Game, 1981; Prostitute Women and AIDS..., 1988; Hooker and the Beak, 1987. **Pres Committees** Co-ord, Legal Action for Women; Mbr, Campaign Against Child Support Act. **Past Committees** Keynote Speaker, Confs 1992: Discovering Women; Haldane Soc; TGWU. **Media Experience** Regular comment TV/radio/press inc Today, BBC News, legal jnls, internat media. **Addits** Organized 1991 Defending Women Conf; profiled in The Independent.

LORD Geoffrey Trustee **ADAPT TRUST, THE** DISABILITY Type: Grant maker. Cameron House, Abbey Park Place, Dunfermline, Fife, Scotland KY12 7PZ Tel:01383-623166 Fax:01383-622149 **Prev Posts** Deputy Chief Probation Officer, Greater Manchester 1974-77; Secretary/Treasurer, Carnegie UK Trust 1978-93. **Prof Background** AIB; MA Bradford University. **Awards/Research** OBE 1989. Auth: The Arts and Disabilities, 1981; FRSA, 1985; Hon Fellow Manchester Metropolitan University 1987. **Pres Committees** Trustee: Home Start UK;Chair, Unemployed Vol Action Fund (Scot); Chair, Pollock Memorial Missionary Trust; Pres, Ctre for Env Interp; Vice Pres, Selcare Trust. **Past Committees** Sec: Carnegie Inq, 3rd Age 1989-93;Cttee of Inq, Arts and Disabled People 1985-88; Vol. Arts Network.

LOUGHRAN Brendan Chief Executive **NATIONAL FEDERATION OF YOUNG FARMERS' CLUBS** SOCIAL Type: Fundraiser; Service provider. YFC Centre, National Agricultural Centre, Stoneleigh Park, Kenilworth, Warks CV8 2LG Tel:01203-696544 Fax:01203-696559.

LOVE Frances Director **MARRIAGE COUNSELLING SCOTLAND** SOCIAL Type: Service provider; Confidential counselling: marriage, relationships. 105 Hanover Street, Edinburgh EH2 1DJ Tel:0131-225 5006 Fax:0131-220 0639 **Expertise** Organizational and industrial consultancy; community education. **Prev Posts** Librarian, Children's Library 1960-68; General Secretary, Playgroup Movement, Scottish Pre-school Playgroups Association 1977-87. **Prof Background** Tutor and lecturer; Human Relations counselling course; Mbr, Scottish Institute of Human Relations (SIHR); Community Education/Adult Cert. **Pres Committees** Assoc Chief Offs of Scott Vol Orgs;Policy Bd & Mngmt Cttee Scott Cncl Vol Orgs;Confed of Scott Counselling Agencies;Stepfamily Scot Pastoral Fndtn;UK Marriage

Orgs Grp. **Past Committees** Independent Broadcasting Authority Appeals Committee 1985-88.

LOVETT Keith Chairman **SOCIETY FOR THE AUTISTICALLY HANDICAPPED - SFTAH** Type: Fundraiser; Service provider. 199/201 Blandford Ave, Kettering, Northants NN1 9AT Tel: 01536-523274 Fax:01536-523274 **Expertise** Autism: Organisation/running training workshops and seminars for professionals & carers. **Prof Background** Company Director. **Awards/Research** Autism News quarterly journal **Past Committees** Inter-Agency Autism Project, Northants, 7 years.

LOWE Marion I. Director of UK Operations **BRITISH RED CROSS** MEDICAL/HEALTH Type: Fundraiser; Service provider. 9 Grosvenor Crescent, London SW1X 7EJ Tel:0171-235 5454 Fax:0171-235 7447 **Expertise** Management; policy development on family care; women's work status. **Prev Posts** Lecturer, Social Studies, West London Inst Higher Education 1979-80; Asst Director, Cleveland SSD 1984-87. Dir, National Foster Care Assoc 1987-95. **Prof Background** Qualified Social Worker; BSC Social Administration; MSc Applied Social Studies; MA History; CQSW. **Awards/Research** Status of Childminders; Womens Role in Vol. Sector early 20 Cent. Various articles/publ family poverty, women and employment, foster care. **Past Committees** Chair, Assoc of Chief Execs of National Vol Orgs (ACENVO); National Children's Bureau; United Response.

LOWNDES R W General Manager **WESSEX AUTISTIC SOCIETY** DISABILITY Type: Fundraiser; Service provider; Campaigning; Social Care Education. 39 Bargates, Christchurch, Dorset BH23 1QD Tel:01202-483 360 Fax:01202-483 171 **Expertise** Development & Delivery of Services to People with Autism and Carers. **Prev Posts** Group Manager, National Autistic Society, 1994-95; Development Officer, National Autistic Society, 1990-95; Service Manager, Devon & Cornwall Autistic Community Trust, 1985-90. **Prof Background** Certificate in Social Service (CSS). **Media Experience** Trained in Facing the Media.

LUCAS Bill Director **LEARNING THROUGH LANDSCAPES** CONSERVATION/ENVIRONMENT Type: Service provider; Membership, Training, Research. 3rd Floor, Southside Offices, The Law Courts, Winchester, Hants SO23 9DL Tel:01962-846258 Fax:01962-869099 **Expertise** Education; Environment; Landscape; Children; Voluntary Sector - Management; fundraising. **Prev Posts** Head of Arts Faculty 1985-1988; Deputy Headteacher 1988-1990. **Prof Background** Arts/Education; MA (Oxon) English Language & Literature; Post-graduate Certificate of Education, Oxford. Teacher since 1980. **Awards/Research** Numerous pubs inc. Series Ed, Oxford Playscripts; Bright Ideas in the Outdoor Classroom; articles for var newspapers/journals, eg Times Education Supplement, Landscape Design. **Pres Committees** Board Mbr, Learning through Landscapes; Chairman of Board, Pegasus Theatre, Oxford; Advisory Bd, Evergreen Fdn Canada; Programmes Cttee WWF-UK. **Past Committees** Southern Arts - Combined Arts Panel. **Media Experience** Prod/adviser 3 videos. Interviews: TV BBC1/BBC2, Radios 1/4. **Addits** Auth:children's plays & textbooks.

LUTHER Anne Director General **ACTION RESEARCH** MEDICAL/HEALTH Type: Fundraiser; Grant maker. Vincent House, North Parade, Horsham, West Sussex RH12 2DP Tel:01403-210406 Fax:01403-210541 **Expertise** Grant Administration. **Prev Posts** PA House Governor, Westminster Hosp 1969-71; Director of Research, Action Research 1982-90. **Prof Background** BSc Physiology/Chemistry; Hospital Administrator; Kings Fund Trainee. **Pres Committees** Trustee Charity Common Investment Fund (Schroders) 1991 to date. **Past Committees** Prince of Wales Adv Gp on Disability 1990-95; Exec Cncl Assoc Med Res Charities 1992-95; Trustee Snowdon Award Scheme 1990-95. **Media Experience** Radio, TV, Press. **Addits** Hon Sec to Assoc Med Res Charities 1982-87.

LYNCH Lynn Business Development Manager SS **GREAT BRITAIN PROJECT** CONSERVATION Type: Fundraiser. Great Western Dock, Gas Ferry Road, Bristol, Avon BS1 6TY Tel:0117-926 0680 Fax:0117-925 5788 **Expertise** Fundraising & marketing. **Prev Posts** Marketing Manager, Newport & Gwent Enterprise 1992-95; Fundraising Manager, RNIB, S Wales 1995. **Prof Background** B.Ed (Hons), DipM, MICM, MICFM.

LYNCH Margaret Director **WAR ON WANT** SOCIAL Type: Int Charity linked to trade union movement. Fenner Brockway House, 37-39 Great Guildford St London SE1 OES Tel:0171-620 1111 Fax:0171-261 9291 **Expertise** Social & economic development; democracy building; women's equalit; workers and human rights. **Prof Background** MA (Hons), Glasgow University. **Awards/Research** Editor of: The Forgotten Workforce : Child Labour in Scotland; Payline; Switching onto Safety; A Multi Option Referendum for a Scottish Parliament; UPFRONT. **Media Experience** Experience with TV and radio (current affairs programmes).

LYSTER Dr Simon Director General **WILDLIFE TRUSTS** ANIMAL/WILDLIFE Type: Fundraiser; Service provider; Campaigning; manages over 2,200 UK nature reserves. 72 Wilton Rd, London SW1V 1DE Tel:0171-931 0744 Fax:0171-931 0025 **Prev Posts** Secretary, Falklands Islands Foundation 1982-86; Head of Conservation Policy, WWF-UK 1986-95. **Prof Background** PhD Cambridge University; Solicitor. **Awards/Research** Auth: International Wildlife Law, 1985. **Media Experience** Frequent radio & TV interviews.

M

MACARTHUR Francesca Chief Executive **CHILDREN NATIONWIDE MEDICAL RESEARCH FUND** CHILDREN/YOUTH Type: Fundraiser; Grant maker. Nicholas House, 181 Union Street, London SE1 0LN Tel:0171-928 2425 Fax:0171-928 0154 **Prev Posts** Barrister 1986-88; Corporate Finance Executive, Henry Ansbacher 1988-90; Corporate Finance Executive, Lazard Brothers 1990-91. **Prof Background** LLB from Southampton University; Barrister at Law - Grays Inn, London.

MACAULAY Anita Executive Director **JENNIFER TRUST FOR SPINAL MUSCULAR ATROPHY** MEDICAL/HEALTH Type: Fundraiser; Service provider; Grant maker. 11 Ash Tree Close, Wellesbourne, Warks CV35 9SA Tel:01789-842377 Fax:01789-842377 **Expertise** Development of self-help; support; outreach; networks; bereavement of parents losing babies & children. **Prev Posts** Company Microbiologist, Food Industry 1976-84; Quality Assurance Officer, County Council 1988-89; Group Technical Manager, Food Industry 1989-92. **Prof Background** Food Science. **Pres Committees** Panel Member, Joseph Patrick Memorial Trust. **Past Committees** Executive Committee Member, CVS Warwick District; Chairman, National Committee, Jennifer Trust for SMA 1988-92. **Media Experience** Extensive & varied experience with radio, TV and press.

MACAULAY Pat Chief Executive Officer **AIDS CARE EDUCATION AND TRAINING - ACET** MEDICAL/HEALTH Type: Service provider. PO Box 3693, London SW15 2BQ Tel:0181-780 0400 Fax:0181-780 0450

MACDIARMID Duncan Director **SUNLEY (BERNARD) CHARITABLE FOUNDATION** SOCIAL Type: Grant maker. 53 Grosvenor St, London W1X 9FH Tel:0171-409 1199 Fax:0171-409 7373 **Expertise** Administration; finance and accounts; investment. **Prev Posts** Various finance & accounts posts in British Petroleum Company Plc 1985-1989; Director of Finance, Help the Aged 1990-1992. **Prof Background** Chartered Accountant; Member of Institute of Chartered Accountants of Scotland.

MACDONALD Barry Director of Finance & IT **NATIONAL LOTTERY CHARITIES BOARD** SOCIAL Type: Statutory Body. St Vincent House, 30 Orange Street, London, WC2H 7HH Tel:0171-747-5247 Fax:0171-747 5311 **Expertise** Finance, Planning, IT. **Prev Posts** Gen Mgr/Finance Director, Reuters Television 1984-93; Director of Finance & Planning, SCOPE 1994-95. **Prof Background** BEng; MA Business Studies; FCMA. **Past Committees** Trustee, Kent Opera 1984-90. **Media Experience** PR for Reuters TV.

MACDONALD Rev Fergus General Secretary **NATIONAL BIBLE SOCIETY OF SCOTLAND** RELIGIOUS Type: Fundraiser; Service provider; Grant maker. 7 Hampton Terrace, Edinburgh EH12 5XU Tel:0131-337 9701 Fax:0131-337 0641 **Expertise** Biblical Studies; Communication. **Prev Posts** Minister, St Andrew's Church, Lima, Peru 1962-66; Minister, Cumbernauld Free Church 1967-81. **Prof Background** MA; BD Edinburgh Univ. **Awards/Research** Various articles in eg. New 20th Century Encyclopedia of Religious Knowledge; Dict of Scottish Church History; World Evangelism. **Pres Committees** Relig Adv Cttee, Scottish TV; Lausanne Cttee for World Evangelism; United Bible Socs Trust Assoc; International Forum of Bible Agencies. **Past Committees** United Bible Socs Europe Middle East Cttee.

MACDONALD J.D. General Secretary **EARL HAIG FUND SCOTLAND - SC** SOCIAL Type: Fundraiser; Service provider; Grant maker. New Haig House, Logie Green Road, Edinburgh EH7 4HR Tel:0131-557 2782 Fax:0131-557 5819

MACDONALD Kelvin Director **NATIONAL HOUSING AND TOWN PLANNING COUNCIL** HOUSING/ENVIRONMENT Type: Campaigning. 14-18 Old Street, London EC10 9AB Tel:0171-251 2363 Fax:0171-608 2830 **Expertise** Planning for Housing; Development Partnerships. **Prev Posts** Asst Director, TCPA 1979-84; Principal Planning Officer, Brighton BC 1984-88; Principal Lecturer, Univ of Westminster 1988-95. **Prof Background** BSc in Town Planning; Fellow of the Royal Town Planning Institute (FRTPI); FRSA. **Awards/Research** Contrib: The Crisis of London, Routledge 1992; Partnership Agencies in British Urban Policy, UCL Press 1995; Columnist on Planning newspaper. **Pres Committees** Mbr, Accreditation Panel, Royal Town Planning Inst; Mbr, Steering Cttee, Dept of Employment Discipline; Network in Town Planning. **Media Experience** Press articles on housing, planning & local gov; TV & radio appearances.

MACFARLANE Wendy Chief Executive **SCOTTISH PRE-SCHOOL PLAY ASSOCIATION - SPPA** CHILDREN/YOUTH Type: Service provider; Vol org in Pre-school childcare & education. 14 Elliot Place, Glasgow G3 8EP Tel:0141-221 4148 Fax:0141-221 6043 **Expertise** Childcare; Pre-school Care & Ed; Mgmt; Consultancy; Mgmt of Change. **Prev Posts** Project Leader, Langlees Family Centre 1983-86; Senior Mgr, Aberlour Childcare Trust 1986-95. **Prof Background** BSc Ord, University of Glasgow; Diploma in Social Work, University of Stirling; CQSW awarded by CCETSW. **Awards/Research** Publications - Pictures of Practice: Vol 1: Chap 5 - Langlees Family Centre NISW 1989; The Aberlour Model of a Family Ctr: Newsletter, Nat Childrens Bur, Scottish Gp, Vol 12 1986. **Pres Committees** Exec Cttee of the Scottish Early Years & Family Network; Nat Steering Gp on Servs for Children under 8; Mbr of Nat Inst of Social Work Scottish Network Dev Gp. **Past Committees** Chair, Scott Assoc of Family Ctrs 1984-90;

Mbr of Early Yrs Forum - Scottish Child & Family Alliance (Children in Scotland) 1987-92. **Media Experience** Radio, TV & Press. **Addits** Associate Nat Inst of Soc Work; Cont to Post Qualifying Social Work Course.

MACGILLIVRAY Cathy Secretary **WOMEN'S ENGINEERING SOCIETY** Type: Fundraiser; Service provider; Professional Association. Imperial College of Science & Technology, Dept of Civil Eng. Imperial College Rd, London SW7 2BU Tel:0171-594 6025 Fax:0171-594 6026 **Expertise** Administration; Women in Engineering. **Prof Background** Administration/Secretarial.

MACGREGOR Elizabeth A. Director **IKON GALLERY** ARTS Type: Service provider. 58-72 John Bright Street, Birmingham B1 1BN Tel:0121-6430708 Fax:0121-6432254 **Expertise** Contemporary visual arts. **Prev Posts** Curator, Scottish Arts Council Travelling Gallery 1982-85; Visual Arts Officer, Arts Council of Great Britain 1985-89. **Prof Background** Stromness Academy, Orkney; MA History of Art, Edinburgh University; Post-graduate Diploma in Museum Studies, Manchester University. **Pres Committees** Board of Kokuma Dance Theatre, Birmingham; Trustee, Public Art Development Trust, London; Trustee, Pier Arts Centre, Stromness, Orkney. **Past Committees** Member of Turner Prize Jury, 1995. **Media Experience** Contributor to Kaleidoscope and other TV and radio arts programmes. **Addits** Fellow of the Royal Society of Arts.

MACGREGOR Ian Chief Investment Officer **WELLCOME TRUST** SOCIAL Type: Grant maker. 210 Euston Road, London NW1 2BE Tel:0171-611 8611 Fax:0171-611 8622 **Expertise** Investment, finance, taxation, legal & information systems activities. **Prev Posts** Director of Finance, Engineering Industrial Training Board 1981-84. **Prof Background** Fellow, Institute of Chartered Accountants of England & Wales (1960). **Pres Committees** Trustee, Legislation Monitoring Service for Charities; Chairman, CTRG; Chairman, ECCVAT; Trustee, GHN Foundation; Governor, Frensham Heights Educational Trust Ltd.

MACKECHNIE-JARVIS Iain Director **EMMAUS UK** Type: Fundraiser; Service provider; Campaigning. 4 Salisbury Villas, Station Rd, Cambridge CB1 2JF Tel:01223-576103 Fax:01223-576203 **Expertise** Homelessness. **Prev Posts** Senior Partner, Miller & Co Solicitors 1971-95. **Prof Background** Solicitor. **Pres Committees** Trustee, Wray Charity; School Governor, St Bedes School, Cambridge. **Media Experience** Radio Interviews; Press statements.

MACKENZIE Rear Admiral D.J. Director **ATLANTIC SALMON TRUST** ANIMAL/WILDLIFE Type: Fundraiser; Service provider; Grant maker. Moulin, Pitlochry, Perthshire PH16 5JQ Tel:01796-473439 Fax:01796-473554 **Expertise** General administration. **Prev Posts** Royal Navy to Rear Admiral 1943-1983. **Awards/Research** CB. **Pres Committees** Observer to North Atlantic Salmon Conservation; Observer to ICES; Tay District Fishing Board; Council of FBA. **Media Experience** Considerable experience radio and TV interviews, before and after Royal Navy.

MACKIE Prof Karl Chief Executive **CENTRE FOR DISPUTE RESOLUTION - CEDR** Type: Service provider; Professional association. 7 St Katharine's Way, London, E1 9LB Tel:0171-481 4441 Fax:0171-481 4442 **Expertise** Mediator, Professor in ADR, University of Birmingham. **Prev Posts** Director, Centre for Legal Studies, University of Nottingham 1987-92. **Prof Background** Barrister, Gray's Inn; Chartered Psychologist. **Awards/Research** Co-author - Commercial Dispute Resolution, (Butterworths); Editor, A Handbook of Dispute Resolution, (Routledge). **Pres Committees** CEDR Board; Editorial Boards for various journals. **Past Committees** Specialisation Committee, Law Society. **Media Experience** Contributed to various videos/radio programmes on dispute resolution.

MACLEAN-BRISTOL The Hon. Mrs Lavinia Director **PROJECT TRUST** CHILDREN/YOUTH Type: Fundraiser; Service provider. The Hebridean Centre, Ballyhough, Isle of Coll, Argyll PA78 6TE Tel:01879-230444 Fax:01879-230357 **Expertise** Administration. **Prev Posts** Administrator, Project Trust 1972-95. **Prof Background** Administration.

MACLEAN-BRISTOL Nicholas Founder and Chairman **PROJECT TRUST** CHILDREN/YOUTH Type: Fundraiser; Service provider; Grant maker. The Hebridean Centre, Ballyhough, Isle of Coll, Argyll PA78 6TE Tel:01879-230444 Fax:01879-230357 **Expertise** Educ new UK generation to understand life in other countries, particularly in the developing world. **Prev Posts** Regular Army Officer 1955-71; **Prof Background** RMA Sandhurst 1953-55 **Awards/Research** OBE, 1994. DL, 1996. Hebridean Decade 1761-1771 (1982); Warriors & Priests: The Clan Maclean 1300-1570 (1995).

MACLEOD J.Robertson- Chief Executive **RALEIGH INTERNATIONAL** CHILDREN/YOUTH Type: Service provider. Raleigh House, 27 Parsons Green Lane, London SW6 4HS Tel:0171-371 8585 Fax:0171-371 5116 **Prev Posts** Marketing Consultant, Markham Group 1985-90; Commercial Dir, Operation Raleigh 1990-92. **Prof Background** British Army 1970-80; Ashridge Management College, numerous management courses.

MACNAMARA Libby Director **ASSOCIATION OF BRITISH ORCHESTRAS** ARTS Type: Service provider; Conferences, Seminars, Training, Publications. Francis House, Francis Street, London SW1P 1DE Tel:0171-828 6913 Fax:0171-931 9959 **Prev Posts** Administrator of The Shell - LSO Music Scholarship 1979-89; Has held a number of other posts in the classical music field. **Prof Background** Music degree from Birmingham University. **Pres Committees** Chair of Board, Nat Campaign for the Arts; Vice-Chairman, Int Alliance of Orchestral Assocs; Executive Member of Nat Music Council of Great Britain. **Media Experience** Taken part in many radio discussion programmes, panels, etc..

MADDOX Ronald PRI President **ROYAL INSTITUTE OF PAINTERS IN WATER COLOURS** ARTS Type: Service provider; Professional Association. 17 Carlton House Terrace, London SW1Y 5BD Tel:0171-930 6844 **Expertise** Artist; Consultant; Designer; Illustrator: Pres/Chief Exec, RI representing British Watercolour painting. **Prev Posts** Vice President, RI; Exhibitions Secretary, RI; Currently, Hon Member Royal Watercolour Society. **Prof Background** Hertfordshire College of Art and Design/St Albans; London College of Printing & Graphic Art; Designer/Illustrator Painter. **Awards/Research** Profiled in: Who's Who; People of Today; Who's Who in Art; European Biographical Directory. **Pres Committees** Governor, Federation of British Artists; Council, Royal Inst of Painters in Water Colours; Jury, Royal Soc of Arts Design Bursary Awards; Trustee: RI Watercolours Ltd, RA British Institution Fund. **Past Committees** Governor, Hertfordshire College of Art and Design. **Addits** Reviews articles on design painting in watercolour, Illustrating Britain. Laing Art Comp Snr Assr; Designer of British stamps.

MAGONET Jonathan Rabbi Prof Principal **LEO BAECK COLLEGE** RELIGIOUS Type: Service provider; Religious education. 80 East End Road, London N3 2SY Tel:0181-349 4525 Fax:0181-343 2558 **Expertise** Hebrew Bible, Interfaith dialogue. **Prev Posts** Head of Dept of Bible, Leo Baeck College 1974-85. **Prof Background** MB.Bs, London University; Rabbinic Ordination (Leo Baeck College 1971) PhD Heidelberg 1974. **Awards/Research** Author: A Rabbi's Bible, Bible Lives, A Rabbi Reads The Psalms; Editor: Jewish Explorations Of Sexuality; Co-Editor: Forms of Prayer (3 vols), How to Get Up When Life Gets You Down. **Pres Committees** Vice-President, World Union for Progressive Judaism. **Media Experience** Frequent broadcaster, BBC World Service; BBC TV Series (The Good Book).

MAGUIRE J. Rev. MHM National Director **EPISCOPAL AGENCY OF THE APOSTLESHIP OF THE SEA** RELIGIOUS Type: Fundraiser; Grant maker; Campaigning. 'Stella Maris' 66 Dock Rd, Tilbury, Essex RM18 7BX Tel:01375-845641 Fax:01375-843736 **Expertise** Spiritual and material welfare of Seafarers. **Prof Background** Roman Catholic Priest, with special emphasis on missionary activities. **Pres Committees** Merchant Navy, Welfare Board; Island Retreats, Hosanna House. **Media Experience** Interviews, talks etc.

MAHER Chrissie Founder Director **PLAIN ENGLISH CAMPAIGN** SOCIAL Type: Campaigning PO Box 3, New Mills, Stockport SK12 4QP Tel:01663-744 409 Fax:01663-747 038 **Expertise** Plain English; Researcher. **Prev Posts** Founder of Plain English Campaign 25 years ago. **Prof Background** MS. Community work, SEAN. MA (Hon) McUniversity. **Awards/Research** Awards: OBE. Auth: The Plain English Story; Small Print; A-Z of Alternative Words; Utter Drivel; Language on Trial; How to write letters & reports in Plain English; Gobbledygook. **Pres Committees** Founder Member, Better English Campaign; Founder Member, Plain English Campaign; Founder Member, National Consumer Council. **Media Experience** Vast experience in radio, TV, video and press. **Addits** Awarded: Rosemary Delbridge Award.

MAIN Carol Director **NATIONAL ASSOCIATION OF YOUTH ORCHESTRAS** Type: Fundraiser; Service provider; Grant maker; Campaigning; Statutory Body. Ainslie House, 11 St Colme St, Edinburgh EH3 6AG Tel:0131-539 1087 Fax:0131-539 1069 **Expertise** Music; Journalism; Broadcasting. **Prev Posts** Simultaneously: Director (Scotland), LIVE MUSIC NOW since 1984;Classical Music Editor, The List since 1985. **Prof Background** Edinburgh University B.A. **Pres Committees** Scottish Arts Council Music Cttee;Board of Directors, Edinburgh Fringe Festival; European Union Cultural Forum. **Past Committees** SALVO (Scottish Arts Lobby); Camerata of St Andrew. **Media Experience** Extensive in radio/press.

MAKEPEACE-WARNE Maj-Gen Antony Director **ARMY MUSEUMS OGILBY TRUST** CONSERVATION Type: Fundraiser; Service provider; Grant maker; Campaigning. 58 The Close, Salisbury, Wilts SP1 2EX Tel:01722-332188 Fax:01772-334211 **Expertise** The British Army, its regimental system, history & traditions. **Prev Posts** Regular Infantry Officer 1957-92; Commandant Joint Service Defence College 1990-92. **Prof Background** Staff College 1970; Royal College of Defence Studies 1985; Joint Service Defence College 1990; BA. **Awards/Research** CB, MBE. Auth: Exceedingly Lucky - A History of The Light Infantry 1968-93 (1993), The Army Today & Tomorrow 1993-94 (1993) & The Light Infantry - A Brief History (1994). **Pres Committees** Council Member, Association of Independent Museums; Council Member, Taunton School Council; Trustee, Godolphin School Performing Arts Centre Trust. **Past Committees** Chairman, Salisbury Civic Society Development Committee 1994-95. **Addits** Also author of Brassey's Companion To The British Army (1995).

MAKIN Claire Chief Executive **ROYAL INSTITUTION OF CHARTERED SURVEYORS** CONSERVATION/ENVIRONMENT Type: Professional association. 12 Great George Street, Parliament Square, London SW1P 3AD Tel:0171-334 3701 Fax:0171-222 5074 **Expertise** Valuation; rating; property management; strategy, organization issues in public/private sectors. **Prev Posts** Richard Ellis, Incl creation/mngmt of landlord/tenant leg dept 1978-90; Price Waterhouse, asset valuation in E Europe 1990-91; DTZ Debenham Thorpe, Dir Consultancy Div 1991-95. **Prof Background** Qualified chartered surveyor (Coll of Estate Management); MBA (City Business School). **Awards/Research** Property strategies for govt agency, colleges, charity. Est real estate practices in Budapest, Prague, Warsaw.

MALLEY Sheila Jane Northern Ireland Coordinator **BBC CHILDREN IN NEED** CHILDREN/YOUTH Type: Fundraiser; Grant maker. Broadcasting House, Ormeau Ave, Belfast BT2 8HQ Tel:01232-338221 Fax:01232-338922 **Expertise** Grant-making & community development. **Prev Posts** Team Leader, N. Belfast, Voluntary Service Belfast 1975-83; Freelance Consultant 1987-90. **Prof Background** Community Development. **Pres Committees** Member, Youth Council for Northern Ireland; UK Grants Committee, Charity Projects; Northern Ireland Voluntary Trust Advisory Group; Youth Demonstration Project. **Past Committees** Youth Action N.I..

MANN Joe General Secretary **NATIONAL LEAGUE OF THE BLIND & DISABLED** DISABILITY Type: Service provider. 2 Tenterden Rd, London N17 8BE Tel:0181-808 6030 Fax:0181-885 3235.

MANSFIELD Nicholas Director **NATIONAL MUSEUM OF LABOUR HISTORY** SOCIAL/CONSERVATION Type: Service provider. 103 Princess Street, Manchester M1 6DD Tel:0161-228 7212 Fax:0161-839 6027 **Expertise** Labour history, museums. **Prev Posts** Assistant Curator, Norfolk Rural Life Museum, Gressenhall 1980-86; Curator, Cyfarthfa Castle Museum, Merthyr Tydfil, Mid Glamorgan 1986-89. **Prof Background** BA Politics and Modern History, Manchester University; BPhil Exeter University; Diploma of the Museums Association. **Awards/Research** Around 20 articles on social and labour history, museums etc. **Pres Committees** Advisory Bd: National Peace Museum; Manchester Police Museum; Manchester Holocaust Museum; Archives Sub Cttee, Scty for Study of Labour History; Mem Registration Cttee Museums & Galleries Commission. **Media Experience** Some experience of radio, TV, press.

MANSFIELD Dr Peter Director **TEMPLEGARTH TRUST** Type: Service provider; Research. PO Box 6, Louth, Lincs LN11 8XL Tel:01507-327655 Fax:01507-327955 **Expertise** The Nature and 'Practice' of Health. **Prev Posts** General Practitioner NHS 1970;-96; Medical Adviser, The Soil Association Ltd Magazine & New Living Magazine. **Prof Background** Educated: Caius College Cambridge: University College Hospital Medical School. **Awards/Research** Author of: The Good Health Hand Book (Grafton 1988); & Chemical Children (Century 1986). **Pres Committees** President, National Pure Water Association. **Past Committees** Council of Soil Association; Founder, Doctors in Britain Against Animal Experiments. **Media Experience** Adviser, Radio Humberside (BBC) & Presenter, The Health Experiment (Anglia TV).

MAPLE Mr Leslie Honorary Secretary **LONG DISTANCE WALKERS ASSOCIATION** SPORT Type: Service provider; Sports Council recognised governing body. 21 Upcroft, Windsor, Berkshire SL4 3NH Tel:01753-866685.

MARNO Ann Director **ENERGY ACTION SCOTLAND** CONSERVATION/ENVIRONMENT Type: Service provider. 21 West Nile St, Glasgow G1 2PS Tel:0141-226 3064 Fax:0141-221 2788 **Expertise** Manages a small team promoting energy efficiency and affordable warmth throughout Scotland. **Prev Posts** Strathclyde Regional Council 1984-1986; Operations Manager, Heatwise Dunbarton 1987-1992; Sen Dev Officer, Energy Action Scotland 1992-1993. **Prof Background** Originally trained as a photographer working in West of Scotland, then moved to public/voluntary sector. **Pres Committees** Board, Right to Warmth; Board, Neighbourhood Energy Action; Watt Committee, Domestic Energy & Affordable Warmth; Scottish Council for Vol Orgs. **Media Experience** Radio & TV regarding fuel poverty, VAT on fuel & energy policy.

MARRIAGE Dr Alwyn Director **FEED THE MINDS** RELIGIOUS Type: Fundraiser; Funding overseas literacy/communications projects. Robertson House, Leas Rd, Guildford, Surrey GU1 4QW Tel:01483-577877 Fax:01483-301387 **Expertise** Philosophy; aesthetics; theology; poetry. **Prev Posts** Associate Lecturer, Surrey Univ 1976-91; Lecturer, West Surrey College of Art and Design since 1991. Currently Gen Sec, United Soc for Christian Literature. **Prof Background** PhD in Philosophy. **Awards/Research** Rockefeller Schol 1993. Auth: Beautiful Man 1977; Life-Giving Spirit 1989; New Christian Poetry 1990; The People of God 1995. Editor, Christian journal. **Pres Committees** Churches Together in Guildford; Diocesan Council for Missions and Unity; CCBI. **Past Committees** Philosophy Examiner, AEB; Gen Studies Standing Cttee for Assoc Examining Bd; Validation for English Degrees, Surrey Univ & Colleges. **Media Experience** Regular broadcaster & writer. **Addits** Regular preacher and lecturer at cathedrals, univs and V&A Museum.

MARSDEN Alan Douglas Chief Executive **ROYAL NATIONAL MISSION TO DEEPSEA FISHERMEN - RNMDSF** SOCIAL Type: Fundraiser. 43 Nottingham Place, London W1M 4BX Tel:0171-487 5101 Fax:0171-224 5240 **Expertise** All areas of charity policy and administration. **Prev Posts** Dir, Brompton Management 1981-83; Sales Admin Manager, Western Glass Int 1983-85; RNMDSF Asst Secretary 1986-88. **Prof Background** Sandhurst; Staff College; National Defence College; FBIM. **Awards/Research** Fishing industry problems. **Pres Committees** Merchant Navy Welfare Board; Parish Councillor. **Media Experience** Press interviewee. **Addits** President, St Mary Bourne Cricket Club; tennis player; gardener.

MARSDEN John Executive Secretary **LINNEAN SOCIETY OF LONDON** SOCIAL Type: Learned Society. Burlington House, Piccadilly, London W1V 0LQ Tel:0171-434 4479 Fax:0171-287 9364 **Expertise** Biochemistry. **Prev Posts** Head of Dept, 1974-86; Dean 1986-88. **Prof Background** C.Chem, FRSC; C.Biol, FIBiol. **Awards/Research** Inborn Errors of Metabolism. **Pres Committees** ARCOS; Population Concern.

MARSH Lt Col Tymothy Director **NATIONAL GARDENS SCHEME CHARITABLE TRUST** SOCIAL/CONSERVATION Type: Fundraiser; Grant maker; Supports nursing charities. Hatchlands Park, East Clandon, Guildford, Surrey GU4 7RT Tel:01483-211535 Fax:01483-211537 **Expertise** Director, Charitable Trust. **Prev Posts** Management Consultant British Rail 1992-94. **Prof Background** MA CDipAF, Oxford University 1963-66; Army (The Parachute Regiment) 1966-91.

MARSHALL Mrs Jose F. Director **BUTTLE TRUST, THE** CHILDREN/YOUTH Type: Grant maker. Audley House, 13 Palace Street, London SW1E 5HS Tel:0171-828 7311 Fax:0171-828 4724 **Expertise** Children and young people. **Prev Posts** Headmistress: Dodderhill School 1978-84; Truro High School 1984-92. **Prof Background** MA Modern Languages, Girton College, Cambridge 1960; teaching and headships thereafter. **Media Experience** Local radio, interviews on education topics.

MARSHALL Anne Director **ADFAM NATIONAL-NATIONAL CHARITY FOR FAMILIES AND FRIENDS OF DRUG USERS** SOCIAL Type: Service provider. 5th Floor, Epworth House, 25 City Rd, London EC1Y 1AA Tel:0171-638 3700 **Expertise** Families and drug use; fundraising; helplines. **Prev Posts**

Media and marketing posts; Fundraiser, Comic Relief 1987-88. **Prof Background** BA Hons (Eng); Voluntary Sector Management (Open University Business School). **Awards/Research** Editor of ADFAM National Publications; Newsletters; annual reports; various articles for press and journals. **Pres Committees** Telephone Helplines Assoc; Standing Conference on Drug Abuse (SCODA); Board of European Fed of Drug Helplines. **Media Experience** Various and regular, including TV, radio and press.

MARSTON Jerry Managing Director **COMIC RELIEF/CHARITY PROJECTS** SOCIAL Type: Fundraiser; Grant maker; Education and Communication. 74 New Oxford Street, London, WC1A 1EF Tel:0171-436 1122 Fax:0171-436 1541 **Expertise** Organisation Management, Internat Grants Progs, Employee Volunteering, European Corporate Citizenship. **Prev Posts** Employment Manager, Nottingham CVS 1983-84; Employment and Economic Development Officer, Leicester City Cncl 1984-86; Community Affairs Manager, Allied Dunbar Assurance 1986-94. **Prof Background** MA (Hons) Cantab, Modern Languages. **Awards/Research** Various articles on corporate and employee community involvement. **Past Committees** Chair: Bootstrap Enterprises Swindon; Thamesdown CAB; Corporate Citizenship Europe; Gov, Wootton Bassett School.

MARTIN Alan C. Chief Executive **YARDLEY GREAT TRUST** SOCIAL Type: Service provider; Grant maker. Old Brookside, Yardley Fields Rd, Stechford Birmingham B33 8QL Tel:0121-7847889 Fax:0121-7851386 **Expertise** Housing management. **Prev Posts** Housing Manager, Harden Housing Association 1988-91; Regional Manager, Harden Housing Association 1991-94; Systems Implementation Manager, Harden Housing Association 1994-95. **Prof Background** Fellow, The Chartered Institute of Housing; Educated at Central Grammar School, Birmingham. **Pres Committees** Assistant Leader, 6th Shirley (St James) Cub Pack (Solihull). **Past Committees** Chairman, Solihull Handicapped Children's Assoc 1991; Gov, Hasluck's Green Junior School, Solihull 1992-96.

MARTIN Laurence Director **ROYAL INSTITUTE OF INTERNATIONAL AFFAIRS - RIIA** SOCIAL Type: Service provider; Research. Chatham House, 10 St James's Square, London SW1Y 4LE Tel:0171-957 5700 Fax:0171-957 5710 **Expertise** International affairs. **Prev Posts** Professor, Kings College, London 1968-78; Vice Chancellor, University of Newcastle 1979-90. **Prof Background** Academic, BA/MA Cambridge; PhD, Yale. **Awards/Research** Knight Bachelor. **Pres Committees** Cncl, School of Slavonic Studies University of London; Various Editorial Boards. **Past Committees** Trustee, UCH Hospitals; Board, Tyne Tees Television; Committee of Vice Chancellors. **Media Experience** Considerable experience with radio/TV/video/press.

MARTIN Noel National Chairman **UNIVERSITY OF THE THIRD AGE - U3A** THE ELDERLY Type: Service provider. 26 Harrison Street, London WC1H 8JG Tel:0171-837 8838 Fax:0171-837 8845 **Expertise** Educational, cultural & leisure activities for retired men & women (self-organised, self-financed basis).

MARTIN Peter Chief Executive **ASSOCIATION FOR PREVENTION OF ADDICTION - APA** MEDICAL/HEALTH Type: Service provider. 67-69 Cowcross Street, London EC1M 6BP Tel:0171-251 5860 Fax:0171-251 5890 **Expertise** Services for people with drug and alcohol problems. **Prev Posts** Regional Dir, Phoenix House Housing Assoc 1984-90; Community Development Officer, Croydon Corporation 1982-1984. **Prof Background** Journalism; protracted experiential placements in drugs field 1965-76; Cert in Youth Community Wk, Goldsmiths Coll Lond Univ. CQSW; DMS; Dip M. **Awards/Research** Churchill Fellow 1986 - Research Drugs/AIDS USA; Churchill Trav Fellowship; Fellow of the Royal Society of Arts. **Pres Committees** Mbr, Parole Board (appt 1994); Advisory Council for the Misuse of Drugs; ACMD Drug Prevention & the Environment. **Past Committees** Witness, EC Rpt on Drug Use in Mbr States 1986; ACMD HIV/AIDS Rpt 1986; ACMD 1988; ACMD Crim Justice Wking Gp; SCODA Exec; City Rds. **Media Experience** Numerous news and documentary programmes. **Addits** Lectured India for Brit Council - counselling and rehab.

MARTIN Robin D.S. Administrator **ROWCROFT HOSPICE FOR TORBAY AND SOUTH DEVON** MEDICAL/HEALTH Type: Fundraiser; Service provider; Hospice. Rowcroft House, Avenue Rd, Torbay, Devon TQ2 5LS Tel:01803-211656 Fax:01803-299065 **Expertise** General Management. **Prev Posts** Royal Marines Officer 1972-90; Dir, Training Company 1990-93.

MARTINS Lorraine Interim Director **SIA** SOCIAL Type: Service provider. Winchester House, 9 Cranmer Rd, Kennington Park, London SW9 6EJ Tel:0171-735 9010 Fax: 0171-735 9011.

MASON Timothy Director **MUSEUMS AND GALLERIES COMMISSION** ARTS Type: Service provider; Grant maker; Statutory Body. 16 Queen Anne's Gate, London SW1H 9AA Tel:0171-233 4200 Fax:0171-233 3686 **Expertise** Administration. **Prev Posts** Director, Scottish Arts Council 1980-90; Consultant: Office of Arts & Libraries, Arts Cncl of GB 1990-91; Chief Executive, London Arts Board 1991-95. **Pres Committees** BBC General Advisory Council 1990.

MASSIE Bert Director **ROYAL ASSOCIATION FOR DISABILITY AND REHABILITATION - RADAR** DISABILITY Type: Information\campaigning\support for disab people. 12 City Forum, 250 City Road, London EC1V 8AF Tel:0171-250 3222 Fax:0171-250 0212 **Expertise** Matters affecting physically disabled people. **Prev Posts** RADAR: Executive asst to the Director, 1978-85; Asst Dir, Disablement Services 1985-89. **Prof Background** BA; CQSW; MIMgt; FRSA. **Awards/Research** OBE; Auth: Employers' Guide to Disabilities; Choosing a Wheelchair; Day Care Centres for Young Disabled People; Seat Belts and Disabled People; Social Justice and Disabled People. **Pres Committees** Disabled Persons Transport Advisory Committee; Nat Adv Cttee on the Employment of People with Disabilities; Nat Disability Cncl; HABINTEG HA, and others.

MASTERS Sarah Director **GREENNET** CONSERVATION/ENVIRONMENT Type: Service provider.

393-395 City Road, London EC1V 1NE Tel:0171-713 1941 Fax:0171-833 1169.

MATHESON Susan Chief Executive **SACRO** SOCIAL Type: Fundraiser; Service provider; Grant maker. Campaigning. 31 Palmerston Place, Edinburgh EH12 5AP Tel:0131-226 4222 Fax:0131-225 1024 **Prev Posts** Senior Research Officer, Scottish Office Central Research Unit, 1975-88; Director, Family Mediation Scotland 1988-96. **Prof Background** BSc Social Science. **Awards/Research** Pubs: Children in Divorce, 1984; The Scottish Family Conciliation Service, 1986; Family Mediation in Scotland, ADR in Scotland 1995. **Past Committees** Scot Wking Pty of All Pty Parl Gp on Child Abduction; One Parent Families Scot; Stepfamily Scot; Assoc of COs of Scot Vol Orgs. **Media Experience** BBC Radio Scotland; BBC Radio 4/5; BBC Scotland; STV News; Nat & Local Papers.

MATTHEWS John Burr Lumley Secretary **SCOTTISH ASSOCIATION FOR MARINE SCIENCE -SAMS** ENVIRONMENT Type: Professional Association. PO Box 3, Oban, Argyll PA34 4AD Tel:01631-562244 Fax:01631-565518 **Expertise** Marine Science. **Prev Posts** Professor Marine Biology, Bergen Univ, Norway 1978-84; Dunstaffnage Marine Laboratory: Dep Dir 1984-88, Dir 1988-94. **Prof Background** Zoology; Research Training; University Teaching; FRSE. **Awards/Research** Articles and papers in marine scientific journals; Editorial Work. **Pres Committees** Scottish Natural Heritage (South West Region); University Highlands & Islands Project Board & Academic Council; Secretary IABO; Secretary MARS. **Past Committees** NCC Scotland; NERC Marine Science Committee; Council MBA. **Media Experience** Radio & Press Interviews.

MAWDSLEY Mrs Anne H. Director **RAYNAUD'S AND SCLERODERMA ASSOCIATION** MEDICAL/HEALTH Type: Fundraiser; Self Help Group. 112 Crewe Road, Alsager, Cheshire ST7 2JA Tel:01270-872776 Fax:01270-883556 **Expertise** Distribution of medical information for Health Professionals and sufferers of Raynaud's & Scleroderma. **Prev Posts** Teacher 1963-69; College Lecturer 1969-72; Teacher 1977-87. **Awards/Research** MBE. Publ: Raynauds - A Handbook for Patients; Scleroderma - A Handbook for Patients; Raynauds - There are More Questions than Answers. **Media Experience** Many interviews on nat radio/TV, articles in nat press.

MAXWELL Robert J. Chief Executive **KING EDWARD'S HOSPITAL FUND FOR LONDON KING'S FUND** MEDICAL/HEALTH Type: Service provider; Grant maker. 11-13 Cavendish Square, London W1M OAN Tel:0171-727 0581 Fax:0171-727 7603 **Expertise** International comparisons in health care; urban deprivation and health; management ethics. **Prev Posts** Principal, McKinsey and Co. 1966-75; Administrator to the Special Trustees, St Thomas' Hospital 1975-80. **Prof Background** BA/MA Oxon;MA Penn Univ;PhD LSE;Dipl Hlth Eco Tromso Univ;Fllw Inst Cost & Mngmnt Accts;Hon D Univ Brunel;Hon D Litt West of Eng Univ;Hon Fllw Royal Col GP;Assn Anaesthitists Hon Mbr Royal Col Physcns **Awards/Research** CBE; Auth: Health Care The Growing Dilemma, McKinsey and Co, 1974; Health and Wealth, 1981. **Pres Committees** Lewisham NHS Trust; United Medical & Dental Schl; Medical Defence Union; Prince of Wales' Advisory Group on Disability; Joseph Rowntree Fndtn. **Past Committees** London School of Hygiene & Tropical Medicine. **Addits** JP, Inner London - family and youth courts.

MAYER R. Anthony Jeffrey Chief Executive **HOUSING CORPORATION, THE** SOCIAL Type: Grant maker. 149 Tottenham Court Road, London W1P 0BN Tel:0171-393 2000 Fax:0171-393 2111 **Expertise** General management and policy administration. **Prev Posts** Assistant Secretary, Department of Environment 1980-85; Managing Director (Finance and Administration), Rothschild Asset Management 1985-91. **Prof Background** BA Politics and Econ. St Edmund Hall, Oxford University. **Past Committees** Housing Finance Corporation Board.

MAYO John Director General **HELP THE AGED** THE ELDERLY Type: Fundraiser.   St James's Walk, Clerkenwell Green, London EC1R 0BE Tel:0171-253 0253 Fax:0171-250 4474 **Prev Posts** Colonel - General Staff Head of Public Information, British Army of the Rhine and Northern Army Group 1979-83. **Prof Background** Kings College, Taunton; commissioned into Royal Regiment of Artillery, 1951; served Malta, N Africa, Malaya, Germany; commanded 17th Training Regiment 1972-75. **Awards/Research** OBE, 1976. Miscellany of articles on military matters, ageing & international vol work. **Pres Committees** Trustee: HelpAge India, New Delhi; HelpAge Sri Lanka, Colombo; HelpAge Kenya, Nairobi; Exec Cttee HelpAge Int; Cranfield Trust; Benevolent Cttee, Brit Legion; Welfare Adv Cttee, SSAFA. **Media Experience** Experienced broadcaster, including TV. **Addits** Trustee: Ex-Services Mental Welfare; Global Cancer.

MAYS Deborah Honorary Secretary **SOCIETY OF ARCHITECTURAL HISTORIANS OF GREAT BRITAIN** CONSERVATION/ENVIRONMENT Type: Professional society. 16 Hart Street, Edinburgh EH1 3RN **Expertise** Architectural History.

MAZIERE Michael Director **LONDON ELECTRONIC ARTS** ARTS Type: Service provider; Professional Association. 3rd Floor, 5-7 Buck Street, London NW1 8NJ Tel:0171-284 4588 Fax:0171-267 6078 **Expertise** Video and New Media. **Prof Background** MA (RCA) Film & TV; Film-maker and Video Artist. **Awards/Research** Awarded: Arts Council Production Award (1996). **Pres Committees** Chairman, Pandemonium BOD (London Festival of the Moving Image). **Past Committees** London Film-Makers Co-operation.

MCALLISTER Judy Buhler- Director **FINDHORN FOUNDATION** CONSERVATION/ENVIRONMENT Type: Fundraiser; Service provider; Education - mainly for adults. The Park, Forres, Morayshire IV36 0TZ Tel:01309-691620 Fax:01309-691663 **Expertise** Ecological Building/Awareness raising. **Pres Committees** Director of New Findhorn Directions; Trustee of Findhorn Fndtn.

MCANDREW Gerri Executive Director **NATIONAL FOSTER CARE ASSOCIATION** CHILDREN/YOUTH Type: Service provider; Carers. 5-7 Marshalsea Road,

London SE1 1EP   Tel:0171-828 6266 Fax:0171-357 6668

MCBAIN Ian G. Director **CAPABILITY SCOTLAND** DISABILITY Type: Service provider. 22 Corstorphine Road, Edinburgh EH12 6HP   Tel:0131-337 9876 **Expertise** Finance and management. **Prev Posts** Sales Manager, Hoover Ltd 1959-63; Director for Scotland, Mercantile Credit 1963-85. **Prof Background** Fettes College, Edinburgh; McClelland Kerr and Co, Chartered Accountants. **Awards/Research** OBE **Pres Committees** Exec Cttee: Federated Pensions Servs Ltd; ICPS; Horizon Housing Assoc Ltd; Scot Spastics Trading Co. **Past Committees** CP-ISRA; Lanark Spastics Assoc; Scott Centre for Children w Motor Impairments. **Media Experience** Participant on specific issues.

MCCALL Ian Director Advisory Service; Dir Scotland. **GAME CONSERVANCY TRUST** ANIMAL/WILDLIFE Type: Fundraiser; Service provider; Professional Association. Couston, Newtyle, Perthshire PH12 8UT   Tel:01828-650543 Fax:01828-650560 **Expertise** Research, Information, Education, Advice and Management. **Prev Posts** Adviser South of England 1975-87. **Prof Background** BSc (Hons) Agricultural Economics; 3 Year Conservation Training with Trust. **Awards/Research** Annual Review, Spring & Autumn Newsletters; Green Management Guides, Fact Sheets. **Pres Committees** Scottish Landowners, Recreation & Environment Cttee; Upland Research Group, Planning Cttee; Scottish Lowland Research Project, Planning Cttee. **Media Experience** Grampian TV Country Matters; Radio Scotland Farming & Wildlife Progs. **Addits** Contributor to Field, Shooting Times, Shooting Gazette & Others.

MCCAWLEY Michael J. Chief Executive **CATS PROTECTION LEAGUE, THE** ANIMAL Type: Fundraiser; Service provider; Grant maker. 17 Kings Road, Horsham, West Sussex RH13 5PN   Tel:01403-221900 Fax:01403-218414 **Expertise** Administration, Fund Raising. **Prev Posts** Admin. Manager, Royal Horticultural Society 1989-90; Assistant Director, The Cats Protection League 1990-92; Deputy Chief Executive, The Cats Protection League 1992-93. **Prof Background** 'A' Level Grammar School; Chief Superintendent - Metropolitan Police (1959-89). **Awards/Research** Serving Brother Order of St. John of Jerusalem. **Pres Committees** Trustees Committee of The Cats Protection League; Council of The Cats Protection League. **Past Committees** Various Committees at Senior Level in Metropolitan Police; Involved with force reorganisation (1985-88). **Media Experience** Experience of radio, TV and press interviews in Police and C.P.L..

MCCLELLAN John F. Director **SCOTTISH INTERNATIONAL EDUCATION TRUST** SOCIAL Type: Grant maker. 22 Manor Place, Edinburgh EH3 7DS Tel:0131-2251113   Fax:0131-2251113   **Prof Background** Civil Servant in Scottish Office (Under-Secretary). **Pres Committees** Hanover Housing (Scotland) Association Ltd (Association for the provision of sheltered homes for the elderly).

MCCLELLAND Neil Director **NATIONAL LITERACY TRUST** SOCIAL Type: Service provider. Swire House, 59 Buckingham Gate, London SW1E 6AJ Tel:0171-828 2435   Fax:0171-921 9986 **Expertise** Education Change; Links with wider communities; Inner City education; UK: Via Links. **Prev Posts** Director of Education, Greenwich, 1989-93; Deputy Director of Schools, ILEA, 1986-89. **Prof Background** University of London, LSE; University of Oxford, Department of Education. **Awards/Research** Teaching & Learning in Cities (Whitbread 1993), Joint Editor/Contributor. **Past Committees** Executive Committee, National Association of Governors & Managers; Director, South Thames Training & Enterprise Council. **Media Experience** Substantial experience of TV & Radio spots & links with press.

MCCONCHIE I. Chartered Secretary **NATIONAL PISTOL ASSOCIATION**   Type: Fundraiser; Service provider; Grant maker; Campaigning; National Sporting Body. 21 The Letchworth Gate Centre, Protea Way, Pixmore Ave, Letchworth, Herts SG6 1JT Tel:01462-679887   Fax:01462-481183 **Expertise** Chartered Secretary. **Prev Posts** Chief Exec of Sir John Cass Halls of Residence Assoc 1986-92. **Prof Background** Degree in Hotel & Catering Administration. **Media Experience** Represent National Pistol Assoc in Media.

MCCONNELL Charlie Chief Executive **SCOTTISH COMMUNITY EDUCATION COUNCIL** SOCIAL Type: Service provider; Quango. 9 Haymarket Terrace, Edinburgh EH12 5EZ Tel:0131-313 2488 Fax:0131-313 6800 **Expertise** Community development & community education. **Prev Posts** Lecturer in Community Education, Dundee College 1973-85; Senior Policy/Devt Officer, Nat Consumer Council, 1985-88; Dir of Public Affairs, Community Devt Fndtn 1988-93. **Prof Background** BA Hons, Politics; M Phil, Community Development. **Awards/Research** Books: Community Development and Europe (92) Co-Ed; Community Development & Urban Regeneration (93) Co-Ed; Scottish Reader on Community Education (95) Ed. **Pres Committees** Scottish Urban Regeneration Forum; Scottish Journal of Adult & Continuing Education; Community Development Journal. **Past Committees** St Georges House Cttee on Mngmt Training for Vol Org; European Citizens Action Serv; European Social Action Network, Vice President **Media Experience** General experience of all media.

MCCRACKEN Bevan R Headmaster **ROYAL SCHOOLS FOR THE DEAF** DISABILITY Type: Fundraiser; Service provider; Non-maintained Schools. Stanley Road, Cheadle Hulme, Cheadle, Cheshire SK8 6RQ Tel:0161-437 5951 Fax:0161-437 7282 **Expertise** Deaf Education; Special Educational Needs; Legislation with reference to Special Education. **Prev Posts** Head of External Services for the Hearing Impaired, Sheffield, 1978-81; Advisor/Head of Service, Special Educational Needs County of Avon, 1981-90. **Prof Background** Qualified teacher of the Deaf; Degree in Arts & Educational Management. **Awards/Research** Auth: Work Books for Children. **Pres Committees** European Deaf Childrens' Trust; British Soc for Mental Health & Deafness; National Conference for Heads of Schools & Serv for Hearing Impaired Children; British Assoc of Teachers of the Deaf.

WHO'S WHO IN THE VOLUNTARY SECTOR - 94

MCCREADY Donald Chief Executive **ROMANIAN ORPHANAGE TRUST** CHILDREN/YOUTH Type: Fundraiser; Grant maker; Technical Assistance (Overseas). 21 Garlick Hill, London EC4V 2AU Tel:0171-248 2424 Fax:0171-248 5417 **Expertise** Overseas development; technical assistance. **Prev Posts** VSO Field Officer, Sudan 1985-87; VSO Field Director, China 1987-90. **Prof Background** MA (Oxon) Philosophy, Politics, Economics; Commission in RAF; Social Work; Teaching English as a Foreign Language.

MCDONALD John Director (UK) **ORBIS INTERNATIONAL** SOCIAL Type: Fundraiser. Garden Suite, Newton Court, Kensington Church St, London W8 4BD Tel:0171-937 4552 Fax:0171-938 4034 **Expertise** Fundraising, media relations. **Prev Posts** Appeals Manager, Oxfam Scotland 1988-90; Fundraising Manager, Orbis 1990-92. **Prof Background** BSc, Aberdeen University; ICFM **Media Experience** Limited exposure

MCDONNEL Michael A. Secretary **SCOTTISH ACCIDENT PREVENTION COUNCIL** MEDICAL/HEALTH Type: Service provider; Campaigning. Slateford House, 53 Lanark Road, Edinburgh EH14 1TL Tel:0131-4557457 Fax:0131-4439442 **Expertise** Accident prevention & road safety. **Prev Posts** Primary Teacher, Strathclyde Regional Council 1976-90; Assistant Road Safety Officer, Strathclyde Regional Council 1990. **Prof Background** Teaching (Primary School); Degree in Divinity. **Pres Committees** Scottish Road Safety Campaign. **Media Experience** ROSPA spokesperson on road safety issues in Scotland. **Addits** Road Safety Manager (Scotland), ROSPA (while Secretary of SAPC).

MCEWAN Roy James Managing Director **SCOTTISH CHAMBER ORCHESTRA** ARTS Type: Service provider. 4 Royal Terrace, Edinburgh EH7 5AB Tel:0131-5576800 Fax:0131-5576933 **Expertise** Arts administration & music. **Prev Posts** Manager, Whitechapel Art Gallery 1978-79; Administrator/Director, MacRobert Arts Centre, Stirling 1979-91; Director, Arts Development, Northwest Arts Board, Manchester 1991-93. **Prof Background** BSc (Econ) London School of Economics; Diploma in the Administration of the Arts, Recreation & Leisure, Polytechnic of Central London. **Pres Committees** Brd Mbr (Managing Dir), Scottish Chamber Orchestra; Brd Mbr, Assoc of British Orchestras; Brd Mbr, Scottish Arts Lobby; Cttee Mbr, Scottish Arts Cncl, Combined Arts Cttee. **Past Committees** Brd Mbr & Chairman, Federation of Scottish Theatres 1983-91; Cttee Mbr, Scottish Arts Cncl, Drama Cttee. **Media Experience** Experience with interviews for radio & press.

MCGEOUGH Brian Thomas Treasurer **HENRY SMITHS CHARITIES** SOCIAL Type: Grant maker. 5 Chancery Lane, Cliffords Inn, London EC4A 1BU Tel:0171-320 6215 Fax:0171-320 6275 **Prev Posts** Solicitor, 1960; Partner, Denton Hall 1963-92; Clerk, Henry Smiths Charities 1972-89, Tre 1989-; Mnging Trustee, Equit Charitable Trust 1984-. **Prof Background** St Chads College, Wolverhampton; BA, Trinity Hall, Cambridge University.

MCGETTIGAN Anna Director **COMMUNITY SELF BUILD AGENCY** SOCIAL Type: Service provider. 40 Bowling Green Lane, London, EC1R 0NE Tel:0171-415 7092 Fax:0171-415 7142 **Expertise** Self build housing, particularly working with the unemployed. **Prev Posts** Area Mgr, London & Quadrant H.T. 1976-79; Housing Mgr & Assoc Secretary, Stonham H.A. 1979-83; Housing Consultant, Ken Walker & Partners 1983-89. **Prof Background** Diploma in Housing and Management; Certificate in Housing Finance. **Pres Committees** National Committee Member, Urban Forum; UK National Committee Member, UN City Summit - Habitat II. **Past Committees** Local Councillor - LB of Southwark; Mbr NFHA working party on housing management standards. **Media Experience** Various radio interviews.

MCGHEE Elaine General Secretary **NATIONAL ASSEMBLY OF WOMEN** SOCIAL Type: Campaigning organisation. 13 Smedley Lane, Cheetham Hill, Manchester M8 8UJ Tel:0161-205 5920 **Expertise** Social work; specialising with drug addicts, alcoholics, adolescents. **Prev Posts** Director, Regina Coeli House Ltd; Manager, Gloucester Night Shelter. **Prof Background** Dip. Soc.Admin (Oxford); Dip.Statistics (Oxford). **Awards/Research** 2 Peace Awards. 6 months research in USA on Poverty in Downtown USA; Life sentencing; Sex offenders. **Pres Committees** Company Sec, Charitable Co; Citywide Rep, Education Forum; Rep, Local Consortium Education Forum; Women National Commission. **Past Committees** Parent Rep on Warnock Report; Management Partners of Prisoners (responsible for recruiting/training court volunteers). **Media Experience** Local TV and radio. **Addits** 30 years as volunteer with voluntary organisation.

MCGOWN Archie Director **SCOTTISH PRE-RETIREMENT COUNCIL** THE ELDERLY Type: Service provider; Campaigning. Alexandra House, 204 Bath Street, Glasgow G2 4AL Tel:0141-3329427 **Expertise** Pre-retirement education & provision of courses. **Prof Background** Proprietor & MD of various companies. **Pres Committees** Past Chairman/Trustee, Royal Scottish Automobile Club; Tres, Scottish Adult Ed Voluntary Org Forum (SAEVOF); Pre-retirement Assoc of G.B. & N.I. (P.R.A.). **Past Committees** Royal Scottish Automobile Club; Scottish Provision Trade Association. **Media Experience** Experience in radio (phone-in programmes).

MCGRATH Laura Executive Officer **SCOTTISH MARRIAGE CARE** SOCIAL Type: Service provider. 50 Greenock Road, Paisley PA3 2LE Tel:0141-849 6183 Fax:0141-849 6183 **Expertise** Counselling; Supervising & Training in Counselling. **Prof Background** BSc; Teacher Trained; Counselling Trained.

MCGREEVY Mark Director **DEPAUL TRUST** SOCIAL Type: Fundraiser; Service provider. 24 George St, London, W1H 5RB Tel:0171-935 0111 Fax:0171-935 6561 **Expertise** Director of all activities. **Prev Posts** Cardinal Hume Centre 1989-90; Deputy Director, Depaul Trust 1990-92. **Prof Background** BA Dunelm (Durham University) General Arts; Post Graduate Certificate in Management Studies. **Pres Committees** Trustee, Alone in London Board; Passage Management Committee; Westminster Diocesan Pastoral Board. **Media Experience** Experience in radio, TV, video and press.

MCGREGOR REID Dr Gordon Director **NORTH OF ENGLAND ZOOLOGICAL SOCIETY** ANIMAL/ WILDLIFE Type: Zoological Society. Chester Zoological Gdns, Caughall Rd, Upton-by-Chester, Chester, Cheshire CH2 1LH Tel:01244-380280 Fax:01244-371273 **Expertise** Zoology & Ichthyology. **Prev Posts** Keeper of Natural History, Horniman Museum 1985-91; Curator-in-Chief, North of England Zoological Society 1992-95. **Prof Background** BSc Zoology with Psychology; PhD Comp Anatomy & Systematics; FIBiol; CBiol. **Awards/Research** Over 100 publications covering varied aspects of zoology & ichthyology; Field work in Africa; Regularly review and edit scientific papers; Various awards, grants, sponsorship received **Pres Committees** Cncl Mbr, Linnean Soc of London; Fauna & Flora Int; Fed of Zoos (UK & Eire); Inspector of Zoos (DoE); Mbr of Int Union of Directors of Zoological Gardens. **Past Committees** Elected Officer Executive & Editorial Cttees, Biology Curators Grp; Mbr of Steering Cttee, Int'l Aquatic Conservation Network. Varied.

MCINTOSH Neil Chief Executive **CENTRE FOR BRITISH TEACHERS** SOCIAL/TRAINING Type: Service provider; Grant maker. Tel:01734-523900 Fax:01734-523926 1 The Chambers, East Street, Reading, Berks RG1 4JD **Expertise** Education Management. **Prev Posts** Director, Shelter 1977-84; Director, VSO 1985-90. **Prof Background** BA Politics; MSc Industrial Relations. **Awards/Research** The Right to Manage? (Macdonalds); Housing and the Economy (Shelter); The Management of Deprivation, (Polytechnic of the South Bank). **Pres Committees** Treasurer, Freedom of Information Campaign; Trustee, Stonham Housing Association. **Past Committees** Founder/Chairman, Homeless Int; Vice President, Building Societies Assoc; Member, Duke of Edinburgh's NFHA Inquiry into Brit Housing. **Media Experience** Varied experience in radio, TV, video and press.

MCKEAN Charles Head of School/Prof of Architecture **DUNCAN OF JORDANSTONE COLLEGE** SOCIAL/TRAINING Type: Service provider; Professional Institute. University of Dundee, 13 Perth Rd, Dundee DD1 4HT Tel:01382-223261 Fax:01382-227304 **Expertise** Admin, architecture, public speaking, writing, providing advice to clients & architects on commissioning. **Prev Posts** RIBA: Eastern Region Secretary 1970-79; Projects Officer 1976-79; Sec/Chief Exec, RIAS 1980-94. **Prof Background** BA Hons (Bristol), Philosophy English & French. **Awards/Research** Building Jnlst of the Year 1983; Thomas Ross Awd 1993; Gordon Ricketts Mem Awd 1980. Many publ inc: architect guides to London, E Anglia, Scotland; Scottish Renaissance; 1930s. **Pres Committees** Architectural Heritage Soc, Scottish Museums Resource, National Trust for Scotland, Council and Buildings Cttee. **Past Committees** Edinburgh Common Purpose, Thirlestane Trustees, Workshops & Artists Studio Provision, SAC Exhibs Panel, CRM Society **Media Experience** Freelance contrib all media inc Times 1977-83, Scotland on Sunday 1986-88. **Addits** IBP Awd Architectural Journalist of the Year 1970, 1983.

MCKECHNIE Sheila Chief Executive **CONSUMERS ASSOCIATION** SOCIAL Type: Service provider; Campaigning. 2 Marylebone Road, London NW1 4DF Tel:0171-830 6000 Fax:0171-830 6220 **Expertise** Consumer issues. **Prev Posts** Health and Safety Officer, Assoc of Scientific and Managerial Staffs 1976-85; Director, Shelter 1985-94. **Prof Background** MA Politics and History, Edinburgh Univ; MA Industrial Relations, Warwick Univ. **Awards/Research** Numerous articles in newspapers and current affairs journals. **Pres Committees** Foyer Federation for Youth; Architecture Foundation. **Media Experience** Weekly contributions/interviews/comment.

MCKITTRICK David Field Officer & Organiser **PROTESTANT AND CATHOLIC ENCOUNTER - PACE** SOCIAL Type: Cross community work in mutual understanding. 174-184 Ormeau Road, Belfast BT7 2ED Tel:01232-232864 **Expertise** Facilitation of group meetings on issues which divide Catholics and Protestants. **Prev Posts** Community Education Officer, Ulster People's College, 1986-87. **Prof Background** MA, Philosophy of Religion & Ethics; Medical Counselling; Teachers Certificate. **Awards/Research** Rogerian Encounter Group in Mutual Understanding work (research supervised by Queens University); Dance in the Middle Years of Schooling (Macmillan 1970); Articles for Pace Journal. **Media Experience** Talk Back, BBC; Sunday Sequence; Interviews given on behalf of PACE.

MCLACHLAN Peter Chief Executive **BRYSON HOUSE** SOCIAL Type: Service provider; Campaigning. 28 Bedford St., Belfast BT2 7FE Tel:01232-325835 Fax:01232-439156 **Expertise** Environment; developing voluntary action; community care;mediation; crosscultural issues; victimology. **Prev Posts** Projects Manager, Peace People CT 1976-80; MD Agricultural Machinery & Engineering Co 1974-76; NI Assembly 1973-74. **Prof Background** Classics, Oxford University. **Awards/Research** Articles on NI cultural differences, mediation. Eisenhower Fellow, OBE. DL. **Pres Committees** Trustee, Buttle Trust, Victoria Homes Trust, Cecil King Memorial Foundation, Committee member of many charities and housing associations; Mbr Medical Research Council. **Past Committees** Member Eastern Health and Social Services Board (NI); Member Board of Visitors HMP Maghaberry; Vice chair NI Hospice 11 years. **Media Experience** Extensive, 2 years presenter community radio programme.

MCLEAN Colin Director **SCOTTISH MUSEUMS COUNCIL** CONSERVATION/ENVIRONMENT Type: Fundraiser; Service provider; Grant maker. County House, 20-22 Torphichen Street, Edinburgh EH3 8JB Tel:0131-229 7465 Fax:0131-229 2728

MCLEAN Sally Director **DISABILTY LAW SERVICE** SOCIAL Type: Service provider; Legal advice. 2nd Floor, Rm 241, 49-51 Bedford Row, London WC1R 4LR Tel:0171-831 8031 Fax:0171-831 5582 **Prev Posts** Solicitor, private practice - Merle Leman Hudson & Co 1988-1989; Solicitor, Disability Law Service 1989-1993. **Prof Background** BA; LLB **Awards/Research** Community Care Legislation briefing notes, Open University; Contrib: Legal help article in The Carers' Guide 1994. **Past Committees** Convenor of Special Needs Group of ELAS (Education Lawyers Association). **Media Experience** Link programme, ITV, November 1992.

MCLEOD Helen R. Brigade Secretary **GIRLS' BRIGADE IN SCOTLAND** CHILDREN/YOUTH Type: Voluntary Youth Organization. Boys' Brigade House, 168 Bath Street, Glasgow G2 4TQ Tel:0141-332 1765 **Prof Background** Diploma in Youth and Community Work. **Pres Committees** Girls' Brigade: National Committees; Chief Executive Officers Group, SSCVYO. **Past Committees** Moray House, Curriculum Group; Secretary, Strathclyde Voluntary Youth Organizations.

MCLEOD Mrs Joss National Officer **NATIONAL FEDERATION OF SHOPMOBILITY - NFS** DISABILITY Type: Service provider; Advisory and coordinating body. 85 High Street, Worcester, WR1 2ET Tel:01905-617761 Fax:01905-617761 **Expertise** Support and advice for new and existing shopmobility schemes. **Prev Posts** MD, Torquil Designs 1989-92; Manager, Shopmobility Worcester 1992-95. **Prof Background** BA (Hons) English and Related Literatures; Diploma in Management - pending. **Awards/Research** NFS Guidelines. **Past Committees** Worcester and District Community Health Council.

MCLEOD Ruth Chief Executive **HOMELESS INTERNATIONAL** SOCIAL Type: Fundraiser; Grant maker; Campaigning. Guildford House, 20 Queens Road, Coventry CV1 3EG Tel:01203-632802 Fax:01203-632911 **Expertise** Urban development; housing/housing rel community activities; Women & construction esp in dvlpng countries **Prev Posts** Dir, Construction Res & Devlpmnt Ctre, Jamaica 1982-89; Co-ord Womens Construction Collective, Jamaica 1982-89; Head of Science Trench Town Comprehensive, Jamaica. **Prof Background** BA Social & Political Science; MA (CANTAB); Diploma of Education, University of The West Indies. **Awards/Research** 'Daughters of Sysiphus' Publ United Nations Centre for Human Settlements; Various papers in devlpmnt journals. 'The Womens Construction Collective/SEEDS Publ, New York. **Pres Committees** Member: UK delegation to the UN Commission on Human settlements; Sec to the UK Habitat II National Council. **Past Committees** Mbr, Habitat Int Coalition Women & Shelter Gp; UNCHS Panel of Experts Gov Steering Cttee for Habitat II;Jamaican delegate to UNCHS. **Media Experience** Video production & journalism specialising in urban & housing issues.

MCMARTIN William National Officer **INTERNATIONAL RESCUE CORPS - IRC** MEDICAL/HEALTH Type: Fundraiser; Service provider; Disaster rescue service. Office 2B, 1 Kerse Road, Grangemouth, Stirlingshire FK3 8HW. Tel:01324-665011 Fax:01324-666130 **Expertise** Rescue work. **Prev Posts** Joined IRC in 1981. **Prof Background** Fire service for 25 years;life boat training 1969 and 1993.

MCMULLIN Meta Regional Services Manager **DEAFBLIND AND RUBELLA ASSOCIATION NI - SENSE - NI** DISABILITY Type: Fundraiser; Service provider. Knockbracken Healthcare Park, Saintfield Road, Belfast BT8 8BR Tel:01232-705858 Fax:01232-705688 **Expertise** Dual and multiple sensory impairment and general disability issues. **Prev Posts** Education Adviser, Regional Co-ordinator Assoc for Spina Bifida and Hydrocephalus. **Prof Background** Certificate in Education, BSc in Maths and Systems Analysis, Diploma in Educational Computing (Special Needs). **Pres Committees** SNAG.

MCVEIGH Jane Director **CONTACT THE ELDERLY** THE ELDERLY Type: Service provider. 15 Henrietta St, London WC2E 8QH Tel:0171-240 0630 Fax:0171-379 5781.

MCWHINNEY Jeff Chief Executive **BRITISH DEAF ASSOCIATION** DISABILITY Type: Fundraiser; Service provider; Campaigning. 1-3 Worship Street, London EC2A 2AB Tel:0171-588 3520 Fax:0171-588 3527 **Expertise** Disability rights, deafness & sign language campaigns; organisational culture & change management. **Prev Posts** Head of SL Community Services, Disability Resources Team 1987-91; Sen Economic Dev Off, L B Wandsworth 1991-94; Director, Greenwich Association of Disabled People 1994-95. **Prof Background** CIM, Kingston University; DMS. **Awards/Research** Author of numerous articles on deaf consciousness & identity. **Pres Committees** Board of Directors, SIGN. **Past Committees** Committee on Employment of People with Disabilities (Dept of Educ & Employment), S London; Human Aids to Communication Wkng Gp. **Media Experience** Experience with TV and radio (BBC and Channel 4). **Addits** Scholarship, Kingston University 1993.

MEAD Deryk Chief Executive **NCH ACTION FOR CHILDREN** CHILDREN/YOUTH Type: Fundraiser; Service provider; Campaigning. 85 Highbury Park, London N5 1UD Tel:0171-226 2033 Fax:0171-226 2573 **Prev Posts** Deputy Director, Social Services, Cumbria 1986-91; Director, Social Services, Gloucestershire 1991-96. **Prof Background** Professional qualifications in social work (child care and psychiatric) MSc. **Pres Committees** Various NCH Action for Children Committees. **Media Experience** Media experience as Director of Social Services.

MEADE Chris Director **POETRY SOCIETY** ARTS Type: Fundraiser; Service provider; Campaigning. 22 Betterton St, London WC2H 9BU Tel:0171-240 4810 Fax:0171-240 4818 **Prev Posts** Co-ordinator, Opening the Book Festival Sheffield Libraries 1984-89; Principal Officer, Arts and Marketing, Birmingham Library Services 1990-94. **Prof Background** Working in Literature and Libraries to promote creative reading and writing. **Awards/Research** Author of plays, reviews, books. George Orwell Award 1984 for creative writing. **Media Experience** TV interviews: Big Breakfast, The Late Show, BBC News; Press/radio Nat/local.

MEADOWS Pamela Director **POLICY STUDIES INSTITUTE** SOCIAL Type: Independent Research Institute. 100 Park Village East, London NW1 3SR Tel:0171-468 0468 Fax:0171-388 0914 **Prev Posts** Chief Economic Adviser, Dept of Employment; Home Office; National Institute of Economic and Social Research. **Prof Background** BA, Durham Univ; MSc (Econ), University of London (Birkbeck College). **Awards/Research** Numerous publications concerned with the labour market. **Media Experience** Various, particularly radio.

MELCHETT Lord Peter Executive Director **GREENPEACE UK** CONSERVATION/ENVIRONMENT Type: Campaigning; anti-nuclear. Canonbury Villas, London N1 2PN Tel:0171-865 8100 Fax:0171-865 8200 **Prev Posts** Government Minister 1976-79; Chair, Greenpeace UK 1986-89.

MENDEL Paul D. Director **COUNCIL OF CHRISTIANS AND JEWS - CCJ** RELIGIOUS Type: Fundraiser; Religious/Educational. Drayton House, 30 Gordon Street London WC1H OAN Tel:0171-388 3322 Fax:0171-388 3305 **Expertise** Christian Jewish relations. **Prev Posts** Deputy Director DEF and group relations board; assistant then Deputy Director CCJ 1985-92 **Pres Committees** Interfaith Network Executive; National Executive Committee Association of Jewish Ex-service Men and Women. **Media Experience** TV, radio and newspapers.

MEYER Christopher J. Director **HEARING CONCERN** DISABILITY Type: Fundraiser; Service provider; Campaigning. 7/11 Armstrong Road, London W3 7JL Tel:0181-743 1110 Fax:0181-742 9043 **Expertise** Strategic Management. **Prev Posts** Attache, Moscow 1986-88; Dir Conventional Arms Control (Europe) 1988-90; UK Liaison Officer to US Strategic Command 1990-93. **Prof Background** Naval Officer, (Captain, RN); Operational Command at sea. **Awards/Research** Numerous articles and short stories published; Research into Hard of Hearing Problems; OBE. **Pres Committees** United Kingdom Council for the Deaf, Trustee; International Federation of the Hard of Hearing (Europe) Board. **Past Committees** American Red Cross, Field Services. **Media Experience** Extensive experience in USA and Great Britain. Russian and German interpreter.

MEYER Paul Director **NATIONAL HOSPITAL DEVELOPMENT FOUNDATION** MEDICAL/HEALTH Type: Fundraiser. The National Hospital, Queens Square, London WC1N 3BG Tel:0171-278 3945 Fax:0171-278 2252 **Expertise** Capital fundraising. **Prev Posts** SENSE 1990-92. **Prof Background** Chartered Secretary. **Pres Committees** Chairman, Roxwell Festival; Essex County Council School Governor. **Past Committees** CBI Companies Committee.

MIDGLEY Christine Head of Information **COUNCIL FOR ENVIRONMENTAL EDUCATION - CEE** CONSERVATION/ENVIRONMENT Type: Educational charity. University of Reading, London Road, Reading, RG1 5AQ Tel:01734-756061 Fax:01734-756264 **Expertise** Information work. **Prev Posts** Information Officer, Physical Education Association of GB and NI 1983-89. Currently: Project Manager, Building Support for Environmental Educ - R&D prog into info provision. **Prof Background** BA (Hons) French, University of Birmingham; MA Library & Information Studies, Loughborough University; Member of the Institute of Information Scientists. **Awards/Research** Ed: Sport & Recreation Inf Group Bulletin 1984-89; British Jnl of Physical Educ 1987-89; Ed, Annual Review of Env Education. **Pres Committees** Environmental Information Forum Committee. **Past Committees** Sport & Recreation Information Group Committee 1984-89.

MILBURN Anthony Executive Director **INTERNATIONAL ASSOCIATION ON WATER QUALITY - IAWQ** CONSERVATION/ENVIRONMENT Type: Service provider; Professional Association. Duchess House, 20 Mason's Yard, Duke Street St James', London SW1Y 6BU Tel:0171-839 8390 Fax:0171-839 8299 **Expertise** Volunteer organisation management. **Prev Posts** Technical Secretary/Editor, International Water Supply Assoc 1973-1975; Training Manager, Nat Water Council 1975-1979; Project Manager (Indonesia), Nat Water Council 1979-1980. **Prof Background** B.Tech Civil Engineering; M.Sc. Hydraulics; Chartered Engineer; MICE, MIWEM, Diploma in company direction. **Awards/Research** Water pollution research and control (joint editor) Biennial 1982-92. **Pres Committees** St. Matthews School; Court of Assistants, Company of Water Conservators; Nominating Ctte, Stockholm Water Prize; Mbr, Int Union of Assocs; Mbr Bd of Govs World Water Council. **Past Committees** Vice-Pres, COWAR - Committee on Water Research of International Council of Scientific Unions. **Media Experience** Little.

MILES Lieutenant Commander Director **ROYAL NATIONAL LIFEBOAT INSTITUTION - RNLI** SOCIAL Type: Service provider. West Quay Road, Poole, Dorset BH15 1HZ Tel:01202-663000 Fax:01202-663167 **Prev Posts** RNLI: Staff Officer Operations 1978, Deputy Director 1982. **Prof Background** Reeds School, Surrey; HMS Conway Merchant Navy Cadet School; Served ten years in P&O Shipping Company, Cadet then Deck Officer, before joining RNLI in 1964. **Awards/Research** CBE; RD; FNI; CIMgt; RNR. **Pres Committees** All RNLI Cttees: Cttee of Management; Executive Cttee and all those reporting to the Executive; Chair of Trustees, Friends of Dolphin; Chair of Directors of Poole Arts Centre Trust. **Media Experience** Interviewee on TV and radio.

MILLBANK Joan Director **CAMBRIDGE HOUSE AND TALBOT** SOCIAL Type: Service provider; Development Agency. 131-9 Camberwell Road, London SE5 0HF Tel:0171-703 5025 **Expertise** Management; community development. **Prev Posts** Community Development Worker 1977-83; Manager of Neighbourhood Office 1985-88. **Prof Background** BA (Hons) Applied Social Studies; CQSW; Diploma in Industrial Relations (Trade Unions). **Pres Committees** Management committees of various local organizations. **Past Committees** Chair, Exec Committee BASSAC (Brit Assoc of Settlements and Social Action Centres). **Media Experience** Limited participation.

MILLIS Susan M. Honorary Secretary **SOCIETY OF EQUESTRIAN ARTISTS** ARTS Type: Professional Association 30 Buxton Close, Lordswood, Chatham, Kent ME5 8UP Tel:01634-668138 **Expertise** Pyrographic artist. **Prev Posts** Honorary Treasurer, Society of Women Artists. **Prof Background** Artist, qualified Book-Keeper. **Awards/Research** 'A Burning Art' Popular Crafts May 1989. Presently engaged in researching for a book on Pyrographic Art. **Pres Committees** Executive committee, The Society of Equestrian Artists; Council, The Society of Women Artists.

MILLS Derek Founder/Director **NATIONAL MUSIC FOR THE BLIND - NMFTB** DISABILITY Type: Fundraiser; Service provider; Grant maker - Grants to Registered Blind only. 2 High Park Rd, Southport, Merseyside PR9 7QL Tel:01704-28010 Braille Fax **Expertise** Creating simulated radio station programme on tape. **Prev Posts** Founder of National Music for the Blind, 1972. **Prof Background** RA AcmY. **Media Experience** Local FM Radio Dune.

MILLS Dian Information Officer **INSTITUTE FOR OPTIMUM NUTRITION** MEDICAL/HEALTH Type: Fundraiser; Service provider; Educational charity trust; nutrition education. 13 Blades Court, Deodar Road, London SW15 2NU Tel:0181-878 9993 Fax:0181-887 9980 **Expertise** Nutrition in preconceptual care; Pain alleviation through nutrition; Endometriosis; Female hlth problems. **Prev Posts** Head of Home Economics & Nutrition, Brighton 1983-87; Trustee, Endometriosis Society 1989-93; Tutor and Lecturer at ION, 1992 to date. **Prof Background** Cert Ed. (Home Ec & Nutrition) Victoria Univ, Manchester; BA (Ed & Psych) Open Univ; Dip ION (Nutritional Med) Institute for Optimum Nutrition; MA Health Ed (Eur) (Nutrition) Univ of Brighton. **Awards/Research** MA: The Role of Nutrition in Preconceptual Care; The Value of Nutrition in The Management of Pain; The Role of Self-Help Groups in Mngmt of Pain - Endometriosis, Parthenon Press 1995. **Pres Committees** Group Co-ordinator of the Endometriosis Society. **Past Committees** Trustee, The Brit Nat Endometriosis Society 1989-94; Eastbourne Cmmty Health Council, Women & Children's Cttee 1990-95. **Media Experience** Extensive experience in a range of TV and radio broadcasts. **Addits** Writing a book on Endometriosis & Infertility with Dr Michael Vernon.

MILLS Elizabeth Director **RESEARCH INTO AGEING** MEDICAL/HEALTH Type: Fundraiser. Baird House, 15-17 St Cross St, London EC1N 8UN Tel:0171-404 6878 Fax:0171-404 6816 **Expertise** Fundraising; charity administration. **Prev Posts** Manager, David Braga Assoc, HK 1977-81; MD, Archer Medical Ltd, HK 1981-84; Administrator Research into Ageing 1985-89. **Prof Background** Secretarial training; Conservative Party Agent. **Pres Committees** Nat Exec, Assoc of Med Rsrch Charities 1992-; Age Concern England 1992-; Cncllr, LB of Hammersmith and Fulham 1994-; Nth Thames Reg Hlth Auth Hlth of Older Pple R&D Grp; Gov Mayfield-St Leonards Sch. **Media Experience** Many appearances spkng for Res into Ageing. **Addits** Liveryman Grocers' Co 1988-.

MILLS Robert Anthony Chief Executive **HANDICAPPED CHILDREN'S PILGRIMAGE TRUST & HOSANNA HOUSE** DISABILITY Type: Fundraiser; Service provider. 100a High Street, Banstead, Surrey SM7 2RB Tel:01737-353311 Fax:01737-353008 **Expertise** Management/Training. **Prev Posts** Youth & Community Worker/Tutor, 1987-91; Training Officer, 1991-92. **Prof Background** Theology; Management; Training. **Past Committees** Development of 'Spectrum' for Youth Leader Training. **Media Experience** Worked with BBC on Songs of Praise

MILNE Yvonne President/Founder (Hon. position) **UK RETT SYNDROME ASSOCIATION - UKRSA** MEDICAL/HEALTH Type: Self-help group. 29 Carlton Rd, London N11 3EX Tel:0181-361 5161 Fax:0181-361 5161 **Expertise** Rett Syndrome, parent of a girl with Rett Syndrome. **Prev Posts** Marketing product manager; lecturer in marketing. **Prof Background** BSc Hotel and Catering Administration, Surrey Univ. **Awards/Research** Midlands Region Whitbread Volunteer Action Awds 1995; Finalist, Guardian Jerwood Awd 1995; BMA film/video educational merit award as director of video: Care Today - Cure Tomorrow. **Pres Committees** Various Malvern committees relating to disability; UKRSA executive committee. **Media Experience** Interviews on radio, national and local press. **Addits** Runner-up Worcs Woman of the Year Award.

MILTON Brian General Secretary **NATIONAL ASSOCIATION FOR ENVIRONMENTAL EDUCATION (UK) - NAEE** CONSERVATION/ENVIRONMENT Type: Teacher Organisation. University Of Wolverhampton, Walsall Campus, Gorway Road, Walsall WS1 3BD Tel:01922-31200 Fax:01922-31200 **Prof Background** Head teacher.

MILTON Lucy Co-Director **ARTISTS' AGENCY** ARTS Type: Service provider. 18 Norfolk St, Sunderland, Tyne & Wear SR1 1EA Tel:0191-5109318 Fax:0191-5652846 **Expertise** Arts administration (organising artists' residencies in social settings). **Prev Posts** Director, Lucy Milton Gallery, London 1971-75; Exhibitions Organiser, Spectro Arts Workshop 1979-82; Artists' Agency 1983-. **Prof Background** BA English Language & Literature (Hons) Trinity College Dublin; PGCE, Whitelands College, London. **Awards/Research** Various articles in art magazines; Co-ordinator of various Agency publications. **Past Committees** Board of Management, Tyne & Wear Foundation, Advisory Group, British Health Care Arts Centre. **Media Experience** Various interviews/features in national & local TV and press.

MINTER Susan Curator **CHELSEA PHYSIC GARDEN** CONSERVATION/ENVIRONMENT Type: Fundraiser; Service provider. 66 Royal Hospital Road, London SW3 4HS Tel:0171-352 5646 Fax:0171-376 3910 **Expertise** Medicinal Plants; Perfumery Plants; Tropical Plants. **Prev Posts** Supervisor, Palm House, Royal Botanic Gardens, Kew, 1984-91. **Prof Background** MA (Hons) History; National Diploma, Horticulture. **Awards/Research** Auth: The Greatest Glasshouse: The Rainforests Recreated, 1990; contrib to RHS Dictionary of Gardening; articles include: Rainforests at Kew, 1990. **Pres Committees** Member, Floral C Committee, Royal Horticultural Society; Member, Council of the Herb Society. **Media Experience** Experience of all media.

MITCHELL Andrew W. Deputy Director **EARTHWATCH EUROPE** CONSERVATION/ENVIRONMENT Type: Grant maker; Education; vol field assistants; Science fndn. 57 Woodstock Road, Oxford, OX2 6HJ Tel:01865-311600 Fax:01865-311383 **Expertise** Conservation & environ issues;marketing & corp sponsorship;trop forests;broadcasting. **Prev Posts** Scientific Co-ord, Scientific Expl Society 1975-81;TV Producer 1983-88;BBC Science & Ftrs ;BBC Nat History Unit;

Mkting Dir Earthwatch (USA) 1989-90. **Prof Background** BSc Hons Zoology Bristol Univ; 20 years managing frontline research expeditons in earth, life & human sciences; Prod/Dir Science Environ TV progs; Dep Dir Earthwatch 6 years; Ext int exp. **Awards/Research** Finalist Sir Peter Kent Conservation Book Prize 1990; Pioneered use of aerial walkway systems for tropical forest canopy research. **Pres Committees** Trustee Scientific Exploration Society; Orang Utang Foundation. **Media Experience** Presenter Ch4 Series; 2 series for Radio 4; reg broadcaster;author 7 books.

MITCHELL Mrs Sally Founder President **THYROID EYE DISEASE ASSOCIATION - TED** MEDICAL/HEALTH Type: Fundraiser; Service provider; Grant maker; Campaigning. Lea House, 21 Troarn Way, Chudleigh, Devon TQ13 0PP Tel:01626-852980 **Expertise** Thyroid eye disease. **Prev Posts** Restauranteur 1983-87. **Prof Background** Cordon Bleu Diploma. **Awards/Research** Contributions to Medical Journals (The Practitioner, Royal College of General Practitioners Reference Book 1995). **Pres Committees** TED Executive Committee; Thyroid Federation International. **Media Experience** BBC Radio 5 Health Programme;BBC TV1 Morning Surgery.

MONKMAN Sally Director **SOS SAHEL INTERNATIONAL (UK)** SOCIAL/OVERSEAS Type: Fundraiser; Service provider; Overseas Aid Agency. 1 Tolpuddle Street, London N1 0XT Tel:0171-837 9129 Fax:0171-837 0856 **Expertise** Strategic planning & management, Programme design & Organisational management. **Prev Posts** Director, Africa & Arab World Programmes, Marie Stopes International 1991-95. **Prof Background** MA (Econ) Development Studies; Dip, Management Studies (DMS); BA (Hons) Social Policy & Administration. **Awards/Research** Author of: The Relationship Between Population, Growth & Development In Sub-Saharan Africa: With Reference To The Zimbabwe Experience; African Debt: Its Impact On The Poor. **Media Experience** Radio & TV experience (ref. overseas aid, fam planning, environmental issues).

MONTGOMERY A. Operations Director **INTERNATIONAL STUDY CENTRE** SOCIAL/TRAINING Type: Service provider; Professional Association; Education. Herstmonceux Castle, Herstmonceux, E Sussex BN27 1RP Tel:01323-834463 Fax:01323-834499 **Expertise** Hotel & Catering Resources; Administration; Site Supervision; Start up/Renovation admin. **Prev Posts** Gen Mgr, H & C Services, Cable & Wireless 1990-92; Gen Mgr, H & C Services, Univ of Brist ol 1992-94. **Prof Background** Hotel & Catering, Member HCIMA; OTT & GTT Training Qualification. **Pres Committees** Secretary, Herstmonceux Castle Enterprises Ltd; SEETB Commercial Mbrs Cttee.

MOODLEY Rev Ronnie Director **AFRICA REFUGEE HOUSING ACTION GROUP - ARHAG Ltd** SOCIAL Type: Service provider. 2nd Floor, St Margarets, 25 Leighton Rd, London NW5 2QD Tel:0171-482 3829 Fax:0171-482 3829 **Expertise** Housing. **Prev Posts** Leisure Centre Attendant, London Casino Group;Architect/Surveyor's Asst, LB Tower Hamlets; Tutor, London University. **Prof Background** BSc (City of London Univ); MSc, International Relations; MST Diploma, Inst of Housing. **Awards/Research** Awds: Black Achiever in Housing 1993. Publ: Refugee Forum Manifesto for Europe; South Africa in Crisis, 1981; Community of Clowns, 1988. **Pres Committees** New Islington & Hackney HA; Kingsland Community Enterprise; Refugee Forum, National Cttee; FBHO. **Past Committees** Cncl of Black Housing Assocs; Refugee/Migrant Housing Forum. **Media Experience** BBC Documentary on refugees; Songs of Praise for refugees. **Addits** Strong campaigner for refugee housing.

MOORE John Director **CAS ARCHITECTS LTD** CONSERVATION/ENVIRONMENT Type: Service provider. 58 Fox St, Glasgow G1 4AU Tel:0141-248 7737 Fax:0141-221 5914 **Expertise** Community architects specialising in working with the 3rd sector, special needs & child care. **Prev Posts** Architect, Technical Services Agency 1988-90; Community Architecture (Scotland) 1990-92. **Prof Background** Chartered Architect.

MOORE Nigel General Secretary **SQUASH RACKETS ASSOCIATION** SPORTS Type: National Governing Body of Sport. 33-34 Warple Way, London W3 0RQ Tel:0181-746 1616 Fax:0181-746 0580 **Expertise** Sponsorship, Public Relations & Events. **Prof Background** BA (Hons), MSc, Army Staff College, Milam (Dip), Telecommunications.

MOORHOUSE John Director **SCOTTISH BUSINESS IN THE COMMUNITY - SBC** SOCIAL Type: Service provider. Romano House, 43 Station Road, Corstorphine, Edinburgh EH12 7AF Tel:0131-334 9876 Fax:0131-316 4521 **Expertise** Economic development, partnership building. **Prev Posts** Advertising Manager 1965-73; Marketing Manager 1977-82; Public Affairs Manager, Shell UK 1982-90. **Pres Committees** Board: CTF Training; Scottish Ballet; Craigmillar Initiative; Greater Easterhouse Development Co; Capital Enterprise Trust; UK 2000 Scotland; Crime Concern Scotland; Young Enterprise Scotland.

MORAES Claude Director **JOINT COUNCIL FOR THE WELFARE OF IMMIGRANTS - JCWI** SOCIAL Type: Service provider; Legal protection/advice/lobbying/media analysis. 115 Old St, London EC1V 9JR Tel:0171-251 8708 Fax:0171-251 5110 **Expertise** Immigration, refugees, parliamentary lobbying. **Prev Posts** House of Commons Adviser; TUC National Official. **Prof Background** LLB Dundee University; MSc London University, Birkbeck College, LSE. **Awards/Research** Articles and chapters on immigration, citizenship and refugee matters. **Past Committees** Exec Mbr/Nat Asst Sec, Anti-racist Alliance. Exec Mbr: Immigration Law Practitioners Assoc; Standing Conf on Race Equality in Europe **Media Experience** Extensive national media and press experience.

MOREHEN David Secretary **ROTARY INTERNATIONAL IN GREAT BRITAIN & IRELAND** SOCIAL Type: Service provider; Grant maker; Association of private members clubs. Kinwarton Road, Alcester, Warwickshire B49 6BP Tel:01789-765411 Fax:01789-765570 **Expertise** Active Managing Officer. **Prev Posts** Superintendent, Metropolitan Police 1980-85;

Asst/Deputy Secretary Rotary Int. 1985-95; Curently also Secretary, Rotary Foundation (UK). **Prof Background** Educated Crypt Grammar School, Gloucester; First Class Civil Service exam; Member Institute of Administrative Management 1983. **Awards/Research** Police Long Service/Good Conduct Medal;Paul Harris Fellow. **Past Committees** General Council of Rotary Int;RIBI: Finance Cttee;Constitutions/Resolutions Cttee;Main Service Cttee;Executive Cttee. **Media Experience** BBC TV That was the week that was; interviews local radio.

MORLAND Brigadier Anthony Chief Executive **ANTHONY NOLAN BONE MARROW TRUST (The)** MEDICAL/HEALTH Type: Service provider. Unit 2, Heathgate Buildings, 75-87 Agincourt Road, London NW3 2NT Tel:0171-284 1234 Fax:0171-284 8226 **Expertise** Management; fundraising. **Prev Posts** British Army 1955-89, Retd as Brigadier. **Prof Background** Staff College; National Defence College; Spanish linguist. **Awards/Research** Awds: MBE; Enconomiendo de Orden Civil (Spain). **Pres Committees** Mbr, European Bone Marrow Transplantation Group; World Marrow Donor Program. MD, Anthony Nolan Marketing. **Media Experience** Considerable.

MORLEY Robert C. Executive Vice President **BRITISH TRUST FOR CONSERVATION VOLUNTEERS - BTCV** CONSERVATION/ENVIRONMENT Type: Service provider. 36 St Mary's Street, Wallingford, Oxfordshire OX10 0EU Tel:01491-839766 Fax:01491-839646 **Expertise** Environmental issues; management; working with government and private sector; Europe and Eastern Europe. **Prev Posts** BTCV: Operations Director 1983-86; Chief Executive 1986-92. **Prof Background** Twenty years in industry before joining environmental voluntary sector. **Pres Committees** Board of Groundwork Foundation.

MORPETH Ros Director **NATIONAL EXTENSION COLLEGE TRUST LTD - NEC** SOCIAL Type: Service provider. 18 Brooklands Ave, Cambridge CB2 2HN Tel:01223-316644 Fax:01223-313586 **Expertise** Adult learning especially open and distance learning. **Prev Posts** Head of Projects, National Extension College 1978-80; Publishing Director, NEC 1980-87. **Prof Background** MA (Cantab) Social Anthropology. Honorary Doctorate Open University 1994. **Awards/Research** Publ: Annual reports; newsletters; articles on adult learning; book reviews. **Pres Committees** Trustee, International Extension College. **Past Committees** BBC Continuing Education Advisory Committee; Management Committee Member, Denman College. **Media Experience** Press interviews.

MORRIS James Chief Executive **SCOTTISH SOCIETY FOR THE PREVENTION OF CRUELTY TO ANIMALS - SSPCA** ANIMAL/WILDLIFE Type: Fundraiser; Service provider. Braehead Mains, 603 Queensferry Rd, Edinburgh EH4 6EA Tel:0131-339 0222 Fax:0131-339 4777 **Expertise** Administration. **Prev Posts** Career with Royal Air Force: Director of Operational Requirements (Air 1) MoD 1986-89; Air Officer, Scotland & NI 1989-91; Retd Air Vice Marshall 1991. **Prof Background** BSc (Edinburgh Univ); RAF Staff College. **Awards/Research** Awds: OBE 1977; CBE 1984. **Pres Committees** President, Royal Air Force Association Scottish Area; Chair Scottish Union Jack Assoc; Commr Queen Victoria School; Chair Scotland & N Ireland Region ATC. **Past Committees** RAF Service Committee. **Media Experience** Formal TV Course - 2 days.

MORRIS Richard Director **COUNCIL FOR BRITISH ARCHAEOLOGY** CONSERVATION/ENVIRONMENT Type: Service provider; Grant maker; Educational; Statutory Consultee. Bowes Morrell House, 111 Walmgate, York YO1 2UA Tel:01904-671417 Fax:01904-671384 **Expertise** Archaeological study of churches, buildings, settlement history. **Prev Posts** Research Officer, CBA 1978-1988; University Teacher, University of York 1988-1991. **Prof Background** MA Oxford University; Member, Institute of Field Archaeologists; Fellow, Society of Antiquities of London. **Awards/Research** Frend Medal Soc Antiq 1992;Ch4 Award ed film script 1988;Hon Vis Prof Univ York.Auth:many arts/books inc:Church in Brit Archaeology 1983;Churches in Landscape 1989;Guy Gibson 1994 **Pres Committees** Ancient Monuments Advisory Cttee England; City of London Archaeology Trust; Standing Conf on London Archaeology; Commr English Heritage. **Past Committees** Executive Committee of Council for the Care of Churches. **Media Experience** Contribs on radio/TV/press; educational videos. **Addits** Yorkshire Post, runner up best first non-fiction book, 1979.

MORRISSEY Margaret Public Relations Officer **NATIONAL CONFEDERATION OF PARENT-TEACHER ASSOCIATIONS - NCPTA** CHILDREN/YOUTH Type: Service provider. 2 Ebbsfleet Industrial Estate, Stonebridge Rd, Gravesend, Kent DA11 9DZ Tel:01474-560618 Fax:01474-564418.

MORROW Rev. John W. Lecturer **IRISH SCHOOL OF ECUMENICS** RELIGIOUS Type: Ecumenical adult education and dialogue. 36 College Park Avenue, Belfast BT7 1LR Tel:01232-329055 **Expertise** Lecturer and tutor in continuing education. **Prev Posts** Chaplain, Queens University 1976-80; Leader, Corrymeela Community 1980-93. **Prof Background** BSc; M Agr; PhD Theology; Minister of Presbyterian Church in Ireland, ordained 1960. **Awards/Research** Auth: articles on peace, reconciliation, ecumenism, etc. and pamphlets for InterChurch Group on faith and politics. **Pres Committees** Chair, InterChurch Group on Faith and Politics; some boards and cttees of Presbyterian Church in Ireland, and all cttees within Corrymeela Community. **Past Committees** Northern Ireland Peace Forum; Irish Council of Churches. **Media Experience** R4 presenter, Thought for the Day; TV/radio programmes inc Services of Worship.

MORTIMER John Chairman **ROYAL SOCIETY OF LITERATURE OF THE UNITED KINGDOM** ARTS Type: Service provider. 1 Hyde Park Gardens, London W2 2LT Tel:0171-723 5104 Fax:0171-402 0199 **Awards/Research** CBE; QC. Awarded: The Benson Medal, The W H Heinemann award and the Winifred Holtby award.

MOSER Michael Edward Dr Director **WETLANDS INTERNATIONAL** ANIMAL/WILDLIFE Type: International NGO. Po Box 7002, 6700 CA Wageningen,

Netherlands Tel:(31) 317 474711 Fax:(31) 317 474712 **Expertise** Wetlands Ecology, conservation and management; Waterfowl, Conservation and management. **Prev Posts** British Trust for Ornithology: Estuaries 1983-86, Director of Development, 1986-88. **Prof Background** BSc (Hons) 1st Class, Durham University 1978; PhD Ecology, Durham University 1983. **Awards/Research** Jt Auth: Wetlands Facts on File, 1991; 30+ scientific papers. David Lack Studenship (for PhD). **Pres Committees** Board, Foundation Tour du Valat, France; Council, Wildfowl and Wetlands Trust UK; Scientific Council, Bonn Convention. **Media Experience** Numerous radio, TV and press coverage/articles.

MOSLEY Martin Development Director **ROYAL LIVERPOOL PHILHARMONIC SOCIETY** ARTS Type: Fundraiser; Service provider. Hope St, Liverpool L1 9BP Tel:0151-709 2895 Fax:0151-709 0918 **Prev Posts** Director of Leisure & Arts, South Somerset DC 1990-95. **Prof Background** Leisure Management.

MOUNT Dr John Chief Executive **ST CATHERINE'S HOSPICE** MEDICAL/HEALTH Type: Service provider. Malthouse Road, Crawley, West Sussex RH10 6BH Tel:01293-547 333 Fax:01293-611 977 **Expertise** General Management. **Prev Posts** Director of Clinical Operations, Homerton Hospital, 1994-95; Divisional Gen Manager, St Bartholomew's Hosp, 1992-94; Director of Pathology Servs, St Bartholomew's Hosp, 1990-92. **Prof Background** Clinical Biochemist; PhD; MSc; MHSM; Recently completed City Universities Health MBA; General Manager. **Awards/Research** Organisational Development and Change Management.

MUDDIMAN Noel MOTABILITY DISABILITY Type: Fundraiser; Service provider; Grant maker; Royal Chartered Body. Goodman House, Station Approach, Harlow, Essex CM20 2ET Tel:01279-632010 Fax:01279-632002 **Expertise** Mobility for disabled people; driver training; transport; logistic and organisational planning. **Prev Posts** Principal Logistic Planner, British Forces Germany 1987-89; Distrib Dir, British Army of the Rhine 1990-92; Commandant, Army School of Mechanical Transport 1992-95. **Prof Background** Regular Army Officer 1965-95; Army Staff College 1975; National Defence College 1981; Royal College of Defence Studies 1992. **Awards/Research** OBE 1994; CBE 1992. Co-Auth: Blackadder's War, 1995. **Pres Committees** Secretary, Tenth Anniversary Trust. **Past Committees** Trustee, Museum of Army Transport 1992-95; Logistic Training Management Board, 1992-95; Humberside Training Enterprise Council, 1995 **Media Experience** Radio, TV and press exposure.

MUIJEN Dr M Director **SAINSBURY CENTRE FOR MENTAL HEALTH** MEDICAL/HEALTH Type: Grant maker; Research & Development Organisation. 134-38 Borough High Street, London SE1 1LB Tel:0171-403 8790 Fax:0171-403 9482 **Expertise** Clinical Psychiatry & Community Care; Development of mental health services. **Prev Posts** Lecturer in Psychiatry, Inst of Psychiatry, 1989-91; Researcher, East London, 1986-89; Trainee Psychiatrist, Cambridge, 1983-86. **Prof Background** London School of Hygiene & Tropical Medicine, MSc Epidermology; London University, PhD; Honorary Consultant Psychiatrist for St Thomas's Hospital. **Awards/Research** Research of mental health services; Publication of wide range of journals; Numerous book chapters. **Pres Committees** Trustee, Primary Care Counselling Trust; Member of Steering & Advisory Grps. **Media Experience** Regular appearances on the media.

MULGAN Dr Geoff Director **DEMOS** SOCIAL Type: Service provider. 9 Bridewell Place, London EC4V 6AP Tel:0171-353 4479 Fax:0171-353 4481 **Expertise** Public policy, Technology, Employment. **Prev Posts** Lecturer at University of Westminster 1988-90; Policy Adviser to Gordon Brown MP, Shadow Chancellor 1990-92; Fellow British Film Institute 1992-93. **Prof Background** BA Hons (1st) Oxford University 1982; PhD University of Westminster (Communications)1990; Visiting Professor, University College London. **Awards/Research** Politics in Anti-Political Age (1994), Communication & Control (1991). **Pres Committees** Trustee: The Photographer's Gallery, Political Quarterly & Crime Concern. **Media Experience** Writes for Guardian, Independent & THES; BBC Radio 4 & BBC2 presenter.

MULLAN Robin Director, Northern Ireland **NATIONAL LOTTERY CHARITIES BOARD** SOCIAL Type: Grant maker; Statutory Body. 2nd Floor, Hildon House, Hill St, Belfast BT1 2LB Tel:01232-551455 Fax:01232-551444 **Expertise** Poverty and disadvantage links to ill health, criminal justice, human rights. **Prev Posts** Chief Executive, Disability Action 1984-93; Chief Executive, Western Isles Health Board 1993-95. **Prof Background** BA (Hons) Queens University Belfast; M. Philosophy (Criminology), Cambridge; Diploma in Social Work, (CQSW), University of Edinburgh. **Past Committees** Standing Advisory Commission on Human Rights (Northern Ireland). Northern Ireland Council for Voluntary Action; Board of Prison Visitors, Maze Prison.

MUMBY Tim Chief Executive **DRIVE FOR YOUTH** CHILD/YOUTH Type: Service provider. Celmi Centre, Llanegryn, Tywyn, Gwynedd LL36 9SA Tel:01654-710454 Fax:01654-712326 **Prev Posts** Police Officer with Metropolitan Police (Last rank superintendent prior to retirement in April 1996) 1966-96. **Prof Background** Police Superintendent; BA Social Sciences. **Media Experience** Experience with radio, TV, video and press with Police.

MUNDAY Jill Director **REACH** SOCIAL/THE ELDERLY Type: Intermediary organization; Voluntary work for retired people. Bear Wharf, 27 Bankside, London SE1 9ET Tel:0171-928 0452 Fax:0171-928 0798 **Expertise** Volunteers and volunteering, especially retired business and professional people. **Prev Posts** Personnel Officer, May and Baker 1961-64; Organizer, Canterbury Volunteer Bureau 1972-85. **Prof Background** BA (Hons) History, Southampton University; DipPM LSE; formerly, Member of Institute of Personnel Management. **Awards/Research** Council for Europe Travel Fellowship, 1984, to study volunteers' work with physically handicapped people in France. **Pres Committees** Board member, Age Resource. **Past Committees** Volunteer Centre UK, board member 1979-88, vice chair 1985-88. **Media Experience** Various radio interviews; REACH video 1991; Skillshop BBCTV 1992.

MUNRO Dr David M Director **ROYAL SCOTTISH GEOGRAPHICAL SOCIETY** CONSERVATION/ENVIRONMENT Type: Service provider; Grant maker; Educational charity. Graham Hills Building, 40 George Street, Glasgow G1 1QE Tel:0141-552 3330 Fax:0141-552 3331 **Expertise** Geographical reference publishing and historical geography. **Prev Posts** Research Fellow, Univ of Edinburgh 1984-89; self-employed geographical reference editor 1989-96. **Prof Background** BSc (Hons) Ecology; PhD Geography; Honorary Research Fellow, Univ of Edinburgh. **Awards/Research** Chambers World Gazetteer (ed) 1988; Oxford Dictionary of the World (ed) 1995; Loch Leven & the River Leven - a landscape transformed 1994; papers/reports on land use in Cent America. **Pres Committees** Chairman: Kinross-shire Civic Trust; Michael Bruce Trust; Mbr of Cncl: National Trust for Scotland. **Media Experience** Various radio programmes & articles published in national newspapers. **Addits** Leader of various research expeditions to Central America.

MURDOCH John Director, Company Secretary **SAMUEL COURTAULD TRUST** Type: Educational Charity. Courtauld Institute Galleries, Somerset House, Strand, London, WC2R ORN Tel:0171-875 2538 Fax:0171-873 2589 **Expertise** History of Western Art. **Prev Posts** Deputy Director, Victoria and Albert Museum, 1989-1993. **Prof Background** Magdalen College, Oxford, BA 1966; Kings College London M.Phil 1970. **Awards/Research** Publ inc: The English Miniature, 1981; Discovery of the Lake District, 1984; David Cox, 1970; Byron, 1974; Seventeenth Century Portrait Miniatures (forthcoming). **Pres Committees** Trustee: William Morris Gallery, Walthamstow; Wordsworth Library & Museum, Dove Cottage, Grasmere; Comite International de L'Historic de L'Art; Walpole Society.

MURPHY Foster Chief Executive **ABBEYFIELD SOCIETY** THE ELDERLY Type: Nat office of 600 local Abbeyfield Socs. Abbeyfield House, 53 Victoria St, St Albans, Herts AL1 3UW Tel:01727-857536 **Expertise** Management within the voluntary sector. **Prev Posts** Sec, Youth Dept, British Council of Churches 1967-72; Div Head/Deputy Dir, NCVO 1972-81; Dir, The Volunteer Centre UK 1981-92. **Prof Background** BA Classics, Trinity College, Dublin 1962; BA Theology, Cambridge Univ 1964. **Awards/Research** Global Family Award for Advancement of Volunteering, 1990. **Pres Committees** Chair Innisfree HA;Chair, Citizens Advice Notes Trust; Mbr, Advisory Cncl, Centre for Voluntary Organizations, LSE. **Past Committees** Sec, Goodman Cttee on Charity Law; Churches Action on Unemp; Sec, Handy Cttee on Charity Effectiveness; Mbr, Carnegie 3rd Age Enq. **Media Experience** Radio - You and Yours, Woman's Hour; speeches given worldwide.

MURRAY Peter Trustee **ORMISTON TRUST** CHILDREN/YOUTH Type: Grant maker. 10 Abercorn Place, London NW8 9XP Tel:0171-289 8166 Fax:0171-286 2531 **Expertise** Children & Families **Prof Background** FRICS **Pres Committees** Trustee: Paddington Charities, YAPP Trusts, Ormiston Children & Families Trust, Kerrison Trust; Paddington Old People's Housing Assoc; Cttee Mbr, Westminster Volunteer Bureau.

N

NAGLER Neville Chief Executive **BOARD OF DEPUTIES OF BRITISH JEWS** RELIGIOUS Type: Service provider; All matters connected with Jewish community. Commonwealth House, 1-19 New Oxford Street, London WC1A 1NF Tel:0171-543 5400 Fax:0171-543 0010 **Prev Posts** Head of Drugs Branch, Home Office 1983-1988; Head of Finance Division, Home Office 1988-1991; Chief Executive, Board of Deputies 1991-today. **Prof Background** History degree at Cambridge University; various training assignments during Civil Service career 1967-1991. **Awards/Research** Various articles on drug policy. **Past Committees** Council of the United Synagogue; United Nations Commission on Narcotic Drugs; Chair, Council of Europe Drug Co-operation Group.

NAISH Peter Chief Executive **EQUAL OPPORTUNITIES COMMISSION** SOCIAL Type: Statutory Body. Overseas House, Quay Street, Manchester M3 3HN Tel:0161-833 9244 Fax:0161-835 1657 **Expertise** Organisation change; Strategic planning. **Prev Posts** English Churches Housing Gp 1977-89; Res Dev for Psychiatry 1989-91; CLS Care Services 1991-94. **Prof Background** Housing Management. **Pres Committees** Muir Housing Gp. **Past Committees** Chair, Nat Fed of Housing Assocs; Chair, Housing Assocs Charitable Trust; Duke of Edin enquiry into Housing; Soc Sec Adv Cttee.

NAUMANN Laurie Director **SCOTTISH COUNCIL FOR SINGLE HOMELESS** SOCIAL Type: Campaigning and research body. 9 Forrest Road, Edinburgh EH1 2QH Tel:0131-226 4382 Fax:0131-220 3107 **Expertise** House campaigning; project devlpmt; voluntary sector management. **Prev Posts** Soc Work Inspector, Scottish Office, 1992-95; Director, SCSH, 1978-92; Soc Worker & Asst Project Leader, Edinburgh Corp/Lothian Regional Cncl, 1973-78; PO, Leeds City Cncl 1970-73 **Prof Background** Home Office Probation & After-care Certificate, Leicester University. **Pres Committees** Kingdom Housing Association; Old Town Housing Association; Garvald Training Centre.

NAYLOR John Secretary/Treasurer **CARNEGIE UNITED KINGDOM TRUST** SOCIAL Type: Grant maker. Comely Park House, Dunfermline, Fife KY12 7EJ Tel:01383-721445 Fax:01383-620682 **Expertise** Managing voluntary organizations; youth work; outdoor education; unemployment; housing; residential work. **Prev Posts** Dir, YMCA Nat Centre, Lakeside, Cumbria 1975-80; Dep Nat Sec, Nat Cncl of YMCAS 1980-82; Nat Sec, Nat Council of YMCAs 1982-93. **Prof Background** MA, Clare College, Cambridge; CIMgt; FRSA. **Awards/Research**

OBE. Chaired working party which produced: Using Residential Experience in the Youth Opportunities Programme. **Pres Committees** Chair Brathesey Exploration Group Trustees. **Past Committees** Chair: Assoc Heads Outdoor Centres 1979-80;DES Youth Serv Innovatory Grants Adv Gp 1986-92. Nat Adv Cncl Youth Serv 1985-88. **Addits** Steering Cttee, Ministers Confs on Youth Servs 89-92. NCVYS V-Chair 85-88.

NEALE Anne Co-Founder/Spokeswoman **WAGES DUE LESBIANS - WDL** SOCIAL Type: Campaigning voluntary organization. Crossroads Womens Centre, PO Box 287, London NW6 5QU Tel:0171-482 2496 Fax:0171-209 4761 **Expertise** Rights of lesbian women/mothers; value of women's unwaged work; rep/res deportation/rape/violence issues. **Awards/Research** Contrib: Right to be Here, GLC Wking Gp 1985. Co-Auth: Policing the Bedroom, 1991. **Pres Committees** Co-ord, lobbying EC Parliament for women's unwaged work to be inc in GNP. **Past Committees** Mbr: NGO Housewives in Dialogue Del, UN Conf Nairobi 1985; Mbr, Internat WDL Del, Nat Lesbian Conf Atlanta 1991. **Media Experience** Regular appearances on TV/radio/press. **Addits** Successful campaign re unfair dismissal (Sect 28) of local teaching staff. .

NEEDS Enid & Ivor Joint Secretaries **JUSTICE FOR ALL VACCINE-DAMAGED CHILDREN UK** CHILDREN/YOUTH Type: Campaigning. Erins Cottage, Fussells Bldgs, Whiteway Rd, St George, Bristol BS5 7QY Tel:01179-557818 **Expertise** Vaccine damage. **Awards/Research** Fact sheets. **Media Experience** World in Action, Nationwide BBC HTV.

NEVILLE Yvonne Secretary/Treasurer **BIELD HOUSING TRUST** SOCIAL Type: Fundraiser; Grant maker. 22 Windsor St, Edinburgh EH7 5JR Tel:0131-557 0888 Fax:0131-557 6327 **Expertise** Care & housing for the elderly, stroke rehabilitation & terminal care. **Prev Posts** Research & Intelligence Unit, Scottish Home & Health Dept 1964-75; Housing Advisory Off, Age Concern, Scot 1977-82; Gen Administrator, Prince & Princess of Wales Hospice 1982-84. **Prof Background** BA (Hons) Arts & Social Science (Upper Second). **Pres Committees** Board of Management, Development Services Committee & Management Services Committee: Bield Housing Association.

NEWMAN Carole Director **GREATER LONDON FORUM FOR THE ELDERLY** THE ELDERLY Type: Development & support to local Forums. 54 Chalton Street, London NW1 1HS Tel:0171-383 4008 Fax:0171-383 4008 **Expertise** Knowledge of Nat and (Lond) Regional issues Re:older people. Education & training; Art; Chairing. **Prev Posts** Org, Home Tutor Scheme for Housebound Elderly LB H'smith & Fulham, 1985-92;Head of Youth Dept, London Vol Serv Cncl, 1980-85; Head of Centre, Adult Education Inst (ILEA), 1974-80. **Prof Background** Qualified Teacher & Youth Worker; London Univ Teacher's Diploma, Diploma in Dramatic Art; Central School of Speech & Dram Teacher's Diploma. **Awards/Research** Articles & Book reviews in Voluntary Voice, Jnl of the Assoc for Educational Gerontology; Research for Age Concern London into the potential for Activity in Residential Homes. **Pres Committees** Trustee, Exec Cttee of Lond Voluntary Serv Cncl; Co-opted member, Camden Youth Cttee; Trustee, Exec Cttee of Camden Age Concern; JP on Adult, Youth & Family Panels; Gov, Special Needs Sch in Camden. **Past Committees** Vice-Chair, Kingsway College of Further Education; Governor, Primary & Secondary School. **Media Experience** Radio, TV & Press; now arrange for elderly to speak for themselves. **Addits** Public Speaking; Film Reviewer.

NEWTON DUNN Charles Executive Secretary **GURKHA WELFARE TRUST** SOCIAL Type: Fundraiser. Room 017, Ripley Block, Old Admiralty Building, Spring Gardens, London SW1A 2BE Tel:0171-218 4395 Fax:0171-218 0601 **Expertise** Fundraising; administration; grant making; aid to developing countries. **Prev Posts** Pestalozzi Children's Village Trust: Marketing Director 1989-90, Overseas Director 1991. **Prof Background** Royal Military Academy Sandhurst 1964; Army Staff College; 25 years in the army with the Gurkhas.

NICHOL David National Development Officer **NATIONAL COUNCIL FOR THE CONSERVATION OF PLANTS AND GARDENS - NCCPG** CONSERVATION/ENVIRONMENT Type: Service provider, Garden plant conservation. The Pines, Wisley Garden, Woking, Surrey GU23 6QP Tel:01483-211465 Fax:01483-211750 **Expertise** Management. **Prev Posts** Director, Garden Centre Association 1978-93. **Prof Background** MA (Cantab) Mechanical Sciences. **Pres Committees** Trustee, Ocean Cruising Club.

NICHOLAS Michael Chief Executive **ROYAL COLLEGE OF ORGANISTS** Type: Fundraiser; Service provider; Grant maker; Academic Institution. 7 St Andrew Street, Holborn, London EC4A 3LQ Tel:0171-936 3606 Fax:0171-353 8244 **Expertise** Organ Playing; Choir Directing; Music Teacher (including academic work); Administrator. **Prev Posts** Organist for; Louth Parish Church 1960-64; St Matthew's Church, Northampton 1965-71; Norwich Cathedral 1971-94. **Prof Background** Organ Scholar Jesus College Oxford 1957-60 (BA) 1960 (MA) 1964;Fellow of the Royal College of Organists 1958;Hon DMus, Uni of East Anglia 1995;Eastern Orchestral Bd (Exec Cttee 1980-84, Chair 1984-89. **Awards/Research** Sightsinging, RSCM, 1966; Various compositions published by Elkin, Cramer, Banks, Novello & Lorenz (USA). **Pres Committees** Church Music Society (Executive); Organists' Benevolent League (Executive);Eastern Orchestral Board (Exec cttee 1980-94, Chair 1984-89). **Past Committees** Royal Sch of Church Music (Cncl 1978-87); Royal College of Organists (Cncl 1980-94); Norfolk & Norwich Festival (Board 1990-94). **Media Experience** Many Radio/TV Broadcasts; CD recordings; appearances in Radio, TV & Press. **Addits** Musical Dir Allegri Singers;Organist/Dir Music All Saints Church Blackheath.

NICHOLSON Liz Director **SHELTER SCOTLAND** SOCIAL Type: Campaigning and housing services. 8 Hampton Terrace, Edinburgh EH12 5JD Tel:0131-313 1550 Fax:0131-313 1544 **Expertise** Citizen Advice, research, active participation. **Prev Posts** Research Associate, Edinburgh University; Housing Campaign Worker, Shelter, 1989-92; Deputy Chief Executive,

Citizens Advice, Scotland, 1992-95.

NICHOLSON Marian Director **HERPES VIRUSES ASSOCIATION** MEDICAL/HEALTH Type: Fundraiser; Service provider; Patient Support Group; Research & Study. 41 North Road, London N7 9DP Tel:0171-607 9661 **Expertise** Counselling; Media Liaison; Research; Talks; Workshops; Lectures; Seminars; self-help & drug treatment. **Prev Posts** Administrator, Appleton & Robinson 1989; Production Asst, LifeTime Video 1992. Currently: Director Shingles Support Society. **Awards/Research** Editor & Contributor to SPHERE (Journal of the HVA), Herpes Simplex and You, Herpes Simplex - A Guide (3 editions). **Pres Committees** HVA Executive Management Committee. **Media Experience** Experience in all media. **Addits** Author of Shingles - The Herpes Varicella-zoster Virus;

NICKSON John Director **ROYAL ACADEMY TRUST** ARTS Type: Fundraiser. Burlington House, Piccadilly, London W1V 0DS Tel:0171-494 5697 Fax:0171-287 6312 **Expertise** Corporate fundraising, individual fundraising, public relations, marketing and fundraising strategy. **Prev Posts** Director, Information and Business Relations, ENO 1987-89; Director of Development ENO 1989-93; Director of Public Affairs, ENO 1993-96. **Pres Committees** General Council of The United World College of the Atlantic. **Media Experience** Interviews/articles for radio, TV & press; PR Directorship (ENO & Brit Cncl).

NIGHTINGALE (John) Nicholas National Secretary **YMCA ENGLAND** CHILDREN/YOUTH Type: Fundraiser. 640 Forest Rd, Walthamstow, London E17 3DZ Tel:0181-520 5599 Fax:0181-509 3190 **Expertise** Leadership; Management **Prev Posts** Solicitor, Slaughter and May 1970-74; Exec Director/Co Sec, Rowntree Mackintosh 1975-89; Co Sec, Tate & Lyle 1989-93. **Prof Background** BA, LLB, Trinity College, Dublin; AMP, Harvard Business School. **Pres Committees** Director: (non-exec) Cookie Jar; (non-exec) Ellis Patents; Cripplegate Foundation. **Past Committees** Chair, Service 9, Bristol Cncl of Soc Serv. Dir: Tom Smith Crackers; Original Cookie Co. Vice Chair, York Rural Community Cncl. **Addits** Former Vice Chair, Yorkshire Rural Community.

NOBLE Geoff General Manager **COT DEATH SOCIETY** MEDICAL/HEALTH Type: Fundraiser; Service provider. 1 Browning Close, Thatcham, Berks RG18 3EF Tel:01635-861771 Fax:01635-861771

NOBLE Lillias Director **LEAD - SCOTLAND** DISABILITY Type: Service provider. Queen Margaret College, Clerwood Terrace, Edinburgh EH12 8TS Tel:0131-3173439 Fax:0131-3397198 **Expertise** Education, disability. **Prev Posts** Guidance teacher, Wester Hailes Educ Centre 1980-85; Project Leader, Save the Children Fund 1985-88. **Prof Background** B.Ed Teaching. **Pres Committees** Vice-Chairman, Mental Welfare Commission for Scotland, Chairperson, Scottish Adult Education Voluntary Organisations Forum; Board Member, LEAD-Telematics Ltd (subsidiary co of LEAD-Scotland).

NORRIS Roy Director for Wales **NATIONAL LOTTERY CHARITIES BOARD** SOCIAL Type: Grant maker. Wales Office, Ladywell House, Newtown, Powys SY16 1JB Tel:01686-621644 Fax:01686-621534 **Prev Posts** Head of Voluntary Sector Branch, Welsh Office 1993-95; Welsh Office Agriculture Dept 1985-93. **Prof Background** BA (Hons) Social Administration; Diploma in Management Studies; Mbr, Institute of Management.

NORTON Dianne Information & Policy Officer, Res/Educn **AGE CONCERN ENGLAND** THE ELDERLY Type: National Organization. Astral House, 1268 London Rd, London SW16 4ER Tel:0181-679 8000 Fax:0181-679 6069 **Expertise** All aspects of education and leisure and older people; writing, editing and publishing. **Prev Posts** U3A: Executive Secretary 1981-90; Editor, Third Age News 1982-94; Acting Chief Executive 1990-91; Publications & Publicity Officer 1991-94. **Awards/Research** Ed: Age Concern Educ & Leisure Newsletter. Contrib: Univ of The Third Age: Mutual Aid Univ, 1984. Auth: Bibliography on education and older adults. **Pres Committees** Leisure sub-ctte, RNIB; Board of Directors: Brewery Arts, Cirencester; European Education Network; NIACE: Older & Bolder, Steering Gp. Also, MD/Founder, Third Age Press.

NORTON Jim Chief Executive **ARTHRITIS & RHEUMATISM COUNCIL** Type: Fundraiser; Grant maker, Med research; Private comp, charitable status. PO Box 177, Chesterfield S41 7TQ Tel:01246-558033 Fax:01246-558007 **Expertise** General management. **Prev Posts** Local government 1950-61; Armed Forces 1961-1981. **Prof Background** Finance, FCIS. **Pres Committees** AMRC, TRENT R & D, BSR. **Media Experience** Radio, TV and press.

NORTON Michael Founder **CENTRE FOR INNOVATION IN VOLUNTARY ACTION** SOCIAL Type: Service provider; project development; infrastructure of charities. 9 Mansfield Place, London NW3 1HS Tel:0171-431 1412 Fax:0171-431 3739 **Expertise** Charity; law; tax; fundraising; trustee matters; corporate giving; Indian voluntary sector. **Prev Posts** Managing director, BPC Publishing, Direct Mail Div. 1969-71; Founder, Directory of Social Change. **Prof Background** MA Natural Sciences, Kings College, Cambridge 1960-63. **Awards/Research** Auth: Tax Effective Giving; Writing Better Fundraising Applications; Raising Money from Trusts; Raising Money from Industry; Corporate Donor's Handbook. **Pres Committees** Asha Foundation; Exec Chair, Changemakers; Fndg Trustee, Books for Change, India. **Past Committees** Cncl for Charitable Support; Legislation Monitoring Service for Charities; Charity Fair. **Addits** Auth: The World-wide Fundraisers Handbook.

NURSE Paul Director-General **IMPERIAL CANCER RESEARCH FUND - ICRF** MEDICAL/HEALTH Type: Fundraiser; Service provider; Grant maker. PO Box 123, Lincoln's Inn Fields, London WC2A 3PX Tel:0171-269 3436 Fax:0171-269 3610 **Expertise** Yeast Molecular Biology and Genetics; Cell Cycle Control. **Prev Posts** Iveagh Prof of Microbiology,Univ of Oxford 87-91;Napier Res Prof, Royal Society Univ of Oxford 91-93;Dir of Res Laboratories,ICRF & Head,Cell Cycle Labs 93-96. **Prof Background** BSc, PhD Cell Biology/Biochemistry;

EMBO;FRS;CIBA Medal of UK Biochemical Soc/Feldberg Prize Anglo/German Med Res 91;Louis Jeanter Prize Med in Europe (Switz); Gairdner Fndtn Int Award 92. **Awards/Research** Over 150 publications in scientific journals/books;speaker at over 200 seminars in res institutes world-wide. **Pres Committees** Editorial Board Mbr of a number of scientific journals;Mbr:Academia Europaea. **Past Committees** Cttee Mbr:UK Genetical Soc 85-88;EMBL Sci Advisory Cttee 89-95;Pres,UK Genetical Soc 90-94;Pres Brit Asscn Biology Section 94-95. **Addits** Royal Soc Wellcome Medal UK,Jimenez Diaz Memorial Award & Medal 93.

NURSEY Caroline Director **WUS (UK)** OVERSEAS DEVELOPMENT Type: Fundraiser; Grant maker. 14 Dufferin Street, London EC1Y 8PD Tel:0171-426 5820 Fax:0171-251 1315 **Prev Posts** Overseas Director WUS (UK) 1994-1995; Overseas Projects Manager YCare International (1992-94) VSO - Various (1985-1991). **Prof Background** BA History; Teacher trained; Management Qualifications. **Pres Committees** Clerk of Quaker Peace and Service Central Cttee; ICD Advisory Cttee; Trustee Ratclif and Barking Trust and Funded Properties. **Media Experience** Some radio and print.

O

O'CONNOR Michael Director of Policy & Corporate Affairs **MILLENNIUM COMMISSION** SOCIAL Type: Grant maker. 2 Little Smith Street, London SW1P 3DH Tel:0171-340 2001 Fax:0171-340 2000 **Expertise** Policy & Corporate Affairs. **Prev Posts** Director, Coronary Prevention Group 1989-93; Director, Developed Economies: Consumers International 1994-96. **Prof Background** BSc; Msc; DIC; FRSA; MIPR. **Pres Committees** Board of Directors, Action on Smoking. **Media Experience** Experience in radio, TV, video and press.

O'LEARY Father Francis Director **ST JOSEPH'S HOSPICE ASSOCIATION** MEDICAL/HEALTH Type: Fundraiser; Service provider; Campaigning; Caring for chronic and terminally ill. La Casa de San Jose, Ince Rd, Thornton, Liverpool L23 4UE Tel:0151-924 3812 Fax:0151-931 5727 **Expertise** Caring for the sick. **Prev Posts** Director for St Joseph's Hospice Association 1962-95. **Prof Background** Ordained as a Priest in 1956; Graduate MA, Glasgow University 1960; MHM. **Awards/Research** MBE 1996. Newsletters; Annual Reports. Daniel Carrion Medal, Lima, Peru, 1973. **Pres Committees** Management Committee, St Joseph's Hospice Association. Occasional appearances on television and in the press.

O'NEILL Maureen Director **AGE CONCERN SCOTLAND** ELDERLY Type: Fundraiser; Service provider; Grant maker; Campaigning. Leonard Small House, 113 Rose Street, Edinburgh EH2 3DT Tel:0131-220 3345 Fax:0131-220 2779 **Expertise** Older People. **Prev Posts** Principal Officer, Policy and Information Scottish Assoc for Mental Health, 1987-93; General Secretary, Edinburgh YWCA 1982-87. **Prof Background** BA (Hons), Diploma in Management Studies; Administration in Medical School; Polytechnic & Prof and nursing associations prior to involvement in voluntary sector. **Pres Committees** Chairman, Edinburgh Council of Voluntary Organisations; Member, Scottish Council of Voluntary Organisations Policy Committee; Scottish Council of Voluntary Organisations Management Board **Past Committees** Voluntary sector management boards covering problems of alcohol, youth, transport for disabled, homelessness. **Media Experience** Spokesperson for Age Concern Scotland.

OAKLEY Michael Chief Executive/Secretary **GIRLS' PUBLIC DAY SCHOOL TRUST** CHILDREN/YOUTH Type: Service provider. 26 Queen Anne's Gate, London SW1H 9AN Tel:0171-222 9595 Fax:0171-222 8771 **Expertise** General management skills. **Prev Posts** Asst

Bursar of Eton College. **Prof Background** Blundells School. **Awards/Research** Awds: TD. **Pres Committees** OFSTED Consultative group; Chair Great Ormond Street Hospital School; Trustee Elizabeth Fitzroy Homes. **Past Committees** Independant Schools Jt Cncl; Chair Indep Schools Bursars Assoc.

OGILVIE Dr Bridget M. Director **WELLCOME TRUST, THE** MEDICAL/HEALTH Type: Grant maker. 183 Euston Road, London NW1 2BE Tel:0171-611 8888 Fax:0171-611 8735 **Prev Posts** Staff member, Medical Research Cncl, National Inst for Medical Research, London 1966-80; Staff member, Wellcome Trust since 1981. **Prof Background** Bachelor of Rural Science, Univ of New England 1960; Doctor of Philosophy, Cambridge Univ 1964; Doctor of Science, Cambridge Univ 1981. **Awards/Research** Various articles on the immunology of parasitic infections. **Pres Committees** Trstee Nat Museum Science & Tech;Mbr UK Cncl Science & Tech;Pres Assoc Science Educ;Mbr Commwth Schol Cmmssn of Assoc of Cmmnwlth Univs;Non-exec Dir Lloyds TSB Grp plc;Fdn for Science and Tech. **Past Committees** Chair, Research for Health Charities Group; Pres Assoc for Science Ed.

OLASHOR Ms Ibukun Administration Officer **ORGANISATION OF BLIND AFRICAN CARIBBEANS -OBAC** DISABILITY Type: Service provider. 24 Mayward House, Benhill Rd, London SE5 7NA Tel: 0171-703 3688 Fax:0171-252 5866.

OLIVER Geraldine Administrator **BRITISH DIGESTIVE FOUNDATION** MEDICAL/HEALTH Type: Fundraiser; Service provider; Grant maker. 3 St Andrews Place, Regents Park, London NW1 4LB Tel:0171-486 0341 Fax:0171-224 2012 **Expertise** Charity Administration and Fundraising. **Prev Posts** Information Mgr, WATT Cttee on Energy 1987-92; Fundraising and Adminstrative Officer, Hearing Research Trust 1992-94. **Prof Background** Business Studies. **Media Experience** Press.

OLIVER Quintin Director **NORTHERN IRELAND COUNCIL FOR VOLUNTARY ACTION - NICVA** SOCIAL Type: Intermediary; umbrella body; development agency. 127 Ormeau Road, Belfast BT7 1SH Tel:01232-321224 Fax:01232-321204 **Expertise** Management; community development; poverty; non-profit sector; Europe. **Prev Posts** Welfare Rights Adviser, Strathclyde Regional Council 1979-84. **Prof Background** MA (Ancient Greek); Dip. Management Studies (Open University) **Awards/Research** Auth:Community Develop in Areas of Political Conflict, 90;New Focuses in Fight Against Poverty & Marginalisation, 91;Poverty in Europe, 92;Euro White Paper on Soc Policy - analysis 94 **Pres Committees** Secretary, European Anti-Poverty Network 1993-94 (President 1991-92). **Past Committees** British Youth Council 1978-81; Neighbourhood Energy Action (UK) 1985-90. UTV Telethon 1988-92. **Media Experience** Regular contrib: BBC Radio Ulster; BBCTV N Ireland; UTV; STV; Radio 4; RTE. **Addits** Pres Mary Robinson's Personal Appointee to Cncl of State of Ireland.

OPPENHEIM Gerald Director UK Grants & Corporate Planning **NATIONAL LOTTERY CHARITIES BOARD** SOCIAL Type: Grant maker; Statutory Body. St Vincent House, 30 Orange St, London WC2H 7HH Tel:0171-747 5254 Fax:0171-747 5297 **Expertise** 16 Years Experience Funding Voluntary Organisations. **Prev Posts** Head of Housing Grants Unit, Former GLC 1980-85; Director, London Boroughs Grants Unit (principal adviser to 33 councillors) 1985-95. **Prof Background** BA History, University of Bristol 1973. Diploma, Management Studies, Southbank Univ 1976. Graduate Entry to Admin Grades at former GLC, 1973. **Past Committees** Board Mbr: Providence Row Housing Assoc; North Lambeth Day Centre (for the single homeless); Info Services Charity Ltd. **Media Experience** Regular press interviews, plus national and local radio.

ORCHARD Dr Stephen Director **CHRISTIAN EDUCATION MOVEMENT - CEM** RELIGIOUS Type: Service provider. Royal Buildings, Victoria Street, Derby DE1 1GW Tel:01332-296655 Fax:01332-343253 **Expertise** Religion; education; social policy. **Prev Posts** Asst General Secretary, British Council of Churches 1982-86. **Prof Background** MA; PhD Cambridge (Trinity College), URC Minister in Local Charge 1968-82. **Awards/Research** Bks: Christian Appreciation of Welfare State '84; Our Commonwealth, Christian View of Taxation '87; Pursuit of Truth, Christian View of Education '92; History of Lewes Post Office '93 **Pres Committees** Chair, British & Foreign Schools Society; Govnr, Cheshunt College Fndtn; V Chair, UK Temperance Alliance; Chair, United Reformed Church History Society; Adviser, John Templeton Fndtn. **Past Committees** Frythe Ethics Cttee (Smith Kline Beecham); Schl Curric & Assessment Authority: Monitoring Gp for RE; Brit Churches Trust for Ch 4. **Media Experience** Live interviews representing BCC and CEM. **Addits** Writer of hymns, prayers and educational materials for churches.

ORTON William T. Dr Honorary Secretary **INSTITUTE OF SPORTS MEDICINE, THE** MEDICAL/HEALTH Type: Fundraiser; Grant maker; Campaigning Burlington House, Piccadilly, London W1V OLQ Tel:0171-277 5269 **Expertise** Public Health Medicine. **Prev Posts** Deputy Medical Officer of Health, Willesden 1960-68; Deputy Medical Officer, Haringey 1968-74; District Community Physician, Haringey 1974-81. **Prof Background** MB; BCh; BAO; Queens University Belfast 1948; DPH Queens University 1951; MFCM (Now MFPHM) 1972. **Awards/Research** Articles: Sport and Health 1986, Journal of the Royal Society of Health 106, 56-59. **Pres Committees** Board, Inst of Sports Medicine; Cncl, Society of Public Health; Medical Commission on Accident Prevention;V Chair, Brit Standing Cttee of Euro Union for School & University Health & Medicine. **Media Experience** Radio, TV, video, press: Health Education. **Addits** Fellow of the Faculty of Community Health.

OSBALDESTON Michael David Chief Executive **ASHRIDGE MANAGEMENT COLLEGE,** SOCIAL/TRAINING Type: Fundraiser; Service provider; Educational trust. Ashridge Management College, Berkhamsted, Herts HP4 1NS Tel:01442-843491 Fax:01442-841002 **Expertise** Management education, research and consultancy. **Prev Posts** Researcher, Merritt Cyriax Assoc; consultancy, teaching and research on human resource management; Ashridge Management College: Director of Studies 1985-88; Dean 1988-90. **Prof**

Background BSc Hons (Biochemistry); MBA (Business Administration); FIPD; CIMgt; FRSA. **Awards/Research** Publ: The Way We Work 1979; numerous research projects, reports and articles. **Pres Committees** Dir: Ashridge Consulting Ltd; Ashridge Strategic Mgt Centre; Tres, Assoc of Business Schools; Trustee, Bridgewater Trust; Dir, Europen Fndtn for Management Dvlpmt. **Past Committees** Constable Enquiry into Mgt Education in UK; Research Brd of Inst of Mgt. **Media Experience** Radio interviews, frequent articles.

OSBORNE Douglas Executive Director **LEUKAEMIA RESEARCH FUND** MEDICAL/HEALTH Type: Fundraiser; Service provider; Grant maker. 43 Great Ormond Street, London WC1N 3JJ Tel:0171-405 0101 Fax:0171-405 3139 **Expertise** General Management voluntary branches. **Prev Posts** Director, Action for Blind People 1979-83;Administrator, Leukaemia Research Fund 1983-89. **Prof Background** Fellow, Chartered Inst of Secretaries and Adminstrators (FCIS). **Awards/Research** Co-editor, Charities Administration, ICSA Publishers. **Pres Committees** Deputy Chair, ICSA Charities Panel; Trustee, Metropolitan Society for the Blind.

OSBORNE Michael Director **ROYAL SCOTTISH FORESTRY SOCIETY** CONSERVATION/ENVIRONMENT Type: Service provider. The Stables, Dalkeith Country Park, Dalkeith, Mid Lothian EH22 2NA Tel:0131-6609480 Fax:0131-6609490 **Expertise** Forestry/woodland management. **Prev Posts** Head Forester, Haddington Estates, Dunbar 1981-93; Technical Consultant, Ronaash Rootrainers Ltd 1988-91. **Prof Background** BSc (Forestry); Member, Institute of Chartered Foresters (ICF) (MICFor). **Pres Committees** Acting Secretary, RSFS Forest Trust Company (SC024112); Acting Secretary, Central Forestry Examination Board. **Past Committees** Regional Secretary, Lothians & Borders Regional Committee (RSFS) 1985-92; Regional Secretary, Borders Region Committee ICF 1987-89.

OSBORNE Robert Director **TREE COUNCIL** CONSERVATION/ENVIRONMENT Type: Fundraiser; Service provider; Grant maker; Campaigning. 51 Catherine Place, London SW1E 6DY Tel:0171-828 9928 Fax:0171-828 9060 **Expertise** Administration. **Prev Posts** HM Forces (Army): Chair, Army Board, Military Agency for Std HQ NATO, 1987-90; Defence & Military Attache, Cairo, 1983-86. **Prof Background** Regular Army Officer, 1955-90; Final rank Colonel. **Pres Committees** Tree Council Management Committee.

OTTON Helen Chief Executive **TOMMY'S CAMPAIGN** MEDICAL/HEALTH Type: Fundraiser; Grant maker. 7th Floor, North Wing, St Thomas' Hospital, London SE1 7EH Tel:0171-620 0188 Fax:0171-928 6628 **Expertise** Major donor development; fundraising. **Prev Posts** Business Development Mngr, IBC Legal Studies & Servs Ltd 1987-92; Major Donor Development Manager, NSPCC 1992-94. **Prof Background** State Registered Nurse; Conference production. **Past Committees** Non-Exec Vice Chair, RTR NHS Healthcare Trust; JP.

OVERTON John L. Chief Executive **ACORNS CHILDREN'S HOSPICE** CHILDREN/YOUTH Type: Fundraiser; Service provider; Campaigning. 103 Oak Tree Lane, Selly Oak, Birmingham, West Midlands B29 6HZ Tel:0121-628 0210 Fax:0121-628 0211 **Expertise** Finance & Administration (Chartered Accountant); General Management; Marketing and Publicity. **Prev Posts** Regional Director, Reed Group 1973-76; Managing Director, Bernard Hodes Overton 1976-91; MD, Overton Executive 1991-93. **Prof Background** Grammar School/Chartered Accountant/International Commerce/Executive Recruitment. **Pres Committees** Sec, Forum of Chairmen of Independent Hospices; Trustee & V-Chair, Children's Hospice Assoc for the South East; Trustee, Health Management Trust; Trustee, Birmingham Playing Fields Association. **Past Committees** Trustee (Chairman of Founding Appeal) none National; Acorns Childrens Hospice (1983-91). **Media Experience** Radio/TV/video/press/mainly regional/local.

OWEN Dr Myrfyn Director General **WILDFOWL & WETLANDS TRUST, THE** ANIMAL/WILDLIFE Type: Fundraiser; Service provider. Slimbridge, Gloucestershire GL2 7BT Tel:01453-890333 Fax:01453-890827 **Expertise** Research and conservation. **Prev Posts** Wildfowl & Wetlands Trust: Res Officer various levels 1967-88; Dir Res and Cons 1988-92. **Prof Background** BSc Wales University 1964; PhD Leeds University 1967. **Awards/Research** Auth: Wildfowl of Europe, 1976; Wild Geese of the World, 1980; Wildfowl in Great Britain, 1986; Waterfowl Ecology, 1990. Also over 100 scientific papers. **Pres Committees** Two DoE Working Groups. **Past Committees** Cncl of British Ornithologists' Union; Wildlife Committees various. **Media Experience** Regular and frequent.

OWENS Commander Jeremy Chief Executive **ROYAL NAVAL BENEVOLENT TRUST** SOCIAL Type: Fundraiser; Service provider; Grant maker; Residential care. Castaway House, 311 Twyford Ave, Portsmouth PO2 8PE Tel:01705-690112 Fax:01705-660852 **Expertise** Law, personnel, administration & skiing. **Prev Posts** Supply Officer, Royal Navy 1962-94. **Prof Background** Barrister (called 1977); Commander, Royal Navy.

OWERS Anne Director **JUSTICE** SOCIAL Type: Service provider; Policy and research. 59 Carter Lane, London EC4V 5AQ Tel:0171-329 5100 Fax:0171-329 5055 **Expertise** Legal, immigration and asylum. **Prev Posts** Joint Council for the Welfare of Immigrants, Research Worker 1981-86;Gen Sec 1986-92. **Prof Background** BA (Hons). **Awards/Research** Many leaflets, briefings and articles. **Pres Committees** Chair of Trustees, Refugee Legal Centre; Member, Advisory Council National Council of Voluntary Organisations. **Media Experience** Wide variety of experience.

OXLEY Julian C. Director General **GUIDE DOGS FOR THE BLIND ASSOCIATION, THE - GDBA** DISABILITY Type: Fundraiser; Service provider. Hillfields, Burghfield, Reading, Berkshire RG7 3YG Tel:01734-835555 Fax:01734-835433 **Expertise** General and financial management. **Prev Posts** Director/Sec, Williams James PLC 1971-84; Director of Administration/Sec, GDBA 1984-89. **Prof Background** MA (Oxon); FCA. **Pres Committees** Chair, International Fed of Guide Dog Schools; Chair, Dogs for the Disabled.

P

PACKARD Mrs Ann Director **ADAPT TRUST** DISABILITY Type: Fundraiser; Service provider; Grant maker. Cameron Hse, Abbey Park Place, Dunfermline, KY12 7PZ Tel:01383-623166 Fax:01383-622149 **Prev Posts** PR Mgr, Forth Ports plc, 1987-92; Project Off, British National Corpus of English Lang, 1993-94; Devmt Off, Assoc for the Protection of Rural Scotland 1993-96. **Prof Background** Member of IPR. **Pres Committees** DTI Appointee to Post Office Users Council for Scotland. **Past Committees** Home Office Appointee to Scottish Advisory Council of Independent Broadcasting Authority; Council of Edinburgh Civic Trust. **Addits** Prev Mbr: Professional Development Cttee, BACB.

PAINE L.H.W. Director **PSYCHIATRY RESEARCH TRUST** MEDICAL/HEALTH Type: Fundraiser. University of London, De Crespigny Park, London SE5 8AF Tel:0171-703 6217 Fax:0171-703 5796 **Expertise** Mental illness; mental handicap; brain disease. **Prev Posts** Editor in the Health Care field; House Governor, Bethlem Royal & Maudsley Hospitals. **Prof Background** MA (Oxon); Management; Journalism; Writing; Editing. Mbr, Chartered Inst of Journalists. **Awards/Research** OBE. Publ: Numerous articles in professional journals. Auth: Know Your Hospital; Health Care in Big Cities; The Psychiatric & Psychosocial Aspects of Aids. **Pres Committees** General Council, The King's Fund; Council, International Glaucoma Association; Council, Blindcare. **Past Committees** Chairman, Adult Education Service, Bromley, Kent 1983-93; Management Committee, King's Fund 1984-89. **Media Experience** Regular contrib to local/national press, eg The Times since 1982.

PALMER Richard General Secretary **BRITISH OLYMPIC ASSOCIATION** SOCIAL Type: Sports body 1 Wandsworth Plain, London SW18 1EH Tel:0181-871 2677 Fax:0181-871 9104 **Expertise** Sports Administration. **Prev Posts** General Secretary, British Universities Sports Federation 1969-1974. **Prof Background** Diploma in Physical Education; Master of Education. **Awards/Research** OBE. **Pres Committees** Vice-Pres, Association of European National Olympic Committees (AENOC); Exec Committee Member, Association of National Olympic Committees (ANOC).

PANKHURST Louise Director **CHILD PSYCHOTHERAPY TRUST** CHILDREN/YOUTH Type: Fundraiser; Advisory/research. Star House, 104-108 Grafton Rd, London NW5 4BD Tel:0171-284 1355 Fax:0171-284 2755 **Expertise** Safety of children; social policies. **Prev Posts** Corporate planning; local authority policy planning for children; equal opportunities; Director, Child Accident Prevention Trust 1987-95. **Prof Background** Town planning. **Awards/Research** OBE. Various publications/articles on child accident prevention. **Pres Committees** Voluntary organizations concerned with child welfare. **Media Experience** Radio interviews, TV appearances and press articles.

PAPE Tim Director General **SHAW TRUST** DISABILITY Type: Fundraiser; Service provider. Shaw House, Epsom Square, White Horse Business Pk, Trowbridge, Wilts BA14 0XJ Tel:01225-716300 Fax:01225-716334 **Expertise** Training, rehabilitation, employment of disabled people. **Prev Posts** Deputy Head Master 1971-80; Head Master 1980-89. **Prof Background** BSc Honours, Zoology & Geology; Education Training. **Awards/Research** OBE. **Pres Committees** Mbr, IPWH (International Provision of Work for Handicapped Persons); Nat Advisory Cncl, Employment of People with Disabilities; Chair, Wilts CEPD; Vice-Chair, Wilts TEC; Vice-Pres, Wilts Comty Cncl. **Past Committees** Chairman, Wiltshire Community Council; Vice-Chairman, Wiltshire Education Business Partnership. **Media Experience** Experience with radio, TV and press. **Addits** Governor, New College, Swindon.

PARASKEVA Janet Director for England **NATIONAL LOTTERY CHARITIES BOARD** SOCIAL Type: Grant maker. 7th Floor, St Vincent House, 30 Orange St, London WC2H 7HH Tel:0171-747 5300 Fax:0171-747 5214 **Expertise** Personal; social and health education; youth & community; equal ops; management development. **Prev Posts** Inspector, Youth & Adult Educ, ILEA 1981-83; HMI Schools 1983-88; Director of National Youth Bureau 1988-90; Director, National Youth Agency 1990-95. **Prof Background** Cert. Education, Worcester College; BA (Open); Studies towards MA Adult Education. **Awards/Research** Robert Schuman Silver Medal for European Unity. Contrib: Youth Policy in the 1990s: The Way Forward; range of articles in youth work press, TES, Education. **Pres Committees** ChildLine; Fosse Health Trust, Nat Bd for Crime Prevention; Make a Difference Team. **Past Committees** Inst for the Study of Drug Dependence; Wyggeston 6th Form College Governor; Islington 6th Form College. **Media Experience** Radio interviews; television inc: Question Time and Any Questions panellist. **Addits** Justice of the Peace.

PARKER John Secretary **WIRELESS FOR THE BEDRIDDEN SOCIETY** DISABILITY Type: Fundraiser; Service provider. 159a High Street, Hornchurch, Essex RM11 3YB Tel:01708-621101 Fax:01708-620816 **Expertise** Company Secretary; Chief Executive since 1975. **Prof Background** Stockbroker, London. **Awards/Research** Bedside World.

PARKIN Ann Secretary & Chief Executive **STANDING CONFERENCE ON SCHOOLS' SCIENCE AND TECHNOLOGY - SCSST** CHILDREN/YOUTH Type: Educational charity. 1 Gildspur St, London EC1A 9DD Tel:0171-294 2431 Fax:0171-294 2442 **Prev Posts** Headmistress, Colston Girls School, Bristol 1981-89; Secretary, The Girls Schools Association 1989-94 **Prof Background** BSc Joint Hons Chemistry and Pure Maths. **Past Committees** DTI Action for Engineering Committee.

PARKIN B. Head of Public Relations **ROYAL PHARMACEUTICAL SOCIETY OF GREAT BRITAIN** MEDICAL/HEALTH Type: Statutory Body; Professional association. 1 Lambeth High Street, London SE1 7JN Tel:0171-735 9141 Fax:0171-735 7629

PARKINSON Joseph Philip ROYAL LEICESTERSHIRE, RUTLAND & WYCLIFFE SOCIETY FOR THE BLIND DISABILITY Type: Fundraiser; Service provider; Campaigning. Margaret Road, off Gwendolen Road, Leicester, Leics LE5 5FU Tel:0116-249 0909 Fax:0116-273 9483 **Expertise** Visual impairment, administration & community work. **Prev Posts** Youth & community worker 1968-71; General Secretary, Leicester CVS 1971-73. **Prof Background** Youth Work Diploma. **Pres Committees** Joint Strategy Group Physical & Sensory Disability. **Past Committees** Member, Joint Consultative Committee; Advisor, Social Services Committee. **Media Experience** Experience with local radio (regularly). **Addits** Justice of the Peace Deputy Chairman Leicester Bench.

PARRY Edward Director **RELIEF FUND FOR ROMANIA** SOCIAL Type: Fundraiser; Service provider; Grant maker. 54-62 Regent Street, London W1R 5PJ Tel:0171-439 4052 Fax:0171-437 5908 **Expertise** Project creation and management; fundraising; networking. **Prev Posts** Marketing Manager, Palace Video 1986-88; Assoc Publisher, Munday Perry 1988-90. **Prof Background** Humanities education; film and TV distribution; marketing and sales. **Pres Committees** Parliamentary Commission on Mental Health in Romania (founded with Parliamentary Human Rights Group). **Media Experience** National TV and press articles on Romania.

PARTRIDGE Nick Chief Executive **TERRENCE HIGGINS TRUST - THT** MEDICAL/HEALTH Type: Fundraiser; Service provider; Health education information. 52-54 Grays Inn Road, London WC1X 8JU Tel:0171-831 0330 Fax:0171-242 0121 **Expertise** Media; treatments and trials. **Prev Posts** THT: Media Liaison Officer 1987-90; Deputy Chief Executive 1990-91. **Media Experience** Numerous.

PASCAL Julia Artistic Director **PASCAL THEATRE COMPANY** ARTS Type: Service provider; Theatre Co. guaranteed against loss. 35 Flaxman Court, Flaxman Terrace, London WC1H 9AR Tel:0171-383 0920 Fax:0171-383 0920 **Expertise** Theatre & dance. **Prev Posts** Associate Director, Orange Tree Theatre 1979-80. **Prof Background** E15 Acting School; BA (Hons) English, London University. **Awards/Research** Awarded Lisa Ullman Travelling Scholarship & Oppenheimer-John Dowes Award; Editor: Women in Theatre - Contemporary Review (Harwood Press); Stage Plays (pub. Faber). **Pres Committees** Drama Advisor, London Arts Board; Director, Pascal Theatre Company. **Past Committees** Director, Central London Arts. **Media Experience** Freelance writing for nat broadsheets & contributer to BBC radio arts progs. **Addits** Theatre Director & Playwright.

PASCOE Ian Philip Chairman & Chief Executive **SCOTTISH ENVIRONMENTAL EDUCATION COUNCIL** CONSERVATION/ENVIRONMENT Type: Fundraiser; Service provider; Networking & Information Provider. Airthrey Annexe, University of Stirling, Stirling FK9 4LA Tel:01786-467867 Fax:01786-467864 **Expertise** Geography, Geology & Environmental Education. **Prev Posts** Teacher in Bristol & Singapore; Bingley College of Education 1966-70; H.M. Inspector of Schools 1970-94. **Prof Background** BA, Geography (Class 2:1) Cambridge University; P.G.C.E., London University. **Pres Committees** Chair of the Brd of Dirs, The Scottish Environmental Educational Cncl; Mbr, Promotion & Education Cttee of the Scottish Wildlife Trust; Chair, Royal Botanic Garden (Edinburgh) Education Group. **Past Committees** Secretary of State for Scotlands Working Grp on Environmental Education (1991-93); Council of the Scottish Wildlife Trust (1980-86).

PASHA Dr Syed Aziz General Secretary **UNION OF MUSLIM ORGANIZATIONS OF UK AND EIRE - UMO** RELIGIOUS Type: Service provider; Representative body of the British Muslims. 109 Campden Hill Road, London W8 7TL Tel:0171-229 0538 **Expertise** International Law and Islamic Law. **Prev Posts** Adviser, Indian Delegation to UN 1961-62; International Law Consultant 1964-65. **Prof Background** BSc, BL Madras University 1945-55; Advocate, Madras High Court; LLM Wisconsin University, USA 1960; SJD, New York University, USA 1963;British Citizen since 1969. **Awards/Research** Auth: Korean Prisoners of War and International Law, 1962; SJD Thesis, Columbia River Controversy and International Law. **Pres Committees** Gen Sec, UMO; Chairman, UMO Trust; Secretary, NMEC; Chairperson, UMO Youth Council. **Media Experience** Interviews on radio, TV and in press.

PATERSON Alison Director **VICTIM SUPPORT SCOTLAND** SOCIAL Type: Fundraiser; Service provider; Campaigning. 14 Frederick Street, Edinburgh EH2 2HB Tel:0131-225 7779 Fax:0131-225 8456 **Expertise** Organisational managment, Criminal Justice issues, mediation, training, PR. **Prev Posts** Director, Nucleus (counselling services) Lothian 1984-91; Mediator, Lothian Family Mediation 1984-91. **Prof Background** Arts Graduate (Aberdeen) trained and qualified Social Worker (CQSW) and accredited mediator. **Pres Committees** Lothian Family Mediation Service (Board); Nat Crime Prevention Cncl. **Past Committees** Sutherland Cttee (Sec of State Cttee investigating miscarriages of justice in Scotland). **Media Experience** Radio/TV/press/training videos.

PATERSON David Fundraising Manager **FINDHORN FOUNDATION** RELIGIOUS/ENVIRONMENTAL Type: Fundraiser. The Park, Forres, Morayshire IV36 0TZ Tel:01309-691620 Fax:01309-691663 **Expertise** Fundraising; education; research. **Prev Posts** Secretary to the Trustees, Bowthorpe Community Trust, Norwich; Chief Examiner, City Guilds Examination Board. **Prof Background** MA(Cantab); MPhil(Sussex); FRSH; FLS; MIBiol; CBiol; MBIM.

PATERSON Lorna M. General Secretary **CHURCH OF SCOTLAND WOMAN'S GUILD** RELIGIOUS Type: Service provider. Church of Scotland Offices, 121 George St, Edinburgh EH2 4YN Tel:0131-225 5722 Fax:0131-220 3113 **Expertise** Church administration. **Prev Posts** School teacher 1960-66; Academic

Administrator, University of Strathclyde 1966-68; Academic Administrator, University of Stirling 1968-79. **Prof Background** MA University of Aberdeen; Dip. Rel. Ed., Aberdeen Teacher Training College; Art 39 Qual in English and History. **Pres Committees** Assembly Council Forum, Office Management Cttee and Nominations Cttee for the Church of Scotland; The Novum Trust; Vice Chairman Linlithgow Arts Guild; Elder, St Michael's Parish Church, Linlithgow. **Past Committees** Commissioner to Church of Scotland's General Assembly. **Media Experience** BBC TV & radio in Scotland: Thought for the Day programmes and interviews. **Addits** Involved with Women's National Commission assisting Guild's representative.

PATTISON Graham Plant Conservation Officer **NATIONAL COUNCIL FOR THE CONSERVATION OF PLANTS AND GARDENS - NCCPG** CONSERVATION/ENVIRONMENT Type: Service provider; Garden Plant Conservation. The Pines, Wisley Garden, Woking, Surrey GU23 6QP Tel:01483-211465 Fax:01483-211750 **Expertise** Horticulturist, plant conservation. **Prev Posts** Supervisor, Royal Botanic Garden Kew 1968-81; Curator, Botanic Garden, Xalapa, Mexico 1981-86. **Prof Background** Horticulture; Kew Diploma Horticulture. **Awards/Research** Plant conservation, articles, conference papers, booklets in Spanish & English. **Pres Committees** Royal Horticultural Society, Woody Plant Committee **Past Committees** Various in Mexico.

PATTISON Michael Director **SAINSBURY FAMILY CHARITABLE TRUSTS** SOCIAL Type: Grant maker. Red Lion Court, London EC4A 3EB Tel:0171-410 0330 **Expertise** Management; administration; representation. **Prev Posts** Chief Exec Royal Institution of Chartered Surveyors 1985-95; Var Govt posts incl: First Sec UK perm mission to UN, NY 1974-77; Priv Sec to successive PMs 1979-82. **Prof Background** BA Hons Sussex Univ. **Pres Committees** Pro Chancellor Greenwich Univ. **Past Committees** Battersea Arts Cntre Comm Trst;Adv Bd: Camb Univ Careers Synd; Nottingham Univ Inst of Engineering, Surveying Space Geodesy. **Media Experience** Periodic interviewee for radio, TV and press.

PATTON Marcus Director **HEARTH REVOLVING FUND** SOCIAL/CONSERVATION Type: Housing. Arts Council Building, 185 Stranmillis Rd, Belfast BT9 5DU Tel:01232-381623 **Expertise** Restoration of historic buildings. **Prof Background** Architect/Planner. **Awards/Research** OBE. Central Belfast (UAHS, 1993). **Pres Committees** Ulster Architectural Heritage Society; South Belfast Resident Planning Group. **Media Experience** Interviews on radio, TV etc.; Articles in press.

PEACOCK Geraldine Chief Executive **NATIONAL AUTISTIC SOCIETY** DISABILITY Type: Fundraiser; Service provider; Campaigning; Carer/User support. 276 Willesden Lane, London NW2 5RB Tel:0181-451 1114 Fax:0181-451 5865 **Prev Posts** Course co-ordinator, Health and Social Welfare, The Open University 1979-82; Snr lecturer Queens Coll, Glasgow 1983-86; Deputy Director LBTC, Tavistock Place, London 1986-89. **Prof Background** BA(Soc); CQSW; Pgrad Dip applied soc wk studies; med social wkr; wkd with people with disabilities; trainer; cnsltnt to Scot Office on Childrens Hearing (panel mbr training); lecturer, writer, snr mgr **Awards/Research** Articles on social work/training; Panel Mbr Training Manual:Children's Hearing System in Scotland, 1986; co-auth: The Haunt of Misery; Social Work and Received Ideas, 1990. **Pres Committees** Mbr, Reg Homes Tribunal; Governor, Whitefields School (Special Educational Needs); Chair, ACENVO (Assoc of Chief Execs of Nat Vol Orgs). **Past Committees** Member, Child Care and Family Law Training Group (Social Services Inspectorate). **Media Experience** Numerous TV and radio appearances; prev invlvd in making TV progs for Open Univ

PEARCE Brian Director **INTER FAITH NETWORK FOR THE UK** RELIGIOUS Type: Service provider; Umbrella Organisation. 5-7 Tavistock Place, London WC1H 9SS Tel:0171-388 0008 Fax:0171-387 7968 **Expertise** Administration. **Prev Posts** Under Secretary, Civil Service Dept 1976-81; Under Secretary, HM Treasury 1981-86. **Prof Background** BA 1959; M Litt 1992. **Pres Committees** Exec Cttee, World Congress of Faiths; Exec Cttee, Council of Christians & Jews.

PEARCE Peter H. Director **LANDMARK TRUST** CONSERVATION/ENVIRONMENT Type: Building Preservation. Shottesbrooke, Maidenhead, Berks SL6 3SW Tel:01628-825920 Fax:01628-825417 **Expertise** Historic Property Management; Land Agency. **Prev Posts** Land Agent, The National Trust, East Midlands 1982-88; Land Agent, The National Trust, Southern Region 1988-95; Project Director, Restoration of Uppark 1989-95. **Prof Background** BSc Estate Management (Land Agency & Agriculture); Assoc Mbr of the RICS. **Awards/Research** Various awards for Uppark. **Media Experience** Radio, TV, Video, Press.

PEARCE Rosemary Director **CRUSE BEREAVEMENT CARE** SOCIAL Type: Service provider; Counselling. Cruse House, 126 Sheen Road, Richmond, Surrey TW9 1UR Tel:0181-940 4818 Fax:0181-940 7638.

PEARSON Richard Director **INSTITUTE FOR EMPLOYMENT STUDIES** SOCIAL Type: Service provider; Research institute. Mantell Building, Falmer, Brighton BN1 9RF Tel:01273-686751 Fax:01273-690430 **Expertise** Employment policy. **Prof Background** Economist; BSc; MSc. **Awards/Research** University Challenge; IES, 1996 Labour Markets; Education & Training; Human Resource Management. **Pres Committees** Univ. Sussex Careers Service; Governor, Lewes Tertiary College; Fellow, Manpower Society; Fellow, RSA. **Media Experience** Extensive experience with press, radio and TV. **Addits** Consultant to OECD & European Commission gvmt depts, agencies & cos.

PEARTON Mrs J.F. General Secretary **BRITISH NATURALISTS' ASSOCIATION** ANIMAL/WILDLIFE Type: Fundraiser; Service provider; Natural History Society. 48 Russell Way, Higham Ferrers, Rushden, Northants NN10 8EJ Tel:01933-314672 Fax:01933-314672 **Expertise** Administration. **Prev Posts** 20 years water industry. **Prof Background** Own business for 13 years. **Awards/Research** Bronze Award to the Association for Blake Shield; Queen's 40th Anniversary Challenge.

PECK Richard L. Director **CHURCHES CONSERVATION TRUST** CONSERVATION/ENVIRONMENT Type: Conservation. 89 Fleet St, London EC4Y 1BH Tel:0171-936 2285 Fax:0171-936 2284 **Expertise** Overall direction and management. **Prev Posts** Commander, 19th Infantry Brigade 1981-83; Director, Personnel (Tri-Service) 1985-87; Engineer in Chief, Army 1988-91; Major General. **Prof Background** Army Royal Engineers: BSc (Eng) London Univ Civils; CEng; FICE; FRGS; Liveryman, Co of Eng; RMA Sandhurst; Army Staff College; Royal College of Defence Studies. **Awards/Research** Awds: CB. **Pres Committees** Lord Kitchener National Memorial Fund; Mnging Trustee, Gurkha Welfare Trust; Col Comdt RE; Col, Queen's Gurkha Engineers. **Past Committees** Chair: Defence Educ & Training Cttee; RE Ops Req Cttee. Vice Chair, Milit Engineer Cttee. Training Studies Steering Gp. **Media Experience** Occasional. **Addits** MCC; Royal Mid-Surrey Golf Cttee; Past-chair, Army Football & Cricket.

PECK Stephen Chief Executive **ENDEAVOUR TRAINING** SOCIAL Type: Service provider. Sheepbridge Centre, Sheepbridge Lane, Chesterfield, Derbyshire S41 9RX Tel:01246-454957 Fax:01246-261865.

PEERS P.J. Secretary **BIRMINGHAM HOSPITAL SATURDAY FUND MEDICAL CHARITY & WELFARE TRUST - BHSF** MEDICAL/HEALTH Type: Service provider. Gamgee House, 2 Darnley Road, Birmingham B16 8TE Tel:0121-454 3601 Fax:0121-454 7725 **Expertise** General Management & Corporate Affairs. **Prev Posts** Director & Gen Manager, WM Aitkenhead Ltd 1978-81; Director, R.A. Lister Farm Equt Ltd 1980-84; Industrial Consultant 1984-86. **Prof Background** Incorporated Engineer; Member/Chartered Inst. of Marketing; Member/Inst. of Mechanical Incorporated Engineers; Member/Inst. of Management. **Pres Committees** Trustee, Birmingham Amenities & Welfare Trust. **Past Committees** South Birmingham Community Health Council; Oldham Engineering Group Training Assoc Ltd.

PELLEW Dr Robin Director **WORLD WIDE FUND FOR NATURE - WWF UK** ANIMAL/WILDLIFE Type: Fundraiser; Grant maker; Campaigning. Panda House, Weyside Park, Godalming, Surrey GU7 1XR Tel:01483-426444 Fax:01483-426409.

PERNAK Derek Director of Finance **NATIONAL DEAFBLIND AND RUBELLA ASSOCIATION - SENSE** DISABILITY Type: Service provider. Finance Centre, 122 Westgate, Wakefield, West Yorks WF1 1XP Tel:01924-298000 Fax:01924-200117 **Expertise** Charity finance. **Prev Posts** Company Secretary 1972-84; Partner in Accountancy Practice 1984-87. **Prof Background** Ten years intensive specialization into charity finance and taxation. **Pres Committees** Representative at Charity Finance Directors Group.

PERRY Baroness Perry of Southwark President **LUCY CAVENDISH COLLEGE CAMBRIDGE UNIVERSITY** SOCIAL Type: Service provider; Cambridge College. Lady Margaret Rd, Cambridge CB3 0BU Tel:01223-332192 Fax:01223-332178 **Expertise** Education. **Prev Posts** Her Majesty's Chief Inspector, Dept of Education & Science 1970-86; Vice Chancellor South Bank University 1987-93. **Prof Background** Girton College, Cambridge, MA (1956). **Awards/Research** 3 Books; Contrib chapters to 9 other books; Numerous articles. **Pres Committees** PMs Advsry Pnl Citizen's Chrtr;Chair DTI Sctr Grp Exports Ed Trng;Bd Patrons Royal Soc Appl;Ho of Lords Slct Cttee Scrutiny Delegated Pwrs;VP City Guilds London;VP Wmns Eng Soc. **Past Committees** Economic & Social Research Council; Board of Directors of South Bank Centre; Foundation for Business-Education Partnerships. **Media Experience** TV: Question Time, Any Questions, etc. Press: Reg columnist. **Addits** VP Soc Rsrch Higher Ed;VP Alzheimers Rsrch Trst;VP BritYth Opera.

PERRY Lyn Executive Secretary **MEDICAL WOMEN'S FEDERATION - MWF** MEDICAL/HEALTH Type: Service provider. Tavistock House North, Tavistock Square, London WC1H 9HX Tel:0171-387 7765 Fax:0171-387 7765 **Expertise** Equal opportunities for women; health/medical; drug users. **Prev Posts** Snr Training Advisor, Maputo Univ Documentation Centre, Mozambique 1979-81; Deputy Director, Release 1982-87; Computing Administrator, London Business School 1989-91. **Prof Background** BA (Hons) Philosophy, University of Manchester; PG Diplomas: Librarianship; Informations Systems/Technology. **Awards/Research** Women and drug use; An Unfeminine Dependency, 1988. Serials Management; A complete training course, 1990.

PETERS Miss Samantha General Secretary **BRITISH YOUTH COUNCIL** CHILDREN/YOUTH Type: Charity for The Voice of Young People. 57 Chalton Street, London NW1 1HU Tel:0171-384 7559 Fax:0171-353 3545 **Expertise** Management, Public Relations, Fundraising. **Prev Posts** Press Officer, National Council of YMCA's 1992-95; Press & Public Affairs Manager, Nation al Council of YMCA's 1995-96. **Prof Background** BA Hons English Language & Literature, Hull University. **Pres Committees** Executive Committee, National Council for Voluntary Youth Services (NCVYS) 1995. **Past Committees** National Executive Committee, National Union of Students, Part-time Executive 1990-1; General Secretary 1991-2.

PHILLIPS Alan Director **MINORITY RIGHTS GROUP** SOCIAL Type: Educational Charity. 379 Brixton Road, London SW9 7DE Tel:0171-978 9498 Fax:0171-738 6265 **Expertise** Group rights and peaceful co-existence; minorities, international human rights. **Prev Posts** General Secretary, World University Service UK 1973-81; Deputy Director, British Refugee Council 1982-88. **Prof Background** Degree in physics; systems analysis training. **Awards/Research** Auth: British Aid for Overseas Students; Education for Refugees; Minorities and Politics (Central Europe). **Pres Committees** NGO Working Group on British Aid, Human Rights and Development. **Past Committees** Commission Chair, World Congress on Human Rights; University of Warwick Council. **Media Experience** Various radio interviews, press comments and briefings on minorities. **Addits** Expert/NGO adviser to UK Gov CSCE Delegations-Copenhagen/Geneva/Helsinki.

PHILLIPS David Chief Executive **HOLIDAY CARE SERVICE** DISABILITY Type: Service provider. Imperial Buildings, Victoria Road, Horley, Surrey RH6 7PZ Tel:01293-771500 Fax:01293-784647 **Expertise** Tourism; General Mgmt; Marketing; PR. **Prev Posts** Mktg & Mngmnt posts w Brit Tourist Auth; Sen Acct Mgr, Biss Lancaster (PR Agcy) 1980-81; Bus Mgr/Copywriter - Writers in Business 1981-88; Asst Mktg Dir, Eng Tourist Brd 1988-94. **Prof Background** MA Hons French Language & Literature, University of St Andrews; Fellow of the Tourism Society. **Awards/Research** Numerous articles for trade and consumer press. **Pres Committees** Tourism for All Advisory Cttee; Hotel & Holiday Consortium; EU Independent Living Tourism for All Cttee. **Past Committees** Director, Cornwall Tourism Devt action programme. **Media Experience** Many press and radio interviews.

PHILLIPS Emma Secretary **SAVE BRITAIN'S HERITAGE** CONSERVATION/ENVIRONMENT Type: Service provider. 68 Battersea High Street, London SW11 3HX Tel:0171-228 3336 Fax:0171-223 2714 **Expertise** Buildings at risk; Currently: Hon Treasurer, Friends of the City Churches. **Prof Background** Administration; MA (Hons) Art History. **Awards/Research** Compiler, Bargain Buildings, 1993; Beauty or the Bulldozer, 1994; The City Churches Have a Future, 1994; Mind over Matter, 1995; Hospitals - a Medical Emergency, 1996. **Pres Committees** Industrial Archaelogy S.E. Committee, BTA Heritage Committee, Friends of Gibraltar's Heritage Society Committee; Friends of the City Churches; Trustee, Ymddirieddaeth Treftadaeth Caernarfon. **Media Experience** Local radio interviews, national TV & numerous press contacts; journalist.

PHILLIPS Marc Chief Executive **TENOVUS** MEDICAL/HEALTH Type: Fundraiser; Service provider; Grant maker. 11 Whitchurch Road, Cardiff CF4 3JN Tel:01222-621433 Fax:01222-615966 **Expertise** Cancer research; counselling. **Prev Posts** Regional Organiser, Urdd Gobaith Cymru 1977-86; Director, Dyfed Assoc of Voluntary Services 1986-95. **Awards/Research** Numerous articles on charity issues in the Welsh language press. **Pres Committees** BBC Wales Appeals Advisory Committee (Member). **Past Committees** HTV Wales Telethon Trust, Trustee; Wales Council for Voluntary Action, Committee Member; Wales Rural Forum, Chair. **Media Experience** Extensive media coverage in English & Welsh.

PHILLIPS Maurice Director **PESTALOZZI CHILDREN'S VILLAGE TRUST** CHILDREN/YOUTH Type: Service provider. Sedlescombe, Battle, East Sussex TN33 ORR Tel:01424-870444 Fax:01424-870655 **Expertise** General management, policy development, child care. **Prev Posts** Deputy Chief Inspector, Social Service Inspectorate, Dept of Health 1988-94; Director, Project Finance 1988-90; Director, Care Consultants 1990-today. **Prof Background** B Soc.Sci; CASS. **Awards/Research** Numerous articles in magazines. **Past Committees** Chair, two DOH Cttees which produced two publications: Social work decision making in child care; Working Together. **Media Experience** Radio/TV/video/press. **Addts** Consultant to HAs & LAs on service transfers/comm care/QA/complaints.

PHILPOTT Dr John Director **EMPLOYMENT POLICY INSTITUTE** SOCIAL Type: Think Tank. Southbank House, Black Prince Road, London SE1 7SJ Tel:0171-735 0777 Fax:0171-793 8192 **Expertise** Economics; employment policy. **Prev Posts** Dir, Employment Inst 1987-92; EPI 1992-. **Prof Background** BA; D Phil (Oxon). **Awards/Research** Research, labour market issues, Ed and Contrib Economic Report. **Past Committees** Cnsltnt: incl Org for Economic Co-op & Devt (OECD); Internat Labour Org; UN; Specialist Advisor UK Hse Cmmns Select Cttee on Emplmnt **Media Experience** Commentator on employment matters.

PHILPOTT Stephen Chief Executive **ULSTER SOCIETY FOR PREVENTION OF CRUELTY TO ANIMALS - USPCA** ANIMAL/WILDLIFE Type: Fundraiser; Service provider. Unit 4, Boucher Business Park, Apollo Road, Belfast BT12 6HP Tel:01232-660479 Fax:01232-381911

PICKARD David General Manager **ORCHESTRA OF THE AGE OF THE ENLIGHTENMENT** ARTS Type: Service provider. 5th Floor, Westcombe House, 56-58 Whitcombe Street London, WC2H 7DN Tel:0171-930 0646 Fax:0171-930 0626 **Expertise** Music & arts administration. **Prev Posts** Managing Director, Kent Opera 1989-90; Asst Director, Japan Festival 1990-91; Artistic Administrator, European Arts Festival 1992-93. **Prof Background** M.A. (Hons) Cantab (Music Degree). **Pres Committees** Board Member, Clicktrack.

PICKERING Caroline Grant and Policy Advisor **LONDON HOUSING FOUNDATION** SOCIAL Type: Grant maker. United House, North Road, London N7 9DP Tel:0171-609 9491 Fax:0171-700 7599 **Expertise** Relief of single homelessness. **Prev Posts** Director, Housing Corporation 1975-91; Managing Director, Circle 33 Housing Trust. **Pres Committees** Chair, Community Housing Association; Solicitor, Disciplinary Tribunal; Cttee Mbr, Merseyside Improved Houses. **Media Experience** Radio interviews whilst at Housing Corporation.

PICKERING Dr Errol Director General **INTERNATIONAL HOSPITAL FEDERATION** MEDICAL/HEALTH Type: Professional Association. 4 Abbots Place, London NW6 4NP Tel:0171-372 7181 Fax:0171-328 7433 **Expertise** Health service management, health policy, quality assurance. **Prev Posts** Executive Director, Australian Council on Hospital Standards 1973-80; National Director, Australian Hospital Association 1983-87. **Prof Background** BA (Hons) Dip. Hospital Administration; PhD. **Awards/Research** Numerous journal articles on health service issues and association management. **Pres Committees** Medisend (U.S. charity); Carelift (U.S. charity); European Society of Association Executives (Management Committee). **Past Committees** Past Chairman, UNICEF Australia. **Media Experience** Spokesman on hospital issues, Australian news media.

PIFF Christine Founder **LET'S FACE IT - SUPPORT GROUP FOR THE FACIALLY DISFIGURED** DISABILITY Type: Service provider. 10 Wood End, Crowthorne, Berks RG45 6DQ Tel:01344-774405

Fax:01344-762925 **Expertise** All forms of facial disfigurement. **Prev Posts** Founded LFI in 1984. **Prof Background** Children's nurse; author; patient; lecturer. Winston Churchill Fellow (lecturing in Sweden & USA). **Awards/Research** Pol Roget Award; Paul Harris Rotarian. Auth: Cancer Upper Jaw; Let's Face It; numerous articles and newsletters. **Pres Committees** LFI Trustees; Honorary Member, Institute Maxillo Facial Technologists. **Media Experience** Frequent national TV, radio and press.

PIGG Iain Director **DISABILITY LAW SERVICE** DISABILITY Type: Service provider. Room 241, 2nd Floor, 49-51 Bedford Row, London WC1R 4LR Tel:0171-831 8031 Fax:0171-831 5582 **Prev Posts** National Secretary, National Union of Students UK 1992-3; Campaigns Officer, Shelter 1993 4; Head of Campaigns, Shelter, The National Campaign for Homeless People 1995-6. **Prof Background** BA (Hons) English Literature & Language, University of Newcastle upon Tyne 1992. **Awards/Research** Shelter's Campaign on the 1995 Housing White Paper: A Case Study (conference paper, FEANTSA, 1995); How Charities Influence Public Policy (Seminar paper, FEANTSA, 1996). **Past Committees** Steering Cttee, Churches Nat Housing Coalition; Board Member, Dalston City Partnership; Council Member, Campaign for Freedom of Info. **Addits** Also sat on Steering Cttee, Nat Union of Students 1990-93.

PIGGOT Mary-Anne Chief Executive **BRITISH INSTITUTE OF RADIOLOGY** MEDICAL/HEALTH Type: Learned Society. 36 Portland Place, London W1N 4AT Tel:0171-580 4317 Fax:0171-255 3209 **Expertise** General Management. **Prev Posts** Royal College of GPs 1984-87; Factory Mutual Insurance Company 1987-88. **Prof Background** BSc (Strathclyde); Henley Mgt Diploma; MBA with distinction from the International Mgt Centres Buckingham.

PIPER Suzanne Maree President **CENTRAL COUNCIL FOR BRITISH NATURISM - CCBN** Type: Fundraiser; Service provider; Grant maker; Campaigning. 30-32 Wycliffe Road, Northampton, NN1 5JF Tel:01604-20361 Fax:01604-230176 **Expertise** Sociology of Naturism, health, history. Has been the main 'public face' of naturism since 1989. **Prev Posts** Public Relations Officer 1991-94; Research and Liaison Officer 1991-92, 1995-; Promotions and Publicity Sub Group 1989-. **Prof Background** Qualified Nurse specialising in Mental Handicap & Mental Illness; Qualified Aromatherapist/Masseuse; Member Royal Society Health. **Awards/Research** Holiday articles & health issues for British Naturism; comments on naturism for BN; Nude and Natural, Health & Efficiency, NZ Naturust, INF Bulletin, JOTS. Naturist of the Year Awd. **Pres Committees** British Naturism, President; Shabden Leisure Ltd, Director and Company Sec; H&E International Fun Fund, Company Secretary. Countless radio & TV programmes inc: Jamesons; Open Space; What's My Line.

PITKEATHLEY Jill Director **CARERS' NATIONAL ASSOCIATION** SOCIAL Type: Support and lobbying. 20-25 Glasshouse Yard, London EC1A 4JS Tel:0171-490 8818 Fax:0171-490 8824 **Expertise** Carers. **Prev Posts** Senior Research Officer, National Consumer Council 1982-86. **Prof Background** BA Economics; CQSW.

Awards/Research OBE; articles/books on volunteering & voluntary sector inc. It's My Duty Isn't It? 1989, The Plight Of Carers; Only Child How to Survive Being One, 1994; Age Gap Relationships, 1996. **Pres Committees** Health Advisory Service; Rural Development Commission, Social Policy; Community Council for Berkshire; Board of Governors, National Institute of Social Workers. **Past Committees** Griffiths Review of Community Care. **Media Experience** Frequent interviews and articles.

POLLOCK David Director **CONTINENCE FOUNDATION** MEDICAL/HEALTH Type: Service provider. 2 Doughty St, London WC1N 2PH Tel:0171-404 6875 Fax:0171-404 6876 **Expertise** Charity administration & campaigning. **Prev Posts** Adminstration & staff planning, National Coal Board 1964-90; Director, Action on Smoking Health (ASH) 1991-95. **Prof Background** BA (Literal Humaniores) Oxford. **Awards/Research** Publications : Tobacco Advertising - The Case For A Ban, (ASH, 1996); Forty Years On, (The Tobacco Industry's Survival), (British Medical Bulletin, 1996). **Pres Committees** Chairman, Rationalist Press Association; Member, Education Committee, British Humanist Association; Member, Hackney LEA Standing Advisory Council on Religious Education. **Past Committees** Secretary, Charity Law Reform Committee (1970's). **Media Experience** Extensive radio, TV and press experience with ASH. **Addits** Auth of Objective, Fair & Balanced (Religion in Schools), Brit Hum Assoc.

POND Chris Director **LOW PAY UNIT** SOCIAL Type: Service provider; Research, advice and advocacy. 27-29 Amwell Street, London EC1R 1UN Tel:0171-713 7616 Fax:0171-713 7581 **Expertise** Economics of poverty and inequality; labour markets, social policy and taxation. **Prev Posts** Economics lecturer, Civil Service College 1978-79; Visiting lecturer, Kent Univ 1981-82. Hon Visiting Prof University of Middlesex. **Prof Background** BA Hons Social Sciences (Economics), Sussex Univ. Fellow, Royal Soc of Arts (RSA). **Awards/Research** Co-Auth: To Him Who Hath: Poverty and Taxation, 1977; Taxation and Social Policy, 1980; Hidden Army: Children at Work in the 1990s. **Past Committees** Policy Review Group (Labour Party) Taxation and Social Security; Unemployment Unit Management Committee; CPAG Executive. **Media Experience** Regular participation. **Addits** Parliamentary candidate (Welwyn Hatfield) 1987; Gravesham 1996/7.

POPPLE Richard Hon General Secretary **INCORPORATED ASSOCIATION OF ORGANISTS** ARTS Type: Education for organists of all levels of ability. 11 Stonehill Drive, Bromyard, Herefordshire HR7 4XB Tel:01885-483155 Fax:01885-488609 **Expertise** Organist & Choirmaster. **Prev Posts** Independent Mngmt Consultant, 1986-present; Senior Personnel Management posts in the Public Sector, 1978-85; Commissioned Service, RAF Administrative Branch, 1952-78. **Prof Background** Grad, RAF Staff Coll; Fellow, Inst of Dir; Fellow, Inst of Personnel & Devt; Mbr, Inst of Mngnt Cons; Certified Mngmnt Cons; Assoc of the Royal Col of Organists & Choirmaster Diploma. **Awards/Research** MBE 1976. Articles in: Training & Development, Personnel Management, Consulting (IMC Yearbook); Managing Ed/Contrib: Organists Review (Quarterly journal of the IAO). **Pres Committees** National Council,

Institute of Management Consultants; Midlands Region Chairman; National Council, Institute of Personnel & Development. **Past Committees** Birmingham Area Chairman, Royal School of Church Music 1983-93. **Media Experience** Contributor to BBC NI Documentary; Occ Radio/TV interviews; Ex Officio.

POWELL Kenneth Director **TWENTIETH CENTURY SOCIETY** CONSERVATION/ENVIRONMENT Type: Fundraiser; Service provider; Campaigning. 70 Cowcross Street, London EC1M 6BP Tel:0171-250 3857 Fax:0171-250 3022 **Expertise** Publicity; Campaigning; Strategy; Policy Making. **Prev Posts** Sec, SAVE Britain's Heritage 1984-87; Architecture Correspondent, Daily Telegraph 1987-93; Freelance Writer, 1995 to date. **Prof Background** BA Hons, History; MA Architecture, Manchester. **Awards/Research** Many articles/books, subjects include Richard Rogers, Edward Cullinan, Michael Graves, Norman Foster. **Pres Committees** Member of Academy Forum; Committee Member at SAVE; Trustee, The Buildings at Risk Trust; Member, Art & Architecture Committee; Westminster Cathedral (RC) etc. **Media Experience** Various.

POWELL Stephen Chief Executive **SIGN CAMPAIGN FOR DEAF PEOPLE** DISABILITY Type: Service provider; Campaigning. 21 Stratton Road, Beaconsfield, Bucks HP9 1HR Tel:01494-680308 Fax:01494-680432 **Expertise** Organisational Development; Fundraising; Health Care. **Prev Posts** Head of Voluntary Sector, British Diabetic Association 1982-89; Director, ME Association 1989-90 **Prof Background** Educator. **Awards/Research** Articles published in variety of magazines on subjects to do with charities, voluntary organisations. **Pres Committees** Treasurer, ACENVO; Cttee member: CFC; British Soc Mental Health & Deafness. Advisory Cttee member, NHS Health Advisory Service; School Governor. **Past Committees** ICFM Cttee **Addits** Conf Speaker eg Dept Health/Environ; At Home in the Community.

PRAILL David Chief Executive **HELP THE HOSPICES** MEDICAL/HEALTH Type: Fundraiser; Grant maker. 34-44 Britannia Street, London WC1X 9JG Tel:0171-278 5668 Fax:0171-278 1021

PRATT Ivan W. Secretary **STROKE ASSOCIATION** MEDICAL/HEALTH Type: Fundraiser; Service provider; Grant maker. CHSA House, Whitecross Street, London EC1Y 8JJ Tel:0171-490 7999 Fax:0171-490 2686 **Prev Posts** Chief Executive: Amateur Rowing Association 1982-90.

PRESTON George D.C. Secretary/Treasurer **QUEEN'S NURSING INSTITUTE (SCOTLAND)** MEDICAL/HEALTH Type: Service provider; Grant maker; Projects in community nursing care & training. 31 Castle Terrace, Edinburgh EH1 2EL Tel:0131-229 2333 Fax:0131-229 0443 **Expertise** Administration. **Prev Posts** Fettes College, Housemaster 1969-81; Snr Master 1981-91. **Prof Background** MA Gonville and Caius College, Cambridge; retired schoolmaster. **Pres Committees** Old Fettesian Association. **Past Committees** Governor, Fettesian Lorettonian Boys Club; Director, Fettes Enterprises.

PRICE Maurice Director **BOURNE TRUST** SOCIAL Type: Service provider. Lincoln House, 1-3 Brixton Rd, London SW9 6DE Tel:0171-582 1313 Fax:0171-735 6077 **Expertise** Criminal Justice, especially prisons. **Prev Posts** Senior Probation Officer 1987-90; Home Manager, Vulnerable Homeless Teenagers 1991-94. **Prof Background** Qualified as Probation Officer 1980; Background in charities caring for homeless ex-offenders. **Pres Committees** Executive Committee (Trustee), Federation of Prisoners Families Support Groups; Social Welfare Committee, Catholic Bishops' Conference. **Media Experience** Interviews for radio, TV and press. **Addits** The Trust is only provider of professional counselling for remand prisoners.

PRICE Rev. Canon Peter B. General Secretary **UNITED SOCIETY FOR THE PROPAGATION OF THE GOSPEL - USPG** RELIGIOUS Type: Service provider; Grant maker; Mission Agency. Partnership House, 157 Waterloo Road, London SE1 8XA Tel:0171-928 8681 Fax:0171-928 2371 **Prev Posts** Vicar, St Mary Magdalene, Croydon 1980-88; Canon Chancellor, Southwark Cathedral 1988-91. **Prof Background** Teaching; industrial training; ministerial education; mission studies. **Awards/Research** Auth: The Church as Kingdom, 1987; Research into Evangelisation and Alternative Church Structures, London University; Seeds of the Word, 1996. **Pres Committees** Board of Mission. **Media Experience** Contrib: BBC Wld Service/R2; Consult: Christianity in Today's World, BBC Educ.

PRICE Roland Chairman **GUILLAIN-BARRE SYNDROME SUPPORT GROUP OF THE UK** MEDICAL/HEALTH Type: Fundraiser; Service provider. Lincolnshire CC Offices, Eastgate, Sleaford, Lincs NG34 7EB Tel:01529-304615 **Expertise** Administration. **Prev Posts** Has become deeply involved in charity work since retirement. **Prof Background** Qualified linguist. **Pres Committees** National Executive Committee of Guillain-Barre Syndrome Support Group of the UK. **Media Experience** Local radio interviews; Group's own video.

PRICE Susan Executive Director **GROUNDWORK MERTHYR & CYNON** ENVIRONMENT Type: Fundraiser; Service provider. Fedw Hir, Llwydcoed, Aberdare, Mid Glamorgan CF44 0DX Tel:01685-883880 Fax:01685-879990 **Expertise** Project Devt & Resourcing for/with the community on environmental improvement & education. **Prev Posts** District Planning Officer, 1980-85; Principal Planning Officer, 1974-80. **Prof Background** BSc Economics; Dip TP, Professional qualification & early career in Town Planning; Developed & Managed Groundwork Trust since 1985. **Pres Committees** Prince of Wales Cttee, Overall Policy & Mngmt Cttee; Merthyr Tydfil Heritage Trst, Mngmnt Cttee; Cynon Valley Bus Ptnrshp Team, Exec Cttee; Merthyr Safer Cities Initiative, Chair Steering Cttee. **Past Committees** Brecon Beacons National Park Management Cttee (3 years).

PUGHE Anne Chief Executive **SEQUAL TRUST** DISABILITY Type: Fundraiser; Service provider. Ddol Hir, Glyn Ceirog, Llangollen, Clwyd LL20 7NP Tel:01691-718331 Fax:01691-718331

PUZEY John Director **SHELTER CYMRU** SOCIAL Type: Service provider; Campaigning and information provision. 25 Walter Road, Swansea SA1 5NN Tel:01792-469400 Fax:01792-460050 **Expertise** Lobbying; housing law and rights. **Prev Posts** Manager, Hull Housing Aid Centre 1983-89. **Prof Background** BA (Hons) Politics: Dip. Politics and Economics, Wales Univ. **Pres Committees** Wales European Anti-Poverty Network; Tenants' Participation Advisory Service Executive; N. Wales NACAB Management Cttees; Cardiff Institute of Higher Education Housing Consultative Cttee. **Media Experience** Frequent contributor to radio/TV and press on housing matters.

Q

QUIGLEY Peter S. Executive Director **ACTION CANCER** MEDICAL/HEALTH Type: Fundraiser; Service provider; Grant maker; Campaigning. 1 Marlborough Park, Belfast BT9 6HQ Tel:01232-382455 Fax:01232-683931 **Expertise** Charity administration, Public Relations, Campaigning and Fundraising. **Prev Posts** Asst Dir, Age Concern NI 1983-85; Administrative Dir, NI Hospice 1985-91; Exec Dir, City of Belfast YMCA 1992-93. **Prof Background** Minister of religion; Member of Inst of Charities Fundraising Mngrs (ICFM); Member of the Inst of Public Relations (MIPR); Fellow of the Inst of Directors (FlnstD). **Awards/Research** Charity Magazines. **Pres Committees** Assoc of Chief Officers of Voluntary Organisations in NI (ACENVO-NI); NI Council on Voluntary Action. **Past Committees** Belfast Education and Library Board (BELB). **Media Experience** Radio/TV/press on issues effecting charities.

CHARITIES-ON-LINE

THE NEW DATABASE REFERENCE SERVICE FOR AND ABOUT THE VOLUNTARY SECTOR.

From 1997 you can dial direct into this on-line facility for detailed information about charities, voluntary organisations and associated bodies.

Annual subscription to this service comes complete with easy-to-use software to make your access to the information fast and precisiely targetted to your needs.

CHARITIES-ON-LINE keeps all your phone bills down and efficiency levels high.

For full details call AURELIAN on 0181-960 7918

R

RAFFERTY John Director, Scotland. **NATIONAL LOTTERY CHARITIES BOARD** SOCIAL Type: Grant maker; Statutory Body. 36 Kings Stables Rd, Edinburgh EH1 2EJ Tel:0131-221 7100 Fax:0131-221 7120 **Expertise** Financial Mgt, Strategic Planning, Mental Health. **Prev Posts** Volunteer Centre, 1978-88; Scottish Foundation for Economic Development 1988-1992. Archdiocese of Glasgow 1992-1995. **Past Committees** Trustee: Pastoral Care Trust, Rosemary Scanlon Trust Dir: Archway Devs, Chapter House Investments. Chair, Glasgow Housing Appeals Tribunal. Dir: Prince's Trust Volunteers; Glasgow IT Centre; Scottish Fndtn for Economic Research. **Media Experience** Experienced with all media.

RAFFERTY Robina Director **CATHOLIC HOUSING AID SOCIETY - CHAS** SOCIAL Type: Service provider. 209 Old Marylebone Rd, London NW1 5QT Tel:0171-723 7273 Fax:0171-723 5943 **Expertise** Housing policy; homelessness; church and social policy. **Prev Posts** Admin Officer, Justice and Peace Commission 1970-76; Housing Adviser, CHAS 1976-80; Asst director CHAS 1980-87. **Prof Background** BA English Language and Literature. **Awards/Research** Regular articles in church press and periodicals; drafted housing chapters of:Faith in the City, and Living Faith in the City. **Pres Committees** South London Family Housing Association; Christian Action; Churches National Housing Coalition. **Past Committees** Campaign for Single Homeless People; Archbishop's Committee on Urban Priority Areas 1983-85. **Media Experience** Radio interviews.

RAMSAY Andrew Vernon Secretary **CHARTERED INSTITUTION OF BUILDING SERVICES ENGINEERS** Type: Fundraiser; Service provider. Delta House, 222 Balham High Rd, London SW12 9BS Tel:0181-675 5211 Fax:0181-675 5449 **Expertise** Professional Institution Administration. **Prof Background** Chartered Electrical Engineer; Chartered Secretary.

RANDALL Adrian J.L. Trustee **SOS CHILDREN'S VILLAGES UK** CHILDREN/YOUTH Type: Service provider, UK & overseas. c/o Moores Rowland, Cliffords Inn, Fetter Lane, London EC4A 1AS Tel:0171-831 2345 Fax:0171-831 6123 **Expertise** Finance. **Prev Posts** Worked 16 yrs for Tate & Lyle and The Hays Group; Dir, Finance & Resources, Cancer Research Campaign 1987-94. Co-Found/Chair, Charity Finance Directors Gp 1988-92. Currently Visiting Prof, Charity Finance, South Bank University. **Prof Background** Chartered Accountant 1968; BSc (Econ) 1971. **Awards/Research** Charity Finance Directors Handbook 1991-92; Charity Finance Handbook 1992-93; numerous articles professional jnls on charity accounting, strategic planning and taxation. **Pres Committees** Mbr, Charity Cmmsn Wkng Pty to Review SORP 2; Inst Chart Accs Charity Accs Wkng Pty; Charity Commission, Charity Monitoring Consultation Gp; Trustee: Rainbows & Unicorns; **Past Committees** Chair, Charities Tax Reform Gp 1992-94; ICAEW Career Develop Gp 1988-92; Treas, Charity Forum; NCVO Charity Law Reform Gp 1990-92. **Addits** Past pres, Essex Soc of Chart Accts 1988-89; Ex-financial adv ICFM Conf.

RASHBASS Dr Barbara Director and Secretary **WOLFSON FOUNDATION, and WOLFSON FAMILY CHARITABLE TRUST** MEDICAL/HEALTH Type: Grant maker. 18-22 Haymarket, London SW1Y 4DQ Tel:0171-930 1057 Fax:0171-930 1036 **Expertise** Health; medicine; science; education. **Prev Posts** Principal Medical Officer, HQ Staff Medical Research Council. **Prof Background** MB, BS Lond Univ 1958; Dip (Child Health) Eng 1961; Dip (Public Health) Eng 1968; FRLP 1995; Barrister-at-law. **Pres Committees** Member, Medico Legal Society; Fellow, Royal Society of Medicine.

RATHBONE William Director **ROYAL UNITED KINGDOM BENEFICENT ASSOCIATION** ELDERLY Type: Fundraiser; Service provider; Grant maker; Serving the Elderly. 6 Avonmore Road, London W14 8RL Tel:0171-602 6274 Fax:0171-371 1807 **Expertise** General management; voluntary work. **Prev Posts** Director, Ocean Inchcape Ltd 1974-79; Exec Director, Gastransco Ltd 1979-88. **Prof Background** MA Oxon (Hons) PPE; Business School Diploma, IMEDE, Lausanne. **Pres Committees** Vice Chair/Trustee, Queen's Nursing Institute; Pres,Community & District Nursing Assoc; Vice Pres, Christ Church United Clubs; Court Mbr, New England Co; Trustee, Eleanor Rathbone Charitable Trust.

RAUPRICH Susanne General Secretary **NATIONAL COUNCIL FOR VOLUNTARY YOUTH SERVICES** NCVYS CHILDREN/YOUTH Type: Service provider. 11 Bride St, London EC4A 4AS Tel:0171-353 6909 Fax:0171-353 2369.

REA Flick General Secretary **PEDESTRIANS ASSOCIATION** Type: Service provider. 126 Aldersgate Street, London EC1A 4JQ Tel:0171-490 0750 Fax:0171-490 0750 **Expertise** Government/Local Authority liaison; fundraising; project management; public speaking. **Prof Background** Extensive experience in voluntary sector; Drama Diploma, RADA; Guildhall School Music & Drama. **Awards/ Research** Various Environmental/Transport Magazines. **Pres Committees** London Borough of Camden Council; Hampstead Theatre Board; Camden Arts Centre; London Centre for Transport Planning. **Past Committees** London Regional Passengers Committee; London Transport Passengers Commitee; Shaw Theatre. **Media Experience** TV, on various consumer programmes; Radio. **Addits** Local Authority Councillor since 1986.

REA PRICE John Director **NATIONAL CHILDREN'S BUREAU** CHILDREN/YOUTH Type: Advice/information/training/research. 8 Wakley Street, London EC1V 7QE Tel:0171-843 6000 Fax:0171-278 9512 **Prev Posts** Community Development Project, Home Office 1969-72;

Director of Social Services, LB Islington 1972-90. **Awards** OBE.

REARDON Rev. John General Secretary **COUNCIL OF CHURCHES FOR BRITAIN AND IRELAND** RELIGIOUS Type: Co-ordinating body for all churches. Inter-Church House, 35-41 Lower Marsh, London SE1 7RL Tel:0171-620 4444 Fax:0171-928 0010 **Expertise** Ecumenism, justice and peace. **Prev Posts** Minister, Trinity Congregational Church, St Albans 1968-72; Church and society secretary, United Reformed Church 1972-90; Moderator of Gen Assembly, United Reform Church 1995-96. **Prof Background** BA (Hons) English, London Univ; Postgraduate Cert. Education, Kings College, London; Roll of Ministers Exam, Congregational Church. **Awards/Research** Ed: Leaves From The Tree Of Peace; Threads of Creation; Contrib: More Everyday Prayers. **Pres Committees** Board of Christian Aid; Free Church Federal Council. **Past Committees** Exec. Committee, United Reformed Church; Assembly of the British Council of Churches. **Media Experience** Articles/interviews in religious press; many radio interviews; TV preaching.

REARDON Ruth Secretary **ASSOCIATION OF INTERCHURCH FAMILIES - AIF** RELIGIOUS Type: Fundraiser; Service provider. Inter-Church House, 35-41 Lower Marsh, London SE1 7RL Tel:0171-620 4444 Fax:0171-928 0010 **Expertise** Ecumenism; Mixed Marriages. **Prev Posts** Sussex Churches' Ecumenical Officer, 1984-89; Co-ordinator, One World Week 1990-91. **Prof Background** Modern History (London); Religious Studies (Louvain). **Awards/Research** Sharing Communion 1983. **Pres Committees** RC Bishops' Committee on Marriage & Family Life; Churches Together for Families.

REES Eirian Director **WELSH COUNCIL ON ALCOHOL AND OTHER DRUGS** Type: Church based; Education & Youth work; Drop-in Centre. 112 Albany Rd, Cardiff CF2 3RU Tel:01222-493895 Fax:01222-257057 **Expertise** Alcohol & other education (Univs, Schs & Colls); Pastoral Training (church workers) & caring. **Prev Posts** Teacher 1964-84; Congregational Church Minister. **Prof Background** Degrees in Economics & Theology; Minister of Religion/Teacher. **Awards/Research** Author of articles in Magazines/Journals in Wales. **Pres Committees** Board Member, United Kingdom Temperance Alliance Ltd; Founder Member, Eurocare; Management Cttee of Unions of Welsh Independents. **Past Committees** Executive Member, Hope UK. **Media Experience** Regular broadcasting for radio and TV.

REEVES Helen Director **VICTIM SUPPORT** SOCIAL Type: Fundraiser; Service provider; Grant maker; Campaigning. Cranmer House, 39 Brixton Rd, London SW9 6DZ Tel:0171-735 9166 Fax:0171-582 5712 **Prev Posts** Probation Officer, Inner London Probation Service 1967-74; Senior Probation Officer, Inner London Probation Service 1974-79. **Prof Background** BA (Hons) Social Administration, University of Nottingham; Home Office Probation Training. **Awards/Research** OBE. **Pres Committees** Trustee, Kidscape; Secretary, European Forum for Victim Services; Vice-President, World Society of Victimology. **Past Committees** National Board for Crime Prevention; Crime Concern. **Media Experience** Frequent contributor to radio, TV, video and press.

REEVES Rudi Manager **ADVICE INFORMATION & MEDIATION SERVICE FOR RETIREMENT HOUSING - AIMS** THE ELDERLY Type: Service provider. Walkden House, 3-10 Melton St, London NW1 2EJ Tel:0171-383 2006 Fax:0171-383 3614 **Expertise** Mediator in disputes between leaseholders of priv sheltered housing and their managers/builders. Spec ADR **Prev Posts** Officer, Cmty Health Cncl 1993-94; Adv Panel Mbr, Jewish Arbit/Medi Serv 1995-. **Prof Background** LLB (Hons). **Pres Committees** V-Chair IVF Medethics Cttee, Holly Hospital 1990-; Mbr, Charities Advisory Panel, Centre for Dispute Resolution 1989-.

REID Donald J Chief Executive **ASSOCIATION FOR PUBLIC HEALTH** MEDICAL/HEALTH Type: Fundraiser. Campaigning, Professional Association. Hamilton House, Mabledon Place, London WC1H 9TX Tel:0171-413 1896 Fax:0171-388 6079 **Expertise** Health Promotion; Anti-Smoking Campaigns. **Prev Posts** Director of Programmes, Health Education Authority, 1987-93; Director of Education & Training, Health Education Council, 1984-87. **Prof Background** Teacher: Head of Science Faculty in Secondary School. **Awards/Research** Auth:Is Health Education via Mass Communications Effective? (1996); Tobacco Control-Overview (1996); Reducing the prevalence of smoking in youth in Western Countries: an int review. **Past Committees** Executive Director of Health Education Authority; Non-Executive Director of Action on Smoking & Health. **Media Experience** Extensive radio, TV and press experience.

REITH Lorna Director **DISABILITY ALLIANCE, EDUCATION AND RESEARCH ASSOCIATION** DISABILITY Type: Service provider; Campaigning. Universal House, 88-94 Wentworth Street, London E1 7SA Tel:0171-247 8776 Fax:0171-247 8765 **Prev Posts** Team leader, LB Hackney 1983-86; Campaign Officer, CHAR 1986-91. **Prof Background** BA Politics, Lancaster University 1975. **Pres Committees** Tottenham Legal Advice Centre; local residents group. **Past Committees** SHIL-Single Homeless in London; Chair, Law Centre Federation; Chile Solidarity Campaign Exec. Cttee. **Media Experience** Participant, all media branches. **Addits** Tenants' activist, Haringey; ex mbr Haringey Borough Housing Cttee.

REMINGTON Stephen Chief Executive **ACTION FOR BLIND PEOPLE** Type: Fundraiser; Service provider; Grant maker; Campaigning. 14-16 Verney Road, London SE16 3DZ Tel:0171-732 8771 Fax:0171-639 0948 **Prev Posts** Chief Executive, Sadler's Wells 1979-94. **Prof Background** Trinity College Dublin, Mental & Moral Science. **Awards/Research** Chevalier Dans L'Ordre des Arts et des Lettres. **Pres Committees** Chair, Method & Madness (Cambridge Theatre Co).

RENOLD Richard General Secretary **NATIONAL ASSOCIATION OF ROUND TABLES OF GB AND IRELAND** SOCIAL Type: Fundraiser; Service provider; Grant maker; Association of young men's clubs. Marchesi House, 4 Embassy Drive, Edgbaston, Birmingham B15 1TP Tel:0121-456 4402 Fax:0121-456 4185 **Expertise** Administration; financial control. **Prev Posts** GKN Group

1970-83; Sussex County Cricket Club 1983-87. **Prof Background** Degree in Mechanical Engineering, UMIST; Diploma in Business Administration, Manchester Business School. **Past Committees** Test and County Cricket Board (as representative of Sussex CCC).

RENSHAW Virginia Director **LIVE MUSIC NOW!** SOCIAL Type: Service provider. 4 Lower Belgrave Street, London SW1W 0LJ Tel:0171-730 2205 Fax:0171-730 3641 **Expertise** Music. **Prev Posts** Teacher at Yehudi Menuhin School 1975-86; Musicians' Manager at Harold Holt Ltd 1986-87; P.A. to John Ogdon 1987-88. **Prof Background** LRAM; Cello; BA (Hons) Italian/French; TEFL Diploma. **Awards/Research** FRSA; ARAM.

REYNOLDS Fiona Director **COUNCIL FOR THE PROTECTION OF RURAL ENGLAND - CPRE** CONSERVATION/ENVIRONMENT Type: Campaigning. Warwick House, 25 Buckingham Palace Road, London SW1W 0PP Tel:0171-976 6433 Fax:0171-976 6373 **Expertise** General environmental. **Prev Posts** Secretary, Council for National Parks 1980-87; Assistant Director, CPRE 1987-91. **Prof Background** MA, Geography and Land Economy 1979, and M Phil, Land Economy 1980, Cambridge University. **Awards/Research** UNEP Global 500 Award 1990. **Pres Committees** UK Representative, European Environmental Bureau. **Past Committees** Member, National Parks Review panel 1989-90. **Media Experience** Frequent participant on TV, radio and in national press.

REYNOLDS J.L. Trust Executive Officer **WHITE HORSE CARE TRUST** SOCIAL Type: Fundraiser; Service provider. PO Box 1263, Swindon, Wilts SN1 5RW Tel:01793-532113 Fax:01793-532114 **Expertise** Administration & Financial Control Systems & Procedures. **Prev Posts** Banking 1967-77; O&M Analyst/Systems, Analyst/Accountant 1977-88; Internal Auditor 1988-90; Trust Executive Officer 1990-today. **Prof Background** Institute of Administrative Management, Diploma (with distinction); Institute of Facilities Management; Various Professional Training Courses. **Media Experience** Press releases, radio/TV interviews.

REYNOLDS Jane Chief Executive **ROYAL MASONIC BENEVOLENT INSTITUTION - RMBI** SOCIAL Type: Fundraiser; Service provider; Grant maker. 20 Great Queen Street, London WC2B 5BG Tel:0171-405 8341 Fax:0171-404 0724 **Expertise** Service for older people and for people with learning disabilities. **Prev Posts** Dir, Westminster Mencap 1983-87; Hospital Manager, Leavesden Hospital, Abbots Langley 1987-91. **Prof Background** 26 years working in organizations providing residential care and other services for different client groups; Diploma, Management Studies; Fellow, Inst of Mngmt. **Pres Committees** Sec: Hannay Masonic Residential Trust; Masonic Fndtn for the Aged and Sick. Founder/Chair, Life Opportunities Trust. Mbr: Registered Homes Act Tribunal Panel; Westminster City Cncl Complaints Panel.

RICE J. Susan Chief Executive Officer **ISSUE (THE NATIONAL FERTILITY ASSOCIATION)** MEDICAL/HEALTH Type: Fundraiser; Service provider; Campaigning. 509 Aldridge Rd, Great Barr, Birmingham B44 8NA Tel:0121-344 4414 Fax:0121-344 4336 **Expertise** Knowledge of infertility; administration and management. **Prev Posts** Administrator, Construction Industry 1973-80; ISSUE, Vice Chair 1986-89, Chair 1989-95. **Prof Background** BSc Hons Economics/Business Administration; numerous study courses. **Awards/Research** Articles in ISSUE magazine and medical journals. **Media Experience** Considerable experience in last 10 years.

RICH Judith Director **CARDS FOR GOOD CAUSES** SOCIAL Type: Donating Charity. 5/6 City Business Centre, Hyde Street, Winchester SO23 7TA Tel:01962-862272 Fax:01962-842747 **Expertise** Training, executive management. **Prev Posts** Asst Purser, Union-Castle Line 1957-62; Challoner Service 1964-66; Trouble shooter, Alfred Marks Bureau 1966-74. **Prof Background** MIEC FICFM; Hon Fellow, Polytechnic of Central London. **Awards/Research** Awds: OBE. **Pres Committees** Trustee, Brit Diabetic Assoc; Monitoring Project WP, Charity Commission; Advisory Cttee Charities Act Part II, VSU Home Office. **Past Committees** ICFM; Trustee, Cambridge Talking News; Chair, Cambridge Civic Society; Governor, Barnsbury School. **Media Experience** Numerous TV appearances.

RICHARDS Jim M. Director **CATHOLIC CHILDREN'S SOCIETY (WESTMINSTER), THE** CHILDREN/YOUTH Type: Service provider. 73 St Charles Square, London W10 6EJ Tel:0181-969 5305 Fax:0181-960 1464 **Expertise** Child care: legislation and residential; Juvenile delinquency; adoption and related family care issues. **Prev Posts** ITO, LB Lambeth 1974-77; Principal Off, Children's Servs LB Hounslow 1977-81; Deputy Principal Adviser LBCRPC 1981-90. **Prof Background** Dip. Soc Admin; Dip. Applied Soc. Studies; MA Social and Public Administration, Brunel University; Probation and child care. **Awards/Research** Training tapes on GALS & court reports; Co-auth: guidance on S.II reports in adoption. Var reports on under-18s, GAL/RO in adoption. Researched reports of GALs 1990; Surrogacy 1995. **Pres Committees** Cardinal Hume Centre; Chair, Professional Issues Cttee of Catholic Child Welfare Council. **Past Committees** Mgmt Cttee, FRG;Adv. Cttees DoH Intermed Treatment;Children Act Implementation Gp; Chair, BASW Wking Pty on Mnging Child Sex Abuse. **Media Experience** Regular contact press/TV/radio; articles in professional/legal jnls. **Addits** Chair, Parkway Spec School Governors; Past Mbr 3 nat cttees reviewing GALS.

RICHARDSON Colin Ryder Hon. Secretary **NEW APPROACHES TO CANCER** MEDICAL/HEALTH Type: Service provider. 5 Larksfield, Egham, Surrey TW20 0RB Tel:01784-433610 **Expertise** Helping those with cancer through the assistance of Complementary Medicine. **Prof Background** Experienced cancer and survived. **Awards/Research** Auth: Mind over Cancer. **Pres Committees** Trustee, British Wheel of Yoga. **Past Committees** Various **Media Experience** Experienced with various media forms.

RICHARDSON Mrs Margaret Curator **SIR JOHN SOANE'S MUSEUM** ARTS Type: Museum. 13

Lincoln's Inn Fields, London WC2A 3BP Tel:0171-405 2107 Fax:0171-831 3957 **Expertise** Architectural conserv/drawings/history (Soane, Lutyens, arts/crafts movement, 20th Cent). **Prev Posts** Assistant Curator: RIBA Drawings Collection 1963-85, Sir John Soane's Museum 1985-95. **Prof Background** University College London, BA Hons (Latin); Courtauld Institute of Art. **Awards/Research** Hon. Fellow, RIBA; Editor of Vol ABC-FS for RIBA Catalogue series; publ inc. Edwin Lutyens 1973; Architects Arts/Crafts Movement 1983; Sketches by Lutyens 1994. **Pres Committees** Pres, 20th Cent Soc; Dir, Sir John Soane's Museum Soc;Trustee Save Britains Heritage,Pell Wall Preservation Trust;Chair/Trustee Lutyens Trust; Cttee Mbr, Guildford Cathedral Fabric Cttee. **Media Experience** Radio/press

RICHES Valerie Director **FAMILY AND YOUTH CONCERN** CHILDREN/YOUTH Type: Fundraiser; Service provider. 322 Woodstock Rd, Oxford OX2 7NS Tel:01865-556848 **Expertise** Family welfare and policy. **Prev Posts** Worked for last 20 years for FYC. **Prof Background** Social work. **Awards/Research** Auth: Sex and Social Engineering; Who Cares for Children? Contrib: book chapters; articles in national newspapers. **Pres Committees** Family Education Trust; Congress for the Family; School Governing Board. **Media Experience** Frequent.

RIDLEY Brig Nicholas Director & Director of Fundraising **FLORENCE NIGHTINGALE FUND** MEDICAL/HEALTH Type: Fundraiser. St Thomas's Hospital, Lambeth Palace Road, London SE1 7EH Tel:0171-922 8057 Fax:0171-928 7964 **Expertise** Hospital fund-raising and appeals. **Prev Posts** Military career 1959-93; Appeal Director 1994-95; Fundraising Consultant 1995-96. **Prof Background** Postgraduate training in general and technical management; Study of American hospital fund-raising techniques. **Awards/Research** OBE & MBE **Pres Committees** Florence Nightingale Trust. **Past Committees** Living Image Appeal Committee; Cranfield Institute of Technology Faculty Board; Eastern District Management Board. **Media Experience** 5 yrs as PR officer; Senior mngment course on TV & radio interview techniques.

RIGGE Marianne Director **COLLEGE OF HEALTH** MEDICAL/HEALTH Type: Service provider; Campaigning. St Margaret's House, 21 Old Ford Rd, London E2 9PL Tel:0181-983 1225 Fax:0181-983 1553 **Expertise** Health, Patient Information, Patient Rights. **Prev Posts** Researcher, Nat Consumer Council 1974-77; Director, Mutual Aid Centre 1977-83. **Prof Background** BA (Hons) University College London. **Awards/Research** Guide to Hospital Waiting Lists, 1984-92; many articles. **Pres Committees** Clinical Outcomes Group; Patient's Charter Group; Quality in Health Care Brd; King's Fund Comparative Database Initiative, Royal Coll Psych Guidelines Gp. **Past Committees** King's Fund Institute, King's Fund Quality Assurance Cttee; Patient Empowerment Focus Group. **Media Experience** Radio/TV/video/press extensive.

RITCHIE Cyril Executive Director **INTERNATIONAL STANDING CONFERENCE ON PHILANTHROPY - INTERPHIL** SOCIAL Type: Fundraiser; Service provider; Consultancy; Network. CIC Case 20, CH-1211 Geneva 20, Switzerland 22-733 6717 22-734 7082 **Expertise** Non-governmental organisations. **Prev Posts** Exec Dir, Int Council of Vol Agencies 1964-78; President, Federation of International Institutions in Geneva 1978-96. **Awards/Research** Order of the Smile, Warsaw. **Pres Committees** Board Member, Union of International Associations; Chairman, InterAid International; President, Society for International Development (Switzerland). **Past Committees** Exec Committee, Environment Liaison Centre Int; Governing Board, Int Schools Assoc; Sec, Foundation of the Int School of Geneva.

ROBERTS Ceridwen Director **FAMILY POLICY STUDIES CENTRE** SOCIAL Type: Independent research/policy centre. 231 Baker Street, London NW1 6XE Tel:0171-486 8211 Fax:0171-224 3510 **Prev Posts** Lecturer in Industrial Sociology, Trent Polytechnic 1975-78; Snr/Principal Research Officer, Dept of Employment, Economic and Research Division 1978-92. **Prof Background** BA (Hons) Sussex Univ; Postgrad Diploma Bristol Univ; Postgrad Research at Industrial Sociology Unit, Imperial College, London Univ. **Awards/Research** Auth (with Jean Martin): Women and Employment: A Lifetime Perspective, 1984. **Pres Committees** Sociology Dept Advisory Board, Surrey Univ;Adv Cttee, Centre for Educ Sociology, Edinburgh Univ; Council of UK Assoc for the International Year of the Family; Trustee, Family Budget Unit. **Past Committees** Executive of Social Research Association. **Media Experience** Various.

ROBERTS Eirlys Chairman **EUROPEAN RESEARCH INTO CONSUMER AFFAIRS - ERICA** SOCIAL Type: Research Organisation 8 Lloyd Square, London WC1X 9BA Tel:0171-837 2492 Fax:0171-482 6376 **Expertise** Consumer Research; Currently plain language in Europe & Biotechnology. **Prev Posts** Editor of Which magazine; Head of Research, Consumers' Association 1958-73. **Prof Background** Classics Degree, Girton College, Cambridge, followed by Journalism. **Awards/Research** Consumers (Pitman) 1966. Awards: CBE. **Past Committees** Economic & Social Committee of the European Community; Foundation for the Improvement of Living & Working Conditions (Dublin).

ROBERTS Elfed Director **ROYAL NATIONAL EISTEDDFOD OF WALES** SOCIAL Type: Annual Welsh Language Festival. 40 Parc Ty Glas, Llanishen, Cardiff CF4 5WU Tel:01222-763777 Fax:01222-763737 **Prev Posts** North Wales organiser of the National Eisteddfod of Wales 1986-93.

ROBERTS Jeffrey John (Major) Director of Public Relations **SALVATION ARMY** SOCIAL Type: Fundraiser; Service provider; Religious organisation. 4 Buchanan Court, Buchanan Business Park, Cumbernauld Road, Stepps, Glasgow G33 6HZ Tel:0141-779 5000 Fax:0141-779 5011 **Expertise** PR; Fundraising; Evangelism; Youth Work & Scout Assoc; Refugee Work (overseas) & Third world admin. **Prev Posts** Regnl Commdr, Malawi 1990-92; Field & Propty Sec, Philippines 1988-90, Training Pncpl/Yth Sec, S Africa 1981-85; Yth Sec, Liverpool/N Wales 1972-3; Yth Sec, Pakistan 1968-72. **Prof Background** Wm Booth Training College,

London; Lab Course, Korle Bu Hospital, Ghana; Assoc Mbr Brit Pharm Industries; Cert. in Refugee studies, York University; Mbr, Inst of Charity Fundraising Managers. **Pres Committees** Exec Sec, SA West Scotland Advisory Board; Exec Sec, SA Inverclyde Advisory Board; Glasgow Rotary Club Internat Cttee; SA Divisional Finance & Business Brd. **Media Experience** Extensive radio, TV & press exp incl interviews, ed progs overseas & in UK. **Addits** Prev Posts: Youth Sec, Ghana 1965-68; Health Centre Mngr, Ghana 1962-65.

ROBERTS Michael National Director **LIFE EDUCATION CENTRES** MEDICAL/HEALTH Type: Fundraiser; Service provider; Health Education; Drug Prevention. 20 Long Lane, London EC1A 9HL Tel:0171-600 6969 Fax:0171-600 6979 **Expertise** Fundraising. **Prev Posts** HM Forces 1959-88; Chief Administrator BHF 1989-91; Director of Fundraising BHF 1992-96. **Prof Background** Military/business. **Past Committees** Chairman, Aylesbury Division Inst of Mgmt 1992-94. **Media Experience** Radio, TV & Press interviews.

ROBERTS Peter John Chief Executive **HOMELIFE (Distressed Gentlefolks Aid Association) - DGAA** ELDERLY Type: Fundraiser; Service provider; Grant maker. 1 Derry Street, London W8 5HY Tel:0171-396 6700 Fax:0171-396 6734 **Expertise** Care of elderly people; relief of poverty. **Prev Posts** Managing Director, Torlink Ltd 1987-1993; Franchise Director, Clarks Shoes 1991-1993. **Prof Background** MA Cantab; IEDP INSEAD. **Pres Committees** Trustee, Bishop Simeon CR Trust for Education of Young South Africans; Chair, VOICES (Voluntary Organisations in Care of Elderly Sector). **Past Committees** Chair: Strode Coll Govs 89-93; Somerset Relate Marriage Guidance 79-82/87-90; Nat Cncl 79-94. Tres, Property Mkt Reform Gp 92-94. **Media Experience** Interviews: World in Action, Money Programme, ITN, local radio & TV. **Addits** Ran campaign against VAT on children's shoes: Westminster 1984-85, EC 1987-9.

ROBERTSON Jane A. Director **SOCIETY FOR WELFARE AND TEACHING OF THE BLIND** DISABILITY Type: Service provider; Grant maker. 12/14 Hillside Crescent, Edinburgh EH7 5DZ Tel:0131-557 1004 Fax:0131-557 4001 **Expertise** Social work and rehabilitation for blind people. Child Care. **Prev Posts** Housemother children's home, Grampian Regional Council 1977-80; Coventry Social Services: Deputy in Charge, Adolescent Unit 1981-84; Social Worker for the blind 1984-89. **Prof Background** Aberdeen Academmy; RGIT, Aberdeen; CQSW, Royal Blind Sch, Edin. - Social Welfare for Blind People; Strathclyde Univ, MBA in prog 1994-96. **Awards/Research** Community Care. **Pres Committees** Exec Cttees: RNIB; NALSUI; SNFWB. RNIB: Educ, Training Employmt Standing Cttee, Scottish Advisory; Diabetics Association, Edinburgh.

ROBERTSON Paul Director **FIRST KEY** CHILDREN/YOUTH Type: Service provider. Oxford Chambers, Oxford Place, Leeds LS1 3AX Tel:01132-443898 Fax:01132-432541 **Expertise** Young people leaving local authority care, and their rights. New technology and evaluation. **Prev Posts** Principal Policy and Evaluation Officer, Bury SSD 1984-92; Evaluation/Development Manager NW NSPCC 1992-93. **Prof Background** BA (Social Work); CQSW; MSc (Social Services Management). **Awards/Research** Res/Auth: Young people's experience of abuse in public care (pub early 1995). Making care systems work. **Media Experience** Various TV & Press interviews/articles.

ROBERTSON Sue Director **ONE PARENT FAMILIES SCOTLAND** SOCIAL Type: Service provider. 13 Gayfield Square, Edinburgh EH1 3NX Tel:0131-556 3899 **Expertise** Project management; service development; legal welfare and housing rights of single parents. **Prev Posts** Co-ordinator, Scottish Womens Aid 1978-83; Training officer, Scottish Council for Single Parents 1983-88. **Prof Background** BA Politics and Economics, Oxford University; MSoc Sc African Studies, Birmingham University. **Pres Committees** National Cttee, Cairn Housing Assoc. **Pres Committees** Extensive experience of press, radio and TV interviews.

ROBERTSON Sue Chief Executive **LONDON ARTS BOARD** ARTS Type: Grant maker. Elme House, 133 Long Acre, London WC2E 9AF Tel:0171-240 1313 Fax:0171-240 4580 **Expertise** Arts education, funding & administration. **Prev Posts** Senior Education Officer, Arts Council of Great Britain 1983-86; Director, Education Programmes, South Bank Centre 1986-92; Executive Director, Southern Arts Board 1993-96. **Prof Background** BA (Hons) English & Related Literature, York University 1971-74; P.G.C.E. University of Nottingham 1974-75; Dip. Arts Administration, City University 1979-80. **Pres Committees** Sits on numerous committees. **Past Committees** Wide range of committees.

ROBINSON Roger Director **ARTSLINE** DISABILITY Type: Fundraiser; Service provider; Campaigning, Access for disabled people to arts. 54 Chalton St, London, NW1 1HS Tel:0171-388 2460 Fax:0171-383 2653 **Expertise** Fundraising, Campaigning, Representing at Government level. **Prev Posts** Labour Party Head office, Head of Admin & Personnel 1976-87; Fedn of Master Builders, Director of Industrial Relations 1987-89. **Prof Background** Fellow of Institute of Personnel Development (FIPD); JP. **Awards/Research** Auth several guides to: Recruitment & selection, Health & Safety at work, Retirement. **Pres Committees** Adv Cttee, Access for Disabled People to the Arts (Shadow Min for Disab People); Capital Access Cttee; Vol Action Camden; Gov, Ruskin Coll; Adv Cttee, Tate Gallery Access; Bd/Treas, Graeae Theatre Co. **Past Committees** Exec Cttee, London Vol Service Cncl; Adv Cncl, Nat Campaign for the Arts; Mbr, Ind Tribunals Eng & Wales; Camden Cncl School Gov. **Media Experience** Represented Artsline on TV and in local & national media. **Addits** Sec/Trustee, Robert Addy Hopkinson Educational Trust; Exec Cttee NACVS.

ROBINSON Steve Chief Executive **ENVIRONMENT COUNCIL** ENVIRONMENT Type: Fundraiser; Service provider; Environmental solutions through consensus building. 21 Elizabeth St, London SW1W 9RP Tel:0171-824 8411 Fax:0171-730 9941 **Prof Background** MSc Management Studies; BSc; Diploma Fisheries Management. **Pres Committees** IUCN, World Conservation Union, Commission on Environmental

Strategies & Planning; Dept of the Environmental Action Fund Grants Panel; Capel Manor Horticultural & Environmental Centre. **Media Experience** Some experience in radio, TV, video and press.

ROBSON Derek Education Secretary/Chief Executive **METHODIST CHURCH** RELIGIOUS Type: Service provider; Grant maker. Methodist Colleges & Schools, 25 Marylebone Road London NW1 5JP Tel:0171-935 3723 Fax:0171-224 0702 **Expertise** Educational administration & advice. **Prev Posts** Headmaster, Culford School, Bury St. Edmunds 1971-92; Senior Lecturer & Warden, City of Leeds & Carnegie College. **Prof Background** M.A. (Cantab); P.G.C.E.. **Pres Committees** Governor of 14 schools & 2 Higher Education colleges; Number of ecumenical church committees; G.B.A. Executive. **Past Committees** H.M.C. **Media Experience** Experience in local radio & regional TV.

ROBSON Howard Training Director **MOBILITY AID AND GUIDE DOG ALLIANCE - MAGDA** DISABILITY Type: Fundraiser; Service provider. 1 Palmer Road, Carlisle CA2 7NE Tel:01228-39523 **Expertise** Training guide dogs and blind people in their use and care. Social work with the visually impaired. **Prev Posts** Guide dog mobility instructor, GDBA 1955-1965; Social Worker for the blind 1965-1980; Guide dog mobility instructor and training director 1980-today. **Prof Background** MA; B.Ed; Dip SW; CQSW. **Awards/Research** Churchill Fellow - GSM (Malaya). Author of books and articles on guide dog training and on social work with the blind. **Pres Committees** Mobility of the Blind Association; Institute of Military, Police and Civilian Dog Trainers (IMPACDT). **Past Committees** National Association of Orientation and Mobility Instructors (NAOMI). **Media Experience** Contributor to local radio, TV and press.

ROE Jane Campaign Manager **ABORTION LAW REFORM ASSOCIATION - ALRA** SOCIAL Type: Pressure group. 11-13 Charlotte St, London W1P 1HD Tel:0171-637 7264 **Expertise** Campaigning on abortion law and services. **Prev Posts** Information officer, Birth Control Trust. Currently Co-ordinator, Pro-Choice Alliance (umbrella group of organizations favouring liberal abortion laws). **Prof Background** Journalism and public relations. **Pres Committees** Steering committee, Pro-Choice Alliance; Executive committee, ALRA.

ROGERS Alison Director **BRITISH LIVER TRUST** MEDICAL/HEALTH Type: Fundraiser; Service provider; Grant maker; Campaigning. Central House, Central Ave, Ransomes Europark, Ipswich IP3 9QG Tel:01473-276326 Fax:01473-276327 **Expertise** General Management, Fundraising, Financial. **Prev Posts** Thorndike Theatre 1988-89; Sail Training Association 1989-92. **Prof Background** BA Hons English Lit & Lang; MA Women in Literature; Trainee chartered accountant. **Media Experience** Radio, TV, Video, press experience.

ROGERS Fergus J. Director **NATIONAL ANKYLOSING SPONDYLITIS SOCIETY - NASS** MEDICAL/HEALTH Type: Fundraiser; Service provider; Grant maker; Education of patients. 3 Grosvenor Crescent, London SW1X 7ER Tel:0171-235 9585 Fax:0171-235 5827 **Prev Posts** Accountant: 10 years in company management; 10 years with own small business financial advisory service. Joined NASS in 1980. **Prof Background** Management Advisory Accountant; suffered from ankylosing spondylitis since 1960. **Awards/Research** Several on the society - ed: NASS newsletter;Illustrator/Jt ed: A Guidebook for Patients; Fight Back physiotherapy video; section ed: Jnl of Medical Biography. **Pres Committees** President, National Ankylosing Spondylitis International Federation (ASIF); Mbr, Brit League Against Rheumatism Bd; Wking Cttee on AS treatment, Chartered Soc of Physiotherapists. **Media Experience** Numerous TV/radio appearances in 6 countries.

ROGERS Patricia Shepheard Director **COUNCIL FOR EDUCATION IN WORLD CITIZENSHIP** SOCIAL Type: Service provider; Education. Weddel House, 13 West Smithfield, London EC1A 9HY Tel:0171-329 1711 Fax:0171-329 1712 **Expertise** Education for international understanding and citizenship; mathematics education. **Prev Posts** UK Co-ordinator, Council of Europe N-S Campaign 1987-1988; Press Officer, Sight Savers 1989-1990. **Prof Background** MA (Hons Cantab); PGCE (London). **Awards/Research** Sand Harvest, computer simulation of life in a Sahel village for 14+; Water Game, educat computer simulation on the use and supply of water; Let's Visit South Korea; many articles. **Pres Committees** UNICEF-UK Ctte; All Party Group on Overseas Development; Trustee, Int Broadcasting Trust; Trustee, Dev Ed Assoc; UK UNESCO SO Cttee; Adv Bd, Safer World; UNA (Tun Wells). **Past Committees** Founder/Dir 1981-85 CWDE (Worldaware) computer mats prog.Chair, UK Cncl of Europe N-S quadrilogue; Local Gov Int Bureau. **Media Experience** Radio mathematics programme for OU; presenter, 50 Eng-lang Korean TV progs. **Addits** Lived/taught/wrote for some years in Nigeria, Pakistan & South Korea.

ROPER Rev Geoffrey H General Secretary **FREE CHURCH FEDERAL COUNCIL** RELIGIOUS Type: 27 Tavistock Square, London WC1H 9HH Tel:0171-387 8413 Fax:0171-383 0150 **Expertise** United Reformed Minister. **Prev Posts** Minister, Trinity, Ifield, Crawley 1965-71; Streatham 1971-78; Seaford 1978-85; Christ Church Chelmsford 1985-95. **Prof Background** MA, Magdalen & Mansfield Colleges, Oxford. **Past Committees** Secretary, United Reformed Church Deployment Committee 1978-84.

ROSE D. Michael Admin-Trustee/Solicitor **MACKINTOSH FOUNDATION, THE** ARTS Type: Grant maker; Privately funded foundation. Watchmaker Court, 33 St John's Lane, London EC1M 4DB Tel:0171-405 2000 Fax:0171-814 9421 **Expertise** Admin & Legal Affairs Trustee; Specialist in theatre & entertainment law. **Prof Background** Solicitor LL.B Hons, London; solicitor to Sir Cameron Mackintosh and his group of companies 1977 to date. **Awards/Research** Various articles on theatre law and practice; Regular columnist in 'The Stage'; Seminar speaker. **Pres Committees** Chairman, Allied Cavendish Properties Ltd 1985 to date. Chairman of Trustees, The Charles Green Settlement. Partner in Tarlo Lyons (solicitors) - Head of Ent Law Unit in Media & Comms Dept. **Media Experience** Columnist in various theatre related journals and books. **Addits** Firm is rated No 1 in theatre law in current edition of The Legal 500.

ROSE Howard Administrator **YORKSHIRE CHILDREN'S HOSPITAL TRUST** CHILDREN/YOUTH Type: Fundraiser, Grant maker. Croft House, Earswick Village, Earswick, York YO3 9SL Tel:01904-750334 Fax:01904-766346 **Expertise** Voluntary group development; fundraising; marketing; training; PR. **Prev Posts** District Sales and Marketing Manager, 1980-90; N Sales Manager, 1990; Senior Management Consultant 1990-91; National Group Development Manager, Research Into Ageing. **Prof Background** Member: Institute of Charity Fundraising Managers (ICFM); Institute of Management (MIMgt); Fellow, Institute of Sales and Marketing Management (FInstSMM). **Pres Committees** Chair, Yorks Branch Inst. of Charity Fundraising Managers; Adviser, ARP/O5O. **Past Committees** National Cttee, Round Table; Chair, Arthritis and Rheumatism Council (Coventry).

ROSIE Morag Director **FRIENDS FOR YOUNG DEAF PEOPLE - FYD** DISABILITY Type: Fundraiser, Service provider. Head Office, East Court Mansion, Council Offices, College Lane, East Grinstead, Sussex RH19 3LT Tel:01342-323444 Fax:01342-410232 **Expertise** Deaf since birth; leadership and training, inc. employment training/communication. **Prev Posts** Director of FYD since 1979. **Awards/Research** MBE; FRSA. **Pres Committees** Trustee, Deaf-Tel; Employers' Forum for Disability; Changing the Attitudes Group; Sports Council, Youth and Sports Forum; ACENVO; NCVO, Training and Education Group. **Past Committees** Surrey CC Vol Orgs; Duke of Edinburgh Awd Scheme; Nat Adv Cncl and Youth Serv; Brit Sports Assoc for the Disab; ILEA Youth Serv. **Media Experience** TV, video and press participation.

ROSS Andrew Chief Executive **CHILDREN'S TRUST** MEDICAL/HEALTH Type: Fundraiser; Service provider. Tadworth Court, Tadworth, Surrey KT20 5RU Tel:01737-357171 Fax:01737-373848 **Prev Posts** Director of Marketing, The Spastics Society 1982-88; Director, Birthright 1988-92. **Prof Background** Sevenoaks School, 1959-64; MA Modern Languages, Emmanuel College, Cambridge; MBA, INSEAD, Fontainebleau; Fellow, Institute of Charity Fundraising Managers. **Pres Committees** Chair, Standards Cttee ICFM; Trustee, The Generation Trust for Paediatric Research, Guys Hospital. **Past Committees** Exec Cttee, ICFM (Chair/Hon Treas); Exec Cncl, Assoc of Medical Research Charities; Mbr, Cncl for Charitable Support.

ROTH Mr R.P.B. Charity Secretary **ARCHITECTS BENEVOLENT SOCIETY** SOCIAL Type: Grant maker. 66 Portland Place, London W1N 4AD Tel:0171-580 2823 Fax:0171-580 7075 **Expertise** Overall administration. **Prev Posts** Company Secretary, Plantations 1960-82. **Prof Background** MA; FCIS. **Awards/Research** Awds: General Service Medal (Cyprus).

ROWLANDSON Dr Piers H. Consultant Paediatrician & Director **DAVID HIDE ASTHMA & ALLERGY RESEARCH CENTRE** MEDICAL/HEALTH Type: Service provider; Research. St. Mary's Hospital, Newport, Isle of Wight PO30 5TG Tel:01983-524081 Fax:01983-822928 **Expertise** Child health: Asthma & Allergy. **Prev Posts** Lecturer in Child Health, Cardiff 1983-88; Consultant Paediatrician, Swindon 1988-95. **Prof Background** Guy's Hospital Medical School; Great Ormond Street; Oxford. **Awards/Research** Fellow of the Royal College of Physicians; Research in the area of general paediatrics. **Pres Committees** Trustee of the David Hide Asthma & Allergy Research Centre; Education Committee (Wessex Child Health). **Media Experience** Experience with radio, TV, video and press.

RUANE Gloria Secretary/Treasurer **INTERNATIONAL BILLIARDS & SNOOKER FEDERATION** SPORTS Type: Professional association. House of Sport, Longmile Road, Dublin 12, Ireland Tel:3531-4509850 Fax:3531-4502805 **Expertise** Billiards & Snooker; administration & refereeing. **Awards/Research** Rules of Billiards & Snooker 1995. **Pres Committees** Republic of Ireland Billiards & Snooker Association.

RUSSELL Andrew Executive Director **SPINA BIFIDA AND HYDROCEPHALUS, ASSOCIATION FOR - ASBAH** DISABILITY Type: Service provider; Research. ASBAH House, 42 Park Road, Peterborough, Cambridge PE1 2UQ Tel:01733-555988 Fax:01733-555985 **Expertise** Service management and development. **Prev Posts** Divisional General Manager, Eastern Division, Royal MENCAP 1985-91. **Prof Background** MA (Cantab) Natural Sciences and English.

RUSTON George Executive Director **HOPE UK** MEDICAL/HEALTH Type: Service provider. 25(F) Copperfield Street, London SE1 0EN Tel:0171-928 0848 Fax:0171-401 3477 **Expertise** Management, policy training, international liaison. **Prev Posts** Community Unit Administration, Islington Health Authority 1982-85. **Prof Background** BSc (Hons) Geography, Bristol University 1974; Health Service management 1974-85. **Awards/Research** Auth: Alcohol and Other Drugs. **Pres Committees** Int Blue Cross Federation; Sec, Prevention Commission and Euro Union Co-ordinating Gp.

RYAN Alison Director **HORTICULTURAL THERAPY** MEDICAL/HEALTH Type: Service provider. Goulds Ground, Vallis Way, Frome, Somerset BA11 3DW Tel:01373-464782 Fax:01373-464782 **Expertise** General management; horticultural therapy and elderly people. **Prev Posts** Deputy Commercial Director, Atomic Energy Establishment, Winfrith, Dorset 1979-85. **Prof Background** MA (Oxon) Philosophy, Politics and Economics; MIMgt. **Awards/Research** Auth: Gardening & Elderly People, 1992; EEC Conf Address 1987 - Environment et handicap, une Realite; Conf Paper: Horticultural Therapy in a Community Context, 1994. **Pres Committees** Chair, Institute of Management, Bath/SW region. **Media Experience** Frequent radio interviews: local and Radio 4; articles in national/local press.

RYDER Lady Ryder of Warsaw Founder **SUE RYDER FOUNDATION, THE** DISABILITY Type: Fundraiser; Service provider; Caring for sick and disabled in UK and overseas. Sue Ryder Home and Headquarters, Cavendish, Sudbury, Suffolk CO10 8AY Tel:01787-280252 Fax:01787-280548 **Expertise** Disability; the elderly; cancer (terminal/convalescent); Huntington's Disease; MS Motor Neurone Disease. **Prev Posts** Served with Polish Section of the Highly Secret Special Operations Executive

1940-45. **Prof Background** Benenden School. Brit Univ Hon Degrees: LL.D: Liverpool 1973; Exeter 1980; London 1981; Leeds 1984; Kent 1986; Cambridge 1989. D.Litt Reading 1982; Doctor of University, Essex 1993. **Awards/Research** OBE 1957; Companion of the Order of St Michael and St George 1976; Baroness Ryder of Warsaw in Poland 1978. Order of Smile (Poland) 1980. Auth: Child of My Love. **Pres Committees** Foundation's Council and variety of other committees in connection with the work. **Media Experience** All branches of the media at various times, and Remembrance (Foundation jnl). **Addits** Awds:Poland, Yugo inc Pol. Golden Ord Merit '76,Cmdrs X Ord Pol Restit '92.

RYDER Michael James Chairman **MUSICAL MUSEUM** Type: Service provider. 368 High Street, Brentford, Middx TW8 0BD Tel:0181-560 8108 **Expertise** Accounting and Management. **Prof Background** Accountant; University Lecturer; Civil Servant; MPhil; F.C.A. **Awards/Research** Various. **Media Experience** Several Radio & TV interviews.

S

SAKNE Allan Business Manager **BRITISH PSYCHOLOGICAL SOCIETY** MEDICAL/HEALTH Type: Service provider; Learned Society. St. Andrews House, 48 Princess Road East, Leicester LE1 7DR Tel:0116-2549568 Fax:0116-2470787 **Expertise** Management of voluntary groups. **Prev Posts** Technical Director, Davlan Electronics Ltd 1965-73; Managing Director, Merilect Ltd 1973- 6. **Prof Background** Electronics Systems Analysis (MSc), Distribution Management, General Management. **Pres Committees** Director of Associate Companies. **Past Committees** Royal Society of Arts Information Technology Committee (Chair); YTS Certification Board. **Media Experience** Mainly print.

SALAMON Esther Co-Director **ARTISTS' AGENCY** ARTS Type: Service provider. 18 Norfolk St, Sunderland, Tyne & Wear SR1 1EA Tel:0191-5109318 Fax:0191-5652846 **Expertise** Arts Administration (organising artists' residencies in social settings). **Prev Posts** Community worker, Gateshead Libraries & Arts Dept 1980-83; Project worker, The Bridges Project 1983-87; Artists' Agency 1987- **Prof Background** Newcastle Polytechnic; Michigan State University. **Awards/Research** Articles in Artists' Newsletter and 'Mailout' arts journals; Chapters in /Sniffing Solutions\publ by Nat Children's Bureau, /Art with People\publ by AN Publ amongst others. **Pres Committees** Board member: AN Publications, South Tyneside Arts Studio and Committee Member of North Tyneside Art Studio. **Media Experience** Various interviews/features in national and local TV and press.

SALLEY Sylvia Administrator **INTERNATIONAL BLACK WOMEN FOR WAGES FOR HOUSEWORK** SOCIAL Type: Campaigning. Crossroads Womens Centre, PO Box 287, London NW6 5QU Tel:0171-482 2496 Fax:0171-209 4761 .

SANDBROOK J. Richard Executive Director **INTERNATIONAL INSTITUTE FOR ENVIRONMENT AND DEVELOPMENT - IIED** CONSERVATION/ENVIRONMENT Type: Service provider; Development. 3 Endsleigh Street, London WC1H 0DD Tel:0171-388 2117 Fax:0171-388 2826 **Expertise** Institutional development; environment; development. **Prev Posts** Director, FOE Ltd 1974-75; Programme Director, IIED 1976-85; Dep Director IIED 1985-89. **Prof Background** BSc Biological Sciences; Fellow of Institute of Chartered Accountants. **Awards/Research** Various publications; Global 500 Award; OBE. **Pres Committees** FOE Trust; Earthscan Publications Ltd. **Past Committees** British delegation to Earthsummit, OECD. Development Assistance Committee (Environment Working Group); various international boards. **Media Experience** Radio, TV and press interviews.

SARWAR Ghulam Director **MUSLIM EDUCATIONAL TRUST** RELIGIOUS Type: Service provider; Educational. 130 Stroud Green Road, London N4 3RZ Tel:0171-272 8502 Fax:0171-281 3457 **Expertise** Education; relief; community work. **Prev Posts** Lecturer in Business Management for 1st degree students 1966-69. **Prof Background** B.Comm (Hons) & M. Comm in Management; Fellow, Royal Society of Arts. **Awards/Research** Islam - Beliefs and Teachings; The Children's Book of Salah; British Muslims and Schools; Sex Education - The Muslim Perspective. **Pres Committees** Trustee, Muslim Aid and International Council for Islamic Information (ICII). **Past Committees** Treasurer, Vice-Chairman (Admin & Finance); Trustee, Islamia Schools Trust. **Media Experience** Panorama, 1984; numerous radio, TV and newspaper interviews.

SAUMAREZ SMITH Charles Robert Director **NATIONAL PORTRAIT GALLERY** ARTS Type: Service provider; Educational. St Martin's Place, London WC2H 0HE Tel:0171-306 0055 Fax:0171-306 0064 **Prev Posts** Christie's Research Fellow In Applied Arts, Christ's College Cambridge 1979-82. V&A: Asst Keeper, V&A/RCA MA Course in History of Design 1982-90, Head of Research 1990-94. **Prof Background** BA Camb (1st cl. History of Art) 1972-1976; Henry Fellow, Harvard Univ. 1977; PhD Warburg Institute 1978-1986. **Awards/Research** Auth: The Building of Castle Howard 1990; Eighteenth-Century Decoration: Design and the Domestic Interior in England, 1993. **Pres Committees** London Library 1992-today. Trustee: Soane Monuments Trust 1988-today; Charleston 1993-today. **Past Committees** Design History Soc 1985-89; Soc of Architectural Historians 1987-90; Assoc of Art Historians 1990-94.

SAUNDERS Matthew Secretary **ANCIENT MONUMENTS SOCIETY** CONSERVATION/ENVIRONMENT Type: Service provider; Statutory Consultee. St Ann's Vestry Hall, Church Entry, London EC4V 5HB Tel:0171-236 3934 Fax:0171-329 3677 **Expertise** Architectural conservation and history. **Prev Posts** Secretary, SAVE Britain's Heritage 1975-77. **Prof Background** History and History of Architecture, Cambridge Univ. **Awards/Research** Auth:Historic Home Owners Companion, 87;Biog of SS Teulon, architect;Chapter:Railway Architecture (ed M. Binney);Jt Auth: Banking on Change, Current Account of Britain's Historic Bank **Pres Committees** Hon Dir, Friends of Friendless Churches; Sec, Jt Cttee of the National Amenity Socs; Trustee, Historic Chapels Trust; Mbr, Places of Worship Cttee, Heritage Lottery Fund; V-Pres, Ecclesiological Soc.

SAVILL Rosalind Joy Director **WALLACE COLLECTION** ARTS Type: Art gallery. Hertford House, Manchester Square, W1M 6BN Tel:0171-935 0687 Fax:0171-224 2155 **Prev Posts** Ceramics Dept V&A Mus, 1973-74; The Wallace Collection Mus Asst 1974-78; Asst to Dir 1978 -92. **Prof Background** BA Hons Univ of Leeds 1972; Study Centre London Dip in Fine & Decorative Arts 1973. **Awards/Research** FSA 1990, FRSA 1990, Nat Art Colls Award Schol 1990. Treas Houses of Brit 1985; Boughton Hse 1992; Versailles:tables royales 1993 (all contrib); Wllce Coll Cat Sevres Porcelain 1988. **Pres Committees** Member National Trust Arts Panel 1995-; Governor, Camden School for Girls, 1996-. **Past Committees** Mbr Cncl Attingham Trust 1980-92; Chair French Porcelain Soc 1988-94.

SAYER Su Chief Executive/Co-Founder **UNITED RESPONSE** DISABILITY Type: Service provider. 113-23, Upper Richmond Road, London SW15 2SL Tel:0181-780 9686 Fax:0181-780 9538 **Expertise** Governance; management; strategic planning; health and safety; voluntary sector issues. **Prev Posts** ICI Fibres (marketing); with United Response since 1973. **Prof Background** BSc Chemical Physics; FRSA; Fellow, Royal Soc of Health. Scholarships: (USA) Loss Control Management; Accredited Safety Auditors; Runner Up, Women Mean Business 1993. **Awards/Research** Auth: Playing Safe; Health and Safety Handbook for Residential Care Homes. Awds: Safety Officer of Year, RoSPA 1987; Runner Up, Insight Manager of Year 1990. **Pres Committees** ACENVO Mngmnt & Governance Task Force; Soc Servs Inspectorate Mngmt Dev Gp; Chair, Dev Cttee, Southern Housing Gp; Dir, Assoc for Residential Care; Trustee, Community Network. **Past Committees** Chair, ACENVO; Dir, Lifecare Charitable Trust; Trustee, Roy Kinnear Trust; Wkng Pty, Planning for Partnership. **Media Experience** Radio and Press; some TV. **Addits** Previously Chair, Wking Pty, A Partnership in Caring.

SCARISBRICK Prof J.J. Hon. National Chairman & Trustee **LIFE** MEDICAL/HEALTH Type: Service provider; Membership organisation. Life House, Newbold Terrace, Leamington Spa, Warks CV32 4EA Tel:01926-421587 Fax:01926-336497 **Expertise** Pro-life action and care. **Prev Posts** Co-founder of LIFE, First National Chairman since 1970 (to date). **Prof Background** Emeritus professor of History, University of Warwick. **Awards/Research** Booklets, leaflets, position papers on pro-life issues. **Pres Committees** Chairman/Trustee, LIFE Hospital Trust. **Past Committees** Opened 1st LIFE Health Centre, Liverpool summer 1994, inc. Zoe's Place (hospice for babies up to 4 yrs old). **Media Experience** Regular media exposure over the period 1970 to present.

SCHAFFER Carol Chief Executive **KITH AND KIDS** CHILDREN/YOUTH Type: Self help group. c/o Haringey Irish Centre, Pretoria Rd, London N17 8DX Tel:0181-801 7432 **Expertise** Meeting needs of people with a learning disability. **Prof Background** Teacher/Therapist/Advocacy.

SCHLUTER Michael Dr Director **RELATIONSHIPS FOUNDATION** SOCIAL Type: Research/practical initiatives in social policy. Jubilee House, 3 Hooper Street, Cambridge CB1 2NZ Tel:01223-566333 Fax:01223-566359 **Expertise** International Economic Development and British Social Policy. **Prev Posts** Consultant, Eastern Africa Division, World Bank 1979-85; Research Director, Newick Park Initiative 1986-91; Director, Keep Sunday Special Campaign 1985-95. **Prof**

Background PhD Agricultural Economics, Cornell University , USA, 1973; BA Economies and Economic History, Durham University, 1968. **Awards/Research** The R Factor, Hodder and Stoughton 1993; Contributor to Relational Justice, Waterside Press 1994; Keeping Sunday Special, Marshall Pickering, 1987. **Media Experience** Extensive: radio, TV, press.

SCHOFIELD Mrs C. Director **CHILDREN'S COUNTRY HOLIDAYS FUND** CHILDREN/YOUTH Type: Service provider. 42/3 Lower Marsh, London SE1 7RG Tel:0171-928 6522 Fax:0171-401 3961

SCOTHERN Mark Director **CRISIS** SOCIAL Type: Fundraiser; Service provider; Grant maker; Research agency. 7 Whitechapel Road, London E1 1DU Tel:0171-377 0489 Fax:0171-247 1525 **Expertise** Expert knwldge servs for single homeless people, emphasis innovative schemes & research, effects of leg. **Prev Posts** Co-ordinator, Thamesdown Housing Link 1985-88; Campaign Wkr, CHAR (Housing Campaign for Single People) 1987-90. **Prof Background** A-levels; studied Theology at Heythrop College, London University. **Awards/Research** Occasional papers for CHAR on single homelessness issues, contributor to housing press. **Pres Committees** Trustee, Empty Homes Agency (re-use of empty properties); DoH Interdeptal Working Grp on Tuberculosis; Gateway Ed Trust; ACENVO Bd. **Past Committees** DSS Advisory Steering Group; NFHA Homelessness Working Party. **Media Experience** Interviewee for most current affairs programmes. **Addits** Interested in effective, good quality services for single homeless people.

SCOTT David Michael Director **ALMSHOUSE ASSOCIATION** SOCIAL Type: Fundraiser; Service provider; Grant maker. Advisory body, non statutory. Billingbear Lodge, Wokingham, Berks RG11 5RU Tel:01344-52922 Fax:01344-862062 **Expertise** Administration of almshouses housing corporation procedures. **Prev Posts** District Manager, Gateway Building Society 1970-75. **Prof Background** Banking; building societies; professional fundraising with Wells Management Consultant. **Awards/Research** Auth: Standards of Almshouse Management. Ed: Almshouses Quarterly Magazine. Awds: Cross of Merit from Sovereign Military Order of Malta 1989. **Pres Committees** Brd of Mngmt, Servite Houses Housing Assoc. Trustee: Order of Malta Homes Trust; Orders of St John Trust; Centre for Sheltered Housing Studies. **Past Committees** DoE, Housing Assoc Grant Working Gp; Age Concern England, Wking Pty on Sheltered Housing; Exec Cttee, Assoc of Landowning Charities. **Media Experience** Local & national radio interviews on almshouse history. Previously on Brd of Mngmt, Salvation Army Housing Assoc.

SCOTT Dr Gordon Chair of Board **SCOT-PEP** MEDICAL/HEALTH Type: Service provider. 21a Torphichen Street, Edinburgh EH3 8HX Tel:0131-229 8269 **Expertise** Sexual health in prostitution. **Prev Posts** Consultant Physician & Head of Department, Genito-Urinary Medicine, Edinburgh Royal Infirmary 1988 to date. **Prof Background** Medicine: BSc 1976;MBCHB 1979; MRCP 1984; FRCP 1993. **Awards/Research** Outreach STD Clinics For Prostitutes In Edinburgh; Contrib: International Journal of STD and AIDS 1995. **Media Experience** Experience in radio, TV, video & press.

SCOTT Mrs Hannah Secretary/Administrator **AIREY NEAVE TRUST** SOCIAL Type: Grant maker. House of Commons, London SW1A 0AA Tel:0171-495 0554 Fax:0171-491 1118 **Expertise** Administration; accountancy; short-listing of candidates. **Prev Posts** Personal Assistant 1960-64; Company Secretary/Director since 1964. **Prof Background** RSA Certificates in commercial studies. **Pres Committees** Airey Neave Trust: Advisory Cttee, Refugee Sub-Cttee, Refugee Vetting Cttee.

SCOTT Jackie Chief Executive **DEAFBLIND UK** DISABILITY Type: Fundraiser; Service provider; Grant maker; Advisory body; Campaigning. 100 Bridge St, Peterborough PE1 1DY Tel:01733-358100 Fax:01733-358356 **Expertise** Communications; management of change; marketing; youth; publishing; developing grant schemes/awards. **Prev Posts** Assistant Director (Communications), National Youth Agency 1991-1993; Programme Director, National Youth Agency 1993-1994. **Prof Background** Journalism. **Awards/Research** CRE Race in the Media Awds: 1993 runner-up (specialist magazine), 1994 Winner Special Youth Awd. Editor, Young People Now Magazine 1989-94. Editor/writer, Youth in Society. **Pres Committees** RNIB Executive. **Past Committees** Steerg Cttee Whitbread Vol Action Awards; Vol Task Gp, European Year of Older People; Leics. Careers & Guidance Service. **Media Experience** Journalist for 8 years; managed press activity for Youth Work Week; radio.

SCOTT Judith Margaret Chief Executive **BRITISH COMPUTER SOCIETY - BCS** Type: Professional Association 1 Sanford Street, Swindon, Wilts SN1 1HJ Tel:01793-417417 Fax:01793-480270 **Expertise** Information Systems. **Prev Posts** Director Product Mktg, Gandalf Technologies 1980-84; Director Corporate Planning, Gandalf Technologies 1984-87; Managing Director, Gandalf Digital Comms Ltd 1987-95. **Prof Background** BSc Mathematics; Diploma in Computer Science; CEng FBCS. **Pres Committees** BCS Policy & Resources Cttee; BCS Finance & Ops Cttee; Board of Govs, Ranelagh School, Bracknell. **Past Committees** Office Systems Interchange Cncl; Canada/UK Chamber of Commerce. **Media Experience** Press interviews - technical press.

SCOTT Sheila Chief Executive **NATIONAL CARE HOMES ASSOCIATION - NCHA** Type: Campaigning, Professional Association. 5 Bloomsbury Place, London WC1A 2QA Tel:0171-436 1871 Fax:0171-436 1193 **Expertise** Community Care - Social Security, Registered Homes Act. **Prev Posts** Director of Nursing 1973-83; Proprietor, Residential Care Hotels 1983-87. **Prof Background** State Registered Nurse. **Pres Committees** Member, Registered Hotels tribunal Panel. **Past Committees** Member, Dept of Health Community Care Support Force. **Media Experience** Experience: TV, radio, video, press.

SCOTT Vanda Director General **BEFRIENDERS INTERNATIONAL** SOCIAL Type: Service provider;

Campaigning, Umbrella Organisation. 23 Elysium Gate, 126 New Kings Rd, London SW6 4LZ Tel:0171-731 0101 Fax:0171-731 8008 **Expertise** Organisational Development; Suicide Prevention. **Prof Background** MSc (Econ) in Social Policy & Administration. **Awards/Research** Role of Volunteers in preventing suicide (in Crisis Journal). **Past Committees** London School of Economics Alumni Association; International Association for Suicide Prevention. **Media Experience** TV/press/radio interviews: HK/India/Sri Lanka/UK/Singapore/N Zealand/Poland.

SENIOR Peter Director **ARTS FOR HEALTH** MEDICAL/HEALTH Type: Service provider. Manchester Metropolitan University, All Saints, Oxford Road, Manchester M15 6BY Tel:0161-236 8916 Fax:0161-247 6390 **Expertise** Art and design. **Awards/Research** MBE. NACF Award. Publ: Helping to Heal - The Arts in Healthcare. **Pres Committees** Chairman, Partnership Art Ltd (Environmental Arts Organisation). **Past Committees** Attenborough Committee of Enquiry; Advisor to ACGB % for Art Committee.

SHAFIK D.J. Chief Executive **KEYCHANGE** RELIGIOUS Type: Service provider. Head Office, 5 St George's Mews, 43 Westminster Bridge Rd, London SE1 7JB Tel:0171-633 0533 Fax:0171-928 1872 **Prev Posts** Joint Managing Director, Construction Company. **Prof Background** Quantity Surveyor; Associate, Guild of Surveyors; Member, Institute of Management.

SHARP Imogen Director **NATIONAL HEART FORUM** MEDICAL/HEALTH Type: Service provider; Health Alliance. Tavistock House South, Tavistock Square, London WC1H 9LG Tel:0171-383 7638 Fax:0171-387 2799 **Expertise** Health Policy, Health Promotion, Coalitions. **Prev Posts** University Teacher, Behavioural Sciences, Univ Hong Kong 1983-87; Assist Editor, Eurasia Media Publ 1982-83. **Prof Background** BSc (Hons) Human Sciences, Univ of Sussex; MSc Health Planning & Financing, Univ of London; Hon Lecturer, Public Health & Policy, Univ of London. **Awards/Research** Publ incl - Physical Activity: An Agenda for Action 1995; Coronary Heart Disease: Are Women Special? 1994; Food for Children, 1994; Nutritional Guidelines for School Meals, 1992. **Pres Committees** Chair, Tobacco Control Alliance; Secretary, School Meals Campaign. **Past Committees** Chair, HK Cncl of Women; HM Gov Cttee on Health of the Nation; Workplace Task Force; Nutrition Task Force Project Teams. **Media Experience** Radio/TV/Press on Health policy issues, various articles. **Addits** Previously: Physical Activity Task Force Sub Gp.

SHARP Les Secretary **BRITISH ACTIVITY HOLIDAY ASSOCIATION - BAHA** SOCIAL Type: Service provider. Orchard Cottage, 22 Green Lane, Hersham, Walton-on-Thames, Surrey KT12 5HD Tel:01932-252994 Fax:01932-252994 **Expertise** Administration. **Prev Posts** Percival Tours: Manager, London Office 1975-85; Managing Director 1985-91. **Prof Background** 40 years practical experience in various aspects of the travel business.

SHAW Charles General Secretary **COMMUNITY AND YOUTH WORK ASSOCIATION - YDA** CHILDREN/YOUTH Type: Service provider; Grant maker; Professional Association for Youth Workers. c/o Oldham CVYS, 122 Rochdale Road, Oldham OL1 1NT Tel:01457-834943 **Expertise** Youth work, education & social welfare; insurance & financial services. **Prev Posts** Youth Service Develop Wkr, Oldham MBC 1974-80; Youth & Community Officer Tameside CRE 1981-84; Financial Planning Associate 1982-84; Financial Planner 1984-90. **Prof Background** Associate, College of Preceptors 1973, Cert, Youth & Community Work 1974; Post-Grad Dip Man. Studies CNAA 1983; Nat Dr 1988; Dr of Philos (HC) (OIUCM Sri Lanka) 1992.Fellow, Soc of Teach in Bus Educ. **Awards/Research** Numerous business and finance awards **Pres Committees** Chair, Insurance Inst Manchester Mktg Ctte; Regional Youth Service Unit NW Training Committee; Chair, NW Gp of Councils for Vol Youth Servs;Chair, Stalybridge & Hyde Constit; Chair, Mossley College. **Past Committees** Mbr: Comty Hlth Cncl 1980-81; Family Prac Ctte/Family HSA 1985-91; Oldham Silver Jubilee Cttee 1976-8. Chair: Youth Wk Consult Cttee **Media Experience** Local media; Radio debates. **Addits** Currently also Gen Sec, Oldham Coucil for Vol Youth Services.

SHAW Revd Michael Executive Director **JOHN GROOMS ASSOCIATION FOR DISABLED PEOPLE** DISABILITY Type: Fundraiser; Service provider. 50 Scrutton St, London EC2A 4PH Tel:0171-452 2000 Fax:0171-452 2001 **Expertise** Generalist. **Prev Posts** Team Vicar, Redcar and Kirkleatham 1974-76; Youth Officer, St Albans Diocese 1976-91. **Prof Background** Diploma in Adult Education, London University; Lichfield Theological College. **Awards/Research** Training games and exercises, Diocese of St Albans. **Pres Committees** Chairman, Prince's Trust, Herts; Chairman of Governors, Townsend Church of England School; Chair, Voluntary Organizations Disability Group. **Past Committees** MSC Manpower Area Board; General Synod Board of Education (Youth and Children); National Council for Voluntary Youth Services. **Media Experience** Blue Peter; Hooked on Kids; Radio 4. **Addits** Music and sailing.

SHAW Stephen Director **PRISON REFORM TRUST** SOCIAL Type: Service provider; Campaigning and information provision. 2nd Floor, The Old Trading House, 15 Northburgh Street, London EC1V 0AH Tel:0171-251 5070 Fax:0171-251 5076 **Expertise** Penal and criminal justice policy; economics. **Prev Posts** Lecturer, Mid-Kent College of Technology 1976-79; Research Officer, NACRO 1979-80; Research Officer, Home Office 1980-81. **Prof Background** BA (Hons) Economics and Politics; MA (Distinction) Economic History; PhD Economic and Social History. **Awards/Research** Many contrib to books and articles in journals. **Media Experience** Frequent media involvement.

SHEBBEARE Tom Executive Director **PRINCE'S TRUST AND THE ROYAL JUBILEE TRUSTS, THE** CHILDREN/YOUTH Type: Grant maker. 18 Park Square East, London NW1 4LH Tel:0171-543 1234 Fax:0171-543 1200 **Prev Posts** World University Service, 1973-75; British Youth Council 1975-80; Council of Europe 1980-88.

SHELLARD Maj-Gen M.F.L. Chief Executive **REGULAR FORCES EMPLOYMENT ASSOCIATION** SOCIAL Type: Service provider. 49 Pall Mall, London SW1Y 5JG Tel:0171-321 2011 Fax:0171-839 0970 **Expertise** Helping service-leavers with more than 3 years in the ranks and rates to find employment. **Prev Posts** Maj General, Royal Artillery 1989-92; Senior Defence Adviser, Shorts Missile Systems Ltd 1992-94. **Prof Background** Army Officer, commissioned from RMA Sandhurst 1957. **Awards/Research** CBE 1989 NYHL. **Pres Committees** Chairman, Royal Artillery Historical Affairs; Member, Army & Navy Club Committee (Finance); Governor, Queen's College Taunton.

SHELMERDINE David J. C. Chief Executive **SCOUT ASSOCIATION, SCOTTISH COUNCIL** Type: Fundraiser; Service provider; Youth Organisation Fordell Firs, Hillend, Dunfermline KY11 5HQ Tel:01383-419073 Fax:01383-414892 **Expertise** Exec responsibility for dev and implementation of policies and mgmt of the Assoc's affairs in Scotland. **Prev Posts** British Telecom 1966-78; Overseas Sec, The Scout Assoc London 1978-82; Assistant Director (Communications) World Scout Bureau, Geneva 1982-87. **Prof Background** BSc Physics; Fellow, Inst Personnel Dev. **Awards/Research** Being Young in Scotland (Scottish Cmty Ed Cncl) 1994; Cmty Ed & LAs - discussion paper 1995. **Pres Committees** Scott Youth Work Frm, Scott Cmty Ed Cncl; Chair, Dollar Cmty Cncl; Bd of Govs, Dollar Acad; Adv Cttee, Effectiveness of Youth Work with Vulnerable Young People. **Past Committees** Mgmt Cttee, Youth Link Scotland; Principal Cmty Ed Officers, Work with Young People Gp; Cmty Ed Working Party, Conv of Scottish LAs. **Media Experience** Radio, TV, Press interviews & Media Mgmt.

SHEPHERD Tony Chief Executive **OTTO SCHIFF HOUSING ASSOCIATION** Type: Service provider. Central Office, The Bishops Ave, London N2 0BG Tel:0181-209 0022 Fax:0181-201 8089 **Expertise** Providing care to the Refugee Jewish Community; Change Management; Residential Care. **Prev Posts** Senior General Manager/Chief Nurse, 1993-95; Hospital Director, 1988-1993; Hospital Gen Mngr, 1985-88. **Prof Background** Registered Nurse; Nurse Tutor. **Pres Committees** North London NHS Training Consortium. **Past Committees** Deputy Chair, London East AIDS Network. **Media Experience** Radio interviews and articles for professional journals.

SHEPPARD Major General Peter JF Controller **SOLDIERS', SAILORS' AND AIRMEN'S FAMILIES ASSOCIATION FORCES HELP - SSAFA FORCES HELP** SOCIAL Type: Fundraiser; Service provider. Queen Elizabeth, The Queen Mother House, 19 Queen Elizabeth Street, London SE1 2LP Tel:0171-403 8783 Fax:0171-403 8815 **Prev Posts** Distinguished service career, culminating as Chief of Staff, Headquarters Quartermaster General 1996. **Prof Background** Professional soldier. **Awards/Research** Awds: OBE 1982, CBE 1991, CB 1995. **Past Committees** Several during service career. **Media Experience** Some media experience.

SHERLOCK Maeve Executive Director **COUNCIL FOR INTERNATIONAL EDUCATION - UKCOSA** SOCIAL Type: Service provider; Education/International. 9-17 St Albans Place, London N1 0NX Tel:0171-226 3762 Fax:0171-226 3373 **Expertise** International education; student and academic mobility; broad, further and higher education. **Prev Posts** National Union of Students: Treasurer 1986-88, National President 1988-90. Dep Director, UKCOSA 1990-91. **Prof Background** BA (Hons) Sociology, Liverpool Univ.Fellow, RSA. Mbr: Court of Warwick Univ; Assembly of Greenwich Univ; Exec Bd of European Assoc for International Education. **Past Committees** Director, Endsleigh Insurance Services Ltd 1986-90; Editorial Advisory Board, New Socialist. **Media Experience** Frequent inc: Question Time, Any Questions, Today, Woman's Hour, Breakfast TV.

SHERRIFF Carol Director **CHILD ACCIDENT PREVENTION TRUST - CAPT** CHILDREN/YOUTH Type: Advocacy, research, child daycare/parents needs. Clerks Court, 18-20 Farringdon Lane, London EC1R 3AU Tel:0171-608 3828 Fax:0171-608 3674 **Expertise** Education and Training; Women in the Labour Market. **Prev Posts** Occupational Guidance Officer, Department of Employment 1977-80; Snr Policy Officer, TUC 1980-94; Director, Daycare Trust 1994-96. **Prof Background** BA(Hons) History and Politics **Awards/Research** Publ inc: Working in Partnership for Quality Training, 1993; Opportunities for All 1992; Positive Action Programmes for Women 1987; Women in the Labour Market, 1985. **Past Committees** Management Boards: The Further Education Staff College; Further Education Unit; Workbase Training; RSA Examinations Board. **Media Experience** Experienced on radio and television.

SHIMMON Ross Chief Executive **LIBRARY ASSOCIATION** ARTS Type: Professional Association. 7 Ridgmount St, London WC1E 7AE Tel:0171-636 7543 Fax:0171-436 7218 **Expertise** Promotion of high quality library and information services. **Prev Posts** Deputy Librarian, Preston Polytechnic, 1975-79; Head, Library Studies Section, Admin College of Papua New Guinea 1979-84; Dir, Prof Practice, The Library Assoc 1984-92. **Prof Background** Librarian **Awards/Research** Various articles in professional press; A reader in library management (editor), Clive Bingley 1976. **Pres Committees** Brit Library Adv Cnc; Bd of Library Assoc Publ; Brit Cncl Libraries Adv Cttee; Bd of Book Aid Int; Brd of Book Industry Communication; Nat Book Cttee. **Past Committees** Papua New Guinea Library Council; Papua New Guinea Book Development Council. **Media Experience** Frequent interviews on TV/local and national radio on library issues. **Addits** Honorary Life Member of Papua New Guinea Library Association.

SHREEVE David Executive Director **CONSERVATION FOUNDATION** CONSERVATION/ENVIRONMENT Type: Fundraiser; Service provider; Grant maker; Project management; information provision. 1 Kensington Gore, London SW7 2AR Tel:0171-823 8842 Fax:0171-923 8791

SIEDERER Nigel Director **ASSOCIATION OF CHARITABLE FOUNDATIONS - ACF** SOCIAL Type: Service provider; Umbrella organisation for grantmakers. 4 Bloomsbury Square, London WC1A 2RL Tel:0171-404 1338 Fax:0171-831 3881 **Expertise** Umbrella organisations. **Prof Background** CVS Development Worker, London Vol Service Cncl 1975-78; Co-ord, Lambeth Umbrella Group 1978-85; Co-ord, LDA Development Fund 1986-90. **Awards/Research** Annual reports, various newsletter articles, book reviews. **Past Committees** Fed. of Independent Advice Centres, Treasurer 1983-85; Advice Services Alliance, Chair 1985. **Media Experience** Some articles. **Addits** Active in Inter-Country Adoption bodies, adopted Romanian son 1990.

SIMANOWITZ Arnold Chief Executive **ACTION FOR VICTIMS OF MEDICAL ACCIDENTS** MEDICAL/HEALTH Type: Service provider. Bank Chambers, 1 London Road, Forest Hill, London SE23 3TP Tel:0181-291 2793 Fax:0181-699 0632 **Expertise** Medical negligence; accountability of health professionals. **Prev Posts** Solicitor, partner: Armstrong and Co 1969-75; Simanowitz and Brown 1975-82. **Prof Background** Law diploma, Cape Town University; Attorney's Professional Examination, Cape Town; Solicitor's Qualifying Examination, London. **Awards/Research** Contrib:No Fault Compensation-Short Term Panacea or Long Term Goal; Medical Audit and Accountability; Powers & Harris-Medical Negligence Agencies; Medical Accidents-Vincent & Ennis. **Pres Committees** Department of Health Working Party on Mediation; Lord Woolf Steering Group; Executive Cttee Assoc of Personal Injury Lawyers; Editorial Board Clinical Risk. **Past Committees** Chair: Croydon Community Relations Council; Wandsworth Prison Board of Visitors. **Media Experience** Numerous TV/radio appearances, eg. Raw Deal BBC2. **Addits** Former Labour councillor, London Borough of Croydon.

SIME Martin Director **SCOTTISH COUNCIL FOR VOLUNTARY ORGANISATIONS -SCVO** SOCIAL Type: Representative Umbrella. 18-19 Claremont Crescent, Edinburgh EH7 4QD Tel:0131-556 3882 Fax:0131-556 0279 **Prev Posts** Manager, Sprout Market Garden 1983-85; Scottish Assoc for Mental Health: Principal Officer 1986-88; Director 1988-91. **Prof Background** Graduate; Social History Researcher; Sheep Farmer. **Pres Committees** Secretary, Scottish Civic Assembly; Trustee, NCVO. **Media Experience** Mostly Scottish current affairs.

SIMMONS Mrs J.A. Secretary **AID FOR CHILDREN WITH TRACHEOSTOMIES - ACT** CHILDREN/YOUTH Type: Fundraiser; Service provider. 215A Perry Street, Billericay, Essex CM12 0NZ Tel:01277-654425 Fax:01277-654425 **Expertise** Information on/medical equipment for caring for children with tracheostomies. **Prev Posts** Office Manager in Personnel Department, London Residuary Body 1984-86. **Prof Background** Qualifications in Business Studies, Interviewing - selection and counselling. Ten years in various Personnel Departments of the Greater London Council. **Pres Committees** ACT Committee; Parent Governor for a Special School. **Media Experience** Provider of information to media.

SIMMONS Sir Michael Secretary **COUNCIL OF JUSTICE TO ANIMALS & HUMANE SLAUGHTER ASSOCIATION** ANIMAL/WILDLIFE Type: Animal welfare/educational. 34 Blanche Lane, South Mimms, Potters Bar, Herts EN6 3PA Tel:01707-659040 Fax:01707-649279 **Prev Posts** All military (Royal Air Force).

SIMON Dr Sybil Director **TAY-SACHS AND ALLIED DISORDERS** MEDICAL/HEALTH Type: Fundraiser; Service provider; Screening for genetic and metabolic disorders. Rm 26 Giving for Living Res Ctr, Royal Manchester Childrens Hospital, Pendlebury, Manchester M27 4HA Tel:0161-794 4696 X2384 **Expertise** Genetic/neurological/biochemical disorders; Dir Manchester Tay-Sachs and Gauchers Screening/Research Ctr. **Prev Posts** Clinical genetics, 5 years; Senior Clinical Medical Officer in Child Health 8 years. **Prof Background** Manchester Medical School. Posts at all three paediatric hospitals in Manchester in general paediatrics, and neurology and biochemical/metabolic disorders. **Awards/Research** Medical Research Council Scholarship in Medical Genetics **Pres Committees** Adviser, Research Trust for Metabolic Diseases In Children. **Past Committees** Chair, Medical friends of the Hebrew University, Jerusalem. **Media Experience** Local radio/press interviews to raise awareness of genetic disorders/screening. **Addits** Lectures on Tay-Sachs & allied disorders to schools etc; fundraising events.

SIMPSON David A. Administrator **CHILDREN WITH AIDS CHARITY** MEDICAL/HEALTH Type: Fundraiser; Service provider; Grant maker. 2nd Floor, 111 High Holborn, London WC1V 6JS Tel:0171-242 3883 Fax:0171-242 3884 **Expertise** Fundraising, Public Relations, Administration. **Prev Posts** Dep. Advertising Manager, Mindmaster Publications Ltd 1990-92; General Manager, Milburgh Hall HIV/AIDS Care Centre and Hospice 1992-94. **Prof Background** St. Lawrence College (Junior & Senior) 1972-84; St. Andrews University 1984-87 MA Hons in French & International Relations. **Media Experience** Radio & press interviews; TV broadcasts (news & chatshows).

SIMPSON Miss Julia B. National Secretary **ROYAL BRITISH LEGION WOMEN'S SECTION** SOCIAL Type: Fundraiser; Grant maker. 48 Pall Mall, London SW1Y 5JY Tel:0171-973 7214 Fax:0171-839 7917 **Expertise** Conference organisation, project management, administration & personnel management. **Prev Posts** Royal Naval Officer 1963-96 (promoted Captain RN 1988, final appointment Director Naval Environment & Safety). **Prof Background** BSc; CEng; MBCS; FRSA.

SIMPSON T.S. Chief Executive **COUNCIL FOR THE ADVANCEMENT OF COMMUNICATION WITH DEAF PEOPLE - CACDP** DISABILITY Type: Nat exam brd in sign lang & other communications. Pelaw House, School of Education, University of Durham, Durham DH1 1TA Tel:0191-374 3607 Fax:0191-374 3605 **Expertise** Social policy and administration; policy and provision for deaf people. **Prev Posts** Lecturer, Business Studies, Carlisle Tech College 1968-74; Lecturer, Social Policy, Moray House College of Educ 1974-79; Director, Communication Skills Project 1979-81. **Prof Background** Churchill Travelling Fellow 1982; BA Social Studies, Durham Univ; MSc (Econ) Social Administration & Social Work Studies, LSE; Teacher training, College of Venerable Bede, Durham Univ. **Awards/Research** Publ:

Articles in journals concerned with policy and practice related to deafness and communication. **Pres Committees** RNIB; Deafblind Sub-committee; IAEDB Working Party; Hon Fellow School of Education, University of Durham. **Past Committees** Chairman, Cumbria Deaf Association 1989-92. **Media Experience** Occasional radio, television and press.

SIMS Ruth Chief Executive **MILDMAY MISSION HOSPITAL** MEDICAL/HEALTH Type: Fundraiser; Service provider. Hackney Road, London E2 7NA Tel:0171-739 2331 Fax:0171-613 5689 **Expertise** General management and Aids palliative care. **Prev Posts** District Nursing Manager, Southend HA 1986-87; Gen Mnger/Chief Nurse, Mildmay MH 1987-92. Current: Dir Mildmay Internat Aids (Aids Care & Educ Progs in E/Cent Africa, spons ODA). **Prof Background** RGN. Cert Ed, Cert Counselling, Snr Mngrs Devlp Prog, Kings Fund Coll 1989; Top Mngrs Prog, Kings Fund 1991. Elizabeth Clark Awd 1984; Help the Hospice Travel Flwshp 1987; Fl. N'gale Schlshp 1991. **Awards/Research** OBE 1995. Jt auth: Community Nursing Mngmnt of Patients with Ulcerating/Fungating Malignant Breast Disease; Terminal Care for People with Aids. Res: Aids & Hospice Care. **Past Committees** Sch Gov, Thorpe Jnr Sch; RCN Aids Nursing Guidelines Cttee; Mngmt Brd, Fairhavens Hospice Southend; Aids Nursing Forum RCN. **Media Experience** Continuous involvement since 1987 with all media; nursing jnl articles. **Addits** Now exploring start of Aids palliative care in Uganda.

SINGH Prof Harmindar Secretary **SIKH DIVINE FELLOWSHIP** RELIGIOUS Type: Mainly religious, social & welfare. 46 Sudbury Court Drive, Harrow, Middlesex HA1 3TD Tel:0181-904 9244 **Expertise** Interfaith dialogue, race relations, religious education & information on Sikhism. **Prof Background** MA, English; Dip, Journalism; Dip, French; Honours, Punjabi. **Awards/Research** Awarded Shirimani Award by Vice-President of India (1979) for services rendered to the community in the UK; Contributions to various articles. **Media Experience** Experience with radio & TV with ref to religious ed, race relations & Sikhism.

SINGLETON Roger Senior Director **BARNARDO'S** CHILDREN/YOUTH Type: Fundraiser; Service provider. Tanner's Lane, Barkingside, Essex IG6 1QG Tel:0181-550 8822 Fax:0181-551 6870 **Expertise** Corporate management. **Prev Posts** Assistant Director of Social Services, 1971-74; Deputy Director, Dr Barnardo's 1974-84. **Prof Background** MA; MSc; Dip. Social Studies; Certificate in Education. **Awards/Research** Contributions to professional journals. **Pres Committees** Trustee & Hon Treas, National Cncl for Voluntary Child Care Orgs; Treasurer, Advancement of Residential Child Care; Member, Deregulation Task Force. **Past Committees** National Children's Bureau; Nat. Youth Bureau; Central Council for Education and Training in Social Work; Committees of Inquiry. **Media Experience** National media participant.

SINNETT Mrs Rae Hon. Secretary & Treasurer **CAT WELFARE, SUSSEX** Type: Service provider; National organisation. 53 Braeside Avenue, Patcham, Brighton, Sussex BN1 8RL Tel:01273-553054 **Expertise** Neutering of cats by subsidising the costs plus rescue work. **Prev Posts** Took over from previous voluntary workers.

SISTER AGNES Superior Provincial **LITTLE SISTERS OF THE POOR** Type: Fundraiser; Service provider. St Peters Residence, 2a Meadow Road, London SW8 1QH Tel:0171-735 0788 Fax:0171-820 9647 **Expertise** Care of the elderly of modest means in residential homes. **Prev Posts** Manager of home for the elderly, Leeds & London, 1986-88, 1984-86, 1978-84. **Prof Background** RGN. **Pres Committees** Member, Trustee Co of the Little Sisters of the Poor. **Past Committees** Those within the Congregation of the Little Sisters of the Poor. **Media Experience** Video, Hands of Love.

SIZER John Chief Executive **SCOTTISH HIGHER EDUCATION FUNDING COUNCIL** Type: Grant maker. Donaldson House, 97 Haymarket Terrace, Edinburgh EH12 5ND. Tel:0131-313 6500 Fax:0131-313 6501 **Prev Posts** Loughborough Univ of Technology, Founding Head of Dept of Mngmt Studies 1971-84; Dir of Business Sch 1991-92; Snr Pro Vice-Chanc 1980-82; Prof of Fin Mngmt 1970-96. **Prof Background** Grimsby Coll of Technol; BA, Univ of Nott; DLitt, Loughboro; FCMA; Teaching Fell, then Lectr, Univ of Edin; Snr Lectr, Lond Grad Sch Busn Studies; FIMgt; FRSA. **Awards/Research** CBE. Articles/Publ incl: An Insight into Mngmt Accntng, var eds; Case Studies in M.A. 1974; Perspectives in M.A. 1981; Jt Auth: Resources & Higher Ed; A Casebook of Brit M.A. **Pres Committees** Nat Forum Mngmt Ed & Dev, Sci & Engrg Base Co-ord Cttee; Mbr, Pub Sect and Not-for-Profit Cttee, Accounting Standards Bd; Vice Pres, Soc for Res into HE; Mbr, Tech Foresight Prog Strng Gp. **Past Committees** Mbr VGC 84-89;Ch Bus & Mngmt stud, Mbr NI Cttee UFC 89-93;Mbr Cncl CIMA 1981-88;Nat Forum Mngmt Ed & Dev 1989-95;Ch Soc Res into HE. **Addits** Auth: Instinctual Responses to Fin. Reductions in Univ Sector 1987.

SKENE Prudence Director **ARTS FOUNDATION** ARTS Type: Grant maker. Countess of Huntingdon's Chapel, The Vineyards, The Paragon, Bath, Avon BA1 5NA Tel:01225-315775 Fax:01225-317597 **Expertise** Arts Administration. **Prev Posts** Administrative Director, Ballet Rambert 1975-86; Executive Producer, English Shakespeare Company 1987-92 **Pres Committees** Mbr, Arts Council of England; Chair, Arts Council Lottery Panel. **Past Committees** Chair, Dancers Resettlement Trust 1988-92; President, Theatrical Management Association 1991-92.

SMART Jane Director **PLANTLIFE** CONSERVATION/ENVIRONMENT Type: Fundraiser; Campaigning; Nature Conservation. Natural History Museum, Cromwell Road, London SW7 5BD Tel:0171-938 9111 Fax:0171-938 9112 **Expertise** Plant conservation issues; all matters concerning wild plants, nature and conservation. **Prev Posts** London Wildlife Trust, 1989-90; London Ecology Unit, 1986-89; GLC Ecology Unit, 1983-86. **Prof Background** PhD on Plant Ecology of Raised Bogs, in particular the effects of Peat Extraction. **Awards/Research** Various articles on Plant Ecology of Raised Bogs; Habitat Management and Creation; Plant Conservation, eg. Plantlife magazine. **Pres Committees** Chairman, Wildlife & Countryside Link. **Past Committees** Plantlife Board, Vice Chair 1989-90. **Media Experience** Various media contribs on behalf of Plantlife.

SMEATON John National Director **SOCIETY FOR THE PROTECTION OF UNBORN CHILDREN - SPUC** MEDICAL/HEALTH Type: Education/lobbying/counselling. Phyllis Bowman House, 5/6 St Matthew St, Westminster, London SW1P 2JT Tel:0171-222 5845 Fax:0171-222 0630.

SMITH Mrs Jacqui National Contact **MICROCEPHALY SUPPORT GROUP** MEDICAL/HEALTH Type: Parent support network. 43 Randall Rd, Kingsley, Northants NN2 7DG Tel:01604-722407 **Addits** Helped organise successful national conference 1995.

SMITH Jef General Manager **COUNSEL AND CARE THE ELDERLY** Type: Advice giving; campaigning. Twyman House, 16 Bonny Street, London NW1 9PG Tel:0171-485 1550 Fax:0171-267 6877 **Expertise** Older people. **Prev Posts** Director of Social Services, Ealing Borough Council 1983-87; Director of Personnel, Haringey Health Authority 1987-89. **Prof Background** BA History, Durham University; Dip. Soc Sci, Liverpool University; Community Work and Social Planning, National Institute for Social Work; Management, Institute of Local Government Studies. **Awards/Research** Frequent articles in professional press since 1963; Council of Europe Fellowship. **Pres Committees** Executive Committee, Age Concern London; Executive Committee, Association of Charity Officers. **Past Committees** Aves Committee on Volunteers in the Social Services; Cook Committee on Clients' Rights. **Media Experience** Frequent contributor to news and features programmes.

SMITH Keith Chief Executive **BROADCASTING SUPPORT SERVICES** SOCIAL Type: Service provider; Media charity. Villiers House, The Broadway, London W5 2PA Tel:0181-280 8000 Fax:0181-810 0169 **Prev Posts** Export Mngr, Wm Collins publ 1970-74; Research Assoc, Sussex Univ 1974-75; Marketing Mngr Third World Publ 1975-76; Publisher/Consult, Inter-Action Trust 1976-83. **Prof Background** BA (Hons) Philosophy, Bedford College, London University; Open Business School, Open University. **Awards/Research** SYP Award 1977; Auth: Publishing in the Third World, 1978; Marketing for Small Publishers, 1980, 1993; Co-Auth: Charitable Status - A Practical Handbook, 1980. **Past Committees** Trtee Cncl Oxfam 1991-3;Trtee Drinkline-Nat Alc Helpline;Strg Grp O/s Adoption Helpline;Childline Cncl;Trtee Spare Tyre Thtre Proj. **Media Experience** Various. **Addits** Prev: Chair, Nat Assoc for Patient Participation 1986-88.

SMITH Michael Chief Executive **ST LOYE'S COLLEGE FOUNDATION** DISABILITY Type: Fundraiser; Service provider. Topsham Road, Exeter EX2 6EP Tel:01392-55428 Fax:01392-420889 **Expertise** Training, administration and fundraising. **Prev Posts** Public Service. **Prof Background** Open University; Cranfield University; Staff College Camberley; Defence College Rome; MIMgt; MIPD. **Awards/Research** Equal Opportunities in Sport; Cost Effective Use of Resources. **Pres Committees** Governor: Priory School; Exeter College. Chair, East Devon SSAFA. Devon & Cornwall Training & Enterprise Cncl (TEC). **Media Experience** Appearances on TV and radio, press. **Addits** Presentations at major conferences.

SMITH Peter General Secretary **ASSOCIATION OF TEACHERS AND LECTURERS** SOCIAL/TRAINING Type: Service provider. 7 Northumberland Street, London WC2N 5DA Tel:0171-930 6441 Fax:0171-930 1359 **Expertise** Education. **Prev Posts** MA, Oxford, English Language & Literature. **Media Experience** Extensive experience with radio, TV, video and press.

SMITH Robert D Executive Director **UNITED KINGDOM COMMITTEE FOR UNICEF - UNICEF** CHILDREN/YOUTH Type: Fundraiser. 55 Lincolns Inn Fields, London WC2A 3NB Tel:0171-405 5592 Fax:0171-405 2332 **Expertise** Overall direction - special responsibility for all external relations. **Prev Posts** Freelance fundraising and public affairs consultant 1968-74; Director, East Midlands Arts 1974-80. **Prof Background** MA Modern Languages, Cambridge; fundraising training and experience with Wells Management Consultants. **Pres Committees** Standing Group of National Committees for UNICEF (International) 1984-87 and since 1991. Treasurer, Childrens Rights Development Unit (UK) since 1992. **Past Committees** Regional Cncl, Arts Cncl of GB; Regional Cttee, Crafts Cncl and Brit Film Inst; Sec/Chair, Standing Cttee, Regional Arts Assoc. **Media Experience** Many interviews all media on overseas devmt/children's affairs; documentaries.

SMITH Roger Director **LEGAL ACTION GROUP - LAG** SOCIAL Type: Service provider. 242-244 Pentonville Road, London N1 9UN Tel:0171-833 2931 Fax:0171-837 6094 **Expertise** Legal aid and services policies. **Prev Posts** Solicitor, Camden Law Centre 1973-75; Director, West Hampstead Law Centre 1975-79; Solicitor, Child Poverty Action Group 1980-86. **Prof Background** Solicitor. **Awards/Research** Auth: Children and the Courts, 1981; Rights Guide to Non Means Tested Benefits, 1982-86; Co-Auth: Strategy for Justice, 1992; Shaping the Future: New Directions in Legal Services 1994 **Media Experience** Varied. **Addits** Hon Prof, Kent Law School 1995-.Co-Auth: Achieving Civil Justice 1995.

SMITH Roger Secretary/Chief Executive **ROYAL INSTITUTE OF PUBLIC HEALTH & HYGIENE** MEDICAL/HEALTH Type: Service provider; Educational Standard Setter. 28 Portland Place, London W1N 4DE Tel:0171-580 2731 Fax:0171-580 6157 **Expertise** Vocational Training & Education; Management (Planning & Strategy). **Prev Posts** RAF Base Administrator 1982-85; Gp Capt, RAF Ground Training, 1985-87; Dep Director, RAF Training & Education 1987-90. **Prof Background** Mod Lang (German) Degree; Civil Serv Intrprtr (1st Class); Adv RAF Staff Course; CPD, Training Design; Dir Staff on RAF Mgment Courses; Training Policy Direction at MOD; inc RAF new mngmt strategy. **Awards/Research** Articles: National Food Hygiene Training Policy; Food Hygiene Management; Choosing Auditors. Handbooks: Hygiene & Safety for Mortuary Technicians. Also for Food Business Supervisors. **Past Committees** Euro/NATO Training; Working Group on Training Technology (Chairman 1987-90); NVQ Steering Group, Public Protection.

SMYTH Julian Director **BRADFIELD FOUNDATION** SOCIAL/TRAINING Type: Fundraiser; Grant maker.

Bradfield College, Reading, Berks RG7 6AU Tel:0118-9744916 Fax:0118-9744330 **Expertise** Fundraising: major gifts, corporate sponsorship, legacy campaigns, trading subsidiaries, event mngmt etc. **Prev Posts** Orchestral Manager, London Symphony Orchestra 1985-90; Director of Fundraising, Royal Ass in Aid of Deaf People 1990-92; Director of Development, Linacre College, Oxford 1992-94. **Prof Background** BA (Hons) Nottingham University; MPhil, Lancaster University, MICFM; APRS.

SNELL Patricia Chief Executive **UK SKILLS** SOCIAL Type: Fundraiser; Service provider. 1 Giltspur St, London EC1A 9DD Tel:0171-294 2420 Fax:0171-294 2430 **Prev Posts** Assistant Director, City and Guilds 1987-89. **Prof Background** BA (Hons) Modern Languages, Bristol University.

SOMERVILLE Lynda M. Director **MENTAL HEALTH FOUNDATION SCOTLAND** MEDICAL/HEALTH Type: Fundraiser; Grant maker; Campaigning; Falicitator inter-agency initiatives. 24 George Square, Glasgow G2 1EG Tel:0141-221 2092 Fax:0141-204 2606 **Expertise** Management, marketing and public relations. **Prev Posts** Director, Mackay Somerville Healthcare Consultancy 1983-86; Manager, Marketing, Britannia Life Ltd 1986-91. **Prof Background** Registered General Nurse; State Certificated Midwife; Business Administration. **Pres Committees** Scottish Users Network Advisory Cttee; The Caledonian Foundation, Grants Council. **Media Experience** Wide range of pro-active and reactive media experience.

SOMERVILLE Stephen Director **REUTER FOUNDATION** SOCIAL Type: Service provider; Grant maker. 85 Fleet Street, London EC4P 4AJ Tel:0171-542 7015 Fax:0171-542 8599 **Expertise** Journalism, financial services. **Prev Posts** Director, UK & Ireland, Reuters Ltd; Deputy Managing Director, Asia, Reuters Ltd 1985-91; Director of Corporate Affairs, Reuters Ltd 1991 to date. **Prof Background** MA (Cambridge). **Pres Committees** Member of Council (Trustee), Newspaper Press Fund; News Agency Committee Member, International Press Institute. **Past Committees** Trustee, Visnews Trust Fund. **Media Experience** Reuters, Foreign Corresp & Sen Editor (Africa, Vietnam, M. East & Europe).

SOUTH Colin General Secretary **CHRISTIANS ABROAD** RELIGIOUS Type: Service provider. 1 Stockwell Green, London SW9 9HP Tel:0171-737 7811 Fax:0171-737 3237 **Expertise** NGO management, action research in education, international secondary education. **Prev Posts** International experience as teacher in secondary school. **Prof Background** BSc Hons; Dip Ed; Dip Careers Education & Guidance; Cert Relig Studies. **Pres Committees** Chairman, Colchester Quaker Housing Association; Trustee and Hon Treasurer, Friends Therapeutic Community Trust. **Past Committees** Governor, Centre for International Briefing; Trustee, Cath Students International Chaplaincy; Trustee, SCM Finance Cttee.

SPEED Brian Director **SCOTTISH LANDOWNERS' FEDERATION - SLF** CONSERVATION/ENVIRONMENT Type: Service provider. Representative body. 25 Maritime St, Leith, Edinburgh EH6 5PW Tel:0131-555 1031 Fax:0131-555 1052 **Expertise** Directing the work of the Federation. **Prev Posts** 35 years service in the Royal Air Force. **Prof Background** French Air Force Staff Course, Air Commodore RAF. FIMgt, Member Institute of Linguists. **Awards** OBE.

SPENCE Christopher President **LONDON LIGHTHOUSE** MEDICAL/HEALTH Type: Service provider. 111-117 Lancaster Road, London W11 1QT Tel:0171-792 1200 Fax:0171-229 1258 **Prev Posts** Var roles eg Dir, Task Force, etc 1964-70; Priv Sec to Spker of Ho of Commons 1970-76; freelance consult/trainer/counsellor/ writer 1976-86. **Prof Background** Bromsgrove School, Worcs; Dip. Counselling Skills, South West London College. **Awards/Research** MBE 1992; Publ: On Watch: Views from the Lighthouse (Cassel 1996). **Pres Committees** Founding Chair, Pan London HIV/Aids Providers Consortium.

SPENCE Jacky Campaign Director **WAR ON CANCER** MEDICAL/HEALTH Type: Fundraiser; research & treatment. 21 Claremont, Bradford, W. Yorks BD7 1BG Tel:01274-383294 Fax:01274-383298 **Expertise** Marketing. **Prev Posts** Marketing Services Controller, Poundstretcher Ltd 1986-94. **Prof Background** Marketing & Marketing Services Positions for past 10 years. **Pres Committees** Member, AMRC. **Media Experience** Production & appearances for radio, TV, video and press.

SQUIRES Dorothy National Chairman **NATIONAL COUNCIL FOR THE DIVORCED AND SEPARATED - NCDS** SOCIAL Type: Service provider; Caring organization promoting social activities. PO Box 519, Leicester LE2 3ZE Tel:0116-270 0595 **Expertise** Management; welfare; organization. **Prev Posts** NCDS: Branch Chair 1980-; Midland Regional Chair/Vice Chair 1984-90; Nat Sec 1985-86; Nat Chair 1986-. **Prof Background** Housing officer, Leicester City Council. **Past Committees** NCDS Executive committee. **Media Experience** Radio and TV.

STANBURY David Chair **WALES WILDLIFE AND COUNTRYSIDE LINK - WALES LINK** CONSERVATION/ENVIRONMENT Type: Service provider;Co-ordinates wk of envir, conserv and access NGOs. Bryn Alderyn, The Bank, Newtown, Powys SY16 2AB Tel:01686-629194 **Expertise** Biologist; educationalist. **Prev Posts** Headmaster, Forest Hill School London 1977-88; Retired 1988. **Prof Background** BSc; ARCS; FLS; FRGS; FZS. **Awards/Research** MBE. **Pres Committees** Nat Trust Cttee Wales;RSPB Cttee Wales;CPRW Cncl;Island Cttee, Dyfed Wildlife Trust (Skokholm);Reg Adv Cttee, Forestry Comm; Envir Ed Cncl for Wales, Steering Cttee. **Past Committees** Education Cttee, Zoological Society of London; Exec Cttee FSC Prince of Wales Cttee Env Study Gp. **Media Experience** TV series: Voyage of Charles Darwin. **Addits** Patron, London Narrow Boat Project.

STANDEN Clive Principal Chief Executive **BRITISH SCHOOL OF OSTEOPATHY** MEDICAL/HEALTH Type: Educational. 1-4 Suffolk Street, London SW1Y 4HG Tel:0171-930 9254 Fax:0171-839 1098 **Expertise** Practising osteopath; Higher education; Professional development. **Prof Background** Diploma in Osteopathy 1978,

MA in Ethics - Healthcare 1882; King's Fund Top Manager's Programme 1995. **Awards/Research** Various professional articles; Book contributions. **Pres Committees** Chairman, Council of Independent Colleges' Research Institutions; Member, Validation Board of the Open University. **Media Experience** Extensive Radio and Press as well as some TV experience.

STANFORD J.K.E. Director General **LEONARD CHESHIRE FOUNDATION, THE** DISABILITY Type: Service provider. 26-29 Maunsel Street, London SW1P 2QN Tel:0171-828-1822 Fax:0171-976-5704 **Prev Posts** Chair/MD, Brooklands Aviation Group 1975-84; Baring Brothers Corp Finance 1985-91; Exec Chair, David Brown Corp Plc 1987-90.Vice-Chair since December 1996, Holiday Care Service. **Prof Background** Rugby School, Warwickshire; RMA Sandhurst. **Media Experience** Frequent interviews radio/press on Foundation work/Lord Cheshire/disability.

STATHAM Daphne Director **NATIONAL INSTITUTE FOR SOCIAL WORK** SOCIAL Type: Research/development/information provider. 5-7 Tavistock Place, London WC1H 9SN Tel:0171-387 9681 Fax:0171-387 7968 **Expertise** Children and families; women; social work and social care development. **Prev Posts** CCETSW, Social Work Educ Advisor 1972-81; Ruskin College Oxford, Social Work Lecturer 1981-87. **Prof Background** Social Administration and Applied Social Work Diploma, LSE; MA Oxford Univ; Home Office Letter of Recognition in Child Care. **Awards/Research** CBE. Publ: Radicals in Social Work 1978; Co-auth: Women and Social Work, 1988. **Pres Committees** President, NACVS; St Pancras Housing Assoc. Trustee, NCVO. External Examiner (Masters/PhD). **Past Committees** Chair: NACVS; Thames Valley CSS Scheme. JUC/SWEA Research Cttee; CCETSW Council. **Media Experience** Interviews/contrib as Dir of Inst and on vol work with single parents group. **Addits** Visiting Professor, Goldsmiths College, University of London.

STAYT David W. Chairman & Director/Chairman of Trustees **CONCERN FOR FAMILY & WOMANHOOD - CAMPAIGN FOR THE FEMININE WOMAN - CFW** WOMEN Type: Service provider. Campaigning. Springfield House, Chedworth, Cheltenham, Glos GL54 4AH Tel:01285-720454 **Expertise** Radio & TV broadcaster, writer & editor. **Prev Posts** Pilot, Royal Air Force; Senior Planning Officer, Local Government 1956-84. **Prof Background** Town Planner & Valuer; M.I.A.S.; A.S.V.A.. **Awards/Research** Founder & Editor of Vive la Difference; Author of: Concern for Family & Womanhood (pamphlet); many articles in national & regional newspapers & magazines. **Pres Committees** Chairman, CFW General Council; Director, CFW Trustees; Chairman of Trustees of David W. Stayt Charitable Trust. **Media Experience** Extensive TV, radio and press experience (loc & nat). **Addits** Writer, Dir & Prod, BBC TV documentary: Campaign for the Feminine Woman.

STEBBINGS Andrew Clerk to the Trustee **JOHN LYON'S CHARITY** SOCIAL/EDUCATION Type: Grant maker. 45 Pont Street, London SW1X 0BX Tel:0171-589 1114 Fax:0171-589 0807 **Expertise** Charity Law & education organisations in particular. **Prev Posts** Solicitor: Partner, Lee & Pembertons 1979 to date; Clerk to Harrow School & The John Lyon School 1983 to date; Clerk to John Lyon's Charity 1991 to date. **Prof Background** Solicitor. MA (Oxon). **Pres Committees** Trustee: Symposium Mammographicum, Mason le Page Charitable Trust, Peter Stebbings Mem Trust; Cncl Mbr, Masonic Trust for Girls & Boys; Exec Cttee, The Harrow Mission; Brd of Mgmt, Harrow Club W10. **Past Committees** Chair, Charity Law Assoc Working Party on Charity Registration. **Addits** Brd of Trustees, Notting Dale Urban Studies Centre.

STENNING T. W. Secretary **FAMILY TREE MINISTRY - FTM** RELIGIOUS Type: Service provider. 67 Old Kennels Lane, Olivers Battery, Winchester, Hants SO22 4JT Tel:01962-855963 Fax:01962-854791 **Expertise** Promotion of Christian healing approach especially regards Anorexia Nervosa & related problems. **Prof Background** Retired Metallurgist. FTM Counsellor **Awards/Research** Relevant books by Dr R Kenneth McAll: Healing the Family Tree; A Guide to Healing the Family Tree. **Pres Committees** Secretary to FTM Trustees.

STEPHEN Col George McLaughlin Vice President of International Affairs **INTERNATIONAL LEAGUE FOR THE PROTECTION OF HORSES - ILPH** ANIMAL/WILDLIFE Type: Fundraiser; Service provider; Grant maker. Anne Colvin House, Snetterton, Norwich, Norfolk NR16 2LR Tel:01953-498682 Fax:01953-498373 **Expertise** Management; fundraising; public relations; overseas liaison. **Prev Posts** Lt-Col and CO, 13/18 Royal Hussars RAC 1978-81; Lt-Col, Staff College, UK and Australia 1981-84; Colonel, MOD 1984-88. **Prof Background** Epsom College, Surrey; HM Forces 1957-1988. **Awards/Research** Contributor to military and equine jnls. Awds: OBE 1979. **Pres Committees** Chair, Heavy Horse Breed Society. **Past Committees** Pres, British Percheron Society 1992; Mbr: National Equine Welfare Cncl; Queens Body Guard for Scotland, Royal Co of Archers 1987. **Media Experience** Considerable experience of all media forms.

STEPHENS Daniel A.P. Secretary **RICHARDS (ADMIRAL OF THE FLEET SIR FREDERICK) MEMORIAL FUND** SOCIAL Type: Grant maker. 86 Cottenham Park Road, London SW20 0TB Tel:0181-946 9541 **Expertise** Secretary and Treasurer. **Prof Background** Midshipman to Commander, Royal Navy 1940-72; Qualified Chartered Secretary 1973; Commerce 1973-today. **Awards/Research** Freeman of City of London; BIM Certificate of Merit 1992. **Pres Committees** General Secretary/Treasurer, Queen Adelaide Naval Fund since 1972. **Past Committees** Nat Cncl/London Branch Cncl, Inst of Chartered Secretaries & Administrators; City of London Branch Ctte, British Inst of Management.

STEPHENSON Jenny Director **FAMILY HOLIDAY ASSOCIATION - FHA** SOCIAL Type: Grant maker. 16 Mortimer Street, London W1N 7RD Tel:0171-436 3304 Fax:0171-436 3302 **Expertise** Fundraising; communications; lobbying; development of networks. **Prev Posts** Amnesty Internat British Section; Trade Union Officer 1981-85; Target Sectors Officer 1985-90. **Prof Background** BA/MA English, St Hilda's College, Oxford; Office Skills; Diploma in Labour Studies, PCL; Training

Courses in Public Speaking; Management; Fundraising. **Awards/Research** Produced publications for Amnesty International; Trade Union News; Student News; Youth Magazine; Articles in New Law Journal; various in house journals; FHA newsletter and reports. **Pres Committees** FHA Executive Committee; Tourism for All. **Past Committees** Council of Amnesty International, British Section; National Committee ACTS. **Media Experience** Woman's Hour; Local radio stations; BBC World Service; Religious Broadcasting.

STEVENS Robin Central Stewardship Officer **CENTRAL BOARD OF FINANCE OF THE CHURCH OF ENGLAND** RELIGIOUS Type: Financial advisory body for Church of England. Church House, Great Smith Street, London SW1P 3NZ Tel:0171-222 9011 Fax:0171-799 2714 **Expertise** Promotion of Christian giving. **Prev Posts** Marconi Communication Systems Ltd 1967-79; Thames Television Plc 1979-91. **Prof Background** Chartered Electrical Engineer; Reader in the Church of England. **Pres Committees** None outside the Church of England.

STILES Madeline Chief Executive **HISTORICAL ASSOCIATION, THE - HA** CONSERVATION/ENVIRONMENT Type: Fundraiser; Service provider; Grant maker; Subject-teaching association. 59a Kennington Park Road, London SE11 4JH Tel:0171-735 3901 Fax:0171-582 4989 **Expertise** Management; administration; computer applications; publishing. **Prev Posts** Fire Records Officer, Fire Protection Association 1972-75; Cost Control Engineer, Petrochemical Construction 1975-79. **Prof Background** Wide experience including librarianship, publishing, youth training, and with the Voluntary Sector for the last 14 years. **Pres Committees** Ms Stiles avoids committee membership. **Media Experience** Provides information by phone to the media regularly.

STOCKER Les Founder/Chairman **ST TIGGYWINKLES, THE WILDLIFE HOSPITAL TRUST** ANIMAL/WILDLIFE Type: Teaching hospital for sick/injured wildlife. Aston Road, Haddenham, Aylesbury, Bucks HP17 8AF Tel:01844-292292 Fax:01844-292640 **Prev Posts** Accountant 1959-78; Founder & Chairman European Wildlife Rehabilitation Association since 1991. **Prof Background** MBE (Hons) 1992; Emanuel Public School 1954-59. **Awards/Research** Rolex Award for Enterprise 1990. Many publ inc: We Save Wildlife 1986; The Complete Hedgehog 1986; Hedgehog and Friends 1990; The Complete Garden Bird 1991; The Complete Fox 1994. **Pres Committees** International Wildlife Rehabilitation Cncl (USA); National Wildlife Rehabilitators Assoc (USA). **Media Experience** Radio phone-in on LBC; corresp Wildlife Rehab Today (USA); videos.

STOKES Geoff Secretary **NATIONAL SOCIETY OF ALLOTMENT AND LEISURE GARDENERS LTD** CONSERVATION/ENVIRONMENT Type: National representative body for allotments. O'Dell House, Hunters Road, Corby, Northants NN17 5JE Tel:01536-266576 Fax:01536-264509 **Expertise** Allotment legislation and allotment matters. **Prev Posts** General commerce to 1980; Self-employed 1980-88. **Media Experience** Occasional articles; radio/TV appearances.

STOKES Mrs Sue Managing Director **REACH - ASSOCIATION FOR CHILDREN WITH HAND/ARM DEFICIENCY** DISABILITY Type: Fundraiser; Support. 12 Wilson Way, Earls Barton, Northants NN6 0NZ Tel:01604-811041 Fax:01604-811041 **Expertise** Children with upper limb deficiency; support and advice for families. **Prof Background** Parent of upper limb deficient child; former trustee of Reach. **Awards/Research** Fact Sheets relevant to upper limb problems in children; Quarterly Newsletter, within Reach.

STONE Judith Chief Executive **NATIONAL EARLY YEARS NETWORK (FORMERLY VOLCUF)** CHILDREN/YOUTH Type: Umbrella/intermediary group. 77 Holloway Road, London N7 8JZ Tel:0171-607 9573 Fax:0171-700 1105 **Prev Posts** Dir, UK Assoc. for Internat Year of the Child 1978-80; Dir, Hammersmith and Fulham Assoc of Community Organizations 1980-88. **Prof Background** BA Philosophy, Politics and Economics, Oxon. Teaching Certificates: London University and National Froebel Foundation. **Awards/Research** Auth: The Parent's Schoolbook, 1976; Handbook for Parents with a Handicapped Child, 1977; Vandalism in Schools, 1977. **Past Committees** Taylor Committee of Inquiry on the government of schools (DES), 1975-77; Trustee, Thames Telethon Trust 1980-88. **Media Experience** 1970-78 - Extensive radio, TV inc phone-ins eg, Tuesday Call. **Addits** 1970-78 - contrib: Education Guardian, Observer and Sunday Times.

STONEHAM Martin W. Secretary **BENEVOLENT FUND OF THE INSTITUTE OF HEALTH SERVICES MANAGEMENT** MEDICAL/HEALTH Type: Fundraiser; Grant maker. 139 Hever Avenue, West Kingsdown, Sevenoaks, Kent TN15 6DT Tel:01474-853014 Fax:01474-853014 **Expertise** Computer systems consultant, training & installation; specialist purchasing projects; company secretary. **Prev Posts** Divisional Supplies Manager, NHS 1984-91; Contracts Manager, NHS 1991-93. **Prof Background** Fellow, Institute of Health Services Management (IHSM); Dip 1977 FHSM; Member, Chartered Institute of Purchasing & Supply, Dip 1977 MCIPS; Member, Institute of Management (MIMgt). **Awards/Research** Author : Total Quality Management, S E Thames Regional Health Authority 1990; Quality Assurance to Total Quality Management NAHCSM Yrbook 1992; Software Selection NAHCSM Yrbook 1994. **Pres Committees** Secretary, Benevolent Fund, Institute of Health Services Management; Secretary, Executive & National Council, IHSM; Company Secretary, IHSM Consultants. **Past Committees** Nat Cncl Mbr & Dir, IHSM; Cncl Mbr & Dir, Chartered Inst of Purchasing & Supply; Cncl Mbr, NAHCSM (Nat Ass of Health Care Supp Mgr. **Addits** Professional adviser to Kent Air Ambulance Trust.

STONELEY Kenneth Secretary **WOODROFFE BENTON FOUNDATION** SOCIAL Type: Grant maker. 11 Park Avenue, Keymer, Hassocks, West Sussex BN6 8LT **Expertise** Company secretary and administration. **Prev Posts** Director, Nat Assoc for Vol Hostels 1966-77; Vice Pres since 1994;Manager, Company Sec Servs Dept, Ernst & Young, Chrtd Accts 1977-84; Co Sec, Energy Shipping 1984-1994. **Prof Background** Dulwich College; JP; MSc; FCIS; FFA; ATII. **Awards/Research** Auth: Establishing a

Hostel, and papers on residential care. Awds: Winston Churchill Fellowship 1973 to N America to research organization and function of residential care. **Pres Committees** Mbr Worshipful Co of Bakers (Master 1975); JP for Surrey since 1959; Trustee, Woodroffe Benton Foundation since 1989. **Past Committees** Carshalton UDC 1947-57(Chr 56/7);Westmin/Kens/Chels Cmnty HC 1974-7;Surrey/Lond Cit Probat Cttees 1972-7;Reg Rep, Cncl ICSA 1986-91. **Addits** Co Sec, South Bank Polytechnic Enterprises 1989-91.

STRANGE Kit Director **WORLD RESOURCE FOUNDATION** ENVIRONMENT Type: Campaigning. Bridge House, High Street, Tonbridge, Kent TN9 1DP Tel:01732-368333 Fax:01732-368337 **Prev Posts** Environmental Consultant, Middle East 1984-86; Senior Public Affairs Manager, British Gas plc 1989-93. **Prof Background** BSc Biochemistry; MSc Environmental Research. **Media Experience** Extensive experience in TV, radio & press.

STREET Margaret Dobson Chairman of Council **SALTIRE SOCIETY** SOCIAL Type: Fundraiser; Campaigning; Cultural promotion. 9 Fountain Close, 22 High St, Edinburgh EH1 1TF Tel:0131-556 1836 Fax:0131-557 1675 **Expertise** Conservation; Maintenance of traditional values. **Prev Posts** Ministry of Labour & National Insurance 1938-47; Freelance articles on household subjects conservation 1947-48; voluntary work thereafter. **Prof Background** Civil servant. **Awards/Research** Andrew Fletcher Award for Service to Scotland, Saltire Society. **Pres Committees** Trustee, Robert Hurd Memorial Fund; Convenor, Friends of North Carr Lightship. **Past Committees** Leith Civic Trust; formerly Edinburgh Health Council; National Trust for Scotland Council 1986-95.

STREET Phil Director **COMMUNITY EDUCATION DEVELOPMENT CENTRE - CEDC** SOCIAL Type: Fundraiser; Service provider. Lyng Hall, Blackberry Lane, Coventry CV2 3JS Tel:01203-638660 Fax:01203-681161

STUART John Secretary General **SCOTTISH EPISCOPAL CHURCH** RELIGIOUS Type: Church. 21 Grosvenor Crescent, Edinburgh EH12 5EE Tel:0131-225 6357 Fax:0131-346 7247 .

STUBBS Mrs Sukhvinder Chief Executive **RUNNYMEDE TRUST** SOCIAL Type: Research & information body. 133 Aldersgate Street, London ED1A 4JA Tel:0171-600 9666 Fax:0171-600 8529 **Expertise** Racial equality policies & projects. **Prev Posts** Director, Corporate Affairs, Community Development Foundation; English Partnerships; British Dyslexia Association; Prisoners Abroad; British Telecom. **Prof Background** MA Oxon,Geography, Postgraduate; Marketing Economic Development. **Pres Committees** Black Country Development Corporation; Queen Marys NHS Trust; Greenwich International Festival.

STUCHFIELD H. Martin Honorary Secretary **MONUMENTAL BRASS SOCIETY** ARTS Type: Learned Society. Lowe Hill House, Stratford St Mary, Suffolk CO7 6JX Tel:01206-337239/0181-520 5249 Fax:0181-521 8387 **Prev Posts** Company Director. **Awards/Research** Jt Auth: Repair of Monumental Brasses 1981; series - Monumental Brasses of..(series): Bedfordshire, 1992; Berkshire, 1993; Buckinghamshire, 1994; Cambridgeshire, 1995; Cheshire 1996. **Pres Committees** Consultant on Monumental Brasses to Chelmsford Dioc Adv Cttee for the Care of Churches, 1990; Consltnt on Mon Brasses to St Edmundsbury & Ipswich Dioc Adv Cttee 1993;V-Chr Essex Arch & Hist Congress. **Addits** Chr, Walthamstow Hist Soc 1994; Vice-Chr Friends of Wm Morris Gallery 1989.

STURGE Michael Deputy Director **JOSEPH ROWNTREE FOUNDATION** SOCIAL Type: Grant maker. The Homestead, 40 Water End, York YO3 6LP Tel:01904-629241 Fax:01904-620072 **Expertise** Finance and Housing associations. **Prev Posts** Regional Finance Officer, The Housing Corporation 1976-80. **Prof Background** Bristol University; Fellow of Institute of Chartered Accountants (qualified with Price Waterhouse). **Pres Committees** Chair, Pensions Trust; Audit Committee, University of York; Chair, Cober Hill Ltd.

SUGDEN Major General Francis Chairman **ROYAL HOMES FOR OFFICERS' WIDOWS & DAUGHTERS** SOCIAL Type: Service provider. Queens Alexandra's Court, St Mary's Rd, London SW19 7DE Tel:0181-946 5182 **Expertise** Chairman of Management Committee. **Prev Posts** Lieutenant Governor and Secretary, Royal Hospital Chelsea since 1992. **Prof Background** HM Forces. **Awards/Research** CB; CBE. **Pres Committees** Royal Hospital Chelsea; Royal Engineers Museum; Royal Engineers Finance and Investment Policy; Royal Cambridge Home for Soldiers' Widows; Royal Patriotic Fund.

SUMMERS Andrew W. G. Chief Executive **DESIGN COUNCIL** ARTS Type: Non-departmental pub body incorp by Royal Charter. Haymarket House, 1 Oxendon Street; London SW1Y 4EE Tel:0171-208 2121 Fax:0171-839 6033 **Prev Posts** Marketing Dir & Managing Dir, JA Sharwood & Co 1975-85; Commercial Dir & Managing Dir, RHM Foods Ltd 1986-90; Chief Executive, Management Charter Initiative 1991-94. **Prof Background** Mill Hill School (Exhibitioner); MA Natural Sciences & Economics, Fitzwilliam College, Cambridge; ISMP, Harvard Business School 1987; FRSA 1991. **Pres Committees** DTI European Trade Committee; Chairman, France Country Group. **Past Committees** Food from Britain, Export Council 1982-86.

SUPPLE Barry Director **LEVERHULME TRUST** SOCIAL Type: Grant maker. 15-19 New Fetter Lane, London EC4A 1NR Tel:0171-822 6938 Fax:0171-822 5084 **Prev Posts** Reader, Recent Social & Economic History, Oxford Univ 1978-81; Prof, Economic History, Cambridge Univ 1981-1993; Master, St Catharine's College, Cambridge 1984-1993. **Prof Background** BSc Economics, LSE 1949-52; PhD, Cambridge Univ 1952-55. **Awards/Research** Rise of Big Business (1991); Modern Industrial & Economic History; History of British Coal Industry 1913-46 (1987); Royal Exchange Assurance 1720-1970 (1970). **Past Committees** Social Science Research Council; President, Economic History Society.

SVENDSEN Dr Elisabeth D. Administrator **DONKEY SANCTUARY** ANIMAL/WILDLIFE Type: Fundraiser;

Service provider. Slade House Farm, Salcombe Regis, Sidmouth, Devon EX10 0NU   Tel:01395-578222 Fax:01395-579266 **Expertise** Fundraising; overall administration incl. of Veterinary Dept. **Prev Posts** Business Consultant/Director, Ponsharden Shipyard 1963-66; Director, Salston Hotel 1966-82; Administrator, Donkey Sanctuary since 1969. **Prof Background** Brighouse Grammar School; Rachel McMillen Training College (1st Class Froebel). **Awards/Research** Awds: MBE 1980; Hon Doctorate DVMS 1992. 19 books inc. compiler of Professional Handbook of the Donkey. **Pres Committees** Administrator, International Donkey Protection Trust; Hon Administrator/Trustee: Slade Centre, Elisabeth Svendsen Trust. **Media Experience** Extensive participation in all aspects of media.

SWINDELLS Major-General G.M.G. Controller **ARMY BENEVOLENT FUND** SOCIAL Type: Fundraiser; Grant maker.   41 Queens Gate, South Kensington, London SW7 5HR   Tel:0171-584 5232 Fax:0171-584 0889 **Expertise** Senior executive officer. **Prev Posts** Chief Joint Services Liaison Organization, Bonn 1980-82; Director, Management and Support of Intelligence, MoD 1982-85. **Prof Background** Army Officer. **Awards/Research** Awds: CB.

SYDDIQUE Eric Mahmood Secretary **ELECTORAL REFORM SOCIETY** SOCIAL Type: Service provider; Pressure group for proportional representation. 6 Chancel Street, Blackfriars, London SE1 0UU Tel:0171-928 1622 Fax:0171-401 7789 **Expertise** Electoral systems; electoral law and good practice in the conduct of public and private elections. **Prev Posts** Electoral Reform Society: Assistant Secretary 1972-80; Research and Information Officer 1980-91. **Prof Background** St Dunstans College, London; BSc (Econ) London Univ. **Awards/Research** Occasional contrib: Representation (Society publication). **Pres Committees** London Branch Cttee, Assoc of Election Administrators; Council mbr, Hansard Society; Secretary, Electoral Reform (Ballot Services) Ltd; Secretary, Electoral Reform (International Services). **Media Experience** Occasional appearances on TV and radio. **Addits** Justice of the Peace for Kent.

T

TAYLOR Mark Director **MUSEUMS ASSOCIATION (THE) - MA** CONSERVATION/ENVIRONMENT Type: Arts Professional Body. 42 Clerkenwell Close, London EC1R 0PA Tel:0171-608 2933 Fax:0171-250 1929 **Expertise** Chief executive. **Prev Posts** Hotel management 1981-84; Conference manager 1984-89. **Prof Background** BA History, Birmingham Univ; Hotel Management Postgraduate Course, Leeds Polytechnic. **Pres Committees** National Campaign for the Arts; Judges' Panel, Gulbenkian Awards; Museum Training Institute; Network of Euro Museum Orgs (NEMO). **Media Experience** Radio interviews and press comments.

TAYLOR Michael H. Director **CHRISTIAN AID** SOCIAL Type: Aid development agency. PO Box 100, London SE1 7RT Tel:0171-620 4444 Fax:0171-620 0719 **Expertise** Social ethics and theology. **Prev Posts** Baptist Minister: North Shields 1960-66; Birmingham 1966-69; Principal, Northern Baptist College, Manchester 1970-85; Lecturer, Ethics/Theology, Manchester Univ. **Prof Background** Manchester Univ and Union Theological Seminary, New York. **Awards/Research** Auth: Sermon on a Mount, 1982; Learning to Care, 1983; Good for the Poor, 1990; Christianity and the Persistence of Poverty, 1991; Not Angels but Agencies 1996. **Pres Committees** ODI Cncl; WCC Service and Sharing Programme; Exec, Assoc of Protestant Devmt Agencies in Eur (APRODEV); Internat Affairs Cttee; Brd for Soc Responsibility, CofE.

TAYLOR Robert Director **AGE CONCERN CYMRU** THE ELDERLY Type: Fundraiser; Service provider. 4th Floor, 1 Cathedral Road, Cardiff CF1 9SD Tel:01222-371566 Fax:01222-399562 **Expertise** Development work; negotiation; information. **Prev Posts** Tutor, South Glamorgan Training Support Unit 1980-82; Director, Age Concern South Glamorgan 1982-89. **Prof Background** CQSW. **Pres Committees** Chair, NACAB All-Wales Steering Gp; Chair, NACAB South Wales Area Committee. **Past Committees** WCVA, Volunteering in Wales Fund; UK Advisory Panel - European Year of Older People 1993. Chair, Cardiff Central CAB, 1992. **Media Experience** Radio & TV interviews; frequent press interviews/comments.

TEDDER Lt Col James Director **NOT FORGOTTEN ASSOCIATION, THE** DISABILITY Type: Fundraiser; Service provider. 158 Buckingham Palace Road, London SW1W 9TR Tel:0171-730 2400 Fax:0171-730 0020 **Expertise** Administration, management, fundraising. **Prof Background** Regular army 1958-95. **Pres Committees** Member, Institute of Welfare Officers.

TEMPEST Ron Mission Director **HELP INTERNATIONAL** SOCIAL Type: Fundraiser; Service provider. Campaigning. Nettle Hill, Brinklow Road, Ansty, Coventry, W Midlands CV7 9JL Tel:01203-611244 Fax:01203-611288 **Prev Posts** Marketing & Sales Manager. **Prof Background** Marketing Degree. **Pres Committees** Help International Trustee. **Past Committees** Covenant Ministries International, Trustee.

THEWLIS Sarah General Manager **ROYAL COLLEGE OF GENERAL PRACTITIONERS** MEDICAL/HEALTH Type: Professional Association. 14 Princes Gate, Hyde Park, London SW7 1PU Tel:0171-581 3232 Fax:0171-225 3047 **Prev Posts** Royal College of Physicians, Deputy Secretary 1991-94. **Prof Background** BA MIPD **Pres Committees** Company Secretary: Medicines Surveillance Organisation; RCGP Enterprises Ltd; College Council; Council Executive Cttee. **Addits** Trained Counsellor; Personnel Adviser to Diocese of Southwark.

THODY Norman Carl Chief Executive/Co-Founder **DISABLED HOUSING TRUST** DISABILITY Type: Fundraiser; Service provider. First Floor, Market Place, Burgess Hill, West Sussex RH15 9NP Tel:01444-239123 Fax:01444-244978 **Expertise** Disability issues, housing provision; Care in the Community; rehabilitation of victims of head injuries. **Prev Posts** Several union management posts within the insurance industry prior to 1979. **Prof Background** ACII; ACIArb **Pres Committees** Trustee, Disabled Enterprises Trust; Ex officio board member, Brain Injury Rehabilitation Trust. **Media Experience** TV and radio appearances.

THOMAS Anthony D. Director **FIELD STUDIES COUNCIL - FSC** CONSERVATION/ENVIRONMENT Type: Service provider. Preston Montford, Montford Bridge, Shrewsbury, Shropshire SY4 1HW Tel:01743-850674 Fax:01743-850178 **Expertise** Environmental Education 5-19; Geography and Science Coursework; Out of Classroom Activity; Field Centres **Prev Posts** Warden & Director of Studies, Rhyd-y-Creuau (Betws-y-Coed) 1975-76, Slapton Ley 1976-83. **Prof Background** Degree in Geography and Politics; PGCE; Academic Diploma in Education **Awards/Research** Co-auth: 'Reaching Out' Living Earth; Brit Cncl Project: Environmental Educ & Citizenship (Hungary), PHARE Project in Slovakia; Env Educ/Awareness develop of trails & support handbook **Pres Committees** Exec Cttees, Cncl for Env Educ & Nat Assoc of Urban Study Centres; Educ Cttee, Geog Assoc; Field Studies Wkg Gp; Treas, UK Cncls for Learning/Educ & Trng Out of Doors; Str Gp for Env Educ Cncl Wales. **Past Committees** SEAC Geog Cttee;Nat Curric Cncl, Geog Consult Cttee;Schl Exam & Assess Cncl; Curric Cncl Wales, Env Educ Non-Stat Guidance Wkg Pty. **Media Experience** Local radio-Shropshire, Cumbria, Devon. Times Educat. Supplement. **Addits** FCS Central Europe (Hung/Czech/Slovak/Slovenia-EKHF); Brit Cncl Plsh Schls Initiative.

THOMAS Christina Chief Executive **EARTHKIND** Type: Service provider; Animal Welfare, Environ Protection, Wildlife Rescue. Humane Education Centre, Bounds Green Rd, London N22 4EU Tel:0181-889 1595 Fax:0181-881 7662 **Prev Posts** Secretary, BVA Animal Welfare Foundation 1993; Consultant/Practice Manager, MCA 1993-94. **Prof Background** Zoology Degree (second class honours), University of Nottingham.

THOMAS G.E. Director **NATIONAL BACK PAIN ASSOCIATION** MEDICAL/HEALTH Type: Fundraiser; Grant maker. 16 Elmtree Road, Teddington, Middlesex TW11 8ST Tel:0181-977 5474 Fax:0181-943 5318 **Expertise** General management, consultancy. **Prev Posts** Senior Executive in NHS; Director, Enterprise Agency; Managing Director, Ophthalmic Company. **Prof Background** C. Eng., M.I Mech. E., M.I.M **Media Experience** Many TV and radio interviews.

THOMAS Jenni T. Director **CHILD BEREAVEMENT TRUST** Type: Fundraiser; Service provider; Grant maker; Training. 1 Millside, Riversdale, Bourne End, Bucks SL8 5EB Tel:01628-488101 Fax:01628-488101 **Expertise** Training in bereavement counselling skills; Supporting professional carer in loss & grief related issues. **Prof Background** Bereavement, Communication, Training. **Awards/Research** Brit. Medical Awards for videos (1994 & 1995). **Media Experience** TV programme shown on BBC and Carlton.

THOMAS John P. R. Chief Executive **CROSSROADS (SCOTLAND) CARE ATTENDANT SCHEMES** Type: Social Care. 24 George Square, Glasgow G2 1EG Tel:0141-226 3793 Fax:0141-221 7130 **Expertise** High quality respite care to carers and clients across Scotland. **Prev Posts** General Manager Mental Health, then Director of Planning & Contracts, Borders 1987-96; Original Member of Community Care Implementation Unit, Scottish Office 1992-93. **Prof Background** BA History; Assoc.Hlth.Serv.Mgrs. **Pres Committees** Member, Scottish Health Advisory Service Panel.

THOMAS Nicholas C. Chair & General Secretary **ANTHROPOSOPHICAL SOCIETY IN GREAT BRITAIN** SOCIAL Type: Service provider; Educational. Rudolf Steiner House, 35 Park Road, London NW1 6XT Tel:0171-723 4400 Fax:0171-724 4364 **Expertise** Electrical engineering; computers; projective geometry; physics and astronomy. **Prev Posts** Engineer Officer, Royal Air Force 1962-79; Programme Manager, Northern Telecom 1982-85; **Prof Background** Engineering training; Royal Air Force Technical College, Henlow; MIEE (1972) and C.Eng. **Awards/Research** Auth: Interaction of Space and Counter Space, Mathematische Korrespondenz, Dornach, Switzerland; Bk: The Battle for the Etheric Realm.

THOMAS Wendy Director **POPULATION CONCERN** MEDICAL/HEALTH Type: Int family planning & reproductive health charity. 178-202 Great Portland Street, London W1N 5TB Tel:0171-631 1546 Fax:0171-436 2143 **Expertise** Adolescent sexuality. **Prev Posts** Co-ordinator, Women's Employment Project 1983-88; General Manager, London Brook Advisory Centres 1988-94. **Prof Background** BSC Sociology. **Pres Committees** Trustee, IBT; Executive Committee Member: Birth Control Trust; London Marriage Guidance Council. **Past Committees** Chair, Play Association; Chair, Governing Body, Hackney. **Media Experience** Extensive experience of all media.

THOMPSON Prof Noel B.W. Chief Executive **ENGLISH FOLK DANCE AND SONG SOCIETY** ARTS/CULTURAL Type: Fundraiser; Service provider. Cecil Sharp House, 2 Regent's Park Rd, London NW1 7AY Tel:0171-485 2206 Fax:0171-284 0523 **Expertise** Education and Training Policy; Educational Management; Voluntary Sector Management. **Prev Posts** Under-Sec, Dept of Education & Science 1980-88; Chief Exec, Nat Cncl for Educational Technology 1988-92; Visiting Professor, Faculty of Mngmt, Univ of Luton 1993 to date. **Prof Background** MA (Cantab); MSc (London) PhD (London); Chartered Engineer; Policy Maker, Ministerial Adviser, Senior Manager in government 1965-88; University researcher & teacher 1956-65. **Past Committees** Leader, UK delegation to EC, OECD & Council of Europe Education Cttees 1986-88; Member, High Council, European Univ Institute 1980-8 **Addits** Member of British Computer Society (MBCS).

THOMPSON Pauline Executive Director **DISABLEMENT INCOME GROUP, THE - DIG** DISABILITY Type: Campaigning charity. Unit 5 Archway Business Centre, 19-23 Wedmore Street, London N19 4RZ Tel:0171-263 3981 **Expertise** Financial consequences of disablity. **Prev Posts** Local authority social worker, 1969-74; Regional Director, MENCAP 1974-79. **Awards/Research** Auth: A Home of My Own? 1991; Short Changed by Disability, 1990; Not the OPCS: Being Disabled Costs More Than They Said, 1989. Many articles/conf papers on economics of disability. **Past Committees** Trustee/Vice Chair, The Independent Living Fund. **Media Experience** Contrib radio/TV re costs of disab, inc Today, Does He Take Sugar? Moneybox etc

THOMSON Mrs G. M. Chairman **EDINBURGH AND S.E. SCOTLAND DYSLEXIA ASSOCIATION** Type: Service provider; Professional Association. The Flat, 7 Napier Road, Edinburgh EH10 5AZ Tel:0131-229 1865 Fax:0131-229 1865 **Expertise** Dyslexia (Advisory). **Prof Background** Trained specialist in P.E. **Awards/Research** Awarded MBE (for work in connection with dyslexia). **Pres Committees** President & Director, The Scottish Dyslexia Association; Chairman, The Edinburgh & S.E. Dyslexia Association.

THOMSON Ms Kirsteen Executive Director **EDINBURGH OLD TOWN RENEWAL TRUST** CONSERVATION/ENVIRONMENT Type: Service provider; Grant maker. 8 Advocate's Close, 357 High Street, Edinburgh EH1 1PS Tel:0131-2258818 Fax:0131-2258636 **Expertise** Urban renewal. **Prev Posts** Consultant 1980-89; Economic Development Manager, Stirling District Council 1989-92; Project Executive, Edinburgh Old Town Renewal Trust 1992-95. **Prof Background** Architecture & Planning.

THOMSON Raymond E.B. Chief Executive **SCOTTISH CENTRES (Scottish Environmental & Outdoor Education Centres Assoc)** CONSERVATION/ENVIRONMENT Type: Service provider. Loaningdale House, Carwood Road, Biggar, Scotland ML12 6LX Tel:01899-221115 Fax:01899-220644 **Prev Posts** College Secretary, Teacher Training College 1980-86 **Prof Background** MA, BCom, Edinburgh. **Pres Committees** Scottish Council for Outdoor Education Training and Recreation; Scottish Mountain Leader Training Board. **Past Committees** Secretary of State Working Group on Environmental Education.

THORNE Alison Director **BRITISH VASCULAR FOUNDATION** MEDICAL/HEALTH Type: Service provider. Griffin House, West St, Woking, Surrey GT21 1EB Tel:01483-726511 Fax:01483-726522 **Expertise** General management; healthcare; international expertise. **Prev Posts** Managing Consultant, Leading Edge Consultancy Servs since 1992. Dir, British Liver Trust 1990-92. **Prof Background** SRN (Guy's Hospital, London); career as int businesswoman, healthcare specialist; Diploma in Mandarin Chinese (Chinese Univ, HK); Counselling Diploma (CTA); FRSA. Mbr, IoD; ICFM; ACENVO. **Awards/Research** Articles on charity management/fundraising/women. Column in Connections magazine. Profiles in Best of British Women Directory (Charity Section) & Debretts. **Pres Committees** Chair, City Women's Network; Adv Panel, Going Int, Women in Business; Adv Panel, Opportunity 2000. Bd Mbr: The International Alliance; Fair Play for Women, London. Bd Mbr, HK Business & Professional Women; Mbrship Cttee, Women in Management; Mktg Cttee, City Women's Network. **Media Experience** Press/TV/Radio.

THORNE David Director General/Secretary General **COMMONWEALTH TRUST/ROYAL COMMONWEALTH SOCIETY** Type: Service provider; Commonwealth Liaison Unit. 18 Northumberland Ave, London WC2N 5BJ Tel:0171-930 6733 Fax:0171-930 9705 **Expertise** Administrator. **Prev Posts** Army Officer, Director of Infantry 1986-88. **Prof Background** Army Officer, RMA Sandhurst, Army Staff College. **Awards/Research** KBE; CVO. **Pres Committees** Non Exec Director, West Suffolk Hospital Trust; Chairman (Trustee), Royal Norfolk Regiment Museum Trustees.

THORNE John V. Director General **MACINTYRE FOUNDATION, THE** DISABILITY Type: Grant maker; Care serv provision, spec needs housing, UK/o'seas. 29 Crawford Street, London, W1H 1PL Tel:0171-723 5676 Fax:0171-723 1761 **Expertise** Special education, special needs building design, innovative project development. **Prev Posts** Asst archtct Stone Toms & Ptnrs;housemstr Dunhurst Bedales Sch; Dep Head (delinqs) Lond 1969-74;Dir Barnardos New Mossford Cntr 1974-82; MD MacIntyre Care 1982-95 **Prof Background** Architecture; education; theology; management. Speaker (on provision of special needs services) at seminars and conferences. **Awards/Research** Fellow of the Philosophical Society of GB. **Pres Committees** Chair and co-founder, Stackpole Trust; Vol Orgs for Disabiltiy Gp; Chair, MacIntyre International; Dir, MacIntyre Housing Assoc; Disability NGOs in Europe & East Africa. **Past Committees** Chair, Redbridge Association of Disabled People 1976-82; Dir, ARC 1982-90;Standing Cttee for progressive ed;EU Disability & the Env. **Media Experience** Radio, TV and press interviews; videos on disability and the disadvantaged. **Addits** Mt expeds inc Kilimanjaro & Himalayas w int disab teams 1991/3.

TICKELL Clare Chief Executive **PHOENIX HOUSE HOUSING ASSOCIATION** SOCIAL Type: Service provider. 47-49 Borough High St, London SE1 1NB

Tel:0171-407 2789 Fax:0171-407 6007 **Prev Posts** Dep Director, Centrepoint 1986-89; Director, Riverpoint 1989-92. **Pres Committees** London and Quadrant Housing Trust, Supported Housing Cttee; Chair, Homeless Network. **Media Experience** Varied participation on TV/radio and newspapers.

TILBROOK Andrew Secretary **BRITISH NUCLEAR ENERGY SOCIETY** SOCIAL Type: Learned Society; Organise Conferences and Seminars. c/o Institution of Civil Engineers, 1-7 Great George Street, Westminster, London SW1P 3AA Tel:0171-665 2241 Fax:0171-799 1325 **Prev Posts** Volunteer Coordinator, Multiple Sclerosis Society 1986-90; Crown Prosecution Service, Administration 1994-95. **Prof Background** Law Degree. **Awards/Research** Society produces bi-monthly journal to members and subscribers; conference proceedings. **Pres Committees** Secretary to Society's Committees: Main board, Meetings, Editorial, General purposes.

TIMMS Judith Director **INDEPENDENT REPRESENTATION FOR CHILDREN IN NEED - IRCHIN** CHILDREN/YOUTH Type: Service provider. Campaigning children's charity. 1 Downham Road South, Heswall, Wirral, Merseyside L60 5RG Tel:0151-342 7852 Fax:0151-342 7852 **Expertise** Children's representation - child care law & practice; rights & welfare; health & social services. **Prev Posts** Lecturer in Socio-Legal Studies 1978-81; Independent Social Worker 1977-84; Guardian ad Litem 1984-94. **Prof Background** MA Econ Diploma Applied Social Studies; Certificate in Social Administration; AIMSW CCO Family Caseworker; Hon Research Fellow, Faculty of Law, University of Liverpool. **Awards/Research** Children's Representation - A Practitioner's Guide (Sweet & Maxwell) 1995; Dept of Health Manual of Practice Guidance for Guardians ad Litem & Reporting Officers (HMSO) 1992. **Pres Committees** Trustee, Social Workers Benevolent Trust; Non-Executive Director, Wirral Health Authority. **Past Committees** Chair, BASW/Macmillan - jt venture co, BASW & Macmillan Magazines Ltd 1987-93; Trustee, ASC, Advoc, Adv & Rep Service for Children. **Media Experience** Radio, TV and Press as Director of IRCHIN & Chair of BASW; contrib IRCHIN jnl. **Addits** Chair - British Association of Social Workers, 1987-88.

TINDALE Mrs Sibylla Consultant Director **UNIVERSITY OF CAPE TOWN TRUST** YOUTH Type: Fundraiser; Grant maker. c/o 7 Fairbourne, Cobham, Surrey KT11 2BT Tel:01932-865242 Fax:01932-867362 **Expertise** Marketing, Fundraising & Publicity. **Prev Posts** Senior Product Manager, Fish & Meals, Birds Eye Walls 1980-82; Marketing Manager, Hair, Skin, Perfumery, Elida Gibbs Ltd (Unilever) 1982-89. **Prof Background** MBA (1977); BSc Chemistry; 13 yrs Professional in Marketing, Unilever Group of Companies. **Awards/Research** Co-author of research paper for Journal of Water Pollution Control, 1974. **Pres Committees** Chairman, Friends of Danes Hill School; Consultant Director, University of Cape Town Trust; Owner, Sibylla Tindale Associates, Marketing Consultants. **Media Experience** Production & briefing of advertising and PR for radio, TV, video & press.

TIPPEN Wing Commander M.W Secretary & Executive Director **HISTORIC CHURCHES PRESERVATION TRUST, INCORPORATED CHURCH BUILDING SOCIETY** CONSERVATION/ENVIRONMENT Type: Fundraiser; Grant maker. Fulham Palace, London SW6 6EA Tel:0171-736 3054 **Expertise** Operational/Managerial. **Prev Posts** Royal Air Force Officer 1954-90. **Prof Background** Air Defence Operations Officer in RAF leaving as Wing Commander.

TISCHLER Lydia Chair **BRITISH ASSOCIATION OF PSYCHOTHERAPISTS** SOCIAL Type: Service provider; Teaching. 37 Mapesbury Road, London NW2 4HJ Tel:0181-452 9823 Fax:0181-452 5182 **Expertise** Child Psychotherapy. **Prev Posts** Principle Child Psychotherapist, Cassel Hospital 62-85; Principle Child Psychotherapist, Redbridge Centre 86-88; Consultant, Student Counsellng Service, City of E.London College. **Awards/Research** Articles inc: Role of Child Psychotherapist in an In patient setting, July 1964; Some problems of Treating Children in an In patient setting, July 1967; Treatment of Families as In P **Pres Committees** European Secreaty/Exec Mbr, Assn of Child Psychotherapists. **Past Committees** Hon Sec, European Fed for Psychoanalytic Psychotherapy; Training Council/exec Cttee, Assn of Child Psychotherapists.

TISHLER Gillian Chief Executive **YOUNG WOMEN'S CHRISTIAN ASSOCIATION OF GREAT BRITAIN - YWCA** SOCIAL Type: Service provider. Clarendon House, 52 Cornmarket Street, Oxford OX1 3EJ Tel:01865-726110 Fax:01865-204805 **Prev Posts** Priv Sec to Parliamentary Sec, Min of Ag, Fish and Food 1985-87; Parliamentary Officer, RNIB 1987-89; Head of Public Affairs, RNIB 1989-92. **Prof Background** Modern Languages degree, St Anne's College, Oxford; joined MAFF as fast stream trainee; 5 months with European Commission in Brussels. **Past Committees** Exec Cttee, NCVO. **Media Experience** Regular local radio broadcasts/interviews.

TOBIN Noel Director **NATIONAL CAMPAIGN FOR FIREWORK SAFETY - NCFS** SOCIAL Type: Service provider. National campaign. 118 Long Acre, London WC2E 9PA Tel:0171-836 6703 **Expertise** Administration; campaigning. **Prev Posts** Theatre Lighting Designer, Prime Presentations since 1966; NCFR from 1970; Sec, Covent Garden Forum since 1975. **Prof Background** MA, Trinity College, Dublin. **Awards/Research** International Firework Report 1976-77 and 1984. **Pres Committees** Trustee, Covent Garden Area Trust; St Paul's Charities Covent Garden. **Past Committees** Chair, Covent Garden Forum, Housing/Education/Environment/Planning. **Media Experience** Nat TV: frequent interviews & full length prog since 1971, & press articles.

TODD Daphne President **ROYAL SOCIETY OF PORTRAIT PAINTERS** SOCIAL Type: Service provider. 17 Carlton House Terrace, London SW1Y 5BD Tel:0171-930 6844 Fax:0171-839 7830 **Expertise** Portrait painting. **Prev Posts** Self employed Portrait Painter, since 1986; Director of Studies, Heatherley School of Fine Art, 1979-86. **Prof Background** Slade School of Fine Art; U.C.L. Undergraduate & Postgraduate (H.D.F.A London); FRSA. **Awards/Research** Sitters incl: HRH The Grand Duke of Luxembourg, Lord Adrian, Lord Pennock, Dame

Janet Baker DBE, Lord Bishop of Hereford; Awds:1st Prize, Hunting Group National Art Award. **Pres Committees** Director, Thomas Heatherley Educational Trust; Director, The Royal Society of Portrait Painters; Director, Board of Governors, Federation of British Artists. **Media Experience** Occasional interviews for TV & Radio. **Addits** Award: 2nd Prize, John Player Portrait Award, NPG.

TODD Jessie YOUTH CLUBS SCOTLAND YOUTH Type: Fundraiser; Service provider; Grant maker; Youth development. 19 Bonnington Grove, Edinburgh EH6 4BL Tel:0131-5542561 Fax:0131-5555223 **Expertise** Personnel, training, idea generating, youth & adult development. **Prev Posts** Senior Lecturer, Business Studies & Consultancy 1983-88; Training Manager, Scottish & Newcastle Breweries 1988-90. **Prof Background** MIPH; SHND Business Studies; PostGrad, Pers Management. **Awards/Research** Awarded Catherine Luyster Award.

TOMBS Sebastian Martineau ROYAL INCORPORATION OF ARCHITECTS IN SCOTLAND - RIAS CONSERVATION/ENVIRONMENT Type: Service provider; Professional Institute. 15 Rutland Square, Edinburgh EH1 2BE Tel:0131-229 7545 Fax:0131-228 2188 **Prev Posts** RMJM Edinburgh 75-6;Roland Wedgwood Edinburgh 76-7; Fountainbridge Housing Assoc 77-78; Housing Corp 78-81; Edinburgh Dist Cncl Ho Dept 82-86; RIAS Dep Sec 86-94. **Prof Background** Bryanston; Cambridge Univ, B Arch; Dip Arch (Cantab); FRIAS; ACIArb. **Pres Committees** Chair, Assoc of Planning Supervisors (APS); Chair, Scottish Ecological Design Assoc (SEDA). **Past Committees** Chair, Parents Council, Edinburgh Rudolf Steiner School; Planning Committee, Merchiston Community Council.

TOMEI Anthony Director **NUFFIELD FOUNDATION** SOCIAL Type: Grant maker. 28 Bedford Square, London WC1B 3EG Tel:0171-631 0566 Fax:0171-323 4877.

TOMKINS Dr Alan Director **INTERCHANGE TRUST** SOCIAL Type: Service provider. Dalby Street, London NW5 3NQ Tel:0171-267 9421 Fax:0171-482 5292 **Expertise** Management in the voluntary sector, arts, education, social services and local government. **Prev Posts** Local government officer; university lecturer. **Prof Background** PhD in Education. **Awards/Research** Publ: Open University books. **Past Committees** Chief Arts Strategy Officer, Greater London Council.

TONNER John Chief Executive **HOSPITALLER ORDER OF ST JOHN OF GOD** SOCIAL Type: Fundraiser; Service provider. St Clares, Scorton, Richmond, N Yorks DL10 6EB Tel:01748-811535 Fax:01748-818194 **Expertise** Occupational Psychology. **Prof Background** Director of Admin 1982-90; Centre Mgr 1990-94; Director of Human Resources 1994-96. **Prof Background** Accountancy, Economics, Psychology with Bus. Admin, Strathclyde Univ; BA Psychology/Philosophy, Durham University; MSc Psychology, Hull University. **Awards/Research** Care in the Community; Attraction to Religious Life. **Pres Committees** Hospitaller Order of St John of God. **Past Committees** Chair, Housing Association Cttees. **Media Experience** Radio, TV, Video, Press.

TORRANCE Mr D. Richard Chairman **SCOTTISH GENEALOGY SOCIETY** SOCIAL Type: Service provider. 15 Victoria Terrace, Edinburgh EH1 2JL Tel:0131-2203677 Fax:0131-2203677 **Expertise** Scottish genealogy. **Prev Posts** Deputy Chairman, Scottish Genealogy Society 1981-88. **Prof Background** BSc, Quantity Surveying; P.G.C.E.. **Awards/Research** Author of: Scottish Personal & Place Names (bibliography); The McClellans in Galloway (2 vols); Scottish Trades & Professions (select bibliography); various smaller works & articles. **Pres Committees** Internal Sub-Committee of: Council, Publishing, Conference, Building/Library, Glenfiddich Award; Representative on: Scottish Association of Family History Societies Council. **Addits** Author of Dictionary of Weights & Measures for the Scottish Family Historian.

TRAER Robert General Secretary **INTERNATIONAL ASSOCIATION FOR RELIGIOUS FREEDOM** RELIGIOUS Type: Service provider; Grant maker; Campaigning. 2 Market Street, Oxford OX1 3EF Tel:01865-202 744 Fax:01865-202 746 **Prof Background** Ordained Christian Minister Presbyterian Church 1969 (USA).PhD Grad Theo Union; JD Sch Law, Univ Calif; DMn Div Sch Univ Chicago; BA Carleton Coll Northfield Minnesota. **Awards/Research** BA magna cum lauda(distntn) Phi Beta Kappa;Amer Juris Awd Excell in Admin Law;Colo Assoc of Sch Bds Ldrshp Awd;PhD (distntn).Publ incl:A Confessnl Apprch to Interfaith Cooperation. **Addits** Publ : Faith in Human Rgts:Support in Relig Traditions for a Global Struggle.

TRAMPLEASURE John Director **SHELTER, NATIONAL CAMPAIGN FOR HOMELESS PEOPLE** SOCIAL Type: Fundraiser; Service provider. 88 Old Street, London EC1V 9HU Tel:0171-505 2000 Fax:0171-505 2169 **Expertise** Fundraising, marketing, management. **Prev Posts** Marketing Manager, Shelter 1991-94; New Product Development Manager, HP Information 1986-91; Sales Manager, PNA Services 1981-86; Sales Executive, Haymarket Publishing 1980-81. **Prof Background** BA (Hons) History/Geography. **Media Experience** Various articles in charity, direct marketing and national press.

TRAVERS William Director **BORN FREE FOUNDATION** ANIMAL/WILDLIFE Type: Fundraiser; Service provider; Grant maker. Coldharbour, Dorking, Surrey RH5 6HA Tel:01306-712091 Fax:01306-713350 **Expertise** Wildlife conservation projects; public awareness projects - Africa **Prev Posts** Wildlife documentary film maker 1980-84. **Awards/Research** Jt Ed, Beyond the Bars; Ed, Wildlife Times. **Pres Committees** Chair, Board Species Survival Network; Mbr, Elephant Wkng Gp SSN (Mbr: IUCN SSC Reintroduction Specialist Gp). **Media Experience** Freq contrib local/nat/int TV, radio, newsletters & articles. **Addits** Patron: Captive Animals Protection Society.

TRIBBLE Col Trevor O.W. Secretary for Social Services Programme **SALVATION ARMY SOCIAL SERVICES** SOCIAL Type: Service provider. 105-109 Judd Street, Kings Cross, London WC1H 9TS Tel:0171-383 4230

Fax:0171-383 2562 **Prev Posts** Salvation Army: Provincial Officer 1978-85; Secretary for Personnel and Training 1985-90; Asst Social Services Secretary 1990-94. **Prof Background** Teaching Certificate. Diploma in Social Studies, London Univ. **Pres Committees** Salvation Army Trustee Company; Territorial Executive Council; International Council on Social Welfare.

TRUSTRAM EVE Mrs Pipyn Manager **CHARTERED SURVEYORS TRAINING TRUST** Type: Fundraiser; Service provider; Grant maker. 9 Bentinck St, London S1M 5RP Tel:0171-224 0205 Fax:0171-224 0328 **Expertise** Managing and counselling. **Prof Background** Counselling and Work Experience. **Pres Committees** Vice Chair of Centec Providers. **Past Committees** Chair of Centec Providers.

TUCKETT Alan Director **NATIONAL INSTITUTE OF ADULT CONTINUING EDUCATION - NIACE** SOCIAL Type: Fundraiser; Service provider. 21 De Montfort St, Leicester LE1 7GE Tel:01533-551451 Fax:01533-854514 **Expertise** Political advice; fiscal management; access to learning for marginalised groups; ethnic minority issues. **Prev Posts** Principal, Friends Centre, Brighton 1973-81; Principal, Clapham/Battersea Adult Education Institute, ILEA 1981-88. Adult Education Adviser, Palestine National Authority. **Prof Background** BA (Hons) Eng & American Lit, DES Major Studentship, E Anglia Univ; Visiting Prof: Warwick Univ 1993, Univ of Technology, Sydney 1993; helped shape adult literacy campaigns 1970s-80s. **Awards/Research** OBE, 1995. Churchill Travelling Fellows 1981; many publ inc: Towards a Learning Workforce 1991; Jewel in the Crown 1988; research/many articles on adult learning. **Pres Committees** Dir, Basic Skills Agency; Governor, Ruskin College; ex-officio all NIACE Cttees; European Assoc for the Education of Adults; Trustee, National Extension College. **Past Committees** Educ Broadcasting Cncl BBC; Educ for Adults Cttee IBA/ITC; Pres Int League Soc Commit Adult Educ; Carnegie Inq 3rd Stage Educ Ctte. **Media Experience** TV & radio experience incl: Presenter of Education Matters, Radio 5.

TUMIM Winifred L. Chair **COUNCIL FOR THE ADVANCEMENT OF COMMUNICATION WITH DEAF PEOPLE** DISABILITY Type: Service provider. Pelaw House, School of Education, University of Durham, Durham DH1 1TA Tel:0191-374 3607 Fax:0191-374 3605 **Expertise** Deafness; disability; governance of charities. **Prev Posts** Chair, RNID 1985-92; Cncl Mbr, Vol Cncl for Handicapped Children 1982-89; Mbr, Hammersmith and Fulham Dist Health Auth. Currently: Chair, NCVO. **Prof Background** BA (Hons) Pol/Philos/Econ, Lady Margaret Hall, Oxford 1958; Dip Soc Studies, Dip Linguistics, London Univ; FRSA. **Awards/Research** OBE. Auth: Weekly Boarding-Why and How, 1974; Parents as Partners, 1980; Pre-School for Deaf Children and Parents, 1981; Notebook for Sch Leavers with Spec Needs (IYC) 1985. **Pres Committees** Mbr, GMC; Trustee: City Parochial Fdtn;Nat Portrait Gallery;Non-Exec Dir, Parkside Health; Mbr, CC Adv Cttee on Trusteeship. **Past Committees** Many eg. Gov, City Literary Inst; Gov Cttee Enq on Educ of Handicapped Children (Warnock) 1974-8; Nat Adv Cncl on Emp of Disab People 1987-91; Ind Living Fund; Carlton TV Trust;Chair, Sec of State, Youth Treatment Serv Gp; **Media experience**TV/radio appearances re deafness/disability; contrib educational press and jnls

TUNNAH John E. Director **NATIONAL PLAYING FIELDS ASSOCIATION (SCOTLAND)** CONSERVATION/ENVIRONMENT Type: Fundraiser; Service provider; Grant maker; sport. 20 Queen St, Edinburgh EH2 1JX Tel:0131-225 4307 Fax:0131-225 5763 **Expertise** Mountaineering; game fishing and team sports. **Prev Posts** RAF Officer (Search & Rescue Service) 1957-1984; Oil Industry Emergency Services Officer 1984-1986; Local Government Emergency Planning Officer 1986-1993. **Prof Background** Engineer with emergency services specialisation. Engineering graduate - Major Disaster Management. Inst. of Management; Inst. of Civil Defence. **Awards/Research** British Empire Medal for mountain rescue operations in Scotland. Internat. Mountain Rescue Handbook contributor. Articles: Winter Survival Techniques. **Pres Committees** Community Education Service Committee Outdoor Activities Adviser (Fife). **Media Experience** Articles; stories and features in all media.

TURNBULL Graham Director **LONDON WILDLIFE TRUST** ANIMAL/WILDLIFE Type: Service provider. 80 York Way, London N1 9AG Tel:0171-278 6612 Fax:0171-837 8060 **Expertise** Marketing; organizational needs. **Prev Posts** Marketing Manager: HSS Hire Shops 1985-88; Sussex Wildlife Trust 1988-91. **Prof Background** Dip. Mus. MICFM, MIPR. **Pres Committees** Heritage Lottery Fund Task Team. **Past Committees** RSNC: Corporate Strategy Project Team; Marketing Subcommittee. **Media Experience** All media. **Addits** Seminar/Training session leader.

TURNER Clive Acting Chief Executive **STONHAM HOUSING ASSOCIATION LTD** SOCIAL Type: Service provider; Registered special needs housing assoc. Octavia House, 235-241 Union St, London SE1 0LR Tel:0171-401 2020 Fax:0171-633 9901

TWEEDY Colin Director General **ASSOCIATION FOR BUSINESS SPONSORSHIP OF THE ARTS - ABSA** ARTS Nutmeg House, 60 Gainsford Street, Butlers Wharf, London SE1 2NY Tel:0171-378 8143 Fax:0171-407 7527 **Expertise** Arts/business sponsorship. **Prev Posts** Manager, Thorndike Theatre, Leatherhead 1976-78; Corporate Finance Officer, Guinness Mahon 1978-80; Asst Director, Streets Financial PR 1980-83. **Prof Background** City of Bath Boys School; MA St Catherine's College, Oxford; FRSA. **Awards/Research** A Celebration of Ten Years Business Sponsorship of the Arts, 1987. **Pres Committees** Dir, ABSA Consulting; V Chmn, CEREC; Mbr, Nat Cinema Centenary Cttee; Mbr, Cncl for Charitable Support; Trustee, Serpentine Gallery; Dir, Oxford Stage Co; Dir, Covent Gdn Int Festival; Dir, Crusaid. **Past Committees** Mbr, UK National Cttee European Cinema & TV Year 1988-89; Mbr, Council Japan Festival 1991. **Addits** Freeman, City of London.

TWEEDY Roberta Director **NEUROFIBROMATOSIS ASSOCIATION** MEDICAL/HEALTH Type: Fundraiser; Service provider; Campaigning. 82 London Rd, Kingston-Upon-Thames, Surrey KT2 6PX Tel:0181-547

1636 Fax:0181-974 5601 **Expertise** PR/Administration. **Prev Posts** Headhunter, Head of Research/Co Secretary 1989-94; Management/PR Consultant 1994-95. **Prof Background** Roedean school. **Past Committees** Neurofibromatosis Assoc 1984-92. **Media Experience** Articles, stories and features in all media.

TWINE Derek Chief Executive **SCOUT ASSOCIATION** YOUTH Type: Fundraiser; Service provider; Youth work, training. Baden-Powell House, Queen's Gate, London SW7 5JS Tel:0171-584 7030 Fax:0171-590 5103 **Expertise** Organisational devt; Education and training. **Prev Posts** Executive Commissioner The Scout Assoc (1986-96); Dir of Programme The Scout Assoc (1979- 86). **Prof Background** 1st Class Honours Degree (BA); Fellow of Institute of Personnel and Devt. **Awards/Research** Urbanisation of Rural Education 1974. **Past Committees** National Youth Agency Education & Training;National Cncl for Vol Yth Services Trng Managers Grp; RSA Comm and Vol Sector Panel. **Media Experience** Extensive interviews across all media.

TYLER Andrew Director **ANIMAL AID** ANIMAL Type: Campaigning & Education. The Old Chapel, Bradford St, Tonbridge TN9 1AW Tel:01732-364546 Fax:01732-366533 **Prev Posts** Freelance journalist and author writing mostly for The Independent and The Guardian until December 1994. **Prof Background** Journalist since mid 1960s. **Awards/Research** Special awards for journalism from several animal campaign groups, a series of investigations on the use and abuse of animals published by national newspapers. **Media Experience** Consultant for TV & radio programmes; numerous radio, press & TV interviews.

U

UNDERHILL Chris Chief Executive **INTERMEDIATE TECHNOLOGY** SOCIAL Type: Development Agency. Myson House, Railway Terrace, Rugby, Warwickshire CV21 3HT Tel:01788-560631 Fax:01788-540270.

UPTON Robert Secretary General **ROYAL TOWN PLANNING INSTITUTE** CONSERVATION/ENVIRONMENT Type: Professional association. 26 Portland Place, London W1N 4BE Tel:0171-636 9107 Fax:0171-323 1582 **Prev Posts** Director of Planning, Hong Kong Government 1989-91; Chief Executive, Rushmoor Borough Council 1992-96. **Prof Background** BA Hons, MA Magdalene College, Cambridge; Program for Management Development, Harvard Business School.

URSELL Frank Business Manager **REGISTERED NURSING HOME ASSOCIATION** MEDICAL/HEALTH Type: Professional Association. Calthorpe House, Hagley Rd, Edgbaston, Birmingham B16 8QY Tel:0121-454 2511 Fax:0121-454 0932 **Expertise** Provision of nursing home care. **Pres Committees** Health Services Advisory Committee.

V

VALLANCE Russell Director **WISHBONE TRUST, THE** MEDICAL/HEALTH Type: Fundraiser; Grant maker. 35-43 Lincoln's Inn Fields, London WC2A 3PN Tel:0171-242 6986 Fax:0171-404 2082 **Expertise** General management; fundraising. **Prev Posts** Director, Fight for Sight Special Appeal 1987-89; Head of Marketing & Fundraising, I Can 1989-90. **Prof Background** BA, Warwick Univ; AB (Pt 1), Chicago Univ; Italian Cert, Venice; Pract Ind Relats, Warwick Univ; Structured Fundraising, DIRAS; Direct Mkting, Dublin; charity finance courses . Mbr:ICFM, IoD, ACENVO; FRFA. **Awards/Research** Numerous articles on employment issues, equal opportunities and fundraising. **Past Committees** Chair, SW Reg HA Staff Cttee;Jt Sec, Univ Tech Staff Reg Appeal Panel;SW Mngmt Centre Cncl;1983 NGO Delegate, UN Human Rights Comm. **Media Experience** Radio, TV, video, and press contrib, plus management of PR function. **Addits** Lecturer on charity fundraising in UK, Holland, Canada and US.

VASEY Terry Director **BRITISH LEPROSY RELIEF ASSOCIATION - LEPRA** MEDICAL/HEALTH Type: Leprosy control programmes; Leprosy research. Fairfax House, Causton Road, Colchester, Essex CO1 1PU Tel:01206-562286 Fax:01206-762151 **Prev Posts** Co-ordinator, UNAIS Bolivia/Brazil 1985-90; Desk Officer, Christian Aid 1990-91; Desk Officer, LEPRA 1991. **Prof Background** Degrees in Philosophy and Theology; CQSW, Dip. Social Work.

VENABLES Robert M C Commissioner & Head of Legal Division **CHARITY COMMISSIONERS FOR ENGLAND AND WALES** SOCIAL Type: Statutory Body. St Alban's House, 57-60 Haymarket, London SW1Y 4QX Tel:0171-210 4419 Fax:0171-210 4604 **Expertise** Law/Charity. **Prev Posts** Assistant Treasury Solicitor: Conveyancing Dept, 1987-89; Energy Dept 1985-87; Establishment/Finance Dept, 1983-85. **Prof Background** Solicitor of the Supreme Court. **Awards/Research** Professional journal articles. **Pres Committees** Council of the Law Society of England & Wales; Standards & Guidance Committee of the Law Society; City of Westminster Law Society. **Past Committees** National Executive Association of First Division Civil Servants; Brd of International Nuclear Law Association. **Media Experience** Some experience.

VENNING Philip Secretary **SOCIETY FOR THE PROTECTION OF ANCIENT BUILDINGS - SPAB** CONSERVATION/ENVIRONMENT Type: Service provider; Statutory Consultee. 37 Spital Square, London E1 6DY Tel:0171-377 1644 Fax:0171-247 5296 **Expertise** Education and training in building conservation. **Prev Posts** Times Educational Supplement, Journalist then Assistant Editor 1970-81. **Prof Background** MA (Cambridge) Economics; Fellow of the Society of Antiquaries. **Pres Committees** Nat. Trust Cncl; William Morris Craft Fellowship Cttee; Conf. on Training in Architectural Conservation; Joint Cttee of Nat. Amenity Socs.

VENTHAM Ian Head of Fundraising & Marketing **ROYAL NATIONAL LIFEBOAT INSTITUTION - RNLI** SOCIAL Type: Fundraiser; Service provider. West Quay Rd, Poole, Dorset BH15 1HZ Tel:01202-663208 Fax:01202-663238 **Expertise** Marketing/Fundraising. **Prev Posts** Silver Jubilee Manager, Help the Aged 1984-86; National Appeals Manager, NSPCC(1986-90); Royal Artillery 1968-77; RMA Sandhurst 1966-68. **Prof Background** Regular Army 1966-77; Marketing Manager Linotype-Paul Ltd 1977-82. **Pres Committees** ICFM Standards Committee. **Past Committees** Chairman ICFM Executive 1992-94. **Media Experience** Interviews on radio, TV and for press.

VERNELLI Toni Campaigns Co-ordinator **PEOPLE FOR THE ETHICAL TREATMENT OF ANIMALS** ANIMAL/WILDLIFE Type: Campaigning; Animal Rights Group. PO Box 3169, London NW1 2JF Tel:0171-388 4922 Fax:0171-388 4925

VINCENT Michael Trading Director **OXFAM** SOCIAL Type: Fundraiser; Service provider; Grant maker; Overseas; relief and development. 274 Banbury Road, Oxford OX2 7DZ Tel:01865-311311 Fax:01865-313163 **Expertise** Marketing and business management. **Prev Posts** Kraft Foods UK: Cheese Mkting Mngr 1986-88; Frozen Foods Dir 1988-89; Kraft General Foods Marketing Development Director 1989-92. **Prof Background** BA (Second Class Hons) Economics and Marketing, Lancaster Univ.

VINCENT Rev. Dr John James Director **URBAN THEOLOGY UNIT - UTU** RELIGIOUS Type: Service provider; Educational; training and support. 210 Abbeyfield Road, Sheffield S4 7AZ Tel:01142-435342 Fax:01142-435342 **Expertise** Urban problems; urban Policy; urban mission. **Prev Posts** Visiting Prof of Theology: Boston Univ, New York Theol Seminary 1969-70; Drew Univ 1977; Adjunct. Prof of Theol, New York Theol Seminary 1979-88. Hon Lecturer, Sheffield Univ. **Prof Background** Richmond College; London Univ (BD 1954); Drew Univ USA (STM 1955); Basel Univ, Switzerland (DTheol 1960); Sgt, RAMC 1948-1949. **Awards/Research** Publ inc:Christ in a Nuclear World, 1962;The Race Race, 1970;Into the City, 1982;Britain in the 90s, 1989;Petition of Distress from the Cities, 1993; British Liberation Theology, 1994 **Pres Committees** Urban Mission Trng Assoc; Trustee Savings Bank Depositors Assoc (& Litigant in High Court and H of L, TSB v Vincent) 1986; Dir, Brit Liberation Theol Project 1991-; Jt Chair, Comm on the Cities, 1995 **Past Committees** Chair, NW Campaign for Nuclear Disarmament 1957-1963; Alliance of Radical Methodists 1970-1976. **Media Experience** Radio, television and press.

VON MALACHOWSKI Virginia Deputy Regional Director **SENSE-WEST (NATIONAL DEAF-BLIND AND RUBELLA ASSOCIATION)** DISABILITY Type: Service provider. 4 Church Road, Edgbaston, Birmingham B15 3TD Tel:0121-456 1564 Fax:0121-452 1656 **Expertise** Sensory impairment; challenging behaviour; severe learning disabilities. **Prev Posts** Beech Tree School, Head Teacher 1985-87; FE Dept SENSE - Midlands, Deputy Head 1987-89, Head 1989-92. **Prof Background** Teacher, BEd (Hons) Education SLD Children (children/young adults with challenging behaviour/sensory loss/learning disabilities); Cert, counselling skills; Direct trainer/ assessor (CP Guilds/NVQ) **Awards/Research** Regular lectures and courses in education esp challenging behaviour and learning disabilities. **Pres Committees** Governing body, EUCO Unit; Staff Training Subcommittee, IAEDB. **Media Experience** PR and training videos.

W

WADHAM John Director **LIBERTY (NATIONAL COUNCIL FOR CIVIL LIBERTIES)** SOCIAL Type: Campaigning for civil liberties & human rights. 21 Tabard St, London SE1 4LA Tel:0171-403 3888 Fax:0171-407 5354 **Expertise** Campaigning human rights law. **Prof Background** Solicitor. **Media Experience** Frequent speaker on TV, radio and to press.

WAKELIN Rev Mark National Secretary **METHODIST ASSOCIATION OF YOUTH CLUBS - MAYC** CHILD/YOUTH Type: Service provider; Youth service. 2 Chester House, Muswell Hill, London N10 1PR Tel:0181-444 9845 Fax:0181-365 2471 **Expertise** Youth work.

WALDEN Ian Director **INTERNATIONAL SPINAL RESEARCH TRUST** MEDICAL/HEALTH Type: Fundraiser; Grant maker. 100 Crossbrook Street, Cheshunt, Herts EN8 8JJ Tel:01992-641999 Fax:01992-640641 **Expertise** Management; fundraising; PR; administration. **Prev Posts** Administrator, St Pauls Church, Camberley 1989-91; Campaign Manager, St John Ambulance 1992-93. **Prof Background** Royal Marines Officer 1958-89; educated at Haileybury; attended Army Staff Course and National Defence College Course. **Awards/Research** MBE. **Past Committees** Trustee, Royal Sailors Rests. **Media Experience** Responsible for MOD TV briefing system.

WALKER Claire Secretary **FIGHT FOR SIGHT** MEDICAL/HEALTH Type: Fundraiser; Grant maker. Institute of Ophthalmology, Bath Street, London EC1V 9EL Tel:0171-490 8644 Fax:0171-490 8635 **Expertise** Fundraising: companies, trusts, legacies; administration: grants. **Prev Posts** Administrator, Cancer Research Campaign 1989-91. **Prof Background** PhD; MICFM **Pres Committees** Trustee, Blindcare; Trustee, Covent Garden Cancer Research Trust. **Media Experience** Experience with radio and press.

WALKER Derek Director **WORLDAWARE** SOCIAL Type: Educational Charity 31-35 Kirby St, London EC1N 8TE Tel:0171-831 3844 Fax:0171-831 1746 **Expertise** Communication of complex ideas at a popular level. **Prev Posts** Deputy Editor, The British Weekly 1957-66, Educ Officer, Voluntary Committee on Overseas Aid & Development 1966-76; Director, Worldaware 1977-to date. **Prof Background** BSc (Econ), London School of Economics, trained as a journalist. FRSA. **Awards/Research** Auth: The Ancient Enemies, 1961; Power to End Poverty, 1969. **Pres Committees** Trustee, Pictorial Charts Educational Trust. **Past Committees**

Chair, Exec Cttee European Develop. Education Curriculum Network 1982-92; Hon Sec, Nat Org Ctte, Cncl Europe North-South Campaign. **Media Experience** Former Deputy Editor British Weekly; freelance contrib journals & radio.

WALKER Lesley National Contact **FRAGILE X SOCIETY** DISABILITY Type: Fundraiser; Service provider. 53 Winchelsea Lane, Hastings, East Sussex TN35 4LG Tel:01424-813147 **Media experience** Frequent contrib. to radio, TV and press.

WALLACE Marjorie Chief Executive **SANE** MEDICAL/HEALTH Type: Fundraiser; Service provider. 2nd Floor, 199-205 Old Marylebone Road, London NW1 5QP Tel:0171-724 6520 Fax:0171-724 6502 **Prev Posts** Research/Reporter, Frost Programme 1965-69; Reporter/Dir, BBC Current Affairs 1969-72; Snr reporter, Sunday Times 1972-89, Times 1985-86; regular lecturer/broadcaster/author. **Prof Background** BA Hons Psychology and Philosophy, London; Guardian Research Fellow 1989-91, Nuffield College, Oxford. International Emmy 1979; Campaigning Jnlst 1982, 1986; Snowdon Special Award 1988. **Awards/Research** Book Trust Awd 1986; Medic Jnlst 1988; Evian Health Awds 1991, 1995. Publ inc: On Giants Shoulders 1976 (joint); Suffer the Children 1978 (joint); The Silent Twins 1986 (& screenplay) **Pres Committees** Mbr: Inst of Psychiatry, Management Cttee & Ethical Cttee (Research); Chair, Open Air Theatre Friends. **Media Experience** Ex reporter/producer. Auth drama-doc; presenter, Byline Whose Mind Is It? 1988. **Addits** Presenter: Circles of Madness 1995.

WALLIS Stewart Deputy Director & Director, International Div. **OXFAM** SOCIAL Type: Fundraiser; Grant maker; Overseas: relief and development agency. 274 Banbury Road, Oxford OX2 7DZ Tel:01865-312177 Fax:01865-312511 **Expertise** General management/development economics. **Prev Posts** Economist/project officer, World Bank USA 1976-83; Gen Mngr, Robinson Special Products 1983-86; Managing dir, Robinson Packaging (£33 million turnover) 1987-92. **Prof Background** MA Geology, Cambridge; MSc Economics and Business Studies, London Business School. **Pres Committees** OXFAM Corporate Management Team (5 person executive team managing OXFAM). **Past Committees** Chair, Robinson Packaging Board; Member, Operating Board, Robinson (Parent Co). **Media Experience** Various with both Oxfam and Robinson Packaging. **Addits** Led culture change in Robinson Packaging; Training Tutor, Leadership Trust.

WALNES Gillian Executive Director **ANNE FRANK EDUCATIONAL TRUST - AFET UK** SOCIAL Type: Fundraiser; Service provider. Garden Floor, 43 Portland Place, London W1N 3AG Tel:0181-950 6476 Fax:0181-420 4520 **Expertise** Co-ord fundraising; Touring and admin educ exhibs; Distr educ mats; Organ nat educ projs; Pbl Speaking. **Prev Posts** Anne Frank House, Amsterdam, UK representative 1989-91. **Prof Background** Human Rights Diplomatic Lobbyist and Campaigner for six years (1983-89). **Awards/Research** Research into Racial and Religious Discrimination. Published an annual journal. **Pres Committees** Anne Frank Educational Trust UK. **Past Committees** Women's Campaign for Soviet Jewry, Bournemouth & District Represetative Council. **Media Experience** Much experience in radio and TV (local and national). Undertake liaison with prof & UK gov organs to ministerial level.

WANDLESS David Executive Director **REAL LIFE OPTIONS** DISABILITY Type: Service provider. Tayson House, Methley Rd, Castleford, West Yorks WF10 1PA Tel:01977-556917 Fax:01977-557915 **Expertise** Developing servs for multiple disabled/head injured/severe learning disab/challenging behaviour, forensic. **Prev Posts** Unit Administrator, NHS 1982-86; Assistant General Manager, NHS 1986-88; Director & General Manager 1988-91. **Prof Background** General Manager; B.Sc (Hons) Social Studies; M.Sc Health Management. **Awards/Research** Articles in Nursing Mirror, Nursing Times on staff development, training, Regional Secure Units and forensic services, learning disabilities and multiple disabilities. **Pres Committees** Board of Management, Director Real Life Options; Trustee, ARC. **Media Experience** Year of Disabled, radio broadcasts and BBC 2 Disability programme 1994.

WARD Col A. C. Warden/Chief Executive **WHITELEY HOMES TRUST** THE ELDERLY Type: Service provider. Whitely Village, Walton-on-Thames, Surrey KT12 4EH Tel:01932-842360 Fax:01932-828952 **Expertise** Care of elderly, management & budget setting. **Prev Posts** Fellowship, Washington (DC) 1991-91; Director, Manpower Audit (Army) 1992-96. **Prof Background** Army Staff College (PSC); Overseas Defence College. **Awards/Research** Geo-political strategy; Awarded OBE & FIMgt. **Pres Committees** Trustee, Queens Royal Surrey Regt Assoc, Walton Weybridge Old Peoples Welfare; Surrey Residential Homes Assoc Cttee; Surrey Cnty Cncl Advisory Cttee (Elderly). **Past Committees** Army Establishment Committee. **Media Experience** Extensive experience in radio, TV, video and press (national & local).

WARD Mrs Elizabeth Despard Founder President **BRITISH KIDNEY PATIENT ASSOCIATION, THE BKPA** MEDICAL/HEALTH Type: Fundraiser; Grant maker. Bordon, Hampshire GU35 9JZ Tel:01420-472021 Fax:01420-475831 **Expertise** Public relations. **Prev Posts** Local rep, SAAFA; volunteer, After Prison Care Service. **Prof Background** Cheltenham Ladies College. **Awards/Research** Auth: Timbo - A Struggle For Survival; Awds: MBE, 1978; Hon LL D, 1990; OBE 1992. **Pres Committees** BKPA Council Meeting, biannual. **Past Committees** BKPA Investment Trust. **Media Experience** Constant and regular participant. **Addits** JP 1974-83.

WARD Les Director **ADVOCATES FOR ANIMALS** ANIMAL/WILDLIFE Type: Campaigning/pressure group for animal protection. 10 Queensferry Street, Edinburgh EH2 4PG Tel:0131-225 6039 Fax:0131-220 6377 **Expertise** All areas of animal protection, esp. animal experiments/blood sports/farm animals/companion animals. Currently: Company Secretary, St Andrew Animal Fund. **Prof Background** Dunbar Grammar School; RAF. **Awards/Research** Churchill Travelling Fellowship, 1984. **Pres Committees** Home Secretary's Animal Procedures Committee; Treasurer: Cttee for the Reform of Animal Experiments; Farm Animal Welfare Co-ordination

Executive. **Media Experience** Participated in many programmes and contributed to various press articles.

WARDMAN Anna National Director **PLAN INTERNATIONAL UK** SOCIAL Type: Fundraiser. 5-6 Underhill St, London NW1 7HS Tel:0171-485 6612 Fax:0171-485 2107.

WARREN Andrew Director **ASSOCIATION FOR CONSERVATION OF ENERGY** CONSERVATION/ENVIRONMENT Type: Fundraiser; Service provider. Westgate House, 2A Prebend St, London NW1 8PT Tel:0171-359 8000 Fax:0171-359 0863 **Expertise** Energy Conservation. **Prof Background** BA Politics **Awards/Research** Successful campaign to pass Home Energy Conservation Act 1995; Many articles on energy conservation policy. Energy Journalist of the Year 1986. **Pres Committees** Buildings Energy Efficiency Confederation. **Media Experience** Frequent Broadcaster, Columns published in every broadsheet paper. **Addits** Monthly column Energy In Buildings and Identity.

WARREN Dr P.T. Executive Secretary **ROYAL SOCIETY (THE)** CONSERVATION/ENVIRONMENT Type: Grant maker; Science. 6 Carlton House Terrace, London SW1Y 5AG Tel:0171-839 5561 Fax:0171-930 2170 **Prev Posts** Science Section, Cabinet Office, Whitehall 1972-76; Safety Adviser, Natural Environment Research Council 1976-77; Deputy Executive Secretary, Royal Society 1977-85. **Prof Background** MA; PhD (Cantab) Natural Sciences (Geology). **Awards/Research** Publ: Geology of the county around Rhyl and Denbigh. **Pres Committees** Council, Girls' Public Day School Trust; Board, Council of Science and Technology Institutes. **Past Committees** Council, Institution of Geologists.

WATCHMAN David Chief Executive **ROYAL ACADEMY OF DANCING** CHILDREN/YOUTH Type: Arts educational organization. 36 Battersea Square, London SW11 3RA Tel:0171-223 0091 Fax:0171-924 3129 **Expertise** General management and marketing. **Prev Posts** Chief Exec, Wesgo PTY Ltd 1975-80; Dir, Atkins Bros plc 1980-90. **Pres Committees** Exec Cttee of Cncl for Dance Education & Training. **Past Committees** Dir: The Cartner Group Ltd, Mors SA. **Media Experience** Interviewed by TV, radio & press worldwide.

WATSON Niall Macleod Executive Officer **FOOD FOR THE HUNGRY/UK** SOCIAL Type: Fundraiser. 58 Beulah Road, Tunbridge Wells, Kent TN1 2NR Tel:01892-534410 Fax:01892-534410 **Expertise** Rural & Community Development. **Prev Posts** Field Co-Ordinator, Lutheran World Federation, Uganda 1991-93; Dep Director, Food for the Hungry International, Mozambique 1993-95. **Prof Background** Agriculturalist; NDA, MRAC, The Royal Agricultural College, Cirencester. **Pres Committees** Food for the Hungry, UK Board.

WATTERS David General Secretary **PRIMARY IMMUNODEFICIENCY ASSOCIATION** MEDICAL/HEALTH Type: Fundraiser; Service provider; Grant maker; Campaigning. Alliance House, 12 Caxton St, London SW1H 0QS Tel:0171-976 7640 Fax:0171-976 7641 **Prev Posts** Threshold Centre 1973-78; Alone in London Service 1978-81; Haemophilia Society 1981-93. **Awards/Research** Haemophilia Society 1991. **Pres Committees** Trustee: Bruce Trust, International Patient Organization for Primary Immunodeficiency (IPOPI); Churchwarden, All Saints Tooting; Justice of the Peace. **Past Committees** Chair SSAT's to 1983; Trustee, Piccadilly Advice Centre. **Media Experience** Radio/TV/Video/press: Extensive for Haemophilia Soc HIV Compensation Campaign.

WEBBER Howard Head of Voluntary & Community Division **DEPARTMENT OF NATIONAL HERITAGE** CONSERVATION/ENVIRONMENT Type: Grant maker; Statutory Body. 2-4 Cockspur Street, London SW19 5DH Tel:0171-211 2800 Fax:0171-211 2807 **Expertise** Policy Devmt & Grant-giving; Monitory & evaluation; Co-ordinator of Govmt Policies on voluntary sector. **Prev Posts** Manager of National Arts & Media Strategy, Arts Council of Great Britain, 1990-93; Director of Incentives Fundary, Arts Council of Great Britain, 1988-1990. **Prof Background** Birmingham University, Bachelor of Law; Harvard University USA, Master of Public Administration. **Awards/Research** Auth: A Creative Future (1993). **Pres Committees** Observer on boards of voluntary organisations funded by VCD. **Media Experience** Radio & press interviews.

WEBSTER Richard Chief Executive **STARLIGHT FOUNDATION** CHILDREN/YOUTH Type: Fundraiser; Service provider; Grant maker; Entertainment/wishes granted for very ill children. 8a Bloomsbury Square, London WC1A 2LP Tel:0171-430 1642 Fax:0171-430 1482 **Expertise** Leadership, management, corporate fundraising. **Prev Posts** Managing Dir, Securiguard Services (London) Ltd 1989-92; President, Service Link Holdings Corp Inc (USA) 1992; Managing Dir, Custodial & Escort Services Ltd 1992-93. **Prof Background** Haileybury College 1948-52; R.M.A Sandhurst 1953-55; Staff College, Camberley 1966-67; National Defence College, Latimer 1974-75; Prof military career 1953-89 from private soldier to brigadier. **Media Experience** Local radio; TV BBC Morning News; Dimbleby Gulf War prog; Nick Owen Show. **Addits** Aide de Camp to HM the Queen 1988-89.

WEDEKIND Grace President **NATIONAL COUNCIL OF WOMEN OF GREAT BRITAIN - NCW** WOMEN Type: Educational charity. 36 Danbury Street, Islington, London N1 8JU Tel:0171-354 2395 Fax:0171-354 9214 **Expertise** Consumer affairs; transport and road safety; women's issues. **Prev Posts** NCW; Vice President (Policy); Chair of Work Liaison Cttee co-ordinating work with affiliated orgs; Chair of NCW Transport Wkng Party 1982-92; Berks CC Envir Forum 1991-93. **Pres Committees** Chair: ICW(GB), representing NCW at International Council of Women and Financial Forum for Women.

WEINSTOCK Anne Chief Executive **RATHBONE SOCIETY, THE** DISABILITY AND HANDICAP Type: Service provider. 1st Floor, The Excalibur Building, 77 Whitworth St, Manchester M1 6EZ Tel:0161-236 5358 Fax:0161-236 4539 **Expertise** Education and training for people with learning difficulties. **Prev Posts** Principal Officer, Nat Assoc for the Care and Resettlement of Offenders 1973-9; Mbr, Home Office Parole Board 1980-84. **Prof Background** BA (Hons) Economic and

Social Science, Manchester University 1972. **Awards/Research** CBE, 1992. Auth: Performance Indicators for People with Special Needs, 1990; TECs and People with Special Training Needs, 1991; Employers and People with Disabilities, 1992. **Pres Committees** M/Cr Training & Enterprise Cncl; BBC Ed Broadcasting Cncl for UK; HMI/Audit Commission, Adv Gp Review of Sp Ed Needs; Dept of Emp G10 Sp Needs Adv Gp; Industrial Soc Cncl; NCVO Access Forum. **Media Experience** Radio, TV, video and press participant. **Addits** Currently Governor, City College Manchester.

WEIR Hilary (Lady) Secretary **ARCHITECTURAL HERITAGE FUND, THE** CONSERVATION/ENVIRONMENT Type: Grant maker; Loanmaker. 27 John Adam Street, London WC2N 6HX Tel:0171-925 0199 Fax:0171-930 0295 **Prev Posts** HM Diplomatic Service 1969-86. **Prof Background** BA, BA Litt, English Language and Literature, Oxford Univ. **Awards/Research** Auth: Articles on Medieval Cairo; Medieval Cairo: A Visitor's Guide; How to Rescue a Ruin by Setting Up a Buildings Preservation Trust; contrib: Egypt in 1800. Ed: AHF annual reports. **Pres Committees** Vice Chair, Brooke Hospital for Animals; Chair, Ramses Wissa Wassef (UK) Exhibition Foundation; Mbr, Nat Cttee, UK Association of Building Preservation Trusts.

WELLS Dr Robin J. Executive Director **AFRICA EVANGELICAL FELLOWSHIP - AEF** RELIGIOUS Type: Fundraiser; Service provider; Recruitment and training of missionaries. 30 Lingfield Rd, Wimbledon, London SW19 4PU Tel:0181-946 1176 Fax:0181-944 5282 **Expertise** Science. **Prev Posts** Snr Advisor, Water Research Commission (South Africa) 1975-79; General Secretary, Universities & Colleges Christian Fellowship 1979-91. **Prof Background** MSc University of Pretoria; PhD Imperial College, London. **Pres Committees** Council, Evangelical Missionary Alliance.

WEST Alison Chief Executive **COMMUNITY DEVELOPMENT FOUNDATION** SOCIAL Type: Service provider. 60 Highbury Grove, London N5 2AG Tel:0171-226 5375 Fax:0171-704 0313 **Expertise** Economic development, adult education, community development, equal opportunities. **Prev Posts** Head of Economic Development & Head of Women's Unit, LB Waltham Forest 1986-91; Head of Corporate Policy, LB Camden 1991-93. **Prof Background** MA English Literature; M. Litt on Wallace Stevens; M. Ed in Community Education & Development; Secondary Teaching Diploma; Dip Ed; CIMA Stage I. **Awards/Research** Various articles on community-based economic regeneration. **Pres Committees** Trade Union Resource Centres. **Past Committees** Women's Management Group; Various Trade Union Centres. **Media Experience** VSTV interview, Women's Hour, Third Sector, Guardian, etc.

WESTGARTH Peter Chief Executive **YOUNG ENTERPRISE** CHILDREN/YOUTH Type: Fundraiser; Service provider. Ewert Place, Summertown, Oxford OX2 7BZ Tel:01865-311 180 Fax:01865-310 979 **Expertise** Youth Devmt; Enterprise Educ; Small Business Devmt; Voluntary Networks; Int Networks; Student Activity. **Prev Posts** UK Director, Livewire, 1986-90; Public Relations Manager, NE Coop, 1982-86; Fundraising Manager, MIND, 1978-82. **Prof Background** Secondary Teacher; Professional Fundraiser; Public Relations Professional; Small Business Development Training; Promotional and Training Video Production. **Awards/Research** Awarded Investors in People Status. **Pres Committees** President, Young Enterprise Europe; Director, YE Scotland and YE Isle of Mann; UK Delegate, Junior Achievement International. **Media Experience** Wide range of media involvement.

WESTLAND Peter Chairman **BROADCASTING SUPPORT SERVICES** SOCIAL Type: Service provider; Media Charity. Villiers House, The Broadway, London W5 2PA Tel:0181-280 8000 Fax:0181-810 0169 **Prev Posts** Dir Social Services, LB Hammersmith and Fulham 1971-80; Undersec, Social Services, Assoc of Metropolitan Authorities 1980-94; currently research consultant. **Pres Committees** Commission on Future of London's Health Service; Non-exec Dir, Wandsworth Community Health NHS Trust; Trustee, National Aids Trust. **Past Committees** Wandsworth Health Authority 1984-90; Chair, King's Fund Primary Care Cttee 1986-92; Trustee, NACRO; Kings Fund Centre Cttee.

WEYMAN Anne Chief Executive **FAMILY PLANNING ASSOCIATION** MEDICAL/HEALTH Type: Health promotion. 2-12 Pentonville Road, London N1 9FP Tel:0171-837 5432 Fax:0171-837 3042 **Expertise** Strategic planning, management, sex education, children's rights, organisational change and development. **Prev Posts** Head of Finance & Administration, International Secretariat, Amnesty International 1977-8 ; Director of Information & Public Affairs, National Children's Bureau 1986-96. **Prof Background** FCA, BSc (Physics) BSc (Sociology). **Awards/Research** Co-author: Modern Brit. Society: A Bibliography 1977, The Soc Behaviour Assessment Schedule & Starting and Running a Voluntary Grp; Articles on Health, Mental Health & Sex Ed. **Pres Committees** Trustee, The Children's Rights Development Unit; Chair, The Sex Education Forum. **Media Experience** Radio, TV & press comment on sexual health issues.

WHARTON B.A. Director General **BRITISH NUTRITION FOUNDATION** Type: Service provider; Professional association. High Holborn House, 52-54 High Holborn, London WC1V 6RQ Tel:0171-404 6504 Fax:0171-404 6747 **Expertise** Developmental nutrition. **Prev Posts** Consultant Paediatrician, Birmingham 1973-88; Rank Professor of Human Nutrition, Glasgow 988-92. **Prof Background** Medicine, Science and Business administration (BA, MBA, MD, FRCP, FIFST). **Awards/Research** Numerous publications concerned with developmental nutrition including pregnancy, the newborn, infants and children. **Past Committees** Committees concerned with child nutrition in government (Whitehall & Brussels) and in professional association (UK and Europe). **Media Experience** Occasional experience with radio, TV, video and press.

WHEATER Professor Roger J. Director **ROYAL ZOOLOGICAL SOCIETY OF SCOTLAND** ANIMAL/WILDLIFE Type: Service provider. Scottish National Zoological Park, Corstorphine Rd, Edinburgh

EH12 6TS   Tel:0131-334 9171   Fax:0131-316 4050 **Expertise** General and operational. **Prev Posts** Chief Warden, Murchison Falls National Park Uganda 1961-70; Dir, Uganda National Parks 1970-72. **Prof Background** Brighton Technical College; Police College, Hendon. C Biol; FIBiol; FRSA; FRSE; William Thyne Scholar 1975; Hon Professor, Edinburgh University 1993. **Awards/Research** OBE. Consultancy in zoo and wildlife management; Consultant World Tourist Organisation (UN) since 1980. **Pres Committees** Patron, Dynamic Earth Appeal;Trustee, Dian Fossey Gorilla Fund;Pres, Assoc Brit Wild Animal Keepers;Chair,Euro Assoc of Zoos/Aquaria;Chair, Access Forum; Mbr: Scot Nat Heritage; Scientific Adv Cttee. **Past Committees** Pres, Int Union Dirs of Zoological Gdns;Chair, Wkng Pty Zoo Licensing Act; Scot Nat Trust;Chair, Fed Zoo Gdns of GB & Ireland. **Media Experience** Regular broadcaster radio & TV & contributor to press. **Addits** Chair, Ed Brd World Zoo Conservation Strategy 1990-93.

WHEELER Colin Chief Executive **SOCIETY OF LICENSED VICTUALLERS** SOCIAL Type: Fundraiser; Trade/Educational Charity. Elvian House, Nixey Close, Slough, Berks SL1 1NQ Tel:01753-814555 Fax:01753-810529 **Expertise** Administration/organization and management. **Prev Posts** Private practice surveyor; Estates Manager, Society of Licensed Victuallers. **Prof Background** Surveying. **Pres Committees** Licensed Victuallers' Schools Boards; Editorial Board, The Licensee and Morning Advertiser. **Media Experience** Presentation skills.

WHISKIN Nigel Chief Executive **CRIME CONCERN** SOCIAL Type: Fundraiser; Service provider. Signal Point, Station Road, Swindon, Wilts SN1 1FE Tel:01793-514596 Fax:01793-514654 **Expertise** Community safety and crime prevention. **Prev Posts** Probation officer 1965-71; Regional Dir, NACRO 1971-82; Asst Dir, NACRO 1984-88. **Prof Background** Probation service. **Awards/Research** Awds: MBE (Services to Offenders). **Pres Committees** Dir, Internal Centre for Crime Prevention (Montreal). **Past Committees** Morgan Working Party, European Analytical College; Community Safety (1990); Crime Prevention & Urban Security 1992-93. **Media Experience** TV, radio and press contributor.

WHITAKER Ben Director **CALOUSTE GULBENKIAN FOUNDATION (UK)** SOCIAL Type: Grant maker.   98 Portland Place, London   W1N 4ET Tel:0171-636 5313   Fax:0171-637 3421   **Expertise** Executive Director. **Prev Posts** Junior Minister for Overseas Devmt 1969-70; MP for Hampstead 1966-70; The UK Member, UN Human Rights Sub-Commission 1975-88; Executive Director, Minority Rights Group 1971-88. **Prof Background** Barrister at law; BA History, Oxford. **Awards/Research** Lieutenant, Order of Merit (Portugal); Author of: the Foundations, The Police in Society, A Bridge of People, The Global Connection, etc. **Pres Committees** Trustee of Allen Lane Foundation. **Past Committees** Chmn, Foundations Forum 1994-96; Goodman Cttee on Chrty Law Reform (auth of dissenting report); Speaker's Commission on Citizenship. **Media Experience** Over 200 broadcasts (TV & radio); author of numerous articles and reviews.

WHITAKER John Deputy Director **OXFAM** SOCIAL Type: Fundraiser; Service provider; Grant maker; Campaigning. 274 Banbury Rd, Oxford OX2 7DZ Tel:01865-312467   Fax:01865-312600   **Expertise** Campaigning; Communication; Fundraising; Marketing. **Prev Posts** Managing Director, AGB Market Information 1986-90; Consultant 1990-92. **Prof Background** MA Cantab (History).

WHITBOURN Dr Philip Secretary **INTERNATIONAL COUNCIL ON MONUMENTS AND SITES - ICOMOS** UK CONSERVATION/ENVIRONMENT Type: Research & Education. 10 Barley Mow Passage, Chiswick, London W4 4PH Tel:0181-994 6477 Fax:0181-747 8464 **Prof Background** FSA, FRIBA, FRTPI, Architect/Planner. **Awards/Research** OBE.

WHITBY Heather Executive Secretary **MATHEMATICAL ASSOCIATION** ARTS Type: Service provider; Professional Association. 259 London Road, Leicester LE2 3BE Tel:0116-270 3877 Fax:0116-244 8508 **Expertise** Management/administration. **Prev Posts** Administrative Officer, The Association of Teachers of Mathematics 1981-90. **Prof Background** BSc Management Science, UMIST; DMS (Distinction), Trent Polytechnic (Nottingham Trent University). **Awards/Research** DMS dissertation on Management in Voluntary Organisations 1988; Article in Mathematics Teaching, The Output of Voluntary Organisations. **Pres Committees** Council & Sub-committees, M.A. (in advisory capacity). **Past Committees** Council & Sub-committee, ATM (in advisory capacity).

WHITE Caroline Chief Executive **ENGLISH CHURCHES HOUSING GROUP** SOCIAL Type: Service provider.   Sutherland House, 70-78 West Hendon Broadway, London NW9 7BT   Tel:0181-203 9233 Fax:0181-203 0092 **Expertise** Housing and care. **Prev Posts** Director Soho Housing Association 1986-89; Development Director Church Housing 1989-91. **Prof Background** BSc (Hons) Durham; MCIOH Member Chartered Institute of Housing. **Pres Committees** Church Housing Trust (fundraising). **Past Committees** Centrepoint, Youth Homeless Charity; Joseph Rowntree Housing Research Cttee; NFHA, Inquiry into the Governance of Housing Assocs. **Media Experience** Some experience with radio, tv, video and press.

WHITLAM M.R. Director General **BRITISH RED CROSS** MEDICAL/HEALTH Type: Fundraiser; Service provider. 9 Grosvenor Crescent, London SW1X 7EJ Tel:0171-235 5454   Fax:0171-235 5194   **Expertise** Voluntary sector management; role of volunteers; juvenile offenders; fundraising. **Prev Posts** Director, Hammersmith teenage project (NACRO) 1974-78; Director, UK Child Care, Save the Children 1978-86; Chief Executive, RNID 1986-90. **Prof Background** M Phil Social Policy; trained as teacher (biology), then further training to become Assistant Governor, HM Prison Service. **Awards/Research** M Phil Thesis: Voluntary Sector Management (Cranfield); numerous articles. **Pres Committees** ACENVO (Assoc. of Chief Execs of Nat. Vol Orgs); numerous Red Cross boards and cttees; several advisory boards. **Past Committees** Too numerous to detail. **Media Experience** Regular TV/radio participant, inc

Newsnight, South Bank Show, & A Good Read.

WIDDOWSON Bob Consultant Director **HOUSING CENTRE TRUST - HC** SOCIAL Type: Educational charity. 356 Holloway Rd, London N7 6PA Tel:0171-700 0100 Fax:0171-700 8128 **Expertise** Voluntary sector at director level. **Prev Posts** Dir, Shelter, (Housing Services) 1985-87; Dir, SHAC (The London Housing Aid Centre) 1988-95; Consultant Dir, Housing Centre Trust 1995 to date. **Prof Background** Housing Advice & Information.

WIGLEY David L. Chief Executive **METHODIST HOMES FOR THE AGED AND METHODIST HOMES HOUSING ASSOCIATION** THE ELDERLY Type: Fundraiser; Service provider. Epworth House, Stuart Street, Derby DE1 2EQ Tel:01332-296200 Fax:01332-296925 **Expertise** General management. **Prev Posts** Dir, Product Development, Proctor & Gamble Italia 1969-77; Technical Manager, Product Development, Proctor & Gamble Latin America 1977-82. **Prof Background** MA, MSc (Chemistry), New College, Oxford 1952-56; FRSA. **Pres Committees** Chair of Governors, Rydal Penrhos School, Colwyn Bay. **Media Experience** TV/radio/video/press experience.

WIGLEY Linda J Director **GARDEN HISTORY SOCIETY** CONSERVATION/ENVIRONMENT Type: Service provider; Campaigning; Nat Amenity Society; Educ/Historical. 77 Cowcross Street, London EC1M 6BP Tel:0171-608 2409 Fax:0171-490 2974 **Expertise** Garden history; museum devt; textile history and technology. **Prev Posts** Devt Manager Bath Royal Lit & Scientific Inst (1994-96);Curator Trowbridge Museum Wiltshire (1989-94);Curator Science Museum London (1985-89). **Prof Background** BA Hons Combined Arts Leicester Univ; Museums Assoc Diploma (AMA). **Awards/Research** Churchill Fellow 1991; Mus & Galls Eur Travel Awards Romania & Belgium;Wyndham Deedes Mem Flshp Israel; Shugborough Hall Pk & Gdns 1984 (rsch);Publ: Arts on Mus in Mus Jnl & Mus Devt. **Pres Committees** South West Federation of Museums and Galleries Cttee Mbr & Hon Editor; Officer on Cncl & Mngmt Cttee Garden History Society. **Past Committees** Officer on Bd of Trustees of the Bath Royal Literary & Scientific Inst 1994-96. **Media Experience** Interviews. **Addits** Freelance Museum Consultant.

WIGMORE Hazel Director **NATIONAL CHILDREN'S CENTRE** CHILDREN/YOUTH Type: Service provider. Brian Jackson Centre, New North Parade, Huddersfield, West Yorkshire HD1 5JP Tel:01484-519988 **Expertise** Management; child care; race awareness. **Prev Posts** Junior executive in industry 1963; own business 1964-68; Advisory teacher 1972-74. **Prof Background** B Ed Hons; Cert Ed. **Pres Committees** BBC Appeals Adv Cttee; Hospital Manager. **Past Committees** Chair, VOLCUF; Chair, Children in Need NE; Non-exec Dir, W Yorks HA; W Yorks Community Care Commission. **Media Experience** Contrib: Other Peoples Children Series, Making A Living Series.

WILCOX Paul Director **COVENANTERS** RELIGIOUS Type: Service provider. 11-13 Lower Hillgate, Stockport, Cheshire SK1 1JQ. Tel:0161-474 1262 Fax:0161-474 1300 **Expertise** Church based youth work. **Prof Background** Regional Co-ordinator for Scripture Union;Secondary Sch Teacher; BA(Hons) Wales. **Pres Committees** Evangelical Alliance Children's Committee.

WILDER John Director **PSYCHIATRIC REHABILITATION ASSOCIATION -PRA** MEDICAL/HEALTH Type: Service provider; Promotion of rehabilitation concepts. The Groupwork Centre, Bayford Mews, Bayford Street, London E8 3SF Tel:0181-985 3570 Fax:0181-986 1334 **Expertise** Community care catalyst and educator. **Prev Posts** Journalism 1945-57; Probation 1957-59; Rehabilitation 1959-today. **Prof Background** Trade Union Courses, Ruskin College Evening Classes; LSE & Home Office Training in Law; Sociology; Psychology; Psychiatry. Established PRA in 1959 using innovative groupwork techniques. **Awards/Research** OBE. National Community Care Awd for therapeutic art technique. Paper to UN Congress on Crime; Social research in E London. Auth: An Aid to Community Care 1980; numerous articles. **Pres Committees** Mbr of many health & local gov cttees on mental health/community care. Consultant on community care progs overseas inc Malta, China, Greece and Mexico. British Rep on EU Cttee for rehabilitation. **Past Committees** Chairman, Rehabilitation International Conference (mental health). Co-Founder, Parliamentary Mental Health Committee. **Media Experience** Various TV and radio programmes and articles in press. **Addits** Composed: Forward with Courage, for the Year of Disabled People.

WILKIN J D Chairman **GOOD GARDENERS ASSOCIATION** SOCIAL Type: Fundraiser; Service provider; Campaigning, Professional Association. Pinetum, Churcham, Gloucester GL2 8AD Tel:01452-750402 Fax:01452-750402 **Expertise** Ecology; Human and Animal health; Natural growing - The No Dig method. **Prev Posts** Dir, Complete Gardeners Ltd 61-95; Birdcage Entertainments 65-75; Courtyard Arts Trust 79-89; Cumulus Organics Ltd 84-92. **Prof Background** Landscaping - Construction ind - Arts. **Awards/Research** Trace Element content of organic and non organic vegetables -its effect on diet and subsequently health. **Pres Committees** Good Gardeners Association Council and Fundraising committees. **Past Committees** Courtyard Arts Trust; Complete Gardeners Ltd. **Media Experience** TV and Radio.

WILKINS David B. Director **EUROGROUP FOR ANIMAL WELFARE** ANIMAL/WILDLIFE Type: Lobbying organization in the European Union. Rue Boduognat 13, 1000 Brussels, Belgium 02 231 13 88 **Expertise** Animal Welfare. **Prev Posts** Partner, Veterinary Practice Horsham UK 1970-77; Chief Veterinary Officer, RSPCA 1977-92. **Prof Background** Veterinary Surgeon, qualified Cambridge Univ Veterinary School 1963. **Awards/Research** Awds: Royal College of Veterinary Surgeons Livesey Medal 1991. **Pres Committees** Secretariat to European Parliament's Intergroup on Welfare & Conservation of Animals; European Conference Group on the Protection of Farm Animals. **Past Committees** Brd of Govs, Ditcham Park Schl, Hants; Cncl of Europe Standing Cttee, Convention on Protection of Animals Kept for Farming Purposes

WILKINS Nichola Director **CARE AND REPAIR** SOCIAL Type: Service provider; Nat co-ordinating body - Home Improvement Agencies. Castle House, Kirtley Drive, Nottingham NG7 1LD Tel:0115-979 9091 Fax:0115-985 9457 **Expertise** Social welfare provision in the voluntary sector. **Prev Posts** Development Officer, Mencap 1985-1989; Regional Officer, Age Concern England 1989-1993. **Prof Background** BA (Hons) Philosophy; M.Med.Sci. in Community Medicine. **Awards/Research** Growing Old in Spain, 1993. Care to Listen, 1987. Birth Plans, 1985. Participation in Health, 1983. Various articles. **Media Experience** Radio interviews, television and press; work in local radio.

WILLIAMS Catriona Director **CHILDREN IN WALES - PLANT YNG NGHYRMU** CHILDREN/YOUTH Type: National Umbrella Childrens Organisation in Wales. 7 Cleeve House, Lambourne Crescent, Cardiff CF4 5GY Tel:01222-761177 Fax:01222-747934 **Expertise** All aspects of Child welfare and childrens issues; Promotion of UN Convention on Rights of the Child. **Prev Posts** Child Protection Co-ordinator (1989-92). **Prof Background** Social Worker; Research and Lecturing. **Awards/Research** Children in Wales publish material. **Pres Committees** Chair, UK Group of The European Forum for Child Welfare; Children's Rights Office; Wales Youth Agency Ed & Training Sub-Cttee; Wales Children in Need Advisory Cttee; Play Wales Mngmt Cttee. **Past Committees** Effective Govt Structures for Children - Advisory Group. **Media Experience** Considerable media experience. **Addits** Health & Social Gain for Children (Welsh Office).

WILLIAMS Brother Gregory Director **LASALLIAN DEVELOPING WORLD PROJECTS** Type: Fundraiser; Service provider; Grant maker (Overseas NGOs only) La Salle House, 405 Beulah Hill, London SE19 3HB Tel:0181-670 1612 Fax:0181-761 7357 **Expertise** Education - Development Education in particular. **Prev Posts** Teacher Prep Sch, Ipswich 1961-64; Boarding House Master, Ipswich 1964-74; Head of R.E. Dept - Year Head, Basildon 1974-88. **Prof Background** BA; PGCE; MA Educational Research. **Awards/Research** MA Thesis relating to attitudes among cross section of school to authority. **Pres Committees** Mgmt Cttee, Lasallian Developing World Projects. **Past Committees** Board of Mgrs, St Williams Cmty Home Sch 1981-92; Prov Cncl, De La Salle Brothers 1977-96. **Media Experience** Occasional Radio & TV interviews; Exec Producer of Video - Brother.

WILLIAMS Grenville National Organiser **CAMPAIGN FOR PRESS AND BROADCASTING FREEDOM - CPBF** SOCIAL Type: Campaigning. 8 Cynthia Street, London N1 9SF Tel:0171-278 4430

WILLIAMS Liz Company Secretary **ADVISORY CENTRE FOR EDUCATION (ACE) LTD - ACE** SOCIAL Type: Service provider. 1B Aberdeen Studios, 22-24 Highbury Grove, London N5 2DQ Tel:0171-354 8318 Tel:0171-354 9069

WILLIAMS Raymond J. General Administrator/Secretary **ASSOCIATION OF INDEPENDENT RAILWAYS & PRESERVATION SOCIETIES** CONSERVATION/ENVIRONMENT Type: Service provider. 16 Woodbrook, Charing, Ashford, Kent TN27 0DN Tel:01233-712130 **Expertise** Policy and administration. **Prev Posts** Secretary, Tenterden Railway Co. since 1985. **Pres Committees** Council of ARPS. **Media Experience** Provides information/comment to all media.

WILLIAMS Rev Trevor Leader **CORRYMEELA COMMUNITY** RELIGIOUS Type: Christian community for reconciliation. 8 Upper Crescent, Belfast, Northern Ireland BT7 1NT Tel:01232-325008 **Prev Posts** Queens University Chaplain, 1977-80; Producer, BBC Northern Ireland 1980-88; Rector, St Johns, Newcastle 1988-93. **Prof Background** Ordained priest of Church of Ireland. **Pres Committees** General Synod of Church of Ireland; Broadcasting Cttee of Church of Ireland; Exec Cttee Irish Council of Churches. **Media Experience** Producer TV and radio (BBC NI); freelance producer Ulster TV 1992-93.

WILLIAMSON Andrew Honorary Secretary **ASSOCIATION OF DIRECTORS OF SOCIAL SERVICES** Type: Professional Association. Social Services Dept, County Hall, Topsham Road, Exeter, Devon EX2 4QR Tel:01392-384947 Fax:01392-384984

WILSON Brenda Admin/Finance Officer **NATIONAL CENTRE FOR PLAY - NCP** CHILDREN/YOUTH Type: Service provider; Information; Training & Research. Moray House Institute, Cramond Campus, Cramond Rd, Edinburgh EH4 6JD Tel:0131-312 8088 Fax:0131-312 8979 **Expertise** Secretary IPA Scotland. **Prev Posts** Employed at Moray House for 11 years. Currently SCOTVEC contact; Secretary, IPA Scotland. **Pres Committees** Secretary, Policy Advisory Group; Playwork Centres Network.

WILSON Rev Cecil H. General Secretary **CHURCH MISSIONARY SOCIETY IRELAND - CMSI** RELIGIOUS Type: Overseas Mission & Development. Church of Ireland House, 61-67 Donegal St, Belfast BT1 4QH Tel:01232-324581 Fax:01232-321756 **Expertise** Management; Ordained Ministry; Conference organising and speaking. **Prev Posts** Northern Secretary CMSI 1986-87; Youth Secretary CMSI 1976-81; Minor Canon, Dromore Cathedral 1972-76. **Prof Background** Church of Ireland Theological College Dublin 1966-69 **Pres Committees** Church of Ireland Council for the Church Overseas; Irish Council of Churches Board of Overseas Affairs CMS (Britain) Standing Comm. **Media Experience** Annual TV broadcast on RTE TV Dublin.

WILSON Morna Administrator **BRITTLE BONE SOCIETY** DISABILITY Type: Fundraiser; Service provider; Grant maker. 30 Guthrie Street, Dundee DD1 5BS Tel:01382-204446 Fax:01382-206771 **Expertise** Fundraising; National Appeals; Trusts Office Management; Conference Organisation. **Prof Background** NEBSM Diploma in Management; HNC Computing. **Pres Committees** Brittle Bone Society Management Committee; OIFE Governing Body. **Media Experience** BBC Scotland interviews; local and national press.

WILSON Paul Chief Executive **CARR-GOMM SOCIETY** SOCIAL Type: Service provider; Special Needs

Housing Association. Duke House, 6-12 Tabard St, London SE1 4JU Tel:0171-397 5300 Fax:0171-397 5301 **Expertise** Housing; voluntary sector management. **Prev Posts** Community Enabler, Bexley London Borough 1974-81; Dir, Council for Social Responsibility, 1981-88. **Prof Background** Associate of Kings College, London 1967; Diploma in Community Studies 1972. **Past Committees** Chair, Victim Support 1984-88.

WILSON Peter Chief Executive **TIMBER GROWERS ASSOCIATION - TGA** CONSERVATION/ENVIRONMENT Type: Service provider; Trade association; Political representation. 5 Dublin Street Lane South, Edinburgh EH1 3PX Tel:0131-538 7111 Fax:0131-538 7222 **Expertise** British Forestry Policy; Information Services; Tropical Silviculture. **Prev Posts** Tech Co-op Officer, O/seas Development Admin Solomon Islands 1984-88; Land Use & Environment Officer/Tech Dir TGA 1988-93. **Prof Background** BSc (Hons) Forestry, University of Wales; MSc Forestry & its relation to land use, Univ of Oxford. MICFor (Member Institute of Chartered Foresters). **Awards/Research** Various research publications by Solomon Islands Govt, numerous articles in press and trade media. **Pres Committees** Home Grown Timber Advisory Committee (statutory cttee);Chair, ICF Policy & Legislation Cttee;ICF Council; UK rep, CEPF - Confed of European Forest Owners. **Media Experience** Frequent contributor to press and radio, some TV.

WINCOTT Elizabeth Chief Executive **HOMOEOPATHIC TRUST FOR RESEARCH AND EDUCATION** MEDICAL/HEALTH Type: Service provider. Hahnemann House, 2 Powis Place, London WC1N 3HT Tel:0171-837-9469 Fax:0171-278 7900 **Expertise** Management; strategic planning; equal opportunities; staff development. **Prev Posts** Adv Soc Wkr, Mt Sinai Hosp, NY USA 70-77; Prncpl Off, Health, Lothian Reg Cncl 77-85;Asst Dir, Field, NACAB 85-89; CE, Brit Deaf Assoc 89-94. Currently Sec, Fac of Homoeopathy. **Prof Background** Dip. Applied Social Studies, LSE; Cert Social Studies, Edinburgh University. **Awards/Research** Papers and reports on social work, haemophilia care and management development in UK & USA; presentations at national and international conferences. **Pres Committees** Chair, Project Group on Assisted Reproduction. **Past Committees** Fnd/Ch:Prncp Offs Ch, Panel of 4. **Media Experience** Numerous radio, some TV and press interviews. **Addits** Co-founder, Special Int Gp, Social Workers in Haemophilia (UK).

WITTS Diana Katharine General Secretary **CHURCH MISSION SOCIETY - CMS** RELIGIOUS Type: Mission Society. Partnership House, 157 Waterloo Road, London SE1 8UU Tel:0171-928 8681 Fax:0171-401 3215 **Expertise** Educationalist,introduced co-educ to Gordonstones Sch,senior/1st house mistress 1971-75;invol in Sudan. **Prev Posts** CMS Regional Secretary W Africa, Sudan, Zaire 1985-95;CMS Mission partner Kenya, Zaire 1975-85;Vocational training/setting up Theological Education by Extension (Zaire). **Prof Background** BSc Physics-Bristol University. **Awards/Research** Cross of St Augustine. **Pres Committees** Trustee: Africa Educational Trust; Cttee: Bd of Mission (Church of England); Partners for world mission;International/Development Affairs. **Past Committees** Africa Cttee, Christian Aid;Churches Comm on Mission, Africa Forum;Jt Christian Ministry W Africa;Prj Christian Muslim Relats in Af. **Addits** Member of Sudan Church Association.

WOOD Arthur M.M. General Secretary and Chief Executive **ROYAL SCOTTISH SOCIETY FOR PREVENTION OF CRUELTY TO CHILDREN - CHILDREN 1ST** CHILDREN/YOUTH Type: Fundraiser; Service provider. Melville House, 41 Polwarth Terrace, Edinburgh EH11 1NU Tel:0131-337 8539 Fax:0131-346 8284 **Prev Posts** Law Assistant 1960-61; Deputy Secretary, RSSPCC 1961-1968. **Prof Background** Legal training 1955-1960; Graduate MA LLB 1960 at Edinburgh University. **Awards/Research** OBE. **Media Experience** Regular involvement.

WOOD Christopher Charles Head of Information Services **HORTICULTURAL RESEARCH ASSOCIATION** ENVIRONMENT C/o Horticulture Research International, Wellesbourne, Warwick CV35 9EF Tel:01789-470382 Fax:01789-470552 **Expertise** Scientific Information, Public Relations. **Prev Posts** Liaison Officer Royal Botanic Garden, Edinburgh 1974-83. **Prof Background** BSc Botany 1967 (first class Hons) University of Newcastle-upon-Tyne; PhD 1971 University of Newcastle-upon-Tyne; FLS 1972 (Fellow of Linnean Society). **Pres Committees** Coventry University, Biological Sciences Advisory Panel; Worcester College of Higher Education, Industrial Liaison Panel. **Media Experience** Consultant Channel 4 production Plant Life.

WOOD Michael A. Director **ULSTER CANCER FOUNDATION** MEDICAL/HEALTH Type: Fundraiser; Service provider; Grant maker; Health advocacy. 40-42 Eglantine Avenue, Belfast, NI BT9 6DX Tel:01232-663281 Fax:01232-660081 **Prev Posts** Royal Navy 1952-64; ICI Marketing 1964-71; Ulster Cancer Foundation since 1971. **Prof Background** Health education; Public relations and marketing. WHO International Health Consultant. Hon MSc Ulster University 1994. **Awards/Research** MBE. **Pres Committees** Chair, International Union Against Cancer Worldwide Tobacco Programme. **Media Experience** NI & Internat Agencies Health spokesman on Cancer/Tobacco for 23 years.

WOOD Dr Stephen J.T. Medical Director **BRITISH INSTITUTE FOR BRAIN INJURED CHILDREN - BIBIC** MEDICAL/HEALTH Type: Fundraiser; Service provider. Knowle Hall, Bridgewater, Somerset TA7 8PJ Tel:01278-684060 Fax:01278-685573 **Expertise** Paediatric neurology and ear, nose and throat medicine. **Prev Posts** NHS Principal in General Practice 1979-86; Consultant Physician in Occupational Health 1986-89. **Prof Background** Read Medicine at Birmingham Medical School. **Awards/Research** MB; ChB; COH; Current research into treatment of children with cerebral palsey. **Media Experience** Some experience with radio and press.

WOODD Charles National Director **COMMUNITY MATTERS** SOCIAL Type: Fundraiser; Service provider. 8-9 Upper Street, Islington, London N1 0PQ Tel:0171-226 0189 Fax:0171-354 9570 **Prev Posts** Director, Bede House Assoc 1972-80; General Sec, Voluntary Action Westminster 1980-86. **Prof Background** BA Econ, Jesus College, Cambridge; Diploma, Social Admin, LSE. **Pres**

Committees Charity Commission's Advisory Cttee on Trusteeship; NCVO Trustee Services Unit Advisory Gp; Meeting Point (local charity, advice centre); Chair, Volunteers in Action Southwark. **Past Committees** NCVO/Charity Commission Working Party on Trustee Training; Exec Cttee, Standing Conf for Community Development.

WOODWARD Robert Founder **CANCER AND LEUKAEMIA IN CHILDHOOD TRUST, THE - CLIC** MEDICAL/HEALTH Type: Fundraiser; Service provider; Grant maker. 12-13 King Square, Bristol BS2 8JH Tel:0117-924 8844 Fax:0117-924 4505 **Prev Posts** Snr Partner, Woodward Brothers 1962-84; Snr Partner, Wotton Mosaics 1975-85; Founded CLIC 1976. **Awards/Research** Auth: Listen My Child Has A Lot Of Living To Do, 1990; Hon LLD, Bristol University 1987; European Architectural Award 1975 (Market St, Wotton-Under-Edge);Co-Ed: The Wootton Mosaic. **Pres Committees** ACT, Assoc for Children with life-threatening or Terminal conditions and their families, Exec Council; Brd of Govs, Inst of Child Health; CLIC SW; CLIC UK; Patron, Bristol Univ Resource Campaign. **Media Experience** Radio/TV and newspapers.

WOOLMER Dr Tim Director **WESTMINSTER PASTORAL FOUNDATION** SOCIAL Type: Service provider. 23 Kensington Square, London W8 5HN Tel:0171-937 6956 Fax:0171-937 1767 **Expertise** Group analyst; administrator. **Prev Posts** Principal, Edwardes College, Peshawar 1982-87; Head of Continuing Education, Roehampton Institute 1989-91. Currently: Director, Counselling in Companies. **Prof Background** MA (Oxon); PGCE and Ac Dip Ed (London); MEd and EdD (Massachusetts). **Awards/Research** Educational philosophy; psychodynamic theory. **Pres Committees** Registration Board, UK Council of Psychotherapy; Member, National Lead Body for Advice, Guidance and Counselling. **Addits** Magistrate (Inner London Juvenile Courts) for 10 years until 1982.

WORTHINGTON Ann Founder/Organiser **IN TOUCH** MEDICAL/HEALTH Type: Service provider. 10 Norman Road, Sale, Cheshire M33 3DF Tel:0161-905 2440 **Awards/Research** MBE.

WRIDE Vanessa Executive Director **IRIS FUND FOR PREVENTION OF BLINDNESS** DISABILITY Type: Fundraiser; Grant maker; Campaigning. 2nd Floor, York House, 199 Westminster Bridge Rd, London SE1 7UT Tel:0171-928 7743 Fax:0171-928 7919 **Expertise** Ophthalmic Research: **Prof Background** M.C.S.P. **Pres Committees** Battersea Crime Prevention Panel.

WRIGHT John Administrator **INDEPENDENT PANEL FOR SPECIAL EDUCATION ADVICE - IPSEA** CHILD/YOUTH Type: Service provider. 4 Ancient House Mews, Woodbridge, Suffolk IP12 1DH Tel:01394-382814 Fax:01394-380518 **Expertise** Indep advice on local education authorities; legal duties towards children with special educ needs.

WYLIE Tom Chief Executive **NATIONAL YOUTH AGENCY** Type: Service provider; Grant maker; Campaigning. 17-23 Albion Street, Leicester LE1 6GD Tel:0116-285 6789 Fax:0116-247 1043 **Expertise** Youth work; Education. **Prev Posts** Her Majesty's Inspector of Education 1979-95. **Prof Background** Teaching; Youth Work. **Awards/Research** Editor of various HMI publications. **Pres Committees** Various youth related bodies. **Media Experience** TV, radio and press.

WYSE JACKSON Peter S. Secretary General **BOTANIC GARDENS CONSERVATION INTERNATIONAL** CONSERVATION/ENVIRONMENT Type: Fundraiser; Service provider. Descanso House, 199 Kew Road, Richmond, Surrey TW9 3BW Tel:0181-332 5953 Fax:0181-332 5956 **Expertise** Plant conservation; botanic garden development. **Prev Posts** Curator, Univ of Dublin Botanic Garden 1981-87; Programme Director, Botanic Gardens Conservation International 1987-93. **Prof Background** Trinity College, Dublin: BA (Mod) Botany; MA; PhD.

Y

YELDING David Director **RESEARCH INSTITUTE FOR CONSUMER AFFAIRS - RICA** SOCIAL Type: Fundraiser; Research Organisation. 2 Marylebone Road, London NW1 4DF   Tel:0171-830 7516 Fax:0171-830 7679

YEO Diane Chief Executive **MALCOLM SARGENT CANCER FUND FOR CHILDREN** MEDICAL/HEALTH Type: Fundraiser; Service provider; Grant maker.   14 Abingdon Rd, London W8 6AF Tel:0171-937 4548 Fax:0171-376 1193 **Expertise** Charity management. **Prev Posts** Charity Commissioner 1989-95; Director, ICFM 1992-95. **Prof Background** London University; Institut Français de Presse. **Pres Committees** Consultant, Ctre for Volun Org, LSE; Consultant, Ctre for Charity & Trust Research, South Bank Univ; Advisory Cncl, CNVO; Advisory Brd, Voluntary Sector TV; Political Advertising Working Party, ASA. **Past Committees** Charity Appointments 1985-86; NCVO/Charity Commission Trustee Training Working Party 1991-4; Charity Standards Cttee 1990-4. **Media Experience** Extensive experience in radio, TV and press. **Addits** FICFM; FRSA.

YOUNG Barbara S. Chief Executive **ROYAL SOCIETY FOR THE PROTECTION OF BIRDS - RSPB** ANIMAL/WILDLIFE Type: Conservation charity. The Lodge, Sandy, Bedfordshire SG19 2DL Tel:01767-680551 Fax:01767-692365 **Expertise** Management and management development; strategy. **Prev Posts** Dist Admin, Haringey Health Auth 1982-85; Dist Gen Mngr, Paddington and N Kensington HA 1985-88; Dist Gen Mngr, Parkside HA 1988-91. **Prof Background** MA (Hons) Classics, Edinburgh; Dip. Inst of Health Services Mngmnt; Patron, Inst of Ecology & Environmental Mngmnt 1993; Hon Degree, Doctor of Univ of Stirling, 1995 in recognition of work for RSPB. **Pres Committees** Trustee, Brd on NCVO 1993; Birdlife Int World Cncl 1994; UK Round Table on Sustainable Devt (Dept of Environment) 1995; Commission on the Future of the Vol Sector 1995 to date. **Past Committees** Cncl, Inst of Hlth Services Mngmnt 1985-91; BBC Gen Adv Cttee 1983-88; Cttee, King's Fnd Inst 1986-90; Going for Green (DoE) 1994-6. **Addits** Committee on the Public Understanding of Science (COPUS), 1996 to date.

YOUNG Bernard Chief Executive **SAINT ANN'S HOSPICE - MANCHESTER** MEDICAL/HEALTH Type: Fundraiser; Service provider. Appeals Office, 2 Finney Lane, Cheadle, Stockport SK8 3DQ Tel:0161-283 6600 Fax:0161-283 6601 **Expertise** Management, nursing, training & development. **Prev Posts** Director of Nursing Services (Board Level) 1987-91; Director, Operational Services (Board Level) 1991-93; Regional Nurse 1993-95. **Prof Background** Registered General Nurse. **Awards/Research** Awarded Territorial Decoration (TD); Major (TA); RAMC (V). **Past Committees** Trent RHA Task Force on Jr Drs; Mbr, Nat NHS Qual Grp; Mbr, Reg Research & Dev Cttee; Mbr, Nat Clinical Coordinators Ad Grp to NHS. **Media Experience** Experience in TV, radio and press.

YOUNG David B.P. General Manager **SCOTTISH ELECTRICAL CHARITABLE TRAINING TRUST** SOCIAL Type: Service provider.   Bush House, Bush Estate, Midlothian EH26 0SB   Tel:0131-4455659 Fax:0131-4455661 **Expertise** Management & Finance. **Prev Posts** General Manager, Caledonian Bank, Standard Property Investment plc 1977-92. **Prof Background** Chartered Accountant.

YOUNG Kate Executive Director **WOMANKIND WORLDWIDE** SOCIAL Type: Fundraiser; Grant maker. 3-4 Albion Place, Galena Rd, London W6 0LT Tel:0181-563 8607   **Expertise** Anthropology, Development studies. **Prev Posts** Fellow, IDS, University Sussex 1975-88.   **Prof Background** PhD London University.   **Awards/Research** Planning Development with Women, Macmillan; Of Marriage & the Market (ed) Routledge; Serving Two Masters (ed) Allied. **Pres Committees** CIIR Executive Committee.

YOUNG Major M.J. Bursar **PARTIS COLLEGE** CHILD/YOUTH Type: Service provider.   Newbridge Hill, Bath, Avon BA1 3QD Tel:01225-421532 **Expertise** Administration, care & catering. **Prev Posts** Lay Administrator, Exeter Cathedral 1983-85; Managing Director, Elmwood Residential Home, Colyford Devon 1985-87; Assistant Accountant, Hoechst Ceramtec UK Ltd 1987-96. **Prof Background** Army Officer; Royal Signals (10 yrs); Army Catering Corps; Final post Staff Officer (Major).

YOUNG Nicholas Chief Executive **CANCER RELIEF MACMILLAN FUND**   MEDICAL/HEALTH Type: Fundraiser; Service provider; Grant maker; Campaigning 15-19 Britten Street, London SW3 3TZ   Tel:0171-351 7811 Fax:0171-376 8098 **Expertise** Community care. **Prev Posts** Solicitor & Partner in Turner Martin & Symes (Law firm) 1979-85; Secretary for Development, Sue Ryder Foundation 1985-90; Dir, UK Operations, British Red Cross 1990-95. **Prof Background** Commercial lawyer; Birmingham University LLB; Cabinet Office Top Management Programme 1993.   **Pres Committees** Vice-Chair, Nat Council for Hospice & Specialist Palliative Care Services; Mbr, ACENVO Policy & Research Task Group. **Past Committees** Various local & professional committees. **Media Experience** Various radio, TV, video, press.

CHARITIES ON DISK - *DATA DIRECT*

*IMMEDIATE ACCESS TO
7000+ UK National Charities
& Voluntary Organizations*

*Your instant database
- no research required*

*With monthly updates
- no need for you to revise*

*Categorised by subject
- easy to sort/search*

*Registered charity numbers
- positive identification*

*Phone, fax and address
at your fingertips*

*Runs on your in-house
database system*

DATABASE SERVICE - CHARITIES ON DISK

Information is continually checked and revised; subscribers receive full updated data disks every month.

Disks are issued in formats to fit all mainstream database systems and so can be loaded onto your own database to meet all your reference and mailing needs.

MAILING SERVICE

Mailing disks for your use can be prepared to your exact specifications. Alternatively, can place an insert in our regular mailings direct to *7000+* charities.

For all details & prices call Aurelian direct on 0181-960 7918/0171-794 8609.

EXECUTIVE NOTICEBOARD ❑
1996-97 Training Sessions and Meetings for Charity Management

THE CHARITY FORUM

The Charity Forum aims to be the leading interactive exchange between member organisations within the voluntary sector and individuals by providing a service of training, focus groups and educative seminars which will maximise their effectiveness, develop tailored professional skills and facilitate successful business outcomes.

A full programme of lunchtime meetings and half-day seminars will be held during 1997, and it is intended that the topics will include:

- **PR and Fundraising - Power Struggle or Power Sharing?**
- **Approaches from the Media - Opportunity or Threat?**
- **SORP - Dealing with Gifts in Kind**
- **Employment Practice**
- **Saying "Thank You" - The Personal Touch in Fundraising**
- **Coping with Increased Activity - Spreading the Workload**
- **Setting Individual Budgets**
- **Evaluation of Meetings - When to Accept and When to Decline**

For details of events, contact the Director of the **Charity Forum**, Graham Allen:
Tel: 01483 281766. Fax: 01483 281767

THE VOLUNTARY SECTOR
☞ HANDS ON ☜ INTERNET TRAINING SESSIONS

Tutors include: Howard Lake - author of *Direct Connection's Guide to Fundraising on the Internet*, and fundraiser for Amnesty International, British Section. Sandra Vogel - now working as an Internet journalist and trainer, previously of LVSC and Shelter. Currently writing *First Steps on the Internet: a Practical Guide.*

Courses are hosted at Internet Cafes. With a maximum of 12 people per PC you will learn through your own hands-on experience. As the cafes offer UK-wide public access to the Internet, you can continue to work on it even if your organization is not yet connected.

Courses are taking place throughout the UK in Spring/Summer 1997.
For details of dates in your area, please call **Aurelian:** Tel: 0181-960 7918. Fax: 0171-794 8609.
All half-day courses commence at 9am, conclude approx 12.30; coffee and pastries included.
Price per person £55.00 + VAT.

Course titles:
- **Introduction to Internet Fundraising**
- **Powers and Uses of E-Mail**
- **Information on the Internet - Getting Your Message Across**

EXECUTIVE NOTICEBOARD ☐
1996-97 Training Sessions and Meetings for Charity Management

ACENVO - Association of Chief Executives of National Voluntary Organisations

Evening Workshops: sponsored by Clark Whitehill

21 Nov 1996   Marketing Your Cause
5 Feb 1997   From Traffic Jam to Super Highway: A Crash Course in Recent IT Development

Cost: £20 to ACENVO members/supporters; £20 to non-member CE's of National Voluntary Organisations

Day Seminars: sponsored by Barclays Bank

31 Jan 1997   Leadership Skills for Chief Executives
11 March 1997 Dealing with Difficult Staff

Cost: £70 to ACENVO members; £95 to non-members. Open to CE's of National Voluntary Organisations only

Action Learning Sets: sponsored by VCD, Department of National Heritage
(each set comprises 6 separate days, commencement date only given below)

4 Dec 1996   Broad Theme: Managing Changing Relationships with Staff and Trustees

Cost £195 to ACENVO members; £320 to non-members. Open to CE's of National Voluntary Organisations only.

Course for New/Nearly New Chief Executives: sponsored by VCD, Department of National Heritage
(6 day course - 1 day per month - in Central London for 12 new Chief Executives)

2 Dec 1996   Financial Matters
15 Jan 1997   Chief Executive as Ambassador
5 Feb 1997   Fundamentals of Fundraising
5 Mar 1997   Strategic Planning

Cost for 6 days: £200 to ACENVO members; £320 to non-members. Open to CE's of National Voluntary Organisations only

All enquiries to Dorothy Dalton: ACENVO, 31-33 College Road, Harrow, Middx HA1 1EJ
                                    Tel: 0181-424 2334; Fax 0181-426 0055

MAGAZINES & NEWSLETTERS ❑
Specialist Charity Publications in the United Kingdom and Overseas

ACE Bulletin 1(b) Aberdeen Studios, 22-24 Highbury Grove, London N5 2DQ
American Benefactor - http://www.AmericanBenefactor.com
ARVAC Bulletin 60 Highbury Grove, London N5 2AG
Association Executive AssociAction Publications, PO Box 10, Epping, Essex
Big Issue Fleet House, 57-61 Clerkenwell Rd, London EC1M 5NP
Business in the Community 44 Baker St, London W1M 1DH
Caritas ICSA, 16 Park Crescent, London W1N 4AH
Charities Management Mitre House, The Clifton Centre, 110 Clifton St, London EC2A 4HD
Charity Magazine Centurion House, 34-36 High St, Rickmansworth WD3 1ER
Charity Times 408 The Fruit & Wool Exchange, Brushfield St, London E1 6EP
Charity World 70 Queen's Head St, London N1 8NG 0171-359 1934
Chronicle of Philanthropy (USA) - chronicle-request@nonprofit.com
Circulation NACVS 177 Arundel St, Sheffield, S Yorks S1 2NU
Common Ground Unison, 1 Mabledon Place, London WC1H 9AJ
Community Care Quadrant House, The Quadrant, Sutton, SM2 5AS
Conservator BTCV 36 St Mary's St, Wallingford, Oxon OX10 0EU
Corporate Citizen Directory of Social Change, 24 Stephenson Way, London NW1 2DP
Funding Digest - http://www.fundraising.co.uk/fundraising/mags/fdigest.html
Fundraising Ireland 55 Whitecliff, Rathfarnham, Dublin 16.
Journal of Nonprofit and Voluntary Sector Marketing Henry Stewart Publications, Russell House, 28/30 Little Russell St, London WC1A 2HN
Home and Country Women's Institute Magazine, 104 New Kings Road, London SW6 4LY
Young People Now National Youth Agency, 17/23 Albion St, Leicester LE1 6GD
NCVO News NCVO, Regents Wharf, 8 All Saints St, London N1 9RL
NonProfit Times - http://haven.ios.com/~nptimes/index.html
Philanthropy News Digest - http://fndcenter.org/phil/philmain.html
Planned Giving Today - http://www.scn.org/ip/pgt/
Professional Fundraising Magazine 4 Post Office Walk, Hertford, Herts SG14 1DL
Raiser's Edge Quarterly Newsletter Blackbaud, Claremont Centre, 39 Durham Street, Glasgow G411BS
Social and Charitable Cause Marketing - michael@yrkpa.kias.com
tCF Now Charity Forum, Stovolds, 191 The Street, West Horsley, Surrey KT24 6HR
Third Force News - SCVO, 18/19 Claremont Crescent, Edinburgh EH7 4QD
Third Sector 4 Assam St, London E1 7QS
Trust and Foundation News Association of Charitable Foundations, 4 Bloomsbury Square, London WC1A 2RL
Trust Monitor - Directory of Social Change, 24 Stephenson Way, London NW1 2DP
UPDATE - ICFM Creative Communications, 77 Alma Rd, Clifton, Bristol BS8 2DP
Voluntary Voice - LVSC 356 Holloway Rd, London N7 6PA
Volunteer - Volunteer Centre Magazine, Carriage Row, 183 Eversholt St, London NW1 1BU

CONSULTANTS & SERVICES

Directory of Management & Development Resources for Charities

COMPUTER SERVICES

AURELIAN INFORMATION

Database information suppliers; voluntary sector mailing lists.

129 Leighton Gardens
London NW10 3PS
Tel: 0181-960 7918 Fax: 0171-794 8609

CONTACTS: Paul Petzold, Kim Worts

Aurelian maintains a continually updated database of information on national charities and voluntary organizations. The database is currently available on annual subscription in the UK. Regular updates are provided. We also run an on-line service for off-site reference.

To facilitate networking throughout the sector we operate a permanent system of monitoring and survey. We also undertake specific research projects for charity clients.

Our information is used by organizations of all sizes and in every area of activity in the voluntary sector.

MINERVA COMPUTER SYSTEMS plc

Computer Systems/Software

21/22 Imperial Square
Cheltenham GL50 1QZ
Tel: 01242-511232
Fax: 01242-221640

CONTACTS: Una Cadien, Hanif Patel

Minerva Computer Systems provides hardware, software, consultancy, system design and development, training, maintenance and other support services to meet both broad based business needs for those in the 'not-for-profit' and selected specialist market place.

CHARITY CLIENTS: Barnardos, World Vision, English Heritage, RNID, National Trust Enterprise, Battersea Dogs Home.

OTHER CLIENTS: Air London, Royal College of Anaesthetists, CBI, Eeiba (Electronic & Electrical Industries Benevolent Association).

Free initial consultation. Negotiable Rates

CONFERENCE & EXHIBITION FACILITIES

MANCHESTER CONFERENCE CENTRE

UMIST P O Box 88
Manchester M60 1QD
Tel: 0161-200 4100
Fax: 0161-200 4090

CONTACTS: Helen McGlashan, Richard Handscombe

The Manchester Conference Centre offers year round conference facilities for up to 300 delegates. During vacations conferences of 500 may be comfortably accommodated. 800 en suite bedrooms as well as 900 standard rooms are available. City centre location with special deals for associations and charities.

CHARITY CLIENTS: National Childbirth Trust, Red Cross, NCVO, British Dyslexia Assoc, British Diabetic Assoc.

OTHER CLIENTS: British Society of Gastroenterology. Royal Society of Chemistry, Library Assoc, NFHA, Assoc of Graduate Recruiters.
Free initial consultation.

DESIGN & PRINT

AUTUMN DESIGNS

Lee Valley Technopark
Ashley Road
London N17 9LN

Tel: 0181-880 4530
Fax: 0181-880 4531
E-mail: autumn@cygnet.co.uk

CONTACT: Steve Harvey

Autumn Designs is a design consultancy specialising in the production of dynamic corporate material that gets results. Whether it is fundraising material, exhibitions or annual reports, our work conveys the personality and energy of our client. We work solely within the public sector, with many charities and housing associations.

CHARITY CLIENTS: Christian Aid, NSPCC, National Foster Care Association, Peabody Trust, Centrepoint, Many Housing Associations, apa - Drugs and community alcohol initiatives, Body Positive, CHAR.

DIRECT MAIL SERVICES

AURELIAN INFORMATION

Voluntary sector mailing lists.

129 Leighton Gardens
London NW10 3PS
Tel: 0181-960 7918 & 0171-794 8609

CONTACTS: Paul Petzold, Kim Worts

Call us for detailed and targetted mailing lists of the UK voluntary sector - we provide labels or disks selected by geography, size or subject to the precise area of the sector you wish to contact.

For less than half the price of the postage - you can join one of our quarterly mailings which go direct to over 7000 national charities and voluntary organizations. Space is limited in the joint mailings so early bookings are recommended.

Our contact information is used by organizations of all sizes and in every area of activity in the voluntary sector.

DIRECT MAIL SERVICES

CAMBERTOWN MAILING

Direct Mail Consultants, Marketing

Unit 21, Goldthorpe Ind Estate
Goldthorpe, Rotherham, South Yorkshire S63 9BL
Tel: 01709-898989 Fax: 01709-897787

CONTACTS: Steve Rudd, Jacki Beardsley

Established 11 years ago, Cambertown is a full service direct marketing agency with a track record of helping charities make the most of mailing/membership budgets. We also do database management, membership processing and merchandise order processing and fulfilment. DMA/DMARC approved.

CHARITY CLIENTS: We work for various environmental and other charities (References Available)

OTHER CLIENTS: Our other clients vary from major financial services and manufacturing plcs to small local traders.

Free initial consultation. Negotiable rates.

ROETARN LTD

Computer systems/Software, Direct Mail Consultants, Direct Marketing Services, List Brokers

17/19 Emery Rd
Brislington
Bristol BS4 5PF
Tel: 0117-972 4400
Fax: 0117-972 4501

CONTACTS: John Stringer, Nick Heath

The complete marketing service bureau for today's professional fundraisers. Services include: List broking, Data entry, Data processing, Data Base management, Response handling. Donation handling, Promotional fulfilment, Laser printing, Mail Order fulfilment, the response and enclosing and Machine enclosing.

CLIENTS: Government, Financial and Mail Order

Free initial consultation.

FINANCIAL SERVICES

CCLA INVESTMENT MANAGEMENT LIMITED

St Alphage House, 2 Fore Street
London EC2Y 5AQ
Tel: 0171-588 1815
Fax: 0171-588 6291

CONTACT: Richard Coulson

Charity Investment Services. Common Investment Funds available to any registered charity.

CLIENTS: Around 16,000 charities currently using the funds.

CLARK WHITEHILL

Accountancy/Management Consultancy

25 New Street Square
London EC4 3LN

Tel: 0171-353 1577
Fax: 0171-583 1720

CONTACTS: Andrew Pianca/Michael Caudrey

A leading firm of advisers with a substantial and specifiic knowledge of the Not-For-Profit sector, including financial reporting, restructuring selection and the implementation of information systems, interim management, auditing, taxation and VAT.

Our high level of personal service is reflected in our unusually high ratio of partners to staff.

For the latest trends and views in the charity sector start subscribing to the specialist magazines. See listing on p. 156.

FINANCIAL SERVICES

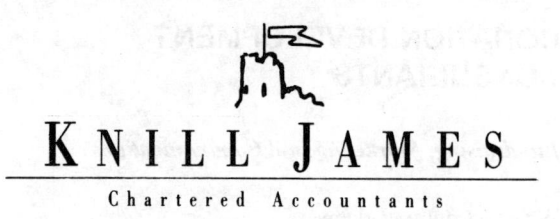

KNILL JAMES
Chartered Accountants

Charity Accounts
We can help!

Auditing and Reporting
(including implementing the new Charity SORP)
Accounts Preparation
Business Planning
Taxation
VAT

For a FREE initial consultation and quotation
contact Susan Foster or Nicholas Rawson

78, High Street, Lewes 01273 480480

FUNDRAISING

Action Planning
The Charity Specialists

ACTION PLANNING

Fundraising and Management

Mid-Day Court, 30 Brighton Road,
Sutton, Surrey SM2 5BN
Tel: 0181-642 4122 Fax: 0181-770 2090

CONTACTS: *David Saint, Sam McGuire*

A well-established, multi-disciplinary fundraising and management consultancy, we are experienced in strategic and business planning, fundraising strategies, reviews and feasibility studies for capital or revenue requirements, and all aspects of communications. Combining insight and imagination with integrity, we solve problems and develop opportunities. If you have either, talk to us.

CLIENTS: Amnesty International, Carers National Association, Imperial Cancer Research Fund, London Zoo, Royal London Society for the Blind, Cafod, St Johns Ambulance, Shaftesbury Society, Charities Aid Foundation.

FUNDRAISING

DONATION DEVELOPMENT CONSULTANTS

Fundraising, Marketing and Communications

Weltech Centre, Ridgeway,
Welwyn Garden City, Herts AL7 2AA
Tel: 01707-871518 Fax: 01707-331175

CONTACTS: C.B.W. Eames, Alan Willett

Donation Development Consultants are a full service fundraising, marketing and communications consultancy working only for charities and the voluntary sector. DDC and its predecessors have been in practice for 25 years and are associated with raising in excess of £1,000,000,000 in voluntary funds for 200 clients.

CLIENTS INCLUDE: Army Benevolent Fund, Assise Animal Charities Foundation, BLESMA, Church Housing Trust, Combat Stress (Ex-Services Mental Welfare Society), EEIBA (Electrical & Electronic Industries Benevolent Association), Fire Services National Benevolent Fund Homeless Fund, National Eye Research Centre, National Hospital for Neurology & Neurosurgery Development Foundation, RAF Benevolent Fund, REACH, Wessex Medical Trust.

MARTIN SHAW AND ASSOCIATES

Fundraising

64 The Grove, Edgeware
Middlesex HA8 9QB
Tel: 0181-958 6885
Fax: 0181 905 3417
Email: mshaw@dircon.co.uk

CONTACTS: Martin Shaw

Direct and indirect fundraising including training sessions for staff and volunteers. Specialising in statutory grants in the UK and the European Commission, Martin Shaw offers a cost-effective service to all charities - small or large. Other services include fund-raising on the internet.

CLIENTS: During the past year Martin Shaw has worked with over 50 UK and European charities.

Special charity rates available.

**Direct Connection's Guide to
FUNDRAISING ON THE INTERNET
by Howard Lake**
"Informative, inspirational" Voluntary Voice
Paperback, £12.99. Order now on 0181-960 7918.

FUNDRAISING

PENNY CLOVER

Exhibition/Conference Organiser, Fundraising, Marketing/Public Relations, Event/Project Management

4 West Saint Helen Street
Abingdon OX14 5BL

Tel: 01235-520404

CONTACTS: Penny Clover

Experienced in market research and Public Relations. Flexible, cost effective service to charities needing short term additional resources to help develop corporate fundraising opportunities, Payroll Giving, and event management.

Development of sponsorship proposals and maximising income from projects a speciality.

CHARITY CLIENTS: UNICEF, Institute of Charity Fundraising Managers, National Back Pain Association etc.

Free initial consultation. Negotiable Rates

INFORMATION

·AURELIAN·

CHARITIES-ON-LINE *EXPRESS*

Aurelian Information Ltd
129 Leighton Gardens
London NW10 3PS

Tel:0181-960 7918 Fax: 0171-794 8609
E-mail: aurelian@geo2.poptel.org.uk.

A full database of information on the UK voluntary sector is now just a phone call away. Annual subscribers receive our easy-to-use software package. You simply type in your query - what children's charities are based in Birmingham, what is the address of the LVSC, which fundraising charities are working for the environemnt, etc - then watch the screen while your computer dials into the database, asks your question and comes back to you with the answers.

No more queuing on the Internet, no more expensive phone bills, our software takes you direct to the source, retrieves the information and clears your phone line in seconds. Call us today for details.

INTERNET SERVICES

ON-LINE PUBLISHING LTD

World Wide Web Designers

Omnibus Business Centre
41 North Road
London N7 9DP

Tel: 0171-700 7611
Fax: 0171-607 2166
E-mail: info@olp.co.uk
Web: http://www.olp.co.uk

CONTACTS: Jeraint Hazan, Steve Bridger

On-line Publishing provide professional design services for the Web. Services include: original graphic creation, scanning, compression, layout and structural design. Technical services include programming, scripts, Java, animation and multimedia. Strong understanding of specific needs within Voluntary sector. Specialise in larger, complex web sites.

CHARITY CLIENTS: ASH, Royal Court Theatre, England's Regional Arts Boards

CLIENTS: The Labour Party, TUC, British Telecom (Environmental Issues), Wedgwood, Royal Shakespeare Company, Royal Albert Hall, National Film Theatre, English National Ballet.

Free initial meeting/consultation.

VOIS - VOLUNTARY ORGANISATIONS INTERNET SERVER

Internet Publishing Services

1 Eton Garages, Belsize Park,
London NW3 4PE
Tel: 0171-435 5787 Fax: 0171-435 8144
Sales: 0171-976 1977
Email: info@vois.org.uk
WWW: http://www.vois.org.uk

CONTACTS: Olabisi Akiwumi, Michael Whiteley

INTERNET SERVICES

VOIS offers a dedicated publishing service to the voluntary sector and supports charities in getting their message across, relationship marketing and networking. The VOIS solution is interactive and simple to use. The complete VOIS solution includes training and telephone support.

For news and information about courses, events, jobs, general information and commercial services for and about the voluntary sector on the Internet, visit Eton Garages (the VOIS online magazine) and the VOIS Resource Centre at http://www.vois.org.uk

CHARITY CLIENTS: Help the Aged, Shelter, Action for Blind People, Volunteer Centre NCVO.

Free initial meeting/consultation.

LEGAL ADVISERS

SINCLAIR TAYLOR & MARTIN

Category: Solicitors

9 Thorpe Close
London W10 5XL
Tel:0181-969 3667 Fax: 0181-969 7044

CONTACTS: James Sinclair Taylor, Lindsay Driscoll, Christina Moreton, Christine Rigby.

The firm has, from its inception, particularly specialised in work for the voluntary sector. Key areas of involvement include contracting, employment issues, property, trading subsidiaries, tax and intellectual property. Litigation and training for staff and trustees also form part of our work.

CHARITY CLIENTS: National Charities, The Civic Trust, Residential and care providing trusts, Afghanaid, Development Trusts, The Bible Lands Society, Disability Charities, Arts and Community organizations.

NON-CHARITY CLIENTS: Housing Associations, Schools, Local Authorities, manufacturing and service companies.

HANDS-ON INTERNET TRAINING SESSIONS
are being held throughout the UK in 1997 by the *Internet-for-All* training team. Call 0181-960 7918 for details of the next session in your area.

MANAGEMENT SERVICES - ADMINISTRATION/LOGISTICS

THE CRANFIELD TRUST

Management/Transport and Logistics

Bluegates Farm, Ashwell, Nr Baldock
Hertfordshire SG7 5JE
Tel: 01462-743022 Fax: 01462-742335

CONTACTS: Sue Mortimer

To provide specialist voluntary help to other charities needing assistance with specific problems of short-term tasks, primarily in management, logistics, engineering/technology, disaster assessment, agriculture & general aid/ development projects.

CLIENTS: Arthritis Care, Feed the Children, Save the Children Fund.

Free service to charities meeting the Trust's objectives - travel, out-of-pocket expenses only.

SCOTTISH COUNCIL FOR VOLUNTARY ORGANISATIONS (SCVO)

Umbrella body

18-19 Claremont Crescent
Edinburgh EH7 4QD
Tel: 0131-556 3882 Fax: 0131-556 0279

CONTACTS: Martin Sime (Director), David Kelly (Head of Membership Services)

SCVO is the umbrella body for the voluntary sector in Scotland. It seeks to promote the interests of voluntary bodies and improve their effectiveness. SCVO offers a range of administrative services carefully designed to meet the needs of the voluntary sector. These include: pensions, payroll, office supplies, printing and advertising.

CLIENTS: Barnardos, Oxfam, Save the Children.

MANAGEMENT SERVICES - ADMINISTRATION/LOGISTICS

WL PARTNERSHIP

WL Partnership
The trustees advisory service

Management

2 Recreation Road, Bourne End
Bucks SL8 5AD
Tel/Fax: 01628-531329 or 01666-823452

CONTACTS: Linda Laurance, John Wheatley

Helping trustees and senior management of not-for-profit organisations work together successfully. WL Partnership offers advice on: Effective Governance, Accounting, Reporting and Monitoring, Human Resource Management, Roles and Responsibilities, Working Relationships, Planning for the Future, Dispute Resolution and aims to provide a high level of personal attention at competitive prices, with assured quality.

CLIENTS: Action Research, Friends of the Elderly, Hertfordshire Society for the Blind, One Small Step Trust, The Children's Society, ACRE.

Operates solely for NFPs.

PROMOTIONAL GOODS

AAA BADGES OF QUALITY

Fundraising

Tumbleweed House, Hamsterley, Bishop Auckland,
Co Durham DL13 3RA
Tel: 01388-488733
Fax: 01388-488048

CONTACTS: Brad P. Hallett

We are a British producer of QUALITY enamel badges, keyrings, cuff links and tie bars, produced in quantities from 100 to 10 million. Products produced to your design/specification.

CLIENTS: Marie Curie, Cancer Relief Macmillan Fund, Scope, Amnesty International, British Heart Foundation, Roald Dahl Foundation, Wildlife Trusts, St Tiggywinkles, etc.

Special prices and special credit terms for charities.

PUBLICATIONS

CHARITY TIMES

408 The Fruit & Wool Exchange
Brushfield St
London
E1 6EP

Tel:0171-426 0101
Fax:0171-426 0123

CONTACT: David Marsh

Charity Times is the leading full colour business magazine for UK charities focussing on issues ranging from law, investment management and insurance, through to fundraising and technology.

The magazine is essential reading for trustees, finance directors and fundraising managers.

CommunityCare
FOR EVERYONE IN SOCIAL CARE

COMMUNITY CARE

Publication

Reed Business Publishing
Quadrant House
The Quadrant, Sutton
Surrey SM2 5AS

Tel: 0181-652 8071 Fax: 0181-652 3989

CONTACTS:
Jacki Leslie, Marketing Manager
Tel: 0181-652 8071
Paul Stephens, Advertisement Manager
Tel: 0181-652 4763
Fax: 0181-652 8923

Community Care is a completely independent magazine with an undisputed reputation for editorial excellence. It's editorial reflects the importance of the voluntary sector, with research showing Community Care to be the most useful publication to those employed in the voluntary sector.

Community Care now has a significant circulation in the voluntary sector and is the first choice of many advertisers.

PUBLICATIONS

INTERNET-FOR-ALL SERIES

Aurelian Information
129 Leighton Gardens
Londfon NW10 3PS

Tel: 0181-960 7918
Fax: 0171-794 8609
E-mail: aurelian@dircon.co.uk
Http://www.dircon.co.uk/books/

A new series of books developed specifically to introduce the voluntary sector to using the Internet to its fullest potenial.

Is the Internet a complete waste of time? Or is it an invaluable tool transforming your office, speeding up your communications and halving your postage bills?

It all depends on how you use it. Let our team of experts show you how.

Titles include:
 Direct Connection's guide to Fundraising on the Internet
by Howard Lake   £12.99
First Steps on the Internet for Voluntary Organisations
by Sandra Vogel (published Spring 1997)   £12.99

AURELIAN INFORMATION

Producers of
CHARITIES-ON-DISK
CHARITIES ON LINE - *EXPRESS*

Purveyors of
MAILING LISTS, DISKS, LABELS

Publishers of
**WHO'S WHO
IN THE VOLUNTARY SECTOR**
**Direct Connection's Guide to
FUNDRAISING ON THE INTERNET**

CHARITIES ADDRESS BOOK - UK

AURELIAN INFORMATION

- serving the voluntary sector

Tel: **0181-960 7918**
Fax: **0171-794 8609**
E-mail: **aurelian@dircon.co.uk**

INDEX BY ORGANISATION
Organisations listed A-Z with their Main Entry references

1990 TRUST	JASPER Mr Lee
AA FOUNDATION FOR ROAD SAFETY RESEARCH	FAIRCLOTH Kenneth G.
ABBEYFIELD SOCIETY	MURPHY Foster
ABERLOUR CHILD CARE TRUST	BARLOW Joy
ABERLOUR CHILD CARE TRUST	GRIEVE William
ABORTION LAW REFORM ASSOCIATION	ROE Jane
ACCADEMIA ITALIANA	LETTS Rosa Maria
ACCEPTANCE HELPLINE FOR PARENTS OF LESBIANS AND GAY MEN	GREEN Mrs J.
ACORNS CHILDREN'S HOSPICE	OVERTON John L.
ACROSS TRUST	HIGGS John
ACTION CANCER	QUIGLEY Peter S.
ACTION FOR BLIND PEOPLE	REMINGTON Stephen
ACTION FOR DYSPHASIC ADULTS	COLES Ruth
ACTION FOR M.E.	ARMSTRONG George
ACTION FOR SICK CHILDREN	HOOPER Cheryl
ACTION FOR VICTIMS OF MEDICAL ACCIDENTS	SIMANOWITZ Arnold
ACTION RESEARCH	LUTHER Anne
ACTION WATER	BATTERSBY Neil
ACTIONAID	BATTEN Dr John R.
ADA COLE MEMORIAL STABLES	BURTON Lt Col B. M.
ADAPT TRUST, THE	LORD Geoffrey
ADAPT TRUST	PACKARD Mrs Ann
ADFAM NATIONAL-NATIONAL CHARITY FOR FAMILIES AND FRIENDS OF DRUG USERS	MARSHALL Anne
ADVENTIST BUSINESS & PROFESSIONALS ASSOCIATION	BALDERSTONE David
ADVICE INFORMATION & MEDIATION SERVICE FOR RETIREMENT HOUSING	REEVES Rudi
ADVISORY CENTRE FOR EDUCATION (ACE) LTD	WILLIAMS Liz
ADVOCACY PARTNERS	BEECHER John
ADVOCATES FOR ANIMALS	WARD Les
AFRICA EVANGELICAL FELLOWSHIP	WELLS Dr Robin J.
AFRICA NOW	KAUSSARI Shala
AFRICA REFUGEE HOUSING ACTION GROUP	MOODLEY Rev Ronnie
AGE CONCERN CYMRU	TAYLOR Robert
AGE CONCERN ENGLAND	NORTON Dianne
AGE CONCERN ENGLAND - THE NATIONAL COUNCIL ON AGEING	GREENGROSS Sally (Lady)
AGE CONCERN SCOTLAND	O'NEILL Maureen
AGENCY FOR COOPERATION AND RESEARCH IN DEVELOPMENT	JAZAIRY Idriss
AID FOR CHILDREN WITH TRACHEOSTOMIES	SIMMONS Mrs J.A.
AID TO THE CHURCH IN NEED	KYRKE-SMITH Neville
AIDS CARE EDUCATION AND TRAINING	MACAULAY Pat
AIDS EDUCATION AND RESEARCH TRUST	KANABUS Annabel
AIR LEAGUE EDUCATION TRUST	COX Edward R.
AIREY NEAVE TRUST	SCOTT Mrs Hannah
AIRLINE AVIATION AND AEROSPACE CHRISTIAN FELLOWSHIP	BROWN John
ALCOHOL CONCERN	APPLEBY Eric
ALEXANDRA ROSE DAY	GREENWOOD Gillian Patricia
ALL-PARTY WATERWAYS GROUP	HART Frances
ALLIANCE OF PARENTS & SCHOOLS	BALL Patricia A.L.
ALLIED DUNBAR CHARITABLE TRUST	BICKELL John
ALMSHOUSE ASSOCIATION	SCOTT David Michael
ALZHEIMER SCOTLAND - ACTION ON DEMENTIA	JACKSON Jim
ALZHEIMER'S DISEASE SOCIETY	CAYTON Harry
AMNESTY INTERNATIONAL (UK)	BULL David
ANCIENT MONUMENTS SOCIETY	SAUNDERS Matthew
ANGLICAN FELLOWSHIP IN SCOUTING AND GUIDING	DAVIES J.
ANGLICAN PACIFIST FELLOWSHIP	HINKES The Revd. Sidney

WHO'S WHO IN THE VOLUNTARY SECTOR - 165

ANIMAL AID	TYLER Andrew
ANIMAL HEALTH TRUST	FREMANTLE Edward V.E.
ANIMAL HEALTH TRUST	HIGGINS Dr Andrew James
ANNE FRANK EDUCATIONAL TRUST	WALNES Gillian
ANTHONY NOLAN BONE MARROW TRUST (The)	MORLAND Brigadier Anthony
ANTHROPOSOPHICAL SOCIETY IN GREAT BRITAIN	THOMAS Nicholas C.
ANTI-SLAVERY INTERNATIONAL	DOTTRIDGE Mike
APEX TRUST	ALLEN Godfrey
ARAB HORSE SOCIETY	CARINE James
ARCHITECTS BENEVOLENT SOCIETY	ROTH Mr R.P.B.
ARCHITECTURAL HERITAGE FUND, THE	WEIR Hilary (Lady)
ARMY BENEVOLENT FUND	SWINDELLS Major-General G.M.G.
ARMY MUSEUMS OGILBY TRUST	MAKEPEACE-WARNE Maj-Gen Antony
ARNOLFINI	JACKSON Tessa
ARTHRITIS & RHEUMATISM COUNCIL	NORTON Jim
ARTHRITIS CARE	GUTCH Richard
ARTHROGRYPOSIS GROUP	ANDERSON Mrs J.
ARTISTS' AGENCY	SALAMON Esther
ARTISTS' AGENCY	MILTON Lucy
ARTS COUNCIL OF NORTHERN IRELAND	FERRAN Brian
ARTS COUNCIL OF NORTHERN IRELAND	GREENFIELD Tanya
ARTS COUNCIL OF WALES	JENKINS Emyr
ARTS FOR HEALTH	SENIOR Peter
ARTS FOUNDATION	SKENE Prudence
ARTSLINE	ROBINSON Roger
ASHRIDGE MANAGEMENT COLLEGE	OSBALDESTON Michael David
ASSOCIATION FOR BUSINESS SPONSORSHIP OF THE ARTS	TWEEDY Colin
ASSOCIATION FOR CONSERVATION OF ENERGY	WARREN Andrew
ASSOCIATION FOR ENVIRONMENT CONSCIOUS BUILDING	HALL Keith
ASSOCIATION FOR JEWISH YOUTH	FINESTONE Eric
ASSOCIATION FOR PREVENTION OF ADDICTION	MARTIN Peter
ASSOCIATION FOR PUBLIC HEALTH	REID Donald J
ASSOCIATION FOR RESEARCH IN THE VOLUNTARY AND COMMUNITY SECTOR	BOLD Maria
ASSOCIATION FOR RESIDENTIAL CARE	CHURCHILL James
ASSOCIATION FOR THE PROTECTION OF RURAL SCOTLAND	GARLAND Mrs Elizabeth
ASSOCIATION OF BRITISH ORCHESTRAS	MACNAMARA Libby
ASSOCIATION OF CHARITABLE FOUNDATIONS	SIEDERER Nigel
ASSOCIATION OF CHARITY OFFICERS	BARROW Valerie J.
ASSOCIATION OF CHIEF EXECUTIVES OF NATIONAL VOLUNTARY ORGANISATIONS	DALTON Dorothy
ASSOCIATION OF CHIEF OFFICERS OF PROBATION	HONEYBALL Mary
ASSOCIATION OF COMMUNITY HEALTH COUNCILS FOR ENGLAND AND WALES	HARRIS Toby
ASSOCIATION OF DIRECTORS OF SOCIAL SERVICES	WILLIAMSON Andrew
ASSOCIATION OF INDEPENDENT RAILWAYS & PRESERVATION SOCIETIES	WILLIAMS Raymond J.
ASSOCIATION OF INNER WHEEL CLUBS IN GREAT BRITAIN AND IRELAND	DOBSON Jane
ASSOCIATION OF INTERCHURCH FAMILIES	REARDON Ruth
ASSOCIATION OF JEWISH REFUGEES IN GREAT BRITAIN	DAVID Ernest
ASSOCIATION OF MEDICAL RESEARCH CHARITIES	GARNHAM Diana
ASSOCIATION OF MUNICIPAL ENGINEERS	HUXFORD Robert
ASSOCIATION OF ROYAL NAVY OFFICERS	OOMBES Lt Cdr I.M.P.
ASSOCIATION OF TEACHERS AND LECTURERS	SMITH Peter
ATLANTIC SALMON TRUST	MACKENZIE Rear Admiral D.J.
BABY LIFE SUPPORT SYSTEMS	KAY Judy
BANKSIDE GALLERY	BLAKE Eleanor
BANKSIDE GALLERY	DIXEY Judy
BAPTIST UNION OF GREAT BRITAIN, THE	JONES Revd Keith G.
BAPTIST UNION OF GREAT BRITAIN, THE	COFFEY Revd David R.
BARNABAS TRUST	HORSNELL Graham J.
BARNARDO'S	SINGLETON Roger
BBC CHILDREN IN NEED	LEWIS Jenny
BBC CHILDREN IN NEED	MALLEY Sheila Jane
BBC CHILDREN IN NEED APPEAL	KAUFMANN Julia
BEACON CENTRE FOR THE BLIND	FIELDING Mr Holroyd
BEAFORD CENTRE	BUTLER Mr R.F.
BEAVERBROOK FOUNDATION	FORD Miss J.
BEFRIENDERS INTERNATIONAL	SCOTT Vanda
BEN-MOTOR AND ALLIED TRADES BENEVOLENT FUND	ATKINSON Geoffrey C.
BENEDICTINE SISTERS OF OUR LADY OF GRACE & COMPASSION/HOUSE OF HOSPITALITY	GARSON Mother Mary
BENEVOLENT FUND OF THE INSTITUTE OF HEALTH SERVICES MANAGEMENT	STONEHAM Martin W.

Organisation	Contact
BIELD HOUSING TRUST	NEVILLE Yvonne
BIRMINGHAM HOSPITAL SATURDAY FUND MEDICAL CHARITY & WELFARE TRUST	PEERS P.J.
BIRTH DEFECTS FOUNDATION	BROWN Mrs Sheila
BLACK EUROPEAN COMMUNITY DEVELOPMENT FEDERATION	HINES Vince
BLIND BUSINESS ASSOCIATION CHARITABLE TRUST	CALLIS Sidney
BLUE CROSS, THE	KENNARD Alan
BMA FOUNDATION FOR AIDS	CURTIS Hilary
BOARD OF DEPUTIES OF BRITISH JEWS	NAGLER Neville
BOOK AID INTERNATIONAL	HARRITY Sara
BOOTSTRAP ENTERPRISES	EVANS Helen
BORN FREE FOUNDATION	TRAVERS William
BOTANIC GARDENS CONSERVATION INTERNATIONAL	WYSE JACKSON Peter S.
BOURNE TRUST	PRICE Maurice
BOYS' BRIGADE, THE	JONES Sydney
BRADFIELD FOUNDATION	SMYTH Julian
BRAINWAVE	DAVIES David G.
BRANDON CENTRE	BARUCH Geoffrey
BREAK	DAVISON Geoffrey M.
BREAK	DAVISON Judith Ann
BREAKTHROUGH TRUST DEAF/HEARING INTEGRATION	HYSLOP David S.
BREAST CANCER CARE	AL QADHI Samia
BRIB - working with blind people	DIXIE David
BRITISH ACTIVITY HOLIDAY ASSOCIATION	SHARP Les
BRITISH ASSOCIATION FOR COUNSELLING	BARON Judith
BRITISH ASSOCIATION FOR EARLY CHILDHOOD EDUCATION	BOON Barbara
BRITISH ASSOCIATION FOR LOCAL HISTORY	COWAN Michael
BRITISH ASSOCIATION FOR THE ADVANCEMENT OF SCIENCE	BRIGGS Dr Peter
BRITISH ASSOCIATION OF PSYCHOTHERAPISTS	TISCHLER Lydia
BRITISH CARTOGRAPHIC SOCIETY	ATHERTON Mr J.K.
BRITISH CARTOGRAPHIC SOCIETY	HILL Mr R. W.
BRITISH COMPUTER SOCIETY	SCOTT Judith Margaret
BRITISH COUNCIL FOR PREVENTION OF BLINDNESS	CHESTERMAN David
BRITISH CYCLING FEDERATION	HENDRY Jim
BRITISH DEAF ASSOCIATION	MCWHINNEY Jeff
BRITISH DENTAL ASSOCIATION	HUNT John
BRITISH DIABETIC ASSOCIATION	COOPER Michael J.
BRITISH DIGESTIVE FOUNDATION	OLIVER Geraldine
BRITISH EPILEPSY ASSOCIATION	LEE Philip
BRITISH EVANGELICAL COUNCIL	GIBSON Alan
BRITISH FEDERATION OF FILM SOCIETIES	BROWNLIE Thomas
BRITISH FEDERATION OF YOUNG CHOIRS	LANSDALE Susan
BRITISH FIELD SPORTS SOCIETY	HANBURY-TENISON Robin
BRITISH FRIENDS OF RAMBAM MEDICAL CENTRE	ALEXANDER-PASSE Anita
BRITISH HEART FOUNDATION	LIVINGSTONE Michael G.
BRITISH HORSE SOCIETY	BOS Frances
BRITISH HUMANIST ASSOCIATION	ASHBY Robert
BRITISH HYPNOTHERAPY ASSOCIATION	BRIAN Mr R. K.
BRITISH INSTITUTE FOR BRAIN INJURED CHILDREN	WOOD Dr Stephen J.T.
BRITISH INSTITUTE OF RADIOLOGY	PIGGOT Mary-Anne
BRITISH KIDNEY PATIENT ASSOCIATION, THE	WARD Mrs Elizabeth Despard
BRITISH LEAGUE AGAINST RHEUMATISM	BAILLIE Kate
BRITISH LEPROSY RELIEF ASSOCIATION	VASEY Terry
BRITISH LIMBLESS EX SERVICEMEN'S ASSOCIATION	HOLLAND Raymond Reginald
BRITISH LIVER TRUST	ROGERS Alison
BRITISH LUNG FOUNDATION	GOVENDIR Ian
BRITISH NATURALISTS' ASSOCIATION	PEARTON Mrs J.F.
BRITISH NUCLEAR ENERGY SOCIETY	TILBROOK Andrew
BRITISH NUTRITION FOUNDATION	WHARTON B.A.
BRITISH OLYMPIC ASSOCIATION	PALMER Richard
BRITISH ORGAN DONOR SOCIETY	EVANS John A.
BRITISH ORT	KING Peggy Ann
BRITISH PREGNANCY ADVISORY SERVICE	JONES Ian Huntley
BRITISH PSYCHO-ANALYTICAL SOCIETY,THE/INSTITUTE OF PSYCHO-ANALYSIS,THE	LAYLAND Dr W. Ralph
BRITISH PSYCHOLOGICAL SOCIETY	SAKNE Allan St.
BRITISH RECORDS ASSOCIATION	HUGHES Elizabeth
BRITISH RED CROSS	WHITLAM M.R.
BRITISH REFUGEE COUNCIL	HARDWICK Nick
BRITISH SCHOOL OF OSTEOPATHY	STANDEN Clive
BRITISH TRUST FOR CONSERVATION VOLUNTEERS	MORLEY Robert C.
BRITISH TRUST FOR CONSERVATION VOLUNTEERS	FLOOD Tom
BRITISH UNIVERSITIES SPORTS ASSOCIATION	GREGORY-JONES G.
BRITISH VASCULAR FOUNDATION	THORNE Alison
BRITISH WHEELCHAIR SPORTS FOUNDATION	HOWARTH David

BRITISH YOUTH COUNCIL	PETERS Miss Samantha
BRITTLE BONE SOCIETY	GRANT Mrs Margaret T.J.
BRITTLE BONE SOCIETY	WILSON Morna
BROADCASTING SUPPORT SERVICES	WESTLAND Peter
BROADCASTING SUPPORT SERVICES	SMITH Keith
BROOK ADVISORY CENTRES	JONES Margaret A.
BROOK HOSPITAL FOR ANIMALS	ABEL Christine
BROOMFIELD SANCTUARY	JUPE Miss E.A.
BRYSON HOUSE	MCLACHLAN Peter
BUSINESS IN THE COMMUNITY	CLEVERDON Julia
BUTTLE TRUST, THE	MARSHALL Mrs Jose F.
CAF CERT	KEEGAN Catherine
CALEDONIAN FOUNDATION	BINNIE Prof Frank
CALOUSTE GULBENKIAN FOUNDATION (UK)	WHITAKER Ben
CALVERT TRUST, KESWICK	CROSBIE John
CAMBRIDGE HOUSE AND TALBOT	MILLBANK Joan
CAMBRIDGE RESEARCH INSTITUTE, THE BETHANY TRUST	CURTIS-PRIOR Dr Peter
CAMPAIGN FOR FREEDOM OF INFORMATION	FRANKEL Maurice
CAMPAIGN FOR PRESS AND BROADCASTING FREEDOM	WILLIAMS Grenville
CAMPAIGN FOR PRESS AND BROADCASTING FREEDOM	TREHARNE Jo
CAMPHILL VILLAGE TRUST	HARRIS Anne
CANCER AND LEUKAEMIA IN CHILDHOOD	HEAD Christopher
CANCER AND LEUKAEMIA IN CHILDHOOD TRUST, THE	WOODWARD Robert
CANCER RELIEF MACMILLAN FUND	YOUNG Nicholas
CANCER RESEARCH CAMPAIGN	GORDON MCVIE Prof J
CANCER RESEARCH, INSTITUTE OF	HORWICH Alan
CANOLFAN IAITH GENEDLAETHOL	JAMES Gareth
CAPABILITY SCOTLAND	MCBAIN Ian G.
CARDS FOR GOOD CAUSES	RICH Judith
CARE AND REPAIR	WILKINS Nichola
CARE INTERNATIONAL UK	DAY William
CARERS' NATIONAL ASSOCIATION	PITKEATHLEY Jill
CARNEGIE UNITED KINGDOM TRUST	NAYLOR John
CARR-GOMM SOCIETY	WILSON Paul
CAS ARCHITECTS LTD	MOORE John
CASTEL FROMA HOME FOR PEOPLE WITH PHYSICAL DISABILITIES	CROXON Roy
CAT WELFARE, SUSSEX	SINNETT Mrs Rae
CATHEDRALS FABRIC COMMISSION FOR ENGLAND	GEM Dr Richard David H.
CATHOLIC CHILD WELFARE COUNCIL	GANDY Mrs Mary C.
CATHOLIC CHILDREN'S SOCIETY (WESTMINSTER), THE	RICHARDS Jim M.
CATHOLIC FUND FOR OVERSEAS DEVELOPMENT	FILOCHOWSKI Julian
CATHOLIC HOUSING AID SOCIETY	RAFFERTY Robina
CATHOLIC INSTITUTE FOR INTERNATIONAL RELATIONS	LINDEN Ian
CATS PROTECTION LEAGUE	McCAWLEY Michael J.
CCLA INVESTMENT MANAGEMENT LTD	CHURCHILL Viscount
CELIA HAMMOND ANIMAL TRUST	HAMMOND Celia
CENTRAL BOARD OF FINANCE OF THE CHURCH OF ENGLAND	STEVENS Robin
CENTRAL COUNCIL FOR BRITISH NATURISM	PIPER Suzanne Maree
CENTRE FOR ALTERNATIVE TECHNOLOGY	KELLY Roger
CENTRE FOR BRITISH TEACHERS	McINTOSH Neil
CENTRE FOR DISPUTE RESOLUTION	MACKIE Prof Karl
CENTRE FOR INNOVATION IN VOLUNTARY ACTION	NORTON Michael
CENTRE FOR POLICY ON AGEING	DALLEY Gillian
CENTREPOINT	ADEBOWALE Victor O.
CHARITIES AID FOUNDATION	BROPHY Michael
CHARITIES AID FOUNDATION	HAYWOOD Sir Harold
CHARITIES EVALUATION SERVICES	COOPER Libby
CHARITY CHRISTMAS CARD COUNCIL	BASS Neville
CHARITY COMMISSION	BERRY Lynne
CHARITY COMMISSION	FRIES Richard
CHARITY COMMISSION	BARING Tessa (Teresa Anne)
CHARITY COMMISSION	BONDS John
CHARITY COMMISSIONERS FOR ENGLAND AND WALES	VENABLES Robert M C
CHARITY FINANCE DIRECTORS' GROUP	FRAMJEE Pesh
CHARITY FORUM	ALLEN Graham S.
CHARITY FORUM COUNCIL	BOYD Brenda
CHARTERED INSTITUTE OF ARBITRATORS	HARDING Esq K. R. K.
CHARTERED INSTITUTION OF BUILDING SERVICES ENGINEERS	RAMSAY Andrew Vernon
CHARTERED SURVEYORS TRAINING TRUST	TRUSTRAM EVE Mrs Pipyn
CHELSEA PHYSIC GARDEN	MINTER Susan
CHILD ACCIDENT PREVENTION TRUST	SHERRIFF Carol
CHILD BEREAVEMENT TRUST	THOMAS Jenni T.
CHILD GROWTH FOUNDATION	FRY Tam Mr
CHILD PSYCHOTHERAPY TRUST	PANKHURST Louise

Organisation	Contact
CHILDLINE	HOWARTH Valerie
CHILDLINE UK	HARRISON Hereward Donald McKaig
CHILDLINK ADOPTION SOCIETY	HESSLEGRAVE Caroline
CHILDREN IN SCOTLAND	COHEN Dr Bronwen
CHILDREN IN WALES - PLANT YNG NGHYRMU	WILLIAMS Catriona
CHILDREN NATIONWIDE MEDICAL RESEARCH FUND	MACARTHUR Francesca
CHILDREN WITH AIDS CHARITY	SIMPSON David A.
CHILDREN'S AID DIRECT	GRUBB David H. W.
CHILDREN'S COUNTRY HOLIDAYS FUND	SCHOFIELD Mrs C.
CHILDREN'S TRUST	ROSS Andrew
CHOICES IN CHILDCARE	CLARKE Peter
CHRISTIAN AID	TAYLOR Michael H.
CHRISTIAN CHILDREN'S FUND OF GREAT BRITAIN	EDWARDS Robert Jack Henderson
CHRISTIAN ECOLOGY LINK	COOPER Tim
CHRISTIAN EDUCATION MOVEMENT	ORCHARD Dr Stephen
CHRISTIAN ENDEAVOUR UNION OF GREAT BRITAIN AND IRELAND	CAMPBELL George
CHRISTIAN ENQUIRY AGENCY	BEETHAM Tony
CHRISTIAN RESEARCH	BRIERLEY Dr Peter
CHRISTIANS ABROAD	SOUTH Colin
CHURCH ACTION ON POVERTY	GOGGINS Paul
CHURCH ARMY, THE	JOHANSON Captain Philip
CHURCH MISSION SOCIETY	WITTS Diana Katharine
CHURCH MISSIONARY SOCIETY IRELAND	WILSON Rev Cecil H.
CHURCH OF ENGLAND BOARD OF EDUCATION	DUNCAN Geoffrey
CHURCH OF SCOTLAND WOMAN'S GUILD	PATERSON Lorna M.
CHURCHES ADVISORY COUNCIL FOR LOCAL BROADCASTING	BONSER Jeff
CHURCHES CONSERVATION TRUST	PECK Richard L.
CIBA FOUNDATION	CHADWICK Dr Derek J
CINNAMON TRUST	JARVIS Averil
CITIZEN ADVOCACY INFORMATION AND TRAINING	CARR Sally
CITIZENS ADVICE SCOTLAND	EVANS Martyn
CIVIC TRUST	GWILLIAM Michael C
CLEAN BREAK THEATRE COMPANY LTD	GAULDIE Alison
CLUB FOR ACTS AND ACTORS (incorp Concert Artistes Association)	DANIELS Barbara
COBBE FOUNDATION in association with the National Trust	COBBE Alec
COED CYMRU	JENKINS David
COLLEGE OF HEALTH	RIGGE Marianne
COLLEGE OF PAEDIATRICS & CHILD HEALTH	KEMPTON James
COMIC RELIEF/CHARITY PROJECTS	MARSTON Jerry
COMMITTEE FOR THE REFORM OF ANIMAL EXPERIMENTATION	HOLLANDS Clive
COMMON GROUND	CLIFFORD Sue
COMMON GROUND	KING Angela
COMMONWEALTH HUMAN ECOLOGY COUNCIL	DAYSH Mrs Zena
COMMONWEALTH TRUST/ROYAL COMMONWEALTH SOCIETY	THORNE David
COMMONWEALTH YOUTH EXCHANGE COUNCIL	CRAGGS Vic
COMMUNITY AND YOUTH WORK ASSOCIATION	SHAW Charles
COMMUNITY DESIGN FOR GWENT	BARLOW Sue
COMMUNITY DESIGN SERVICE	HASLAM Geoff
COMMUNITY DEVELOPMENT FOUNDATION	WEST Alison
COMMUNITY EDUCATION DEVELOPMENT CENTRE	STREET Phil
COMMUNITY HEALTH UK (NATIONAL COMMUNITY HEALTH RESOURCE)	DE GROOT Richard
COMMUNITY MATTERS	WOODD Charles
COMMUNITY RELATIONS COUNCIL (NI)	FITZDUFF Dr Mari
COMMUNITY SELF BUILD AGENCY	MCGETTIGAN Anna
COMMUNITY SELF-BUILD SCOTLAND	CHALMERS Robert
COMMUNITY SERVICE VOLUNTEERS	HOODLESS Elisabeth A.
COMMUNITY TRANSPORT	COOPER P.
COMUNN NA GAIDHLIG CAMPBELL Allan	
CONCERN FOR FAMILY & WOMANHOOD - CAMPAIGN FOR THE FEMININE WOMAN	STAYT David W.
CONSERVATION FOUNDATION	SHREEVE David
CONSUMERS ASSOCIATION	MCKECHNIE Sheila
CONTACT THE ELDERLY	MCVEIGH Jane
CONTEMPORARY ART SOCIETY	HEDLEY Gill
CONTINENCE FOUNDATION	POLLOCK Mr David
COOPER ATKINSON CHARITABLE TRUST FOR INDIA	COOPER J. Neville
CORONARY ARTERY DISEASE RESEARCH ASSOCIATION, THE	BURNS Anthony Michael James
CORPORATION OF THE SONS OF THE CLERGY	LEACH R.C.F.
CORRYMEELA COMMUNITY	WILLIAMS Rev Trevor
COT DEATH SOCIETY	NOBLE Geoff
COTTAGE AND RURAL ENTERPRISE LIMITED	DOGGETT T.S.

Organisation	Contact
COTTAGE HOMES	LESIRGE R.
COUNCIL FOR AWARDS IN CHILDREN'S CARE AND EDUCATION	DORRANCE Dr Richard C.
COUNCIL FOR BRITISH ARCHAEOLOGY	MORRIS Richard
COUNCIL FOR EDUCATION IN WORLD CITIZENSHIP	ROGERS Patricia Shepheard
COUNCIL FOR ENVIRONMENTAL EDUCATION	MIDGLEY Christine
COUNCIL FOR INTERNATIONAL EDUCATION	SHERLOCK Maeve
COUNCIL FOR PROFESSIONS SUPPLEMENTARY TO MEDICINE	HALL Michael
COUNCIL FOR SCOTTISH ARCHAEOLOGY	HARDEN Jill
COUNCIL FOR SCOTTISH ARCHAEOLOGY	BEGG Patrick
COUNCIL FOR THE ADVANCEMENT OF COMMUNICATION WITH DEAF PEOPLE	TUMIM Winifred L.
COUNCIL FOR THE ADVANCEMENT OF COMMUNICATION WITH DEAF PEOPLE	SIMPSON T.S.
COUNCIL FOR THE CARE OF CHURCHES	COCKE Thomas Hugh
COUNCIL FOR THE PROTECTION OF RURAL ENGLAND	REYNOLDS Fiona
COUNCIL OF CHRISTIANS AND JEWS	MENDEL Paul D.
COUNCIL OF CHURCHES FOR BRITAIN AND IRELAND	REARDON Rev. John
COUNCIL OF JUSTICE TO ANIMALS & HUMANE SLAUGHTER ASSOCIATION	SIMMONS Sir Michael
COUNSEL AND CARE	SMITH Jef
COUNTRYWIDE HOLIDAYS ASSOCIATION LTD	DOYLE Colin P.
COVENANTERS	WILCOX Paul
CRIME CONCERN	WHISKIN Nigel
CRISIS	SCOTHERN Mark
CROSSLINKS	BOWEN Rev Roger
CROSSROADS (SCOTLAND) CARE ATTENDANT SCHEMES	THOMAS John P. R.
CRUSADERS	KERBEY Alan
CRUSE BEREAVEMENT CARE	PEARCE Rosemary
CRUSE BEREAVEMENT CARE SCOTLAND	HAMPTON Ruth
CRY-SIS SUPPORT GROUP	JORDAN June
CYSTIC FIBROSIS TRUST	BARNES Rosie
DANCE UK	ATTENBOROUGH Jane
DAVID HIDE ASTHMA & ALLERGY RESEARCH CENTRE	ROWLANDSON Dr Piers H.
DAVID LEWIS CENTRE	HANCOCK Robert M.
DAYCARE TRUST/NATIONAL CHILDCARE CAMPAIGN	KELLEHER Colette
DEAFBLIND AND RUBELLA ASSOCIATION NI	MCMULLIN Meta
DEAFBLIND UK	SCOTT Jackie
DEMOS	MULGAN Dr Geoff
DEPARTMENT OF NATIONAL HERITAGE	WEBBER Howard
DEPAUL TRUST	McGREEVY Mark
DESIGN COUNCIL	SUMMERS Andrew W. G.
DEVELOPMENT EDUCATION ASSOCIATION	BOURN Douglas
DIRECTORY OF SOCIAL CHANGE	FITZHERBERT Luke
DISABILITY ALLIANCE, EDUCATION AND RESEARCH ASSOCIATION	REITH Lorna
DISABILITY AWARENESS IN ACTION	HURST Rachel
DISABILITY LAW SERVICE	PIGG Iain
DISABLED CHILDRENS FOUNDATION	HENDERSON Leslie Coultas
DISABLED CHRISTIANS FELLOWSHIP	EDWARDS Miss Jenny
DISABLED DRIVERS ASSOCIATION	CAMPBELL Douglas
DISABLED HOUSING TRUST	THODY Norman Carl
DISABLED LIVING FOUNDATION	BENNETT Susan
DISABLEMENT INCOME GROUP, THE	THOMPSON Pauline
DISABLITY LAW SERVICE	MCLEAN Sally
DOLMETSCH HISTORICAL DANCE SOCIETY	CRUICKSHANK Diana
DONKEY SANCTUARY	SVENDSEN Dr Elisabeth D.
DOWN'S HEART GROUP	GREEN Penny
DRIVE FOR YOUTH	MUMBY Tim
DUNCAN OF JORDANSTONE COLLEGE	MCKEAN Charles
DYSLEXIA INSTITUTE, THE	BROOKS Mrs Liz
DYSTONIA SOCIETY, THE	LENG Alan
DYSTROPHIC EPIDERMOLYSIS BULLOSA RESEARCH ASSOCIATION	DART John
EARL HAIG FUND SCOTLAND SC	MACDONALD J.D.
EARTHKIND	THOMAS Christina
EARTHWATCH EUROPE	MITCHELL Andrew W.
EDINBURGH AND S.E. SCOTLAND DYSLEXIA ASSOCIATION	THOMSON MBE Mrs G. M.
EDINBURGH NEW TOWN CONSERVATION COMMITTEE	GRIFFITH Richard J.
EDINBURGH OLD TOWN RENEWAL TRUST	THOMSON Ms Kirsteen
ELECTORAL REFORM SOCIETY	SYDDIQUE Eric Mahmood
ELIMINATION OF LEUKAEMIA FUND	HALL Martyn
ELIZABETH FITZROY HOMES	EMMERSON David
EMMAUS UK	MACKECHNIE Iain, -JARVIS
EMPLOYMENT POLICY INSTITUTE	PHILPOTT Dr John
ENABLE	DUNNING Norman

Organisation	Contact
ENDEAVOUR TRAINING	PECK Stephen
ENERGY ACTION SCOTLAND	MARNO Ann
ENGINEERING COUNCIL	HEATH Michael Stuart
ENGLISH CHURCHES HOUSING GROUP	WHITE Caroline
ENGLISH COLLECTIVE OF PROSTITUTES	LOPEZ-JONES Nina
ENGLISH FOLK DANCE AND SONG SOCIETY	THOMPSON Prof Noel B.W.
ENGLISH REGIONAL ARTS BOARDS	GORDON Christopher
ENGLISH SKI COUNCIL	KING Diana
ENGLISH TOURING OPERA	HERBERT Katharine
ENVIRONMENT COUNCIL	ROBINSON Steve
ENVIRONMENTAL TRANSPORT ASSOCIATION	DAVIS Andrew
EPILEPSY RESEARCH FOUNDATION	LITTLE Mrs Isabel
EPISCOPAL AGENCY OF THE APOSTLESHIP OF THE SEA	MAGUIRE Rev J.
EQUAL OPPORTUNITIES COMMISSION	NAISH Peter
EQUITY TRUST FUND	HANRECK Carla
EURO BUREAU	HUFF John
EUROGROUP FOR ANIMAL WELFARE	WILKINS David B.
EUROPEAN COUNCIL FOR THE VILLAGE AND SMALL TOWN	DOWER Michael
EUROPEAN RESEARCH INTO CONSUMER AFFAIRS	ROBERTS Eirlys
EX-SERVICES MENTAL WELFARE SOCIETY	DEVINE Wing Commander D.
EX-SERVICES MENTAL WELFARE SOCIETY - COMBAT STRESS	DIXON Brigadier A.K.
EXPLORING PARENTHOOD	DOUGLAS Carolyn
EXTERN ORGANISATION	LOCKHART Dr Bill
FAIRBRIDGE	HAYNES Nigel
FALKLANDS CONSERVATION	BROWN Ann
FAMILIES NEED FATHERS	BERRY Trevor
FAMILY AND YOUTH CONCERN	RICHES Valerie
FAMILY HOLIDAY ASSOCIATION	STEPHENSON Jenny
FAMILY PLANNING ASSOCIATION	WEYMAN Anne
FAMILY POLICY STUDIES CENTRE	ROBERTS Ceridwen
FAMILY RIGHTS GROUP	EDWARDS Dave
FAMILY SERVICE UNITS	EISENSTADT Naomi
FAMILY TREE MINISTRY	STENNING T. W.
FARM AND FOOD SOCIETY	BOWER Joanne
FARM-AFRICA	CAMPBELL David
FATHER HUDSON'S SOCIETY	CAFFREY Kevin
FAWCETT SOCIETY, THE	DIPLOCK Mrs Shelagh
FEDERATION OF BLACK HOUSING ORGANIZATIONS	JULIENNE Louis
FEED THE MINDS	MARRIAGE Dr Alwyn
FESTINIOG RAILWAY TRUST	CHICKEN Mr B.W.O
FIELD STUDIES COUNCIL	THOMAS Anthony D.
FIGHT FOR SIGHT	WALKER Claire
FINDHORN FOUNDATION	MCALLISTER Judy Buhler-
FINDHORN FOUNDATION	PATERSON David
FIRST KEY	ROBERTSON Paul
FLORENCE NIGHTINGALE FUND	RIDLEY Brig Nicholas
FOOD FOR THE HUNGRY/UK	WATSON Niall Macleod
FOREST MANAGEMENT FOUNDATION	BAIRD Nicola
FOUNDATION FOR SPORT AND THE ARTS	ENDICOTT Grattan
FOUNDATION FOR THE STUDY OF INFANT DEATHS	EPSTEIN Joyce
FRAGILE X SOCIETY	WALKER Lesley
FREE CHURCH FEDERAL COUNCIL	ROPER Rev Geoffrey
FRESHWATER BIOLOGICAL ASSOCIATION	JONES Prof John Gwynfryn
FRIEDREICH'S ATAXIA GROUP	GREENHALGH Bob
FRIENDS FOR YOUNG DEAF PEOPLE	ROSIE Morag
FRIENDS OF THE EARTH SCOTLAND	DUNION Kevin
FRIENDS OF THE ELDERLY	LEVETT Mrs Sally
FRONTIER YOUTH TRUST	HARDWIDGE Martin
GABBITAS EDUCATIONAL CONSULTANTS	BROWN Peter M.
GAINSBOROUGH'S HOUSE SOCIETY	BELSEY Hugh
GAME CONSERVANCY TRUST	MCCALL Ian
GARDEN HISTORY SOCIETY	WIGLEY Linda J
GARDENERS' ROYAL BENEVOLENT SOCIETY	BUNCE Colin
GEMMA	BECKETT Elsa
GENETIC INTEREST GROUP	KENT Alastair
GEOLOGICAL SOCIETY	BATEMAN Richard
GEORGIAN GROUP	BURTON Neil
GIRLS FRIENDLY SOCIETY	CROMPTON Mrs Hazel
GIRLS' BRIGADE IN SCOTLAND	MCLEOD Helen R.
GIRLS' BRIGADE NATIONAL COUNCIL FOR ENGLAND AND WALES	BUNTING Mrs Sylvia P.
GIRLS' PUBLIC DAY SCHOOL TRUST	OAKLEY Michael
GLASGOW & WEST OF SCOTLAND SOCIETY FOR THE BLIND	FOSTER Dr A.
GOOD GARDENERS ASSOCIATION	WILKIN J D

Organisation	Contact
GRAND METROPOLITAN PLC	BUSH Geoffrey
GREAT BRITAIN SASAKAWA FOUNDATION	HAND Peter
GREAT ORMOND STREET HOSPITAL FOR CHILDREN NHS TRUST	CREIGHTON Robert
GREATER LONDON ASSOCIATION OF DISABLED PEOPLE	HASLER Frances
GREATER LONDON FORUM FOR THE ELDERLY	NEWMAN Carole
GREATER LONDON FUND FOR THE BLIND	HERINGTON Michael
GREATER SYLHET DEVELOPMENT & WELFARE COUNCIL	HUSAIN Dr M.
GREEN ALLIANCE	HILL Julie
GREENNET	MASTERS Sarah
GREENPEACE UK	MELCHETT Lord Peter
GROUNDWORK FOUNDATION	DAVIDSON John
GROUNDWORK MERTHYR & CYNON	PRICE Susan
GUIDE ASSOCIATION SCOTLAND	ASHTON Pauline
GUIDE DOGS FOR THE BLIND ASSOCIATION, THE	OXLEY Julian C.
GUILD OF CHURCH MUSICIANS	EWINGTON John
GUILLAIN-BARRE SYNDROME SUPPORT GROUP OF THE UK	PRICE Roland
GURKHA WELFARE TRUST NEWTON	DUNN Charles
H.M. FRIGATE UNICORN	FOX Andrew J.A.
HAEMOPHILIA SOCIETY	ARCHER Susan
HALLIWICK ASSOCIATION OF SWIMMING THERAPY	BUCK Michael
HANDICAPPED CHILDREN'S PILGRIMAGE TRUST & HOSANNA HOUSE	MILLS Robert Anthony
HANDIGOLF FOUNDATION	GREASLEY Andrew
HANOVER HOUSING ASSOCIATION	GATWARD John
HARRISON ZOOLOGICAL MUSEUM	BATES Dr Paul Jeremy J.
HEALTHCARE FINANCIAL MANAGEMENT ASSOCIATION	GRIMES Chris
HEARING CONCERN	MEYER Christopher J.
HEARING DOGS FOR THE DEAF	BLUNT Anthony
HEARTH REVOLVING FUND	PATTON Marcus
HELEN ARKELL DYSLEXIA CENTRE	GOEDKOOP Mrs Gail
HELP INTERNATIONAL	TEMPEST Ron
HELP THE AGED	MAYO John
HELP THE HOSPICES	PRAILL David
HENRY DOUBLEDAY RESEARCH ASSOCIATION	GEAR Mrs Jackie
HENRY DOUBLEDAY RESEARCH ASSOCIATION	GEAR Alan
HENRY MOORE FOUNDATION	LLEWELLYN Timothy David
HENRY SMITHS CHARITIES	MCGEOUGH Brian Thomas
HERPES VIRUSES ASSOCIATION	NICHOLSON Marian
HERTFORD COLLEGE, OXFORD	BODMER Sir Walter Fred
HERTFORDSHIRE & MIDDLESEX WILDLIFE TRUST	HINCHLIFFE-WOOD Mieke
HISTORIC CHAPELS TRUST	FREEMAN Jennifer M.
HISTORIC CHURCHES PRESERVATION TRUST, INCORPORATED CHURCH BUILDING SOCIETY	TIPPEN Wing Commander M.W
HISTORIC ROYAL PALACES	BEETON David Christopher
HISTORICAL ASSOCIATION, THE	STILES Madeline
HOCKEY ASSOCIATION	BAINES Stephen
HOLIDAY CARE SERVICE	PHILLIPS David
HOME AND SCHOOL COUNCIL	BULLIVANT Mrs Barbara J.P.
HOME FARM TRUST LTD, THE	CAREY Conan
HOME-START UK	HARRISON Margaret
HOMELESS INTERNATIONAL	MCLEOD Ruth
HOMELIFE (Distressed Gentlefolks Aid Association)	ROBERTS Peter John
HOMOEOPATHIC TRUST FOR RESEARCH AND EDUCATION	WINCOTT Elizabeth
HOPE UK	RUSTON George
HORTICULTURAL RESEARCH ASSOCIATION	WOOD Christopher Charles
HORTICULTURAL THERAPY	RYAN Alison
HOSPICE OF OUR LADY AND ST JOHN	JELL Leslie J.
HOSPITALLER ORDER OF ST JOHN OF GOD	TONNER John
HOUSING CAMPAIGN FOR SINGLE PEOPLE	FITZMAURICE Jon
HOUSING CENTRE TRUST	WIDDOWSON Bob
HOUSING CORPORATION, THE	MAYER R. Anthony Jeffrey
HOUSING SERVICES AGENCY	CRIPPS Alan
HOWARD LEAGUE FOR PENAL REFORM	CROOK Frances
HUMAN SCALE EDUCATION	CARNIE Fiona
HYDE HOUSING ASSOCIATION	ADAMS C.S.
HELPAGE INTERNATIONAL	GORMAN Mark
IKON GALLERY	MACGREGOR Elizabeth A.
IMMIGRATION ADVISORY SERVICE	BEST Keith
IMMUNITY LEGAL CENTRE	HUTTON Ceri
IMPERIAL CANCER RESEARCH FUND	NURSE Paul
IN TOUCH	WORTHINGTON Ann
INCORPORATED ASSOCIATION OF ORGANISTS	POPPLE Richard
INCORPORATED SOCIETY OF MUSICIANS	HOYLE Neil

INDEPENDENT ADOPTION SERVICE	JAMES Mary
INDEPENDENT HEALTHCARE ASSOCIATION	HASSELL Barry
INDEPENDENT PANEL FOR SPECIAL EDUCATION ADVICE	WRIGHT John
INDEPENDENT REPRESENTATION FOR CHILDREN IN NEED	TIMMS Judith
INLAND WATERWAYS ASSOCIATION	EDWARDS Neil
INSTANT MUSCLE LTD	COX Peter
INSTITUTE FOR COMPLEMENTARY MEDICINE	BAIRD Anthony
INSTITUTE FOR EMPLOYMENT STUDIES	PEARSON Richard
INSTITUTE FOR EUROPEAN ENVIRONMENTAL POLICY, LONDON	HAIGH Nigel
INSTITUTE FOR JEWISH POLICY RESEARCH	LERMAN Antony
INSTITUTE FOR OPTIMUM NUTRITION	MILLS Dian
INSTITUTE FOR POLICY ANALYSIS AND DEVELOPMENT	CLAYTON Dr Anthony
INSTITUTE FOR THE STUDY OF DRUG DEPENDENCE	BRADLEY Anna
INSTITUTE OF CHARITY FUNDRAISING MANAGERS TRUST	LEE Stephen
INSTITUTE OF COMMUNITY STUDIES	DARTINGTON Lord Young of
INSTITUTE OF GROUP ANALYSIS	LING Brenda
INSTITUTE OF HORTICULTURE	CLARKE Angela
INSTITUTE OF PAPER CONSERVATION	HAMPSON Clare
INSTITUTE OF SPORTS MEDICINE	ORTON William T. Dr
INSTITUTION OF CHEMICAL ENGINEERS	EVANS Dr T. J.
INSTITUTION OF ENVIRONMENTAL SCIENCES	FULLER R.A. Dr
INSTITUTION OF OCCUPATIONAL SAFETY & HEALTH	BARRELL John
INSTITUTION OF STRUCTURAL ENGINEERS	DOUGILL Dr J.W.
INSTITUTION OF STRUCTURAL ENGINEERS BENEVOLENT FUND	KITCHING H.S.
INSULIN DEPENDENT DIABETES TRUST	KILN Dr Matthew
INSULIN DEPENDENT DIABETES TRUST	HIRST Jenny
INTER FAITH NETWORK FOR THE UK	PEARCE Brian
INTER-ACTION TRUST	BERMAN E.D.
INTERCHANGE TRUST	TOMKINS Dr Alan
INTERHEALTH	LANKESTER Dr Ted
INTERMEDIATE TECHNOLOGY	UNDERHILL Chris
INTERNATIONAL ASSOCIATION FOR RELIGIOUS FREEDOM	TRAER Robert
INTERNATIONAL ASSOCIATION ON WATER QUALITY	MILBURN Anthony
INTERNATIONAL BILLIARDS & SNOOKER FEDERATION	RUANE Gloria
INTERNATIONAL BLACK WOMEN FOR WAGES FOR HOUSEWORK	SALLEY Sylvia
INTERNATIONAL COUNCIL ON MONUMENTS AND SITES	CHITHAM Robert
INTERNATIONAL COUNCIL ON MONUMENTS AND SITES	WHITBOURN Dr Philip
INTERNATIONAL FEDERATION OF MULTIPLE SCLEROSIS SOCIETIES	HAMILTON Richard
INTERNATIONAL GLAUCOMA ASSOCIATION	CRICK Ronald Pitts
INTERNATIONAL HOSPITAL FEDERATION	PICKERING Dr Errol
INTERNATIONAL INSTITUTE FOR ENVIRONMENT AND DEVELOPMENT	SANDBROOK J. Richard
INTERNATIONAL LEAGUE FOR THE PROTECTION OF HORSES	STEPHEN Col George McLaughlin
INTERNATIONAL PLANNED PARENTHOOD FEDERATION	BRUEGGEMANN Ingar
INTERNATIONAL RELIEF FRIENDSHIP FOUNDATION	HAYS Chris D.
INTERNATIONAL RESCUE CORPS	MCMARTIN William
INTERNATIONAL SPINAL RESEARCH TRUST	WALDEN Ian
INTERNATIONAL STANDING CONFERENCE ON PHILANTHROPY	RITCHIE Cyril
INTERNATIONAL STUDY CENTRE	MONTGOMERY A.
INTERNATIONAL VOLUNTARY SERVICE	HARROWER Neil
INTERNATIONAL WAGES FOR HOUSEWORK CAMPAIGN	JAMES Selma
INTERNATIONAL WINE & FOOD SOCIETY	DUNN-MEYNELL Hugo
INTERSERVE SCOTLAND	JACKSON Mr John M.
INVALID CHILDREN'S AID NATIONWIDE	JONES Brian
INVALIDS-AT-HOME	LOMAS Sarah E.
IRIS FUND FOR PREVENTION OF BLINDNESS	WRIDE Vanessa
IRISH SCHOOL OF ECUMENICS	MORROW Rev. John W.
IRONBRIDGE GORGE MUSEUM TRUST	LAWES Glen
ISSUE (THE NATIONAL FERTILITY ASSOCIATION)	RICE J. Susan
JAZZ SERVICES	HODGKINS Chris
JENNIFER TRUST FOR SPINAL ATROPHY	MACAULAY Anita
JEWISH AIDS TRUST	COLLIN Rosalind
JEWISH CARE	CARLOWE Melvyn I.
JEWISH MUSEUM - LONDON'S MUSEUM OF JEWISH LIFE	BURMAN Rickie

Organisation	Contact
JOHN GROOMS ASSOCIATION FOR DISABLED PEOPLE	SHAW Revd Michael
JOHN LYON'S CHARITY	STEBBINGS Andrew
JOHN MUIR TRUST	HAWKINS Nigel
JOHN S COHEN FOUNDATION	HALDANE Duncan
JOINT ASSOCIATION FOR PETROLEUM EXPLORATION COURSES (UK)	FISHER Michael J.
JOINT COUNCIL FOR THE WELFARE OF IMMIGRANTS	MORAES Claude
JOINT EDUCATIONAL TRUST	BAINER Mrs Susan
JOSEPH ROWNTREE CHARITABLE TRUST	BURKEMAN Steven
JOSEPH ROWNTREE FOUNDATION	BEST Richard
JOSEPH ROWNTREE FOUNDATION	STURGE Michael
JOSEPH ROWNTREE REFORM TRUST	FLOWER Antony John Frank
JOSEPHINE BUTLER SOCIETY	CASS Mrs Ruth
JUSTICE	OWERS Anne
JUSTICE FOR ALL VACCINE-DAMAGED CHILDREN UK	NEEDS Enid & Ivor
KARUNA TRUST	JOSEPH Peter
KENRIC CHAIR	
KENWARD TRUST	FEATHERSTONE Godfrey
KEYCHANGE	SHAFIK D.J.
KIDS' CLUBS NETWORK	LONGFIELD Anne
KIDSCAPE	ELLIOTT Michele
KING EDWARD'S HOSPITAL FUND FOR LONDON	MAXWELL Robert J.
KING GEORGE'S FUND FOR SAILORS	APPLETON Martin
KING'S CONSORT	KING Robert
KING'S FUND DEVELOPMENT CENTRE	COULTER Angela
KITH AND KIDS	SCHAFFER Carol
LADY HOARE TRUST FOR PHYSICALLY DISABLED CHILDREN	ATKINSON Jane
LANDMARK TRUST	PEARCE Peter H.
LANDSCAPE FOUNDATION	DARLEY Gillian
LANDSCAPE RESEARCH GROUP	BURGESS Jacquelin
LANGLEY HOUSE TRUST	ADAMS John
LANTERN TRUST	IVES Cyril
LASALLIAN DEVELOPING WORLD PROJECTS	WILLIAMS Brother Gregory
LEAD - SCOTLAND	NOBLE Lillias
LEAGUE AGAINST CRUEL SPORTS	BRYANT John
LEAGUE OF BRITISH MUSLIMS UK	CHAUDHRY Mr B.A.
LEAGUE OF REMEMBRANCE	BARCHARD Betty
LEARNING THROUGH ACTION	COTTERILL Annette
LEARNING THROUGH LANDSCAPES	LUCAS Bill
LEAVENERS	FATEH Mr Eenasul
LEGAL ACTION GROUP	SMITH Roger
LEO BAECK COLLEGE	MAGONET Jonathan Rabbi Prof
LEONARD CHESHIRE FOUNDATION, THE	STANFORD J.K.E.
LET'S FACE IT - SUPPORT GROUP FOR THE FACIALLY DISFIGURED	PIFF Christine
LEUKAEMIA CARE SOCIETY	BROWN Sandra
LEVERHULME TRUST	SUPPLE Barry
LIBERTY (NATIONAL COUNCIL FOR CIVIL LIBERTIES)	WADHAM John
LIBRARY ASSOCIATION	SHIMMON Ross
LIFE	SCARISBRICK Prof J.J.
LIFE EDUCATION CENTRES	ROBERTS Michael
LIMBLESS ASSOCIATION	BURNIE Mrs P.A.
LINK CENTRE FOR DEAFENED PEOPLE	GAILEY Dr Lorraine
LINNEAN SOCIETY OF LONDON	MARSDEN John
LITTLE SISTERS OF THE POOR	SISTER AGNES
LISTENING LIBRARY	HEPWORTH G. Anthony
LIVE MUSIC NOW!	RENSHAW Virginia
LONDON ARTS BOARD	ROBERTSON Sue
LONDON BUSINESS SCHOOL	BAIN Prof George S.
LONDON ELECTRONIC ARTS	MAZIERE Michael
LONDON GUILDHALL UNIVERSITY	FLOUD Roderick
LONDON HOUSING FOUNDATION	PICKERING Caroline
LONDON LIGHTHOUSE	SPENCE Christopher
LONDON VOLUNTARY SERVICE COUNCIL	HOLLOWAY Christine
LONDON WILDLIFE TRUST	TURNBULL Graham
LONG DISTANCE WALKERS ASSOCIATION	MAPLE Mr Leslie
LOW PAY UNIT	POND Chris
LUCY CAVENDISH COLLEGE CAMBRIDGE UNIVERSITY	PERRY Baroness, of Southwark
MACINTYRE FOUNDATION, THE	THORNE John V.
MACKINTOSH FOUNDATION	ROSE D. Michael
MALCOLM SARGENT CANCER FUND FOR CHILDREN	DARLEY Sylvia
MALCOLM SARGENT CANCER FUND FOR CHILDREN	YEO Diane
MALT HOUSE TRUST	CARMICHAEL Brother Michael
MANIC DEPRESSION FELLOWSHIP	FULFORD Myra
MANNA COUNSELLING SERVICE	KENDALL Jeannie
MARIE CURIE CANCER CARE	CARLETON-SMITH Major General M.E.

Organisation	Contact
MARINE SOCIETY, THE	FRAMPTON Lt Cdr Richard M.
MARRIAGE CARE	CORBETT Mary
MARRIAGE COUNSELLING SCOTLAND	LOVE Frances
MARY WARD CENTRE	FREESTONE Patrick
MATERNITY AND HEALTH LINKS	CHAUDHRY Shaheen
MATHEMATICAL ASSOCIATION	WHITBY Heather
MCCARTHY FOUNDATION	BRADLEY Christine Ann
MEDIA TRUST	DIEHL Caroline
MEDIC ALERT FOUNDATION	FRIEND Julie
MEDICAL ACTION FOR GLOBAL SECURITY	HARTOG Martin
MEDICAL COUNCIL ON ALCOHOLISM	ABRAHAM Dr Peter
MEDICAL EMERGENCY RELIEF INTERNATIONAL	BESSE Dr Christopher
MEDICAL WOMEN'S FEDERATION	PERRY Lyn
MENTAL HEALTH FOUNDATION SCOTLAND	SOMERVILLE Lynda M.
METHODIST ASSOCIATION OF YOUTH CLUBS	WAKELIN Rev Mark
METHODIST CHURCH	GAMBLE Rev David
METHODIST CHURCH	ROBSON Derek
METHODIST HOMES FOR THE AGED AND METHODIST HOMES HOUSING ASSOCIATION	WIGLEY David L.
MICROCEPHALY SUPPORT GROUP	SMITH Mrs Jacqui
MIDLANDS ASTHMA & ALLERGY RESEARCH ASSOCIATION	CORDEN Julie
MILDMAY MISSION HOSPITAL	SIMS Ruth
MILLENNIUM COMMISSION	O'CONNOR Michael
MINORITY RIGHTS GROUP	PHILLIPS Alan
MISSIONS TO SEAMEN, THE	JONES Revd Canon Glyndwr
MOBILITY AID AND GUIDE DOG ALLIANCE	ROBSON Howard
MONUMENTAL BRASS SOCIETY	STUCHFIELD H. Martin
MOORES ROWLAND	RANDALL Adrian J.L.
MOTABILITY	MUDDIMAN Noel
MOTHERS' UNION	EAMES Lady (Christine)
MOTOR NEURONE DISEASE ASSOCIATION	LEVVY George
MOUNTAINEERING COUNCIL OF SCOTLAND	HOWETT Kevin
MOUNTAINEERING COUNCIL OF SCOTLAND	DALES Mike
MSF - THE UNION FOR SKILLED AND PROFESSIONAL PEOPLE	BALL Dr Chris
MUSEUM OF SCIENCE & INDUSTRY IN MANCHESTER	GREENE Dr J. Patrick
MUSEUMS AND GALLERIES COMMISSION	MASON Timothy
MUSEUMS ASSOCIATION (THE)	TAYLOR Mark
MUSEUMS JOURNAL	CARRINGTON Lucie
MUSICAL MUSEUM	RYDER Michael James
MUSICIANS BENEVOLENT FUND	FAULKNER Helen
MUSLIM EDUCATIONAL TRUST	SARWAR Ghulam
MYALGIC ENCEPHALOMYELITIS ASSOCIATION	GRENIER Paola
MYASTHENIA GRAVIS ASSOCIATION	KEELING Preston
NABC - CLUBS FOR YOUNG PEOPLE	GROVES Colin
NATIONAL ABORTION CAMPAIGN	KEARY Anne Marie
NATIONAL AIDS TRUST	BODELL Derek
NATIONAL ANKYLOSING SPONDYLITIS SOCIETY	ROGERS Fergus J.
NATIONAL ART COLLECTIONS FUND	BARRIE David
NATIONAL ASSEMBLY OF WOMEN	MCGHEE Elaine
NATIONAL ASSOCIATION FOR CHILDREN WITH LOWER LIMB ABNORMALITIES	BANTON Sue
NATIONAL ASSOCIATION FOR ENVIRONMENTAL EDUCATION (UK)	MILTON Brian
NATIONAL ASSOCIATION FOR GIFTED CHILDREN	CAREY Peter
NATIONAL ASSOCIATION FOR MENTAL HEALTH	CLEMENTS Judi
NATIONAL ASSOCIATION FOR PATIENT PARTICIPATION	ASHCROFT Michael
NATIONAL ASSOCIATION FOR PREMENSTRUAL SYNDROME	HOWE Jackie
NATIONAL ASSOCIATION FOR THE CARE & RESETTLEMENT OF OFFENDERS	EDWARDS Helen
NATIONAL ASSOCIATION OF COUNCILS FOR VOLUNTARY SERVICE	CARLING Christine
NATIONAL ASSOCIATION OF FIELD STUDY OFFICERS	CLATWORTHY Michael James
NATIONAL ASSOCIATION OF LEAGUES OF HOSPITAL FRIENDS	CONWAY Mike
NATIONAL ASSOCIATION OF ROUND TABLES OF GB AND IRELAND	RENOLD Richard
NATIONAL ASSOCIATION OF YOUTH ORCHESTRAS	MAIN Carol
NATIONAL ASSOCIATION OF YOUTH THEATRES	CARNEY Lynne
NATIONAL ASTHMA CAMPAIGN	LETTS Melinda
NATIONAL AUTISTIC SOCIETY	PEACOCK Geraldine
NATIONAL BACK PAIN ASSOCIATION	THOMAS G.E.
NATIONAL BIBLE SOCIETY OF SCOTLAND	MACDONALD Rev Fergus
NATIONAL CAMPAIGN FOR FIREWORK SAFETY	TOBIN Noel
NATIONAL CAMPAIGN FOR HOMELESS PEOPLE	HOLMES Chris

WHO'S WHO IN THE VOLUNTARY SECTOR - 175

NATIONAL CAMPAIGN FOR THE ARTS	EDWARDS Jennifer
NATIONAL CANINE DEFENCE LEAGUE	BALDWIN Clarissa
NATIONAL CARE HOMES ASSOCIATION	SCOTT Sheila
NATIONAL CAVING ASSOCIATION	BAGULEY Frank S.
NATIONAL CENTRE FOR PLAY	WILSON Brenda
NATIONAL CENTRE FOR VOLUNTEERING, THE	KELMANSON Andrea
NATIONAL CHILDMINDING ASSOCIATION	HAYNES Gillian
NATIONAL CHILDREN'S BUREAU	HODGKIN Rachel
NATIONAL CHILDREN'S BUREAU	REA PRICE John
NATIONAL CHILDREN'S CENTRE	WIGMORE Hazel
NATIONAL CONFEDERATION OF PARENT-TEACHER ASSOCIATIONS	MORRISSEY Margaret
NATIONAL COUNCIL FOR EDUCATIONAL TECHNOLOGY	BELL Margaret
NATIONAL COUNCIL FOR HOSPICE AND SPECIALIST PALLIATIVE CARE SERVICES	GAFFIN Jean
NATIONAL COUNCIL FOR THE CONSERVATION OF PLANTS AND GARDENS	NICHOL David
NATIONAL COUNCIL FOR THE CONSERVATION OF PLANTS AND GARDENS	PATTISON Graham
NATIONAL COUNCIL FOR THE DIVORCED AND SEPARATED	SQUIRES Dorothy
NATIONAL COUNCIL FOR VOLUNTARY ORGANISATIONS	ETHERINGTON Stuart
NATIONAL COUNCIL FOR VOLUNTARY YOUTH SERVICES	RAUPRICH Susanne
NATIONAL COUNCIL OF VOLUNTARY CHILD CARE ORGANISATIONS	BURNELL Jan
NATIONAL COUNCIL OF WOMEN OF GREAT BRITAIN	WEDEKIND Grace
NATIONAL CRICKET ASSOCIATION	BATES Terry N.
NATIONAL DEAF CHILDREN'S SOCIETY	DANIELS Susan T.
NATIONAL DEAF-BLIND AND RUBELLA ASSOCIATION	BARKER Adrian
NATIONAL DEAFBLIND AND RUBELLA ASSOCIATION	CLARK Rodney
NATIONAL DEAFBLIND RUBELLA ASSOCIATION	PERNAK Derek
NATIONAL EARLY YEARS NETWORK (FORMERLY VOLCUF)	STONE Judith
NATIONAL EXTENSION COLLEGE TRUST LTD	MORPETH Ros
NATIONAL EYE RESEARCH CENTRE	GAUSSEN Sam
NATIONAL FAMILY MEDIATION	FISHER Thelma
NATIONAL FEDERATION OF CITY FARMS	EGGINTON-METTERS Ian
NATIONAL FEDERATION OF GATEWAY CLUBS	FITZGERALD Julie
NATIONAL FEDERATION OF MUSIC SOCIETIES	JONES Russell
NATIONAL FEDERATION OF SHOPMOBILITY	MCLEOD Mrs Joss
NATIONAL FEDERATION OF THE BLIND OF THE UNITED KINGDOM	KELLY Lesley
NATIONAL FEDERATION OF YOUNG FARMERS' CLUBS	LOUGHRAN Brendan
NATIONAL FENCING TRAINING AUTHORITY	HAYZELDEN K.J.
NATIONAL FOSTER CARE ASSOCIATION	LOWE Marion I.
NATIONAL FOSTER CARE ASSOCIATION	MCANDREW Gerri
NATIONAL GARDENS SCHEME CHARITABLE TRUST	MARSH Lt Col Tym
NATIONAL HEART FORUM	SHARP Imogen
NATIONAL HERITAGE MEMORIAL FUND	CARNWATH Francis
NATIONAL HORSERACING MUSEUM	BRACEGIRDLE Hilary
NATIONAL HOSPITAL DEVELOPMENT FOUNDATION	MEYER Paul
NATIONAL HOUSE BUILDING COUNCIL	ALLEN Anthony
NATIONAL HOUSING AND TOWN PLANNING COUNCIL	MACDONALD Kelvin
NATIONAL HOUSING ASSOCIATION	COULTER Jim
NATIONAL INFORMATION FORUM	DARNBROUGH Ms Ann
NATIONAL INSTITUTE FOR SOCIAL WORK	STATHAM Daphne
NATIONAL INSTITUTE OF ADULT CONTINUING EDUCATION	TUCKETT Alan
NATIONAL KIDNEY FEDERATION (NAT FED OF KIDNEY PATIENT ASSOCS)	JACKSON Margaret
NATIONAL LEAGUE OF BLIND AND DISABLED	MANN Joe
NATIONAL LIBRARY FOR THE BLIND	BENNETT Margaret
NATIONAL LITERACY TRUST	MCCLELLAND Neil
NATIONAL LOTTERY CHARITIES BOARD	PARASKEVA Janet
NATIONAL LOTTERY CHARITIES BOARD	BUBB S J
NATIONAL LOTTERY CHARITIES BOARD	HORNSBY Timothy
NATIONAL LOTTERY CHARITIES BOARD	OPPENHEIM Gerald
NATIONAL LOTTERY CHARITIES BOARD	MULLAN Robin
NATIONAL LOTTERY CHARITIES BOARD	RAFFERTY John
NATIONAL LOTTERY CHARITIES BOARD	NORRIS Roy
NATIONAL LOTTERY CHARITIES BOARD	MACDONALD Barry
NATIONAL MUSEUM OF LABOUR HISTORY	MANSFIELD Nicholas
NATIONAL MUSEUMS & GALLERIES OF WALES/ AMGUEDDFEYDD AC ORIELAU CENEDLAETHOL	FORD Colin John
NATIONAL MUSIC COUNCIL	GOODWIN Jennifer

NATIONAL MUSIC FOR THE BLIND	MILLS Derek
NATIONAL OSTEOPOROSIS SOCIETY	EDWARDS Linda
NATIONAL PISTOL ASSOCIATION	MCCONCHIE I.
NATIONAL PLAYING FIELDS ASSOCIATION	DAVIES Elsa
NATIONAL PLAYING FIELDS ASSOCIATION (SCOTLAND)	TUNNAH John E.
NATIONAL PORTRAIT GALLERY	SAUMAREZ SMITH Charles Robert
NATIONAL RETREAT ASSOCIATION	LANE Paddy
NATIONAL RURAL ENTERPRISE CENTRE	BERRY Simon
NATIONAL SOCIETY FOR CLEAN AIR AND ENVIRONMENTAL PROTECTION	CROSSETT Tom
NATIONAL SOCIETY FOR EPILEPSY	CORSAR Bill
NATIONAL SOCIETY FOR THE PREVENTION OF CRUELTY TO CHILDREN	HARDING James Owen Glyn, (Jim)
NATIONAL SOCIETY OF ALLOTMENT AND LEISURE GARDENERS LTD	STOKES Geoff
NATIONAL SPIRITUAL ASSEMBLY OF THE BAHAIS OF THE UK	ADAMSON Hugh
NATIONAL STEPFAMILY ASSOCIATION	DE'ATH Erica
NATIONAL TRUST	DRURY Martin
NATIONAL TRUST FOR SCOTLAND	DOW Rear-Admiral Douglas
NATIONAL WOMEN'S REGISTER	HICKS Barbara
NATIONAL WOMEN'S REGISTER	KERR Ruby
NATIONAL YOUTH AGENCY	WYLIE Tom
NATURAL MEDICINES SOCIETY	LIU Sato
NCH ACTION FOR CHILDREN	MEAD Deryk
NEA (THE NATIONAL ENERGY ACTION CHARITY)	COOK Andrea
NETWORK OF ACCESS AND CHILD CONTACT CENTRES	HALLIDAY Eunice
NEUROFIBROMATOSIS ASSOCIATION	TWEEDY Roberta
NEW APPROACHES TO CANCER	RICHARDSON Colin Ryder
NEWSTRAID BENEVOLENT SOCIETY	HORWITE Brian
NORTH BRITISH HOUSING ASSOCIATION	ARMITAGE Eric D
NORTH OF ENGLAND ZOOLOGICAL SOCIETY	MCGREER REID Dr Gordon
NORTHERN CONCORD	BAKER Jenny
NORTHERN IRELAND CHEST HEART & STROKE ASSOCIATION	DOUGAL Andrew Patrick
NORTHERN IRELAND COUNCIL FOR VOLUNTARY ACTION	OLIVER Quintin
NORTHERN IRELAND WOMEN'S AID FEDERATION	COURTNEY Angela
NORWICH PLAYHOUSE	BURKE Henry
NORWOOD RAVENSWOOD CHILD/FAMILY SERVICES	BRIER Sam
NOT FORGOTTEN ASSOCIATION, THE	TEDDER Lt Col James
NUFFIELD FOUNDATION	TOMEI Anthony
OCKENDEN VENTURE	BEALE James
OFFICER'S PENSIONS SOCIETY (WIDOW'S FUND)	BONNET P.R.F Major General
OFFICERS' ASSOCIATION, THE	JOHNSON Brigadier Peter Dunbar
ONE PARENT FAMILIES SCOTLAND	ROBERTSON Sue
OPEN SPACES SOCIETY	ASHBROOK Kate
OPPORTUNITY TRUST	CUTHBERT Neil
ORBIS INTERNATIONAL	MCDONALD John
ORCHESTRA OF THE AGE OF THE ENLIGHTENMENT	PICKARD David
ORDER OF ST JOHN, THE	IMRAY Sir Colin
ORGANIC LIVING ASSOCIATION	NIGHTINGALE Mr Dennis C.
ORGANISATION OF BLIND AFRICAN CARRIBEANS	OLASHOR Ibukun
ORMISTON TRUST	MURRAY Peter
OTTO SCHIFF HOUSING ASSOCIATION	SHEPHERD Tony
OUTWARD BOUND TRUST	HOBBS Michael
OVERCOMING SPEECH IMPAIRMENTS	CORKISH Norma
OXFAM	BRYER David Ronald William
OXFAM	VINCENT Michael
OXFAM	WALLIS Stewart
OXFAM	WHITAKER John
OXFAM IN SCOTLAND	HEARLE Marie
PAPWORTH TRUST	KUMAR Harpal S.
PARENTLINE	BAISDEN Carole
PARENTLINE	BURTON Virginia
PARENTS AGAINST INJUSTICE	AMPHLETT Sue
PARENTS FOR CHILDREN	IRVING Mrs Karen
PARENTS' FRIEND	DICKENS Joy
PARKINSON'S DISEASE SOCIETY OF UK	BROOKING Barry A.
PARTIS COLLEGE	YOUNG Major M.J.
PASCAL THEATRE COMPANY	PASCAL Julia
PATIENTS ASSOCIATION	HOWLAND Guy
PAUL HAMLYN FOUNDATION	CORNFORD James
PEDESTRIANS ASSOCIATION	REA Flick
PEOPLE FOR THE ETHICAL TREATMENT OF ANIMALS	VERNELLI Toni
PESTALOZZI CHILDREN'S VILLAGE TRUST	PHILLIPS Maurice
PHAB ENGLAND	GOOCH Peter
PHOBICS SOCIETY	FISHER Harold
PHOENIX HOUSE HOUSING ASSOCIATION	TICKELL Clare

Organisation	Contact
PILKINGTON RETIREMENT SERVICES LTD	BROOKS Marilyn
PLAIN ENGLISH CAMPAIGN	MAHER Chrissie
PLAN INTERNATIONAL UK	WARDMAN Anna
PLANTLIFE	SMART Jane
POETRY SOCIETY	MEADE Chris
POLICY STUDIES INSTITUTE	MEADOWS Pamela
POPULATION CONCERN	THOMAS Wendy
POSITIVELY WOMEN	ELSY Stephanie
PRAMACARE	GREGORY Roger
PRE-RETIREMENT ASSOCIATION OF GB & NI	DAVIES Dr Mary
PRIMARY IMMUNODEFICIENCY ASSOCIATION	WATTERS David
PRINCE'S TRUST - BRO	CALDWELL Neil
PRINCE'S TRUST AND THE ROYAL JUBILEE TRUSTS, THE	SHEBBEARE Tom
PRINCE'S TRUST VOLUNTEERS, THE	CROWTHER-HUNT Elizabeth
PRINCESS ROYAL TRUST FOR CARERS	BUTLER David
PRISON FELLOWSHIP SCOTLAND	GRANT Allan
PRISON REFORM TRUST	SHAW Stephen
PRISONERS ABROAD	LAURENZI Carlo
PROGRESSIVE SUPRANUCLEAR PALSY (PSP EUROPE) ASSOCIATION	KOE Brigadier M.R.
PROJECT SEED EUROPE	GRUNFELD Rabbi J.
PROJECT TRUST	MACLEAN-BRISTOL The Hon. Mrs Lavinia
PROJECT TRUST	MACLEAN-BRISTOL Nicholas
PROTESTANT AND CATHOLIC ENCOUNTER	MCKITTRICK David
PSYCHIATRIC REHABILITATION ASSOCIATION	WILDER John
PSYCHIATRY RESEARCH TRUST	PAINE L.H.W.
QUAKER PEACE & SERVICE	CLARK Andrew C.
QUEEN ELIZABETH'S FOUNDATION FOR DISABLED PEOPLE	CLARK Malcolm B.
QUEEN MARY'S ROEHAMPTON TRUST	BAKER Alan H.
QUEEN'S NURSING INSTITUTE	BAGNALL Pippa
QUEEN'S NURSING INSTITUTE (SCOTLAND)	PRESTON George D.C.
RADIANT LIFE MINISTRIES	CRICK Rev W.
RAILWAY DEVELOPMENT SOCIETY	GARROD Trevor
RALEIGH INTERNATIONAL	MACLEOD J.Robertson-
RARE BREEDS SURVIVAL TRUST	ALDERSON Lawrence
RATHBONE SOCIETY, THE	WEINSTOCK Anne
RAVENSWOOD FOUNDATION	BRIER Norma
RAYNAUD'S AND SCLERODERMA ASSOCIATION	MAWDSLEY Mrs Anne H.
REACH	MUNDAY Jill
REACH - ASSOCIATION FOR CHILDREN WITH HAND/ARM DEFICIENCY	STOKES Mrs Sue
REAL LIFE OPTIONS	WANDLESS David
REDR - REGISTERED ENGINEERS FOR DISASTER RELIEF	LAMBERT Bobby
REGISTERED NURSING HOME ASSOCIATION	URSELL Frank
REGULAR FORCES EMPLOYMENT ASSOCIATION	SHELLARD Maj-Gen M.F.L.
RELATIONSHIPS FOUNDATION	SCHLUTER Michael Dr
RELEASE	GOODMAN Mike
RELIEF FUND FOR ROMANIA	PARRY Edward
REMAP (SCOTLAND)	GOLDER John
RESCARE - NAT SOC FOR MENTALLY HANDICAPPED PEOPLE IN RESIDENTIAL CARE	JACKSON Richard Smith
RESCUE FOUNDATION FOR THE BRAIN INJURED INFANT	LEWIS Miriam
RESEARCH INSTITUTE FOR CONSUMER AFFAIRS	YELDING David
RESEARCH INSTITUTE FOR THE CARE OF THE ELDERLY	JONES Roy
RESEARCH INTO AGEING	MILLS Elizabeth
REUTER FOUNDATION	SOMERVILLE Stephen
RICHARDS (ADMIRAL OF THE FLEET SIR FREDERICK) MEMORIAL FUND	STEPHENS Daniel A.P.
RICHMOND FELLOWSHIP	DRAKE Madeline
RIDING FOR THE DISABLED ASSOCIATION	DAVIES W J
RIGHT OF WAY LAW REVIEW	BRAHAM Margaret Louise
RIGHTS OF WOMEN COLLECTIVE	
ROADPEACE	CHAUDHRY Brigitte
ROMANIAN AID FUND	HORNSBY Valerie
ROMANIAN ORPHANAGE TRUST	MCCREADY Donald
ROTARY INTERNATIONAL IN GREAT BRITAIN & IRELAND	MOREHEN David
ROWCROFT HOSPICE FOR TORBAY AND SOUTH DEVON	MARTIN Robin D.S.
ROY CASTLE CAUSE FOR HOPE FOUNDATION	INGHAM Sylvia
ROYAL ACADEMY TRUST	NICKSON John
ROYAL ACADEMY OF DANCING	WATCHMAN David
ROYAL AERONAUTICAL SOCIETY	KENNETT R J
ROYAL AGRICULTURAL BENEVOLENT INSTITUTION	DUCKETT Richard
ROYAL AGRICULTURAL COLLEGE	JONES Prof Arthur Stanley
ROYAL ANTHROPOLOGICAL INSTITUTE	BENTHALL Jonathan
ROYAL ARTILLERY MUSEUMS LTD/HERITAGE CAMPAIGN	EVANS David

Organisation	Contact
ROYAL ASSOCIATION FOR DISABILITY AND REHABILITATION	MASSIE Bert
ROYAL ASSOCIATION IN AID OF DEAF PEOPLE	EDMOND Brian
ROYAL ASTRONOMICAL SOCIETY	LANE J.E.J
ROYAL BOTANIC GARDENS KEW FOUNDATION	COODE-ADAMS Giles
ROYAL BRITISH LEGION WOMEN'S SECTION	SIMPSON Miss Julia B.
ROYAL COLLEGE OF GENERAL PRACTITIONERS	THEWLIS Sarah
ROYAL COLLEGE OF NURSING	HANCOCK Christine
ROYAL COLLEGE OF OBSTETRICIANS AND GYNAECOLOGISTS	BARNETT Paul
ROYAL COLLEGE OF ORGANISTS	NICHOLAS Michael
ROYAL COLLEGE OF SPEECH AND LANGUAGE THERAPISTS	EVANS Pam
ROYAL GEOGRAPHICAL SOCIETY	GARDNER Dr Rita
ROYAL HIGHLAND AND AGRICULTURAL SOCIETY OF SCOTLAND	DAVIES Hywel
ROYAL HOMES FOR OFFICERS' WIDOWS & DAUGHTERS	SUGDEN Francis Major General
ROYAL HORTICULTURAL SOCIETY	HEARN Donald P.
ROYAL INCORPORATION OF ARCHITECTS IN SCOTLAND	TOMBS Sebastian Martineau
ROYAL INSTITUTE OF INTERNATIONAL AFFAIRS	MARTIN Laurence
ROYAL INSTITUTE OF PAINTERS IN WATER COLOURS	MADDOX Ronald PRI
ROYAL INSTITUTE OF PUBLIC HEALTH & HYGIENE	SMITH Roger
ROYAL INSTITUTION OF CHARTERED SURVEYORS	MAKIN Claire
ROYAL LEICESTERSHIRE, RUTLAND & WYCLIFFE SOCIETY FOR THE BLIND	PARKINSON Joseph Philip
ROYAL LIFE SAVING SOCIETY UK, THE	LEAR Stephen
ROYAL LIVERPOOL PHILHARMONIC SOCIETY	MOSLEY Martin
ROYAL MARSDEN NHS TRUST	CUNNINGHAM Miss Phyllis M.
ROYAL MASONIC BENEVOLENT INSTITUTION	REYNOLDS Jane
ROYAL NATIONAL EISTEDDFOD OF WALES	ROBERTS Elfed
ROYAL NATIONAL INSTITUTE FOR DEAF PEOPLE	ALKER Doug
ROYAL NATIONAL INSTITUTE FOR THE BLIND	BRUCE Professor Ian
ROYAL NATIONAL INSTITUTE FOR THE BLIND	ENNALS Paul
ROYAL NATIONAL INSTITUTE FOR THE BLIND	LANCASTER Mike
ROYAL NATIONAL INSTITUTE FOR THE BLIND	KING Stephen P.
ROYAL NATIONAL INSTITUTE FOR THE BLIND	ASTON Anthony
ROYAL NATIONAL INSTITUTE FOR THE BLIND	GIFFORD Barry Thomas
ROYAL NATIONAL INSTITUTE FOR THE BLIND	COOPER Steven A.
ROYAL NATIONAL LIFEBOAT INSTITUTION	MILES Lieutenant Commander
ROYAL NATIONAL LIFEBOAT INSTITUTION	VENTHAM Ian
ROYAL NATIONAL MISSION TO DEEPSEA FISHERMEN	MARSDEN Alan Douglas
ROYAL NAVAL BENEVOLENT TRUST	OWENS Jeremy
ROYAL PHARMACEUTICAL SOCIETY OF GREAT BRITAIN	PARKIN B.
ROYAL PHILANTHROPIC SOCIETY	COLEMAN Don
ROYAL PHOTOGRAPHIC SOCIETY, THE	LANE Barry John
ROYAL SCHOOL FOR DEAF CHILDREN	GUNNELL Jonathon Charles
ROYAL SCHOOL OF CHURCH MUSIC	KING Charles
ROYAL SCHOOLS FOR THE DEAF	MCCRACKEN Bevan R
ROYAL SCOTTISH ACADEMY	LAIDLAW Bruce
ROYAL SCOTTISH FORESTRY SOCIETY	OSBORNE Michael
ROYAL SCOTTISH GEOGRAPHICAL SOCIETY	MUNRO Dr David M
ROYAL SCOTTISH SOCIETY FOR PREVENTION OF CRUELTY TO CHILDREN - CHILDREN 1ST	WOOD Arthur M.M.
ROYAL SOCIETY (THE)	WARREN Dr P.T.
ROYAL SOCIETY FOR THE PREVENTION OF ACCIDENTS	EDWARDS A.W.(Tony)
ROYAL SOCIETY FOR THE PREVENTION OF CRUELTY TO ANIMALS	DAVIES Peter R C B
ROYAL SOCIETY FOR THE PROTECTION OF BIRDS	YOUNG Barbara S.
ROYAL SOCIETY FOR THE RELIEF OF INDIGENT GENTLEWOMEN OF SCOTLAND	GODDARD George Ferguson
ROYAL SOCIETY OF EDINBURGH	JOHNSTON T.L.
ROYAL SOCIETY OF EDINBURGH	DUNCAN Dr William
ROYAL SOCIETY OF HEALTH	BYRNE Anthony J.
ROYAL SOCIETY OF LITERATURE OF THE UNITED KINGDOM	MORTIMER CBE QC John
ROYAL SOCIETY OF PORTRAIT PAINTERS	TODD Daphne
ROYAL STAR & GARTER HOME FOR DISABLED SAILORS, SOLDIERS & AIRMEN	LASHBROOKE Ian
ROYAL TOWN PLANNING INSTITUTE	UPTON Robert
ROYAL UNITED KINGDOM BENEFICENT ASSOCIATION	RATHBONE William
ROYAL UNITED SERVICES INSTITUTE FOR DEFENCE STUDIES	COBBOLD Richard
ROYAL YACHTING ASSOCIATION	DUCHESNE Peter Robin
ROYAL ZOOLOGICAL SOCIETY OF SCOTLAND	WHEATER Professor Roger J.
RSI ASSOCIATION	KILBRIDE Peter
RUNNYMEDE TRUST	STUBBS Mrs Sukhvinder
RURAL FORUM SCOTLAND	GRIMSON Dermot
RWANDA DEVELOPMENT TRUST	JONES Hugh

SACRO	MATHESON Susan
SAINSBURY CENTRE FOR MENTAL HEALTH	MUIJEN Dr M
SAINSBURY FAMILY CHARITABLE TRUSTS	PATTISON Michael
SAINT ANN'S HOSPICE - MANCHESTER	YOUNG Bernard
SAINT JOHN'S WINCHESTER CHARITY	JACKSON Mr M. I.
SAINT LEONARDS HOSPICE	KAY Janet
SAINT MARTIN IN THE FIELDS CHRISTMAS APPEAL FUND	ALLEN Mrs Sibyl R.
SALISBURY CATHEDRAL SCHOOL	CRAIGIE Andrew John
SALISBURY CATHEDRAL TRUST	GAMBLE R.M.
SALTIRE SOCIETY	STREET Margaret Dobson
SALVATION ARMY	ROBERTS Jeffrey John (Major)
SALVATION ARMY SOCIAL SERVICES	TRIBBLE Col Trevor O.W.
SAMARITANS, THE	ARMSON Simon
SAMUEL COURTAULD TRUST	MURDOCH John
SANE	WALLACE Marjorie
SAVE & PROSPER EDUCATIONAL TRUST	GRANT Duncan
SAVE BRITAIN'S HERITAGE	PHILLIPS Emma
SAVE THE CHILDREN FUND, THE	AARONSON Michael
SCHIZOPHRENIA ASSOCIATION OF GREAT BRITAIN	HEMMINGS Gwynneth
SCHOOLS OUTREACH	BAILEY Gordon
SCHOOLS' ASSOCIATION FOOTBALL INTERNATIONAL BOARD	ALLATT C.S.
SCIENTIFIC EXPLORATION SOCIETY	BLASHFORD-SNELL John
SCOPE	BREWSTER Richard
SCOT-PEP	SCOTT Dr Gordon
SCOTTISH ACCIDENT PREVENTION COUNCIL	McDONNEL Michael A.
SCOTTISH ASSOCIATION FOR MARINE SCIENCE	MATTHEWS John Burr Lumley
SCOTTISH ASSOCIATION FOR MENTAL HEALTH	BARCUS Shona
SCOTTISH BEEKEEPERS ASSOCIATION	BLAIR Mr David B. N.
SCOTTISH BUSINESS IN THE COMMUNITY	MOORHOUSE John
SCOTTISH CENTRES	THOMSON Raymond E.B.
SCOTTISH CHAMBER ORCHESTRA	MCEWAN Roy James
SCOTTISH CIVIC TRUST	FORD John N P
SCOTTISH COMMUNITY EDUCATION COUNCIL	MCCONNELL Charlie
SCOTTISH COUNCIL FOR POSTGRADUATE MEDICAL AND DENTAL EDUCATION	BUCKLEY Dr E.G.
SCOTTISH COUNCIL FOR SINGLE HOMELESS	NAUMANN Laurie
SCOTTISH COUNCIL FOR VOLUNTARY ORGANISATIONS	SIME Martin
SCOTTISH COUNCIL ON ALCOHOL, THE	ALLSOP Douglas T.
SCOTTISH COUNTRYSIDE ACTIVITIES COUNCIL	AITKEN Dr R.
SCOTTISH EDUCATION AND ACTION FOR DEVELOPMENT	GRAY Linda
SCOTTISH ELECTRICAL CHARITABLE TRAINING TRUST	YOUNG David B.P.
SCOTTISH ENVIRONMENTAL EDUCATION COUNCIL	PASCOE Ian Philip
SCOTTISH EPISCOPAL CHURCH	STUART John
SCOTTISH EUROPEAN AID	CUNNINGHAM Michael
SCOTTISH FIELD STUDIES ASSOCIATION	GIMINGHAM Helen
SCOTTISH GENEALOGY SOCIETY	TORRANCE Mr D. Richard
SCOTTISH HIGHER EDUCATION FUNDING COUNCIL	SIZER John
SCOTTISH HISTORIC BUILDINGS TRUST	CLARE John Andrew
SCOTTISH INTERNATIONAL EDUCATION TRUST	MCCLELLAN John F.
SCOTTISH LANDOWNERS' FEDERATION	SPEED Brian
SCOTTISH MARRIAGE CARE	MCGRATH Laura
SCOTTISH MUSEUMS COUNCIL	MCLEAN Colin
SCOTTISH OPERA	JARMAN Richard
SCOTTISH PERMACULTURE	BELL Graham
SCOTTISH PRE SCHOOL PLAY ASSOCIATION	MACFARLANE Mrs Wendy
SCOTTISH PRE-RETIREMENT COUNCIL	McGOWN Archie
SCOTTISH SOCIETY FOR AUTISTIC CHILDREN	LIDDELL Donald J.
SCOTTISH SOCIETY FOR THE PREVENTION OF CRUELTY TO ANIMALS	MORRIS James
SCOTTISH SPORTS COUNCIL	ALSTEAD Allan
SCOTTISH URBAN ARCHAEOLOGICAL TRUST LTD	BOWLER David
SCOUT AND GUIDE GRADUATE ASSOCIATION	HAIGH Dr Paul
SCOUT ASSOCIATION	TWINE Derek
SCOUT ASSOCIATION, SCOTTISH COUNCIL	SHELMERDINE David V. C.
SCRIPTURE UNION - ENGLAND	KIMBER Charles Peter
SEND THE LIGHT LTD	DANBY Keith
SENSE-WEST	VON MALACHOWSKI Virginia
SEQUAL TRUST	PUGHE Anne
SHAFTESBURY SOCIETY	BECKETT Fran
SHAW TRUST	PAPE Tim
SHELTER CYMRU	PUZEY John
SHELTER SCOTLAND	NICHOLSON Liz
SHELTER, NATIONAL CAMPAIGN FOR HOMELESS PEOPLE	TRAMPLEASURE John
SHELTERED HOUSING AND WORKSHOPS PROJECT	HESLOP Michael
SHINGLES SUPPORT SOCIETY	NICHOLSON Marian
SIA	MARTINS Lorraine

WHO'S WHO IN THE VOLUNTARY SECTOR - 180

SIGN CAMPAIGN FOR DEAF PEOPLE	POWELL Stephen
SIKH DIVINE FELLOWSHIP	SINGH Prof Harmindar
SIR JOHN SOANE'S MUSEUM	RICHARDSON Mrs Margaret
SIR OSWALD STOLL FOUNDATION	BRUNWIN Rick
SKILL: NATIONAL BUREAU FOR STUDENTS WITH DISABILITIES	COOPER Deborah
SKILLSHARE AFRICA	ALLUM Cliff
SKIN CARE CAMPAIGN/NATIONAL ECZEMA SOCIETY	FUNNELL Christina M.
SNAP PEOPLES THEATRE TRUST	GRAHAM Andy
SOCIAL CARE ASSOCIATION	CLOUGH Richard
SOCIETY AND COLLEGE OF RADIOGRAPHERS	EVANS Stephen
SOCIETY FOR MUCOPOLYSACCHHARIDE DISEASES	LAVERY Christine
SOCIETY FOR PROMOTING CHRISTIAN KNOWLEDGE	CHANDLER Paul
SOCIETY FOR RADIOLOGICAL PROTECTION	BERRY Tessa
SOCIETY FOR THE AUTISTICALLY HANDICAPPED	LOVETT Keith
SOCIETY FOR THE INTERPRETATION OF BRITAIN'S HERITAGE INTERPRET BRITAIN	HEHIR Lesley
SOCIETY FOR THE PREVENTION OF SOLVENT AND VOLATILE SUBSTANCE ABUSE	EVANS Nancy
SOCIETY FOR THE PROMOTION OF HELLENIC STUDIES	FISHER F.J.
SOCIETY FOR THE PROMOTION OF NEW MUSIC	GRAHAM Cathy
SOCIETY FOR THE PROTECTION OF ANCIENT BUILDINGS	VENNING Philip
SOCIETY FOR THE PROTECTION OF UNBORN CHILDREN	SMEATON John
SOCIETY FOR WELFARE AND TEACHING OF THE BLIND	ROBERTSON Jane A.
SOCIETY OF ARCHITECTURAL HISTORIANS OF GB	MAYS Deborah
SOCIETY OF EQUESTRIAN ARTISTS	MILLIS Susan M.
SOCIETY OF GENEALOGISTS	CAMP Anthony J.
SOCIETY OF LICENSED VICTUALLERS	WHEELER Colin
SOLDIERS', SAILORS' AND AIRMEN'S FAMILIES ASSOC	SHEPPARD Major General Peter
SOS CHILDREN'S VILLAGES UK	FOX Daniel
SOS CHILDREN'S VILLAGES UK	RANDALL Adrian
SOS SAHEL INTERNATIONAL (UK)	MONKMAN Sally
SOUND SENSE	DEANE Kathryn
SOUTH WEST HERTS HOSPICE CHARITABLE TRUST (THE PEACE HOSPICE)	BALL Graham
SOUTHAMPTON COUNCIL OF COMMUNITY SERVICE	ASH Ms. J.
SPARE TYRE THEATRE COMPANY	HANNAH Liz
SPINA BIFIDA AND HYDROCEPHALUS, ASSOC	RUSSELL Andrew
SPURGEONS CHILD CARE	CULWICK David
SQUASH RACKETS ASSOCIATION	MOORE Nigel
SS GREAT BRITAIN PROJECT	LYNCH Lynn
ST ANDREW'S AMBULANCE ASSOCIATION	HEALY B.J.P.
ST CATHERINE'S HOSPICE	MOUNT Dr John
ST CHRISTOPHERS FELLOWSHIP	HITHERSAY Medora Ann
ST DUNSTANS FOR WOMEN AND MEN BLINDED IN THE SERVICES	FROST G.B.
ST JOHN AMBULANCE	LEWIS Martin
ST JOSEPH'S HOSPICE ASSOCIATION	O'LEARY Father Francis
ST KATHARINE & SHADWELL TRUST	DAWES Jenny
ST LOYE'S COLLEGE FOUNDATION	SMITH Michael
ST MUNGO ASSOCIATION CHARITABLE TRUST	LANE John
ST PIERS LINGFIELD	BESAG Dr F.M.C.
ST TIGGYWINKLES, THE WILDLIFE HOSPITAL TRUST	STOCKER Les
ST VINCENT DE PAUL SOCIETY ENGLAND & WALES	FAGAN Dr Austin
STANDING CONFERENCE ON DRUG ABUSE	HOWARD Roger
STANDING CONFERENCE ON SCHOOLS' SCIENCE AND TECHNOLOGY	PARKIN Ann
STARLIGHT FOUNDATION	WEBSTER Richard
STEPPING STONES IN SCOTLAND	LAWSON Isobel
STILLBIRTH AND NEONATAL DEATH SOCIETY	EL-RAYES Mary
STONHAM HOUSING ASSOCIATION LTD	TURNER Clive
STROKE ASSOCIATION	PRATT Ivan W.
SUE RYDER FOUNDATION, THE	RYDER Lady Ryder of Warsaw
SUNLEY (BERNARD) CHARITABLE FOUNDATION	MACDIARMID Duncan
SURVIVAL INTERNATIONAL	CORRY Stephen
SUSTRANS	GRIMSHAW John
SUSTRANS SCOTLAND	GRANT Tony
SUZY LAMPLUGH TRUST, THE	LAMPLUGH Diana
SWIMMING TEACHERS ASSOCIATION/CHARITABLE TRUST	HARVEY A.W.
TAXAID	BRODIE David
TAY-SACHS AND ALLIED DISORDERS	SIMON Dr Sybil
TEAR FUND	BALFOUR Doug
TELEPHONES FOR THE BLIND	IVES Graham
TELEVISION TRUST FOR THE ENVIRONMENT	LAMB Robert
TELEWORK TELECOTTAGE AND TELECENTRE ASSOC	DENBIGH Alan
TEMPLEGARTH TRUST	MANSFIELD Dr Peter
TENOVUS	PHILLIPS Marc
TERRENCE HIGGINS TRUST	PARTRIDGE Nick

Organisation	Contact
THYROID EYE DISEASE ASSOCIATION	MITCHELL Mrs Sally
TIDY BRITAIN GROUP	BINGHAM Dee
TIMBER GROWERS ASSOCIATION	WILSON Peter
TOMMY'S CAMPAIGN	OTTON Helen
TOURISM CONCERN	BARNETT Trisha
TOWN AND COUNTRY PLANNING ASSOCIATION	CORDY Tim
TRANSPORT ON WATER ASSOCIATION	FARAM L.
TREE COUNCIL	OSBORNE Robert
TRELOAR TRUST	LINDSAY Colonel Oliver J.M.
TRIDENT TRUST	COOKE-PRIEST Rear Admiral Colin
TRINITY COLLEGE LONDON	DAVEY John
TRINITY COLLEGE, BRISTOL	GILLETT Rev Canon David
TRUST FOR WESSEX ARCHAEOLOGY LTD	LAWSON Andrew J.
TSB FOUNDATION FOR ENGLAND & WALES	DUNCAN Kathleen N.
TURNING POINT	HEWITT Rex
TWENTIETH CENTURY SOCIETY	POWELL Kenneth
TWINS AND MULTIPLE BIRTHS ASSOCIATION	ELLISON Jane
UK CENTRE FOR ECONOMIC AND ENVIRONMENTAL DEVELOPMENT	COPE David R.
UK FORUM ON YOUNG PEOPLE & GAMBLING	BELLRINGER Paul
UK RETT SYNDROME ASSOCIATION	MILNE Yvonne
UK SKILLS	SNELL Patricia
ULSTER CANCER FOUNDATION	WOOD Michael A.
ULSTER SOCIETY FOR PREVENTION OF CRUELTY TO ANIMALS	PHILPOTT Stephen
UNION OF LIBERAL & PROGRESSIVE SYNAGOGUES	BURMAN Michael
UNION OF MACCABI ASSOCIATIONS IN GREAT BRITAIN AND NORTHERN IRELAND	HERMAN Marc
UNION OF MUSLIM ORGANIZATIONS OF UK AND EIRE	PASHA Dr Syed Aziz
UNITED KINGDOM COMMITTEE FOR UNICEF	SMITH Robert D
UNITED KINGDOM JEWISH AID AND INTERNATIONAL DEVELOPMENT	KAUFMANN Dr Georgia
UNITED KINGDOM VINEYARDS ASSOCIATION	BERWICK I. H.
UNITED NATIONS ASSOCIATION FOR INTERNATIONAL SERVICE	CARTER Jane
UNITED NATIONS ASSOCIATION UK	HARPER Malcolm
UNITED NATIONS ENVIRONMENT & DEVELOPMENT UK	DODDS Felix
UNITED REFORMED CHURCH, THE	BURNHAM Reverend Anthony G.
UNITED RESPONSE	SAYER Su
UNITED SOCIETY FOR THE PROPAGATION OF THE GOSPEL	PRICE Rev. Canon Peter B.
UNIVERSITIES FEDERATION FOR ANIMAL WELFARE	KIRKWOOD James K.
UNIVERSITY OF CAPE TOWN TRUST	TINDALE Mrs Sibylla
UNIVERSITY OF DERBY	GILLIS Richard
UNIVERSITY OF THE THIRD AGE	MARTIN Noel
UNIVERSITY OF WESTMINSTER	COPLAND Dr Geoffrey
URBAN THEOLOGY UNIT	VINCENT Rev. Dr John James
VEGETARIAN SOCIETY UK LTD	FOX Tina
VEGFAM - FEEDS THE HUNGRY WITHOUT EXPLOITING THE ANIMALS	HOWARD F.
VENTURE SCOTLAND	BUSHBY Rob
VICTIM SUPPORT	REEVES Helen
VICTIM SUPPORT SCOTLAND	PATERSON Alison
VICTORIA & ALBERT MUSEUM	BORG Dr Alan
VICTORIAN SOCIETY	FILMER-SANKEY William
VOICE	HORROCKS Christine
VOICE FOR THE CHILD IN CARE	JAMES Gwen
VOICE OF THE LISTENER TRUST	HAY Jocelyn
VOICE OF THE PEOPLE TRUST	CRIPPS Mr N.
VOICES FOUNDATION	DIGBY Susan
VOLUNTARY SERVICE OVERSEAS	GREEN G. David
WAGES DUE LESBIANS	NEALE Anne
WALES COUNCIL FOR VOLUNTARY ACTION/CYNGOR GWEITHREDU GWIRFODDOL CYMRU	BENFIELD Graham
WALES WILDLIFE AND COUNTRYSIDE LINK - WALES LINK	STANBURY David
WALLACE COLLECTION	SAVILL Rosalind Joy
WANDSWORTH OASIS AIDS SUPPORT CENTRE AT SALVATION ARMY	GEEKIE Peter
WAR ON CANCER	SPENCE Jacky
WAR ON WANT	LYNCH Margaret
WARWICKSHIRE INDUSTRIAL LOCOMOTIVE TRUST	GRIFFITHS Mr K.
WASTEWATCH	GEORGESON Ray
WATERAID	LANE Jon
WAVERLEY CARE TRUST	JOHNSON David
WELLCOME TRUST	MACGREGOR Ian
WELLCOME TRUST, THE	OGILVIE Dr Bridget M.
WELSH COUNCIL ON ALCOHOL AND OTHER DRUGS	REES Eirian
WESSEX AUTISTIC SOCIETY	LOWNDES R W

Organisation	Contact
WEST HAUGH CENTRE FOR DISABLED CHILDREN	FISHER Michael Robert
WESTMINSTER PASTORAL FOUNDATION	WOOLMER Dr Tim
WETLANDS INTERNATIONAL	MOSER Michael Edward Dr
WHITE HORSE CARE TRUST	REYNOLDS J.L.
WHITELEY HOMES TRUST	WARD Col A. C.
WHO CARES? TRUST	CHEAL Susanna
WILDFOWL & WETLANDS TRUST, THE	OWEN Dr Myrfyn
WILDLIFE AND COUNTRYSIDE LINK	HILBORNE Stephanie
WILDLIFE TRUSTS	CORNWELL Mary
WILDLIFE TRUSTS	LYSTER Dr Simon
WINGED FELLOWSHIP TRUST	BILLINGTON Andrew
WIRELESS FOR THE BEDRIDDEN SOCIETY	PARKER John
WISHBONE TRUST, THE	VALLANCE Russell
WOLFSON FOUNDATION, and WOLFSON FAMILY CHARITABLE TRUST	RASHBASS Dr Barbara
WOMANKIND WORLDWIDE	YOUNG Kate
WOMEN'S EDUCATIONAL TRAINING TRUST/WOMEN'S TECHNOLOGY SCHEME	DOVE Claire
WOMEN'S ENGINEERING SOCIETY	MACGILLIVRAY Cathy
WOMEN'S ENVIRONMENTAL NETWORK	CRIPPS Diana
WOMEN'S NATIONWIDE CANCER CONTROL CAMPAIGN	BUCHANAN Dr Mary
WOMEN'S ROYAL VOLUNTARY SERVICE	BURTON Gerald
WOMEN'S THERAPY CENTRE	BERRY Sally
WOODLAND TRUST	JAMES John D.
WOODROFFE BENTON FOUNDATION	STONELEY Kenneth
WORKERS' EDUCATIONAL ASSOCIATION	LOCHRIE Robert
WORKERS' EDUCATIONAL ASSOCIATION: SCOTLAND	CONNON Joyce
WORLD ASSOCIATION OF GIRL GUIDES AND GIRL SCOUTS	BRANDON Heather
WORLD MEMORIAL FUND FOR DISASTER RELIEF	CHILDS David J.
WORLD ORTHOPAEDIC CONCERN (UK)	GUY John G.
WORLD RESOURCE FOUNDATION	STRANGE Kit
WORLD UNIVERSITY SERVICE	GREGG Andy
WORLD VISION UK	CLAYTON Charles
WORLD WIDE FUND FOR NATURE	PELLEW Dr Robin
WORLD WIDE LAND CONSERVATION TRUST	BURTON John A.
WORLDAWARE	WALKER Derek
WREN TELECOTTAGE (WARWICKSHIRE RURAL ENTERPRISE NETWORK)	BERRY Jane
WUS (UK)	NURSEY Caroline
YARDLEY GREAT TRUST	MARTIN Alan C.
YMCA ENGLAND	NIGHTINGALE (John) Nicholas
YMCA SCOTLAND	KNOX John
YMCA SCOTQUEST	LANSDELL Nick
YOGA FOR HEALTH FOUNDATION	KENT Howard
YORKSHIRE AGRICULTURAL SOCIETY	KEIGWIN Mr R. T.
YORKSHIRE CHILDREN'S HOSPITAL TRUST	ROSE Howard
YOUNG ENTERPRISE	WESTGARTH Peter
YOUNG PEOPLE'S TRUST FOR THE ENVIRONMENT & NATURE CONSERVATION	LITTLEWOOD Cyril
YOUNG WOMEN'S CHRISTIAN ASSOCIATION OF GB	TISHLER Gillian
YOUNG WOMENS CHRISTIAN ASSOCIATION OF GB - SCOTTISH NATIONAL COUNCIL	CARR Isabel Anne
YOUTH ACTION 2000	ELLISTON Tony
YOUTH CLUBS SCOTLAND	TODD Jessie
YOUTH CLUBS UK	BATEMAN John
YOUTH HOSTELS ASSOCIATION (ENGLAND AND WALES)	LOGAN Colin
YOUTH SPORT TRUST	CAMPBELL Susan
ZITO TRUST	HOWLETT Michael
ZOOLOGICAL SOCIETY	BURGE Mr Richard